THE WHITE WAR

The White War

Life and Death on the Italian Front

1915–1919

MARK THOMPSON

faber and faber

First published in 2008
by Faber and Faber Limited
3 Queen Square London WC1N 3AU

Typeset by Donald Sommerville
Printed in England by CPI Mackays, Chatham, ME5 8TD

A CIP record for this book
is available from the British Library

ISBN 978–0–571–22333–6

2 4 6 8 10 9 7 5 3 1

For Noel, George, and Sanja –
in time and always

Contents

CONTENTS

Illustrations

Maps

'Italians! Go back!'

Some of the most savage fighting of the Great War happened on the front where Italy attacked the Austro-Hungarian Empire. Around a million men died in battle, of wounds and disease or as prisoners. Until the last campaign, the ratio of blood shed to territory gained was even worse than on the Western Front. Imagine the flat or gently rolling horizon of Flanders tilting at 30 or 40 degrees, made of grey limestone that turns blinding white in summer. At the top, Austrian machine guns are tucked behind rows of barbed wire and a parapet of stones. At the bottom, Italians crouch in a shallow trench. The few outsiders who witnessed this fighting believed that 'Nobody who hasn't seen it can guess what fighting is needed to go up slopes [like these].'

This front ran the length of the Italian–Austrian border, some 600 kilometres (almost 400 miles) from the Swiss border to the Adriatic Sea. On the high Alpine sectors, the armies lived and fought in year-round whiteness. As on other fronts, the armies were separated by a strip of no-man's land. Peering at a field cap bobbing above the enemy trench, an Italian soldier reflected on the conditions that made the carnage possible:

We kill each other like this, coldly, because whatever does not touch the sphere of our own life does not exist . . . If I knew anything about that poor lad, if I could once hear him speak, if I could read the letters he carries in his breast, only then would killing him like this seem to be a crime.

If the anonymity was mutual, so was the peril. Better than anyone in the world, the enemy who wants to kill you knows your anguish. The deafening preliminary barrage, the inconceivable tension before 'zero hour', the pandemonium of no-man's land: trench assaults did not vary much in the First World War. Likewise, the patterns of collusion which made life more bearable between the battles – shooting high, staging fake raids, respecting tacit truces to fetch the wounded and bury the dead, even swapping visits and gifts.

Another kind of collusion was so rare that very few instances were recorded on any front. It happened when defending units spontaneously stopped shooting during an attack and urged their enemy to return to their line. On one occasion, the Austrian machine gunners were so effective that the second and third waves of Italian infantry could hardly clamber over the corpses of their comrades. An Austrian captain shouted to his gunners, 'What do you want, to kill them all? Let them be.' The Austrians stopped firing and called out: 'Stop, go back! We won't shoot any more. Do you want everyone to die?'

Italian veterans described at least half a dozen such cases. In an early battle, the infantry tore forward, scrambling over the broken ground, screaming and brandishing their rifles. The Austrian trench was uncannily silent. The Italian line broke and clotted as it moved up the slope until there were only groups of men hopping from the shelter of one rock to the next, 'like toads'. Then a voice called from the enemy line: 'Italians! Go back! We don't want to massacre you!' A lone Italian jumped up defiantly and was shot; the others turned and ran.

A few weeks earlier, in September 1915, the Austrians urged the survivors of an Italian company to stop fighting and go back to their own line, taking their wounded, or they would all die. 'You can see there is no escape!' Eventually the Italians gave up, and the Austrians hurried down with stretchers and cigarettes. The Italians gave them black feathers from their plumed hats and stars from their collars as souvenirs. A year later, a Sardinian battalion attacked positions on the Asiago plateau where, unusually, no-man's land sloped downhill towards the Austrians. As the Italians stumbled over boulders, the enemy machine gunners had to keep adjusting their elevation; this saved the battalion from being wiped out. As the survivors drew close to the enemy trench, an Austrian shouted in Italian: 'That's enough! Stop firing!' Other Austrians looking over the parapet took up the cry. When the shooting stopped, the first Austrian, who might have been a chaplain, called to the Italians: 'You are brave men. Don't get yourselves killed like this.'

If there is any proof that such scenes were played out on other fronts, I have not found it. A Turkish officer may have shouted to the Australians attacking The Nek in August 1915 during the Gallipoli campaign, telling them to go back. Even if he did so, the Turkish machine gunners kept shooting and the Australians kept dying. The following month, German machine gunners may eventually have stopped firing on Hill 70, in the Battle of Loos, when the British columns 'offered such a target as had never been seen before, or even thought possible'. The incidents reported on the Italian front went further than this. To take their measure, bear in mind that there was no shortage of hatred on this front, that soldiers could relish the killing here as much as elsewhere, the Austrians were outnumbered and fighting for their lives, and any officer or soldier caught assisting the enemy in this way would face a court martial.

These deterrents could be overcome only by the spectacle of a massacre so futile that pity and revulsion forced a recognition of oneself in the enemy, thwarting the habit of discipline and the reflex of self-interest. Half a dozen cases over three years might not mean much if other fronts had thrown up examples of the same thing. As it is, they suggest that courage, incompetence, fanaticism and topography combined on this front to create conditions unlike any others in the Great War, and extreme by any standard in history. This is the story of those conditions.

Think of Italy: the clearest borders in mainland Europe. From Sicily by the toe, past Naples and Rome, up to Florence and Genoa, that long limb looks like nothing else on the globe. Further north, the situation is less distinct. Above the basin of the River Po, Alpine foothills rise sharply in the west, more gradually to the east. The eastern Alps do not crown the peninsula tidily; they run parallel to the northern Adriatic shore, curving down to the sea after 200 kilometres. The rivers rising on the south side of these ranges flow through foothills that drop a thousand metres to the coastal plain, some 60 kilometres from the sea. Flying into Trieste airport on a clear day, you see the rivers' stony courses like grey braids: the Piave in the distance, then the Livenza and the Tagliamento. Closest of all, passing only a couple of kilometres from the runway, is the River Isonzo. Rising in the easternmost Alps, the Isonzo follows geological faultlines, piling through gorges only a few metres wide, bisecting steep wooded ridges, then emerging near Gorizia. Its lower course, strewn with rubble from the mountains, follows a wide curve to the sea. The water threads the white detritus like a turquoise ribbon through a sleeve of bones. In dry summers, the ribbon vanishes altogether. East of the river and the airport, a ridge of high ground rises 'like a great wall above the plains of Friuli'. This is the Carso plateau, and it marks the edge of the Adriatic microplate. Further south, this ripple becomes a tectonic barrier, a limestone rampart that cuts south-eastwards for 700 kilometres, as far as Albania.

This corner of the country, between the River Tagliamento and the eastern Alps, hardly seems Italian in the obvious ways. Most of the towns are raw and somehow sad. The hillsides boast no renaissance villas, the museums hold little that is familiar, and the church towers are mostly concrete. No olive groves, rosy brick barns or terracotta tiles, and precious little marble (except in war memorials). Even the food and grape varieties are different. Other languages – Slovenian, Friulan – jostle with Italian on the signposts, sharpening the sense of anomaly. It is, unmistakably, a multiethnic area, a fact that sometimes enraged the architects of Italian unification in the nineteenth century.

In the 1840s, the rulers of Piedmont, in north-western Italy, planned how to amalgamate half a dozen kingdoms, duchies and Habsburg provinces into a nation state. They wanted the northern border to reach the Alpine watershed, or beyond it, all the way from the Swiss border to the Istrian peninsula. When the First World War began, the Austro-Hungarian Empire still straddled the Alps, penetrating far into Italian territory. After months of political turmoil, Italy's rulers joined the Allied war against Germany and Austria-Hungary. They hoped to defeat Austria and finally claim their ideal border. Less publicly, they wanted to control the eastern Adriatic seaboard, where few Italians lived, and become a power in the Balkans.

The Allies, desperate for help against the Central Powers, met these conditions, and agreed as well to award Italy some territory in Albania and the Aegean sea, to enlarge its African colonies and let it share the spoils in Turkey if the Ottoman Empire fell apart. On these hard-nosed terms, Italy launched what patriots called 'the fourth war of independence'. The foremost goal was the capture of this wedge of land around the northern Adriatic, an area smaller than the English county of Kent.[1] It also wanted part of the Habsburg province of Tyrol, from Lake Garda up to the Alpine watershed. Italy's strategy of attacking eastwards meant there was not much fighting around the Tyrol. The army massed in Friuli, below the Carso plateau, and threw itself at the enemy on the ridge above. The general staff expected to be 'in Vienna for Christmas'. It was not to be. Over the next two and a half years, the Italians got nowhere near Trieste, let alone Vienna. Italy's offensives

---

1 Eastern Friuli and Trieste comprised some 3,000 square kilometres. Istria – where no fighting took place, though it was equally an Italian objective – is about 5,000 square kilometres. South Tyrol, comprising what Italians called the Trentino and Alto Adige, has 13,600 square kilometres.

clawed some 30 kilometres of ground – mostly in the first fortnight – at a cost of 900,000 dead and wounded. The epicentre of violence was the Isonzo valley, at the eastern end of the front. In Italy, the names Isonzo and Carso still resonate like the Somme, Passchendaele, Gallipoli or Stalingrad.

In autumn 1917, with German help, the Austro-Hungarians drove the Italians back almost to Venice. It was the biggest territorial reverse of any battle during the war, and the gravest threat to the Kingdom of Italy since unification. A year later, the Italians defeated Austria-Hungary in battle for the first time. Europe's last continental empire collapsed. This is the story of that crisis, recovery and victory.

To the commanders deadlocked on the Western Front, the Italian front was a sideshow, nasty enough but not quite the real thing, waged by armies whose tactics, training and equipment were often second-rate. The Italians reacted to this deprecating attitude in ways that confirmed their Allies' prejudices. During the war, many Italians felt that their allies undervalued their sacrifice. The sense of neglect lingered afterwards, despite or because of the Fascist regime's habit of trumpeting Italy's immortal achievements in the war. British and French indifference was particularly hurtful. A few years ago, two of the country's finest historians grumbled wryly that 'Our entire war is viewed from the other side of the Alps with the vaguely racist superficiality that we ourselves reserve for Turks and Bulgarians.'

Outside Italy and the former Habsburg lands, not much has been written about the Italian front, although it was unique in several ways. Alone among the major Allies, Italy claimed no defensive reasons for fighting. It was an open aggressor, intervening for territory and status. The Italians were more divided over the war than any other people. For a minority, the cause was whiter than white: Italy had to throw itself into the struggle, not only to extend its borders but to strengthen the nation. In the furnace of war, Italy's provincial differences would blend and harden into a national alloy. The greater the sacrifice, the higher the dividends. Not surprisingly, it was a conviction that made no sense to the great majority. This is the story of that conviction: who held it, and who paid for it.

Even by the standards of the Great War, Italy's soldiers were treated harshly. The worst-paid infantry in western Europe were sent to the front sketchily trained and ill-equipped, sacrificed to the doctrine of the frontal assault, ineptly supported by artillery. Italy mobilised the same number of men as mainland Britain, and executed at least three times as many. No other army routinely punished entire units by 'decimation', executing randomly selected men. Only the Italian government treated its captured soldiers as cowards or defectors, blocking the delivery of food and clothing from home. Over 100,000 of the 600,000 Italian prisoners of war died in captivity – a rate nine times worse than for Habsburg captives in Italy. Statistically, it was more dangerous for the infantry to be taken prisoner than to stay alive on the front line.

Finally, Italy's situation after the war was like none of the other victors'. While the war did complete Italy's unification, it was disastrous for the nation. Apart from its cost in human life, the war discredited Italy's liberal institutions, leading to their overthrow by the world's first fascist state. Benito Mussolini's self-styled 'trenchocracy' would rule for twenty years, with a regime that claimed the Great War was the foundation of Italy's greatness. For many veterans, Mussolini's myth gave a positive meaning to terrible experience. This is the story of how the Italians began to lose the peace when their laurels were still green.

Mark Thompson
February 2008

ONE

A Mania for Expansion

My Native Land! I See the Walls, the Arches,
The columns and the statues, and the lone
Ancestral towers; but where,
I ask, is all the glory?
LEOPARDI, 'To Italy' (1818)

Europe before the First World War was rackety and murderous, closer in its statecraft to the Middle East or central Asia than today's docile continent, where inter-state affairs filter through committees in Brussels.[1] It was marked by the epic formation of two large states. When Germany emerged in the 1860s, Italy had taken shape in a process of unification called the *Risorgimento* or 'revival'. Led by Piedmont, a little kingdom with its capital at Turin, the Risorgimento merged two kingdoms, the statelets controlled by the Pope, a grand duchy, and two former provinces of the Austro-Hungarian Empire.

By 1866, the Italian peninsula was unified except for Papal Rome and Venetia, the large northern province with Venice as its capital. Rome could not be liberated until France withdrew its support for the Pope. Against Austria, however, the Italians found themselves with a mighty ally; Prussia's prime minister, Otto von Bismarck, invited them to attack Austria from the south when he attacked from the north. Italy lost the two decisive battles of the war and won the peace. Austrian Venetia became the Italian Veneto.[2] The Italians even gained a fraction of Friuli, but not the Isonzo valley or Trieste.

In the east, the new border ran for 150 kilometres from the Alps to the Adriatic Sea, partly along the courses of the Aussa and the Judrio

1 The gulf between past and present was measured when Yugoslavia fell apart amid bloodshed and lies in the early 1990s. Faced with the savage, nation-building politics of their grandparents' day, Europe's leaders denied the evidence of their eyes, trying to douse the fire with conference minutes and multilateral resolutions.
2 The story of Italy's third war of independence is told in the Appendix.

rivers, hardly more than streams for most of the year. Elsewhere the new demarcation ran across fields, sometimes marked by wire mesh hung with bells. Local people came and went to church or market as they pleased. The customs officers knew which women smuggled tobacco and sugar under their broad skirts, and waved them through all the same. Personal contacts were everything. Austrian border guards looked the other way when Italian nationalists crossed the border for Italian national holidays in Udine or Palmanova. In the language of the day, the new border was cravenly *administrative* instead of nobly *national*. It was makeshift and relaxed, not the absolute perimeter that nationalists dreamed of. Even worse, Austria kept control of the high ground from Switzerland to the sea. Trieste, like south Tyrol, remained a dream. 'Is it possible', lamented Giuseppe Mazzini, the father of liberal nationalism, 'that Italy accepts being pointed out as the only nation in Europe that does not know how to fight, the only one that can only receive what belongs to it by benefit of foreign arms and through humiliating concessions by the enemy usurper?'

The 1866 war could have had a much worse outcome. As Garibaldi, the figurehead of unification, would admit in his memoirs, the alliance with Prussia 'proved useful to us far beyond our deserts'. The legendary warrior heaped contempt on the regular army commanders, whose arrogance and ignorance had negated Italy's massive advantage in strength and dumped the nation 'in a cesspit of humiliation'. And it was Garibaldi who said the best that could be said of the campaign: Italians from all over the peninsula had joined forces for the first time. This was a landmark in national history, though it could not outweigh the military failure, which bequeathed the young kingdom a complex that the Italians could not win anything for themselves. For decades afterwards, foreign leaders winked at Italy's diplomatic achievements: they had to lose badly to make any gains!

The nation's leaders yearned for spectacular victories to expunge the bitter memory of those defeats in 1866. The army was in no condition to provide such solace, even after the command structure was amended on Prussian lines in the 1870s. This thirst for great-power status led to defeats in Ethiopia in 1887 and 1896, and the pointless occupation of Libya in 1911. King Victor Emanuel II's refusal to clarify the army command in 1866 led the next generation of commanders to insist on a unified structure with no ambiguities. His determination to exercise his constitutional role as commander-in-chief, despite being wholly unfitted for that role, would deter his grandson, Victor Emanuel III, from holding his own chief of the general staff to account during the Great War.

Then there were the borders. It was well and good to have Venetia, yet Austria's continuing control of the southern Tyrol meant the newly acquired territory was not secure. Venice was still a hostage, for Austrian forces could threaten to pour down the Alpine valleys and swarm over the plains to the sea. The new demarcation in the far north-east was even worse. Patriots denounced it as humiliating, indefensible, and harmful to Friuli's development.[3] They quoted Napoleon Bonaparte's remark that the natural demarcation between Austria and Italy lay between the River Isonzo and Laibach (now Ljubljana, the capital of Slovenia), taking in parts of Carniola (the Austrian province roughly corresponding to today's Slovenia) and Istria, joining the sea at Fiume (now Rijeka), and his reported comment that the line of the Isonzo was indefensible, hence not worth fortifying. Garibaldi called it an ugly border, and hoped it would soon be moved 150 kilometres eastward.

One of these protesting patriots was Paolo Fambri. Born in Venice, he fought as a volunteer in 1859, became a captain of engineers in the regular army, and then a deputy in parliament and a prolific journalist who ridiculed the new border at every opportunity. Fambri defined the problem by its essentials. What is a border? It may be literal (a river) or symbolic (a pole across a road), but between states with the power and perhaps the will to threaten each other, it must be solid, 'a force and not a formality'. The Alps should serve Italy as its ramparts. Instead, they enclose the country like a wall. As for the new frontier near the Isonzo, 'a more irrational and capricious line was never yet imposed by arrogance or conceded by the most abject weakness'. There was no coherent historical, ethnic, physical, political or military concept behind it. Just as Italy's security in the north was a hostage to the Tyrol, so its security in the east was threatened by three great natural breaches in the Julian Alps: at Tarvis through to Villach (today in southern Austria); at Görz (now Gorizia) and the valley of the River Vipacco (now the

---

3 In fact, Friuli developed on both sides of the border after 1866, as even Italian nationalist historians acknowledged. On the Austrian side, vines and fruit orchards were planted, and groves of mulberry trees fed the silkworms that supplied the textile industry. Gorizia flourished as 'the Nice of Austria' and Grado, with its shining lagoons and sandy beaches, became central Europe's favourite seaside resort. Land reclamation schemes created rich farmland near Monfalcone.

Vipava, in Slovenia), through to Laibach; and up the coast from Fiume and Trieste. Italy could not be secure without controlling all this territory, but the chances of a successful pre-emptive attack were 'worse than bad', because the enemy held all the high ground. The Austrians, by contrast, could stroll over the Isonzo and onto the plains of Friuli 'without a care in the world'. Either Austria or Italy could hold all the territory from Trieste to Trent (now Trento), but they could not share it, so the 1866 border could never become stable.

Giulio Caprin, a nationalist from Trieste, was equally scornful: the new border 'is not a border at all: neither historic nor ethnic nor economic; a metal wire planted haphazardly where nothing ends or begins, an arbitrary division, an amputation . . . alien to nature, law and logic'. Foreign analysts agreed the border would not last. A British journalist wrote in the 1880s that if Italy ever fought Austria without allies, defending the Veneto would be very difficult. Not only would Austria hold the high ground in the east; the southern Tyrol would become 'the most threatening salient', looming above the Italian lines. Further east, where the Alps curve southwards, turning the plains of Friuli into an amphitheatre, Austria's position enjoyed 'peculiar excellence'. Just how excellent would be tested half a century later. Perceptive observers noted another effect of the 1866 border. By putting pressure on the south-western corner of the Austro-Hungarian Empire, this border encouraged Habsburg high-handedness towards Vojvodina and Bosnia, the empire's restive Slavic lands close to Serbia. In this way, Garibaldi's 'ugly border' added a line of gunpowder to the incendiary pattern of 1914.

The abortive bid for Trieste in 1866, when an army corps marched around the northern Adriatic, hoping to capture the Austrian port before Bismarck forced a peace settlement on Italy, fired Italian nationalists on both sides of the new border with fresh enthusiasm. Their watchword became irredentism, coined from the slogan *Italia irredenta*, 'unredeemed Italy'. The irredentists wanted to 'redeem' the southern Tyrol, Trieste, Gorizia, Istria and Dalmatia by annexing them to the Kingdom of Italy. The Christian overtone was anything but accidental: for these nationalists, the fatherland was sacred and their cause was a secular religion.

Formed by cells of disillusioned Garibaldians, Mazzinians and other hotheads gathering in groups such as the Association for Unredeemed

Italy (founded in 1877), they were inspired by ambitions that were almost comically beyond their grasp. Not only were the Austrians determined to stop them spreading their revolutionary ideas; successive governments in Rome were ready to sacrifice them as the price of staying in the good graces of Europe's great powers. Governments could do this because the irredentists swam against the tide of public as well as diplomatic opinion. With the capture of Rome in 1870, most Italians reckoned that Italy was complete.

The human cost of unification since 1848 was around 6,000 dead and 20,000 wounded: as such things went, not excessive for the creation of a nation state with 27 million people. Yet the achievement left a hangover. The compromises entailed by state-creation tasted bitter to the very idealists who had inspired the Risorgimento. Their feeling was caught long afterwards by Valentino Coda, a veteran of the Great War who became a leading Fascist: 'In a nation that was only born yesterday and lacks unitary traditions, irredentism was the only spring of patriotic action, even if the bourgeoisie and the socialists conspired to suffocate it.' Irredentism was the best cause around for disaffected nationalists, at a loss for direction in a country where 'civil society' was a crust of professionals – lawyers, merchants, scholars, administrators, army officers – resting on a magma of industrial workers, peasant farmers and labourers, unenfranchised, extensively illiterate, patchily becoming a political class.

There was more to this bitterness than dislike of the way that Venice and the Veneto had been brought into Italy. Mazzini spoke for many when he denounced the course and outcome of unification. From their point of view, the kingdom had been hustled into existence, leaving two large communities of ethnic Italians outside its borders. Even worse, the pre-1860 élites – the court, landowning aristocracy and professional classes – kept their power, ensuring that their interests were not threatened by broader involvement. There had been no transformation of the political system or culture, nothing like a revolution in values. The House of Savoy blocked the way to progress. The masses were still alienated subjects rather than active citizens.

Other prominent figures made this analysis, but no one was as sharp as Mazzini. The executive, he wrote near the end of his life, governed with 'a policy of expedients, opportunism, concealment, intrigue, reticence and parliamentary compromise characteristic of the languid life of nations in decay'. Like dissident leaders in other times and places, he was tormented by the low means that politicians used to achieve a great purpose, by his own impotence (as distinct from moral stature), and by ordinary people's sluggish reluctance to rise against their oppressors, whether foreign or domestic. Visionary, cadaverous, clad in black, Mazzini in old age seemed more spirit than man, kept alive by a burning will to sustain the people's faith in self-determination. He wanted a strong state, but one that had been transformed by revolutionary idealism.

This prophet of European integration believed Italy had a mission to extend European civilisation into northern Africa. He scorned the 'brutal conquest' that typified European colonialism; foreign engagement should be emancipatory, extending the rights and freedoms that European citizens fought for at home. The fact that politicians do not take the huge risks incurred by foreign adventures without more selfish ends in view did not distract him. He saw Austrian control over the south Tyrol and Trieste as 'the triumph of brutal force' over popular will. On the Tyrol, he was an orthodox nationalist: everything up to the Alpine watershed must be Italy's, including the wholly German areas around Bozen (now Bolzano in the Alto Adige). Yet he was uncertain about the north-eastern border. Sometimes he said it should follow the crest of the Alps down to Trieste, at others, that it should follow the Isonzo. Shortly before his death, he wrote that Istria must be Italian because the poet Dante had ordained it six hundred years before, in lines known to every patriot:

> *a Pola presso del Carnaro*
> *che Italia chiude e suoi termini bagna.*

> to Pola by the Quarnero bay
> washing the boundary where Italy ends.

(The town of Pola is at the southern tip of the Istrian peninsula.) He was never a maximalist, however: he had too much respect for Slavic self-determination to claim that Dalmatia – the eastern Adriatic coast – should be controlled by its tiny Italian minority. His views on Italian–Slav relations were far-sighted: the two peoples should be allies in seizing freedom from their Austrian oppressor. After his death in 1872, the irredentists imitated his style of total dedication to an ideal. His legacy was an ascetic commitment to the fatherland, a radical libertarianism that was ultimately contemptuous of liberalism, with its unavoidable compromises and calculations, its suspicion of state power. This fanaticism was handed down to later generations, including the volunteers of 1915.

The 1870s bore hard on irredentist ideals. When the Emperor Franz Josef visited Venice in 1875, Victor Emanuel assured him that irredentist claims would be dropped, and that Italy's intentions were entirely peaceful. The next year, the King praised the 'cordial friendship and sympathy' between Italians and Austrians. The Austrian occupation of Bosnia and Herzegovina, in 1878, sent shock waves through the Italians of Dalmatia, who were already hugely outnumbered by Croats and now feared they would be swamped by a million and a half more Slavs, pressing at their backs. Anti-Slav prejudice spread up the Adriatic shore to Trieste, but Rome lent no moral or practical support.

This was nothing beside the hammer blows that came in 1882, the *annus horrendus* for nationalists. In May, Italy signed a treaty with Germany and Austria-Hungary. This was the Triple Alliance, which would endure until May 1915, the eve of war. Alliance with the old enemy was so controversial that successive governments denied its existence. (The text was not published until 1915.) Under its provisions, Italy was guaranteed support if France attacked. It also gained security along its border with Austria, good relations with Germany, and the international respectability that went with membership in a defensive great-power alliance. The most significant clause dealt with the Balkans:

Austria-Hungary and Italy undertake to use their influence to prevent all territorial changes which might be disadvantageous to one or the other signatory power. To this end they agree to interchange all information throwing light on their intentions. If, however, Austria-Hungary or Italy should be compelled to alter the status quo in the Balkans, whether by a temporary or by a permanent occupation, such occupation shall not take place without previous agreement between the two powers based on the principle of reciprocal compensation for every advantage, territorial or otherwise.

Any Austrian moves in the Balkans could in principle be leveraged to deliver Trentino and/or Trieste as 'compensation'. Indeed, Italy might even encourage Austrian expansion, for that ulterior purpose.

As well as full recognition of their own borders, Italy's allies got guarantees of mutual and Italian support if France or Russia attacked either of them. Military protocols, added in 1888, specified the Italian support that would be sent to Germany if France attacked. In military terms, Italy's benefit was doubtful, as France was more likely to attack Germany. Politically, it was curious to swap the public renunciation of claims to Tyrol and Trieste (inviting domestic accusations of betrayal) for a conditional clause about compensation. On the other hand, Italy stayed in the alliance for so long because it married realist foreign policy goals with the officer corps' admiration for the Prussian army. Ties with Austria were a price worth paying.

The chief drawback was not obvious in 1882. For it turned out that the alliance removed Italy's freedom to shift as occasion suited between France, Germany and Austria, and hence to punch above its weight. Intended to raise the country's international standing, the Triple Alliance narrowed its scope of action. If Italy was to build an overseas role, it needed significant allies. This is why a Catholic liberal politician, Stefano Jacini, criticised Italy's real motive for entering the Triple Alliance as a 'mania for expansion', which led the country to take on 'an enormous armament quite disproportionate to our resources'.

Out of France's long shadow at last, Italy chased colonial power in the Horn of Africa. In 1885, it occupied a dusty port on the Red Sea, 'where not even the standard of a Roman legion could be re-discovered'; from this seed, the colony of Eritrea would sprout. Further south, the colony of Somaliland took shape over the 1890s. The third profitless prize in the region was Ethiopia; when the Emperor Menelik denounced Italy's protectorate, Italy slid down a path of threats to the exquisite humiliation of Adua, where Ethiopian forces killed 6,000 Italians in a single day in 1896. This did not cure the mania, which eventually led to the attack on Libya, a gambit that would have driven Mazzini and Garibaldi to despair. In September 1911, Rome informed Ottoman Turkey that the 'general exigencies of civilisation' obliged Italy to occupy Libya. Having accomplished this, Italy declared war on Turkey itself. Although the war ended formally in October 1912, when the Ottoman state ceded Libya and let Italy occupy Rhodes and the Dodecanese Islands, local resistance could not be quelled. Unable to assess or affect the attitudes of hostile Libyan tribes, the army clung to the coast, within range of the naval guns. Some 35,000 men had embarked in 1911. By 1914, the commitment had grown to 55,000 men with no victory in sight.

This was all instigated by Giovanni Giolitti, the greatest reforming politician that Italy has ever produced. He wanted to outflank his nationalist critics with a spectacular invasion, and thought Libya would be a stroll. Instead it became a quicksand. Giolitti lied about the costs of the campaign and conjured up imaginary victories. He drew cautionary lessons about plunging the country into war, ill-prepared, but kept them to himself. The ultimate legacy of his cynical adventure was the Fascist invasion of Ethiopia in 1935.

Libya confirmed that the Italian army was incapable of waging effective colonial campaigns. After a flurry of reforms in the 1870s, including universal conscription and the reorganisation of the general staff, successive initiatives to overhaul the military had suffocated in red tape and party-political wrangling. Unhealthy closeness to the royal court undermined professionalism in the officer corps. Measured against Italy's geostrategic vulnerability and colonial ambitions, the reforms were half-baked and the army was still much too small. Bismarck's quip was still true: Italy had 'a large appetite and very poor teeth'.

The second blow to the irredentists in 1882 was the death of Garibaldi on 2 June. In his last years, the great hero kept exhorting the Italians of Tyrol and Trieste not to lose heart. His passing left many of his compatriots feeling bleakly that their country's best days were already behind it. The towering figure that had encouraged and sometimes berated them for almost forty years was gone, and nobody could take his place.

The third blow was another death: the execution of a young man in Trieste, one Guglielmo Oberdan (originally Wilhelm Oberdank: like many nationalist fanatics, his own national identity was ambiguous). Along with other draft-age Habsburg Italians, he fled to Italy in 1878 to avoid being sent to the new Austrian garrisons in Bosnia and Herzegovina. 1882 happened to be the 500th anniversary of Trieste's submission to Habsburg power. The celebrations were scheduled for September, and Franz Josef would be there. Oberdan decided to assassinate the Emperor. Acting either alone or as part of a shadowy network, he re-entered Austria. Arrested near the border with bombs in his baggage, he confessed. The Emperor rejected pleas for clemency, and Oberdan was hanged in a barracks cell on 20 December after refusing religious rites. As he mounted the gallows he cried 'Long live Italy! Long live free Trieste! Out with the foreigners!' He became the only full-blown Italian martyr of Austro-Hungarian brutality. While it failed to derail the Triple Alliance, his act put Trieste on the map. Local patriots sang a rapidly composed 'Hymn to Oberdan'. Within five years, there were 49 'Oberdan societies' in Italy and Austria, defying repression in order to nurse irredentist dreams.

These societies got scant encouragement in the kingdom. Hardest on them was the government of Francesco Crispi, a Sicilian lawyer turned politician with the aura that all Garibaldi's former comrades possessed. As prime minister from 1887 to 1891, Crispi believed Italy had an imperial destiny much larger than the unredeemed lands. The Triple Alliance should be a platform for these endeavours. But he was a realist, too, who knew there was no international support for seizing the southern Tyrol and Trieste. He spent heavily on the military and talked a lot about 'Italian rights in the Mediterranean' while quietly instructing Italian leaders in Trieste to clamp down on their irredentists. As a reformed freedom-fighter, Crispi disliked the new generation of militant idealists and their cause.

Based on the votes of 2 per cent of the population and royal approval, Italian governments were highly unstable. Their make-up was not determined by parties or party loyalties; every cabinet included moderates from Right and Left, dominated by an outsized personality. After Cavour and Crispi, the next such personality was Giovanni Giolitti, prime minister five times between 1892 and 1921. The decade and a half before the Great War is known as the *era giolittiana*, the era of Giolitti. He won and kept power by winning over moderate leftists and Catholic conservatives and by manipulating elections. Rather than working solely to benefit his own class, the Piedmontese élite, however, he was an enlightened conservative with liberal tendencies, pioneering redistributive taxation, improvement of labour conditions, social change through public spending, and electoral reform.

Amid the colourful monomaniacs and profiteers of the day, Giolitti was prosaic on a grand scale. He was a wily calculator, an artist of the possible, a patrician seeking 'to reconcile stability with liberty and progress'. To his detractors, he became the emblem of a political order that was practical but petty, humdrum and sometimes corrupt, 'unworthy' of Italy's achievements and ideals. The nationalists detested him. His project, they said witheringly, was *Italietta*, 'little Italy', shorn of splendour, preoccupied with trivial problems – like the balance of trade deficit, agricultural tariffs, tax collecting, the unruly banking sector, the plight of peasant farmers, the tyranny of absentee landlords, rural emigration, and the use of martial law against strikers in Italy's giddily expanding cities.

Many things improved under Giolitti. Italy ended the tariff war with France, doubled its industrial output over the decade to 1910, and narrowed the trade deficit. Measured by the growth of railways, the navy, education, merchant shipping, electricity consumption and land reclamation, the country was developing at a phenomenal rate. Yet it was still firmly the least of the great powers, and poor by comparison. With 35 million inhabitants, it was Europe's sixth most populous state. (Russia had nearly 170 million, Germany 68 million, Austria-Hungary nearly 52 million, Britain 46 million, and France, 40 million people.) The middle class was very small: only 5 per cent of the population. Some 40 per cent worked on the land (there were 9 million farm labourers with their dependents, living at subsistence level), and 18 per cent were artisans or industrial workers. Health indicators were at pre-industrial levels. The economy was primarily agricultural, with low productivity because farming was unmodernised except in the north. Hence the country was not self-sufficient in staples, importing three times more wheat than it produced. Lacking coal or iron reserves, Italy had little heavy industry; iron and steel, chemicals and engineering were getting under way, but textiles and foodstuffs were still the mainstays of a sector that was also limited by low investment and poor working conditions – though thanks to militant trades unions, industrial salaries had increased steadily since 1890. Even with this recent growth, Italy was not catching up with France, Germany or the United States. Businesses were small or very small: 80 per cent were completely unmechanised and employed two to five people. Most Italians had only the vaguest notion of the state; their lives were local and regional by dialect, custom, labour and experience.

Despite his modernising achievements, the Socialists too often sided with nationalists and democrats against Giolitti, scorning his devotion to 'empirical politics'. Guilty as charged, said Giolitti, '*if* by empiricism you mean taking account of the facts, the real conditions of the country, and the population . . . The experimental method, which involves taking account of the facts and proceeding as best one can, without grave danger . . . is the safest and even the only possible method.' Antonio Salandra, Giolitti's successor in 1914, would shred this liberal credo when he took the country to war against its nominal allies, Austria and Germany.

TWO

'We Two Alone'

It is always the case that the one who is not
your friend will request your neutrality, and
that the one who is your friend will request
your armed support.
MACHIAVELLI, *The Prince* (1532)

How the Government Plotted against Peace

Italy was pulled into the First World War by two whiskery men in frock coats and an anxious, weak-willed king. They were not alone: interventionist passion surged around the higher echelons of society, making up in noise what they lacked in popular support. Yet, without a conspiracy in the highest places, Italy would have stayed neutral.

Prime Minister Antonio Salandra and Foreign Minister Sidney Sonnino were like-minded conservatives and old friends who knew they were backed by an élite of northern industrialists and politicians which supported rearmament and military expansion around the Adriatic Sea. When Salandra finally let parliament debate the international situation, in December 1914, deputies were not allowed to query the government's foreign policy or the army's readiness. The cabinet was not informed about the twin-track negotiations with London and Vienna until 21 April 1915. Five days later, without forewarning parliament, the Prime Minister committed Italy to fight. The deputies rubber-stamped his decision after the fact. With the King's support, he had carried out a coup d'état in all but name.

This process, without parallel in other countries, split the country. Many nationalists believed the war would heal this rift. Instead the fractures widened under the pressure of terrible carnage, undermining morale in the army and on the home front. There would be no equivalent of the French *union sacrée*. Parliament too was damaged. After granting the government decree powers, the Chamber of Deputies became a cipher.

The Socialists, who tried to preserve a watchdog role, could be cowed or sidestepped when the need arose. Historian Mario Isnenghi argues that the interventionist campaign of 1914–15 created a new political force, the 'war party', cutting across traditional loyalties, scornful of institutions and elected majorities, convinced that they alone represented the nation's true identity and interests. This force proved to be durable; parliamentary life had scarcely revived in 1922 when Mussolini's accession – overwhelmingly supported by the chamber – subverted and then destroyed Italy's liberal institutions. In short, the events of spring 1915 struck a blow from which the country would not recover for 30 years.

Early in 1914, Prime Minister Giolitti resigned when part of his coalition crumbled away. Still the most powerful leader in parliament, he persuaded the King to replace him with Antonio Salandra, a lawyer from a rich landowning family in Puglia. Giolitti meant Salandra to be a stopgap while he reshuffled the pack of his actual and potential supporters. His legendary skill at manipulating the blocs of deputies into viable majorities gave every reason to expect his swift return to power. Yet the lawyer from Puglia was more resolute and devious than Giolitti realised.

The constitution gave the monarch overarching power. He appointed and dismissed government ministers; summoned and dissolved parliament; retained ultimate authority over foreign policy; and commanded the armed forces. He could issue decrees with the force of law, and declare war without consulting parliament. But Victor Emanuel III was reluctant to wield this power. Very short in stature and ill-favoured, he did not cut a regal or martial figure. One of his cruel nicknames was *sciaboletta*, or 'little sabre'; he could not wear a full-length sword, and cartoonists drew the tip of his scabbard resting on a little trolley. When the war started, he wanted to cut the figure of a soldier king, but really preferred coin-collecting and photography. One close observer thought he was 'too modern'; in ordinary life he would have been a republican or socialist by temperament, for he had little faith in the future of the monarchy. Insecure and naïve, he was easily led by forceful personalities. Making matters worse, he was in a nervous depression in 1914, precipitated by fear of losing his adored wife's love. Rumour had it that he was considering abdication.

His views on the national question were moderate, like Giolitti's; he thought Italy should have part of the south Tyrol and Friuli as far as the

River Isonzo, but not Bolzano or Gorizia, let alone Trieste. He would probably have accepted a peaceful solution with Austria if Salandra had not panicked him into believing that the alternative to war was revolution. The real revolution was Salandra's own.

When the Habsburg heir was assassinated in Bosnia at the end of June, Salandra was distracted by the aftermath of workers' protests, known as 'red week', in which strikers paralysed most of Italy's cities and were attacked by troops and police. His foreign minister, Antonio di San Giuliano, was a Sicilian aristocrat who felt little hostility to Austria. He knew Giolitti had warned the Austrians that Italy would not support an attack on Serbia, something that looked increasingly likely as Vienna blamed Belgrade for the assassination. Neither Austria nor Germany involved their ally in their summits. Italy was not invited to the all-important talks at Potsdam on 5 July, when Kaiser Wilhelm gave Vienna the fatal 'blank cheque', promising to back any action against Serbia. When they prepared an ultimatum to Belgrade, setting conditions intended to be unacceptable, they kept the text secret from Italy. This violated the letter of the Triple Alliance.

San Giuliano told Vienna on 10 July that Italy would expect all of Italian-speaking south Tyrol as 'compensation' for the slightest Austrian gain in the Balkans. Although they ignored the warning, the Central Powers were confident of getting Italian support. Inside the bubble of their belligerence, the élites in Vienna and Berlin missed a crucial change in Italy during July: the opinion-making classes ceased to accept the idea of fighting alongside Germany and Austria. Several factors encouraged wishful thinking. San Giuliano's ambassadors in Berlin and Vienna exaggerated their government's loyalty to the Alliance. The coincidental call-up of three Italian classes during July was probably misinterpreted. The German general staff did not understand that their opposite numbers in Italy were under civilian control, so may have overrated the pledge by Italy's new chief of the general staff, General Luigi Cadorna, to respect the army's existing commitments. This mightily reassured the Germans, because Cadorna's predecessor, General Pollio, had been a zealot for the Alliance. He even wanted the three allied armies to agree on joint operations and planning, and called on the Allies to 'act as a single state' – a goal none of them would dream of embracing.

In 1912, the demands of the Libyan campaign led Pollio to rescind Italy's old commitment to send six corps and three cavalry divisions to

Germany if France attacked. A year later he partly restored the pledge, offering two corps. The following April, he stunned the German attaché in Rome by raising the commitment to three corps. This force, he said, would tie down as many French troops as possible while German forces were engaged further north. Then he mused whether Italy should send a separate force to help Vienna, if Serbia attacked Austria when France (perhaps backed by Russia) attacked Germany. While the attaché reeled at the thought of Italian troops fighting for the Habsburg empire, Pollio added an even more heretical thought. 'Is it not more logical for the Alliance to discard false humanitarian sentiment, and start a war which will be imposed on us anyway?' Field Marshal Moltke and General Conrad von Hötzendorf, Pollio's opposite numbers in Berlin and Vienna, could not have expressed the Central Powers' catastrophic fatalism more pithily.

'I almost fell off my seat,' reported the attaché. 'How times have changed!' He wondered if Pollio was too good to be true; maybe he was really angling for Trento and Trieste? But there was no ulterior motive. Giolitti and Salandra might also have fallen off their seats if they had been in the room. Whether Pollio had cleared his proposals with the minister of war – his superior in peacetime – is unclear. The wretched communications between the government and general staff would not improve under his successor.

In addition to the usual veneration of Prussia, Pollio had married an Austrian countess. There was even something Viennese about the man himself: handsome, charming, cultured, the author of well-received military histories. He was no genius; his plan to occupy Libya in 1911 took no account of the Arab population, and assumed the Turkish garrison would head for home rather than retreat to the trackless interior. These were grievous mistakes; the Libyan campaign cost almost 8,000 casualties and soaked up half the gross domestic product that year, and not much less in 1912. Yet he had a penetrating and unorthodox mind. Immune to anti-Habsburg feeling, he believed the Alliance was in Italy's best interest and wanted it to work. Moltke had assured Conrad, whose suspicion of Italians matched his loathing of Serbs, that Pollio should be trusted. Even so, they chose not to inform him fully about Germany's plans for a lightning strike against France and Russia.

One of Moltke's advisors, tasked to study the Italian situation, reported in May that Pollio was an excellent fellow, 'a great mind and a trustworthy man', but he faced internal resistance. The King would be led by his government; France still had many friends in Italy; the historic feud with Austria was not forgotten, and Italy's ambitions in the Adriatic were still lively. 'How long will his influence last?' Death answered the question a mere month later. On 28 June, Pollio boarded a train to Turin where a new field mortar was to be tested. Archduke Franz Ferdinand had been shot in Sarajevo a few hours earlier; when Pollio was told, early next morning, he showed no concern. Next day, he was taken ill with myocarditis and died early on 1 July, carried off by a heart attack. His demise seemed so uncannily timed to harm the Central Powers that Germany suspected foul play. While the Italian officer corps generally supported the Triple Alliance, none of the senior generals shared Pollio's dedication. The Germans knew this, and from mid-July urged the Austrians to reach an understanding with Italy over territory. In vain.

When Cadorna became chief of staff at the end of July, Berlin's relief was short-lived. Rome's signals were being received at last. On 30 July, Austria's ambassador in Berlin reported that a 'state of nervousness' was palpable for the first time, due to fear 'that Italy in the case of a general conflict would not fulfil its duty as an ally'. By August, the German high command was putting the best face on a bad situation. Moltke told the government in Berlin that a demonstration of Alliance unity mattered more than Italy's material contribution. A token force would be enough. Yet Berlin would not lean on Rome, judging that it would be counter-productive unless the Austrians made a positive gesture. The Austrians still deluded themselves that resolute action against Serbia would bring Italy to heel. Italy wanted Austria's promise of 'compensation' before it would consider supporting the Central Powers, while Austria wanted proof of support before it would consider giving any territory – and even then, the south Tyrol was out of the question.

By this point, Italian forces were concentrating towards the French border in accordance with Pollio's plans. On 31 July, Cadorna sent the King a memorandum on the deployment towards France and 'the transport of the largest possible force to Germany'. Meanwhile San Giuliano told the cabinet that, in present conditions, Italy could not fight. No one told the King, who approved Cadorna's memo the following day. By now the Austrians knew they had sparked a European war, and they told the Italians that they could expect compensation if they supported their allies. Conrad cabled Cadorna to ask how he intended to co-operate. Too late! It was 1 August, and the wider conflict had begun. Next day, without even informing Cadorna, the government declared neutrality. It was five days after Austria-Hungary had declared war on Serbia, two days after Russia mobilised, and one day after Germany declared war on Russia.

When he heard the news, Cadorna went to Salandra, who confirmed that fighting France was out of the question. 'So what should I do?' the Chief of Staff asked. Salandra said nothing. 'Prepare for war against Austria?' ventured Cadorna.

'That's right,' said the Prime Minister.

Cadorna began a massive re-deployment to the north-east. The switch had to remain low-key, or the Austrians might lash out pre-emptively – or so Salandra claimed to fear, even though Austria's border with Italy was practically undefended and the Austrians were in no position to divert forces from Serbia and Galicia.

San Giuliano's case for not joining Austria and Germany was solid. Apart from the matter of compensation, the Alliance was a defensive treaty and Austria was the aggressor against Serbia. (Austria's 23 July ultimatum was, he said grandly, 'incompatible with the liberal principles of our public law'.) Moreover, Austria and Germany had violated the Alliance by excluding Italy from their discussions. These objections could have been finessed if the public had roared support for the Triple Alliance, but opinion was broadly anti-Austrian. The government and industry feared the effects of a British naval blockade if Italy joined the Central Powers. Italy depended on Britain and France for raw materials and foodstuffs, and almost all of Italy's coal arrived with other imports through routes controlled by the British navy.

For these reasons, and out of respect for British military power, as well as a feeling that Britain's position on the sidelines during July was like Italy's own, the Italians wanted to see which way London would jump. Britain's entry into the war on 4 August calmed those senior figures who had wondered if it was rash not to support the Central Powers. Looking further ahead, the government feared that whether or not the Powers defeated the Allies, Italy was unlikely to get what it wanted. San Giuliano summed up the conundrum: if Austria fails to win convincingly, it will not be able to compensate us, and, if it does win, it will have no motive to do so. The best course was to wait and watch.

Germany urged Austria to offer enough territory to swing the Italians on-side, or at least stop them joining the enemy. Any concession could be revoked after victory. With late-imperial arrogance, Austria refused to believe that Italy's decision would make a difference. Besides, giving away territory would send a dangerous signal to the empire's other nationalities. The Germans kept pressing the Austrians to reconsider their position on the south Tyrol. Vienna answered irritably that the whole purpose of the war was to preserve the empire; it would be a nonsense to give away one of its most faithful provinces.

On 9 August, San Giuliano broached the possibility that Italy might join the fight against Austria when it was certain of winning. 'This may not be heroic,' he wrote to Salandra, 'but it is wise and patriotic.' On the same day, he opened contacts with London. It was the start of a twin-track diplomacy that lasted for nine and a half months. Germany's successes in France in mid-August froze these overtures.

In terms of élite opinion, September was the decisive month. Salandra leaned toward intervention after a secret meeting on 17 September with Sidney Sonnino, who was in the Prime Minister's 'kitchen cabinet' weeks before he joined the government. So, elsewhere on the spectrum, did a young Socialist firebrand called Benito Mussolini. When the Germans failed to break France's resistance on the Marne, in mid-September, San Giuliano recognised that the Central Powers' bid for a crushing victory in the West had failed. The balance of likely victory tipped away from the Central Powers, never to be restored, despite stunning local successes. 'Their famous lightning strike has misfired,' he told a journalist. 'There is no question that our interest is for neither side to win an overwhelming victory.' The ideal outcome, in fact – he added, humorously – would be for both Austria *and* France, the two historic opponents of Italian unification, to lose! Salandra said privately that Italy should use the 'historic cataclysm' to 'resolve some of its principal problems'. He also remarked that the Triple Alliance was morally dead.

Italy's ambassadors in Vienna and Berlin did not share this view; they were exasperated by the government's secrecy and dismayed by its perceptible shift towards the Entente. Even if Italy was not bound to support its allies, it was morally obliged to stand alongside them. They deplored the 'enormous pressure' from 'the noisiest and most turbulent part of public opinion and the press'. Instead of resisting, the government and the sovereign let themselves twist in the wind whipped up by 'a hundred journalists', led by the *Corriere della Sera*. Like Giolitti, these ambassadors failed to see that Salandra was the master of this situation, not its victim. What they saw as weakness was finely calibrated judgement. He now applied shrewd pressure on the King, advising him at the end of September that the government was duty-bound to seize this chance to 'complete and enlarge the fatherland'. He said that the South Slavs, Romania and Turkey would all profit from Austria's defeat or diminishment in the Balkans, and predicted with only partial exaggeration that victory for the Central Powers would mean 'servitude' for Italy, killing the chances of redeeming the south Tyrol and Trieste, let alone expansion further afield. Whatever happened, Italy must not end up on the losing side. Noting that the general staff favoured going to war in the spring, Salandra remarked that 'a real national war' would do wonders for the poor morale of the army.

In mid-October, death removed someone else who might have curbed Salandra's appetite for war. San Giuliano, the foreign minister, had been ailing for months. Lucid to the end, he told a journalist that if Italy intervened, her fate after the war would be dismal: the Central Powers would hate her, blaming her for their defeat, while the Allies would want to forget Italy's contribution, if any. Much of this prophecy would come true. Salandra took over the portfolio for a fortnight, during which he uttered the only phrase for which he is still remembered: *sacro egoismo*, 'sacred egoism'. This principle, he said, must guide foreign policy. His enemies pounced on the phrase; national interests should be decisive, but calling them 'sacred' was a nationalist twist, and branding them as 'egoism' appealed to those who saw politics as a mystical arena where national identities were locked in struggle.

Sidney Sonnino became foreign minister in early November, pledging to uphold 'vigilant neutrality'. Raised as a Protestant by his converted Jewish father and Scottish or Welsh mother, Sonnino was an outsider in Italian politics. He served two brief terms as prime minister before 1914. A taciturn man with no penchant for ideas, he never apologised and certainly never explained. Nevertheless, he rose in the war to become Catholic Italy's most important civilian leader. At this stage, his and Salandra's real objective could not be admitted. Parliament and the public wanted neutrality, as did the Church, and the army was not ready for war.[1] Even so, the Socialists smelled a rat; by early November, the party newspaper *Avanti!* tagged Salandra as 'the minister for war'.

---

1 Many in Rome still saw the Habsburg dynasty – led by 'His Apostolic Majesty', the Emperor – as the mainstay of Catholic values. The leader of the Catholic bloc in parliament, Paolo Boselli, who became prime minister in 1916, even claimed that Austria's aggression against Serbia had not nullified the Triple Alliance.

Berlin sent a senior figure to try to persuade Italy to stay neutral. Prince Bernhard von Bülow, a former chancellor, was convinced the Central Powers had mishandled their former ally. Germany should have foreseen Austria's refusal to take the Italians seriously. This was true, but he arrived with nothing but his good offices, seeking concessions without anything up his sleeve. Franz Josef refused to give up the south Tyrol, but he was very old; the Italians should wait calmly and let nature take its course. Bülow did not see that this was impossible. Europe was being torn apart by a war without precedent; whatever the outcome, and even if the fighting only lasted a few months or a year, as most people still expected, the prewar order would not be restored. Many middle-class Italians were convinced that they *must* strike, now or never.

In January, Sonnino itemised Italy's demands to Vienna. Trentino and Friuli as far as the River Isonzo should be transferred to Italy, while Trieste should be autonomous and neutralised, with no occupying forces. Pretending not to hear, the Austrians said that compensation should only involve Albania, in which Italy did indeed want a stake, as shown by its occupation of the port of Valona (now Vlorë) in December. As Austria did not control Albania, the retort was doubly irrelevant. Bülow did not help by suggesting the Italians would be satisfied by getting a fraction of the south Tyrol, because they accepted that Trieste was Austria's lung. The Austrians suspected the German mediator had gone native.

Early in February, Giolitti went public with his misgivings. Italy could, he said, obtain 'a good deal' of what it wanted without fighting. His statement was mere common sense to most Italians:

I certainly don't consider war to be a blessing, as the nationalists do, but as a misfortune that must only be faced when the honour and great interests of the country require it. I do not think it is legitimate to take the country to war because of feelings about other peoples. Anyone is free to throw his own life away for an emotion, but not the country.

Italy's vital interests were not at stake: the Trentino would drop into its hands sooner or later, the Isonzo would become the north-eastern border and a compromise would be found for Trieste. Why, then, go to war? For Salandra and Sonnino, however, vital interests required mastery of the Adriatic. The south Tyrol, the Isonzo valley and Trieste were only the start; they wanted Istria and Dalmatia, virtual control of Albania, and a strong role in the Balkan hinterland. Austria would never grant these demands; even the Allies might balk at them.

That Giolitti, with all his acumen, did not grasp the scale of Salandra's and Sonnino's ambition gives a measure of their secrecy, and how far from mainstream opinion they wanted to take the country. If they could turn the Adriatic into an Italian lake, they would ensure Balkan and Mediterranean markets, expunge the failures in Africa, and vault into a seat at Europe's top table. Victor Emanuel came to accept that, if parliament stood in the way, it should be bypassed. This freed Salandra from accountability to a broadly hostile chamber. On 15 February, Sonnino notified Vienna that military action in the Balkans without prior agreement on compensation had violated the Triple Alliance. This message was purely for the record, clearing the way to seek counter-offers from the Allies. An envoy was despatched to London the next day.

The opening of parliament in late February 1915 triggered pro- and anti-war rallies around the country. By putting his head above the parapet after the Socialist Party had split over the war, Giolitti became the leading neutralist and the target of ferocious attacks. The press shrieked that neutrality was 'suicide'. Under this pressure, his judgement lapsed. After receiving Salandra's assurance that war was conceivable only as a last resort and he would keep Sonnino on a tight leash, Giolitti urged his followers to trust the government. Nagging ill health, as well as a temperamental inability to ride the nationalist storm, explain his gullibility.

Sonnino told Salandra that 1 March should be the deadline for Austrian offers. On that date, the general staff announced a 'red alert', putting the army on a war footing without the publicity of a mobilisation. Sonnino warned that the Allies were making headway against Turkey (a hopeful reading of the Allied operations in the Dardanelles); this was worrying because he and Salandra wanted a piece of Turkey for themselves. Also, Bulgaria and Greece might intervene at any moment, while 'in London', he added testily, 'we haven't even opened negotiations!'

Their proposal to the Allies was secretly presented in London on 28 February. Italy's reward for joining the Allies should be the south Tyrol up to the Brenner Pass; Trieste and Gorizia; Istria; Dalmatia and most of its islands; Valona, in Albania (which should become 'a small neutralised Muslim autonomous state'), and the Dodecanese Islands, between Greece and Turkey, which Italy already occupied. The coast south of Kotor bay should be 'neutralised'. Acceptance of Italy's interest in the balance of power throughout the Mediterranean should be respected.

Italy should receive territory if the Ottoman Empire were to be dissolved. It wanted a British war loan of £50 million and war indemnities.

News of the proposal reached Berlin and Vienna, whose agents kept them better informed than the Italian cabinet. Nudged again by Germany, the Austrians finally stirred themselves to offer the Trentino and a border on the Isonzo, after the war. When Italy insisted that the territory had to change hands at once, the proposals withered on the table.

The Allies, meanwhile, were unhappy with three of Italy's demands: for Dalmatia, for the Montenegrin and Albanian coast to be 'neutralised', and for a Muslim Albanian statelet. Salandra took stock in a candid letter to Sonnino. They were heading for an open rupture with the Central Powers without the King's consent or any agreement with the Allies. The country did not support them, and the army would not be battle-ready before the end of April, or probably later. They should apply the brakes; neither the King nor parliament was ready to take a clear position, so they should keep parleying with the Central Powers, 'pretending we believe a favourable outcome is possible', until the army was ready and they had agreed terms with the Allies. In the end, he wrote, 'we two alone' would have to decide when 'to play this terrible card'.

The Allies answered formally on 20 March. Dalmatia was the sticking point: the Russians objected that Italy's claims would lead to war with Serbia in future. What Rome called strategic self-defence, Russia denounced as expansion. Sonnino, who always denied any imperialist motive, argued that the western Adriatic coast was indefensible against the deep harbours and myriad islands of the eastern Adriatic. He explained to the British ambassador that military supremacy in the Adriatic had become Italy's main incentive to join the Allies. As Salandra was telling Bülow the same thing, the Central Powers knew where Italy stood. Vienna took this as confirming that negotiations were pointless; if Austria could only buy Italy's neutrality by abolishing itself as an Adriatic power, there was nothing to discuss.

Salandra believed the Allied failure to force the Dardanelles in mid-March had given Italy extra leverage. So it proved when British and French diplomats urged Russia to let Italy have 'effective control of the Adriatic'. It was, they said, a price worth paying. The British foreign secretary, Sir Edward Grey, argued that Italy's intervention 'probably would, in a comparatively short time, effect the collapse of German and Austro-Hungarian resistance'. A fortnight later, he predicted that it would be the turning point of the war, partly by bringing Romania and

Bulgaria off the fence into the Allied camp. (To colleagues in London, he also argued the benefit of preventing a future single 'great Slav power' – meaning Russia – from controlling the eastern Adriatic.) Italy's terms should be accepted without delay. The French were just as enthusiastic; they had poured money into the pro-war campaign, bankrolling Mussolini's new newspaper and paying off the demagogic poet D'Annunzio's debts in Paris.[2]

The Russians were truculent. Italy had ducked the worst of the war, they complained, and Austria-Hungary could now be beaten without its help. They themselves – having come into the war because of Serbia – wanted the Serbs to have free access to the Adriatic after the war. Besides, Dalmatia had more than half a million Slavs and only 18,000 Italians: how could Rome justify its claim? Privately, the British élite was just as contemptuous; ministers felt the Italians had 'blackmailed' them. Prime Minister Asquith remarked that 'Russia is quite right, but it is so important to bring Italy in at once, greedy and slippery as she is, that we ought not to be too precise in haggling over this or that.' Elsewhere he referred to 'that most voracious, slippery and perfidious Power'. This abuse was matched by his navy minister, Winston Churchill, who described Italy as 'the harlot of Europe'. Admiral Fisher, Britain's irascible First Sea Lord, scorned the Italians as 'mere organ-grinders! No use whatever.' To Lloyd George, they were 'the most contemptible nation'.

With rumours circulating that Austria and perhaps Germany were about to reach a separate peace with Russia, Salandra and Sonnino were on tenterhooks. Would they intervene too late to grab their portions of territory? The outlook was not improved when Austria – yielding to German pressure, abetted by bad news from the Eastern Front – agreed on 27 March to cede the south Tyrol (without Alto Adige), make Trieste autonomous, withdraw to the Isonzo, approve the occupation of Valona, and discuss Gorizia. Sonnino rejected this offer – which exceeded his demands in January – as 'dubious and absolutely inadequate'. Fearing that he might have overpriced Italy's support, he dropped the demand for Spalato (now Split), Dalmatia's biggest city,

2 On 1 May, accused by a British journalist of having betrayed the Yugoslavs with this 'wretched "pound-of-flesh" convention', the French foreign minister protested that 'Italy put a pistol to our heads. Think what it means. Within a month there will be a million Italian bayonets in the field, and shortly thereafterwards 600,000 Romanians. Reinforcements as large as that may be worth some sacrifice, even of principle.'

which the proposal had called 'the seat of glorious Latin civilisation and fervent Italian patriotism'. The Allies called on him to let Dalmatia be neutralised. He refused.

The new German Chief of Staff, General Erich von Falkenhayn, urged Conrad to withdraw from the Trentino at once. This would keep Italy neutral and could be revoked after the war. If the Central Powers lost, the territory would go anyway; the urgent thing was to disperse the 'negative constellation' looming over their heads. No, rejoined Conrad, this would not satisfy the ex-allies, who were planning a big offensive against the 'heart of the monarchy'. He was right on both counts. Although unwilling to buy off the Italians, Conrad and his government were too disengaged and contemptuous to wonder what would happen if the traitors in Rome got a better offer elsewhere. Italy kept the illusion alive by not breaking off negotiations.

The Russians finally accepted that Dalmatia south of Split might be neutralised under Serbian sovereignty. Grey announced the good news on 10 April. With the major issues resolved, the diplomats focused on the detail. Salandra, meanwhile, instructed Italy's regional governors to prepare secret reports on popular attitudes to fighting Austria. The result was an extraordinary snapshot of public opinion. In general, people were only ready to accept the prospect of war if it was a struggle for national survival against foreign invaders. Most people's neutralism was spontaneous and passive. Anti-war feeling was strongest among peasant farmers, for whom war was a calamity like famine or plague. Even for middle-class Italians, who provided most of the pro-war passion, strong feelings about Trento and Trieste were the exception. In most places, only the intellectuals were pro-war; business leaders were not.

Neutralist opinion was strongest in the south, including Salandra's home province of Puglia. In parts of Sardinia, the peasants and workers openly criticised the warmongers. In Naples, the governor reckoned that 90 per cent of all social classes were anti-war. As another governor pointed out, nobody had invaded their homeland, the south had no historic scores to settle, the previous year's harvest had been poor, and the European war had blocked emigration – the traditional escape from poverty. The south was suffering already; why should anyone want an unnecessary war? In the north, the Socialists gave a backbone to neutralism, yet a broader vein of anti-Austrian feeling offset this. Only in Bologna did the governor warn that failure to intervene might create unrest. (So much for the danger of revolution.) At the same time, the governors reported high levels of trust in the government – thanks above all to the policy of neutrality which it was about to overturn! If war were declared, people would do their duty. This was the bottom line: the masses would fight.

With the Allies piling pressure on Rome, the final wrinkles were ironed out. As signed on 26 April, the Treaty of London stated that, in exchange for committing all its resources to fighting the enemies of France, Great Britain and Russia within 30 days, Italy 'will receive' all of south Tyrol, Trieste, Gorizia, Istria, Dalmatia down to Trogir, near Spalato, plus most of the islands further south to Dubrovnik. This unconditional promise, not to be found in the Allies' other secret treaties, was a measure of Italy's importance.[3]

These lands were home to some 230,000 German-speaking Austrians and up to 750,000 Slovenes and Croats, far outnumbering the 650,000 native Italians. Additionally, Italy would get Valona, giving her control over the Straits of Otranto, gateway to the Mediterranean; sovereignty over the Dodecanese Islands; and a guaranteed interest in a province of Turkey if the Ottoman Empire disintegrated. If Britain and France enlarged their African colonies, Italy would be 'equitably compensated' with territory for its own colonies: Libya, Eritrea and Somaliland. The loan of £50 million – later described by one of Sonnino's advisors as 'derisory' – was reckoned enough to underwrite the short triumphant campaign that everyone expected.

The treaty pledged its signatories to secrecy. On 1 May, Sonnino called on the cabinet to repudiate the Triple Alliance, so that Italy could seal an agreement with the Allies – an agreement that ministers did not know was already in his pocket. The repudiation followed on 4 May. Next day, the poet D'Annunzio gave a well-trailed, bloodcurdling speech in Genoa. Even though Salandra kept the King and his ministers away from Genoa, the portent was clear to everybody. Cadorna hurried to Salandra's office. 'But this means immediate war!' he said. 'Yes indeed,' said the Prime Minister, 'we have to go to war by the 26th of this month.'

'What! But I don't know anything about it!'

'Well, you should hurry up . . .'

In a last bid to avert war, the Vatican persuaded Vienna to reiterate its offer of 27 March, bolstered with German guarantees. But the

---

3 Probably at Russia's insistence, the port of Fiume was assigned to 'Croatia, Serbia and Montenegro'. This provision would return to poison the peace settlement in 1919.

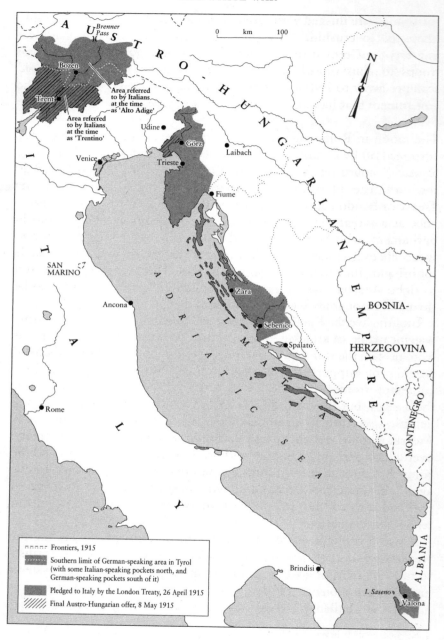

Territory promised to Italy by the Allies in April 1915

Austrians were flushed with recent success over the Russians and more interested in crushing Italy than bargaining. Berlin, too, had lost interest; the German foreign minister wished they only had enough troops 'to rebuff those knaves'. After the first clash, he said, they would scamper away to southern Italy and the people would overthrow the government that had pitched them into a senseless war.

The mood in Rome was so volatile that the Austrian embassy was cordoned off by cavalry and infantry with bayonets fixed. After a long absence, Giolitti returned on 9 May for the opening of parliament on the 12th. The interventionists, both those few who knew about the Treaty of London and the many who did not, saw Giolitti's reappearance as a threat. But he was hailed by a majority of the deputies in parliament, who hoped he would restore the opposition's unity and focus. He told a journalist, off the record, that the ministers responsible for bringing Italy to this pass should be shot. There was no good reason to fight; Austria's last offer was acceptable;[4] Sonnino claimed to be saving the monarchy when it was not in danger.

Giolitti gave the King and Salandra the benefit of his views. The army was incapable of attacking and winning; the Central Powers were far from beaten; the war would last longer than people realised; parliament would not support the London terms; Italy's calculations drew contempt from both sides. ('Our new allies will be pleased for themselves, but they will despise us.') The government should let the deputies overturn its promise to the Allies, then resume talks with Austria. Giolitti did not realise that Italy was bound by a state treaty, over which parliament had no authority to arbitrate. Salandra and the King chose not to inform him. He had overrated the King and now, again, he underrated Salandra, who pushed back the opening of parliament to 20 May and on the 13th, persuaded the entire cabinet to tender its resignation.

It was a brilliant move. Historians still interpret it as proving the weakness of his position. In reality, Salandra was daring the neutralists to take the reins of government in an atmosphere of pro-war hysteria and incipient violence. He believed the neutralists were too divided to accept the challenge; by backing down, they would destroy their

4 He mistakenly believed this offer included Gorizia and some Dalmatian islands. When the journalist corrected him, Giolitti went red in the face and shouted, 'Salandra lied to me! Just like a Puglian!'

[33]

credibility. His gambit fooled almost everyone. Cadorna, out of the picture as ever, was shocked. Again he sought out Salandra. 'What are we doing?' he asked.

'I don't know what to tell you,' said Salandra demurely. 'I may not even be prime minister any longer. Anyway I cannot give you orders.'

'But the whole army is on the move,' Cadorna protested. 'Austria is wide awake to everything.'

Salandra agreed, and shrugged: 'I cannot let you prepare for a war that may not happen.'

'What! Should I call off the mobilisation?' asked Cadorna, referring to the eight corps that he had quietly mobilised on 23 April, and started moving to the north-east on 4 May.

'Yes.'

'But, Excellency, consider what a disaster it will be if Austria beats us to it! Do you really think it is possible to stop the mechanism just like that? At least let me continue the measures in hand; let the mobilisation take its course.'

'No,' said Salandra, 'I cannot do that.' He was determined to break the will of the anti-war deputies, whatever the military cost.

Incredibly, Italy was at war within a fortnight of this conversation. The last months of neutrality could have been used as cover to initiate a discreet mobilisation, allowing Cadorna to explode across the border when war was declared. While this could not have ensured a quick victory, it would have hugely increased Italy's chances of breaking through and seizing Trieste in 1915.

Any appetite Giolitti had felt for a showdown was spoiled when Victor Emanuel argued that the honour of the monarchy was pledged to fulfilling the Treaty of London. If the King and Prime Minister were set on war, he could only oppose them by rallying the opposition into a force that would shout as loudly as its opponents. For this, he lacked both the nerve and the populist skills at a moment when the interventionists, unaware of the Treaty of London, thought Italy might still opt to stay out of the war. The historian George Trevelyan saw 'hundreds of thousands of good people of all classes' filling the streets of Rome and other cities, 'intoning with a slow and interminable repetition, "Death to Giolitti, Death to Giolitti."' Bands of students chanted 'Up with war!', 'Up with D'Annunzio!' Theatres put on anti-neutralist sketches. The press screamed for war. Mussolini, the turncoat warmonger, accused both Giolitti and the government of 'sabotaging the Nation's spiritual preparation for war'. Giolitti decided it was impossible to accept the King's invitation to form a new government. On the 16th, the King rejected Salandra's resignation. The government was reinstated and Giolitti stumped home to Piedmont, complaining about Salandra ('it has all been a trick, in true Puglian style').

Salandra was reinstated and the King threatened to abdicate if parliament opposed intervention. A right-wing commentator described the pending decision in the typical apocalyptic terms that made sober debate impossible:

Either Parliament will defeat the Nation and take up its trade prostituting Her sacred trembling body to the foreigner, or the Nation will overthrow Parliament, overturning the benches of the moneylenders, purifying the dens of the pimps and panders with iron and fire.

On 20 May, parliament ratified the decision to go to war. Two days later, it bound and gagged itself by authorising the government to issue decrees with the force of law on any issues concerning 'defence of the State, maintenance of public order and the urgent needs of the national economy'. The Socialist bloc found itself alone in opposing the bill; resistance from the liberal and Catholic blocs had melted away. Even Filippo Turati, the Socialist leader, sounded beaten: 'Let the Italian bourgeoisie have its war . . . there will be no winners, everyone will lose.'

On 23 May, Italy's Ambassador Avarna in Vienna – who privately fumed against Salandra's 'swinish and faithless' policy – told the Austrian government that Italy would be at war with Austria-Hungary from midnight.[5] 'It is the last war of independence', trumpeted the *Corriere della Sera*. 'Generous Italian blood prepares to trace the fulfilment of our destiny with indelible lines.' In Rome, Cadorna embraced Salandra before cheering crowds at the railway station and set off for his headquarters in Udine. The weather was fine and clear, though still cold in the mountains.

Neutrality was a façade behind which Salandra had played both ends against the middle, a means to something else – but what? Irredentism

5 Italy's decision not to declare war on Germany – hoping against reason to avoid fighting Austria's dreaded ally – was its first violation of the terms of the Treaty of London, and cost the government in Allied goodwill. When German troops were captured on Italian soil, in the Dolomites, the government turned a blind eye. Rome declared war on Berlin in August 1916, after capturing Gorizia.

was the ostensible goal, invaluable for motivating patriots and as a label for Italy's war aims. 'Trento and Trieste!' was the cry that went up from columns of new recruits, the names daubed on troop trains, not 'Dalmatia and Valona!' Italy's plunge to war was decided by a blend of great power ambition and Salandra's belief that a short, victorious war would seal his premiership. For Salandra was not obsessed by territory. He later denied having ever believed that Italy would benefit from gaining Dalmatia or the Tyrol north of Bolzano; they were to be bargaining chips after the war.

His project was something else; he wanted to move Italian politics permanently to the right by building a new anti-Socialist bloc of northern industrialists and southern landowners, who both wanted markets abroad and civic discipline at home. A genuine reactionary, Salandra aspired – as he put it in memoirs that were written, admittedly, under Fascism – to purge liberalism of its democratic 'dross'. In today's terms, he was a neo-conservative, promoting business over social justice while launching military adventures abroad. As has often been observed, intervention was a response to internal pressure, meant as a solution to internal problems. The crisis caused by 'red week' in June 1914 was formative for his premiership, and the advent of the European war a few weeks later was an opportunity that he could not pass up. For 'only a war, with a phase of compulsory peace on the labour front and the militarisation of society, would permit the hierarchical reorganisation of class relations'. The same analysis was made long ago by Italy's great liberal thinker, Benedetto Croce; intervention, Croce argued, was meant to supplant the liberal order with an authoritarian regime, 'a modern plutocracy, unencumbered with ideologies and scruples'.

It was not only élite politicians with ulterior motives who feared standing aside when Europe's fate hung in the balance. Events themselves strengthened the belief that Italy's whole history made war inevitable. When two members of the Garibaldi family died fighting with the French army in December 1914, their funeral in Rome drew 300,000 mourners. The interventionists could argue that their cause fulfilled Italy's republican tradition as well as its national aspirations. In other words, even if fighting Austria proved to be a colossal mistake, it was a *necessary* mistake, one that self-respecting patriots should be ready to commit.[6]

6 Alfredo Panzini, a professor from Pesaro, caught this mood in his diary: 'We know that three-quarters of parliament do not want war, and three-quarters of the nation too: they endure it as an *ananke* [force of destiny]. But it really is an *ananke*: *(continued opposite)*

The interventionist camp was diverse and potentially fractious, what with its neo-conservatives, industrialists wanting new markets as a valve for chronic over-production, doctrinaire nationalists committed to 'Greater Italy', cultural chauvinists, devotees of renewal through bloodshed, proto-fascists shrieking for expansion to accommodate the fertile Italian 'race', democratic anti-imperialists, syndicalist revolutionaries, and Mazzinian idealists. While they bridged their differences to get Italy into the war, their rivals were incapable of such discipline. The Socialists and the Vatican could not make common cause; Giolitti could not forge an anti-war front; nobody could turn neutrality into stirring rhetoric. Italy was full of citizens who did not want to intervene, yet no way existed to leverage their opposition. It is a problem as old as politics, and still intractable.

In the end the Allies wanted Italy *in* the war more than the Central Powers wanted it *out*. One way and another, Austria helped to ensure the outcome that its Chief of Staff always thought was unavoidable. The Triple Alliance was damaged past repair by Austria's refusal to compensate Italy after annexing Bosnia and Herzegovina in 1908. Excluding Italy during July 1914 finished it off. Although the Germans leaned on their allies to make a better offer, they were not surprised by Italy's stance. After all, Moltke had never counted on Italian support; there were no detailed plans for joint mobilisation – just as there were no German–Austrian plans for simultaneous mobilisation against Russia, Serbia and Italy.

Bülow looked back sadly at the whole saga. He bitterly regretted that Germany had not leaned harder ('we have been the horse instead of the rider'). The weird inevitability that overhung the July crisis affected the Powers' treatment of Italy. They acted as if Rome's disloyalty was automatic. Even though Vienna's attack on Serbia released Italy from its obligations, Italy might have been deterred from joining the Allies by an early compromise over Trentino and Trieste. Germany saw more clearly than Austria, perhaps because its vision was not blurred by loathing. But Vienna easily absorbed Berlin's fitful pressure. Half a dozen years earlier, when he was chancellor, Bülow had admitted that Italy might not stand with its two allies in a European conflagration. Yet, in his view, there was no question of the Italians attacking Austria-Hungary;

everyone feels this . . . It is a terrible moment. A nation that isn't provoked, is not attacked, indeed is being flattered, has to find the strength to throw itself into such a conflict!'
(11 May 1915)

they lacked strength or boldness for that. In May 1915, the Italians discovered this boldness.

Two and a half years later, after the disaster of October 1917, a staff officer who served Cadorna loyally throughout the war confided some angry thoughts to his diary. Italy's involvement in the war now looked ill-starred, tainted by falsehood from the outset.

This whole war has been a heap of lies [wrote Colonel Gatti]. We came into the war because a few men in authority, 'the dreamers', flung us into it. They could not accept that you don't do politics by dreaming. Politics is reality. You don't stake the future of a nation on a dream, a yearning for reinvigoration. It is idiotic to imagine that war can be a means of healing.

The chief spokesman of this dreaming – this idiocy – was not a politician at all, or even a soldier. It was, as we shall see, a famous poet.

THREE

Free Spirits

'There's no such thing as a Latin. That is
"Latin" thinking. You are so proud of your
defects.' Rinaldi looked up and laughed.
HEMINGWAY, *A Farewell to Arms* (1929)

D'Annunzio and Mussolini: Demagogues for War

Salandra and Sonnino had no more charisma than the King. Incapable of stirring the crowds themselves, and still needing (as members of a minority government) to keep the extreme warmongers at arm's length, they wanted to turn their conspiracy into a mass movement. Even with the support of the press, the agitators and intellectuals could not reach a broad enough public. Eventually this vital task was contracted to Gabriele D'Annunzio.

Between the death of Verdi in 1901 and Mussolini's march on Rome in 1922, D'Annunzio became the most famous Italian in the world. Born in 1863, he started publishing verse in his teens. By his thirties, he was the country's best-known poet, most acclaimed novelist and glittering dramatist. He had a matchless ear for the mellifluous, incantatory qualities of the language. Artistically bold and highly intelligent, he owned all the talents for a brilliant career. An exuberant, insatiably acquisitive personality, he lived in fine villas and had countless love affairs. Magnetised by his reputation, society ladies reserved rooms in hotels where he stayed, hoping to catch his eye. He was a committed dandy; his collars were the stiffest, his creases the sharpest, his buttonhole carnations the whitest. His greyhounds wore livery tailored by Hermès. His correspondence with his jeweller has been published as a separate volume. Even his debts were legendary.

His status was always controversial. Accusations of plagiarism were hard to shake off. In Rome, the Catholic Church placed his works – rife with decadent sensuality – on the Index of Prohibited Books. In Dublin, the student James Joyce claimed that D'Annunzio had broken new ground in fiction. (He would later call him one of the three greatest natural talents among nineteenth-century writers.) In London – where at least one of his plays was banned – Henry James reviewed his novels. In Paris, the young Marcel Proust hailed him as a great writer. His steadiest biographer, John Woodhouse, catches the glitter of his celebrity before the flight to France in 1910: 'For almost thirty years not a week had passed without D'Annunzio's name appearing in the newspapers, and for almost as long his name had been held before the public thanks to the undeniable fact that his works had been on display in the windows of every bookseller in Italy.' In short, he acquired fame, salted with notoriety, on the scale that Byron and Liszt had enjoyed: glamour of the kind now reserved to film stars, rock musicians or footballers.

If this glamour is now hard to convey, it is partly because his work has become almost unreadable. Love lyrics, idylls on classical themes, patriotic dramas, and trashily plotted novels about supermen figures who are transparently the author himself: D'Annunzio's output was formally varied, but the variety is skin-deep. Mummified at its centre lies an effigy of the poet himself. The hosts of characters in his collected works are, with few exceptions, shadows or silhouettes, denied individuation by the monotonous gaudiness of his language, styled to hypnotise and overmaster a reader. The historical themes and political ideas that he discusses are ciphers of himself, pretexts for rapture. Meanwhile the waves of swooning rhetoric roll on, rising to crescendos of alliteration before subsiding in cycles as incessant and oceanic as the poet's self-regard. It was an ideal style to promote a policy of 'sacred egoism'.

D'Annunzio was a spectacular case of arrested emotional development, arguably a natural fascist. The otherness of other people – a puzzle that haunts modern thought and art – could not fascinate him because other people existed as objects of appetite or will, research opportunities in a quest to investigate the effects of denying himself nothing. The lovers he venerated came to repel him when sex led to expectations that limited his freedom. The actress Eleonora Duse, herself an international celebrity, was lavish with inspiration and money for nine years. Among the surviving shreds of their correspondence is an exchange from summer 1904, when the relationship foundered. Reproached by Duse, who was driven to despair by his infidelities and excuses, D'Annunzio found nothing to regret: 'The imperious needs of a violent, carnal life, of pleasure, of physical risk, of happiness, have kept me from you. And you ... can you cry shame on me for these needs of mine?'

Duse's reply still carries a charge:

Do not speak to me of the imperious 'reason' of your 'carnal' life, of your thirst for 'joyous existence'. I am tired of hearing those words. I have heard you repeat them for years now: I can neither entirely go along with your philosophy nor entirely understand it. What love can you find which is worthy or profound if it lives only for pleasure?

Her question would have made no sense to D'Annunzio, who found a philosophical alibi for egotism in a selective reading of Friedrich Nietzsche. He had no use for Nietzsche the prophet of radical uncertainty, unstitching the assumptions of Western philosophy, the mocker of 'profundity', the ironic psychologist, the teasing critic of repression by grammar. For D'Annunzio, as for the German and Italian fascists after him, Nietzsche was the champion of life as endless expression, the revaluer of good and evil, scorning normal experience, unmasking Christian 'slave morality', and the discoverer of the Will to Power as the wellspring of human motivation.

Above all, he was the author of the concept of the Superman. D'Annunzio's first book to show the impact of Nietzsche's ideas was *The Triumph of Death* (1894). The novel's hero, Giorgio, is haunted by his search for someone who can be 'the strong and tyrannical master, free of the yoke of every false morality, secure in the feeling of his own power ... determined to lift himself above Good and Evil through the sheer energy of his will, capable even of forcing life to keep its promises.' *The Virgins of the Rocks* followed in 1895, replete with Nietzschean insights:

The world is the representation of the sensibility and the thought of a few superior men, who have created and adorned it in the course of time and will go on adding to it and adorning it further in future. The world as it appears today is a magnificent gift bestowed by the few upon the many, by free men upon slaves: by those who think and feel upon those who must labour.

D'Annunzio detested socialism. For him the emancipation of the masses was an absurdity, if not a crime.

While the dust settled long ago on the incestuous and sado-masochistic traces in his work, his career in the First World War has gained a power to appal. The whiff of sulphur around his name has transferred from his sex life and steamy novels to his politico-military career. For he emerged in 1915 as the figurehead of the intervention campaign, and went on to become the country's most publicised and decorated soldier. Daring exploits with aeroplanes and torpedo boats lifted his popularity to new heights; he became a full-blown national hero. The sordid aspects of his past – adulteries, illegitimate children, trails of creditors – were obscured by the blaze of glory conferred by the press, the military and politicians.

D'Annunzio's embrace of war in 1915 was predestined. An outspoken patriot all his life, he attacked Austria as an oppressor of subject peoples, but his real commitment was to Italy's imperial mission in the Adriatic basin and beyond. He loved the idea that Italy should control the entire Dalmatian coast. He complained that Austria was crushing Italy's 'left lung' – its north-eastern territories. Economic or demographic arguments against these maximalist claims could not touch him; for his position rested on faith in 'Latin genius' and the superiority of 'Latin' civilisation.

As Italy was duty-bound to assert itself as a great power, it had to build up its armed forces. In his journalism, D'Annunzio had called since the late 1880s for Italy to develop its navy ('Italy will be a great naval power or it will be nothing'). Favouring war on principle, he was thrilled by the Libyan campaign of 1911, and wrote a series of commemorative poems for *Corriere della Sera*, swiping at Austria as well as Turkey. One poem, 'The Song of the Dardanelles', was censored by the government, on the grounds that its attack on Austria was dangerous to Italy's strategic interests. (In a typical flourish, he likened the double-headed imperial eagle to 'the head of a vulture which vomits the undigested flesh of its victims'.) D'Annunzio did not forgive Prime Minister Giolitti for this affront.

By this point, *Corriere* was his preferred outlet in Italy. Its editor, Luigi Albertini, became a confidant. He paid off some of his debts, and warned that his creditors would take every penny if he returned. During 1913 and 1914, D'Annunzio wrote desultory pieces for *Corriere*, trying to fend off his French creditors. He had tired of his current principal mistress, a Russian countess. In short, he was hankering for change when Germany attacked France, a clash that he saw as 'almost divine' in scope, a 'struggle of races, an opposition of irreconcilable powers, a trial of blood'. He wrote to Albertini at the end of August that 'destiny' appeared to be shaping events 'like a sublime tragic poet'. He refused to leave Paris, instead laying in a stock of tinned food, filing articles to *Corriere* and seeking official permission to visit the front. He hailed the successful French resistance on the Marne as a miracle.

Italy's rightful place, in his view, was with the Allies. He told friends that he would end his 'exile' when Italy declared war, but his confidence in this longed-for outcome wavered. Then, out of the blue, in March 1915, a letter held out an opportunity to return in proper style, giving the countess and his creditors the slip. He was invited to speak at the unveiling of a monument to Garibaldi and his volunteers, on 5 May, at the spot near Genoa where the heroes had set sail to conquer Sicily in 1860. The King and his ministers were to be present. At the same time he was contacted by Peppino Garibaldi, grandson of the great man. Peppino had led a brigade of Italian volunteers fighting with the French. After heavy losses, the brigade was disbanded on 5 March. D'Annunzio was contacted by French government figures to assist with a propaganda project: the surviving volunteers would be re-equipped, given new red (Garibaldian) shirts, and sent back to Italy to shout for intervention.

Providence was taking a hand. He would lead the volunteers home and be flanked by them when he made a glorious speech at Genoa, reclaiming the place in national life that was his due. He recorded his excitement in a notebook: 'To arrive not as an ordinary speaker but as the leader of Youth, mediator between two generations!' Everything *ordinary* carried a pejorative reek, while *youth* was a token of everything vital and masterful. He arranged for *Corriere* to publish the oration on the day of its delivery. The text was also sent to the Prime Minister. Under pressure from the Vatican and the German embassy, which was still hoping the Italians could be bought off, Salandra and his ministers kept a prudent distance from D'Annunzio's calls for the 'enslaved lands' of Trieste, Istria, the Adriatic and Trento to be liberated. Excuses were found for the King to break his engagement.

On 3 May, D'Annunzio boarded a train in Paris. Although Albertini subsidised the trip, he raised more funds by pawning emeralds that Duse had given him. His Italian biographers still see his arrival in Italy in the poet's own grandiose terms: cometh the hour, cometh the man.[1] At the time, however, D'Annunzio expected to return to France after a round

---

[1] Here is a wartime propagandist's hilarious account: 'Almost in voluntary exile, and rapt in his sublime visions, he seemed to have forgotten his beautiful fatherland. But no, as soon as the first signs of the new dawn appeared in the skies of the fatherland, he arose proudly and his heart inflamed his mind with a shudder of love, and he ran to the breast of the great Mother.' Did the author, Stefania Türr, pen this passage before, after, or even while being pleasured by the Bard?

of banquets in Genoa. The trip was to be an excursion, not the start of a new life. Unsure of his reception, he hoped for one outcome but was equally prepared – with the resilience that was one of his less obvious qualities – for disappointment. Warming up for the following day, he spoke to the crowd that welcomed him in Genoa. 'Is it a gift of life that I bring,' he asked, 'that you should surge to meet me?' Without spelling it out, this gift was himself, come to assure his compatriots that 'doubt cannot touch us. We shall not let Italy be dishonoured; we shall not let the fatherland perish.' He tells the crowd that they want 'a greater Italy, not by acquisition but by conquest, not measured in shame but as the price of blood and glory'.

His speech the next morning was relentlessly purple. Churchill at his most orotund was prosy beside D'Annunzio in full flight. Citing the 'holy bronze' of the monument as warrant for claiming Garibaldi's approval, he invoked the spirit of self-sacrifice, rising to a pastiche of the Sermon on the Mount, shot through with his hallmark prurience.

O blessed are they that have, for they have more to give, they can burn more brightly. Blessed are the twenty-year-olds, pure of mind, well-tempered in body, with courageous mothers. Blessed are they who, waiting with confidence, do not dissipate their strength but guard it in the discipline of the warrior. Blessed are they who disdain sterile love-affairs to be virgins for this first and last love. Blessed are the young who hunger and thirst for glory, for they shall be sated. Blessed are the merciful, for they shall have splendid blood to wipe away, radiant pain to bind up.

People caught the gist: now is the time for all of you to find the courage to die for your country. Croce called the speech a piece of buffoonery. Others agreed it was vulgar and grotesque. The big false intimate words that had embittered Duse's heart had yielded to big false political words. More speeches followed 'in a species of lyric frenzy', keeping up the pressure. That evening, toasting 'the martyred cities' on the other side of the Adriatic, the poet told his audience – students for the most part – that they were pilgrims of love, messengers of faith, the intrepid arsonists of the great fatherland, the impetuous sparks of a holy blaze!

After dallying with admirers in his hotel, D'Annunzio travelled on to Rome, where his first speech – from his hotel balcony – invoked the spirit of Garibaldi 'the Liberator' against 'the odour of treachery that has begun to stifle us'. He contrasted Italy's present shame with the glories of the Risorgimento:

No, we are not, we do not want to be a museum, an inn, a holiday destination, a horizon touched up with Prussian blue for international honeymoons, a delightful marketplace for buying and selling, for swindling and bartering. Our Genius calls us to put our stamp on the confused material of the new world.

The roar of acclaim drowned the rest of his words.

His speech the next day to another tumultuous crowd was more sharply focused:

If it is a crime to incite the citizens to violence, then I boast of committing that crime. Today the treachery is blatant. We don't only breathe in its horrid stench, we feel all its appalling weight. And the treachery is being committed in Rome, city of the soul, city of life.

He called on the people to form patrols, a 'vigilant militia', and hunt down the traitors, above all Giolitti. Mixing mystical nationalism with appeals for vigilante violence against liberal opponents, this speech begs fair to be counted as the first fascist oration.

The irony hanging over these blasts against the government's cunning and incompetence is that this government – in which Giolitti played no part – had committed Italy to join the Entente by signing the Treaty of London on 26 April. When Salandra's cabinet resigned, D'Annunzio seemed to believe he had brought down a neutralist cabal single-handedly. Next morning, a member of the cabinet took him aside and told him about the Treaty of London, and that the government had already disowned the Triple Alliance.

D'Annunzio, rarely nonplussed, adjusted at once. That evening (14 May) he told an audience in a theatre about the nullification of the Triple Alliance, assuring them he had known all about it before leaving France. He then resumed his attacks on Giolitti and neutralism. Giolitti, 'the chief evil-doer, whose soul is nothing but a frozen lie', was betraying the King and the fatherland. D'Annunzio was not the first to accuse the neutralists of being *nemici interni*, 'internal enemies', but nobody else gave the accusation such prestige.

In the run-up to parliament's crucial vote on intervention, D'Annunzio intensified his attacks, denouncing the treacherous politicians who had spent months parleying with the enemy, 'clowns camouflaged in the flag'. Who has saved Italy in these dark days if not the genuine people, the profound people? 'Long live our war! Long live Rome! Long live Italy! Long live the Army! Long live the Navy! Long live the King! Glory and victory!' He wrote in his diary that the rabble had been 'sublimated' by its delirium at his words.

On 19 May, he was gratified by an audience with the King. On the evening of the 20th, after parliament voted for war, he spoke triumphantly to the swelling crowds:

The honour of the Fatherland is saved . . . We do not fear our destiny but move to meet it, singing . . . In each of us burns the youthful spirit of the two twin Horsemen who guard the Quirinale.[2] They will descend tonight and water their horses in the Tiber, beneath the Aventine Hill, before riding towards the Isonzo that we shall turn red with barbarian blood.

If that sounded ominous, it was mild beside remarks he made at dawn on the 25th, after celebrating the first day of war:

Our vigil is ended. Our exultation begins . . . The border has been crossed. The cannon roars. The earth smokes. The Adriatic is as grey at this hour as the torpedo boat that cuts across it.

Companions, can it be true? We are fighting with arms, we are waging our war, the blood is spurting from the veins of Italy! We are the last to join this struggle and already the first are meeting with glory . . . The slaughter begins, the destruction begins. One of our people has died at sea, another on land. All these people, who yesterday thronged in the streets and squares, loudly demanding war, are full of veins, full of blood; and that blood begins to flow . . . We have no other value but that of our blood to be shed.

The author of these psychotic remarks was a national hero. Has any artist played a more baleful part in decisions that led to violence and suffering on the largest scale? Yet, however clinical his obsessions now appear, there is a sense in which he truly was – as he claimed – a mouthpiece of the 'national will', defined as the preference of a minority with the power to shape policy. Some of the artists in the Futurist movement anticipated the mass slaughter with equal relish, as we shall see, but none of them had D'Annunzio's rhetorical skill or the megaphone of his international fame. Other interventionists could be withering about D'Annunzio as an artist and personality, yet they were all working to bring about his vision of smoking blood. The decadent fantasist was more perceptive about the coming war than those who took pride in their lucid realism.

At the end of May, Cadorna promised D'Annunzio a commission in the Novara Lancers. Assigned to Third Army headquarters near the Isonzo front, he was authorised to visit any corps and 'witness any action'. As well as his officer's salary, he cajoled a retainer from

2 Colossal statues of mythical twins Castor and Pollux, on horseback, in the piazza in front of the Quirinale palace, then the residence of the royal family, now the seat of the President of the Republic.

Albertini. He became a freelance warrior-reporter, quartered privately in Venice, dipping in and out of battle as he chose, dosing himself with enough danger to pique his appetite, and writing up his adventures and exhortations, as well as penning inspirational odes. Styling himself 'a poet of slaughter', he became the nation's foremost propaganda asset. War was his extreme sport, or extreme therapy. Sometimes the stunts came off; often they led to the death of his associates; and at least once, as we shall see, they led to a fiasco that cost many Italian lives.

Among the crowd in Genoa on 5 May 1915 was a lantern-jawed journalist. The fact that his report did not even mention D'Annunzio or his speech is not as odd as it seems, for Benito Mussolini still insisted he was a socialist. Beyond ideology, the omission may also have been intuitive, hinting at the rivalry that would develop after the war, when D'Annunzio was mooted in proto-fascist circles as a contender for national leadership, and before Mussolini rewarded him lavishly to stay out of politics. ('Two things can be done with a bad tooth,' he quipped. 'Pull it out or fill it with gold.') Mussolini, too, had venerated Nietzsche, whose glorious ideals would only be understood by 'a new species of free spirits' who would be 'fortified in war'. Mussolini wrote that in 1908; in 1915, he was not ready to apply these concepts to the interventionist debate, and he balked at D'Annunzio's erotics of racial bloodletting.

In summer 1914, Mussolini was the Socialist Party's rising star, a journalist and agitator on the extreme left of the party, committed to revolution. He was passionately militant, anti-bourgeois, brave though not reckless, and highly ambitious. When Italy attacked Libya in September 1911, he called on workers to block troop transports by blowing up the railway lines. Sentenced for inciting violence, he used his four months in jail to write racy memoirs that nurtured the image of a wild, uncalculating revolutionary. When Serbia, Montenegro, Bulgaria and Greece attacked Turkey in October 1912, in what became known as the First Balkan War, Mussolini ardently supported the threat by the Socialist parties of the Second International to start a general strike if a European war broke out. Taking over the party newspaper *Avanti!* in December 1912, he almost doubled the circulation within a year. Party membership boomed.

He was disillusioned by the party's prudence during 'red week' in June 1914. Publicly, he respected the party's refusal to support an unlimited general strike; privately, he shared the anarchists' frustration.

He was likewise respectful of the Socialists' anti-war position. On 26 July, he thundered that Italian workers should give 'not a man, not a penny' to the cause of war, nor spill 'one drop of blood' for a cause that had 'nothing to do with it'. If the government failed to declare neutrality, the proletariat would force it to do so.

When the executive committee of the Socialist International met in Brussels on 29 July, the Austrian Social Democrats refused to support a general strike. The workers in Vienna were clamouring for revenge on Serbia, they said, and it was better to be wrong with the working class than right against it. Other parties, too, refused to condemn their own governments. The German Social Democrats held out longest against the war, but in early August they buckled under the pressure. Only the Italian party stuck to an anti-war position. Holding firm, in mid-September 1914 Mussolini lamented (admittedly to a female comrade whom he hoped to get into bed) that his Socialist comrades were switching sides, becoming 'apologists for war! It is a contagion that spares no one. But I mean to hold the rampart until the end.' He drafted a manifesto on the 'profound antithesis' between war and socialism. For war 'amounted to the annihilation of individual autonomy and the sacrifice of freedom of thought to the State and militarism'.

He abandoned the rampart in October. When the party reaffirmed its commitment to neutrality, and denounced the betrayals of socialism in Germany and elsewhere, only Mussolini voted against the resolution. In mid-November he resigned the editorship of *Avanti!* and launched a new newspaper with French and Belgian money. *Il Popolo d'Italia* ('The People of Italy') called for intervention on the Allied side. The other party leaders denounced his treachery, and he was expelled on 24 November.

This switch did not come out of the blue. There was a wobble in his neutralism from the outset, for he always divided the warring countries into aggressors and defenders. This proved to be the thin end of a wedge: by mid-October, he was close to arguing for pre-emptive action against 'possible future reprisals'. As the historian Paul O'Brien argues, Mussolini was latently pro-intervention and – like the government – waited for the outcome of the Battle of the Marne before declaring himself for war. With Germany bogged down in France, the odds had shifted far enough in the Allies' favour for intervention to look sensible.

In the end, Mussolini's about-face was ordained by character. When the balance of energy and likely success favoured intervention – with its inspiring vistas of limitless political tumult – his switch of allegiance was only a matter of time. A former comrade in the Socialist Party later alleged, rightly, that the only cause Mussolini ever recognised 'was his own', and his

only use for ideas was to enable him to dispense with ideas . . . The whole object of his intellectual researches was to collect everything which detracted, or appeared to detract from the reality or binding nature of principles . . . Only action counted, and on the plane of action betrayal did not exist, only victory or defeat.

At first, he claimed to be rescuing Socialism from the 'docile herd' in the party. Defining his position as national but not nationalist, he denounced Salandra's appeal to 'sacred egoism' and continued to invoke anti-imperialism as the basis for intervention. Even for a man with Mussolini's power of self-conviction, anti-Socialist socialism was an uncomfortable stretch. This is why Filippo Corridoni was so important to him. For Corridoni was a trades union leader who wanted Italy to intervene because war would create the best conditions for socialist revolution. The July Crisis found him in prison for fomenting a general strike. Released in August 1914, he threw himself into the pro-war campaign. Italian workers should support the 'revolutionary war'. Only neutered men wanted neutrality, Corridoni cried, for we who oppose the bourgeoisie, the dynasties and the capitalists of all countries – we are ready for battle! When this effort failed, he and others founded the breakaway Italian Union of Labour and borrowed anti-imperialist language to try to stir the masses.

'This is not a dynastic war', he bellowed at the thousands who packed into the cathedral square in Florence on 10 May,

. . . it is not a war to save a ruling house, it is a war of liberty and revolution, a war of the people. And the Italian people, once the old men in Rome have stopped delaying and called it to arms, shall not sheathe its sword before the Austrians have been hunted all the way across the Alps.

He took care to add that this was not a war of hatred against the German and Austrian people. After the war, the masses would have to rejoin the class struggle. For the time being, this struggle was best served in uniform. In fact, politics as such should be suspended. 'For now, there is only one party: Italy. Only one programme: action. Because Italy's salvation means the salvation of every party.'

Mussolini warmed to this millenarian rhetoric. He trailed Corridoni on his later appearances around the country, sometimes joining him on the platform. He was slower to emulate him when war came: Corridoni volunteered at once, whereas Mussolini waited to be called up. In 1933, Mussolini's regime built a monument on the Carso where Corridoni died in October 1915. If the Duce never stopped exaggerating the other man's significance – turning him into a Fascist martyr – it was because he had shown him how to argue that not he but the Socialist Party had betrayed its ideals.

Italy's part in the Great War obsessed Mussolini for the rest of his life. After 1922, he used his dictatorial power to mould and polish a mythical version of events, with intervention marking Italy's birth as a dynamic, self-confident state. Maintaining this version involved much censorship and distortion, yet the Duce was not incapable of uttering blunt truths about the war.

At five o'clock one Saturday afternoon in July 1943, the Fascist Grand Council convened in Rome. Italy had reached a turning point: Allied forces were overrunning Sicily; an attack on the mainland could not be long in coming; and Hitler refused to send more troops. The previous weekend, Allied bombers had struck Rome for the first time. High-level dissatisfaction with Mussolini was growing, and Italy's dithering king – still Victor Emanuel III – was for once not inclined to stand by him: he foresaw his dynasty being dragged into oblivion along with the regime. Mussolini had ignored rumours that a momentous challenge was brewing, so was taken aback when the meeting passed directly to a proposal that the King should replace him as commander-in-chief and prime minister. When someone blamed him for the unpopularity of the war, he saw an opening. 'The people's heart is never in any war,' he protested. 'Was the people's heart in the 1915–1918 war, by any chance? Not in the least. The people were dragged into that war by a minority ... Three men launched the movement – Corridoni, D'Annunzio and myself.' Far from being bound in sacred unity, Italy in 1915 was divided 'in an atmosphere of civil war'. Not even the defeat at Caporetto in 1917 had healed this rift. 'Was the people's heart in a war that produced 535,000 deserters?' he asked.[3] 'It is a law of history that when there are two contrary currents of opinion in a nation, one

3 During the war, 162,563 soldiers were court-martialled for desertion and 101,685 were found guilty. Either Mussolini made up the figure of 535,000 on the spot, or he referred to the propaganda myth – discussed in a later chapter – that most of the 600,000 Italian prisoners of war, taken by the Austrians and Germans, were 'deserters'.

wanting war and the other peace, the latter party is invariably defeated even when, as always happens, it represents the numerical majority.'

He could have added a second law of history: in Italy, the pro-war minority takes no serious interest in the military calculus (tasks-to-resources) that determines actual performance on the battlefield. It was a law that General Cadorna learned the hard way in 1915.

FOUR

Cadorna's Clenched Fist

The Commander stands for the virtues of
wisdom, sincerity, benevolence, courage and
strictness.
    SUN TZU, *Art of War* (c. 512 BC)

Who is Cadorna? What has he done that
Italy's destiny should be placed in his hands?
    COLONEL GIULIO DOUHET, JULY 1916

Of the cadets at military academy in 1866, none was marked by the botched campaign against Austria more strongly than Luigi Cadorna (b. 1850). His father, Count Raffaele, who led the hopeless lunge to Trieste that summer, always warned his son that splitting the army leadership led to disaster. He clenched his fist to show what the command should look like. Repeating the gesture for the last time in 1897, on his deathbed, he gave it the aura of a sacred decree.

Young Luigi was destined for a career in uniform. Civilian life ended in his tenth year, when he was enrolled at the military college in his home city of Turin. Discipline was harsh, but Luigi had less trouble with the occasional nights in a solitary confinement cell than with the regular syllabus. Maths and history were particularly challenging. He was a complex boy: resolute, opinionated, incorruptible, studious, touchy, unforgiving and unsociable, physically robust, never brilliant, yet able to shine through diligence. These characteristics became more marked as he grew. Nothing seemed easy for him, yet his potential was widely noticed. Those who knew him well said his remoteness was due to timidity. Others saw pride or arrogance as the root.

After graduating, he was attached to the general staff. Promotion was steady, not remarkable. Captain in 1880, major three years later, colonel in 1892, major general in 1898, lieutenant general in 1904. He gained a reputation for ferocious discipline and inflexibility. The Ministry of War once wanted a young man in his regiment to take the officers' training course. Cadorna demurred: the man was one centimetre shorter than the minimum height required. The ministry insisted. So did Cadorna: if we start making exceptions, where will it end? When the ministry approved the exceptional admission, Cadorna asked if this authorisation was in fact an order? Colleagues thought he was his own worst enemy, fated by temperament never to reach the highest rank. His caustic comments about Giolitti and strong dislike of the Masonic lodges (influential among the Italian élite) were other indiscretions that boded ill for Cadorna's career.

His Catholic faith was central in his life, yet relations with the Church were often difficult, partly because his father had led the army that liberated Rome from Papal rule in 1870. Luigi was present as a junior officer in an artillery regiment – his only combat experience before 1915, for he was not sent to Libya. Pride in his father's achievement and loyalty to the House of Savoy trumped any qualms that he might have felt at this reduction of the Church's earthly power. His scepticism about professional politicians – fickle, always playing to galleries – was confirmed forever in 1877 when his father learned from the newspapers that he had been retired by the Ministry of War. When it came, the communiqué was disdainfully vague: 'length of service and reasons of state'. What humiliation! In truth, as everyone knew, the government wanted to dilute the Piedmontese presence in the senior ranks of the army, so that more southerners could be promoted. This would have struck father and son as appallingly short-sighted, for Italy's only real military tradition came from Piedmont.

When the Chief of the General Staff fell ill in 1906, opening the question of a successor, Cadorna pushed his interest behind the scenes. The vacancy materialised in 1908, and Cadorna was contacted by one of the King's adjutants. Was it true that he would reject any supervision in the exercise of his command? Cadorna's views were well known and he stood by them now, but he hotly denied ever having called for the King to lose his position as supreme commander. While he would resist the King's assumption of operational command in wartime, he never challenged his constitutional supremacy. In practical terms, the chief of the general staff's power should be absolute, for 'It is absolutely necessary to avoid any recurrence of the rivalries, and worse, of past wars and especially the war of 1866.' The fist must be clenched. The imperative of 'unity of action' meant that authority and responsibility had to have a single address.

Cadorna's refusal to veil his opinion, cost what it may, was admirable. Yet his touchiness was hardening into a persecution complex. The manner of his denial, blasting the 'slanders' that his candidacy had provoked, told against him. The job went to General Alberto Pollio, who was oil to Cadorna's vinegar. Cadorna reckoned that Giolitti and Pollio's Jewish wife had intrigued against him ('everyone knows how much the Jews meddle and conspire'). To old Piedmontese military stock, liberals and Jews were always suspect.

Even if Cadorna had not felt victimised, he and Pollio were too unlike to have seen eye to eye. Cadorna was inordinately proud of his single contribution to tactical thought, a pamphlet called *Frontal Attack and Tactical Training* that started life as an article for the Italian military journal in 1888, was revised in 1895 and further amended over twenty years. He shared the blind commitment to compact infantry offensives, regardless of enemy firepower, that was standard doctrine at that time.

The offensive is profitable and almost always possible, even against mountainous positions that appear to be impregnable, thanks to dead ground that permits (a) advance under cover, (b) deployment towards the flanks or weak points, unseen by the enemy.[1] If the defender holds the crest, he will not see. If he descends to lower ground, his retreat will be very difficult. It is often possible to use diverse lines of fire, obtaining the participation of successive ranks in the attack.

The campaigns on the Isonzo would expose the fallacies in this passage. Where was the dead ground at the foot of Carso escarpments? What would the Habsburg forces not see from their trenches on the summit ridges? Even if the enemy had to retreat, how would their difficulties compare with those of the Italians, attacking uphill all the way?

There were, he stated, two ways to demoralise and defeat the enemy: 'superior fire and irresistible forward movement. Of these, the latter is more important (winning means going forward).' His thinking rested on a truism that hid a tautology: wars are won by offensives, so commanders should go on the offensive. About defensive operations he had nothing to say.

Cadorna sent his pamphlet (3rd edition) to Pollio, whose replies revealed wide differences in their thinking. 'If the defending infantry is concealed behind trenches or other shelters,' wrote Cadorna woodenly, 'the attacker's artillery will only have a limited impact; but when the

1 'Dead ground' is not visible from enemy positions.

infantry advances, the defender must in most cases expose himself if he wants to hit it and the artillery can then take the opportunity to strike the defender with rapid fire.'

'Why so?' asked Pollio. 'Don't any trenches permit fire from close range? If the attacker is very close and the attacking artillery uses indirect fire, the attacking artillery can no longer fire in case it hits its own men.' When Cadorna ordained that 'the attacking side must have superior strength in artillery', Pollio said it all depended on the immediate disposition of forces. 'One can have twice the artillery, but at the place where one attacks, the defender may very well be stronger.' Pollio danced around Cadorna like a picador with a stolid, hard-breathing bull.

But it was the picador that died, leaving the bull to get ready for war. He had to start from scratch, for Pollio had not considered operations against Italy's allies. On 21 August 1914, Cadorna issued a memorandum on fighting the Austro-Hungarian Empire. The south Tyrol salient was well fortified and the Italians lacked the heavy siege artillery for a direct assault, so they would surround the Trentino on three sides and neutralise it with limited incursions. Cadorna's prime targets were Trieste and Gorizia. After engaging and defeating the bulk of enemy forces, the Italians would surge towards Ljubljana and even Zagreb. The left (or northern) flank would capture the high passes leading to inner Austria. The right (or southern) flank would drive to Trieste, then swing inland to rejoin the principal forces on the Slovenian plains. If he attacked across the middle and upper Isonzo valley before the end of October,[2] he believed he could reach 'the heart of the Habsburg monarchy' in a matter of weeks. Either the Italians would steamroll towards Vienna or the Austrians would redeploy substantial forces from Serbia and the Eastern Front to the south-west, in which case Italy would defeat them then and there.

While Cadorna's concept was in line with strategic planning since the 1880s, his confidence in an easy victory was new. Although he conceded that his army might be 'paralysed' by resistance on the Carso, he made no tactical allowance for this possibility. If his optimism was pardonable in August 1914, when Austria's border with Italy was almost undefended, it was inexcusable in May 1915.

2 The upper Isonzo refers to the portion from Flitsch to Tolmein; the middle Isonzo runs from Tolmein to Gorizia; the lower Isonzo runs from Gorizia to the sea.

The government refused to declare a general mobilisation, and Cadorna rejected the Minister of War's compromise idea of partial mobilisation because no plans existed for that. Salandra pretended to be afraid of provoking a pre-emptive attack; in truth, he was undecided on intervention and the fortunes of war still favoured the Central Powers. Always quick to scorn, Cadorna accused the government of lacking martial spirit. The King told him to back down. On 22 September, Salandra challenged Cadorna to say that the army was ready to take the field and win. Cadorna grudgingly agreed that mobilisation should wait until spring. The moment for a rapid attack had passed; winter was too close.[3]

As Sonnino parleyed with Vienna and London, Cadorna prepared the army. Italy's choice of allies mattered less to him than its commitment to fight; his consternation in early August was professional, to do with the practicalities of dragging the troops back from the French border. And there was so much to do. The army had faced huge challenges since 1866; it had to defend the kingdom, with its long borders, against powerful potential enemies; protect the civil order; help build the new nation; and fight overseas wars. And it had to do these things as the instrument of governments that were almost always unstable and often divided, and of a monarchy that was still widely felt as more Piedmontese than Italian. Overseas wars had brought no glory. Efforts to carve out an empire within a few years, with no experience or expertise, lacking knowledge of their opponents, had led to the colonial disasters of the 1890s, leaving a stain that seemed indelible. The occupation of Libya, though not an outright failure, was an expensive distraction that absorbed more troops than the army could spare.

In summer 1914, Italy's army was the weakest of any aspiring great power. Decades of high military spending – averaging almost a quarter of the state budget from 1900 to 1914 – had not overcome the deficits of professionalism and equipment. The army was top-heavy with administration and red tape, burdened with ancillary units (doctors, vets, chemists, engineers) far beyond its needs. Procurement and supply

---

3 Cadorna airbrushed this episode from his memoirs, maintaining that the army was too weak and ill-organised for rapid action in 1914. 'Morally unprepared for war', the nation would have been 'practically defenceless' against a pre-emptive Austrian attack. Salandra's memoirs were equally deceptive; he blamed the parliamentary system and the 'disastrous' condition of the officer corps for forcing him to delay intervention.

problems were endemic. Up to a half of the soldiers were illiterate. The officer corps was badly depleted, lacking as many as 15,000 men. With 27 permanent divisions, Italy's standing force was about half the size of France's and Germany's, and its reserves were much weaker: only 13 divisions could be mobilised for war – about the same size as Britain's home-defence territorial reserve in July 1914 – compared with Germany's 44 reserve divisions. The rail network could not meet a modern army's needs. A decision taken decades earlier to develop fortifications rather than transport had left the country short of track, locomotives and rolling stock. War-games around 1900 had showed Italy losing to Austria in the Trentino and Friuli. As for nation-building, the Piedmontese military had no model for absorbing conscripts from around the country. The most notable step involved mixing troops from different parts of Italy in single brigades. The drawback was that many regional dialects were mutually incomprehensible, and some brigades could not operate without junior officers 'interpreting' between their men.

Pollio had wanted to increase the standing army by 70,000 (to 345,000), modernise the artillery and accelerate the officers' training. The government rejected these plans as too ambitious and costly. Parliament, controlled by anti-war deputies, still refused to increase military spending, and Cadorna only got the go-ahead for these reforms in October. He quickly moved his people into leading positions; General Vittorio Zupelli proved an effective Minister of War, pushing hard for more rifles and ammunition, though not for artillery or machine guns. The army started the war with sufficient manpower, uniforms, cars, rifles and bullets, but dire shortages of the weapons that mattered most. Only 309 of a notional total of 623 machine-gun sections were ready by mid-May 1915. The artillery was in even worse shape, with most batteries at a quarter strength.

In December 1914, Cadorna told Salandra that the army would not be ready to fight before April. He shared the judgement that Germany could not defeat France. With Serbia still defiant and the Eastern Front locked in attrition, the outlook for the Central Powers was deteriorating. He told a journalist off the record that 'if another army were thrown into the fray, it would tip the balance'. Italy's aim, if it were to intervene, should be to smash Austria, in co-ordination with Russia. Sonnino's imperial vision left him cold, because he realised how costly it would be to secure the eastern Adriatic with its maze of inlets and islands on such a tiny demographic basis. Yet, like the Prime Minister, he was thinking big: Trento and Trieste were springboards for a much greater endeavour, leading towards Vienna. The scale of his ambition made him Salandra's natural ally.

One reason why the general staff did not press harder for machine guns and artillery was that lessons from other fronts were not being learned. Cadorna had 25,000 copies of his famous pamphlet distributed to officers in February 1915. In this edition, he claimed bizarrely that the Western Front confirmed his faith in frontal attack and breakthrough tactics. Enemy positions could be captured; the challenge lay in retaining them. He was not entirely wrong; solving this problem, however, called for fresh thinking about the use of reserves. To his mind, a war of attrition was always a hiatus. Since attrition in itself achieved no result, whichever side first 'feels truly stronger than the other' would take the offensive. Hence, 'Manoeuvre will continue to decide the outcome of war.'

This simple-minded thinking was reinforced by the analysis arriving from his military attachés at the Italian embassies in Paris and Berlin. While these men rightly saw that successful French resistance on the Marne portended a reversal of German fortunes, they misinterpreted the stabilisation of trench lines during October. It did not occur to them that events had exposed a fundamental flaw in tactical assumptions. Their reports noted the new technology in use, but missed the tactical implications of barbed wire, trenches and machine guns. Both attachés clung to the faith that gains in defensive strength had merely raised the cost of successful frontal attacks, though not to an unacceptable level. 'Today, as in the past, the offensive retains its superiority over the defensive; victory still requires attack and manoeuvre.' Attrition was a phase, an intermezzo. Like Cadorna, who insisted that 'the possibilities for successful offensives are greater today than in the past', they mistook a tautology for sturdy insight. After visiting the front in February 1915 and seeing that the second and third lines were strongly fortified, the attaché in Paris reported that the only way to break the deadlock would be through a third party 'entering the field with new forces in the sacred name of its own jeopardised interests, and those alone'. No prize for guessing which party he had in mind.

Proof that an open-minded amateur could see more clearly what awaited Italy's army came from Father Agostino Gemelli, the extraordinary Franciscan friar who pioneered the study of military psychology and served as Cadorna's chaplain in Udine. By March 1915, Gemelli realised that the coming war would be fought in trenches, where months would pass without any decisive action. 'Gone are the wars of impetuous assaults and great battles, instead there is the struggle which exhausts with its uniformity.' He gleaned this much from reading press reports and letters from the Western Front, and from a brief stay in Germany during autumn 1914.

A more conventional voice from the general staff reflecting on the Western Front was that of Colonel Angelo Gatti, mentioned in an earlier chapter. A fluent writer, he commented on the war for the (strongly interventionist) daily *Corriere della Sera* from August to December 1914. He warned readers in November that, if military means determined the duration of the war, it would last a long time. Then he assured them that Austria was the weakest of the warring powers. Her citizens were not united behind the army, heart and soul. Unlike Germany, with its 'organic living strength', or infinite Russia, Austria like France possessed only 'the strength to resist'. On the other hand, he granted that Austria possessed remarkable 'powers of recovery'. Just how remarkable, the Italians would discover.

If there was a date when prewar planning ceased to provide guidance to the warlords, it was perhaps 25 November 1914, when Falkenhayn ordered German forces in the West to form defensive positions and hold their ground. Watching trenches spread along the Western Front from the Channel ports to the Swiss frontier, Lord Kitchener, the British minister of war, famously confessed that he did not know what to do. 'This isn't war.' By late December, the lines in France had been static for two months. Manoeuvre had become very difficult, if not impossible. It was hard to see how the situation could change beyond the capture or loss of a few hundred metres of trench.

Gatti's end-of-year summary was grimly poetical: 'All is slow, vast, exhausting in this monstrous conflict, where the lives of men and the fate of nations descend towards death with the majesty and calm of the great American rivers flowing to the sea.' He spoiled the effect by forecasting that Germany would muster all its forces for a supreme effort in spring 1915. If this failed, Germany would collapse in exhaustion. The Allies should pre-empt this titanic offensive, Gatti said in a coded plea for intervention, by pooling their strength. This would lead to battles that dwarfed anything yet seen and finish the war, one way or another. Like many other intelligent analysts, he could not imagine the perpetuation of deadlock. So he contradicted himself: militarily, there could be no quick solution, but there *would* be a military solution the following spring – when, as Gatti knew but his readers did not yet, Italy would almost certainly enter the war itself.

FIVE

The Solemn Hour Strikes

*Let your plans be dark and impenetrable as night and
when you move, fall like a thunderbolt.*
  SUN TZU

*War should be undertaken with forces corresponding
to the magnitude of the obstacles that are to be
anticipated.*
  NAPOLEON, *Military Maxims* (1827)

Yellowed prints of the 1866 border show simple guardhouses beside
stone bridges. Farmers pose, squinting, by the barrier poles alongside
their carts and livestock, while children play at the roadside under
listless flags. Few traces of that frontier can be seen today. On the
outskirts of Cormons, a guardhouse has been adapted into a loggia for
a private home, sheltering an expensive car. Deep in its stony bed, the
River Judrio trickles past the end of the garden. Traffic whines along the
SS356 highway, a hundred metres away, beyond a monument marking
where the first shots were fired in Italy's last war of independence. The
inscription says that on the night of 23/24 May, Italian customs officers
opened fire to stop Austrian reservists from burning the wooden bridge
over the Judrio. A few hours later, the first Italian casualty was brought
back across the bridge on a farmer's cart.

The 23rd was a Sunday, and parish priests along the border warned
their congregations that war was coming. Hostilities officially commenced at midnight. Assuming supreme command, the King overcame
his diffidence and spoke to the people – something he rarely did. The
solemn hour of national claims had struck, he cried, standing on the
balcony of the Quirinale palace and waving a flag. The enemy were
battle-hardened and worthy; favoured by the terrain and by careful
preparations, they would fight tenaciously, 'but your indomitable
ardour will certainly overcome them'. It was an oddly subdued

performance. Even so, according to press reports, the crowd was delirious. With this ordeal behind him, the King hurried to the front; he did not want to miss a moment of his army's dash to glory.

The army was not, however, dashing anywhere. Full mobilisation began on 22 May and was scheduled to take 23 days. It took twice as long; the army was not fully deployed until mid-July. The general staff had prepared for war as if it would occur in peacetime conditions. Little allowance was made for systemic stress and breakdown, all the concomitants that Clausewitz called 'friction'.

When the fighting began, Cadorna had some 400,000 men in the plains of Veneto and Friuli. Yet, these hastily concentrated forces included only two of the army's 17 regular corps – fewer than 80,000 rifles. On the lower Isonzo, the Third Army was to rush to the river, establish bridgeheads and capture Monfalcone. Gorizia was to be isolated by taking the hills that flanked the city. On the middle and upper Isonzo, the Second Army's priority was to take the Caporetto basin and then the Krn–Mrzli ridge. The Fourth Army was supposed to pinch the neck of the Trentino salient by occupying a series of towns in the north: first Cortina, deep in the Dolomite mountains, then Toblach (Dobbiaco) and Bruneck (Brunico). The First Army was deployed defensively around the western side of the salient.

Cadorna should have had the benefit of co-ordinated operations by Russia and Serbia, but the Serbs were in no condition to attack and anyway resented Italian ambitions in the Balkans, while the Russians were paralysed after heavy losses in May and early June. The Italians were on their own, and the long build-up deprived them of surprise. Also, Austrian agents in the border areas had been feeding them disinformation, so they were expecting ambushes and sabotage on the roads to the east.

There was another reason for the Third Army's snail's pace. As it rolled into action, Cadorna replaced its commander, General Zuccari, because he had delayed his arrival at the front or possibly to settle a score. The timing was astonishing; Zuccari's successor, the Duke of Aosta, took up his command on 27 May, exactly when the Third Army should have been smashing the enemy lines. The Italians crept to the Isonzo instead of racing there. The cavalry were ordered to take the bridges above Monfalcone on the morning of the 24th. But their commander, expecting tough resistance, wanted to keep contact with the supporting infantry, so the Austrians had time to blow the bridges that afternoon. Cadorna blamed the men's lack of 'offensive spirit', rather than poor preparation, sheer inexperience, or the enemy's skill at spreading false reports.

The Habsburg secret services scored real successes in April and early May 1915. Italian intelligence reported that the enemy had eight or ten divisions on the Italian border – around 100,000 infantry. In fact, the Isonzo frontier was guarded in mid-May by only two divisions – some 25,000 rifles, supported by around 100 artillery pieces. Intelligence from the Alpine regions was no better. Crucially, Cadorna was unaware that in the Tyrol and the Dolomites the Austrians had withdrawn to a defensive line some way behind the state border, leaving large tracts of territory near Lake Garda and north of Asiago practically undefended.

The Habsburg commander in the Tyrol reported on 20 May:

We are on the eve of an enemy invasion. We have erected a weak line of combat on the border, but we have only 21 reserve battalions and seven and a half batteries along a front of some 400 kilometres. All our proper troops are on the Eastern Front [meaning Galicia]. Only the Trent zone is a bit better fortified and sufficiently garrisoned . . . I don't know what will happen if the Italians attack vigorously, everywhere.

The reservists were mostly labourers who had been building the defences and were then put in uniform, given a rifle and basic training.

There was no vigorous attack. West of the Isonzo, only the Fourth Army under General Nava and the Carnia Corps were deployed to attack, targeting the Puster valley and Villach. With just five divisions, Nava's force was too dispersed to make much impact. They had only one heavy battery and no other means of breaching wire: no gelignite tubes or even wire-cutters.[1] Small wonder that Nava's men advanced so slowly in May and June. An Austrian officer posted in the Dolomites wrote on 23 May that, if the Italians knew their business, they would march overnight and reach the Puster valley inside Austria by morning; nothing could have stopped them. But they did not know their business, and the window closed. The Fourth Army occupied Cortina five days after the Austrians evacuated it, then delayed the offensive proper until 3 June, for no clear reason. This gave the Austrians ample time to

---

1 Known in English as Bangalore torpedoes, the gelignite tubes were iron pipes, around 1.5 metres in length, with gelignite packed in one end. The wire-cutting party would thrust the explosive end under the wire, then light the long fuse with a sulphur match before retreating. When they worked, these devices could blast a gap of 3–5 metres in the wire.

strengthen their line. Lieutenant General Krafft von Dellmensingen, leading the German Alpine Corps on this sector, recalled that the Italians' initial superiority was so great that they could have broken through at will. 'We expected them to do just that, and were more and more astonished when they let two weeks and more pass without moving.' The Italians never got near the Puster valley.

In Carnia, the mountainous hinge of the entire front, the Italian force was, again, too small for its ambitious tasks of breaking through at Tarvis. No artillery was available until 12 June and anyway there were no tracks or roads to bring the batteries close to enemy lines, so it was impossible to attack the well-protected approaches to the passes into Austrian Carinthia.

West of Carnia and the Dolomites, General Brusati, commanding the First Army, was straining at the leash. Although he had only five divisions for a sector of 130 kilometres around Trentino, he was dismayed by Cadorna's decision not to let him attack.[2] So he attacked anyway, achieving no success because he chose the only strongly fortified zone in his sector: the high ground between Trent and the coastal plain. His offensive unfurled as if in slow motion.

With Habsburg troops pouring in from Serbia, the balance was changing every day. By 24 May, the Austrians had 50,000–70,000 men on the Italian front. A further 40 battalions (40,000 men) arrived by the end of the month. By mid-June, there may have been 200,000 Habsburg troops facing the Italians. Nonetheless, Italy had a broad advantage of at least 4:1 in fighting strength for the first month of the war. This disparity was not admitted at the time, or under Fascism. Mussolini would claim that the Italians had faced 221 enemy battalions. The Austrians credited the Italians with 48 divisions (44 infantry, 4 cavalry), instead of 35. Each side overestimated the other's initial strength, but the overestimation had dire consequences for one side only.

Local people had helped the Austrians to erect barriers across the border roads, using trees, glass, barbed wire, and even farm implements. They also warned the advancing Italians about mines, traps and electrified wire barriers that did not exist. Nosing tentatively

2 Cadorna's original plan had foreseen offensives in this sector, but he changed his mind at the last minute, when he decided that offensive efforts should concentrate almost exclusively on the Isonzo.

forward, skirmishing with Austrian patrols but meeting no fierce resistance, the Italians only reached the Isonzo on the 26th. The brunt of Cadorna's attack was planned to take place across the river, between Sagrado and Monfalcone, a distance of 12 kilometres, east of the lower Isonzo. The bridges were all blown. Further days were wasted in exploring the riverbanks. Heavy rain had swollen the Isonzo and its tributaries. What with accurate enemy fire and shortages of bridging equipment, it proved impossible to cross the river until the night of 4/5 June. Once they reached the eastern side, the Italians found that the enemy had flooded the low-lying area between the river and the Carso by closing the sluices on a raised canal. The Italians blew up the sluice gates, but too late to save the troops from being bogged down. This bought the Austrians more time to prepare their defences on the Carso ridge.

The rapture and creeping disillusion of early June were chronicled by Giani Stuparich, a volunteer from Trieste. Stuparich enlisted in the 1st Regiment of Sardinian Grenadiers at the end of May and entrained for the front at once. He was a fastidious man and the company in the crowded carriage ('two Florentines . . . a Roman . . . a Sicilian . . . one from Livorno') soon became tiresome. A sergeant in the reserves made 'loudly incomprehensible speeches about humanity, barbarism, sacrifice, duty and many other muddled concepts'. Looking for distraction from the chatter, Stuparich noticed a silent figure in the corner of the carriage. 'He is not listening or talking, he is the only one rapt in a preoccupation that he cannot account for, but it fevers his expression and stiffens his limbs, paralysing his soul in an intense stupor.' His mouth hung open, his eyes were fixed and shining. He was a peasant in uniform, perhaps leaving home for the first time in his life, probably fluent only in dialect. The nameless man was still far from the front, but even now he could not grasp what was happening. Wrenched from his family and routine for reasons neither explained nor understood, he was in shock. While the writer saw this and was moved, too much separated them for a friendly word to be uttered.

At Mestre station, outside Venice, the men see wounded soldiers waiting for transport away from the front. 'There are thousands of them!' says one of the Tuscans in a trembling voice. (Thanks to censorship, he would have had no idea of the initial casualties.) Smells of blood and iodine seep into the carriage. Like the peasant in the corner, the wounded say nothing. The train moves on towards the front.

[65]

Marching to the border, the men are nervous, starting at shadows by the roadside. Beyond Cervignano, there are tree trunks across the road. Bersaglieri speed past them on bikes, raising trails of dust.[3] A public fountain slakes their thirst. They sleep on their capes under the stars, and awaken spangled with dew. Ordered to carry heavy cauldrons, Stuparich – a bespectacled, intense, 25-year-old intellectual – notes euphorically that his body alone could not have borne the weight; 'my strength is sheer willpower'.

They cross the Isonzo on 5 June, 'a tremendous, foaming azure current cut by pontoons'. His rucksack no longer weighs him down. Near the front, smells of putrefaction emanate from the roadside bushes, but the men are too hopeful to be gloomy. Marching towards Monfalcone on 8 June, they talk excitedly about reaching Trieste within a fortnight. Giani dreams of being one of the first to enter the main square, covered in dust. Next day, he reaches the Carso. The unit is sheltering from Austrian fire in a dyke. They clamber out, and come face to face with a rocky, barren hillside. 'A chilly gust of wind hits me, a bullet whistles over my head, then another, then more buzz past my ears with a softer, keening sound.'

The Carso figures in this story as a landscape, a battlefield, practically a character in its own right. It is a triangle of highland with vertices near the hill of San Michele in the north, Trieste in the south, and somewhere around the town of Vipava – deep inside Slovenia – in the east. To the south and east, it merges into the limestone ranges that reach into Slovenia and Croatia, and ultimately stretch all the way along the eastern Adriatic coast to Montenegro. In the north, it is bounded by the valley of the River Vipacco. It is from the west, however, that the Carso shows its most impressive aspect, at first like a bar of cloud on the horizon, then surging from the ground.

There is a legend about the origins of the Carso. God sent an archangel to take away the stones that stopped people from growing crops. The devil saw the angel flying high over a land with beautiful woods and streams and meadows, carrying a huge sack. Hoping for treasure, the devil approached the archangel from behind and slashed his sack with a knife. Out poured the stones, covering the beautiful

3 The Bersaglieri (literally 'sharpshooters') were mobile light infantry, recognisable by the long black feathers in their wide-brimmed hats. Some units rode bicycles.

country below. God was sanguine: 'No harm is done. The people in that country sheltered the devil instead of praising my name. Let this be a lesson to them. Let this be the kingdom of stone, where men labour to survive. Then they will learn not to trust the devil.' The local people chased the devil away, but too late. The Carso remained a wasteland, as God had ordained.

The Carso only reaches 500 metres in height, like the chalk downs in southern England, but it feels like a world apart. The surface is uneven, pitted with sinkholes where water has drained into the stone. If you stumble, it is easy to break an ankle or cut yourself to the bone. Someone likened the Carso to an immense petrified sponge. It is a hydrologist's laboratory, a potholer's playground; fissures in the surface open into grottoes and caverns that lead deep underground. The largest holes, called dolinas, are conical, steep-sided depressions up to 200 or 300 metres across and 50 metres deep. Formed by water erosion and often plugged with fertile red soil, they were oases of cultivation on the arid plateau, where otherwise only goats could forage.

The Carso was almost trackless, and thinly populated – by Slovenes, not Italians, living in hamlets of limestone blocks, roofed with lichened stone. Habsburg forestation projects had created woodland around the fringes, but the plateau proper was almost treeless, for the natural flora was sub-alpine heathland, with thyme, cyclamen, narcissi, and juniper bushes. The fauna, too, was distinctive: boar, deer, lynx, jackals and horned vipers were all found. The climate is harsh. In winter, the Carso is swept by winds, including a cold, dry north-easterly called the bora that can gust at 100 knots. Rain turns the red clay to gluey mud. Summer turns the Carso into a desert; clouds form over the sea and pass overhead without releasing a drop of rain.

Made of rock that reflects the heat, waterless when not flooded, hard to walk over, let alone run, the Carso might have been designed as the last place on earth for trench warfare. Shellbursts were like volcanoes erupting. When heavy shells hit limestone, the fragments of steel casing and stone could maim soldiers a kilometre away. Trenching was extremely difficult without drills, under fire. Mattocks and picks were no use when solid rock lay on or just below the surface, so both sides built low walls of loose stones, knee-high and easily demolished by incoming shells. Disgust for these dry-stone defences is vividly expressed in war memoirs. The novelist Carlo Emilio Gadda, who fought on the Carso, found a memorably painful image when he wrote of the contending generals who 'scraped their massacred battalions over those hills like matchsticks'.

————————

The day when Giani Stuparich's unit reached the Carso, 9 June, the Sardinian Grenadiers were involved in capturing Monfalcone. With 10,000 people, Monfalcone was the biggest town between Gorizia and Trieste, and it was booming, thanks to shipbuilding and chemical industries. Its capture gave the Italians their first triumph.

While infantry of the Messina Brigade entered the town directly, the Grenadiers circled around the back. If you drive through Monfalcone today, you glimpse a white monument on a low hilltop behind the main square. This is the Rocca, literally 'the Rock', a miniature fortress with a squat limestone tower, 10 metres square, hooped by walls four or five metres high. Fortifications stood here for centuries before the Venetians built this tower some 500 years ago. (The lion of St Mark, its forepaw resting on the Gospel, is still visible on the façade.) It is a superb vantage-point, looking forward over the plains of Friuli and the Gulf of Trieste, and rearward to the Carso. A prehistoric trade route from the Adriatic to the Black Sea passed by this place.

The fight for the Rocca on 9 June was fierce but short. The Austrians pulled back across a valley to a hill called Cosich. At 112 metres, Cosich stands only 30 metres higher than the Rocca, but it was naturally apt for defensive operations. A smug Viennese journalist dubbed it the 'Hotel Cosich'. The Austrians were not budged from it until August 1916.

Stuparich found Monfalcone deserted, 'almost spectral'. The shop-fronts were shuttered. He did not know it, but the Austrians had ordered a complete evacuation on 24 May, and only 3,000 determined Italians stayed behind, sheltering in cellars from the shelling. Then a shutter went up, a head peered out. Rumours spread that a sweet shop had opened, but what the soldiers wanted was liquor. They ransacked the houses for 'souvenirs', stealing pictures, furniture, cutlery, even clothes. For days afterwards, troops wandered around kitted in women's blouses, until these too were infested with lice.

That evening, Giani walks up to the Rocca. The air is fragrant with pine resin. At dawn the next day, the Austrian artillery on Cosich is silhouetted by the slanting light. The Grenadiers feel unaccountably sad; even the officers seem discouraged. A rumour deepens their gloom: other platoons in the battalion may have taken heavy casualties from

Italian artillery. This is soon confirmed; a hundred men have been killed by friendly fire. (The battery commanders did not learn to co-ordinate their fire with infantry advances until the following summer.) This raises the losses around Monfalcone to nearly 300. Giani reports that the terrible accident brings the advance to a halt. He feels the sinews snapping in his breast. He wants to weep but cannot, and has no appetite for supper. Only yesterday Trieste seemed so close, as if they could reach it in one bound. Now it seems so far away.

A few days later, the pinewoods around the Rocca catch fire from the Austrian guns. After the blaze, the ground is carpeted with ash that swirls up and coats the soldiers' faces. Then the rain starts again, and the ground is churned to soaking mud. By mid-June, Monfalcone is in ruins.

On the day the Italians took Monfalcone, the Second Army made its first attack on the little hill of Podgora, to the west of Gorizia. The troops had crossed the river below San Michele with relative ease, but made no headway on Podgora. There was an equally futile attempt on Mount Sabotino, north of Gorizia. By 11 June, Cadorna realised what he was up against. Gorizia was, he admitted, a proper trenched camp buttressed by mighty hills: Sabotino and Podgora west of the Isonzo, Monte Santo and San Gabriele to the east, and then San Michele to the south. These hills were the town's outlying ramparts, rising abruptly some 600 metres from the valley.

Also on 9 June, the Italians clashed for the first time with the Austrians on the lower Isonzo. It happened at Sagrado, a little town south-west of Gorizia. Before dawn, a battalion of the Pisa Brigade crossed a pontoon that had been thrown across the river where a sandy islet in midstream made the work easier. (The islet is still visible today.) The artillery hammered the enemy forward positions beyond the river. The major blew his whistle, the Italians – unaware how vulnerable they now were – jumped up to yell 'Savoy!', the name of the royal family, and ran forward from their improvised bridgehead. Suddenly the Austrian positions erupted with devastating fire. The pontoon was destroyed and the battalion pinned down without supplies or support. The Italians fell back to the river, and used bayonets when their ammunition ran out. As the Austrians closed in, they threw some newfangled weapons that the Italians had never seen – hand-grenades. The Italians waded back to the little island – the water was only a metre and a half deep – and burrowed into the sand as best they could. At nightfall, the handful of survivors floundered back to the western shore, leaving behind some 500 dead.

It was an astonishing blunder. Why was the operation launched with no secure bridgehead on the far side of the river? Why were the obvious risks not anticipated and planned for? These questions were not asked, even though the first massacre on the Isonzo had happened a week before, some 80 kilometres away, on the middle reach of the river, between the towns of Tolmein (now Tolmin) and Karfreit, better known as Caporetto. The Italians had advanced more rapidly on this sector. As elsewhere, they expected stiff resistance but met with almost none. On one of the hilltops above Caporetto, they found nothing but a defiant message scrawled in faulty Italian and stuffed into a bottle. The message ended, 'Thus misfortune will come to our powerful enemies the Italians. Long live Austria! Long live the Emperor!'

By the morning of the 24th the Second Army controlled the western ridges above the valley. What did they see? Except for the weaving line of the Isonzo, the area between Flitsch (now Bovec) in the north and Gorizia in the south – where the river issues onto the plain – was a vast jumble, with no paths on the tops and very little surface water. Picture hills like the highest ranges in Wales or Scotland – around Snowdon, the Ben Nevis massif or the Cuillins of Skye, but with limestone instead of slate, granite or gabbro. The tops are often jagged, though sometimes they undulate like the Pennines. The hills rise a thousand metres and more from narrow valleys. Sheer cliffs drop to remote corries. The hills are linked by ridges that rise and fall, merge and separate like giant waves in a choppy sea. Only the Isonzo valley widens into basins where hamlets or little towns huddle the river, and farmers use every scrap of soil for crops or grazing. A rough road runs beside the river. Tracks lead up to a few higher hamlets with summer pastures. Scrubby undergrowth covers the lower slopes. For the most part, the landscape is a stony wilderness.

The Italians entered the hamlet of Livek, above Caporetto, a few hours after it had been abandoned by the Habsburg military police, who left their shiny new barracks in such a rush that the cooking pots were full of sauerkraut. As in the other 'liberated' villages north of Gorizia, the local people were Slovenes. The only one who spoke Italian was a woman called Katerina Medves. When she offered coffee to an ailing infantryman, he would not touch it before she drank some herself.

By the end of the day, several villages had been occupied on the eastern bank of the river, at the foot of the mountains. By the 24th, only a few Austrian reservists were left in Caporetto, which was taken the next morning. (A Slovene child, seeing the Bersaglieri approaching by bicycle and fascinated by the plumes on their hats, cried out 'Daddy, daddy, look at all the ladies coming here on bikes!') The Italians made their way carefully to the old stone bridge over the Isonzo, which presses through a canyon a few metres wide. Inevitably, the bridge had been blown. Scanning the hillside across the river, they saw several Austrians gazing at them from the undergrowth. Why didn't they open fire? Then they realised these enemies were straw dummies in uniform. The first prisoners of war were taken the following morning.

At this point, inexplicably, the regiments in the Isonzo valley were ordered to sit tight by the corps commander, General di Robilant, based more than 20 kilometres away in Cividale. Up in Livek, the 12th Bersaglieri milled around for four days, gazing into the valley below and at the Mrzli ridge that rose 1,000 metres on the far side of the river. When their commander, Colonel De Rossi, asked Katerina Medves about nearby Austrian positions, she shrugged: there were none. Scanning the motionless landscape with binoculars, he could not be sure she was lying.

De Rossi was baffled by the orders from Cividale, and with reason. The prime objective in this sector was to capture the peaks of Krn and Mrzli and the lofty connecting ridges, in order to outflank the town of Tolmein. If the Italians took Tolmein, they would control the crucial railhead at Santa Lucia; then they could throttle the Habsburg defences all the way from Gorizia to Tarvis. In frustration, De Rossi ordered his sappers to throw a footbridge over the Isonzo on the 27th. When he sent his men across the bridge to prepare positions under Mrzli, on the 30th, he was ordered to pull back to Livek. Other units, he was told, were active on Mrzli.

General di Robilant had unaccountably ordered a reserve division in Cividale to lead the attack on Mrzli ridge. The 26 battalions of Alpini[4] and Bersaglieri stood by and watched as the reservists crept up the flanks of the Krn and Mrzli massifs. The Italians did not realise that Mrzli was unoccupied. Sitting in Tolmein and desperately short of men,

4 The first Alpini companies were formed in 1872 to protect Italy's mountainous northern border. Unlike the infantry brigades (except those from Sardinia), their units were recruited regionally, from the northern parts of the kingdom.

the Austrians had expected the Italians to swarm over the valley and onto Mrzli. When they realised this was not happening, they sent units of a mountain brigade onto the ridge. Later that day, the 28th, the Italians finally tried to take Mount Mrzli, and found themselves fighting one of the strongest units in the Habsburg army: the 4th Bosnian Regiment. They could get no further than a ridge at 1,186 metres on the north-west shoulder of the mountain, still 200 metres below the summit. Ferocious fire made it impossible to secure this ridge, and they fell back.

De Rossi's men were let off the leash on 1 June. They climbed to the ridge below the summit and charged up the steep slope, led by officers brandishing sabres. Machine guns cut swathes through their ranks, but they got within 50 metres of the enemy. That night was mild and clear, and De Rossi crawled to the forward Italian position. The zinc coating on the barbed wire was silvery in the moonlight, which shone on the Austrian line, a rough wall of stones below the summit. The Italians captured this line in a dawn attack. Instead of finding themselves as masters of the hilltop, however, they were stuck. The final slope up to the summit was packed with barbed wire. Pinned down by Austrian fire, De Rossi decided to explore possible routes down to the river on his left, northwards. But another officer jumped up and, in what De Rossi called a fit of madness, ordered his men to attack. This man, Lieutenant Colonel Negrotto, was in the grip of nationalist fever; his letters home described the war as pitting 'luminous Latin civilisation' against 'the barbarous but disciplined German culture'.

Hit in the spine by machine-gun fire as he tried to stop this suicidal attack, De Rossi was paralysed for life. Further north, where Mrzli converges with the Krn massif in a jumble of knife-like ridges and gullies, the Italians hurled themselves towards the summits with no greater success. As well as using their firearms, the Austrians piled boulders into pyramids and rolled them down the mountainside. By 4 June, the Italians had lost more than 2,500 men on this sector, including nearly a hundred officers. Cadorna's judgement on the assaults on Mrzli was succinct: 'heroic but senseless'. The Austrians were so dismayed by the loss of the little ridge at 1,186 metres that officers of the defending battalion were court-martialled. Nevertheless, Austria had got the better of this first engagement on the upper Isonzo.

The Italians had done better further north. Krn itself, which soars like a shark's fin 2,000 metres above Caporetto, was taken in a daring pre-dawn attack by the 3rd Regiment of Alpini on 16 June, with their boots swaddled in sacks of straw to reduce noise. It was a glorious success, the first of the war, presaging others that never materialised. One of the three casualties provided Italy's propagandists with a cult hero. Alberto Picco was a young officer from Tuscany, a handsome boy, the centre-forward and first captain of his home town's team, La Spezia, where the soccer stadium still bears his name. He died in his captain's arms.

Elsewhere the Italians were fatally diffident. They took the hamlet of Plava, halfway between Gorizia and Tolmein, at the end of May, but only managed to cross the river on 9 June. There were two objectives. One was Mount Kuk (611 metres), a couple of kilometres to the south. Looming in front of them was a smaller hill, which, like most of the nameless hills and peaks along the front, was known by its metric height above sea level: Hill 383.

Kuk was swathed with barbed wire, and the Italians were tricked by Austrian camouflage. The trees seemed to rain grenades, and death blazed from the undergrowth. The 37th Infantry Regiment lost half its men and most of its officers before being pulled back to the river. The survivors were ordered to join an attack on Hill 383, defended by a tough Dalmatian regiment, the 22nd Infantry, whose commander urged the men to defend their 'Slavic soil' against the ancestral foe. Decades later, a veteran recalled that the Austrians seemed to know exactly when the Italians would emerge from their positions on 16 June. Given the quality of Habsburg intelligence, they quite likely did possess this information. Even if they did not, the cycle of preparatory bombardment and frontal attack was pathetically predictable.

It was like the end of the world and you would have thought a volcano was erupting. Down below, the Isonzo was boiling. I was wondering how a humble infantryman could come out of this inferno alive. We were going up all the time, under an avalanche of fire; I was praying all the time. There were already big holes in our line . . .

Despite horrific losses – almost five hundred dead, nearly a thousand wounded – the Italians took the hill. The Austrians hid in dug-outs and tunnels along their second line while the Italians celebrated and then slept. Early next day the counter-attack drove the Italians halfway back to the river. Among the prisoners taken was a lieutenant, a deputy in the Italian parliament, who spoke freely about his army's desperately bad medical service and worsening morale.

At the northern end of the Isonzo front was the little town of Flitsch, overlooking broad meadows a dozen kilometres upstream from a dog-leg bend in the river. By early June, the Italians controlled this bend and much of the ridge that runs from here to the Krn massif. Yet, the sector commander did not try to take the town, even though Cadorna's orders were to do just this as quickly as possible. For Flitsch occupied a strategic position. It is dominated by a hulking mountain called Rombon, reaching up almost 2,000 metres from the valley floor. Whichever side held Rombon would have a stranglehold on Flitsch and control the access to the northern passes. The Austrians needed to make Rombon unconquerable; the Italian pause gave them the chance to make it so.

During the first month of war, Italy lost 11,000–20,000 men. Austrian losses were around 5,000. Cadorna's army was incapable of successful offensives against competently defended positions. He had failed to instil the 'offensive spirit' into his senior officers. Circular orders were no substitute for direct exhortation, in person. To close observers, he gave the impression of being only half engaged. What he did do was start a rolling purge of the officer corps that continued throughout his tenure; by October 1917, Cadorna had dismissed 217 generals, 255 colonels and 355 battalion commanders. This ungentlemanly harshness shocked the career officers, who became more frightened of being 'torpedoed' than of carrying out absurd orders or sacrificing their men's lives pointlessly. Combined with Cadorna's intolerance of anything that might smack of insubordination, the sackings discouraged ambitious officers from sharing their thoughts on the course and conduct of the war.

In fairness, his faith in the frontal infantry offensive was no more dogged than Joffre's or Haig's. But he was fighting in terrain that exposed the flaws in this doctrine with utter ruthlessness. The poor quality of organisation and equipment was already having an effect. There were disturbing cases in June of conscripts spitting at the national flag. Many soldiers were disappointed by the local civilians' cool response to their liberators, so unlike the acclaim promised by the newspapers. Instead they were met, for the most part, with shuttered windows and 'hard Friulan faces'. Some of the soldiers began to wonder if their cause was just, after all. Their heroic idea of war was fading, and, in questions of morale, the volunteers were bellwethers; doubts that assailed them were soon felt more widely.

The opening moves in any military endeavour are likely to be clumsy, especially when the attacking army lacks relevant campaign experience.[5] Armies learn as they go, often more quickly than their own commanders. Translating fresh information into tactical thought is a challenge for any staff headquarters in war. Without free-flowing communication, lessons can hardly be learned. It was clear by early June that the channels in this army were badly clogged. Beyond this, the situation facing Cadorna in late May was worse than he had reasonably expected. Allied efforts to break through at Gallipoli had failed, so the Central Powers did not have to bolster the Turks. The Balkan neutrals, Romania and Bulgaria, had not come off the fence. Italy was alone.

By 10 June, Cadorna recognised that matters were not going to plan. He told his family that the advance faced great difficulties and a trench war was looming – a prospect he detested. Salandra was under pressure from warmongers whose euphoria was beginning to curdle. A note of asperity crept into his communications with Cadorna, who warned that the campaign would take a long time, and advised Salandra to inform the public of the real situation. This advice was not taken.

Meanwhile, as the clashes died down in the second week of June, Cadorna's army set about hacking trenches and gun emplacements in the limestone, carving mule-tracks in zigzags up the mountains, and draping the valley with telephone wires and cableways suspended from triangular wooden stanchions that can still be found in the forests that now cover the lower hillsides. Pontoons over the Isonzo were strengthened, swept away by late spring rains, rebuilt. Barracks were built in the rear. Cadorna took over the archbishop's palace in Udine which he named the 'Supreme Command' instead of the traditional 'General Headquarters'. The commanders of the Second and Third Armies set up their headquarters closer to their sectors. By 21 June, Cadorna was ready to start the war in earnest. With over a million men on the plains of Veneto and Friuli – the greatest force ever assembled in Italy – he issued orders for a general advance towards Trieste and Gorizia. The first battle of the Isonzo was about to begin, but the Austro-Hungarian army was better prepared than anyone had thought possible in May.

---

5 For example, the Austrians counter-attacked by night from the start – something the Italians were not prepared for.

SIX

A Gift from Heaven

*Whoever is first in the field and awaits the coming of
the enemy, will be fresh for the fight.*
SUN TZU

*The superiority of the defensive (rightly understood)
is very great, and much greater than may appear at
first sight.*
CARL VON CLAUSEWITZ, *On War* (1832)

In the first days of May 1915, a battalion of the Austrian territorial
militia detrained in a little town in the Puster valley, near the Italian
border. One, two, three, four companies marched out of the station,
complete with machine guns, horses, mules and muddy wagons, and
formed a column. The officers stared at the road ahead. The men were
not young or smart or well-equipped. The boys scampering around
could not get a word out of them. The adults realised that the dreaded
war with Italy must be very close. These men did not look up to much,
yet they were better than nothing and surely others would follow,
maybe with artillery.

The silent column marched westwards to the principal pass over the
mountains into Italy. People lined the road to cheer, and the closer they
drew to the border, the louder the cheers rang out. The soldiers halted
at nightfall near the foot of the pass, without encamping. Under cover
of darkness, they moved off again, quietly – not southwards to the
border, but north. Early next day, four more companies climbed down
from the train at Hermagor. 'Look!', people said, 'we're getting a whole
army!' The men fell in and marched off. At night they rested near the
border before turning their backs on the border and disappearing
northwards. Next day, the same happened again. The trainloads of
arriving soldiers looked wearier and more unkempt as the days passed.
Eventually some onlookers wondered if they were not the same men,

marching more than 40 kilometres each day with full kit, then looping around to the next valley and arriving back in Hermagor each morning. A battalion of the damned, repeating their futile routine day after day, with no hope of release.

If they really were the same men, then the meaning of the deception was all too obvious. The empire had no more or better troops to spare. Italian spies were supposed to report a build-up on the border, so that Cadorna would expect to confront a great battle-hardened army. Whatever the truth about this particular story, it was true that Austria could ill afford a third front. In summer 1914 – spectacularly unprepared for the war it was bent on fighting – Austria-Hungary had put 50 infantry divisions into the field against Russia's 94 and Serbia's 11 divisions. These divisions suffered early losses that almost beggar belief. The standing army's peacetime strength had been around 450,000; this force took some 80 per cent casualties in the first few months. The winter operations against Russia led to 700,000 losses, reducing many infantry divisions to 3,000 or 5,000 rifles, instead of the standard strength of 12,000. The 1914 campaign against Serbia cost the lives of 600 officers and 22,000 men. In other words, the casualties between August 1914 and May 1915 equalled the size of the prewar army. The official history of the war would say that the old professional army 'died in 1914' and was replaced by something quite different, 'a conscript and militia army'. The army that faced Italy in spring 1915 was a different force: 'civilians in uniform' for the most part, who were more easily moved by the nationalist currents washing through the empire.

Universal conscription had been introduced nearly fifty years before, but the army's capacity to draft and train the annual intake was very limited. While the population increased by 40 per cent between 1870 and 1914, military strength grew by only 12 per cent. Lacking weapons and facilities, Austria-Hungary could mobilise fewer men than France, which had a smaller population. In the decades before 1914, military spending in the Habsburg empire had fallen behind that of the other great powers. When Franz Conrad von Hötzendorf became chief of the general staff in 1906, there was a new effort to modernise the armed forces and boost their share of the budget. But military spending, even at its zenith, represented only 21 per cent of the empire's total budget. It was a quarter of Germany's and Russia's spending, less than half of France's, and less even than Italy's.

Still essentially pre-industrial, the empire produced less iron and steel than Belgium. While this lack of economic modernisation probably acted as a political preservative, it did the military no good, entailing permanent shortages. In 1914, Austria had the weakest firepower of any major army. Artillery support averaged only 42 light pieces per division (even the Russians had 48). Even so, they outgunned the Italians in the summer of 1915. Crucially, they had three times as many machine guns. The empire's lack of industrial capacity only became crippling in the war's later stages. Road and rail communications were also pre-modern – though it happened that Austrian rail links to the Italian front were far better than Italy's to Friuli (six railheads compared with two).

The army mirrored the ethnic diversity of the empire. In 1914, a quarter of the infantry were Austro-German; 18 per cent were Magyar-speakers (Hungarians); 13 per cent were Czechs. The rest (some 45 per cent) were Poles, Croats, Slovenes, Serbs, Romanians, Slovaks, Ruthenes, Bosniaks (Muslims from Bosnia), Jews, and also – in the proportion of one or two per cent – Italians. Elaborate procedures were in place to accommodate the multiethnic, polyglot intake. By 1914, the officer corps was still 72 per cent German-Austrian and the language of command remained German, but it comprised only 80 or 90 expressions. For the rest, regiments used whichever of nine other languages – most of them mutually unintelligible – that their men understood. Fewer than half of the 330 regiments were more or less homogenous in ethnic and linguistic terms. Fully half of them used two languages routinely. Officers were expected to learn the language of the troops within three years of joining a regiment. (Reservists who replaced officers lost in the early campaigns were often unable to communicate with their men.)

The high command was gloomily aware that the military could not be immunised against the rise of nationalism. Early in 1914, Conrad – whose opinion of Italians and Serbs verged on racist – sent a memo to the Emperor, ranking the nationalities in terms of their likely loyalty to the army in a war. The only 'completely reliable' elements would be the German Austrians, Croats, Slovenes and Bosniaks. The Serbs and Czechs, by contrast, were 'completely Russophile'. His forecast proved broadly accurate for the first two or three years of the war, until the bonds of loyalty frayed beyond repair for all nationalities. Many Serbs from Bosnia wanted Russia, not Austria, to win. There were summary executions of 'unreliable' Serb soldiers on the Eastern Front. All the

Serbian-language newspapers in the Habsburg province of Vojvodina (now northern Serbia) were banned at the start of the war. As for the Czechs, when two infantry regiments surrendered to the Russians in the spring of 1915, they were officially disbanded. Over the course of the war, the Bohemian Germans, Slovenes and Bosnian Muslims suffered the highest casualty rates – a rough but valid indicator.

Against this background, the high command was astonished when the mobilisation in 1914 proceeded without problems, indeed with fervour. No sooner had the failures against Russia and Serbia burned away the initial enthusiasm than the Italians gave Austrian morale a desperately needed lift. The Emperor's message to his people, announcing Italy's declaration of war, was crafted to stir deep emotions. Italy, he said, had committed a betrayal unique in history. After more than thirty years of alliance, the kingdom had 'abandoned us in the hour of danger' and unfurled its banners on the field of our enemies. But the 'great memories of Novara, Custoza and Lissa, which formed the pride of my youth, and the spirit of Radetzky, Archduke Albrecht and Tegethoff', the Habsburg commanders who had won those famous victories, guaranteed that 'we will also successfully defend the borders of the monarchy in the south'. They had always beaten the Italians in the past, and they would now do so again.

Anti-Italian propaganda pushed at an open door. The German Austrians had a set of prejudices about the uncivilised, unreliable, cowardly Italians that could easily be mobilised.[1] As early as August 1914, Conrad believed that the likely struggle with Italy would hinge on successful appeals to 'the good German and Slav peoples' of the empire, 'still loyal to the Emperor, and determined to fight valiantly for hearth and home'. The Slavic peoples could be encouraged to share the feeling that the Italians were perfidious, sly in the Latin way. This stereotype was a priceless asset; the high command's hope that Slavic soldiers would fight valiantly proved well-founded from the first clashes.[2] A few weeks into the war, the Papal nuncio in Vienna reported that hatred for the Italians was widespread. There were even mutterings that the

---

1 They had a slang word for Italian economic migrants: *Katzelmacher*, 'kitten-maker' or tomcat – sexually promiscuous, with a large family back home, typical of backward peoples. (The same fearful contempt can be heard today when Serbs talk about Albanians from Kosovo.)

2 This hope was also the fear of at least one British Foreign Office mandarin, who predicted in March 1915 that the Treaty of London 'would drive Dalmatia and the Slav countries into the arms of Austria'.

Church in Austria might split away from Rome. The Archbishop of Vienna agreed that anti-Italian passions posed a grave danger to Catholic unity. The Italians, by contrast, had no such universal 'enemy image' to manipulate. Hatred of the Austro-Hungarians was a middle-class emotion, and smart talk about Prussian militarism or the Habsburg prison-house of peoples was for intellectuals only.

General Ludendorff, Germany's First Quartermaster General but in reality the senior strategist, contrasted the Habsburg troops' lacklustre record on the Eastern Front with their ardour against the 'hereditary enemy'. Field Marshal Hindenburg, too, would write that they fought the Russians with their head but attacked the Italians with their whole soul. Czech and Slovak troops who had failed against Russia 'did excellent work against Italy'. Even greater excellence was shown by the Slovenes, Dalmatians (meaning Croats and Serbs from Croatia), and Bosnians, for these peoples – who entered the Yugoslav state together in 1918 – stood to lose most from Italian expansion in the Balkans. The high command played the ethnic card against Italy from the outset. Regiments from Slovenia were deployed to the Italian border in 1914. Dalmatian and Bosnian regiments were later sent where the fighting was fiercest. The front-line troops were supported by reservists from Trieste and Istria. The last Habsburg census before the war showed that some 7 million 'Yugoslavs' (Slovenes, Croats, Serbs and Bosniaks) lived in the empire – around 14 per cent of the total population. In 1914, they formed 11.5 per cent of the armed forces, and 3.1 per cent of the officer corps. By 1917, these proportions rose to 17 per cent and 9 per cent respectively. On the Isonzo front, Yugoslavs were 42 per cent of the Habsburg forces.

With its population of Orthodox Serbs (44 per cent), Muslim Bosniaks (32 per cent) and Catholic Croats (22 per cent), Bosnia compacted the empire's fractious diversity in a little space. The high command tried to ensure that the four Bosnian regiments all reflected the ethnic make-up of Bosnia as a whole. This was impossible to sustain when the purge of many Serbs early in the war reduced the strength of the Bosnian units by a third. Nevertheless, these regiments earned a reputation on the Italian front for supreme valour and toughness.

Conrad never trusted Italian neutrality. He placed the border units on alert in August 1914 and appointed General Franz Rohr to organise the defences so that Austria could resist the Italians 'most resolutely'. With the Habsburg army fully stretched on other fronts, Rohr's forces were a motley collection of training battalions, militia units, border guards and customs officers, armed with old rifles and no artillery to speak of. If they were attacked, they could be crushed in a few hours. (Falkenhayn wrote after the war that the Central Powers could 'scarcely' have held 'another enemy at bay' over the winter of 1914–15.) Rohr's men would not be reinforced by regular units until early 1915, when they were also joined by Tyrolese *Standschützen*, volunteer riflemen with a proud local tradition. Around 20,000 of these 'schoolboys and grandfathers' were soon under arms. (The regular troops from the Tyrol were away in Galicia and Serbia.) Similar units were formed in Carinthia, Slovenia and Trieste.

Conrad realised that Austria could not win a third war. His strategic aim was twofold: to delay an Italian advance towards Vienna, and keep possession of the Tyrol. (He did not believe Trieste could be held.) His first idea was to draw the Italians over the mountains, cut them off, and smash them in the valleys of Carinthia and Slovenia. He reckoned that public opinion in Italy was so divided over the war that this would deal a terminal blow. But it would be very risky, and he needed 10 German divisions. When Falkenhayn refused to deplete German forces on the Western and Eastern Fronts, Conrad was compelled to adopt a purely defensive strategy. His relationship with Falkenhayn, never good, deteriorated.

Conrad announced on 21 April 1915 that no ground should be ceded without a fight. The Austrians faced a much stronger enemy, and neither the quantity nor the quality of their supplies and equipment was likely to improve. On the contrary, it would be a miracle if these did not decline. So they took their stand not at the border but further back on the first high ground. They had learned from their campaign against Serbia, where small units of irregulars who knew the ground well and were supported by the people had defeated a much stronger but poorly informed force. They fortified the western edge of the Carso plateau and the hills around Gorizia, aiming to prevent the Italians penetrating the valleys that led to the interior. Working around the clock, they entrenched the plateau rim, laying landmines and triple rows of barbed wire. Bunkers were prepared for machine guns and artillery. The Italians apparently discovered little about these preparations. By mid-May, the defences around the Tyrol were complete, with wire entanglements 6–12 metres deep, trenches and emplacements excavated and sometimes armoured, magazines prepared, telephone lines laid, and sight-lines cleared of vegetation. Further east, the work in Carnia was delayed by late snowfalls.

The situation on the Isonzo was less satisfactory. Work in some northern sectors was almost complete but further south the defences were still patchy. The positions around Gorizia were mostly ready, though the barbed wire and minefields were not. The Carso and Monfalcone sectors – guarding the route to Trieste – were still sketchy; the Austrians had taken too long deciding where their front line should run. On the coast, they fixed their rear defences near Duino, a few kilometres east of Monfalcone, where their position overlooked open marshes and a deep fast river, the Timavo.[3] By 26 May, Rohr could report that the line on the Isonzo was 'almost completely closed', with two rows of barbed wire, increasing to four rows at decisive points. The first line would be ready by the end of the month, though the second, he warned, could not be finished in the near future.

Conrad reportedly said on 22 May that, if the Italians did not attack at once, it would show they were 'stupid dogs' as well as cowards. When the last Habsburg officials pulled out of Gorizia on 25 May, they told the head of the grammar school to hand over authority to the first Italian troops to enter the city. Two days later, General Erwin Zeidler led the 58th Division into the city. The Italians had missed a chance to capture Gorizia almost without firing a shot. He was soon joined by General Wenzel Wurm, arriving with his corps from Serbia and an order to 'stop the Italians with all methods as early as possible and to slow down their advance by causing them as many casualties as possible'. On his own initiative, Wurm prepared a bridgehead around Gorizia. He and Zeidler, an outstanding engineer, would make a first-rate team. By 1 June, the Austrians realised they were in the fight after all. This is why a Hungarian historian recently described the Italian delay as 'a gift from heaven'.

Conrad organised the five divisions on the Isonzo into a new formation, the Fifth Army, led by a Croatian general – the highest ranking 'Yugoslav' in the empire. On 27 May, the day he assumed command, Svetozar Boroević von Bojna issued a set of fundamental

3 This was the same Duino where the German poet Rilke spent the winter of 1911–12 as the guest of the noble family that still owns the castle. Walking on the battlements one stormy morning in January when 'the water gleamed as if covered with silver', Rilke seemed to hear a voice calling from the air: 'Who, if I cried out, would hear me among the angels' hierarchies?' This became the first line in the sequence of poems called the *Duino Elegies* (1923).

orders. All positions must be held to the last man. Commanders must allocate all manpower not needed in the front line to the *sacred duty* of adapting positions so that counter-offensives could be launched. Defences had to include at least five rows of barbed wire, with the first row camouflaged. If the troops stayed calm and only opened fire when the enemy was less than 100 paces away, they would hold the line. If the enemy broke through, the defenders must not panic but stay in their place while the reserves moved up to contain and reverse the breach. Prisoners should be taken whenever possible, to gain information.

Like Cadorna, Boroević had lived in uniform since the age of ten, had an unremarkable appearance and a reputation for ruthlessness. Unlike the other man, his career was based on achievements in war. First decorated for bravery during the capture of Sarajevo in 1878, he rose to become a corps commander fighting the Russians in 1914–15. Consistently impressive and effective, able to inspire devotion as well as respect, he proved an excellent choice to lead the defence. If the Italians had made all speed in May, they would have caught the Austrians before Boroević set his seal on his new command.

Cadorna's opposite number across the border was Franz Conrad von Hötzendorf (1852–1925), the Austrian chief of staff until March 1917. Near anagrams as well as near contemporaries, the two men were alike in several ways. Their direct experience of war was marginal and long ago (Cadorna at Rome in 1870, Conrad in the Balkans around 1880). Like Cadorna, Conrad 'believed that infantry could advance without adequate artillery support against entrenched positions'. Both men over-rated the capacity of their armies to carry out successful offensives, while underrating their enemies – a blindness that was accentuated by their remoteness from the troops and their almost unaccountable powers. Temperamentally, both were possessed by intense convictions and strong passions, and given to rhetorical boldness that wavered in front of real opportunity.

The differences, too, were striking. Conrad's was a larger, more gifted and complex personality. He was popular and self-confident as well as ambitious, exercising a power to charm and disarm that Cadorna never had. A brilliant linguist who mastered half a dozen languages, he loved the process of 'entering into the spirit of a language . . . coming closer to the mentality of the people'. He assured his Italian mistress that he much admired her people's 'racial characteristics'; he also keenly admired Japanese martial spirit, so much finer than the 'softened whites' of Europe. He shared the Victorian fascination with the laws of nature (without the Victorians' softening faith in Christian morality), the Viennese obsession with imperial decline, and the conservative hatred of liberalism. He was a tactical innovator who came up with new ideas for combat training, mountain warfare and military mapping. He was an inspirational teacher at the War School. He was also, however, a slave to philosophical dogma. For he was a Social Darwinist, convinced that the struggle for existence was an almighty law, the great principle that rules all earthly events. His first sight of corpses on a Bosnian battlefield filled him with 'the conviction of the relentlessness of the struggle for existence'. As we shall see in a later chapter, Social Darwinism was a common belief, but the intensity of Conrad's conviction was exceptional. Believing that non-Germanic peoples belonged to lesser races, such as the Turks in Bosnia with their *criminal physiognomies*, or the *primeval, bestial warriors* he had faced in Herzegovina, he argued that nationalist threats to the empire should be confronted and whenever possible, eliminated.

In practice, he advocated preventive wars against the Serbs and Italians. As incoming chief of staff, he was keen to settle accounts with Italy at the first opportunity. (Kaiser Wilhelm sympathised: it would, he said, give 'lively satisfaction' to join Austria in teaching their nominal allies a 'salutary lesson'.) Italy responded with bristling suspicion until Alberto Pollio became chief of staff in 1908, when military operations against Austria became almost unthinkable. Conrad was still convinced that a showdown was inevitable and had best be launched before nationalism eroded the armed forces beyond utility. In February 1910, he again urged a preventive war against 'Austria's congenital foe'. Franz Ferdinand, the Emperor's heir, shared Conrad's visceral hatred, but the Foreign Ministry and the Emperor did not. When Conrad repeated his call the following year – tempted by Italy's distraction in Libya – he was sacked. This move was naturally welcomed in Rome, just as his recall the following year was deplored. It came at the behest of Franz Ferdinand, who resented Serbia's success in the First Balkan War (1912) and wanted Conrad back at the helm.

Conrad loved the empire's Italian holdings in the way that British colonialists loved India, with a delicious sense of entitlement. As a young man, on the train to Trieste, he suddenly saw – as one still does, approaching from the north or east – the Adriatic spread below. 'The world lay open before me. I was filled with a sense of joy and freedom.' He spent four and a half years there, commanding the 55th Infantry Brigade, followed by a stint as commander in the Tyrol, where, as in Trieste, he despised the Italian agitators who were drawn, as he observed, from 'the intelligentsia, the propertied classes, the middle class, schoolboys, teachers, and a part of the clergy'. The Italian peasantry, on the other hand, were mostly still loyal. He was convinced that the south Tyrol would be an excellent base for attacking Italy.

Conrad's pessimism turned his high-risk programme for imperial renewal into a suicidal drive. Contrasting a *desire* for victory with the *will* to win, he accepted that the Habsburg empire lacked this will, yet believed it was better to risk total defeat than try to adapt. As he wrote to his mistress at the end of 1913, 'Our purpose ultimately will be only to go under honourably ... like a sinking ship.' His actions the following summer showed the same spirit. When Franz Ferdinand was assassinated, Conrad urged immediate war against Serbia; he wrote privately that it would 'be a hopeless struggle, but it must be pursued, because such an ancient monarchy and such a glorious army cannot perish ingloriously'. For he was under no illusion about Austria's ability to win on three fronts (or four, if Romania joined the Entente). When the short, victorious campaign of his public predictions did not come to pass, he blamed the politicians for dragging the empire into war before it was ready.

As for Italy, Conrad was the last person to show facile optimism in 1914 – especially after Pollio's sudden death removed the only Italian general that he almost trusted. On 23 July, when the Austrian foreign minister voiced doubts about Italy, Conrad commented that 'If we also have to fear Italy, then we should not mobilise.' Why did he ignore his own warning? His biographer, Lawrence Sondhaus, suggests that Conrad's carelessness was due to the impossibility of including another variable in his calculations, amid the tumult of July, without losing his mind. Yet there were other reasons why he omitted to reckon on Italy's likely betrayal. He despised the Italians as soldiers; on the other hand, if Austria was doomed to lose in the end, what did it matter if they joined the Allies?

At the same time, Italy was intimately associated for Conrad with love and hope, not war and betrayal. For he was besotted with an Italian woman, the wife of an Austrian industrialist. They had met at a social occasion in Trieste, when Conrad was happily married, but he remembered her when they met in Vienna seven years later. Conrad was now a widower, and Virginia was the mother of six children. Fascinated by his ardour, she recovered from her shock at his avowal of love. Her husband was complaisant, and Conrad became a fixture at the family home, and 'uncle' to her children. He persisted in wanting marriage, despite Catholic morality, his own eminence, and Virginia's horror at the prospect of losing her children, as would happen if she were the cause of a divorce. Conrad fantasised about returning from a triumphant campaign in the Balkans, bolstered with such prestige that he could sweep all obstacles aside and make Gina his wife. Amid the shattering events of September 1914 on the Eastern Front, with the old Habsburg army in tatters around him, he confided to an astonished fellow officer that failure in the field would mean losing Gina: 'a horrifying thought . . . because I would be lonely for the rest of my life'.[4] Rationally convinced that Austria was doomed, but unconsciously bent on engineering a conflagration that would let him smash the chains separating him from the woman he loved – what could be more Viennese, more human, banal and apocalyptic?

4 They married in autumn 1915, after the husband sued for divorce and Gina accepted generous terms for access to her children.

SEVEN

Walls of Iron, Clouds of Fire

*Let your rapidity be that of the wind, your
compactness that of the forest.*
  SUN TZU

*The first principle is, to concentrate as much
as possible. The second principle runs thus –
to act as swiftly as possible.*
  CARL VON CLAUSEWITZ

The First Battle of the Isonzo

Cadorna's first full-scale offensive had several objectives.[1] The Second
Army was ordered to take the summit of Mount Mrzli while enlarging
the bridgehead at Plava, further south, and strengthening its position
around Gorizia. These goals had to be pursued vigorously, aiming for
success 'at all costs'. Further south, the Third Army was to push
forward on the Carso between Sagrado and Monfalcone. For these
tasks, Cadorna committed only 15 of his 35 infantry divisions. The
remainder were distributed around the Alpine sectors further west, or
held in reserve. While the seven reserve divisions were soon moved to
the Isonzo, Cadorna's original decision showed an ominous reluctance
to concentrate his forces, as well as complacency about the prospects of
swift success.

At Plava, eight separate attempts to take Hill 383 on 24 June achieved
nothing. Operations ground to a halt. The offensive around Gorizia
failed due to lack of firepower against the strongest Austrian defences
on the front. General Zeidler, who had been decorated for his

---

1 When the Austrians began to identify the battles on the Isonzo by number, the Italians
followed suit, not guessing that this would play into the hands of enemy propaganda. As
Cadorna launched offensive after offensive from the same positions against the same lines,
the numbering of the battles underscored his failure to break through.

Front lines, 1915–18

fortifications in Bosnia and the Tyrol, ensured that his positions could not be seriously damaged by the Italian artillery. The bridgehead was safe as long as the hills of Sabotino and Podgora, looming above the river to the north and west of the town, were unconquered.

The thrust against Mount Mrzli began on 1 July. Two days of bombardment were followed by an infantry attack. But a poor spring had yielded to a wet and squally summer. Torrential rain had turned the 40-degree hillsides into muddy pistes, exposed to Austrian fire. The mist that sometimes lay in the valley bottom afforded the only cover. Infantry on the higher slopes were unable to dig proper trenches in ground that was too muddy or too rocky. The front line slanted up the hill from Tolmein, so the Italians were exposed to flanking fire from the lower Austrian positions. The attacks fizzled out. On Mount Sleme, halfway between Krn and Mrzli, a battalion of the Intra Brigade struggled up to the enemy wire, losing more than 300 men in the process. The commanding officer who had ordered the attack committed suicide. This operation was not mentioned in the daily bulletins issued by the Supreme Command. Indeed, actions on Mrzli during the rest of the year would mostly take place in official obscurity. Other assaults were tried piecemeal, and failed. The Italians took no ground between Krn and Tolmein.

They were discovering that barbed wire was practically insuperable. The Perugia Brigade tried to breach the wire on Podgora with gelignite tubes on 6 July. Enemy fire was so intense that they could not get close to the wire. When the Italians attacked next day, regardless, the Austrians held their fire until the attackers were 30 paces away, while the artillery opened up against the reserves in the rear. No advance was possible. The only sector where Italian operations avoided a fiasco was around the Carso, where the bombardment started on the 23rd, against enemy lines near Sagrado. The troops of the 19th and 20th Divisions drove the Austrians back and got a foothold on Mount San Michele and Mount Sei Busi. An epic struggle for the westernmost heights of the Carso had begun.

Both sides knew the strategic importance of Mount San Michele. A sprawling, inelegant hill with four distinct summits, it fills the angle where the River Vipacco flows into the Isonzo, south of Gorizia. Its summit rises only 250 metres above the plain, but the northern and western slopes are steep. In the east and south, the gradients are much gentler as the hill merges into the Carso plateau. It formed an Austrian salient, protecting Gorizia and the Vipacco valley on one side and the Carso on the other. Without it, the Austrians' defence on the lower Isonzo might unravel. The Italians were not aware that, on this part of the front, the enemy defences were still shallow. Lacking rock-drills, the Austrians had had time only to hack knee-deep grooves in the rock, then heap rubble and soil into low parapets. With every battalion tasked to prepare 3–5 kilometres of line, they hastily adapted the rocky outcrops, ridges and natural craters, and disguised the barbed wire with branches.

Shortly after midday on 1 July, the Italians advanced from their bridgehead at Sagrado towards the summit of San Michele, with a secondary thrust towards a rounded spur closer to the river, known as

Hill 142. Long afterwards, a junior officer in the Pisa Brigade, Renato di Stolfo, described the first attack. He was supposed to lead his platoon armed with a pistol, but there were no pistols, so he had nothing but his dress sabre, with no cutting edge. The day began with a thunderstorm at 06:00, as the men traversed the wooded flanks of the hill. Renato's waterlogged cape was so heavy that he threw it away. As the men emerged from the woods, the sun rose over the brow of the Carso in front of them, dispersing the clouds; a rainbow arced across the sky.

The men rest for a few hours, trying to dry out. At noon, they form a line, dropping to one knee while the officers stand with sabres drawn. The regimental colours flutter freely. Silence. Then a trumpet sounds, the men bellow 'Savoy!' as from one throat, the band strikes up the Royal March. Carrying knapsacks that weigh 35 kilograms, the men attack up the steep slope, in the teeth of accurate fire from positions that the Italians cannot see. An officer brandishing his sabre in his right hand has to use his left hand to stop the scabbard from tripping him up. The men are too heavily laden to move quickly. Renato remembered the scene as a vision of the end of an era: 'In a whirl of death and glory, within a few moments, the epic Garibaldian style of warfare is crushed and consigned to the shadows of history!' The regimental music turns discordant, then fades. The officers are bowled down by machine-gun fire while the men crawl for cover on hands and knees. The battle is lost before it begins. The Italians present such a magnificent target, they are bound to fail. A second attack, a few hours later, is aborted when the bombardment falls short, hitting their own line. The afternoon peters out in another rainstorm.

Yet these blundering attacks, repeated less disastrously over the following days, pressed the Austrians harder than the Italians knew. On 4 July, the Austrian commander on the Carso reported that his situation was desperate: the last reserves had been pulled into the line. Control of the plateau edge was threatened. The Duke of Aosta, commanding the Third Army, had asked for reinforcements on the 2nd, but Cadorna was non-committal. By the time extra forces arrived on the afternoon of the 5th, the Austrian crisis was past.

On the southernmost sector, around Monfalcone, the Italian mood was gloomy. The first efforts to drive the Austrians off Mount Cosich and the neighbouring heights (Hills 85 and 121) failed badly. Even worse, the counter-attacks created panic. The Italians were taking steady high losses from the machine guns across the valley. The First Battle found Private Giani Stuparich near the Rocca, on the brow of a hill overlooking the bare, rocky valley. (Today the hillsides are thickly wooded, and a motorway passes along the valley.) He spent his days crouching behind a dry-stone wall reinforced with sandbags, facing a jumble of wire, nauseated by the stink of shit; for the men defecated in the open – anywhere, just to be safe from snipers – turning the pine-scented hillside into a dunghill. The constant rain churned the red clay into soapy, clinging muck. At night, he curled up in the muck and sank into sleep that was violent and black, like death.

The Austrians repelled four attacks on Hill 121. A fifth attempt fails when the company assails the wrong part of the line, where there are no gaps in the wire. Nothing goes well, and the forced passivity is a burden. When their commanding officer asks for volunteers to blow a hole in the enemy wire, Giani and his brother Carlo step forward. There is six days' leave for the team that succeeds, but they are not after this reward; they are Habsburg Italians, volunteers from Trieste. 'We are in this war because we wanted it; how can we hide behind silence?' That night, they creep towards the enemy lines carrying gelignite tubes. Unusually, the party succeeds in breaching the wire, but the gaps are repaired before the Italians can exploit them. Giani's spirits sink when the Austrians bombard Monfalcone; at this early stage of the fighting, the targeting of civilian areas shocks the idealistic volunteer.

The first full-scale attack against Cosich began at 02:30 on 30 June, in torrential rain. Austrian counter-battery fire silenced the Italian guns. Yet the dawn assault was not abandoned, as another veteran recalled: 'All at once the cry goes up, with nothing human about it, "Savoy! Savoy!" – which the valleys echo up to the sky, as if invoking God's witness to their martyrdom. But a wall of iron stops them, a cloud of fire envelops them.'

The last veteran of the first battle on the Isonzo was alive and well in a leafy suburb of Rome in 2004. Born in December 1894, Carlo Orelli was conscripted on 24 May 1915 and sent off to the Carso after notional training. Nearly 90 years later, he sat in sharp sunlight beside the opened shutters of his bedroom window. He was very still under his dressing gown, silk scarf and cloth cap; only an index finger moved, tracing a pattern on his leg. His blue eyes were filmy.

Orelli was a Socialist, but in the debate over intervention that raged in Italy in 1914–15, he switched sides, like Mussolini. 'Supposedly it was all secret, but everyone knew the war was coming.' The troop train left from Naples.

It was a lovely day, I remember it well. A great blue sky. We thought we were going to the front to take Trento and Trieste, which were under Austria. We had gone to war to conquer those territories, which were Italian. Austria had taken them from us. Then we would go forward, forward . . . We expected a short war, not one that would last so many years.

Words came awkwardly, in short breaths, as memories surfaced.

Was it a war of conquest or liberation? 'Liberation,' he said firmly. 'We were not taking what was theirs.' Were the troops eager for war? 'Not enthusiastic, no! They thought it was a fine thing to reconquer our lands, *le terre nostre*, but they weren't prepared for what faced them at the front.'

He was a non-commissioned officer in the 3rd Company of the Siena Brigade. Arriving at Sagrado at the end of May in cotton uniforms and berets, with boots of light canvas, the Italians pillaged the linen they found in the houses ('Austrian stuff', said Orelli), as well as blocks of sugar that were left in a factory yard. The men were mostly from Calabria, in the south. 'You could not understand a word they said. Good illiterate peasants. I wrote their letters home for them. Oh, you people today don't know how backwards Italy was in those times. They couldn't read or write, but they never complained. They died in silence.' He did not blame the army for poor training. 'War is not something you teach, you do it and that's all. Attack, fire, take cover when you have to. That's it. And then bring in the dead.'

The Italians were hugely disadvantaged at the outset. 'The Austrians had fine covered trenches, with bunkers. They shot at us from loopholes, while we were in shallow holes, ordered to charge the enemy with bayonets. It was attacks, attacks all the time, from dawn to dusk.' The Austrians on Mount San Michele did not have to shoot much. 'They only had to hold their positions and wait to kill us in the open.'

While the Austrian positions on San Michele during the first battle were not really much better (though they soon became so), Orelli's recollection is true to the Italians' sense of being desperately unprepared. And he was correct about the difference in firepower.

You cannot have any idea what an Austrian 420-millimetre howitzer sounds like. Quite different from what you would expect. It's not like in a film. It was too far away to make a boom. It was more of a rumble, a distant roar, then a whistling that grew louder and louder the closer it came. Then we knew the shell was about to hit. It did not always explode at once. Sometimes it didn't explode at all. That's the lottery of death.

The Italians did not have any 420s, or any 305s for that matter. They had a few 149-millimetre guns at Sagrado, targeting those Habsburg trenches.

The Italians' battle cry was 'Savoy!', while the enemy screamed 'Hurrah!', or 'Živila Austrija!' ('Long live Austria!') if they were Croatians or Bosnians. On Mount San Michele and Mount Sei Busi, the armies were 100 or 200 metres apart. There was a 'tacit agreement' not to make each other's lives even worse than they had to be. Sniping was suspended between attacks.

Did you hate the enemy?

No, no, no! They were under orders, just as we were. War is war, if you try to kill me I'll try to kill you, but there was no hatred. When we took prisoners, they were sent to work the land in Italy for the rest of the war. There was no mistreatment. It was the same with Italians taken prisoner. The Austrians, who had everything, offered our men fine food, because they knew we had nothing. We asked them to taste it first, in case it was poisoned, but it was all good stuff.

'It was a war without hatred,' he repeated, 'not like nowadays, with all this. . .' His attention drifted, following some elusive connection. The pause lengthened. 'There's war everywhere now,' he announced. 'A nation is dying today – the one led by that general with the beard, a prisoner now. What's his name?' He meant Saddam Hussein, the Iraqi dictator, lately captured but not yet executed.

Lightly wounded in the First Battle, Orelli was riddled with shrapnel in the Second. By this point, only 25 men of the 330 who had gone up to the line with him in May were still unharmed. He left the front in September 1915, never to return, so the attitudes that crystallised in him – including the conviction that gentlemanly conduct had persisted – reflected the first months of fighting. Orelli had not seen the spiral down into brutality and perhaps did not believe it ever occurred.

'I remember the mountains,' said Orelli, making a final effort for my benefit, 'places where we fought. I remember my part of the front, at Sagrado, where the artillery was. I remember waking one morning and finding myself in a cemetery! But many things I don't remember any longer,' he finished, with a hint of frustration. Forgetting was a new experience, still resented. Even so, he recognised the names of hills on

[93]

the Carso more quickly than his children's names. He wanted to see those places again, but his legs were not what they had been. His parting handshake was warm and light, like holding a bird. 'Many greetings to your family, and when you visit Rome again, come and see me,' he said, patting the chair. 'I'll be right here.'

There is so much talk nowadays about Trento and Trieste, and the war to liberate them [he told his last interviewer], but nobody really knows what it was like.

He died in January 2005, a month after his 110th birthday.

EIGHT

Trento and Trieste!

When I asked the 109-year-old Carlo Orelli what he had believed he was fighting for, he replied almost testily, 'Why, Trento and Trieste!' Another veteran, perhaps the last still alive at this time of writing, Delfino Borroni, gave the same answer to the same question: 'For Trento. For Trieste. To get what was due to Italy. It was our land. Instead the Germans and the Austrians had chased us away. That wasn't right.'

Their long dead comrades would say the same – if they could identify a reason at all. With an average age of 20 or 21, pulled straight from labour on the land, many or even most had little idea why they were in uniform. Italy's war poets noticed a tragic symmetry between the completeness of their comrades' ignorance and the totality of the sacrifice they were called on to make. Fresh evidence of this came as recently as 2005, in a series of interviews with surviving veterans, all well over 100 years old. Many confessed to having felt bafflement about Italy's aims. 'I did not know why there was a war at all,' said one. 'For that matter they didn't let the troops in on anything. You had to find your reasons for yourself, on the spot.' Introducing these interviews, the historian Lucio Fabi said the old-timers had forgotten the reasons. Given the vividness of their accounts, they were more likely expressing a truth that has not yet become quite palatable. Lectures by officers on Italy's goals and purposes did not necessarily leave the blank-faced conscripts any the wiser. The key word 'irredentism' was mysterious to the majority. After months at the front, Private Mussolini reported in his newspaper that the peasant soldiers remained 'unaware of the existence' of the words 'neutrality' or 'intervention'.

The task of explanation was made no easier by the secrecy that shrouded the Treaty of London. Expansion in the Balkans, the eastern Mediterranean and Asia Minor was hardly the stuff for inspirational talks to the troops, while the elaborate bloodthirsty speeches of D'Annunzio would make no more sense to many officers than to the men. According to Curzio Malaparte, the veteran and journalist, 'The profound ignorance of our masses did not admit historical or

[95]

geographical complexities. When the officers explained to us the ideal reasons of our war and the need to crush the barbarism and militarism of the Central Powers, the soldiers were deeply attentive; but they did not understand a word.'

Trento and Trieste, on the other hand, were actual places, not airy concepts, even if most of the soldiers had never heard of them before. They became the symbols of injustice and a national mission unfulfilled. The keyword in nationalist accounts of Austrian rule was 'domination'. This vague word was paired with another, equally emotive: 'redemption'. Redeeming these two cities for Italy was the most publicised and least controversial of the government's reasons for going to war. Interventionists wore rosettes of red, white and green ribbon around the names of Trento and Trieste. Alliteration evoked a military rhythm: the tongue struck the palate like boots on freedom's road. To the Triestine poet Umberto Saba, it was like diastole and systole: 'the double-name' that beat louder than his own heart.

The Trentino is a mountainous area the size of Devon or Delaware, shaped on the map like a man riding a bull. It reaches from the northern tip of Lake Garda to a line midway between Trento and Bolzano. It is bisected by the River Adige, whose narrow valley has always been one of the main trans-Alpine corridors and is now tinged with smog from traffic pounding up to the Brenner Pass or down to Venice, Verona and points beyond. A century ago its population was overwhelmingly Italian: the 1910 census found that its 383,000 inhabitants included only 13,500 German-speakers. The city of Trento had around 20,000 people. Between the Trentino and the Alps proper lies the region known to Italians as Alto Adige, the 'upper Adige', where the ethnic balance is very different. Its population of 242,000 included 16,500 Italian-speakers at most, and perhaps many fewer. (The 1910 census findings are disputed.) An Italian guide to the 'unredeemed lands' published in September 1915 admitted that the rural parts of the Alto Adige were 'absolutely German'.

When it came under Austrian control in 1815, the Trentino was merged with the Tyrol – a move that local Italians resented. Their demand for autonomy was raised in 1848, the year of revolutions, then periodically up to 1914. The Austrians refused to risk losing control of this sensitive frontier. Their argument, that Trentino formed a natural extension of the Tyrol, admittedly somewhat Italian in character but still part of a Germanic whole, was not tenable if only for ethnic reasons.

For nationalists, Trentino was undeniably Italian, a reasonable claim that was taken, unreasonably, as proving Mother Italy's entitlement to the whole of the south Tyrol. Although the tiny size of the Italian community undermined any ethnic claim to Alto Adige, the strategic claim was paramount. Unless Italy controlled the Tyrolese Alps up to the watershed, Venice and its lowlands would always be vulnerable to Austrian assault. Mazzini did not doubt that Italy must possess everything up to 'the highest circle of the Alps'. The imperative of so-called natural borders trumped the national rights that Mazzini himself generally upheld. The Austrians were equally adamant that the Tyrol was theirs for ever. It had a particular status in their empire; coming under the direct authority of the royal house, it was the apple of Franz Josef's eye. With its cattle and vineyards, felt hats, Lederhosen and dirndl skirts, pine-clad mountainsides and foaming rivers, it was an album of luscious images that summed up Habsburg Austria.

The failure of the 1866 campaign dealt a blow to irredentists in the Trentino. Vienna halted a process of enlightened reform that went back seventy years. Some societies and newspapers were banned. Students were no longer allowed to study at the University of Padua. Austria erected a customs barrier with Italy where there had been none before, hurting commerce across the frontier. In 1903, Italian teachers were banned from the university in Innsbruck, provoking demonstrations in Italy. Italian deputies in the Tyrolese assembly, also in Innsbruck, were outvoted by their German colleagues.

The Trentino's Italian identity could only be dismantled by tyrannical repression, which was not in the Habsburg repertory. Despite the partial repression, extensive concessions were made to the Italians. Except in the army and police, theirs was the official language of local government, courts and schools. In 1890, they founded a National League to defend their nationality. (It was tolerated until 1915.) The community paid for a monument to Dante; unveiled in 1896, the massive statue was a potent reminder of Italy's past greatness and current misfortune. Around this time, an Italian ideologue floated the idea that the German-speaking Tyrolese were Germanised Italians. (This thesis would be exploited under Fascism and even afterwards.) An official counter-offensive of pro-German measures and pan-Germanist propaganda, launched in the 1880s, only hardened the ethnic and linguistic divide. Yet the fact of division did not translate automatically into resistance. As elsewhere, irredentism was a concern of the urban élite. The farmers mostly favoured staying in the empire, for their best market lay to the north. Indifference to nationalist grumbles rested on economic common sense.

The empire persisted in its self-destructive policies. Over the long run, measures to suppress irredentism served to strengthen it. A few Austrian officials realised that economic under-development was fuelling tension, but little was done. When routes to rational progress are blocked, people turn radical, embracing ideologies of salvation. This process was personified by Cesare Battisti, a name familiar to all Italians because of his martyr's death (every town in the land has a via Battisti). Editing magazines, launching cultural initiatives, penning a stream of reports on social and economic conditions, serving as a city councillor, a Socialist deputy in the provincial assembly and then in Vienna, Battisti was the sort of figure who can ignite and organise a political movement almost single-handed. He was a tireless agitator for Italian interests within the Habsburg empire before he became an enemy of that empire. As a councillor, he campaigned for civic issues: the quality of flour, public health. Not an extremist by nature, he was clear-thinking and practical, only driven to violent solutions by Habsburg refusal to reform.

By 1913, when the Italian army secretly hired him to write a military guide to the Trentino, Battisti had given up on Austria. He already knew his native valleys and villages by heart. Using his parliamentary position to get access to Habsburg army maps, he combed the territory anew. The following spring he started to do the same for the Alto Adige, up to the Brenner Pass, when he was abruptly redirected to the Carnian and Julian Alps. When he reached the Isonzo, in early August, an Austrian patrol stopped him and asked why he was examining this particular bridge over the river. Trekking around the mountains, Battisti had no idea that Austria had declared war on Russia and mobilised all men between 20 and 40. He hurried back to Trento and led his family over the border into Italy.

Unlike other leaders in Trento such as the Catholic activist Alcide De Gasperi, who became Italy's prime minister after the Second World War, Battisti realised that the events of August 1914 had destroyed reformist illusions for ever. He was still a socialist, anti-clerical, committed to the equality and liberation of all peoples. Austria's rage to destroy Serbia confirmed that multinational empires had to be dismantled if socialism was to be established in Europe. Only national states could provide the framework of legitimate governance that gives socialist parties a chance to win power. For the Italians of the empire, the hour of destiny had struck. Battisti became the first prominent Italian to call publicly for Austria-Hungary to be abolished.

Over the next six months or so, he spoke at over a hundred public meetings up and down the land, arguing for Italy to intervene. Sometimes he was cheered to the echo; at others, the anti-war faction stopped him reaching the platform or making himself heard. Privately he disagreed with nationalist demands for all of the south Tyrol; publicly he kept the faith, 'because it is not for me, as an irredentist, to deprecate the maximal programme of the irredentists'. His speeches were larded with propaganda. He claimed that Trentino's population was 'entirely Italian', and the only reason why Alto Adige's population was four-fifths German was that 'barbarian irruptions' from the north during the decline of the Roman Empire had driven the 'Romanised elements' away from the Alps. Trentino's mission was to hold back the 'Teutonic elements' and preserve its 'incorruptible Roman-ness'. Everything about Trentino was, he insisted, Italian: the sky, the flora, the climate, the customs, traditions and feelings. Even the criminals were *passionately* delinquent, not like cold-hearted German crooks.

Along with such absurdities, Battisti harshly criticised Rome's official attitude to irredentism since 1866. While the Trentino sank into 'wretched squalor', governments in Rome sacrificed Trento and Trieste to their relationship with the great powers. Whenever Italy ratified its existing borders, it drove another nail into the coffin of patriotic aspirations. After the Treaty of Berlin in 1878, irredentism was dropped from foreign policy. 'Whole generations in Italy not only feel no fraternity with the Italians of Trento and Trieste; they lack the most elementary geographical notion about those lands.' This, Battisti argued, was why the real defender of Italian identity in the Trentino had become – Austria itself! For the brutality and cynicism of repression fanned the fire of rebellion. The more Austria discouraged political awareness among its Italians, the more convinced they grew that Trentino had no future in the empire. He gave political and economic reasons why Trentino should be annexed to Italy, but what he called 'the reason of blood' was paramount. 'All the sons of Italy should be united in a single family.'

Battisti's Trento was recognisably medieval. Craftsmen and merchants bustled along narrow lanes in the shadow of a great castle, overlooked by steep hillsides crowded with vineyards and meadows. There were and still are a dozen places more or less like it on all sides of the Alps. Trieste was very different. The Austrians invented it in the eighteenth century to be their great port, connecting the empire to the seaways of the world.

Trieste lies in the north-eastern corner of the Adriatic Sea, on the upper edge of the Istrian peninsula. It faces north-west, towards the Italian mainland, with its back to the Balkans. The city elders chose Habsburg rule in the fourteenth century to protect themselves against Venice. In 1719, when it was a fishing town with some 7,000 inhabitants, Vienna gave it the status of a Free Port and development began in earnest. The salt pans were filled in and a grid of streets was laid around a short canal, with imposing piazzas, a seafront, and quays reaching into the deep-water harbour. The old castle and cathedral were left on a hilltop in the background, picturesque witnesses to the activity below. When the railway arrived in the 1850s, Trieste grew even faster as the transit port for goods coming from or going to central Europe. After Venice was lost in 1866, it became the empire's naval head-quarters. After 1869, when the Adriatic became a route to the Suez Canal, Triestine prosperity increased again. (Italian trade hardly benefited at all.)

Thriving in their fabricated city, the Triestines were more interested in commerce than politics. Language was a marker of class, not a flag of identity; the Italians filled the wide space between German-speaking merchants, administrators and army or navy officers on one side, and the Slavic peasants drawn in by the promise of paying work on the other. The commercial élite of shipping magnates, bankers and insurers comprised many nationalities. Cultures mixed here, overlapping rather than blending. The Jewish, Greek and Serbian communities all left their stamp on the architecture. They coloured its idiom too: the dialect called *triestino* amalgamates several influences in an Italian matrix.

The city's heyday lasted a quarter of a century, from around 1890. A third harbour was built. Preferential tariffs boosted Trieste's attraction and the eastern Adriatic became the seventh biggest shipbuilding centre in the world. By some indicators, its citizens were the richest in the empire. Including the suburbs, the population grew from 155,000 in 1890 to 230,000 in 1910 and 243,000 in 1914. It was now the third biggest city in Austria, after Vienna and Prague – and ten times more populous than Trento. (In Hungary, Budapest was growing at a similar explosive rate.) Ethnically, 51 per cent of the population in and around the city was Slavic, with Slovenes outnumbering Croats by 20 to 1. Just over a third was Italian. In the city itself, Italians outnumbered Slovenes by more than 4:1, with almost 96,000 as against 22,500. In the suburbs, the Slovenes had a narrower majority: 28,000, compared with 22,000 Italians.

Trieste had an affluent middle class, cafés, newspapers, theatres, and an appetite for culture. Its position between Vienna and Rome, as well as its hospitality to outside influences, made it a channel for ideas as much as trade, a natural home for innovation. Trieste was the crack through which modernism seeped into Italy. Ibsen and Wagner found early champions here. Freudian psychoanalysis entered Italy through Trieste. The young James Joyce came to teach English in 1904 and stayed to write two masterpieces and begin a third, *Ulysses*. (If the Austrians had not forced foreigners to leave in 1915, he would never have gone.) One of his middle-aged pupils, Italo Svevo, invented the psychological novel in Italian, writing in a 'Germanic' style that offended Italy's literary purists. Marinetti, the impresario of Futurism, loved the modern swirl of ideas and ideologies, calling Trieste 'our beautiful powder-keg'.

The city's modern buzz echoed more loudly because there were so few traditions to muffle it. Despite the massive solidity of the Habsburg buildings and the substantial Austrian commitment behind them, there was something rootless about Trieste, provisional, two-dimensional. Whether cultural status is measured by the canonical achievements of Western civilisation or by folklore, Trieste looked eccentric, flamboyantly crammed with different nationalities.

This did not trouble most of Trieste's Italians. These people were certainly patriotic: they celebrated the King's birthday, adored the patriotic operas of Verdi, rallied for an Italian-language university, and resented the censors and narks who pounced on signs of nationalist disaffection. Yet, while there was no shortage of minor 'provocations', Italian extremists were almost unknown. (Guglielmo Oberdan, would-be assassin of the Emperor, was the rule-proving exception.) This lack of zeal troubled some of the brightest middle-class Triestines who were born around 1890. The city's vivid variety was no compensation for its shaming lack of national definition or continuity. The Habsburg Jewish writer Joseph Roth gibed that 'national self-determination' was 'an intellectual luxury for a group that has nothing more serious to worry about'. Of nobody was this more true than Trieste's irredentists.

Benefiting from the city's prosperity while despising its materialism, they were inspired by the heroic story of Italy's unification. Austrian orderliness seemed paltry and banal to 20-year-old intellectuals whose only direct experience of the Kingdom of Italy was a spell at university in Florence or Rome. Their loyalty was to an Italy of the spirit, so imperfectly represented by governments in Rome. Whether they were convinced like Battisti that only a national state could deliver social justice, like D'Annunzio that nationalism was supremely beautiful, or like the Futurists that it was supremely thrilling, they felt, like nationalists in other border societies, more oppressed than the facts of their situation warranted.

As well as exaggerating their oppression, the irredentists overstated the level of support in their community. In the run-up to war, Battisti claimed that all the Italians in Trieste demanded more than economic improvements and political autonomy. ('The people in Trieste want complete liberty. They want to be redeemed from the Habsburg yoke. They, together with all of Venezia Giulia, want to be annexed to Mother Italy.') This was never remotely true. Mario Alberti, a high-profile irredentist from Trieste before he was a high-profile Fascist, recalled that the prewar movement had minimal impact on the villages and little in the towns and cities. It had no following among industrial leaders or bankers, some influence among the middle classes (shopkeepers, craftsmen), and most influence among intellectuals (students, teachers, lawyers, doctors). He estimated that Trieste had about 500 active irredentists and no more than 4,500 sympathisers. One of the former was Giani Stuparich (b. 1891), whom we last saw in a trench above Monfalcone:

Growing up in these parts meant growing up with an unstable heredity, one that constantly needed propping up. Simply going for a walk meant collisions. There was nowhere, not a single place, to repose in contemplation. If you sat on the bank of a stream, in order to lose yourself in its placid flow, a shout would immediately reach you from the other bank, a shout that you had to oppose. If you searched high up for the serenity of the sky which extends above the mountain crests, you found someone already there on the same summit who squared up to defend himself when you drew near and raised his staff, ready to strike.

Compared to this feverish vision, political or economic arguments for annexing the city to Italy were papery. For this, in the end, was irredentism's foundation: an appalled conviction that, wherever you went, you would be challenged by 'a shout that you had to oppose', an alien wielding a stick. It was an obsessive state of mind which James Joyce – who loved Trieste's polyglot, hybrid openness – teased in his prose-poem 'Giacomo Joyce', written a few years before the war: 'Trieste is waking rawly: raw sunlight over its huddled browntiled roofs . . . a multitude of prostrate bugs await a national deliverance.'

The real cause of Stuparich's dread was a factor that loomed very large in Trieste, though it did not exist in the Trentino. This was the threat posed by 'the Slavs'. The German-speakers were not numerous; linked to the Habsburg administration, they would dwindle along with Habsburg power. The local Slovenes were another matter. The irredentists were outraged by Habsburg encouragement of Slav immigration to the eastern Adriatic towns, which was happening anyway for economic reasons. From around 1880, the Slovenes joined the imperial administration in droves, established banks and cultural societies, and won official status for their language in schools and courts. A Slovene middle class was emerging. When universal male suffrage was introduced for parliamentary elections in 1907, Slovenes in the countryside challenged the Italians in the urban centres. The Italians were used to holding disproportionate power in city councils along the coast, and resented its loss. Committed to minimising the Slavic presence in public life, Italian nationalism took on a strongly anti-democratic tint.

Behind the irredentists' hostility stretched a civilisational divide that was centuries old. Stuparich was not a racist; he belonged to an enlightened circle that studied the other subject peoples of the empire, taking their problems seriously. He himself wrote a fine book about the Czechs. Yet the Czechs were comfortably remote; about the Slovenes, his fellow Triestines, he had little to say. Where Battisti made rhetorical hay by likening the modern Austrians to the Hunnish hordes, the Triestine irredentists identified the Slovenes as latter-day barbarians. With no cultural achievements to their name (meaning, none that the Italians knew or cared about), communicating in an incomprehensible tongue, the irredentists' Slavic neighbours – dockers, labourers, servants and nursemaids, but also clerks, teachers and priests – loomed as the first waves of an ocean that would drown the remnants of Italian identity.

These remnants were shrilly celebrated by nationalist writers in Italy. As one of them complained, before the 1860s the mute and anonymous

Slavs of the eastern Adriatic had 'slept the sleep of their prehistory'. How dare the Austrians stir them into consciousness! The Italians of Istria numbered over 130,000 in 1910, and dominated the coast and larger inland towns. In Dalmatia, however, there were only 18,000 Italian-speakers in a population of 610,000. Luigi Barzini, the star reporter of *Corriere della Sera*, described the towns in inland Istria in 1913 as great fortresses under siege. Along the coast, 'Italianism is uncontaminated, full, generous, ardent, and proudly struggling for its millennial life.' Behind the 'invading Slavs' stood 'the full weight of the vast Slavic masses of the empire with its social and financial structures, and its thirst for conquest. Behind the Italians', by pathetic contrast, 'there is no one and nothing. They are alone with their right.' Egged on by the Habsburg authorities, the Slavs, 'an inferior race', were waging 'a bloodless war of extermination'. By carrying this incendiary journalism, the *Corriere della Sera* hoped to stoke public feeling against the Triple Alliance and Socialist internationalism.[1] More likely it narrowed the slender space for liberal debate about nationality politics in the empire.

Beyond the cries of persecution, what alarmed the irredentists was their anxiety that, in the terms that dominated thinking about nations and nationhood, the Slovenes were powered by the unstoppable energy of youth. Many educated Italians worried that their own civilisation was torpid and exhausted; in Trieste, this worry sharpened into paranoid fear. History's next winners would prove their strength by trampling on the has-beens.

People who claim to believe in determinist ideas rarely act on them. Moderate spirits wanted a rational redistribution of power within the empire, letting the non-Germanic peoples organise their own affairs. Nationalists argued, with desperate chauvinism, that Italy could still use force to assimilate the Slovenes. The most extreme wanted a war to bring the empire down; without their imperial sponsors in Vienna, the Slavs could be put in their place.

Stuparich and other young Triestines felt in their souls that Italian identity on the eastern Adriatic could be saved. Dazzled by idealism, they took their city's prosperity for granted. While they dreamed of

---

1 From 1909, Trieste's Italian and Slavic Socialist Parties presented a single slate in local elections. This was consistent with Austrian Socialist anti-nationalism; the party leaders in Vienna wanted to reform the empire into a federation of ethnically-based units.
Nationalism, in their view, was an outgrowth of bourgeois capitalism, a weapon in the class war that should and could be 'put beyond use', if it could not be destroyed.

turning Trieste into a moral example to the world, they ignored the sources of its prosperity. When they remembered economics at all, they called for Trieste to replace Venice as the Queen of the Adriatic. In Rome, Sidney Sonnino, before he started angling to bring Italy into the war, was hard-nosed enough to admit that Trieste would be 'ruined' if it joined Italy. This was a forecast that irredentists could not afford to heed; instead they insisted that if Italy controlled enough of the hinterland, the city could remain buoyant.

Even in Trieste, where socialists outnumbered irredentists, wiser heads saw that severing the city from central Europe would rob it of a future. One such head belonged to Angelo Vivante, a Triestine Jewish journalist who analysed 'Adriatic irredentism' (the title of his classic study) and reached three conclusions. Trieste's economic potential for Italy was very limited. The Slovenes and Croats were entitled to resist assimilation; if the Italians were right to resist Austrian domination, then the Slavs would be right to resist Italy. The third conclusion followed: ethnic or national cohabitation was the only way to ensure the wellbeing of all the peoples concerned. The national issue should be resolved bilaterally; the *partly* Italian identity of this region could be affirmed *without* war, inside the Habsburg empire, to which undeniable economic interests bound the territory. The empire should be helped to evolve into a democratic union of peoples, as a station towards a European socialist confederation.

However utopian his vision, Vivante's practical priority was conciliation and reform. Militant irredentists shouted him down. Ruggero Timeus, who would volunteer for the Italian army in 1915 and die in uniform that September, warned that if Trieste and Venezia Giulia remained in Austria, the Italian minority would be drowned in a sea of Slavs. It followed that Italy should provoke a war and conquer Venezia Giulia by force. This was in Italy's interest in any case, he added, as the young kingdom ought to expand around the northern Adriatic, to become 'master' of the sea.

Among the Triestines who sided publicly with Vivante in 1912 was a young writer and activist called Scipio Slataper. In 1914, he became a warmonger. By the end of 1915, he had died a hero's death on Podgora hill. As we shall see in a later chapter, the story of how a generation of middle-class Italians overcame their liberal doubts is summed up in Slataper's strange career.

From Position to Attrition

Among mountains there are everywhere numerous positions extremely strong by nature, which you should abstain from attacking.
NAPOLEON

The Second Battle of the Isonzo

On 7 July 1915, the last day of Italy's first full-scale offensive, Cadorna was at a conference of Allied commanders in France, to co-ordinate operations. The main purpose was to support the Russians, who had lost ground steadily since the defeats at Gorlice in May. It was hoped that a fresh Anglo-French offensive in August would relieve pressure on the Eastern Front. On the 'Italo-Serbian front', as General Joffre irritatingly called it, the Italians should keep attacking with all their might. The French commander added that, if Germany came to Austria's aid on the Isonzo, the Italians might think of stopping at Laibach and Klagenfurt. A period of consolidation on the plains, with the Alps at their back, would leave them well placed to resume the offensive towards Vienna and Budapest in due course.

Within a few months, this advice would mock the Italians' inability to crack the Isonzo front. At the time, Cadorna took heart from the Allied support for his strategy and tactics. A week and a half later, the mobilisation was complete and Cadorna launched the second offensive. The bombardment began at 04:00 on 18 July along a 36-kilometre front. The Supreme Command took responsibility for co-ordinating the medium-calibre batteries and, instead of showering shells around the Austrian lines, the gunners concentrated on hitting the front line. This improved the results; the Austrians were stunned by the artillery fire, which continued into the afternoon. Yet the Italians still lacked detailed information about enemy positions, and did not realise that in many places the Austrians ducked into well-made underground shelters. The rear positions, on the other hand, were totally exposed, and the reserves took heavy casualties.

The main objective was Mount San Michele, at the northern tip of the Carso. Attacking at 13:00 hours on the 18th, the infantry made good progress, quickly reaching the enemy lines on outlying summits and pressing upwards. The hilltop was stormed on 20 July, but the triumphant Italians were hammered by accurate Austrian fire. The Duke of Aosta asked for reinforcements and, while his request was under consideration, Boroević mustered forces for a counter-attack before dawn on the 21st. After an opening bombardment and two hours' hand-to-hand fighting against a Bosnian regiment brandishing studded maces, the outnumbered Italians fell back to avoid being outflanked. They retook the hill on the 26th, twice, without being able to hold it. Losses on both sides were huge. The Sassari Brigade alone took 2,400 casualties, about 40 per cent of its strength. (It would lose a further 1,200 men during August.)

A dozen kilometres to the south, Giani Stuparich crouches behind a stone parapet, peering through binoculars at the soldiers crawling 'like lines of ants' over the grey flanks of Mount Cosich. He is glad to be distracted from the nauseating heat and stink of faeces, unburied corpses and sulphur. The stones in the trench are scalding. All the men can do is rig sunscreens from lengths of canvas. Another kind of heat is welcome: he notes the relief of ducking into a trench at night that is still warm from other bodies, like a communal bed. His rucksack, too, inspires affection: *canterano* or 'chest of drawers' by day, pillow by night. The men move in shadowy groups around the hillside, outlined by the pale rock.

The order comes to advance. Reddish shrapnel bursts overhead, yellow explosions flare on the ground. Deafened, stumbling into potholes in the limestone, sometimes so deeply that other soldiers have to drag them out, the men look as if they are walking on flames. The ground trembles under their boots. Terrible losses halt the operation on 23 July. The following day, the Third Army suspends all attacks. Stuparich's unit moves to the wetlands south of Monfalcone. Their new trench offers an easy target, and they cannot attack because the ground ahead is too marshy. The captain's hands shake, his eyes are dull. After two straight months at the front, the men's nerves are shot; life seems unendurable.

The Italians made no more headway further north. Successive charges up Mount Sabotino and Podgora hill, around Gorizia, gained little ground against machine-gun enfilades. Marginal progress in the first days was wiped out by counter-attacks. Repeated thrusts at Hill 383, above Plava, were repulsed.

For the soldiers, the Carso quickly became an evil force rather than an inert landscape: an enemy that probed their human frailty, flaying their senses. An Austrian officer remembered the vertical sun,

. . . baking the leaves on the trees to a dark crisp, until they crackle on the branch. It blanches the grass until it shatters at a touch, like the thinnest blown glass. In the glare, trees look black. Beyond, the sea steams, or gleams like steel. Rocks split. Sounds carry far louder and faster. It is as if the sun's rays were multiplied by millions of mirrors, tormenting the soldiers' eyes. There is no escaping the heat. Tongues swell, coated with thick saliva. Fingers swell and dangle clumsily from sticky hands. Eyes inflamed, skin like parchment. The blinding light beats everywhere, penetrating our eyelids. Our flasks are empty, sucked dry by early morning.

The writer, Captain Abel, also left a vivid account of an Italian bombardment:

The incoming shells are visible to the naked eye; they look like black sausages. If their effect were not so terrible, the sight of Carso veterans leaping this way and that to avoid the shells would be ridiculous. Not realising that they must dodge the shells, many of the newcomers are blown up. As soon as the bombardment ends, the Italians rush out of their advance positions – usually very close to our front line – and jump into our trenches.

Bringing their machine guns and sandbags with them, they swiftly convert a conquered trench into a defensive position. 'Their engineering skills are matchless.' The Austrian commanders must prepare a counter-attack at once, or it will be too late. Survivors lie where they fall in the burning sun, not daring to brush away the flies; the slightest movement draws enemy fire.

The battlefield is a vision of hell. The men trample on detritus at every step. The thin soil in the natural craters is pocked with shell holes. Fragments of shell casing have sunk deep into the tree trunks. Unexploded projectiles of every calibre end up in the most unlikely places, half buried, wedged between rocks. Telephone wires are tangled like clumps of exotic grass. Coagulated blood glints on the rock. And everywhere the sickly stink of corpses. Night brings little rest. Patrols search for the wounded, the dead and the buried-alive. Mules bring munitions and victuals up to the line. The daily allowance of a litre of water is delivered, and often finished by daybreak. Sappers and engineers repair the trenches, hating the moonlight that silhouettes them. Throbbing away, unseen, are the rock-drills that are now arriving, 'more important than water, than air, even than the Military Order of Maria Theresa. A rock-drill can eat up a metre and a half of rock in one hour.'

On the upper Isonzo, the climate and conditions were atrocious in different ways that also added to the Italians' difficulties. A junior officer called Virgilio Bonamore (3rd Company, 21st Battalion of Bersaglieri) kept a diary in the first months of the war. His company was stationed above Caporetto. He described nights at 2,000 metres, shivering uncontrollably on paths like goat-tracks where a wrong step meant certain death. On 29 July, he spent 24 hours in a trench between Mounts Krn and Mrzli,

. . . squatting among our own and enemy corpses. The stench was unbearable and on top of that we had to withstand a furious enemy assault and we repelled it. Many of our men fell, hit in the head while they poked out of the trench to fire. The constant stream of bombs also caused some casualties. These are steel cylinders about 30 cm long that the Austrians throw at us with special equipment from up to 300 m away.[1] Their effect is horrific. A poor Alpino lost his legs and had his stomach ripped out. In daytime you can see the bombs coming and dodge them but at night it's serious stuff.

When Austrian artillery caused a cliff to collapse above the Italian line, 20 men were swept into the abyss.

As well as enemy fire and deadly rock-falls, the Bersaglieri had to contend with violent electric storms, freezing winds, and hailstones 'as big as walnuts'. On 2 August, Bonamore wrote: 'It hasn't stopped raining for a single day. The cold was so intense that the whole battalion apart from 50 had to go down with frostbitten feet.' Judging by his diary, the company was not aware that the second offensive was under way, nor were their movements timed to relieve pressure elsewhere. In late July and early August, the company was needed for defensive operations, repelling ferocious Austrian sallies down from the Krn–Mrzli ridge.

1 It was his first experience of trench mortars.

Only in mid-August, when the Carso had been quiet for a week, did the Italians mount a major assault on the upper Isonzo. (Cadorna was trying to break through towards Tarvis.) Bonamore recorded the horror of compact infantry assaults on the cliffs and ravines in a landscape where only well-equipped mountaineers would now venture. At 03:00 on 14 August, the artillery opens up. Under cover of the darkness and thundering guns, the Bersaglieri crawl up the trackless hillside. More than once, Bonamore slithers back 20 or 30 metres. They stop some 200 metres below the enemy line and huddle for warmth. Bonamore sleeps 'for an hour or so leaning on the knees of Sergeant Meda who in turn was leaning against a tree trunk so as not to fall'. The climbing sun reveals them to the Austrians, who rake the mountainside with shrapnel. The Italians press against the rocks, and wait. The wire-cutting detail is highest up the slope.

Around 12:15 the artillery falls silent. Bonamore keeps checking his watch. The order to attack comes at 12:35 precisely. Roaring encouragement, Captain Rossi of 3rd Company races up the hill, with Bonamore and a few others in his wake. They reach the wire through a hail of bullets, overtaking the wire-cutters who go down like ninepins. In desperation, the captain's party tries to tear out the pegs that pin the strands of wire to the ground. It cannot be done. They try to hack through the wire with little hatchets, but the wire is too thick. Others have caught up by now, and men are dying all around. The sappers still lag behind and seem to be hesitating. Looking back down the hillside, they see artillery and machine-gun crossfire sweeping the hillside, 'mowing down everything'. It is carnage. 'The dead are in piles on top of each other. Nearly all the senior officers have fallen.'

The captain's party is quickly reduced to a dozen, 'right beneath the barbed wire. We throw ourselves to the ground.' At least they are safe from the deadly crossfire: the Austrian gunners do not dare to aim so close to their own first line. As they cannot retreat without making themselves easy targets, they wait, firing as rapidly as possible to make the Austrians think there are more of them. When the ammunition runs low, the captain decides to move. One by one, four men crawl away from their enclave by the wire; all are killed. The survivors wait for nightfall. 'It's raining and we're literally sodden in freezing water.' Darkness finally comes and they get back down the hillside, treading on 'innumerable corpses' as they go. 'What a massacre! How many young lives wasted. It's raining non-stop and we lie in the bottom of a ravine to spend the night amid the water and cold.' The scale of the disaster becomes clear next day: 'Except for 50 or so survivors, the 21st Battalion no longer exists.'

Repeated assaults on the Krn–Mrzli sector brought no gains that could be held. At 02:00 on 19 August, the Italians captured the enemy's front line on Mrzli, an unusually well-built trench that snaked below the summit ridge. This was the notorious '*trincerone*' or Big Trench. Under it, the ground fell to the Italian positions. The Austrians only had to push rocks down the mountain at the right moment for an attack to fail. Above the Big Trench, massive boulders interrupted the sight-lines to the summit. Mrzli could not be taken unless the Big Trench was in Italian hands. Yet it was fearsomely difficult to secure; reinforcements had to cross 60 metres of mainly open hillside. Boroević's men, masters of the counter-attack, quickly regained the Big Trench. The Italians almost seized it again at the end of the month, only to be beaten back the following day – as so often by a Bosnian battalion.

On the same day, 29 August, the Second Army tried to capture Mount Rombon, at the northern limit of the Isonzo front. After belatedly occupying Flitsch, the Italians were pinned down by fire from Rombon, towering overhead. Boroević had wisely garrisoned Rombon with the 2nd Mountain Rifles, a regiment that was almost 90 per cent Slovene. The soldiers were fighting to save their nation from Italian domination as well as defending their emperor against traitors. Rombon was a bulwark, guarding over a million Slovenes, and the troops were packed onto the narrow summit, still snowbound in late August. The northern face, looking away from the Isonzo, is almost sheer, so the Italians had no choice but to press upwards directly from the valley. Bent on emulating the glorious capture of Krn in June, two battalions of Alpini managed to capture the little cone of Čukla, a bump on Rombon's flank. When they tried to charge up the steep ridge to the summit, they stood no chance. In the first days of September, the survivors retreated to the valley bottom.

The Second Battle was the first full-scale bloodbath on the front, costing 42,000 Italian casualties. Combined with the 15,000 losses in the first battle, the Italians had lost more than 1 in 20 of their able men. They still advanced in ranked masses, as if for close-order drill, led from the front by junior officers brandishing swords, against entrenched positions where the vastly outnumbered Austrians waited with machine guns and rifles.[2] These officers also led patrols and wire-cutting parties. Their uniforms were clearly recognisable at a distance, making them easy targets. (A new regulation, stipulating that officers' uniforms should be identical to the other ranks', was passed only on 15 July, and could not be implemented quickly.) Disproportionate numbers of young officers died, often left hanging on the wire. The cycle of bombardment and attack was unvarying. The Austrians could usually observe the Italian lines; when the artillery fell silent, they knew the infantry would clamber into view a few minutes later. The gunners still did not know how to support the advancing infantry, leaving it exposed to defensive barrages. Austrian prisoners admitted that shooting at the Italians was better than target practice.

When the Italians occupied Austrian trenches, they were amazed at their quality. They actually zigzagged; they had communication trenches, so the men could move between the lines without exposure; some even had concrete walls. And they were stocked with demijohns of wine! These impressions said more about the standard of Italian positions than about Austrian defences, which, though excellent in some places (including Mrzli and Rombon), were still rudimentary in others. They had not yet learned to use the natural grottoes in the Carso that were impregnable even against the heavy artillery that was beginning to reach Cadorna's army.

This is one reason why Habsburg losses also ran so high: nearly 47,000, according to official sources, exceeding Italian losses for the only time during the war. More effectively targeted than in the first offensive, large numbers of Austrians were killed and wounded as they moved between their front and rear lines, still unprotected by helmets against the splinters that burst from the ground. The other reason for the casualties was Boroević's refusal to cede *any* ground, no matter the odds against keeping it. Tactical withdrawal was out of the question, and positions lost had to be counter-attacked at once.

On the Italian side, anxiety about casualties was mounting. Senior officers began to massage the statistics. General Reisoli of the Second Army, stationed at Plava, ordered that losses should not be reported to higher authorities unless absolutely necessary. In Rome, Foreign Minister Sonnino told a journalist that the war was not going to plan,

2 The Austrian officers, by contrast, led from behind, revolvers at the ready to threaten fainthearts and potential deserters. From January 1916, the Italians were allowed to do the same.

it was turning into something new, a struggle of positions and attrition without decisive manoeuvres. 'Had you not seen what was happening on the other fronts?' asked the journalist sensibly. Sonnino replied as a politician: it was now possible to see more clearly. Cadorna, hypersensitive to criticism from any quarter, tried to head off Salandra's disapproval with a letter on 6 August, explaining that the failure of the second offensive should be blamed on shortages of shells and reserves, and the lack of aerial observation. This was partly true, yet these factors hardly accounted for the dire outcome. Unlike Sonnino, the Supreme Command did not realise that positional war had turned into attritional warfare. The Austrian history of the war, straining for an apt definition of the conflict at this point, settled for calling it 'a war of manoeuvre on the spot'. Cadorna wrote to his son that the war would not be over before 1917.

The condition of the troops after the offensive alarmed some of their commanders. Reports from the Catanzaro and Sassari Brigades noted the physical and moral deterioration caused by continuous weeks and months in the trenches, never far from the enemy. The men's spirits were depressed by continuous anxiety and danger, by lack of sleep, by seeing their comrades fall wounded or dead at every moment. The awful weather obliged them to live in mud and water. They slept – when the lice let them – without straw or blankets on bare, often soaking ground. They were weakened by enteritis, rheumatism and bronchial complaints. Even worse, Habsburg troops had brought cholera from the Russian front, and by mid-August it was spreading along the front. The rations were usually late, cold and not nourishing. Drinkable water was often scarce and brackish.

The gloom was also due to the quality of the Italian positions, which were makeshift for doctrinal reasons as well as due to lack of time. If the whole purpose of war is ceaseless attack, it is a waste of energy to build protective positions that will soon be left behind on the march to victory.

TEN

The Dreaming Barbarian

*O my country O my country etc. what shall
I do I cannot shed my blood for you who do
not exist any more etc. etc. etc. what great
deed shall I do?*
    LEOPARDI (1798–1837)

During the war and for decades afterwards, Italian historians claimed
that Habsburg Italians flocked across the border in their thousands to
join the fight against Austria in 1915. Recent research by Fabio Todero
has exposed this claim as a myth that endured by downplaying the
number of *regnicoli*, who were Italian citizens living in Austria-
Hungary for economic reasons. Some 49,000 *regnicoli* lived in Trieste:
a fifth of the population. They had to return home in 1915 or face
prosecution, so should not be counted as volunteers. From March
1915, they were queuing to get their passports stamped at the Italian
consulate in Trieste. Some 35,000 made the one-way journey. Only
881 Triestines really volunteered for the Italian army: less than 1 per
cent of the city's Italian community, drawn from the middle classes.
The proportion of Tyrolese Italian volunteers was even smaller: 650
from a population of 400,000.

The 'foreign' volunteers were disliked by ordinary Italian soldiers,
for they might be Austrian spies and they actually wanted this foul war.
Patrizio Borsetti, a volunteer from the south Tyrol, wrote home in
August 1915: 'the soldiers look at us as if we were the reason why they
have to fight. How many curses on account of "Trento and Trieste". . . .'
So widespread were the 'mockery and rebukes' directed at volunteers
that in October 1915, the commander of the 65th Division (Second
Army) formally ordered his officers to monitor and punish 'such ignoble
attitudes'.

The volunteers were geeky and bookish, afire with conviction. Giani
Stuparich's brother Carlo marched to war at the age of 21 with Dante,

Homer, the Bible and Mazzini in his knapsack. The brothers were anguished by their comrades' suspicion. 'What more do we have to do to convince them that we are Italians too?' Giani asked his diary. 'Just like them, just like them!' They were not just like them. Highly educated, mostly unmarried and childless, these zealots were ready, even enthusiastic, to lay down their lives. Modelling themselves on Garibaldi's famous redshirts, they were even less prepared for the horror of modern warfare than their working-class comrades, who took revenge in trench songs:

> Cursed be those young students
> full of learning, wanting war
> They put Italy in widow's weeds
> she'll be grieving a century more.

The volunteers' letters and journals are impossibly exalted. Marco Prister, a Triestine Jewish Italian, kept a diary which ends with these lines: '22 November [1915], 13:00: Going into action, maybe I'll soon be dead! Farewell everyone! Long live Italy! I've got the order to advance. I'm ready! My destiny unfolds! Long live Italy! Long live Trieste!'

Antonio Bergamas wrote to his mother from Udine in June 1915:

Tomorrow I am going away, who knows where, almost certainly to death. When this reaches you, I will no longer exist . . . Perhaps you won't understand, cannot understand how, without being forced, I went to die on the battle-field . . . it is a thousand times sweeter to die facing my native land, our sea, for my natural Fatherland, than over there on the frozen fields of Galicia or the stony fields of Serbia, for a Fatherland that was not my own and that I hated. Farewell beloved mother, farewell dear sister, farewell father, and if I die, I do so with your adored names on my lips facing our savage Carso.

He survived for another year, until he was cut down by machine-gun fire trying to cross a third line of barbed wire.

More than 300 Triestine volunteers died in the war: a knucklebone in the hecatomb of the Great War. Yet Mussolini turned them into a full-blown cult, naming streets, squares and schools after them. One of the survivors lived to spell out the tragic irony of their sacrifice:

Everything we hated about Austria, the oppression of different peoples, the suppression of liberty in general and the press in particular, the Church's interference in public life as the established religion of state, the huge power of militarism – all this came back to life in Fascist Italy, in an even worse form.

The cult survives, ghoulishly, in the Risorgimento Museum in Trieste, off the Piazza Oberdan, not far from D'Annunzio Avenue. The custodian did not look up from her newspaper when I walked in. My footsteps echoed among glass cases of faded uniforms, medals, illegible documents, fuzzy photos of the beardless dead. The volunteers' complex ardour could hardly be worse served; the museum is like a second death. Depression only lifted when I read a heartfelt entry in the visitors' book: 'Nationalism – what a deadly infection! Let us hope we're less infected with it today.'

Of all the Italians who volunteered in 1915 and died on the Isonzo front, Scipio Slataper was perhaps the most gifted, the sort of figure who defines a place and a time. To his admirers he was a meteor in the skies above Trieste, alerting all Italy to the new ideas coursing through Europe. Yet he turned into a passionate champion of the values that led to Europe's nemesis in two world wars.

Slataper was born in Trieste in 1888 to middle-class parents. His mother was Italian while his father's roots were Slovene or Croatian. Perhaps as a result, he was keenly alive to his city's uniqueness, with its triple identities – Italian, Germanic and Slavic – woven together by Habsburg power. He loved its anomalies, as he loved its odd location between the limestone uplands of the Carso and the Adriatic Sea. What he did not love was its provincialism; he longed to shake its citizens out of their money-making routines, and help Trieste discover its vocation as Italian culture's gateway to the Germanic and Slavic worlds, stretching to the Baltic and the Black Seas. For he longed to be a heroic educator, even a prophet. 'I was born to give form to clay', he wrote to a friend, with the solemnity of 19 years. 'When they tell the story of my life, they will say: he was a *vivifier* in everything he did.' He was an alpha-male; 'domination is in my character', he airily confessed. Handsome and charismatic, he gathered a following of talented men and women who shared his idealism and were under his spell. His closest acolyte, Giani Stuparich, became his biographer. The three women in the group all fell in love with him. One killed herself on his account; another married him; after his death, the third married his future biographer in a union-by-proxy that could not last.

In 1908, the end of a sentimental affair made Trieste suddenly unbearable. He won a scholarship to study in Florence, which then possessed the sort of cultural glamour in Italy that Paris exerted over Europe as a whole. Florence was part of his inheritance as an Italian, yet he felt like a savage amid its splendours. (From a letter to one of his three muses: 'I am a barbarian who dreams. I have nothing but my pain and the joy of having it.') For other strands completed his inheritance – strands remote from Tuscany's placid landscapes, immemorial cities and the secure achievements of the Renaissance. By these standards, Trieste had no culture. Yet its newness held a promise: Trieste was raw and vital, with the potential to become something. Was not Italy decrepit by comparison?[1] His mind teemed, and being Slataper, he shouted his insights to the nation. A series of 'Triestine Letters' was published in an avant-garde journal called *La Voce* ('The Voice'), published in Florence. Predictably, the bourgeois Italians of Trieste were scandalised, taking as condescension what was meant as a bracing challenge.

The Voice became Slataper's intellectual home soon after he reached Tuscany. He noticed the first issue in a bookshop, read it from cover to cover and soon called on the editors. It was the most exciting cultural and political review in Italy. Irreverent and caustic as well as learned, it had a broad concept of culture and a mighty ambition: nothing less, according to Slataper's biographer, than 'a systematic critical revision of Italian life', renewing national culture by quarrelling with its makers, canons and clichés. While their concerns were national, the editors were moved by a 'yearning for universal culture'. Slataper was the quiet one among the *vociani*, soaking up their ease of allusion and acerbic self-assurance. He never quite became one of them; his background set him apart, and he had no thought of disowning it. He corresponded intensely with his Triestine circle, especially the women. To one of them in particular, Anna Pulitzer, he described his efforts to get over the botched affair that had brought him to Tuscany in the first place.

In the course of these confidences, he grew infatuated with Anna herself. Calling her Gioietta, 'little joy', he said she was 'the most divine woman I could have dreamed of', an ominous tribute. The infatuation was mutual. Slataper poured out passion and opinions in equal measure. 'I don't want to command', he declared not quite convincingly. 'I want to bring people to *their* liberty so that they can find their own

1 James Joyce, that adoptive Triestine, had a similar reaction to Rome in 1906: the Eternal City reminded him of 'a man who lives by exhibiting to travellers his grandmother's corpse'.

way. What stops them is slavery, the terrible slavery of the internal lie.' He sounds like D. H. Lawrence's Adriatic cousin, wrestling with sexual convention. 'All the world should be remade by my desire,' he exulted; but what about the object of that desire? His letters were serial monologues, and they swamped Anna. His worship became oppressive and eventually unbearable. What did it have to do with her as she actually was? How could she live up to his ideal? Anna shot herself in May 1910, standing in front of a mirror. She left a note dedicating her suicide to Scipio's future work.

His reaction confirmed the grounds of her despair. He intensified the torrent of letters to her. 'Letters of pride, of anger, of prayer, of grief, of humiliation,' Stuparich calls them. 'The beloved lived on in his imagination, as she had lived before dying.' The fact of her self-destruction eventually sank in. 'Gioietta's love had made him feel like a god. Her suicide destroyed that.' His self-belief was too strong to be cowed for long. The following year, under the shadow of her loss, he wrote his masterpiece. Il mio Carso ('My Carso') has a triple subject: Slataper's growth and character, his birthplace of Trieste, and the Carso. The first pages evoke a happy childhood, rich in sensuous detail. Young Scipio serves his appetites, recording trials of inner strength with adults and physical endurance with other boys, yearning for mastery. He prays for 'our fatherland' across the sea, traces Garibaldi's campaigns on a map and dreams that Italy 'will liberate us'. He and his pals sing irredentist songs in the street, then scatter when the police give chase. First love is giddy ('I brought her the finest pear on the tree between my teeth'), and ends abruptly, without pain. As he grows, his vision is touched with nationalist paranoia. 'Every step in the city is monitored by spies who pretend not to see anything.' Contact with irredentists leaves him underwhelmed; where is their passion? The story of Oberdan makes his heart pound. 'I wished I could die like him.' At a loose end after school, he becomes a journalist – a modern version of the prophet's calling.

Slataper's Trieste is a thriving port, crammed with goods passing from the Orient, America and Italy towards central Europe. Wagons clatter through the streets, laden with crates of oranges, casks of oil, grey sacks of coffee beans and rice, trailing lines of snow where customs officers have punctured the sacks with their ink-stamps. Colliers hauling fuel on board the steamships pause to hawk and spit on the quayside. 'I move through the streets and am happy that Trieste is so wealthy.' For it is also a bourgeois city; motor cars roll along the Corso, past strollers in fur coats. And it is a city of political tensions. The Bosnian sentries in front of the governor's palace remind Slataper how far away the fatherland really is. He joins the demonstrators marching for an Italian-language university, is arrested and led away but twists free from the Habsburg policeman. It is good sport, but serious too.

Then there is the Carso, rising behind the city, a tramride away. It is a dreamscape, a psychogeography of contradictions. In his half-feral boyhood, he ran with the wind, bounding over the stone walls and juniper bushes, plunging into a stream 'to slake my skin', then flinging himself naked on the heather. Scent of bitter almonds. Gentians (distilling the blue of spring skies) and primroses ('the first sunrays!') amid the weathered rocks. His loneliness is writ large in the Carso's desolation. 'My cape sticks to its rocks like flesh to embers.'

As Slataper strides across the rocky meadows, a Slovene peasant eyes him warily. 'You are barbarous in your soul,' thinks the Italian, but adds that 'selling milk in the city for a few coppers would be enough to soften you'. The peasant could be urbanised, and who is to stop this from happening? Slataper's dislike yields to frank admiration.

You are a Slav, a son of the new race. You came to this land where nobody could live and you made it fruitful. You, a son of the soil, took the Venetian fisherman's nets away from him and made a sailor of yourself. You are steadfast and frugal. Strong and patient. For long years your servitude was flung in your face; but your hour, too, has struck. It is time you were master. For you are a Slav, son of the great future race.

By contrast, the Italians seem anaemic and exhausted, bragging about their 'twenty centuries of culture', unable to channel the Carso's nourishing energy into their city. Their 'vital force' has been sapped. The Slovenes have a place in Trieste's future – perhaps the foremost place.

In *My Carso*, Gioietta remains off-stage, impalpable as mist. 'Filled with grief and death', the author yearns for her. The Carso's petrified expanses fit him like a glove. 'Boulders grey with rain and lichen, contorted, split, whetted.' The cold north-easterly wind called the bora. Fierce sunlight and bristling grass. Grief turns into leave-taking: burn her pale corpse on a pyre of pine branches, cover her grave with junipers. When this mood, too, works itself out, he discovers a work ethic. Her suicide wiped away the petty truths he once lived by. Realising that 'work is a vain quest for something that has been lost', he resolves to be strong and to toil without hope. He blesses the day of

Gioietta's birth and the day she chose to die. A timely southern wind brings health and joy from the green Adriatic. Purged of grief, he can celebrate the Carso again, a landscape that offers no quarter, 'an inferno' – Slataper exults in the Dantesque metaphor that soldiers would use again and again to describe the battlefield a few years later. He returns to Trieste with a new sense of purpose. 'We love and bless you, for we would even be happy to die in your blaze.' It was another ominous tribute.

This sense of purpose led him to support Angelo Vivante against the militants who denounced his peaceful vision for the Habsburg Italians. 'The historic task of Trieste', Slataper said, 'is to be the crucible and propagator of civilisation, three civilisations.' He and his friends decided to try to change the climate of ideas in Italy and Austria by establishing an intellectual centre of 'centripetal energy'. They would tackle the leading problems of the day, starting with the national question. Each of them would study a different language. ('With ten of us, we can cover Europe, if not beyond,' he enthused.) Using Trieste as an 'observatory', they would publish a review called *Europa* to debate 'the general problems of modern civilisation: races, Semitism, feminism, democracy, religion, political activism'.

He fell in love again, with another of his Triestine circle: Luisa Carniel. They married in 1913 and moved to Hamburg, where Scipio worked at the university. The third muse, Elody Oblath, still deeply smitten, trailed after them and shared their quarters for several months, surely an excruciating arrangement. Scipio's mind was fixed on Trieste, as always when he lived abroad. The couple returned home in August 1914. From the outbreak of the Great War until his death in December 1915, he was prolific even by his own standards, as he strove to increase public support in Italy for war.

Until the start of the war, he had refused to take sides on the irredentist question. He thought Italian nationalists underestimated Trieste's economic links with Austria, while socialists like Vivante tended to intellectualise the national question. Yet he believed that conflict between nations was proper, because civilisations do not hold equal rights before history. It is 'morbid and harmful' to concede something to one nation simply because 'another has reached the stage of deserving it'. The Italians stood above 'the Slavs' because they 'have a richer civilisation' and were 'right to affirm it *and fight for it*'. Even so, he would not call for war unless it was in Italy's own interest to fight. August 1914 presented exactly the scenario that would swing his position. He decided that Italy should enter the war with a view to sharing the territorial spoils with Serbia. Italy would take Friuli, Trieste, the Alpine frontier, all of Istria, a Dalmatian island or two, and eventually Albania.

As summer became autumn and Serbia defended itself against immense odds, while Russia attacked the Austrian Empire in the east, the case for Italian intervention became – in Slataper's view – rock solid. Italy should fight for the rights of the non-German peoples of the empire, but also for the territorial claims that stemmed from the Italians' superior civilisation. Avid for a national readership, he wrote for a pro-war newspaper in Bologna (the same one that channelled funds to launch Mussolini's newspaper in November 1914). His despatches were gossipy and vivid. When war broke out, there was confusion in Trieste. 'No one could make head nor tail of it.' The military band played marches in the streets and there was much flag-waving. News of Britain's entry into the war was met with stunned silence in the city stock exchange, broken by a trader who cried 'It's all over!' The city was practically undefended; the garrison had been sent to the Eastern Front. Apart from a few reserve companies on the Carso, only a few hundred Slovenian military police were left. The Austrians evacuated their archives and transferred the regional capital to Gorizia. They were so jittery about a British naval raid that the governor slept outside the city every night. The bank vaults were emptied: strongboxes were loaded onto wagons and pulled by oxen through the deserted city at night. The mass exit of *regnicoli* caused dozens of shops to close; barbers and waiters were particularly hard to find. The cafés were quiet, after losing their clientele as well as their staff. People wandered down to the quays at night, which were empty for the first time, dark and silent. Gas lamps were unlit, to save fuel. Access to border areas was restricted, so rumours of troop movements across the Isonzo could not be verified.

Privately, Slataper was exasperated by the local Italians' 'lack of historical responsibility'. Instead of seizing the chance to throw off the Austrian yoke, they got on with their lives as best they could. Under this pressure, he became a propagandist. An article in December 1914 ended with a steely call to arms: 'For 32 years of forced peace we could not say the name of Oberdan. Oberdan is a duty: he is war. Simply that. We shall sing his name when our soldiers enter the barracks in Trieste where he was hanged.' He assured his readers that Austria's border on the lowlands of Friuli was 'absolutely indefensible'. He came to share the nationalist contempt for Habsburg fighting abilities, claiming that 'the Austrian soldier cannot win because he has no will to win'. One of his last publications was a silly pamphlet predicting that Trieste would be liberated within a few days and Laibach after a few weeks. His old insights into Italian–Yugoslav relations, and Slavic toughness in particular, were forgotten. Yet even now he could be surprising. His last article, datelined 22 April 1915, admitted that the pursuit of nationalist claims would never produce a stable order in Europe, because every success triggers counter-claims by another minority. Only 'healthy liberalism' could provide a 'true guarantee' for Europe's minorities.

By May 1915, he was living in Rome. He volunteered at once and found himself in the Sardinian Grenadiers. The troop train pulled out of Portonaccio station under heavy rain. Slataper wore a red rose in his cap. Wounded in June by friendly fire, he returned to the line as quickly as possible. In November he was sent to Podgora, the hill above Gorizia that the troops called 'Calvary'. Five years earlier, he had foreseen his death:

One day, when I'm still young, when I'm walking on the Carso and the stones and flowers are telling me things I already know, some Slav will hurl an eroded, heavy rock full of sharp edges at me. And that's where I'll fall, up on the Carso. Not in bed, amid tears and stinks and whispers and people walking softly in the room. I want to die at the height of my life, not down there.

His wish was granted on 3 December, when a Croatian or Bosnian bullet killed him during an action that he had volunteered for. He was 27 years old.

Slataper's biographer tried to explain his hero's attitude to the carnage.

He did not approve of so many lives being lost due to lack of planning or resources, but if blood had to be so grievously shed to cement the future history of the fatherland, he could not spare his own with the excuse that the Italian generals were so many contemptible executioners . . . For all those who *did not know why*, it was necessary for someone to go in full knowledge, but with their same humility.

Slataper was a sublime educator, showing by example how the Italian soldiers must go like cattle to the abattoir. His search after Anna's suicide for what he called 'a harder, more heroic and disinterested life' led to what his biographer praised as devotion to 'violent liberty and complete sincerity' – dangerous goals at any time, and fatal for many in 1915. The Slovene peasant who was guardedly admired in *My Carso* became his mortal enemy. Slataper the vivifier finished as an apostle of the twentieth century's worst malady – aggressive ethnic nationalism. A decade after the war, Elody Oblath, his truest soulmate, looked back on the inbred intensity of their group:

We thought we knew all about the horrors of war, but we knew nothing except our own exaltation. Yet we did know with conscious certainty that whatever these horrors would be, none of us would hold back. Our plotting for war really was like [the revolutionaries in] 1848. Thinking today of our inviolable closeness, and everything we tried to do and did do with such effort, I feel admiration and also pity for that limitless and truly heroic enthusiasm. Ours was an ideal co-operation for a collective truth. For the sake of this truth, each of us, I am sure, would have gone to the gallows, just as we consciously instigated and helped all our friends (the best part of ourselves) to go forth and die. Days of mad illusions, faith in a better humanity, which made us exult and demand the deaths of millions of men.

The news of Scipio's death 'shattered our fanaticism for ever'.

ELEVEN

Walking Shapes of Mud

*It is a military axiom not to advance uphill
against the enemy.*
SUN TZU

The Third and Fourth Battles of the Isonzo

Cadorna was in no hurry to start a third offensive. Aware that his
resources lagged behind the nation's ambitions, he needed more heavy
artillery and munitions if his breakthrough strategy was to succeed. He
scraped together medium and heavy guns from far and near, including
some naval batteries, and pushed the government to boost domestic
production. The economy had to be put on a war footing, but the
government still regretted its dream of a short campaign and feared the
public's reaction when it awoke from the same dream. Cadorna's case
was not helped when the Minister of War, Zupelli, criticised his use of
resources, particularly the dispersal of men and artillery.

Cadorna estimated that Italy's arms manufacturers would need the
best part of a year to produce the quantity of heavy artillery that he
wanted. He had no doubts about the ultimate outcome, and urged the
government to prepare for a long haul to victory. But governments are
shy of long hauls when the stakes are so high, and Cadorna's relationship
with Salandra began to sour. He had to put up with a string of high-
profile visitors from Rome, warning that the nation needed a resounding
victory by the end of the year. If they could not have Trieste, what about
Gorizia, the only other city in the 'unredeemed lands' around the
Adriatic? Other pressure came from the Allies. In October, when Britain
and France wanted Italy to relieve the strain on Serbia and the Western
Front, the onus on Cadorna to attack became irresistible.

In the meantime, the Supreme Command assessed its failures to date.
As thousands of dead were collected in raw new cemeteries along the
valley bottoms, where the villages stood empty and the crops rotted,

senior officers drafted memoranda on tactics. These discussions centred on the reasons why Italy's offensives had failed. The theory of attack was clear; the preliminary bombardment had to be heavy enough to wreck the enemy's forward positions, but not so long that reinforcements could be brought up to the attack zone. The 'methodical advance', introduced over the summer, was meant to deter the Austrians from building up their strength at strategic points.[1] Diversionary assaults were timed to prevent the enemy transferring forces to block the main thrust. When the infantry attacked, artillery fire should be lengthened to strike the enemy rear, to block counter-attacks from the second defensive line. The attacking infantry line should be spaced out, with the soldiers a metre apart, except where they poured through the breaches in the barbed wire that had been made the night before by the wire-cutting teams, and widened by the artillery. These teams comprised four or five men with a pair of cutters, some sacks, half a dozen hand-grenades, and gelignite tubes.

In practice, matters had gone very differently. The Italians could not knock out the enemy batteries if they did not know their location; aerial reconnaissance was not yet developed, and even the observers perched at the top of church towers could not see over the brow of the Carso. Co-ordination between the attacking infantry and the supporting batteries was often poor, as was the communication between observers and gunners. The fire was not accurate enough to pinpoint the enemy reserves as they moved up to counter-attack. Rigid fire tables prevented the gunners from reacting flexibly to evolving situations. Shells were in short supply and many guns had been damaged by over use. At the end of August, the Supreme Command set a daily ceiling on use of artillery. This helped to preserve the guns, at the cost of sparing the enemy. New approach roads were constructed, so heavy artillery could be brought closer to the front. Artillery fire was reduced when the infantry attacked, rather than switched off abruptly.

No reliable way had been found to breach barbed-wire entanglements. Heavy artillery could do it, but could rarely be spared for this task. Even when the gelignite tubes exploded (the fuses easily became damp and

---

1 The 'methodical advance' engaged front-line units in raids and other small-scale actions along the front. The purpose was to keep the Austrians in 'continual tension', denying them the advantages that accrued from the Italians' predictable cycles of preparation and attack. However, as these smaller actions were largely fruitless and costly, they also sapped the Italians.

refused to ignite), the gaps were so narrow that they formed deadly bottle-necks when the Italians tried to crowd through – a gift to enemy machine gunners. Unless enough cylinders were used, the explosions failed to break the wire. Even then, the Austrians usually had time to patch over the gaps before dawn. In desperation, weird alternative devices were tried out. A large rectangular shield was fitted with an axle and two wheels that the soldiers pushed in front of them, up to the wire. A wheel was equipped with spiked blades and launched at the enemy lines by catapult. While the blades sliced through the first strands of wire, the wheel got snarled up in the wire. An explosive charge in the wheel hub would then detonate, blasting a wide hole. It worked as well as would be expected. Wire-cutting teams were given portable shields of iron for carrying up to the wire, where they presented a splendidly static target.

Even local successes had exposed crippling defects. When the Italians did manage to break into an enemy trench, after heroic efforts, they seemed at a loss. Their resolve disintegrated at the first burst of gunfire, flurry of grenades, or bayonet charge. The Austrians found they could stampede the Italians back to their own lines quite easily. Cadorna was oblivious to such omens about training and morale. On 9 October, he suspended all leave except for convalescence, a crushing blow to soldiers who had been in the line since June.

The reserves were another problem. Before the Italians could bring theirs into an occupied line, the enemy's had moved up from the second and third lines. The Supreme Command realised that the first wave of attacking infantry had to be supported by second and third waves – and even fourth and fifth waves, entering the fray before the Austrians mounted their inevitable counter-attack. This could not be done unless more reserves were brought up before an attack, especially difficult when communication trenches were lacking in many places. Cadorna's answer was to establish 'men-reservoirs' as close to the front line as possible, like a human munitions dump. Unfortunately this created another problem: how to protect the reserves against well-targeted Austrian artillery?

Then there were the problems of defence. The Italians still lacked rock-drills and explosives to deepen the trenches, so – like the Austrians – they piled up stones into parapets, and piled sandbags on the stones.[2]

2 'Where are the trenches?' asked a junior officer, arriving on San Michele in November 1915. 'Trenches, trenches . . . ' came the wondering reply. 'There aren't any. We've got holes.'

The Austrians could aim almost at will; as a rule, their observers high up on the hills had sight of the front lines and the rear. And Italian losses were increased by sheer carelessness, born of inexperience and also ideology. Many officers disdained to organise their defences properly because they thought the Austrians did not deserve the compliment. Only tragic experience would expunge this prejudice.

In short, the Austrians were masters of the front. By day, their lines were generally quiet, though sharpshooters were quick to fire on Italians who forgot to stay under their parapets. Their artillery was well back, out of Italian view. By night, they kept up intermittent fire while their searchlights played over the Italian lines, interrupting the drilling, digging and provisioning. By October, most sectors on the lower Isonzo front had three main lines, zigzagging in textbook style and linked by communication lines. These defences were deep enough to absorb local breakthroughs, like an airbag in a car crash. During Italian bombardments, the first line was almost empty except for observers. The forward troops waited in deep dug-outs behind the trenches, often six or eight metres deep, swarming with vermin. As soon as the fire lengthened towards the communication lines, the infantry clambered up the ladders and poured out of these dug-outs, quickly joined by units from the second line. They usually reached the front in time to repulse the Italians. Inured to hardship and ferocious discipline, they were skilled and savage at hand-to-hand fighting – the essence of counter-attack – with bayonets, spiked clubs, daggers and knuckledusters.

It was difficult to anchor barbed wire in the Carso rock, a job that could only be attempted at night. Luckily it was even more difficult for the Italians to cut through wire, anchored or not. At the same time, the Austrians were making geology work for them. The second and third defensive lines made good use of grottoes and caverns. When these were not accessible through fissures, holes could be drilled or blasted through the limestone. Lined with planks, creosoted against damp, these shelters accommodated hundreds of soldiers. Although the heaviest shells could not smash through more than a metre and a half of solid stone, prolonged shelling made the cavern walls tremble, inducing panic and claustrophobia – a fear of never seeing sunlight again. But it was better than being blown up.

Bulgaria came off the fence in September – and joined the Central Powers. From mid-October, assailed by Austria from the north and west and Bulgaria from the south-east, Serbia was fighting for its life. Meanwhile the Allied offensives in France were at a bloody standstill. The Allies called on Italy to take some of the heat.

Cadorna believed he had enough artillery and shells for another attack. Trieste had mocked his efforts so far; it was inconceivable that an impressive breakthrough would be achieved in that direction by the end of the year. Gorizia was another matter. It was worth very little strategically, but it lay only one or two kilometres beyond the Italian lines. If he could outflank the city by taking Plava and Tolmein to the north and Mount San Michele to the south, the fanatical resistance of Zeidler's Dalmatian and Hungarian forces in the bridgehead could, Cadorna supposed, soon be reduced. Gorizia and its 15,000 citizens would drop into his hand.

Under General Frugoni, the Second Army prepared to attack Tolmein and Plava, as well as the hills of Podgora and Sabotino. Meanwhile the Duke of Aosta's Third Army would attack Mount San Michele once again and try to drive forward elsewhere on the Carso plateau. Austrian intelligence, helped by talkative Italian deserters, was well informed about these plans.

The offensive started on 18 October, a chilly autumn day, with more than 1,300 Italian guns shelling along a 50-kilometre front, from Krn to the sea. The bombardment was more intense than anything the Austrians had seen on this front.[3] Yet, as before, the brunt of it was fired by 75-millimetre artillery, too light to harm trenches or wire. When the Italians moved out of their trenches on the 21st, they expected large gains. The Austrians, however, were more than ready. Enough machine guns always survived to check the Italians – even when they advanced in armour of steel plates, as they did in some places. Very little was achieved on the northern Isonzo. The Italians had briefly recaptured the 'Big Trench' on Mrzli at the end of September, only to lose it to the usual ferocious counter-attack. They hauled artillery onto Krn to pound the summit of Mrzli and its rear lines from the north while the infantry drove up from the south and west. Assisted in this way, the Salerno Brigade took the Big Trench on 21 October. Success was clinched with

<hr/>

3 The Croatian writer Miroslav Krleža, strolling in Agram (now Zagreb) on 20 October, nearly 200 kilometres away, imagined he could feel the ground vibrating under his feet. 'Subterranean rumblings', he noted in his diary. 'Guns on the Isonzo.' Next day, he reported rumours circulating in the cafés 'that the guns on the Isonzo are audible. The Isonzo has its magnetic field and we all walk around inside its spell.'

bayonets. Losses on both sides were very high. Hundreds of mud-plastered prisoners, including Bosnians with their sky-blue fezzes, were led down to the valley. The front lines were so close that working parties, collecting the dead or bringing up supplies, sometimes found themselves on the wrong side. At dawn on the 24th, the Italians made their first real grab for the elusive summit of Mrzli. They were driven back once, then twice. These failures were mitigated by advances elsewhere on the mountain, pushing the Austrians back towards the summit on either side of the Big Trench. But there was no breakthrough.

The Italians were nowhere near taking Tolmein. Hill 383, looming over Plava, remained impregnable. As for Gorizia, there were 30 assaults on Sabotino and Podgora, often in driving rain. The corps commander on this sector was General Luigi Capello, promoted from divisional commander on the Carso, where his ruthlessness justified the nickname he had earned in Libya: 'the butcher'. This reputation commended him to Cadorna, who otherwise disliked Capello as too political and, especially, too active as a Freemason. Their on-off partnership defined much of the Italian war for the next two years.

On the Carso, control of San Michele switched from one side to another amid savage fighting over three days. The Italians repeatedly overran the Austrian front line, but could not withstand the counter-attack. Again and again, they charged at positions that turned out not to have been seriously damaged. Their assaults were stopped short by intact wire. The Austrians had made good use of the quiet months since the Second Battle. By the time the Italians had taken the first line of enemy trenches, the enemy reserves had reached the second line, which was in better condition than the first line and well able to block any further advance while the Austrians prepared their counter-attack.

Between San Michele and Monfalcone, the Carso escarpment rises and falls without any clear summits. The name given to this limestone wilderness is Monte Sei Busi, which translates as Six Holes Mountain. (To someone walking over the surface, the name could as well be Sixty or Six Hundred Holes.) The Siena Brigade's task in the Third Battle was to take the Austrians' long, well-fortified front line on Sei Busi. On 23 October, the trench was taken after three days of bloody assaults, with all three battalions engaged. The rejoicing was short-lived; that night, the Italians were driven back to their jump-off position. As usual, they had no time to prepare their defence. The next morning, the Austrians called for an hour's ceasefire to tend the wounded and collect the dead.

Soon afterwards the Siena Brigade was replaced with a regiment of Bersaglieri and the Sassari Brigade. Together, these fresh forces retook the trench early in November, and kept it. Yet another massive effort had yielded a 'success' which was scarcely visible on the map.

Bad weather lasted throughout the battle, intensifying at the end of the month. By early November, the trenches were quagmires of filth, the roads almost impassable. The first snowfalls forced the fighting to stop.

The last days of the battle, 3 and 4 November, were extremely violent. Brigade diaries reported fears that some units might crack and desert en masse. The attacks on San Michele were weakening under the internal pressures of exhaustion and hopelessness. The Italians had sustained 67,000 losses along the front. On San Michele, the Catanzaro Brigade alone lost almost 2,800 men and 70 officers between 17 and 26 October, nearly half of each category. The Caltanisetta Brigade, deployed alongside the Catanzaro, took even heavier casualties, losing two-thirds of its men and 63 per cent of its officers between 22 October and 3 November. South of Monfalcone, the 16th Division carried out a frontal attack on Hill 121, the nearest point to Trieste that Cadorna's army had yet reached. This one failed attack cost 4,000 Italian casualties. The battle's only gains were trivial: some ground along the river, south of Plava, and two hills to the west of Podgora, bringing the Italians a hundred metres closer to Gorizia.

The extra artillery and tinkering with infantry tactics had made little difference. One reason was the rigorous centralisation of command and control. Given the poor communications on the battlefield, this made bad decisions inevitable. An episode involving the Lazio Brigade, recovered by the historian Giorgio Longo, illustrates this with tragic clarity.

The brigade was stationed on the northern slope of San Michele. It is the steepest face of the hill, rising 270 metres from the Isonzo within 900 horizontal metres. The 132nd Infantry Regiment (Lazio Brigade, 29th Division, Third Army) was stationed between regiments of the Perugia and Verona Brigades. It faced formidable Austrian defences, guarded by multiple rows of barbed wire and machine-gun nests, backed by batteries to the east. Flanking movements along the river were barred by a redoubt with outlying trenches that the Italians judged to be impregnable. On 21 October, the 132nd Infantry was ordered to take a ridge on the northern slope. Known as Hill 124, this ridge was ringed with barbed wire that had suffered only a few narrow breaches. Efforts to widen the breaches with wire-cutters and gelignite tubes had mostly failed. Inevitably, the attackers suffered heavy losses; over ten days of continuous assaults, the 132nd lost 26 officers and 707 men. The survivors sheltered in muddy holes; their soggy uniforms could not be dried.

On the evening of the 31st, the regiment was ordered to renew its attack the following morning. The commanding officer, Colonel Viola, decided to resist. He reported to the brigade commander, General Schenardi, that attacking in these conditions was impossible: the rain had made the steep slopes too slippery; the paths disappeared under sliding mud; the triple rows of wire were intact; enemy fire turned the assaults into pointless butchery.

Schenardi knew Viola as a courageous CO who would not refuse an order without good reason. Throughout the following day, he urged him to proceed with the attack. The other man bought time by sending out wire-cutting patrols. That evening, Schenardi put the best face possible on the colonel's refusal in a report to his divisional commander, General Marazzi. Wire had blocked the 132nd Infantry's progress, and subsequent wire-cutting patrols had been killed by enfilade fire from above. They would send night patrols to try again, but if these failed to widen the breaches, the next day's attack could only succeed if the Verona Brigade, adjacent to the Lazio, gave timely support. He ended by assuring the general that every effort was being made and every hardship endured to achieve success.

At divisional headquarters in Sdraussina, two kilometres away, Marazzi warned that the men's 'extreme energy' might be undermined by weakness in the officers. Any commander suspected of shortcomings should be replaced. Behind their defences, the enemy were few and disheartened. 'Strike a vigorous blow with every means, and victory shall be ours.' Marazzi was under pressure from the corps commander, General Morrone, who had been stung by a phone call from the Duke of Aosta himself, in his headquarters at Cervignano some 16 kilometres away, regretting that the previous day's action had brought 'no appreciable result'. On the morning of 2 November, Marazzi informed the irate Morrone that 'the most energetic orders' had been given 'to drive the troops forward with the utmost vigour'. Every man would do his duty to the last, at whatever cost.

General Schenardi ordered the attack to take place at 13:00 hours. Colonel Viola protested that the breaches in the wire were still too narrow, due partly to damp fuses in the gelignite tubes. Without support from the Verona Brigade, the 132nd would be massacred again. Once again, zero hour passed without an attack. When Schenardi asked about the Verona Brigade, General Marazzi snapped back: attack at once, never mind the Verona Brigade! A quarter of an hour later, he followed this order with another: if Colonel Viola hesitates for an instant, relieve him of his command.

Viola duly gave orders to advance. As usual, he led from the front. The platoons poured uphill in waves, only to break against the wire, still 'nearly intact' according to the brigade diary. Reinforcements arrived, but the enemy fire was overwhelming. Around 19:00, the regiment fell back. The following day, Viola prepared to lead his men back up the hill, but torrential rain forced a postponement. The same happened on the 4th. The 29th Division was exempted from the next rotations, so the men of the 132nd stayed at their sodden posts. By 10 November, the regiment was stunned by exhaustion, in terrible condition. That evening the steady downpour became a cloudburst, flooding the trenches and turning the paths into foaming streams. Two days later the 132nd was granted a week's leave. Colonel Viola died on 22 November, leading his men in yet another attack against Hill 124.

The Third Battle was suspended on the evening of 4 November, but Cadorna was unreasonably convinced that Boroević's army teetered on the edge of collapse. Knowing that 24 fresh battalions were due to arrive within a week or two, he felt sure Gorizia could still be taken. After a week's pause, the Fourth Battle was launched with a short bombardment. The infantry did their best to charge up the open slopes of Mrzli, Podgora, Sabotino and San Michele, swept by machine-gun fire. The rain pelted down, the temperature sank, and then – on 16 November – heavy snow fell. There would not be a proper thaw until spring 1917, when corpses were revealed after a year and a half.

Thanks to the wire and machine guns, Austrian units that had lost half their men held back Italian advances with three times their own strength. A bit of ground was taken here and there, after huge losses, but nothing decisive. Capello, an intuitive soldier, knew it was impossible to succeed in such conditions, with the men exhausted. He sent a graphic report to General Frugoni, commanding the Second Army. As the rations were cold by the time they reached the men, and short as well, the mud-soaked infantry could not 'restore their strength with hot, abundant rations'. Some units went more than two days without food. They were not so much men as 'walking shapes of mud. It is not the will to advance that's lacking ... what they lack is the physical strength.' Even the reserves had spent days in water and mud, hence were not capable of reinvigorating the first-line troops. Malingering and self-mutilation were serious problems. Malingerers imitated symptoms that doctors found hard to verify. With so many infantrymen presenting tidy wounds to their hands or feet, officers learned to look for telltale scorchmarks. Self-mutilation could be punished with summary execution or jail, but the trend was only reversed much later, when the Supreme Command sent all suspects straight to the front line.

Amid the routine slaughter, 18 November marked a turning point: the Italians shelled Gorizia for three hours. This was the start of 'total war' on the Isonzo. Until now, both sides had mostly refrained from targeting civilians – though Austrian ships and planes had shelled several Adriatic cities in May 1915. Astutely, the Italians had milked the fact that they had less to gain from targeting civilians. In July, Cadorna offered to support a joint commitment against targeting 'open cities'. The Austrians were not interested: they wanted to exploit their superiority in the air.

Gorizia was known as the Austrian Nice, the city of roses or violets. Blessed by a mild climate in winter, with hills behind and the turquoise Isonzo in front, it flourished under the Habsburgs. Long avenues were lined with handsome villas. The public gardens were exceptionally pretty, the medieval castle on the hill was picturesque. The hospitals and convalescent homes were patronised by wealthy Viennese and Bavarians, who formed a German crust on top of the mixed Italian and Slovene population. After May 1915, fighting quickly reached the city's edge. The first wave of refugees brought some 40,000 people through the city, local Italians as well as Slovenes, carrying or dragging whatever they could save from the invaders; many would spend years in internment camps. Although the prewar population of 31,000 soon halved, as citizens fled to safer regions, numbers were kept up by several tens of thousands of Habsburg troops quartered in the city, turning it into a virtual third line. Curtains of reeds were hung across the streets to block enemy snipers' sight-lines; otherwise life continued almost normally. Officers and their wives strolled in the gardens, sat in the cafés, and kept local businesses afloat. Authority passed from the mayor to General Zeidler, legendary commander of the 58th Division, who chose not to evacuate the city, perhaps because the attack was a gift to Habsburg propaganda.

Why did Cadorna abandon the moral high ground now, when he knew that Gorizia could not be taken during this battle? His memoirs offer no clue. Perhaps he decided that civilised restraint had become a luxury, or the spectacle of the city's near-normality so close to the front line harmed his own men's morale. Joffre, who visited the front, may have advised that he could not afford to spare the city. Whatever the reason, Cadorna privately admitted that Gorizia was more a political than a strategic objective, and the shelling brought no advantage to offset the propaganda loss.

The Supreme Command ordered a last offensive on Mount Mrzli and around Tolmein for 23 November. Senior officers were unconvinced. Many of the men could no longer fit their boots onto their swollen feet, and frostbite was a danger. The mud, too, undermined morale: when their uniforms dried out, they were stiff as boards. The sight of Sicilian peasants shivering in a trench, hands purple and swollen, unequipped for climatic extremes that were as inconceivable to them as the war itself, could sow doubt in any observer's mind about continuing the assaults in sub-zero temperatures. But Cadorna was not an observer; he was in Udine, nearly 40 kilometres from Mount Mrzli, surrounded by deferential staff officers.

Even so, on 26 November, the Italians pushed the Austrians back to within 20 metres of the summit. Taking advantage of a rising mist, the counter-attacking Austrians quickly drove the Italians back to the Big Trench. A separate push to take the southernmost end of the ridge, directly above Tolmein, was also repulsed. Inching up the mountain, the Italians eventually found themselves only eight metres below the Austrian front line. Pelted with grenades, rocks, barrels, even tins filled with faeces, they could get no further. It was rumoured that a corps commander shouted at his staff, 'Don't you see I need more dead men, *lots* more, if we're to show the top brass that the action against Mrzli cannot succeed?' By the end of 1915, the losses of two brigades that had served on Mrzli from the start – the Modena and Salerno – exceeded 9,000 men.

Operations petered out in the first week of December, when heavy snowfalls obliterated trenches and wire. The Fourth Battle had added 49,000 Italian casualties to the 67,000 from the Third. Austrian losses were 42,000 and 25,000 respectively. Summarising the reasons for failure, the Italian official history of the war blamed the barbed wire, which was 'practically impossible' to destroy. Many months would pass before the Italians found a remotely effective solution.

TWELVE

Year Zero

Civilians on the Italian Front

Before Cadorna settled into the winter's work of preparing to campaign again in the spring, he helped the government fend off its critics in Rome. Although they dominated parliament, the Liberal and Socialist deputies had been subdued since May. Massive public support for the army made it almost impossible to challenge the government politically. But the failure to gain a breakthrough in 1915 made Prime Minister Salandra more vulnerable, and some opposition deputies tested the water by raising a problem that was genuine and might be eye-catching, but stopped short of implicating the military. This was the government's policy towards civilians in the occupied areas. The deputies were particularly concerned about the internees, men and women arrested on the orders of the Supreme Command without a legal basis and often on flimsy pretexts. The internees were forcibly transferred – sometimes with their children, sometimes by cattle truck – to locations the length and breadth of Italy, where they lived under police surveillance, subsisting on hand-outs, amid suspicious Italian patriots.

On 11 December, having agreed a line with Cadorna, Salandra assured parliament that only 200 or 300 of the internees were Italian citizens. The remainder – numbering no more than 2,000 – were Austrian subjects from the liberated territory. Internment was only used with people whose presence in the occupied territory might, 'even unconsciously and without blame on their part', benefit the enemy. Nevertheless, he promised to review the cases of the Italian citizens and let them return home when security allowed. A week later, the Supreme Command followed up with a soothing (and hollow) assurance that internment would no longer be ordered on the basis of vague allegations. In fact the number of internees was already 5,000 and would rise to 70,000. Internment began as soon as the army marched into eastern Friuli and the Dolomites. As the highest authority in the war zone, the Supreme Command decided who should be interned and on what grounds. There were no fixed criteria for these judgements, and decisions were made by the commanding officer on the spot, or by military police.

The occupation created a golden chance for score-settling. Local nationalists, prone to the intolerance that partners revolutionary idealism, prepared blacklists of their opponents, who were not lacking, for most Habsburg Italians were not nationalist at all. Kinship ties, ethnic origins, hearsay, anonymous letters, the testimony of 'trusted' informants, and sheer malice: all these played a part in the drama of internment. Francesco Rossi, a labourer, was arrested and interned after he was overheard saying that Italy was poor and would never be able to help poor people, as Austria had done. A family of seven was deported to southern Italy for giving their youngest child the 'disrespectful' name of Germana. The infant's godfather was interned as well for good measure. Six men from Villa Vicentina were interned for allegedly criticising the Italian army in a bar. Their offence was 'defeatism', like Leonardo Mian of Aquileia, interned after insulting army officers when in his cups. Another man was reportedly slow to help an Italian soldier who fell in a river, so he was packed off to Puglia at the far end of Italy. Few internees were given any reason for their treatment. Many files contain no allegations at all. Lack of open enthusiasm for the occupation was enough to prompt misgivings. Giuseppe Leghissa, a trader, was banished to Tuscany for being 'notoriously hostile to the cause'.

'Spying' was a standard accusation. Actual espionage did not have to be proven; arrest and internment followed from being in the wrong place at the wrong moment, or asking about Italian strength or intentions. A housewife could be charged with collaboration for hanging sheets out of windows facing the Carso, allegedly signalling to the Austrians. Parish priests were interned for ringing the church bells (and they were rung everywhere when the Italians marched in, because Pentecost fell on 23 May). So bell-ringing was prohibited, along with possession of firearms and keeping pigeons. A Germanic accent and old-world Viennese manners aroused suspicion, as several titled land-owners learned to their cost. Accusations were thickest in the areas where Slovenes lived. In some cases, internment was justified with the single word: 'Slav'.

A powerful factor was the irredentists' animus against the Catholic Church, for Catholicism was still regarded as nearly synonymous with anti-Italianism. When the Ponton brothers, Massimiliano and Giuseppe, were arrested and taken to the main square in Palmanova at the end of May 1915, a local man jumped at Giuseppe 'like a wild animal', according to a witness, screaming, 'We've got you now, you filthy German, you spy! Now you'll pay for your wrongdoings!' He punched Giuseppe hard on the head, then threw him back against a wall. Onlookers cheered as Giuseppe bled. The brothers were led away to join the other internees who had been rounded up, thirty or so altogether, to be handcuffed and shoved into carts (for the peasant farmers) or open carriages (if they were landowners or priests), then taken under military escort to prison, where a crowd was waiting with stones and sticks, led by 'well-dressed men' who shouted, 'Now you'll see who's master! You'll see what happens when you side with the Catholic swine!'[1] The police stood by as blows rained down on the handcuffed men.

The Ponton brothers were pillars of their community. What had they done to deserve this violence? Giuseppe's offence was logged as 'ex-Mayor, Catholic', while Massimiliano's was 'pro-Austrian, member of Catholic associations'. Making matters still worse, their brother Olivo was active in the movement against irredentism, and had fled to Gorizia at the start of the war. This movement was led by the People's Catholic Party of Friuli (PCPF), with a programme that chilled the marrow of Italian nationalists on both sides of the border. For the PCPF argued that Italian identity and rights could thrive within the empire on a basis of strong local autonomy. This was precisely what the irredentists denied. Every Habsburg Italian who believed in a bland constitutional settlement for Italians in the empire had made life harder for the irredentists and now, logically, would do so for the occupying forces. Activists who shared this vision were the worst enemies of the irredentists, rather as, elsewhere in Europe, democratic socialists would soon be the worst enemies of communists. The PCPF was led by a priest from Gorizia, Monsignor Luigi Faidutti, demonised in the nationalist press as a 'renegade'.

The clergy were automatically suspected of supporting the PCPF. Of the 80 priests in the occupied territories, 59 were interned in 1915 on generic grounds of spying, inciting resistance, and 'Austrophilia'. They were replaced by Italian priests in military service, often natives of

1 The irredentists were mostly well educated, town-dwellers. These men in suits had probably fled to Italy before the war and returned with the army.

western Friuli. The Supreme Command described this policy as 'just and praiseworthy', for the local priests had 'always supported the Austrian government, and hence could contribute to a state of mind not at all favourable to the new regime'. This was a slur on many priests, who simply had a different notion of what was good for the Habsburg Italians, but as a policy it made sense. Apart from their loyalty to the Apostolic Majesty in Vienna, most of the clergy were Slovenes, like their flock, and their opinion of the invaders was sharpened by ethnic antagonism. The Habsburgs were defenders of the faith, whereas the Italian army – led by Cadorna's father, as it happened – had conquered the Papal States and confined His Holiness to the Vatican, like jailers. Many saw Cadorna's forces in the darkest terms as profaners and rapists, and warned their congregations accordingly from the pulpit.

Other influential figures in the community were also targeted. Mayors, retired officials, teachers, tradesmen: all were likely to be interned. Some were sent to Udine or the Veneto; others to Piedmont and Lombardy; most ended in Tuscany or further south. All men between 18 and 50 from the 'redeemed' territory were supposed to be confined to the island of Sardinia. Consequently, three-quarters of the internees found themselves in one of the poorest, least healthy parts of Italy, where Habsburg Italians – let alone Slovenes – could make no sense of the impenetrable dialect. Italians sent to Sicily baffled the local people by speaking Italian – the Sicilians assumed that enemy civilians were bound to be German.

The state gave the internees one lira each per day: twice as much as a private in the infantry, but not enough to meet elementary needs. If they managed on their own savings or income, they could choose where to live. While some sank into ruin, most managed to find their feet. Clubs of local patriots would denounce internees to the police, but the police did not always listen and there were open-minded families ready to share food and lend clothes.

As well as internments, Cadorna's Supreme Command ordered mass evacuations. Everyone living within 500 metres of the 'zone of military operations' was supposed to be moved away. Many villages were virtually emptied. In all, more than 40,000 civilians were evacuated during the first year of the war. Some were sent a few kilometres down the road; most ended up unthinkably far from hearth and home, anywhere between Sicily and the French border, until 1919.

Families were given a few hours' notice to collect whatever they could carry, then escorted to collection points at Udine and Palmanova to be registered, disinfected and vaccinated against cholera and dysentery, then moved on to their destinations, where no camps had been prepared and there was no prior co-ordination with local authorities. Only when the Austrian offensive in 1916 drove almost 80,000 Italians off the Asiago plateau did the government realise that provision for refugees should be systematised. Even then, unlike in France or Britain, no central body was set up to organise refugee affairs.

Official and popular suspicion was pervasive; these people might have been 'redeemed', but they were still Austrian subjects. People spat on the evacuees in the streets of Livorno: 'You Germans, coming here to eat our bread.' They were moved around in convoys, under police escort. Their movements were often restricted. In some places, priests and teachers reached out to the evacuee groups. Yet they were practical people, ready to make the best of things – even the baffling foodstuffs. (Pasta and rice were unknown in eastern Friuli before the war.) As well as the daily subvention from the state, they were allowed to take paid work. A March 1916 report on Habsburg Italian evacuees in the southern province of Abruzzo observed that they mourned 'the tranquillity that they have lost and the prosperity they believe is gone for ever. But there is no rancour or hatred.'

Evacuee life was especially tough for the 10,000 or more Habsburg Slovenes who had to move to the interior of Italy. Apart from the shock of displacement, few of them could communicate with local people, who resented them more than the Italian evacuees. The same report from Abruzzo described the Slovenes as 'very submissive and docile' but also 'closed and suspicious'. The adults kept a distance from local people, though the children were more prepared to mix. In some places, the local authorities did not want to accept Slovenes at all.

The Supreme Command set up a new office to manage the evacuations and other civilian matters in the occupied territories. This was the General Secretariat for Civil Affairs, led by a lawyer, Agostino D'Adamo. Although he reported to Cadorna, D'Adamo came from the Ministry of the Interior. He was a key figure, the man who would prepare the full-scale integration of the 'redeemed' territory into the Kingdom of Italy. Cadorna's priority was his army's security. Salandra supported this, but he wanted something else as well: a political revolution to entrench Italian sovereignty over the conquered land. It was a delicate project, for Italy was party to international conventions that forbade occupying powers from imposing permanent changes in territory occupied in war. An occupying regime could only impose its national laws as far as necessary to ensure public order. It was entitled to demand obedience but not loyalty, a fragile distinction.

The Italians now disowned their international obligations, claiming exemption in the name of 'special considerations of law, of political opportunity, and sentiment'. From Rome's point of view, the occupation should *from the outset* mean 'the reality of the redemption, the stabilisation of liberty, and the accomplishment of national solidarity'. Without formally claiming the conquered land, as Bulgaria for example would do with Serbia, Italy laid the foundations for postwar annexation by integrating it into Italian life. D'Adamo spelled out the implications to the Supreme Command in March 1916: the population of the 'occupied territories' must understand that there could be 'no return to the preceding state' and they were subject to Italian sovereignty.

As these areas had been part of the Austrian Empire for four centuries, compared with the Kingdom of Italy's half-century of existence, and the local people had no reason to prefer Italy, it was not easy to induce this understanding. D'Adamo aimed to preserve the form of Habsburg administration while filling it with new national substance. 'Pro-Austrian elements' were to be removed from public life and replaced by individuals with 'Italian sentiments'. The purges were directed at local level by civil commissars. Italian became the sole official language. Slovene-language education was stopped; Italian history and geography loomed large in the new curricula. Army officers taught the lessons, and military chaplains took catechism classes. Pupils celebrated the birthdays of Italy's king, queen, and queen mother. German and Slavic place-names were Italianised in order to 'restore dignity' that had been lost to 'Austrian mangling'. By the end of 1917, some 2,500 toponyms had been changed. A project to impose Italian versions of Slovene surnames was launched.

Yet D'Adamo was a humane pragmatist who did his best for the people. Food and healthcare were provided, and state support was not withheld from families with men serving in the Austrian army. Even the Slovene press, across the border, gave credit where it was due, quoting the villagers' praise for the new regime. And he had a spine: when the government squeezed the local population unreasonably, he spoke up –

as when Rome wanted to force the introduction of Italian currency – for he believed the population should be won over, not simply coerced. This was a rare insight; the government mainly acted as if the locals should have their noses rubbed in the reality of Italian power. Despite a few enlightened policies, there was no systematic effort to convince them of the benefits of the new regime. As often in Italian history, individuals redressed the negligence and callousness of institutions.

D'Adamo's job was made harder by several murderous reprisals against local people. At the end of May 1915, the commander in Villesse believed – mistakenly – that the villagers were shooting at his men. He ordered everyone to be rounded up and kept as hostages. Then he shot six people, including the deputy mayor. The rest were interned. A week later, the Italians carried out a summary decimation of farmers from half a dozen hamlets between Caporetto and Tolmein. The adult males were rounded up and accused of betraying positions to the enemy and sheltering Italian deserters. Their denials were waved away by the commanding officer, a captain, who lined the farmers up and ordered every tenth man to step forward. The unlucky six were shot in the back and buried where they fell, scapegoats for the Italian soldiers' lack of enthusiasm for futile attacks against a much smaller Habsburg force, including many Slovenes, on the Krn–Mrzli ridge.

Compared with the slaughter on the hills above, these were minor mishaps, statistically almost invisible. But they were blatantly unjust, and they echoed around the occupied territory, poisoning local attitudes. A soldier stationed near Tolmein wrote in his diary on 30 June: 'The population is still hostile. Spies are constantly being shot at Caporetto.' In fact the shootings were sporadic; the soldier's impression of incessant executions – like the rumours that spread, for example about Slovene women cutting off the heads of wounded Italians – spoke volumes about the nerve-jangling atmosphere.

The Italians believed the liberated areas were teeming with spies – how else to explain their failure to break through? The other reason for their jumpiness was dismay at their reception by the people who were being 'redeemed'. Expecting fierce resistance, the troops were discomfited by the eerie emptiness of the land that they entered on 24 May. Then they were baffled by the attitude of the civilians. The villages were heavy with fear and distrust; even in towns with a reputation for nationalism, like Cervignano, the streets were empty and the houses shuttered. A deputy who had volunteered wrote to Salandra that 'we are welcomed coldly, with suspicion, often with open antipathy' in every village from the sea to the mountains. Italian commanders were reduced to forcing the local authorities to put on a show of pro-Italian emotion.

The welcome was even chillier in the Dolomites. Some valleys were pro-Austrian, others pro-Italian, depending on their proximity to the border and the trade that flourished along them. On the whole, the Habsburg Italians were loyal to their emperor. Italian nationalists venerated the Alps, their 'natural frontier', as the home of epic virtues: strength, sincerity, simplicity, faith and family. Ironically, these virtues tilted the mountain-dwellers against new-fangled Italy. For nationalism came late to the mountain communities, filtering in with the spread of Alpinism in the last third of the nineteenth century, when Italian and Austrian climbers competed for the honour of first ascents. Soldiers were dismayed to find people even in the southern valleys, closest to Italy, 'very hostile' to the men who were 'fighting to liberate their brothers'. An elderly Italian in Cortina was heard to comment, 'Wonderful! They have come to liberate us. But who will liberate us from them?'

Slovene newspapers reported with glee that the Italians were 'particularly angered' by the local people's attitude. After the wild rhetoric about the mission of Latin civilisation, many soldiers expected 'the Slavs' to hail their deliverance from cultural inferiority. By an irony that eluded them, the Italians were reaping the harvest of state policy towards the Slovene minority on their own side of the border. Since 1866, the Slovenes in Italy had envied the position that their co-nationals (often their blood kin) enjoyed across the border. The Italians did not realise that the terms of the Treaty of London meant – especially when simplified by Austrian propaganda – that they were seen as alien conquerors. Italian propagandists blamed their Austrian counterparts for brainwashing the locals with lies about Italian savagery.

But these people had been living with the war for nearly a year. Their menfolk were fighting in Galicia or Serbia. In the summer and autumn of 1915, the civilians in eastern Friuli saw their world turned upside down. They were dazed by the disappearance of the empire in which they and their forefathers had lived. The *regnicoli*, peaceable immigrants from Italy who in many cases had lived in these villages for decades, were forced out. The dusty lanes were torn up by the first motor vehicles that some of the locals had ever seen. Men and women were drafted into labour gangs to build tracks into the mountains. Fields were seized for barracks, depots, field kitchens, hospitals and airfields. The mortality rate in these villages soared, for the war brought disease.

All this occurred against a background of low-level ethnic distrust. The Slovenes were broadly pro-Austrian, without being aggressively anti-Italian. Their experience of war was exactly what the Italians could not imagine. Behind these misunderstandings lay a deep ignorance of the people who lived around Italy's north-eastern border. North of Gorizia, the population on the Isonzo front was entirely Slovene, mostly smallholding farmers with cows and goats, maize fields and orchards, shod in wooden clogs, ploughing their narrow fields with horses, eating rye bread and polenta, flat cake made with maize flour. The only Italian-speakers were women who had been in domestic service in Trieste. Further north, in Carnia, even the locals who were not Slovene and spoke something a bit like Italian, larded with Germanic and Slavic terms, were quite unlike the Venetians. The first Italian officials to make their way up these valleys after the 1866 war did not know how to classify the locals: were they German or Italian? These settlements shared an Alpine culture that linked them with the north and west; they also lay close to trade routes that connected the Mediterranean with central Europe.

The Austrians had tried to dilute Italian nationalism by encouraging the regional identity of Friuli. There was and is a Friulan identity – as the Italian state has accepted since 1945. Other ethnic identities had survived in the lee of the Alps: the Ladini, who had kept their ancient forms of community life in the high valleys of the Dolomites; the Cimbri on the Asiago plateau, with their Germanic dialect; the Mocheni further west in the Trentino. These particularities held no interest for Italian nationalists. The committed volunteers pouring across the border in 1915 felt they were entering virgin land that was, in a mystical way, destined to be Italian. Amleto Albertazzi, a 2nd lieutenant in the Fusiliers, shinned up a beech tree near the eastern bank of the Isonzo, in the first week of June 1915. His heart leaped to see 'the lands that will soon be ours: a high chain of mountains on the horizon; lower down, a series of hills sloping down to the plain, studded with little villages, growing denser around industrial Monfalcone', then Mount Hermada 'like a colossus' and Duino with its sombre castle, lapped by the sea. On the horizon, there is Trieste, 'white city of our dreams'.

What mattered was the *place*. The inhabitants were décor, not essential. Mussolini's journal shows this outlook perfectly. Moving over the old (1866) border in September 1915, he notices a little boy drawing water at a pump. What is his name? 'Stanko.' Stanko what? The boy does not understand the question, and Mussolini does not realise that Stanko must be a Slovene. Someone tells him the boy's surname is Robančič. 'A completely Slavic name,' notes Mussolini, then changes the subject. This encounter, so revealing of Italian assumptions, needs no comment on his part. In Caporetto a few months later, he notes the 'enigmatic faces' of the Slovenes. They still do not like us, he reflects. 'They submit with resignation and ill-concealed hostility. They think we are only passing through and don't want to compromise themselves in case yesterday's masters return tomorrow.'

For the most part, civilians were not brutally treated. Compared with the sufferings inflicted on Armenians, Belgians, French, Poles, Serbs and Russian Jews, they were fortunate. The Italians' lack of initial planning probably worked in the civilians' favour; mixed with the general population rather than cooped up in camps, like the Austrian evacuees, they had more opportunities to earn a living and integrate with the community. Perhaps, too, the lawful treatment of Slovenes and German-speaking Austrians in the border area reflected a general failure by Italian propagandists to poison the attitudes of ordinary soldiers.

It was different on the other side of the front. Before the war, life for Slovenes had been better in Austria than in Italy. During the war, life was better in Italy – even under occupation. Compared with conditions in the empire, it was easy to survive in occupied Caporetto. Even a week before Italy attacked in May 1915, the Austrian Ministry of the Interior advised people to stay at home, assuring them that full provision had been made in the event of war. Three days later, the villages on the Carso and the Isonzo began to be evacuated. Trieste, Gorizia and Monfalcone were not evacuated, perhaps for propaganda reasons. Many of their inhabitants left of their own will. Half the populations of Trieste and Gorizia moved away. Many villagers, too, took the initiative to go east. By the end of May, 100,000 civilians – Italians, Slovenes and Croats – had moved or been moved to the interior.

As elsewhere, internment was a preventive tool against suspected spies and saboteurs, potential enemy sympathisers, and political opponents (anarchists and socialists). It was the fate of some 3,000 male *regnicoli* of military age who had not left the empire by the end of May. Their wives and children – almost 12,000 individuals – were sent elsewhere in Austria or returned to Italy via neutral Switzerland, with the help of the Red Cross. These families often left their apartments fully furnished, with the floors swept and clean tablecloths on the table, never dreaming they would be gone for years. Life was particularly hard for Habsburg Italian evacuees and refugees in the empire. Statistics are fuzzy, but there were probably well over 20,000 of these. They were victims of the difficulty of proving a negative: how to convince the authorities that they were not covert irredentists? Mistaken for *regnicoli* or political internees, they met with hostility that corroded their loyalty to the empire. They had done nothing wrong, yet they were virtual prisoners far from home, subject to strict order, half starving, denied the chance of work, unable to move far from their camps, suspected by the local people. The camps became hotbeds of Italian nationalism.

Assistance for internees, evacuees and refugees was better organised but less generous than in Italy. In 1915, some of the camps were equipped with schools, churches, baths, laundries and electric light; others were primitive, insanitary barracks. Conditions deteriorated during the war, along with everything else in the empire. By late 1916, food was in short supply. The Ministry of the Interior was responsible but until the end of 1917, helping refugees was a concession, not a legal obligation, made to preserve what the ministry called 'the sense of belonging to a common fatherland'. Like any concession, it was arbitrary; hence the ethnic Italians were treated like 'objects of administration', as one of their leaders complained, 'as if they had no will, no rights of their own'. Matters were hardly better for the Slovenes, who killed time in the camps by singing songs and reciting the verses of Simon Gregorčič, a shy priest from Caporetto, who had foretold the carnage nearly forty years earlier:

> Here at the clash of sharpened blades,
> your waters will be tinged with red:
> our blood will run to you,
> that foe will make your current drag!
> Bright Isonzo, then remember
> what your ardent heart implores . . .

The first historian of the war in Friuli explained why Italy's internees and evacuees were not worth studying: 'They do not stir that sense of the heroic which makes suffering admirable, sacrifice luminous, death honourable and envied.'[2] It was better to omit these elements than spoil a sublime picture. The real history was preserved and transmitted orally, by survivors. Families never forgot the catastrophe of displacement. When the Italian soldiers broke the news, the lanes between the houses rang with screams; some people tried to bury their valuables in the cellar while others beat their heads on the wall, wailing.

One man who lived long enough to inform a new generation of historians was Andrej Mašera of Caporetto, interviewed when he was ninety.

What I think is that the Italian soldiers who came to fight here felt cheated. Because they had been told, 'We're going to liberate our brothers.' But when they spoke to us, nobody understood a word. This is why I think the Italian soldiers really *had* been cheated. Before they came into the war, there was great propaganda about liberating us, but once they got here, they asked themselves 'Where are those brothers of ours? Just what are we doing here?'

---

2 This historian, Giovanni Del Bianco, also argued that the executions at Villesse had been offset by 'the glow of a more radiant future, and new hopes arose, as if to affirm the fluctuations of life and death by which the becoming of peoples is destined to unfold'. Boilerplate dialectics were a convenience for historians under fascism, as for those under communism.

THIRTEEN

A Necessary Holocaust?

*A certain plodding earnestness and strict discipline
may keep up military virtue for a long time, but can
never create it.*
Carl von Clausewitz

At the end of 1915, the volunteer officer Guido Favetti sits in a trench
behind Monfalcone, facing Mount Cosich. Nothing stirs. Amid the
'glacial silence', metaphors for the situation arise in his highly educated
mind. The two warring nations seem to be separated by a silent strip of
death, a tongue of fire. Life is suspended; death hovers in the air, ready
to pounce. The anticipation of atrocity is a terrible burden, yet the
prospect of death is not demoralising; instead, it induces a mild
melancholy, like going to the dentist.

This fine disdain for danger was shared by many middle-class
irredentists, whose faith in what Favetti called 'the religion of the
Fatherland' could not be shaken. It was much harder for ordinary
conscripts to distance themselves from their experience in this way;
intellectual consolation was not available. Remarkably, Favetti – who
deplored the men's lack of idealism – recognised this, and imagined the
state of mind of

... the infantryman keeping watch with his rifle at the loophole while a shell
smashes the trench a few metres away; legs, arms, bits of brain fly through the
air, hitting your face like shrapnel ... someone is screaming because he has lost
his legs, or his stomach is split open, he's raving, he gabbles a prayer, one of
those prayers that make you weep.

Favetti's 'feeble words' can never describe the 'mortal anxiety' of an infantryman under attack or ordered to attack, when 'enthusiasm, patriotism, no
longer exist, or rather, they didn't exist before for these masses of peasants
and workers'. Stepping beyond stock responses, Favetti exclaims to his
diary: 'Is he not a true hero? They are all like this – all of them!'

*

For several months after the Fourth Battle, the army was close to collapse. Cadorna's losses in 1915 ran to 400,000, including 66,000 killed (compared with 28,000 Austrians). To grasp the intensity of destruction, consider the fate of a single brigade, the Casale, known as the Polenta Brigade due to its yellow colours. In May 1915, its strength was 130 officers and 6,000 soldiers. After 440 casualties during June and 800 more in July, it spent three months on Podgora, the steep hill west of Gorizia, where it lost another 2,822 men, including 86 officers – two-thirds of its total strength. During seven months at the front, the Casale lost 154 officers and 4,276 men, dead, wounded and missing.[1] Tens of other brigades suffered equivalent losses.

The survivors' morale was shaky; even for enthusiasts, the jubilation of their 'radiant May' was a mocking memory. The troops were unprepared, in every sense, for the conditions they faced. Lacking weapons, ordered to attack intact barbed wire, struck down by typhoid and cholera, poorly clothed and fed, sleeping on wet hay or mud, the men began to realise that they were 'going to be massacred, not to fight'. Hardly Garibaldian warriors, rather cannon fodder in a new kind of war.

The positions and communications were improvised. Most of the front line was impossibly exposed and highly vulnerable to counter-attack. The trenches were still shallow scrapes, filthy with rubbish. Even on San Michele, the epicentre of the front, there was no real line; hummocks made of sandbags and rubble alternated with stretches of completely open, unprotected ground.

Sweat, dust, mud, rain and sun turned the men's woollen uniforms into something like parchment. Their boots often had cardboard uppers and wooden soles. Lacking better remedies, the men rubbed tallow into their cracked feet. Helmets were in very short supply. The wooden waterbottles were unhygienic. The tents – when they had them – leaked. The wire-cutters were almost useless, and unusable under fire: 'mere garden secateurs', as a Sardinian officer wrote disgustedly in his diary. Ration parties were often delayed by enemy fire. The only hot meal was in the morning, and so poor that soldiers often rejected most of it. The pervasive stench could, anyway, make eating impossible. The effects of such poor nutrition were evident after three or four days in the trenches, and some units sent out raiding parties for food and clothing in trenches that the enemy had abandoned. The soldiers slept on straw pallets, but

1 The Casale Brigade would lose 2,000 more men on the Asiago plateau in May and June 1916, then another 3,000 in the battle for Gorizia in August 1916.

there were not enough to go around. Even in the rear, before proper hutments were built, the men lived in tents that quickly became waterlogged and filthy. Abysmal medical care led to 'a good number of avoidable deaths due to inhuman treatment'. Wounded men were routinely 'shipped on 20 or 30 km ambulance runs on vile roads and then kept waiting for hours outside hospital'.

On the higher positions, the infantry tried not to freeze to death in their dug-outs, heating rations on Primus stoves that made everything taste of petrol. They slept in holes or pits, wrapped in their coats, packed together for warmth, under canvas stretched between boulders. During their brief spells out of the line, they were often drafted into labour platoons. As for recreation, nothing was organised in the rear areas. To the puritanical Cadorna, free time was a regrettable necessity. Men were forbidden to enter cafés or bars during the day, or to be seen in public 'in easy company'. (A soldier might be arrested for strolling arm in arm with his fiancée.) There were no libraries, cinemas, or theatres. The only distractions were alcohol (the soldiers called it their petrol), authorised brothels (separate for officers and men), and saucy literature. The first modern Italian novel to sell more than 100,000 copies was *Mimi Bluette, Flower of my Garden*, by Guido da Verona, the story of a ballerina pure in heart though not in deed, who kills herself at the pinnacle of her renown. The book's huge popularity in the trenches troubled Father Giovanni Minozzi, a priest who believed that immoral literature made the soldiers' souls 'flabby'. The following summer, he set up Soldiers' Houses, where men off duty could relax amid improving books, discuss their worries with priests, and be helped to write letters home. These high-minded places were not much fun, but they did some good.

A senior medical officer with the VI Corps (Second Army) assessed the men's health in early January 1916. Their clothing was of poor quality, torn and crusted with mud. Their feet were frostbitten and swollen. 'Psychic disturbances' were most acute where the trenches were continually exposed to the enemy. 'Standing inert with the prospect of having to attack or be attacked, from one moment to the next, certainly has a great influence on the evolution of these disturbances of the nervous system.'

Morale was also damaged by the callousness of many senior officers, which Cadorna encouraged and even demanded. Regimental commanders vainly objected that men should not be sent against

Prime Minister Antonio Salandra near the front in May 1916, a month before he was forced to resign.

Baron Sidney Sonnino: 'never was a foreign minister more stubborn and unintelligent, or more honest and sincere'.

Captain Gabriele D'Annunzio, talking the talk near Vicenza, 1918.

Benito Mussolini, arrested at an interventionist rally in 1915. Perhaps this was in Rome, in April, when Curzio Malaparte saw Mussolini bellowing as the police dragged him away: 'thin, pale, jaws set hard, his neck straining with effort'.

General Cadorna visiting British batteries in spring 1917.

Looking from the western rim of the Isonzo valley, across to Mount Mrzli. The Italians clawed their way up this 1,200-metre face, but never took the summit. Colonel De Rossi's view in May 1915 was from a lower elevation.

Austro-Hungarian troops rest while building a trench on the Carso.

Looking from the Austro-Hungarian forward positions on Mount San Michele, across the Italian lines and the River Isonzo to the plains of Friuli. Udine is almost visible in the distance on the left.

Trieste and its port in 1919. 'National deliverance' has come at last to the city's 'huddled browntiled roofs' (James Joyce). And the quays are empty.

A farming family in Friuli, probably posing for an officer who was billeted in their home. Other officers can be seen among the oleanders.

Approaching Gorizia, with Podgora hill and Mount Sabotino in the background. The Italians captured them all in August 1916.

Looking from the summit of Mount San Michele towards the Italian lines and the River Isonzo. Ungaretti's regiment was posted in the middle distance when he wrote 'The Rivers'.

The relief. 'What's your regiment / brothers?'

Looking across the mouth of the Travenanzes valley to the flank of Mount
Tofana, held by the Italians, and the Castelletto, a natural fortress 200 metres tall,
held by the Austro-Hungarians until late 1916.

Carso mud and stone: an Italian second-line camp near Mount Fajti.

The so-called 'road of heroes', cut into the sheer face of Mount Pasubio, in the Trentino. Italian military engineering was much admired. What one veteran called the *exhilaration of extreme situations* was easily felt in such surroundings.

unbroken barbed wire. A corps commander on the Isonzo, General Vincenzo Garioni, argued that the massacre of infantry should be seen as 'a necessary holocaust'. The slaughter was therapeutic, a purgative that strengthened the army for future battles, rendering it fit for victory. Whether this nonsense was more a cause or an effect of the senior commanders' indifference to suffering, it is hard to say.

As well as the losses due to poor equipment, countless lives were thrown away because the men lacked elementary training, for example not even being told to keep their heads down when they reached the trenches. A staff officer in Carnia realised in summer 1915 that 'Nobody has a clue how to lay wire, how to throw a hand-grenade, how to attack a trench system.' A rare British witness of the 1915 campaigns was George Barbour, a Scottish Quaker who served with the Friends' Ambulance Unit on the Isonzo after several months in Flanders. He recorded his dismay at the sight of men trying to move along a road to the rear, in November. The road was under fire, and the Italians were clueless how to protect themselves. 'When told to advance, they do so in the most inconvenient manner possible at a slow double and then again expose themselves under cover by lying against the projecting bank at the corner where the shells always fall . . . they seem to be babes in the art of war.' Regular lunch breaks were further evidence of poor professionalism: 'The victor will be he who can put his heart into the thing for 2 successive days – all the Quisca batteries stop for 1½ hrs at lunch time & the Austrians do the same with the same infantile regularity.' This slack custom endured throughout the war.

Something that revolted foreign observers and sensitive Italians alike was the carelessness about latrines. Giani Stuparich's reaction, cited earlier, was dainty compared to Carlo Emilio Gadda's. For the future novelist, then a lieutenant in the 5th Regiment of Alpini, military defecation gave a frightful insight into national character. 'Shit of every size, shape, colour, texture and consistency is scattered everywhere in the vicinity of the camp', he wrote despairingly, 'yellow, black, ash grey, swarthy, bronze; liquid, solid, etc.' Incredibly, the men could not see how needlessly unpleasant they made life for everybody – themselves included – by not using latrines. This chronic inability to grasp the wider effects of their actions was a trait that he dubbed 'the *cretinous egotism of the Italian*'. A British private who spent the last year of the war in Italy was shocked by the appearance of an abandoned camp: 'literally a field of filth. I had never seen such a disgusting sight and wondered what kind of epidemic was being bred amidst the excreta and soiled paper.' With such disregard for basic hygiene, how could the Italians hope to wage war properly?

These humble problems were beneath Cadorna's notice. When in Rome, he grumbled that he felt much better 'at the front'. By this he meant his headquarters, for he rarely ventured closer to the fighting. The Supreme Command, jokily known as the *Commandissimo*, was a world apart. To Rudyard Kipling's visiting eyes, it was like a monastery or laboratory: simple, austere, dedicated. This was not the view of officers up the line, who saw Cadorna's staff lavished with privileges: working in safety, with fine food and drink, their families installed nearby and chauffeurs at the ready; given fast-track promotions, contact with ministers and the King, and unmerited decorations.[2] It was hardly surprising if this pampered coterie did not question 'the boss', as they called him.

Enemy propaganda made good use of Cadorna's lack of progress and carelessness about losses. One leaflet in the autumn printed maps of the paltry territory that the Italians had captured since May, alongside estimates of the casualties they had taken. Another, released over Italian positions from hot-air balloons before the Fourth Battle, reproduced an order of Cadorna that a certain position must be taken regardless of how many lives were lost.

These conditions frayed the bonds of discipline. The first proper mutiny occurred in early December 1915. After four months in the trenches, the 48th Regiment (Ferrara Brigade) was reduced to 700 effectives. Despite losing some 2,300 men, the regiment had just performed well during a month on San Michele. Then, on 11 December, some 200 of these survivors – almost all Calabrians, from the far south of Italy – were granted a spell of rest and recuperation while the remaining 500 were sent back to the front at Tolmein. The men's sense of injustice welled up, and shots were fired. The divisional commanders set up an extraordinary court martial and two soldiers were shot, less than 24 hours after the offence.

2 Lieutenant Ugo Ojetti, a middle-aged art historian doing propaganda work at the Supreme Command, was given the Bronze Medal for Military Valour for entering Gorizia on 9 August 1916, shortly after the first Italian troops. The joke went around that he was then awarded the Silver Medal for Civil Valour, honouring the nerve he had shown by accepting the first medal.

Another incident occurred on 20 December at Kamno, on the middle Isonzo, directly below Krn, when a regiment of the Salerno Brigade was ordered back to the first line. Apparently fuelled by drink, someone fired a shot at the officers' mess. The divisional command surrounded the regiment with four battalions, complete with machine guns and artillery. The following morning, an extraordinary court martial considered the charge of 'revolt in the presence of the enemy' – a dubious charge, as the rebels were not in the line. Eight were sentenced to death, others to hard labour for 20 years. The condemned men wept as they were led away. After witnessing the executions, the regiment was escorted back up the line by carabinieri (military police).

One of the chief grievances was the lack, and irregularity, of home leave. Cadorna believed he could not spare the men from the front during the autumn offensives. The longer they went without leave, and the worse the army's results in the field, the more fearful the Supreme Command became that the soldiers' accounts of life at the front would harm wider support for the war. The censorship of their letters and the press, and the relentlessly upbeat statements issued by Udine and Rome, left the public completely unprepared for realistic accounts of the war. Cadorna had set a trap for himself that time would spring.

With Christmas impending and the front locked down by winter weather, it was impossible to keep postponing the men's home leave. When a fortnight's leave was granted to tens of thousands of soldiers in December, the impact on public spirits was perceptible. Stories circulated about terrible losses on Mount Col di Lana in the Dolomites; entire regiments thrown at positions on the Carso that could not be taken; trenches that could be stormed but not held. The government warned that any soldier on leave who spread 'tendentious or exaggerated rumours' which weakened 'faith in the success of our endeavours' would be returned to his unit. The threat did not work; on 16 January, Cadorna ordered commanding officers to take harsh measures against 'defeatism' among soldiers on leave.

This was not his only political annoyance as the year drew to its end. Salandra wanted visible success – even though other fronts were stagnant too. Having given Cadorna sole charge of the conduct of the war, he was unhappy that a bloody stalemate was his reward. He found the supreme commander personally difficult; Cadorna refused to inform the government of his plans or curb his demands for weapons, ammunition and equipment.

Cadorna stuck to his doctrine; nobody, he declared, not even Napoleon (his favourite precursor) could have obtained better results.[3] The keys to success were resources and sacrifice. He was convinced – not wrongly – that the Austrians were desperately stretched. (Over the winter, they called up 850,000 men, mostly aged 43–50. The oldest Italians in the line at this time were 39.) He saw himself as labouring to persuade a feckless government and a fickle nation that a long, grinding campaign was inevitable. There might be few dramatic breakthroughs, but victory was likely; for the Austrians could never match the Italians in manpower, or prevail in a *Materialschlacht*, a war of material; the Russian Front and the Allied naval blockade would see to that. On top of this, Cadorna had another reasonable grievance. He was unhappy with Sonnino's decision to send two divisions to Albania in early December, as insurance against Allied backsliding on the promises of April 1915. Cadorna was a soldier, not an imperialist, and feared the diversion of resources.

Only one minister had the knowledge or nerve to suggest an alternative strategy. In an explosive memorandum to Salandra, the Minister of War, General Zupelli, pointed out that most of the nation's medium and heavy artillery was not deployed on crucial sections of the Isonzo. Boldly, he proposed that Cadorna should mount a fresh offensive on the Carso in early February. It should start with a bombardment by at least 500 medium or heavy guns on a front no wider than 12 kilometres, giving Cadorna an intensity of firepower resembling that on the Western Front. Delaying the resumption of war until April or later would benefit Austria more than Italy. Zupelli made his case to the cabinet at the end of January. Sonnino, angling to get Cadorna replaced by someone more congenial, urged the establishment of a Council of War as a forum for ministers and generals. This was transparently a gambit to keep tabs on Cadorna. Fearing the general's wrath, Salandra referred the matter to the King, the only person to whom Cadorna was accountable. What did he think? If the army repeated the extensive frontal attacks that had already failed, would they not – insinuated Salandra – be knocking their heads on a wall?

3 In January 1916, Cadorna solicited comments on tactics from senior commanders. The conventional replies showed that no higher wisdom was circulating away from the Supreme Command. On the other hand, free-thinking officers may have kept their real thoughts to themselves.

Cautious Victor Emanuel sent his aide de camp to Udine. Denouncing Sonnino's idea, Cadorna accused the government of trying to provoke his resignation. The King was sympathetic; in his milder way, he shared his general's contempt for Roman shenanigans and his low opinion of Salandra. Cadorna followed up with a strongly worded letter: 'These parliamentary regimes in the Latin style are made to corrupt the country in peace and sweep it to perdition in war. And do not accuse me of anti-liberalism just because events have made me so sceptical.' To his wife, he wrote that his principal enemies were no longer the Austrians.

The army's dismal showing against Albanian guerrillas helped Cadorna; had he not foreseen a fiasco? Then his position was suddenly weakened, when the army lost a piece of territory north of Gorizia. Counter-attacks were beaten back by Croatian and Hungarian regiments. More than 4,000 men were lost, half as prisoners. These were worrying figures, and rumours circulated that the front-line units were going soft. In this pass, Cadorna's staff turned to their contacts in the press. Journalists dubbed Cadorna the *generalissimo*, a title that stuck. The *Corriere della Sera* editorialised that 'Italy has found her *Duce*', her leader: a dramatic claim. D'Annunzio penned an ode, imploring God to aid the '*Duce*' in his mighty task.

> Temper his certainty, O Lord, and
> nail his certainty in our breasts.[4]

The *Idea Nazionale* told its readers that Cadorna was 'the only man Italy still believes in'. The boss was particularly pleased by the compliments in Mussolini's newspaper: 'Who would have believed two years ago that Signor Benito would ever sing my praises.'

With the wind in his sails, Cadorna bore down on the original troublemaker. He had picked Zupelli for the job in October 1914, when he needed a trusted aide in preparing the army for war. Now he had been stabbed in the back. (There was no such thing as constructive criticism; the commission of inquiry after Caporetto found that Cadorna displayed 'intolerance of every judgement and assessment . . . even from persons who had the right and duty to discuss his decisions'.) At the end of February, Cadorna told Salandra that Zupelli had to go or he would resign. The Prime Minister warned Cadorna not to price himself out of work, but with the King's backing and matters in Albania

4 Was this a rhetorical flourish, or had D'Annunzio sensed the irresolution beneath Cadorna's tenacity?

going from bad to worse, the supreme commander was unstoppable. When Salandra offered to resign, the King refused and cajoled Cadorna into backing down. Zupelli's position was untenable, and he resigned. The new minister of war was Paolo Morrone, a biddable general proposed by Cadorna.

The 'government in Udine', as the Supreme Command was becoming known, had trumped the government in Rome. No more was heard of the Council of War, and Zupelli was banished to the front. He had done his job well: machine guns and hand-grenades were being produced in large numbers. Another weapon also began large-scale production. This was the *bombarda*, a primitive trench mortar or bomb-thrower that fired tail-finned shells (30–200 millimetre calibre) in a high trajectory. The Italians finally had something to rend barbed wire, and even blow the entanglements out of the ground.

Back in the war zone, certain lessons had been learned and applied. The forward positions were thinned out, to spare as many men as possible the rigours of winter. The Third Army brought its batteries closer to the front and experimented with ways to make better use of observers. The defences were strengthened on the middle and upper Isonzo. The engineers constructed proper positions on some sectors. The defensive fall-back lines on the River Tagliamento were taken in hand. The forces around Gorizia – VI Corps, under the dynamic and alarming command of General Capello – were placed under the Third Army, linking them with the forces on the Carso.

As the call-up was extended to further conscript classes, 24 new infantry regiments were formed in early 1916, together with two Bersaglieri regiments and 246 battalions of Alpini, specialised mountain troops destined for the Dolomites and the Tyrol. Italy's 35 divisions in May 1915 would increase to 48 by the end of 1916, bringing the total number deployed on the front to one and a half million. The infantry began to be issued with heavy overboots and greatcoats; rubbed with grease, these gave better protection against the elements. Hobnailed leather boots arrived. Much was still amiss with the uniforms – woollen socks were in short supply, and the capes absorbed water – yet by April, the Third Army (at least) was for the first time better equipped than the enemy. Barracks were disinfected. Anti-cholera vaccinations were carried out. The first iron helmets were distributed – prototypes, based on a French model. Over the winter, front-line tours were shortened to

15 days and organised in cycles: units should pass from the first to the second line, then back to the reserves. In practice, the time spent in the line was not standardised.

Finally, concessions were made to the attacking infantry; they could leave their heavy knapsacks behind when they went over the top. In a break with Garibaldian tradition, officers were permitted to direct attacks from behind. This reform was forced on the Supreme Command by the toll on the officer corps in 1915. Best of all, from the infantry's point of view, the Supreme Command ruled that sector commanders should seek to bring their front lines within 50 metres of the enemy's foremost positions. This distance was later reduced to 30 and then 20 metres, trying to minimise the infantry's exposure in the death zone.

Cadorna could outmanoeuvre Italy's government, but not her allies. On 6 December, the Allied commanders met again at Chantilly to decide on strategic priorities for the coming year. It had been a terrible year for the Entente, and Joffre and Haig wanted an overwhelming focus on the Western Front. The Italians, represented by Cadorna's feckless deputy, General Carlo Porro, were left in no doubt that their front was a sideshow. They and the Russians pledged to launch synchronised attacks in the spring, some time after March. This timetable was made irrelevant by the German onslaught at Verdun and the Meuse, starting in late February. By early March the hard-pressed Joffre was calling for his allies to launch supporting offensives. Cadorna wanted to wait for the spring thaw before renewing the attack on Gorizia. Reluctantly, he promised a modest 'offensive demonstration'. Publicly, he gave it a grander name: it would be a 'vigorous offensive' along the length of the Isonzo.

Starting on 11 March with a 48-hour bombardment, the Fifth Battle of the Isonzo concentrated on the middle reach of the river between Tolmein and Mount San Michele. This involved the usual bloodbath on the hill of Podgora, where Zeidler's Dalmatian units resisted with their normal doggedness. A few kilometres away, the Italians gained a hundred metres of altitude on Mount Sabotino – a genuine achievement, made possible by long preparation over the winter, entrenching and sapping up the mountain's western flanks. On San Michele, the Third Army gained ground near the hamlet of San Martino, only to lose it when the Austrians used tear-gas shells. Offensives around Tolmein and on Mount Mrzli met with no better success. Snow in the north and fog in the south forced a cessation. Yet the fighting ran on; the Austrians counter-attacked, tightening their grip on Tolmein and Rombon, while the Italian 18th Infantry Regiment captured an important position south of San Michele, between Mount Sei Busi and Monfalcone.

The Italians took another 13,000 casualties without improving their position much or helping the French in any way. A Croatian newspaper crowed that the fifth offensive had 'ended in the same kind of success as the first four'. Cadorna took the outcome as final proof that he needed much more heavy artillery. His opposite number, Conrad von Hötzendorf, drew a different lesson: that the moment had come to turn the tables.

FOURTEEN

The Return Blow

*The defensive in war cannot be a state of endurance
. . . a defensive, without an offensive return blow,
cannot be conceived.*
CARL VON CLAUSEWITZ

Austria's passivity on the Isonzo did not suit the fiery Conrad, chief of the Austro-Hungarian general staff, who longed to take the battle to the traitors. After Serbia was overrun in mid-November, the Habsburgs were fighting on only two fronts and Conrad believed he had an opening. He cherished two bold ideas for an offensive. One was an attack across the upper Isonzo, between Tolmein and Flitsch. The other was an operation out of the Tyrol towards the sea. As 1915 drew to its end, this second idea became an obsession. If the Austrians surged across the mountains onto the plains of the Veneto, their impetus and the enemy's disarray would make them unstoppable. Reaching the sea near Venice, they would cut Cadorna's supply lines. Even if the Italian reserves improvised defences in front of Padua and Venice, they would not be able to counter-attack effectively. Unless Britain and France sped to the rescue – an unlikely prospect, he thought, given their focus on the Western Front – Rome would have to sue for peace.

Conrad calculated that he needed 16 full-strength divisions – more than 160,000 men – to give him a 2:1 advantage over the Italians in the Trentino. As the Austrians' total strength on the Isonzo front was 147 battalions, each with no more than 1,000 men, they would need Germany's help. Conrad sat down with his German counterpart, Erich von Falkenhayn, on 10 December. While he accepted that the French were the principal enemy, he argued that a decisive success was much more likely in the Italian theatre. If they struck early the following year, before Cadorna built up his strength and materiel, Italy could be eliminated altogether. At the least, the front would be shortened dramatically, freeing 200,000 Austrian troops for deployment elsewhere. Germany was not formally at war with Italy, but if Falkenhayn saw his way to releasing nine Austrian divisions from the Eastern Front, around 100,000 men, he would greatly improve the odds of dealing Italy a terminal blow.

Conrad had the impression that Falkenhayn was not opposed, so he felt let down when Germany said no. Falkenhayn's logic was, however, impeccable. First, Conrad underestimated the strength needed for a successful attack: realistically, he should have 25 divisions, not 16, and finding 25 divisions was out of the question. Second, the Germans would only support the operation if it could knock Italy out of the war; simply pushing the front line back, even to Lake Garda and Padua, would bring no advantage. But Italy was utterly beholden to France and especially Britain, which would not allow her to capitulate. Therefore the operation did not justify the diversion of German forces from the Western Front.

Privately, Falkenhayn thought the Austrians were blinkered by a fixation on their 'own private enemy', and missing the wider picture. Conrad confirmed this insight by taking the rebuff as a personal slight, and the relationship between the two, always difficult, now broke down. Liaison between their staffs virtually ceased. Mirroring more sharply Cadorna's attitude to the French and British, Conrad resented Germany's deprecation of the Italian front. Again like Cadorna, resentment bolstered his stubborn self-righteousness. In late January, encouraged by Austria's conquest of tiny Montenegro, he decided to go it alone against the Italians.

What Falkenhayn had chosen not to mention was that every last German division was needed for a colossal new operation on the Western Front. When Conrad learned about the Verdun offensive, only a few days before it was unleashed on 21 February, he decided to keep the Germans in the dark about his own plan for Trentino. His army's recent stronger showing on the Eastern Front seemed to confirm that significant front-line forces could safely be withdrawn without German substitutes. He informed Archduke Eugen, the commander on the empire's South-Western Front, that Italy would be attacked between the Adige and Sugana valleys. The initial bombardment would last only a few hours before the infantry were unleashed. Cadorna's army would have seen nothing like it.

Boroević was instructed to send four of his best divisions and many of his heavy batteries. By mid-March, there were only 100 Habsburg battalions on the Isonzo; medium or heavy guns were down to 467 from 693. With five divisions and much artillery subtracted from Galicia (against Falkenhayn's express request) and other forces transferred from Serbia, Conrad scraped together 15 divisions: nearly 200 infantry battalions with more than a thousand artillery pieces, including 60 heavy batteries. With nearly 160,000 fighting men, he should still have a powerful advantage in manpower and a 3:1 superiority in medium and heavy guns. Mild temperatures in February led Conrad to propose a mid-April date for the attack. Given that his forces would have to capture peaks and ridges over 2,000 metres high, this was rash. The likelihood that the terrain would be passable by 10 April was always slim. Conrad lost his wager on the weather. Snow began to fall heavily on 1 March, and kept falling. By early April, the invasion routes were under more than two metres of snow, forcing Conrad to postpone the operation.

The Italians registered the enemy build-up in the Trentino without grasping its import or realising the implications for the Isonzo campaign. It was a classic case of a headquarters possessing intelligence without the ability to interpret it.

The sector commander who would face Conrad's onslaught was General Roberto Brusati. By mid-February he sensed that the Austrians were stirring; he asked Cadorna for reinforcements, and was told curtly that he had enough for any need that might arise. A month later, on 22 March, the very day that Conrad's strike force was assembled and ready to move, Brusati reported that a substantial attack could be expected within a few days, striking down from Trento towards Vicenza and the Veneto plains. There would be flanking support along the Sugana valley. 'I have already reported that, in the event of a serious enemy attack, this Army absolutely lacks any reserves.'

As Brusati's tone suggests, his relationship with the Supreme Command had a history. For he had chafed under Cadorna's refusal to pursue offensives in his sector, between the Dolomites and Lake Garda. Dismayed by Cadorna's failure to realise in May 1915 that the Austrians had withdrawn to a defensive line behind the state border, Brusati had tried to compensate ever since by attacking towards Trento, despite Cadorna's order of 24 February to prepare the First Army's main defence on the stronger rearward lines. He had pushed his forces forward over the summer and autumn and now they were strung along advance positions, without reserves or reliable communications. These positions had not been tested in action and were extremely vulnerable. His defensive lines, too, were in poor shape. Yet Cadorna, usually the scourge of free-thinking officers, neither disciplined Brusati nor compelled him to ensure that his defences were in order. Probably he was relieved that a bit of progress was being made.

Cadorna received Brusati's report with scepticism, if not incredulity. Distracted by the aftermath of the Fifth Battle, he saw no need to revise his judgement that the Austrians were fighting a purely defensive war. Why, anyway, would they suddenly go on the offensive when the Russians were attacking in the east?[1] His composure was not disturbed by the detailed testimony of Habsburg deserters, one of whom – an ethnic Italian – even produced documents about the build-up. While consenting to reinforce the First Army with five extra divisions, Cadorna rebuked Brusati for lacking the 'imperious calm' which reigned at the Supreme Command. The enemy movements were, he maintained, a bluff to divert attention from an imminent offensive on the Isonzo.

Brusati made matters worse by committing the extra divisions to his untenable front line rather than his fragile defences. He went to Udine in person, but again failed to persuade Cadorna that the situation in Trentino was unusual. Then a Czech officer deserted with precise information about the impending attack. By mid-April, accurate estimates of the Austrian build-up (though not of the artillery) were appearing in the Italian and French press. Still unmoved, Cadorna added a further reason for scepticism: why would the Austrians attack on this front when the Russians were about to launch a major new offensive? What he did not know was that the Russians had just decided, on 24 April, to postpone their next offensive until June. Cadorna only learned of this decision on 14 May, the day before Conrad's Trentino offensive began. Bad communications between the Allies reinforced Cadorna's obstinacy.

Around this time, reportedly, an officer in the Alpini presented himself at the Supreme Command in Udine, with important information about the situation in Trentino. After a long wait, a captain on Cadorna's staff emerged: 'His Excellency the Supreme Commander of the Army has no need of advice from Lieutenant Battisti.' The officer

---

1 The Russians launched the Battle of Lake Naroch on 18 March 1916, in response to Joffre's appeal for diversionary help.

thus dismissed was Cesare Battisti, the legendary patriot from Trento, who knew every tree and rock in the threatened sector.

Cadorna was not truly so pig-headed as his communications with Brusati and his rudeness to Battisti suggested. Writing to Joffre on 26 April, he warned that an Austrian attack on the rear areas was probably imminent. He coolly asked for French artillery and other help – this, during the Battle of Verdun, perhaps the bloodiest confrontation of the entire war. Three days later, as if to show that he took the omens seriously, Cadorna visited the Trentino front. It was his first inspection since September, and he refused even to meet Brusati, a decision that only makes sense if – as Cadorna's biographer suggests – he was setting the other man up as a scapegoat. Back in Udine, he brushed off Brusati's strained assurances that he had always respected orders. On the contrary, both the lines and the batteries in Trentino were dangerously exposed, in violation of his directive that any offensive actions by the First Army must strengthen its defences. Brusati hit back: the First Army's offensives had conformed to orders, and Cadorna had repeatedly expressed approval. To no avail. The critic of Roman intrigue was himself a merciless political operator. On 8 May 1916, he wrote to the King that Brusati should be replaced. Even though the general's brother Ugo was aide to Victor Emanuel, Cadorna had his way. Brusati was replaced with an elderly general whom he, Cadorna, brought out of retirement and who repaid the kindness with total obedience.[2] Ugo Brusati asked why his brother had been sacked so soon after Cadorna's assurance that he did not believe in an Austrian offensive. The Supreme Commander replied that he had not changed his mind on that point; General Brusati had to go, not because he had neglected the defences but because he had shown 'too little serenity'.

At dawn the next day (15 May), Conrad's guns began to roar. An Austrian journalist gave the offensive a name that stuck: the *Strafexpedition*, or 'punishment expedition'. Punishment was an important concept in the propaganda of the Central Powers. Austria had started the

---

2 On 25 May, Brusati learned from the newspapers that the cabinet had decided to dismiss him from the army. By omitting to say that he had been removed from the Trentino before Conrad's offensive, the bulletin implied that he and not Cadorna was most responsible for the army's lack of readiness. Poisonous rumours now enveloped the disgraced man: he had an Austrian wife (she was American); his son had volunteered for the Austrian army (he was a decorated Italian soldier). When the authorities in Milan could not guarantee his safety against whipped-up public outrage, Brusati went into hiding. He was rehabilitated in 1918, after Cadorna's removal.

war in order to punish Serbia. A phrase coined by a nationalist poet, 'Gott strafe England!', meaning 'May God punish England!', entered the language as a cap-badge slogan, a military salute, a drinking toast. The Italian traitors' chastisement was under way.

In early May, the Germans had asked their Austrian allies to call off the offensive. The delay due to bad weather had, they said, removed the vital element of surprise. For once, the Germans overrated the Supreme Command; Cadorna's cussedness meant that an element of surprise was, against all odds, retained. The Austrians quickly overran the Italian lines on a 20-kilometre front, west of the Asiago plateau, involving the conquest of deep valleys and jagged summits. The Italians fought bravely but in vain; their gunners, withdrawing the batteries prematurely, left the infantry in the lurch.

Rising at last to Conrad's challenge, Cadorna transferred all available units from the Isonzo. Within a fortnight he had formed a new army of 180,000 men in the Trentino. The Fifth Army would guard the valley mouths, where they opened onto the plains of the Veneto. Several new divisions were mustered from new conscript classes. Additionally, he recalled two divisions that Sonnino had sent to Albania – a snub to the foreign minister. By mid-June, more than 300,000 men were deployed on the Trentino sector.

The shock of the attack – the brilliance at the heart of Conrad's scheme – was attested by Giani Stuparich, now a lieutenant in the Sardinian Grenadiers. Transferred to the Trentino in the first wave of reinforcements, he had the usual reaction of infantry when they moved from the lower Isonzo to the mountains. 'How far we are from the convulsed and menacing Carso!' The very sky seems 'carefree'. Can the Austrians really be attacking? His disbelief vanished when a wounded infantryman told him that his unit was wiped out. 'They're up there.' Stuparich squints at a tiny peak, swirling with cloud. 'Up there? That's insane!' But it was true. The infantry struggled uphill against a current of old men, women and children on mules, pushing their belongings on carts, with cows and pigs trailing behind.

On 20 May, Conrad extended the operation eastwards to the Sugana valley. In this second phase, the Austrians swept onto the Asiago plateau. Their forces were still storming ahead, but their chances of reaching the sea shrank with every extra lateral kilometre. Their supply lines were weak, munitions were running low, and the men were exhausted. The Italians fell back to their third defensive line, but could not hold it. Cadorna formed a new corps to defend Asiago. On 27 May, the Austrians captured the town of Arsiero, only a few kilometres from the plains. No defensive line had been prepared, despite the town's strategic importance. The next day, Asiago fell. Cadorna shocked the government by warning that, unless the enemy pressure relented, he would order a full-scale withdrawal behind the River Piave, less than 30 kilometres from Venice. The only good news at the end of May was the Austrians' failure to break out of Vallarsa onto the lowlands.

Cadorna appealed for Russia to attack at once rather than on 15 June, as planned. When Joffre demurred, the King appealed directly to the Tsar. On 1 June, Cadorna learned that the Russians would move on 4 June. This would not stop the Punishment Expedition in its tracks, but it should slow it. In the event, General Brusilov's offensive succeeded better than the Italians could have hoped. Like Brusati's men in the Trentino, the Habsburg forces in Galicia were caught too far forward. After two days, the Russians had driven back the Austrians by 75 kilometres, along a 20-kilometre front. After a week, they had taken 200,000 prisoners and 700 guns.

This relief came at the last possible moment, for on 3 June, the Sardinian Grenadiers were driven off the southernmost peak of the Asiago plateau. It was to be the Austrians' last big achievement of the campaign. By the 8th, the Italians were surging back up the flank of Mount Cengio. That night, the Austrians tried to beat them back. Ferruccio Fabbrovich, a 19-year-old volunteer, described the clash:

Suddenly the alarm sounds, the enemy is out of his trench and coming to attack. Only one voice spoke up: be brave and always go forward! Our loopholes are already open, we were all ready for the counter-attack. The order suddenly comes to fire at will; dear father, if you could only have heard the racket; thousands and thousands of rifles – the whole Pistoia Brigade was there – spewing fire at the barbarous enemy hordes. But the Austrians kept coming; they were only 40 metres away. We kept waiting, because it was impossible to give the Savoy because of the distance, and the mountainside was very steep and rocky. My heart was bursting with emotion, I trembled all over. Ah, father, what terrible minutes those were. Finally the order came: 'Savoy!' At the fateful cry 6,000 Italians leaped out of their burrows like a single man and flung themselves at the Austrians, massacring them and shoving them back into their trenches. I found myself well and safe in the darkness, I don't know how or when: I was stunned. Oh what joy it was, what indescribable joy you feel when you go into the attack with a bayonet . . .

The tide had turned. On 9 and 13 June, Conrad returned two extra divisions that had recently arrived from the Eastern Front. By now the outcome of the offensive was clear. On 16 June, he stopped the Punishment Expedition.

By this point, Cadorna had survived a government bid to unseat him. On 30 May, following the loss of Arsiero and Asiago, Salandra sought the King's backing to oust the Supreme Commander. The King indicated that, if Salandra had full cabinet support, he would not stand in the way. Then Salandra met Cadorna himself, at Vicenza. He told the old general that he would not hear of strategic retreats. If the army pulled back behind the River Piave, the government would fall and subversive revolutionary elements would seize their chance. Cadorna, imposingly calm and self-possessed, said that a retreat was now unlikely, but he was duty-bound to prepare for all contingencies.

Back in Rome, Salandra was uncertain. If he forced Cadorna's removal at the height of the crisis, who would take his place? And with what prospects of saving the day? While he vacillated, the military balance shifted in Italy's favour. The press backed the generalissimo, extolling his dynamism and brilliance. When parliament opened on 6 June, deputies blamed Salandra for the crisis so narrowly averted. The Prime Minister hit back, accusing Cadorna of failing to prepare his defences. Most deputies backed the army, and Salandra lost a vote of confidence. 'Hanged in his own noose,' was Cadorna's pithy comment.

On 25 June, the Austrians withdrew to well-prepared defences. Arsiero and Asiago were ransacked, burned and abandoned, their streets strewn with rubble, faeces and dead horses. Cadorna dissolved the Fifth Army, its task fulfilled. But the Italian counter-attacks were hasty, unco-ordinated, and very costly; only a third to a quarter of the territory lost since 15 May was regained. Among the losses was Cesare Battisti, captured on a mountain, recognised as the famous traitor, and publicly hanged in Trent. Propaganda photographs of his last moments, and of Austrians grinning around the martyr's corpse, caused outrage in Italy and beyond. It was Battisti's last service to the cause.

The Austrians held firm on the northern portion of the Asiago plateau, well inside the 1866 border, mocking Cadorna's promise at the start of the year that the enemy would never set foot on the fatherland's sacred soil. The plateau would be a battleground for the rest of the war, stretching the Austrian forces even more thinly. The Italians had taken around 147,000 casualties, some 50,000 more than the Austrians. The Trentino salient still hung over the army like the sword of Damocles. Cadorna, fixated on the Isonzo, did not contemplate an all-out attack to remove this threat. On the contrary, he seemed to take a perverse pride in his vulnerability. When General Robertson, Chief of the British Imperial General Staff, wondered how the Italians could persevere despite such gaping insecurity, Cadorna felt gratified as if by praise. He even let it be known that he wanted to disprove Napoleon's claim that Austria could only be attacked on the Isonzo if the Trentino was already controlled. For would he not thereby prove that he was greater than Bonaparte?

Cadorna's acclamation as a hero during June says less about him than about the low level of national confidence and the power of the press. As a deputy later protested in secret session, 'Why was Cadorna allowed to celebrate this grievous episode of the war and boast about it as something glorious?' It was a rhetorical question, for who was to stop him? The new government had little credit with the public. The Supreme Command's publicity machine promoted the generalissimo's greatness. The oversights and blunders that preceded the attack and let it drive so deep, and then let the enemy keep so much territory, went unexamined. On the contrary, the *unpredictability* of the attack became axiomatic.[3] The propaganda worked because people were desperate for good news. In this sense, Cadorna was the beneficiary of an appetite for success that his own failures had created. Morale in the country and the army swung down, then up. What General Capello called 'an obscure feeling of mortification because of an insult endured' was rapidly overlaid by euphoria at the narrow escape. If the breakthrough was regrettable, the resistance was unexpectedly successful.

For Conrad, on the other hand, slender gains were no success at all when measured against his original ambition and the disaster in Russia. By 4 June, Conrad knew his original planned strength was inadequate, and the emergency created by Brusilov prevented him from transferring more troops from the Eastern Front. Yet the Russian crisis did not force him to go below that strength and, anyway, the Punishment Expedition had stalled several days earlier. He underestimated the manpower

---

3 This nonsense was parroted by well-meaning foreign visitors such as H. G. Wells, who assured English readers later in the year that, 'There was only one good point about the Austrian thrust. No one could have foretold it.'

necessary for such a broad offensive; underrated Cadorna's energy and resolve; discounted the impact of Russian support; and failed to use Boroević's army for large-scale diversionary action on the Isonzo. Above all, he stuck to traditional tactics in mountain warfare, dragging artillery up cliffs with block and tackle. During the planning, he had clashed with General Alfred Krauss, the able chief of staff at Austria's South-West Front Command, who boldly advocated rapid penetration of the valleys without simultaneous progress on the high ground. If Conrad had accepted this advice, the Austrians could have made faster advances in the crucial first phase. These misjudgements were dictated by personality. The Punishment Expedition was shaped by his Italophobia and 'wretched rivalry' with Falkenhayn. By beating the Italians, the Austrians would finally claim equal partnership with Germany.

Falkenhayn's decision to withhold German support was not personally motivated in this way, though it was perhaps coloured by a hope that, if given enough rope, his vexatious ally would hang himself. Indeed, Conrad's prestige never recovered in Vienna and Budapest, where he was seen as responsible for triggering Brusilov's campaign, which in turn led to Romania's decision to join the Allies in August. By September, when the imperial forces were formally subordinated to German command, Conrad's failure in Trentino had already exacted a heavy price on the Isonzo.

FIFTEEN

Victory's Peak

Once the great victory is gained, the next question is not about rest, not about taking breath, not about considering, not about reorganising, etc. etc., but only of pursuit of fresh blows.
CARL VON CLAUSEWITZ

The Sixth Battle of the Isonzo

By mid-June, Cadorna's mind was back on the Isonzo. His original ambitions had taken such a bruising that he set more modest goals for the next offensive. He told the Duke of Aosta that it would take place as soon as possible, aiming for 'firm possession of the threshold of Gorizia'. He wanted to set the Italians up for a future attack on the city and on Mount San Michele, and to make it impossible for the Austrians to break out of Gorizia. For the first time, he would concentrate his firepower 'in a very narrow space', the short tract of front between Podgora hill and Gorizia. He also accepted the Duke's suggestion to extend the attack down to Mount San Michele in the south. Although it was separated from Gorizia by the valley of the Vipacco, five or six kilometres wide, San Michele was in tactical terms the southern rampart of the Gorizia enclave. Cadorna rightly supposed that the Austrians would not expect a major operation on the Isonzo so soon after the close call in Trentino. Given his previous disdain for the element of surprise, this was another sign that something had been learned.

After the restructuring around Gorizia, the offensive came under the Third Army. The Duke of Aosta made sure the three divisions attacking San Michele had substantial artillery support (though no heavy guns) and the lion's share of reserves, which were never abundant on the Isonzo. This had serious consequences when the attack took an unexpected turn. The task of getting a foothold on the left bank of the Isonzo, on the skirt of land between the river and the city, fell to

VI Corps under General Capello. Capello's orders reiterated Cadorna's aim of capturing 'a small bridgehead' that could be defended by a few men with machine guns.

Capello, bulking larger than life, cultivated renown as a plain-speaking warrior, learned in the arts of war, implacable in attack. He predicted that they would take the bridgehead in four hours and Gorizia in four days. 'Let us not deceive ourselves,' cautioned Cadorna, five times burnt. In this case, Capello's bullish confidence had a foundation: the Italians' excellent preparatory work on Mount Sabotino, a 600-metre hill that fills Gorizia's northern horizon like a scalene triangle. The western side descends steeply but evenly; on the other side of a narrow summit crest, the eastern side falls almost sheer to the Isonzo. Since winter, units of the 4th Division had excavated an intricate grid of trenches, tunnels and caverns in the limestone, often by night, sapping up the western flank of the mountain until the front lines were close enough for the infantry to attack with realistic hope of success. The 4th Division had one of the better commanders, General Luca Montuori, assisted by Colonel Pietro Badoglio, a veteran of Ethiopia and Libya with the knack of inspiring trust in senior commanders. When Sabotino came under the responsibility of VI Corps, Capello became involved.

The divisions that had been transferred to the Trentino were brought back to the Isonzo, along with most of the First Army's artillery, without detection. By early August, over 200,000 men were ready to move against San Michele and Gorizia. The heavy guns were placed in front of Gorizia, shells had never been available in such quantities, and the number of mortars quadrupled over the past year.

The bombardment began early on 6 August, pounding the Austrian lines all the way from Tolmein to the sea, before drawing in to San Michele and Gorizia. Cadorna's gunners had never been so effective. The Austrian lines were shrouded in smoke, their command centres disabled, many observation posts destroyed, and communications wrecked. Boroević telegraphed the Army High Command for urgent reserves and heavy artillery. He had underestimated the enemy build-up, partly because it was well concealed (with Cadorna making highly visible visits to Trentino). The Austrians had assumed that the new government in Rome would want more time before launching its first offensive. What was more, the trickle of deserters that preceded previous offensives had not materialised. But the high command was desperately stretched on the Eastern Front and had nothing to spare for the Isonzo. Boroević

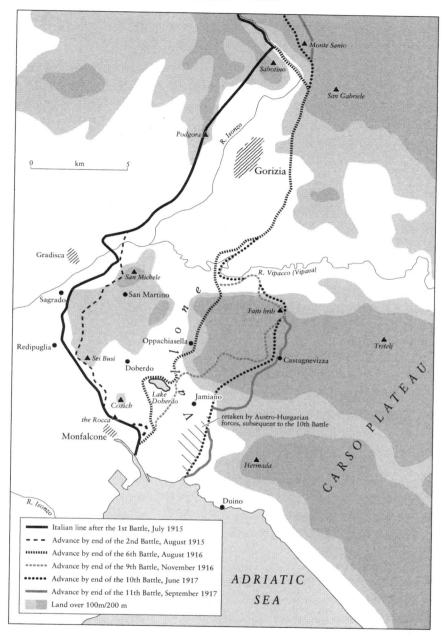

The Carso and the Gorizia sector

would have to manage with what he had, some 102,000 fighting men along the middle and lower Isonzo. Only 18,000 of these were deployed around Gorizia, in a semicircle from Sabotino to the Vipacco valley. The troops and guns that had been lent to the Punishment Expedition were slow to return. Making matters worse, Boroević had sent his own reserves – a scanty six battalions – south to protect the direct approach to Trieste. Retrieving them would take several days. As for artillery, the inferiority was frightful: he was outgunned on the Isonzo by at least 3:1, and in some places around Gorizia by 12:1.

Recognising that previous progress had been made in the first days or even hours, Cadorna curtailed the preparatory bombardment. At 16:00 on the 6th, Capello's first wave of infantry scrambled out of the upper trenches on Mount Sabotino with large white disks tied to their backs. Thanks to this simple device, the battery commanders co-ordinated their fire with an assault for the first time. The Dalmatian troops defending the mountain were hopelessly outnumbered when Badoglio's men stormed the summit, taking it in 38 minutes flat. 'They look like Roman legions!' enthused the King, watching from a hilltop in the rear. When the last defending platoons in the warren of tunnels refused to surrender, the Italians poured petrol into the tunnels and set them ablaze.

It was the best news since the capture of Mount Krn more than a year before. D'Annunzio, the self-styled poet of slaughter, caught the joyful mood in a couplet:

> Swift as the wing that stoops in a streak,
> The first shout rang out from victory's peak.

Further south, across the river, more glory lay in store. Although San Michele had seen no major offensives since the Fourth Battle, the Italian XI Corps had not been idle. As on Sabotino, the 'methodical advance' was conducted diligently until no-man's land was only 50 or even 10 metres wide. When rock-drills arrived at the end of March, proper shelters and tunnels were excavated. Secure emplacements were made for the new trench mortars. Salients were protected with extra wire.

Even without major operations, the attrition on San Michele had been costly. Hundreds of men were lost in the limited actions of the Fifth Battle, and hundreds more during Austrian diversions in May. The following month, the Austrians used a new weapon to loosen the

Italians' grip. On 29 June, a mixture of chlorine gas and phosgene was released above the Italian line. After a stormy night, the wind died away just before dawn and the Austrians had considered aborting the operation. Then a south-easterly breeze picked up, and the 3,000 cylinders were opened. Dirty white clouds rolled towards the mystified Italians, withering the leaves and grass, then smothering the lookouts and the front line. The men keeled over, gasping, glassy-eyed, foaming at the mouth, and died clutching their stomachs. Primitive gas-masks – cotton-wool pads impregnated with alkaline solution, and separate goggles – had been distributed not long before, but many soldiers thought the precaution was needless; their masks were soon lost or damaged. In the second line, men looked around in panic for their gas-masks, not knowing these were ineffective against phosgene. Some 2,000 men of the Brescia and Ferrara Brigades died, and a further 5,000 were injured. Yet, like the Germans at Ypres in April 1915 when lethal gas was first used, the Austrians were too fearful of their weapon to seize the opportunity that it had created. (Fearful with reason: they lost 40 dead and 212 wounded to the gas.) They had bought a little time without improving their strategic position. By the end of the day, Italian counter-attacks had regained the ground lost in the morning.

Survivors and relief units were shocked by the sight of dead men at their post, caught unawares and so quickly that they had not even tried to escape. Corporal Valentino Righetti (19th Infantry, Brescia Brigade) was among those sent up the hill late on the 29th, wondering why his unit was returning to the front line only a day after leaving it. Reaching his trench after dark, he was perplexed to find it full of soldiers. The silence was complete; they must all be asleep. They were still sleeping at first light, so he shook the man next to him. 'Dead! They were all dead! Eyes rolling, foam on their mouths.' The brass stars on their uniforms and the metal of their rifles were discoloured green. Outrage was compounded when studded maces were found in the trenches. These had been used to finish off the gassed victims. The maces were exhibited in schools around Italy to prove the contrast between Habsburg barbarism and Italy's just struggle – what the Supreme Command called the 'sublime goodness' of the war.[1]

*

1 Coincidentally, Cadorna had suggested on 26 June that poison gas should be used to make Podgora 'uninhabitable'. This proved impossible, because the Italians still lacked reliable cylinders.

The assault on San Michele began at 15:30 on 6 August. Though suffering heavy losses, the Catanzaro, Brescia and Ferrara Brigades took the summit while the Pisa and Regina Brigades pushed to the edge of San Martino hamlet. The counter-attacks that night, by Hungarian units, were beaten back. Boroević's reserves were needed to limit the breach at Sabotino; there was nothing left for San Michele.

The whole sector fell the following day. The dreary whaleback hill was firmly Italian at last. Soldiers wandered around the silent summit, dazed at finally being able to set foot among the corpses, cartridge-boxes, spent cartridges, blackened boots, bits of rifles and empty knapsacks. One officer's chief memory was of disgust at the sight of maggots, more than he had ever seen before, apparently sprouting out of the ground, 'white and soft, wriggling towards the motionless bodies, penetrating them, feeding, reappearing in the empty sockets and half-closed mouths'. The conquest of San Michele had cost at least 110,000 Italian casualties over 14 months, including 19,000 dead, on a sector only eight kilometres long.

With Sabotino lost, the 15-kilometre line around Gorizia began to crumble. Most of Podgora hill – insuperable for so long – was overrun on the 6th. Counter-attacks during the night could not roll back the Italian gains. The Austrian artillery had run out of shells, and other sectors on the Isonzo were so sparsely manned that they could only spare half a dozen battalions, nothing like enough to wrest back control of Sabotino. Boroević was startled by the speed of the Italian advance; his reserves could not reach Gorizia before 10 or 11 August – too late to save the city. Nevertheless, he would not hear of a withdrawal, so more counter-attacks were launched, in vain. By sunset on the 7th, the ground between Sabotino and Podgora had fallen. A single Croatian regiment stood between Cadorna and complete control of the Isonzo's right bank. Shortly after midnight, Zeidler told Boroević that the situation was untenable and ordered his men to fall back across the river. Only 5,000 reached the second line behind the city, where the triple peaks of Monte Santo, San Gabriele and San Marco form a barrier even more imposing than Sabotino and Podgora.

Two hours after Zeidler issued his fateful order, Capello reminded his divisional commanders that their task was still to establish 'little bridgeheads wherever possible' on the Isonzo. A commander who reported rumours that Gorizia stood empty, and recommended a vigorous thrust over the river, was told to investigate further. Naturally the commander shrank from sticking his neck out, and troops continued to cross the river in dribs and drabs. As often, the senior commanders' lack of nerve was exposed by a plucky junior officer. Early on the 8th, as the last pockets of resistance on Podgora were being mopped up, a few platoons of the 28th Infantry (Pavia Brigade) gathered on the right bank of the Isonzo, opposite the city. The first Italians to get this far, they had discovered a tunnel under the flank of Podgora and made their way through it, towards the river. Machine-gun fire was incoming from a trench across the river, some 20 metres from the water's edge. As the only intact bridge was under heavy Austrian fire, a young officer, Lieutenant Aurelio Baruzzi, got permission to wade across the Isonzo, carrying an Italian flag.

The water is fast but not very deep; Baruzzi uses the flagpole as a staff to steady himself. Other men are swept downstream, but a hundred or so make it across, clear the trench and seize the bridge. The railway station is visible a few hundred yards away, across a field. Baruzzi knows what to do: 'I *must* cross that field. I have sworn to my flag that it will fly over the houses of Gorizia. Now the flag helps me for the second time. I unfurl it and shake it open. Our gunners see it and lengthen their fire. We run across the field to the station.' The station is protected by wire, but Baruzzi finds a breach and races up the staircase. 'Moments later, the flag is flying from the highest roof-beam under the hot August sun.'

By the afternoon, Gorizia was in Italian hands. The latest bombardment had caused huge damage. All the churches were hit, some several times over. Rubble and shattered trees lay everywhere. The streets were barricaded with barbed wire and heaps of furniture. Some buildings were mined. A last-minute evacuation left only 1,500 civilians, risking everything to save their property.

Grasping the scale of the breakthrough, Capello alerted the Duke of Aosta, who advised Cadorna to chase the Austrians back to their second line and attack the chain of hills behind the city. Cadorna agreed, and brought the Second Army into play, attacking the Plava bridgehead. Everything went well that day; the Italians were unstoppable. Seen from the rear areas, the horizon from San Michele to Podgora was 'wrapped in fire and steel', roaring under a cover of reddish cloud.

On San Michele, the Italians secured the summit and attacked the Austrian second line on the rearward slopes. Here they were stopped for the first time – another testament to Austrian defences. The loss of Gorizia removed the point of sacrificing more Austrian lives for San

Michele. If the Italians maintained their impetus, they might cut off the Austrians' routes back to their second line. Boroević transferred his artillery to new positions several kilometres further east, on the far side of a valley that scored a north–south line across the Carso. This was the Vallone, like a giant trench one or two kilometres wide and 200 metres deep. On 9 August, the troops followed.

The withdrawal from the western Carso – abandoning Mount Sei Busi, Cosich and other battlefields as well as San Michele itself – was perfectly executed. After contesting every pebble and root for 14 months, the Austrians flitted away like shadows. Next morning, the officers on San Michele scoffed at reports that the enemy positions were empty. By nightfall, the Austrian trenches were crowded with incredulous Italians, picking through the detritus for souvenirs. The Supreme Command ordered an immediate attack across the Vallone, but the artillery lagged behind (being too heavy for the pontoons over the river), the men were weary, the Austrian gunners were ready behind their wire, and Boroević's reinforcements had finally arrived. Successive waves were beaten back in a reversion to the old futile pattern, until Cadorna called a halt on 17 August. The Austrians had lost 50,000 men since 6 August, the Italians at least twice as many.

On 9 August, the church bells of Friuli rang out for the first time since 24 May 1915. Patriots declared that a wholly Italian army had defeated a great foreign army for the first time since the fall of the Roman Empire. Italy's allies agreed that the capture of Gorizia was a mighty feat of arms. The enemy had been driven back four to six kilometres, along a 24-kilometre front. It was by far the biggest advance to date.

Coming so soon after the much-trumpeted defeat of the Punishment Expedition, this made Cadorna's position unassailable. He had proved that he could carry out a successful offensive. As Italian morale surged, the Austrian army's slumped. Successful resistance on the Isonzo had created a unique *esprit de corps*. This spirit was potent but highly vulnerable; the first substantial reverse might burst the illusion that the empire could defy all odds, indefinitely. Were this to happen, Habsburg morale could be expected to fray at exponential speed. The Sixth Battle did not deliver this defeat, but it came near.

Cadorna's finest hour confirmed his limitations. Far from exploiting the breakthrough, he clung to his original plan. By the time he awoke to the opportunity, fresh troops, cavalry and munitions could not be brought up in sufficient strength to attack the second line before it was reinforced by Zeidler's retreating battalions and fresh reserves. On 10 August, realising that a golden chance had slipped beyond reach, he censured Capello for his 'slowness' in attacking the high ground behind Gorizia, in line with the 'objectives' that had been assigned to VI Corps. This was disingenuous, for Cadorna had never anticipated capturing the city, let alone any ground beyond it. Capello, for all his show of audacity, was hardly better. Astonishingly, no one seemed to realise that the Vipacco valley, leading to the Slovenian hinterland, lay wide open. The enemy's second line was still weak here, with shallow trenches and wire fixed loosely to the soil.

The Italians had shifted their problems several kilometres eastwards. The challenge ahead was all too familiar: attacking uphill against well-built positions defended to the death by battle-hardened troops. They had spent more than a year besieging San Michele and Podgora. In the next phase, they would hurl themselves at Monte Santo, San Gabriele, Fajti hrib and other obscure heights across the Vallone that soon became household names in Italy.

SIXTEEN

Starlight from Violence

Poetry in the War Zone

As the Sixth Battle peters out, a soldier on Mount San Michele makes his way over boulders, through foliage and insect-buzz down to the turquoise river. Off comes his woollen tunic, lousy, rank with sweat; he unwinds his puttees, unlaces his heavy boots. That night, back in his trench above the valley, he shelters near a tree stump. Moonlight on the river: silver in the distance. The artillery has thumped all day, somewhere to the east. The sector is quiet and his body, relaxing, remembers its sensations in the water. He finds a pencil, tears the corner off a cartridge box and scribbles on it:[1]

> This morning I lay back
> in an urn of water
> and like a relic
> took my rest
>
> The Isonzo's flow
> smoothed me
> like a stone of its own
>
> I hauled myself, this
> bonebag, up
> and off I went
> like an acrobat
> on water . . .

The writer was Giuseppe Ungaretti (1888–1970), a private in the 19th Infantry, Brescia Brigade. A dozen of his poems are still the best-known Italian literature of the Great War. They broke the mould of poetry in his language, freeing it from late romantic rhetoric.

1 With one exception, the translations in this chapter are my own, though indebted to previous versions by Patrick Creagh (in McKendrick's anthology) and Andrew Frisardi. The exception is 'Vigil', which is newly translated by Jamie McKendrick.

This poem, called 'The Rivers' and dated 16 August 1916, has been an anthology piece for decades. After setting the scene, the poet tells how the water of the Isonzo restores him to himself, bearing him back to other rivers in his life. He names the Serchio, a Tuscan river that watered the farmland where his ancestors lived. Then the Nile, from his birthplace in Egypt, and lastly the Seine, for it was Paris that awoke his vocation.

> These are my rivers
> summed up in the Isonzo.

The mood is blissful, almost anthemic. Rivers are ancient symbols of life, and Ungaretti feels his existence being affirmed. The rocks in the riverbed are no harder than his bones. His life is a river, the war is not strong enough to stop it. Why, he can walk on water.

> This is the Isonzo
> and here I best
> recognise myself:
> a yielding fibre
> of the universe
>
> My torment's
> when I
> don't believe myself
> in harmony
>
> But those hidden
> hands
> that soak and blend me
> regale me with
> rare
> happiness

Finally the poem circles back to the hillside, alights like a barn-owl on that 'mutilated tree', folds its wings and gazes at us:

> now that it's night
> and my life looks to me
> a corolla
> of darkness

Soldiers stripping off to bathe recur in English-language poetry of the Great War. The men's pleasure moves the watching officer to pity, sometimes flushed with yearning. Ungaretti's poem evokes a little of this pathos, but with a difference: he is his own spectator. The poet's participation is complete, like his body's immersion in the river.

In a British front-line poet, this focus on himself would seem strange. It cuts against the idea that good poetry from the Great War bore witness to monstrous inhumanity, the epic betrayal of civilised ideals. The scholar Jon Stallworthy has said that well-made poems from the Great War 'move us (as Aristotle said) to pity and terror; also, I suggest, to a measure of fury'. While this is true of Sassoon's and Owen's work, it is much less true of the good poems in Italian. By any standard that emphasises dissent or indignation, Ungaretti's work hardly counts as war poetry at all. For the war is largely the backdrop in a drama about identity and endurance. One of his first critics drew this distinction by observing that Ungaretti had written not *war* poems but a *soldier's* poems. In the Italian context, poetic self-absorption need not be an escape from the reality of war. In Ungaretti's case, it opens a private vista onto a wider truth. For identity was at the heart of Italy's war. The nation was taken to war in the name of political claims that flowed from Italy's history and values, beyond mere politics. The more cynical motives stayed in the shadow, behind the patriotic rhetoric. The interventionists appealed to a highly coloured version of Italy's recent past and its immemorial 'Latin' culture.

The Italians were told by their leaders in spring 1915 that they should not be happy in their own skin – the skin formed by the shape of their country on the map. They were told that it was right to seethe within those unjust confines, and burst through them with weapons. When Ungaretti avowed his happiness in his own skin as a soldier, massaged by the Isonzo, he was speaking about Italian identity as well as his own. If he was where he ought to be, then the Isonzo was the right place for other Italian soldiers. And if this was their proper place, the arguments that triggered their invasion were valid. There is no suggestion that 'The Rivers' points to an alternative way of being, a realm of nature that exposes the futility of war. If anything, the water refreshes the soldier for the struggle.

There had been a vogue for incendiary verse since D'Annunzio published his 'Laus vitae' in 1903, a lurid vision of battle that champions the victors' right to slaughter their foe, lay waste his cities and rape his women. 'We shall ransack the mothers' wombs with fire ...' Italy's attack on Libya in 1911 inspired Italy's unofficial laureate to pen odes to bloody Victory:

> You smile upon the land that is your prey.
> Italy! From the passion that devours me
> a song arises fresher than the morn ...

The start of war in 1914 and 1915 released a wave of patriotic poetry across Europe. In Italy, anthologies with titles like *Songs of the Fatherland* poured off the press. Among hundreds of examples, consider Corrado Govoni's long poem, called simply 'War!' The entire world is turning into 'a long cemetery of trenches'. How lovely to fertilise earth's old carcass with guns! Let savage instinct be our only master! Disorder is order, destruction is being constructed. Half a dozen breathless pages of necrophile ranting lead to a final demented exhortation:

> Burn, burn,
> set fire to this world till it becomes a sun.
> Devastate smash destroy,
> Go forth, go forth, oh lovely human flail,
> be plague earthquake and hurricane.
> Make a red spring
> of blood and martyrdom
> bloom from this old earth,
> and life be like a flame.
> Long live war!

A more intellectual version came from Giulio Barni, a volunteer from Trieste, in verses written in 1914:

> Liberty, liberty,
> if you're a woman
> come, come to me:
> come and sleep with me
> for I want to kill
> peace and lies for you

'Peace and lies': that angry pairing says everything about nationalist feeling – and thinking – as Italy geared up for war.

The vein of ecstatic belligerence did not dry up on contact with real

[181]

horror. Again, examples are legion. A bersagliere called Luigi Granturco published a collection called *Songs of the Bayonet* in 1917.

> O land of Italy, O first among all the lands on the globe,
> here, I see you: the envy of the world . . .
> It is the race created for mastery.

Such stuff was easier to write than to read – which explains why the copy in Oxford's Bodleian Library was still uncut after 90 years. Sometimes the belligerence took a mystical colouring; Vittorio Locchi's best-selling *Sabbath of Holy Gorizia* invoked the sacred mountains as witnesses at a festival of blood and song. Religious motifs were drafted to induce awe and deference:

> all the bayonets
> yield like ensigns
> on the altars of the mountains,
> on the sacred carnage of our dead.

British patriotic poetry was muted beside the Italian kind. On war as escape from tawdry peace, Britain had Rupert Brooke ('To turn, as swimmers into cleanness leaping, / Glad from a world turned old and cold and weary'). On the war in the air, Yeats imagined a pilot following a 'lonely impulse of delight' to 'this tumult in the clouds'; for the Futurist poet Soffici, on the other hand, the firmament in battle reeked of thighs and armpits. Aloft, he could 'kiss the noiseless vulva of the sky'. On war as renewal, there was Charles Hamilton Sorley ('there has come upon the land / The curse of Inactivity'). On the intoxication of battle, Britain had Julian Grenfell ('joy of battle takes / Him by the throat, and makes him blind'). Even these last lines seem reflective, partly regretful, beside the mad euphoria of the Italians. Squibs about hating the Boche are one thing, D'Annunzio's hymning of bloodlust is quite another.

What Wilfred Owen called the pity of war is not much present in Italian war poetry. Perhaps it is the difference between belligerence welcomed as a vocation and martial courage felt as a duty. Yet there were Italian poets ready to record the worst that the war could show. After a long education, Clemente Rebora (1885–1957) had cast around for a direction in life and failed to find one. A religious vocation was stirring; he would eventually enter the Catholic Church and, twenty years after the war, be ordained as a priest. When war came, he was drafted and sent to the Isonzo. He likened military service to a 'mission', like pastoral care, and praised the soldiers' 'patient sweet humanity'. As a soldier and poet, he was determined to spare himself nothing amid the 'seas of mud and freezing bora, and putrefaction'. He was tormented at having to send his men – who '*love* me (that's the right word!)' – to almost certain death. 'What a stench from our unburied dead, while *our own* artillery kills us off by mistake!' he exclaimed, in a letter that slipped past the censor.

On 1 December 1915, shortly before he was invalided away from the front, Rebora wrote to his mother: 'It is a blessing for your peace of mind and comfort that you know nothing about the moral mire, the pity and horror of what's happening; and only know the news through the yellow press that deceives the fatherland – and you mothers!' The physical suffering was awful, but the inward torment was much worse. His poetry excelled at conveying both kinds. One of his best-known poems relates an episode about a wounded comrade screaming for help from no-man's land. Its title is 'Viaticum', the Catholic Eucharist for the dying.

> Oh wounded man in the valley below,
> So loud your pleas
> That three comrades, no less,
> Fell for you who almost aren't there,
> A legless trunk
> Between mire and blood,
> And here comes your wail again,
> Stirring pity in survivors who have not yet
> Drawn our dying breath and time stops,
> The agony quickens,
> You can stop,
> Finding comfort in
> The insanity that cannot go mad,
> While the moment won't end, and
> Sleep hurts my brain,
> Leave us in silence –
>
> Thank you, brother.

The space before the last line measures the man's death, freeing the poet to mutter his gratitude for not causing more soldiers to lose their lives. Nothing in Ungaretti matches this agonised submission to the truth of other men's suffering. Nor does anything by Ungaretti resemble the extraordinary poem by Fausto Maria Martini, called 'Why I didn't kill you', which describes the poet's decision not to kill an Austrian soldier, a terrified boy cowering under his (Martini's) bayonet. The reason was not cowardice; rather, the 'unknown blond enemy's face' reminded him of his own 'leaner, older' face.

> It was not, then, for fear
> that I didn't kill you: it was – not to die myself!
>
> Not to die in you: you were my twin,
> or seemed so in the twinned trench

Too prosy to be high art, the poem is deeply affecting, and may be unique in the language. Like Wilfred Owen's great line, 'I am the enemy you killed, my friend', this recognition of self in the other dissolves the political arguments for organised murder.

Ungaretti's route to the Isonzo was long and meandering. He was born in Alexandria, where his Tuscan parents had emigrated so his father could work on the Suez Canal. After his father's death when he was only two, his pious mother raised Giuseppe in poverty. They visited his father's grave every day. After school, he took menial jobs in Cairo. At 24, he left Africa, intending to study in Paris. He gravitated to avant-garde circles, befriending the poet Apollinaire and eating in the same bistro as Modigliani. Contemporaries recalled a warm, shambling loner with no particular direction; round-shouldered, tousled, with blue eyes half-closed and hardly visible when his face creased in an enormous grin; speaking expressive Italian larded with French. He went to Italy in 1914, perhaps influenced by meeting Italian writers at a Futurist event in Paris, who included some of the most radical propagandists for war. Settling in Turin, he trained as a schoolteacher of French, but soon plunged into the pro-war campaign, more from a sense of cultural solidarity with Paris, '*città santa dell'uomo moderno*', 'the holy city of modern man', than for Trento and Trieste. Never a cautious man, he was arrested at one of the rallies where interventionists and neutralists clashed, and briefly jailed. 'I don't like war,' he said much later, 'and I did not like it then, but it seemed to us that *that* war was necessary. We thought Germany was completely to blame.'

He moved to Milan to concentrate on his exams, but political passion would not let him go. Europe's crisis of nations had sparked a crisis of his own. Like other Italian émigrés at this time, he discovered a yearning to merge with the land of his forefathers, in his case Tuscany – the 'promised land' of childhood fables. 'I'm a lost soul', he confessed to a friend.

Which people do I belong to? Where am I from? I have no place of my own in this world, no neighbours. Wherever I draw close to anyone, I hurt myself. How to live like this, forever shutting myself up like a tomb? . . . Is this my fate? And who should take any interest if I'm suffering? Who could hear me? . . . I talk oddly, I'm a stranger. Everywhere. Am I going to destroy myself in the blaze of my desolation? And what if war ordains me an Italian?

The last question is so important that he rushes at it and stops short, as if hardly daring to hope.

He volunteered for the infantry only to be rejected for active service, being six years older than the first conscripts. Stuck behind a desk, he wrote despairingly to a friend that 'everything is at stake', for the prospect of getting to the front was his 'only joy'. The army relaxed its standards after the first bloodbaths, and by Christmas he was at the front, near Mount San Michele. He would spend two and a half years there. Military service was the most emphatic way of affiliating with Italy, in whose uniform he could – as he wrote in another poem – lie down 'as in my father's cradle'. The war, he would later say, gave him his identity papers, and 'The Rivers' marked a moment when he felt sure of belonging. Much more often the sense of isolation was almost overpowering, perhaps held at bay by the act of composing poetry:

Another night

In this gloom
with frozen
fingers
making out
my face

I see myself
abandoned in endlessness

In the trenches, he grew immune to nationalist passion. 'There is no trace in my poetry of hatred for the enemy, or anyone else,' he said later, truthfully. 'There's an awareness of the human condition, men's brotherhood in suffering, the extreme precariousness of their situation.' His prewar letters sometimes sound a Futurist note; he told a friend in

1913 that he was a Nietzschean, because he wanted 'a more heroic humanity' and a 'new aesthetic'. In his writings from the front, this note is no longer heard. Although he was friendly with some of the most extreme nationalists, he did not lapse into the ranting that poisons so much Italian wartime writing. Like many artists, he was drawn to absolutes of experience; ideology was a means to emotion, not an end in itself. In fact, 'The Rivers' can be read as a humanist redemption of a nationalist motif – the Isonzo itself, named in a thousand bellicose speeches and articles. In May 1915, D'Annunzio told a crowd in Rome that Italian soldiers would soon turn the Isonzo red with barbarian blood. In Ungaretti's poem, by contrast, it is the uniform that is 'foul with war', not the river, which washes the squalor away.

When Private Mussolini reached the Isonzo on 16 September 1915, he recorded the moment for his newspaper, *Il Popolo d'Italia*. 'I have never seen bluer waters. Strange! I bent down over the cold water and drank a mouthful with devotion. Sacred river!'

Ungaretti met Mussolini in late 1914, admired him, and near the end of 1918 would become the *Popolo*'s erratic correspondent in Paris. Profoundly naïve about politics, he joined the Fascist Party in the 1920s, along with so many other disillusioned veterans. The admiration was mutual to some degree, as the Duce wrote an offhand preface for his poems in 1923, a single ambiguous paragraph, devoid of interest beyond its byline. Now and then he petitioned the dictator for favours, and in 1930 chose 'Benito' as his son's middle name. An excruciating letter came recently to light, appealing to the *'carissimo Duce'* for help in gaining election to a prestigious academy. He flattered the dictator's revolutionary vitalism ('*life* is what we need, not people who write to amuse the bourgeoisie'), hailed himself as the best of Italy's younger poets, and signed off as 'your most devoted warrior'. No reply has been found. Mussolini came good in later years, however, getting charges dropped after Ungaretti's several run-ins with the police for criticising the regime and speaking up for a Jewish poet. Desperately chasing regular work, he took his family to Brazil in 1936. The self-styled anarchism of his later years was a twice-burned poet's way of sending all politicians to blazes. His real politics were summed up in lines that end a poem from France in May 1918:

I seek an
innocent country.

In autumn 1915, Ungaretti would probably have read *Il Popolo d'Italia* when it came his way. To be sure, Mussolini's banal veneration is very unlike Ungaretti's private ceremony. For the poet, the river's sacredness is inseparable from the feel of it flowing over weary flesh. For the future Duce, it is automatic, almost abstract. Where he bowed over the river to scoop up the holy water, Ungaretti crouched beside it after his dip, as if taking Holy Communion:

> and like a bedouin
> bent down to receive
> the sun

By smuggling his Egyptian childhood into the scene, he dispels any nationalist atmospherics.

Other poems by Ungaretti come closer to our usual idea of war poetry.

> *Brothers*
>
> What's your regiment
> brothers?
>
> Word trembling
> in the night
>
> Leaf barely born
>
> In the tortured air
> involuntary revolt
> of man facing his
> own frailty
>
> Brothers

This conjures a situation with marvellous economy, far beyond the wordy poetic norms of the day. Columns of infantry swap greetings as they file past each other. These words hang in the air, defying the silence and the risk of drawing enemy fire as new leaves uncurl despite the risk of frost, and as his own words unfurl despite artillery and barbed wire.[2]

2 The leaf is also any soldier likely to die before his time. Transferred to France in summer 1918, Ungaretti wrote a micro-epic called, simply, 'Soldiers': '*Si sta come d'autunno / sugli alberi le foglie*'. (A tone-deaf reduction into English: 'Here like leaves / on autumn trees'.) With Japanese delicacy, these lines renew a comparison that is as old as literature. Homer's Greeks stood before Troy 'as numberless as leaves bred in the spring', *(continued on p. 188)*

These tiny affirmations of shared humanity and common purpose, involuntary because instinctive, hinge on the title-word 'brothers', so rich in meaning for the poet. Politicians and demagogues boasted that the war was bonding Italians together for the first time. Ungaretti lived that process with a rare intensity. In a wartime elegy for an Arab friend who had taken his own life in Paris, Ungaretti suggested that the other man had destroyed himself by getting stranded between nations.

> He loved France
> and changed his name . . .
> but he was no Frenchman
> and no longer knew
> how to live
> in his family's tent.

Identity, like war, is a matter of life and death. Ungaretti had swayed on the brink of losing this crucial knowledge. War was the crucible where he fused with his people.

When brutal details do enter his poetry, their purpose is not documentary.

> *Vigil*
>
> One whole night
> thrown down nearby
> a slaughtered
> comrade his mouth
> rigid and upturned
> to the full moon
> his swollen hands
> delving into
> my silence
> I wrote
> letters full of love
>
> Never have I held
> so hard to life

Many soldiers were haunted by the memory of dead comrades' hands, particularly when they died clutching at barbed wire, and as

and Milton imagined Satan's legions, the fallen angels, lying 'thick as autumnal leaves' (*Paradise Lost*, i. 302). By 1918, the exhausted Ungaretti felt more damned than vernal.

Catholics readily saw such victims as Christ-like. Ungaretti revered the soldiers who, just by being their uncomplicated selves, soothed his insecurity. A letter to a friend, the writer Giovanni Papini, in March 1916 started cheerfully: 'My comrades and I are writing, curled up in our dens in the midst of a racket that has simply become monotonous.' A few months later he wrote, again to Papini: 'The other night I had to march ten km or so in a downpour; I let myself go singing with the other soldiers; I forgot myself; what happiness.' Their kindness moved him deeply ('if my knapsack is hurting, they'll take it off my back and try to take my rifle as well'). They would have thought the old man needed taking care of. He was amused when they called him 'sir', for he was a private like them and insisted on staying one. Many officers wrote about this bond with the men, inevitably with a paternalist awareness of their authority or other advantages over them. Ungaretti's enjoyment of the bond was as free of condescension as it could be. When the army sent him on the officers' training course in 1917, he flunked out; 'unfit for command' was the verdict. Which he was, and wanted to be. He needed anonymity in the ranks. 'The least thing that would have distinguished me from the next soldier would have seemed a hateful privilege,' he explained long after the war.

Pilgrimage

Stuck
in these guts
of rubble
hours and hours
I dragged
my bones
given to mud
like a boot-sole
or a seed
of hawthorn

Ungaretti
man of sorrows
an illusion's enough
to make you brave

A searchlight
over there
makes a sea
in the fog

What was this illusion? Not the interventionists' promise of rapid victory. (Even in his old age, when scathing criticism of the war was commonplace in Italy, Ungaretti preferred not to discuss the 'humbug' that was mixed with the ideals of spring 1915.) It was the beguiling distraction of a visual metaphor – those waves painted on the fog by a searchlight beam. A trick of the light, over in a moment, leaving the soldier no better off but enriching the poet.

Distrust of 'literature' was another lesson of life in the trenches. For if he owed his comrades his education in humanity, he must also have been indebted to them for his plain idiom and staccato rhythm, as well as to his beloved friend Apollinaire, who showed how to quit punctuation. These poems were written when Ungaretti's ears echoed day and night with the speech of peasants and labourers. To Papini, again: 'My dear comrades have looked death in the face without knowing why.' Surely he wanted to write poetry that was true to the unquestioning acceptance that was, for him, the hallmark of his companions' experience. True, that is, to the 'community of suffering' that he felt proud to join. While he shared their disgust at the politicking in Rome, he was no more inclined than they were to oppose the war. Ungaretti's artistic courage was not matched by independent thinking about the calculus that turned so much slaughter into so little gain. His nationalism was conventional. Healing immersion in the life of the troops was what he wanted, and got.

Life at the front encouraged modernist concision; for 'There was no time: the words you used had to be the decisive, absolute words, there was this necessity to express yourself with the fewest words, to cleanse yourself, not to say anything except what had to be said.' With their startling lack of connective tissue, his poems measure a duress that threatens to cancel individuality altogether, drowning out the personal voice – the voice of poetry. They imitate the posture of the infantry, crouching to minimise their exposure. The wondrous musicality of Italian has been internalised, driven inside the word or phrase. Rhythms lie low until the pulse of speech releases them. Syllables are cherished like comrades' lives, and spent reluctantly. These poems skirt the brink of silence: heroically minimal, revealing depth in paucity. Commitment to his material is gauged by devotion to its purity.

They might never have seen print. Ungaretti's first collection was published thanks to a chance encounter. Ettore Serra, a lieutenant with literary interests, was strolling through Versa, 'a fly-bitten, dusty little village' where the 19th Infantry happened to be resting. His eye was caught by a ragged, insouciant soldier who was taking such pleasure in the sunshine that he failed to salute the passing officer. Serra wanted his name, which led to a conversation about a few early poems that Ungaretti had published in a magazine. Asked about his recent work, Ungaretti dug in his pockets for the scraps of paper. Serra took them away and turned them into a book that changed Italian poetry. Not that *The Buried Harbour*, privately printed in Udine late in 1916, made much impact at the time, even on the poet's avant-garde friends in Florence and Rome, except Papini, who announced with relish that Ungaretti had 'strangled rhetoric'. Slipping onstage without benefit of manifestos, the implications of this debut would have been hard to see even without the distraction of war. The poet himself may not have grasped them at the time. For he was not having a quarrel with poetic tradition when he wrote his 'book of desolation', as he called it; he was saving his sanity.

His poems still carry the charge of new expression, minted for new experience. Written as a sort of journal, not meant for publication, they have the self-communing quality of something kept for no one else's eyes. Early in 1917, he wrote to a friend about an enthralling discovery: 'liberty is in us'. Nothing can prevent him 'marvelling at life's marvels', and this compensates for his woes.

I've lain down on muddy stones where mice the size of cats run over me as if I'm one of them, while the lice, charming creatures, tenacious as Germans, chewed on us contentedly. But my imagination had nothing to feed on except contemplation of itself, rejoicing that I'm still myself.

Perhaps Ungaretti kept his status as Italy's foremost war poet because he proved that lyrical transcendence survived on the Carso, shrunken, introverted, but intact. He spared his readers from reflecting on Italy's conduct of the war and imagining the horrors inflicted on the soldiers. More than this: by clinging 'so hard to life' in the midst of death, he partly redeemed those horrors. Half a century later, he identified 'the almost savage exaltation' in his war poems, powered by 'the vital impulse and the appetite to live'. This is the source of consolation in his work. His poetry, he said, 'burst like starlight from violence'. Starlight reaches the eye across gulfs of space and time, aeons from the explosion that creates it. Poetry like Rebora's is more like phosphorus: searing and intolerable.

Ungaretti valued two kinds of calmness and found them both in the war. Away from the trenches, a receptive stillness of soul let him

> yield
> to the drifting
> of the limpid universe

as he wrote early in 1916. The reprieve from danger cast a halo around sunlight on dewy grass, purple shadow thrown by mountains, the carnal pink of sunset, a green glade amid blitzed woodlands above the Isonzo. We hear the din of battle in the white silence around his words. There is a seven-syllable poem, 'Morning', written in the quiet village of Santa Maria la Longa. When the sky is clear, the mountains to north and east serrate the horizon: a glorious view.

> *M'illumino*
> *d'immenso*

became the best-known Italian poem since Dante.[3] Today, it stands on signposts along the main road through the village.

Then there was the endless resignation of the men in the trenches. The word that linked these states of being was *docile*: docile, meek, yielding. After Caporetto, he described the soldiers in retreat: 'They went in silence, meekly, as the Italians go, dying with a smile.' Despite his ready grin, Ungaretti did not impress others as particularly docile. Explosive, rather; truculent; his own man. A friend was working at the Supreme Command when Ungaretti dropped by in June or July 1917. The poet was soon complaining loudly about the soldiers' conditions and plummeting spirits. The friend told him to lower his voice: General Diaz was in the next office. But Ungaretti's nerves were shot after a year and a half on the Carso. 'I'd like to know what's going on in your general's head,' he shouted. 'What's going on in all their heads, here? The soldiers are worn out, they're at the end of their tethers, and as for morale, that's been stagnant for a long time. Where's this all leading? Where?'

Three months later, the Twelfth Battle supplied the answer.

---

3 Clive Wilmer's paraphrase gets the sense: 'I flood myself with the light of the immense.'

SEVENTEEN

Whiteness

*Snow is truly a sign of mourning; I don't know
why the westerners chose black; this is another
thing where the Chinese are more intelligent.
Black makes me feel mystery, fear, the absolute,
infinity, God, universal life; but white gives me
the sense of things ending, the iciness of death.*
PRIVATE UNGARETTI, at the front, early 1917

In the second half of September 1916, snow began to fall on the Alpine front. The winter that followed was one of the harshest on record. It closed down the fighting on the middle and upper Isonzo, where six to eight metres of snow smothered the mountainsides, three times the annual average today. The impact was greatest on the western portions of the front. From Flitsch on the upper Isonzo to the Stelvio Pass on the Swiss border is more than 400 kilometres, much or most of it over 2,000 metres. Five metres of snow fell during the second half of December alone. In this terrain, warfare – like other human activity before man-made fabrics, aviation and electronics – was a hostage to climate.

The Dolomite mountains, midway along the Alpine front, were not a priority for either side. With Italy's consuming focus on the Isonzo, the Fourth Army – responsible for this sector – was not given resources to exploit a breakthrough even if one could be achieved. On the other hand, offensive objectives were defined: the Fourth Army was supposed to drive westwards towards Bozen and the Adige valley; north-west, towards the Brenner Pass; and north-east towards inner Austria. This contradiction between means and ends was always likely to have bloody consequences.

The Austrian forces were spread even more thinly here than elsewhere in the mountains; parrying the Italian thrusts was their only aim. In the decades before 1914, most of the Habsburg budget for renewing and extending fortifications had been devoted to Galicia in the east and Istria on the Adriatic. As chief of the general staff, Conrad neglected the Dolomites in favour of strengthening the south Tyrol as a base for attacking the Veneto. As a result, the defences were second-rate compared with those in Trentino. In May 1915, rather than try to hold the small fortresses against Italian artillery, the sector commander, Major General Ludwig Goiginger, abandoned the forts without a fight and distributed their artillery around the mountains. By dividing up their batteries among more or less isolated positions on the flanks and summits, the Austrians wrung every advantage from the dramatic topography of the Dolomites. Goiginger hoped he could pen the Italians in the southern valleys, away from the strategic passes.

As on the Isonzo, then, the Austrians pulled back from the prewar border to the nearest defensible line. This meant inaccessible cliffs and pinnacles hundreds of metres above the approach roads. Before they became a playground for climbers, hikers and skiers, these mountains were a limestone jungle, a thinly populated frontier where pious farming communities, loyal to the emperor in Vienna, eked a living. For the Italians deployed here between 1915 and 1917, the Dolomites were a terrible place, one that mocked their ambitions and their courage. After touring the front in August 1916, the English writer H. G. Wells reflected this mood in a propaganda report. The 'grim and wicked' Dolomites are

worn old mountains, they tower overhead in enormous vertical cliffs of sallow grey, with the square jointings and occasional clefts and gullies, their summits are toothed and jagged. In the distance rise other harsh and desolate-looking mountain masses, with shining occasional scars of old snow. Far below is a bleak valley of stunted pine trees through which passes the road of the Dolomites.

The prewar border between Italy and Austria looped through the Dolomites just south of Cortina d'Ampezzo, then becoming known as a resort. Cortina lay at the crossroads of the only two highways through the Dolomites. The Emperor's Road linked Toblach (now Dobbiaco) in the north to Belluno and the coastal plains, while the Dolomites Road – the one that Wells surveyed – connected the Julian Alps and the Isonzo valley in the east to Bozen and the Adige valley in the west. Completed a few years before the war, it was a feat of engineering, zigzagging over passes, dropping into broad valleys and skirting the edge of streams.

In May 1915, the Italians did not believe the Austrians would abandon Cortina without a fight, so lost precious days before venturing into the town. Then they waited another week or ten days before pushing north, along the Emperor's Road. The same errors that plagued the early campaigns on the Isonzo were repeated here. For example, they put a token force of Alpini on the flat summit of Mount Piana, neglected to reinforce it, and were driven off by Austrian militia. A miniature war of position ensued; the Austrians lost ground, but clung to the northern edge of the summit. Although casualties were measurable in hundreds rather than tens of thousands, they were incurred with no better result than on the Isonzo. If anything, these lives were spent even more wastefully, for the Italians had not committed the forces that would be needed to exploit a breakthrough. At least, on the Isonzo, Cadorna believed he had sufficient forces to break through eventually. In the Dolomites there was no such belief, yet the Fourth Army was still obliged to attack. As on the Isonzo, these attacks were not concentrated. By mounting simultaneous attacks along the Dolomites sector – some 80 or 100 kilometres – the Italians lengthened the already long odds against their cracking the Austrian grip on the key routes northward.

Rebuffed to the north, the Italians pushed westwards from Cortina, along the arterial road towards the Adige, twisting up through meadows, shadowed by huge cliffs. They crept forward for 10 kilometres or so, reaching the head of the Falzarego valley by mid-June 1915.[1] They approached a feature called the Sasso di Stria, a spike rising a couple of hundred metres like a miniature Matterhorn, forcing the road to swing south-westwards. A secondary route forks north through the Valparola Pass towards the town of Bruneck. The Austrians had fortified the Sasso, on the southern side of the Valparola Pass, and prepared strong positions on the northern side. If the Italians were to have any chance of reaching Bozen and the Brenner Pass, they had to break out of the Falzarego valley.

The first attempt to penetrate the Valparola Pass, on 15 June, was a fiasco. The battalion leading the assault was told that the Alpini had captured the Sasso, on their left flank, and that the wire in front of them had been successfully breached. Both reports proved to be false.[2] Their

---

1 At 2,105 metres above sea-level, the Falzarego Pass is only 140 metres lower than the summit of Krn, the highest peak on the Isonzo. Such were the altitudes on the Dolomites front.

2 In fact the Alpini had seized positions close to the summit, capturing most of the Austrian unit on the Sasso. The Fourth Army commander, General Nava, inexplicably abandoned these positions three days later. The Austrians filled the vacuum, and their hold on the Sasso was not seriously threatened again. Nava was replaced in September.

own artillery support failed to materialise; the gunners on the south side of the valley were afraid of hitting their own infantry. The battalion commander was so bent on glory that he ignored the lack of supporting fire. The bugles sounded, and the battalion – Sardinians of the Reggio Brigade – charged at the wire yelling 'Savoy!' They lost contact with the reserves and were picked off as they scrabbled for shelter behind boulders on the open hillside. Days later, a junior officer wrote in his diary that the battalion's spirits had not recovered: 'No joking, no laughter any more.'

Over the next months, the Sasso di Stria and adjacent positions at the throat of the Valparola valley were occasionally seized, at great cost, but could not be held. A valiant officer led a small unit almost to the top of the Sasso on 18 October. He was shot and his men were captured. It was a pointless gesture. Better results were obtained a couple of kilometres away, where important footholds were captured on the northern rim of the valley. The first counter-attacks were beaten back, but the Italians were not securely placed: the emerging front line was often high above their nearest resources, horribly exposed to enemy fire. The closer the Italians could get to the cliff face, the safer they were. By late autumn they were tucked on ledges hundreds of metres above the valley floor, living in huts pinioned to the rock, supplied by cableways, probing the Austrian lines as and where they could. Donning hemp-soled shoes, they wormed their way up cracks that would challenge a trained alpinist. Easier gradients were overcome by bolting ladders to the rockface. Machine guns and small artillery were hauled by rope to the top of overhangs.

With progress measured in vertical centimetres and no breakthrough in sight, the Italians decided to blast the Austrians off their eyries above the Falzarego valley. This endeavour led to extraordinary feats of engineering: for two years, Italian sappers tunnelled hundreds of metres in order to lay mines under enemy positions. The largest of these mines was laid under the Castelletto or 'little castle', a curious rock formation that looms over the entrance to the Travenanzes valley, an alternative passage northward. When they failed to break beyond the Sasso di Stria, the Italians switched their offensive efforts in this direction. One problem with this fallback plan was that the Travenanzes valley was wild and trackless. Getting and supplying an army through it would be difficult, if not impossible, without control of the surrounding heights – something the Italians never looked likely to achieve.

The other problem was access to the valley, which lay over a pass some 500 metres above the road through the Dolomites. This pass, the Forcella Col dei Bos, was dominated by the Castelletto. Geologically, the Castelletto is a fragment of Mount Tofana, which rears over Cortina d'Ampezzo like a mile-high megalith. Separated from the hulking Tofana by a narrow saddle of scree, the Castelletto rises 200 metres to a jagged crest. On its other (western) side, it falls 400 metres to the threshold of the Travenanzes valley. It is a natural fortress.

During the autumn, the Italians edged upwards from the valley almost to the foot of the Castelletto. They captured Tofana without firing a shot and kept a presence on the summit, dug in and supplied under Austrian fire, in temperatures that sank below minus 30 degrees, hammered by blizzards. They expected the Castelletto to fall into their hands, but it could not be sighted from Tofana's summit and artillery fire did little damage. It could accommodate a platoon in a warren of tunnels and caves. Although it lay 500 metres ahead of the nearest Austrian cover, the rock could be resupplied in darkness. It had to be conquered if the Italians were to secure the Falzarego Pass and get into the Travenanzes valley, leading north to Bruneck, then the Brenner Pass and eventually the Austrian heartland. The sector commanders grew obsessed with the Castelletto, and battered it with everything they could find. To the Austrians, it was the *Schreckenstein* or 'rock of terror'. Italian infantrymen crossed themselves when it was mentioned. Apart from tactical reasons, the Italians argued, army morale demanded its capture.

All the misplaced ingenuity and energy of the Alpine campaign was expressed in the attempt to do just this. Two young officers conceived the plan of mining the Castelletto in late 1915. It involved digging a 500-metre gallery from positions at the foot of Tofana, behind the face of the mountain, under the saddle. The two engineers said they needed 35 tonnes of gelignite to be sure of forcing the Austrians off the rock. This would make it the biggest military mine in history.

The mine should have been ready by the end of May 1916, but rapid progress became possible only in March, when two rock-drills were delivered. Except for the officers, the sappers were not military engineers; they were soldiers in the Alpino units of the Fourth Army who had worked as miners before the war in Germany and Austria. With 120 of these men working in shifts, it was possible to drive five or six metres in 24 hours. By early June, they were still 33 metres short of the objective.

The Austrians were aware of the Italian operation, and had started to dig a countermine. Lacking a rock-drill, they could make little headway and were very unlikely to discover the Italian mine. Even so, by the end of the month, the Italian engineers reckoned that the head of their gallery – the chamber for the gelignite – lay no more than six metres from the nearest countermine. After filling the chamber with explosives, the miners plugged the tunnel with 33 metres-worth of rubble, sandbags and broken furniture: sufficient, they reckoned, to stop the blowback of gas. As they had taken the extra precaution of building right-angles into the tunnel, they were confident that their own troops, poised to move onto the saddle from above and below, would be safe from the massive explosion. Half the Italians were waiting in a subsidiary tunnel inside Tofana, above the saddle of scree linking it to the Castelletto. The membrane of rock at the end of this tunnel would be blown out just after the main detonation, freeing the men to swarm down on the shattered Austrian positions. The remainder were ready below the saddle. Across the valley, the King, Cadorna, and the commander of the Fourth Army peered through binoculars as the minutes ticked down to zero.

In the final stage of digging, aromas from the Austrian rations being prepared in the Castelletto seeped through fissures in the limestone to the Italians below. If the Austrians noticed these air currents, they might release poison gas above the fissures, slowing the tunnelling or even stopping it. Apparently the idea never occurred to the Austrians, who were absorbed by the challenge of keeping their sanity.

The senior officer on the Castelletto was Hans Schneeberger, a 19-year-old ensign in the Austrian Kaiserjäger, the Emperor's Hunters, native Tyrolean soldiers. In early June, he was ordered to lead his platoon up to the Castelletto. A reputation for agility around the mountains had already earned young Schneeberger the nickname of 'the snow-flea', yet his commanding officer explained that the main reasons for his assignment were his age (he was the youngest officer available) and marital status (single). For it was clear that the enemy were preparing to detonate a spectacular mine. The rock was buzzing and trembling under the Austrians' boots. Another drill could be heard behind the surface of Tofana, across the saddle.

Visiting the Castelletto one night, Schneeberger's sector commander, Captain von Rasch, put him in the picture. In the long term, it was impossible to hold the Castelletto. For 'reasons of prestige', the divisional command refused to abandon a single foot of territory without a fight. The situation was hopeless: 'If you do not freeze or starve to death first, you will be blown up', Rasch told the teenaged ensign. There were two ways of averting this outcome: they could drive the Italians off Tofana completely, or foil their plan by discovering and destroying their tunnel. The first option was out of the question: the Italian counter-offensive in the south Tyrol and Brusilov's offensive on the Eastern Front meant that no more men could be spared for the Dolomites. The second option was highly improbable, for the army was unable to provide a rock-drill. The most they could hope for were a few flame-throwers and heavy machine guns.

Schneeberger resisted the impulse to share the bad news. ('For the first time in my life I intuit the secret of authority: knowing, yet saying nothing.') The cavern walls were thin, however, and word quickly got around. The effect on the Austrians' nerves can be imagined. Young Schneeberger's soldierly resolve sometimes wavered. ('When death is certain, it eclipses everything else: every other thought and feeling.') Not so the 30 men under his command. Of Alpine stock themselves, they lived up to the reputation of highlanders for taciturn strength and dependability. Their stoicism shamed and heartened the young ensign. When he asked what they thought of the situation, they shrugged and carried on.

As the days passed, Schneeberger began to find the noise of the enemy drill reassuring: it meant the Italians were not yet ready, and 'as long as they are not ready, we survive'. When the drills fell silent, everyone knew the countdown had started but not when it would end. Schneeberger asked who wanted to be transferred off the rock. Nobody spoke: not Aschenbrenner, with eight children at home, nor the spindly, 52-year-old Latschneider. At midday on 10 July, the Italian guns across the valley below Tofana opened fire on the Castelletto. The intensity of the bombardment suggested the detonation was imminent.

At 03:30 next morning, Schneeberger is in his cavern, trying to sleep. A candle gutters on the table. Outside, the sky is predawn grey. At once the rock shakes, everything goes black and he is flung off his hammock. Coming to, he feels his head roaring, his brains want to burst out of his skull. The air is thick with sulphurous dust. Stones crash around him, men groan. It has come at last. From across the valley, the King sees a tower of flame blaze up between the Castelletto and Tofana. A colossal

noise crashes around the mountain walls. In Cortina, some 10 kilometres away, people think it must be an earthquake.

Schneeberger staggers outside. The sky has vanished in boiling dust.
The saddle is unrecognisable: a crater has been blown in the middle,
'deep as a church tower', fringed with rubble. Turning around, he sees
the southern end of the summit crest has disappeared. Only ten of his
platoon are alive. He sends three men to relieve the observation post
under Tofana and posts two more on the crater's rim. The others search
for survivors in the rubble. High overhead on Tofana, machine guns
chatter at anything that moves.

Then soldiers and black smoke pour out of the tunnel mouth newly
gaping in Tofana. Ignoring the smoke, the Italians make their way
down to the huge crater in the saddle. Then they keel over, one after
another. It is what miners call afterdamp or white damp: refluxing
clouds of carbon monoxide, formed by the explosion and sucked out
of the tunnel. The men waiting below the saddle fare no better. As they
race up the slope, they are skittled over by huge boulders dislodged by
the blast, careering down from the crater. The survivors are driven back
by rifle fire from the surviving Austrians, but Schneeberger knows they
cannot hold the Castelletto without urgent reinforcements. Thanks to
brave Latschneider ('You only die once, sir'), he gets a message to
sector command and a relief platoon arrives 36 hours after the
explosion. The spectral Schneeberger briefs the new commanding
officer, who considers him coolly and wonders if he has not been 'up
here a bit too long?'

The same considerations of morale that motivated the operation
required censorship of the facts about its outcome. The engineers
assessed that 'the mine responded perfectly both in respect of the
calculations made and of the practical effects'. The Supreme Command
used this report to mislead the public about the paltry results.

Next day, the Italians captured the south side of the Castelletto. At
the end of July, they tried to push down the Travenanzes valley. If they
had succeeded, they would have cut off the little Austrian force still
clinging on to the north side of the Castelletto. But the Austrians knew
they were coming and pulled back 500 metres down the valley. They
prepared a new defensive line with no wire, trenches or visible dug-outs.
Nervous but unsuspecting, the Italians walked into an ambush, took
heavy casualties and retreated. Even if they had forced a way through
the Travenanzes valley in summer 1916, it is difficult to see how they

would have broken through to Bruneck, let alone the Brenner Pass. Besides, during the seven months that were needed to mine the Castelletto, the entire front had ground to a halt.

It took the Fourth Army three more months to prise the Austrians off the Castelletto. The savage winter of 1916–17 then put a stop to large-scale operations. Over the following spring and summer, although the Italians managed to press the Austrians a little way down the Travenanzes valley, there was no breakthrough. In frustration, the Fourth Army approved a madcap scheme to bypass the Sasso di Stria by digging a 2,000-metre tunnel directly from the Falzarego Pass into the Valparola valley. The retreat after Caporetto very likely spared the Italians the embarrassment of another failed 'technical fix'.

The worst bloodletting in the Dolomites occurred on Mount Col di Lana (2,450 metres), with twin summits overlooking the highway to Bozen, a few kilometres from the Sasso di Stria. An outcrop of dark volcanic rock amid the granular Triassic limestone, the Col di Lana looks more Scottish than Dolomitic, quite unlike the towering pinnacles all around it. The highway curves below the Col di Lana; with light artillery on its twin summits, the Austrians blocked use of the highway leading west and north. If the Italians were to reach the Adige valley and Trento, they had to take Col di Lana. According to received wisdom, which insisted that high ground had to be taken before all else, this meant frontal assaults.

The first bombardments achieved little. In July 1915, a full month after they reached the foot of the mountain – a hiatus that the Austrians knew how to use – the infantry attacked. Despite horrific casualties, they kept attacking the mountain on three sides throughout the summer and autumn: 12 infantry and 14 alpine companies. Imagine a campaign to capture a cathedral spire by creeping along its roof-ridge, with 45-degree slopes on either side. Eventually they got within 50 metres of the enemy trench that ringed the twin summits. In early November, a ferocious bombardment followed by a storming assault gained the top. Incredulous Austrian observers on Mount Sief, a few hundred metres westwards along the ridge, raised the alarm. Under concentrated artillery fire, the Austrians regained the summit the same evening. The Italians crept back and took the summit again early next day without firing a shot. Under cover of thick mist, they moved along the ridge towards Sief. Austrian resistance was too strong, however, and the Italians were caught by overnight temperatures that sank to minus 15 degrees. Dozens of soldiers suffered frostbite.

Winter did not stop the fighting, which raged on through December. By the end of the year, the Italians had launched more than 90 assaults on Col di Lana. They had plenty of men, but as elsewhere lacked machine guns, mortars, and medium and heavy batteries.

In January 1916, as on Tofana, the Italians resorted to mining. The Austrians dug a countermine, which exploded too far from its target to cause damage. A 5,000-kilogram charge was detonated under the Austrian front line, a heavily protected trench, in mid-April. The commander on the summit felt the mountain implode beneath his feet, then boil up like milk. The jubilant Italians reckoned that 10,000 tonnes of rock were displaced. Almost half the Austrian force was killed; the remaining 140 were taken prisoner when the Italians seized the summit once and for all.

Again, the narrow ridge leading to Sief was desperately defended by Austrian reserves. Over the next year and a half, the Italians edged closer and closer to Sief without conquering it. No amount of courage could overcome the Austrians' natural advantages and, from the strategic point of view, without Sief, the Italians might as well not have Col di Lana. The Austrians still blocked access to the west and north, and threatened traffic on the Dolomites Road as it crawled around the hairpin bends down from Falzarego. In October 1917, the Italian Fourth Army had to retreat, following the breakthrough at Caporetto. By this point, more than 6,000 Italians had died on Col di Lana and Sief for precisely nothing.

The Castelletto and Col di Lana were exceptions. For the most part, due to the landscape, climate, and the lack of men and munitions, combat in the Dolomites was small in scale. After late summer 1915, when the lines settled, this was a front where a single artillery piece would target a single enemy encampment – perhaps a few tents in a meadow – at the same time every day. Offensives were platoon-sized, aimed at capturing an isolated position. A typical operation was a patrol into the no-man's land between trenches and observation posts. When patrols met, firefights erupted. The nature of the front created a peculiar tension that gnawed at these patrols, especially at night, as they moved past dozens or even hundreds of crags and boulders, any of which could conceal a sharpshooter. A platoon could hide in a shadow. Searchlights playing over a mountain were like candles in a catacomb.

Strange weapons were invented for mountain warfare. The Austrians made *Rollbomben*, cast-iron spheres filled with explosive, for dropping down the rockface. (Turkish forces had done something similar at Gallipoli.) The Italians made balls of resin and bitumen, as big as footballs, for lighting and rolling towards enemy lines when, as rarely, these were lower than their own. The soldiers, too, were different. Both sides had special units for mountain warfare. The Italian Alpini had a proud tradition dating back to the 1870s. Recruited from Italy's mountain areas, they were devoutly Catholic and monarchist, less prone to the political turbulence that affected some of the infantry brigades, with their intake from the politicised working class. They were – and still are – famous for their *esprit de corps*, valour and songs. Unlike many of the lowland and southern Italians on the Alpine front, they were not bewildered by fighting over useless, uninhabitable mountains.

For Germany and Austria, the Tyrolese militias were also drawn from the local population. Often middle-aged, its members were hardy, moved around the terrain with the confidence of chamois, and – as hunters – were crack shots. German troops were also present: the Alpine Corps was formed hurriedly in 1915 to bolster the defence in the Tyrol. Unlike the Tyrolese militia, these were well equipped. Thirteen battalions served in the Dolomites under Krafft von Dellmensingen's able leadership until the Austrian line was stabilised. As Italy and Germany were not officially at war until August 1916, they tried to stay north of the prewar border.

The mountain units had to endure fantastically severe conditions. War had never been fought at such heights before, up to 3,500 metres. Fighting in the Sino-Indian war of 1962 and more recently in Kashmir occurred at even greater altitudes, but the soldiers' experience on the Alpine front remains unmatched. In mid-winter, sentries faced temperatures as low as minus 40 or even minus 50 degrees Celsius with woollen greatcoats, scarves and gloves. Freak snowfalls could be heavy even in midsummer. Above the Falzarego Pass in early July 1915, soldiers had to warm their numb hands on the bowls of their pipes as they smoked. By mid-August, higher on the mountains, water froze at night and soldiers were incapacitated with frostbite. On peaks with permanent icefields, such as Marmolada, quarters were excavated in the ice and troops lived there round the year.

Except at Mount Col di Lana and a very few other places, planned offensives stopped from late October until spring – almost half the year. At higher altitudes, the shutdown lasted from mid-September until June. When the snow was really deep, incoming shells would sink in, without exploding. Yet most of the positions remained manned throughout the year, as lookouts. During the snowy months, the more remote positions could only be supplied by cableways up the mountainsides from the nearest roadheads all along the front. In the Alps, these black threads were lifelines.

Alpine conditions exposed the wretched lack of adequate equipment. What was uncomfortable on the Carso could be lethal in the mountains. The lack of camouflage in the first winter was fatal for many: the grey-green uniforms made perfect silhouettes. Winter climbing is now a sport; before the First World War it was unknown, so even the specialist mountain troops had few techniques to minimise the discomforts and dangers, from snow-blindness to avalanches, known as 'white death'. The former could be prevented with the use of slitted aluminium goggles. Against the latter, nothing could afford protection except experience and prudence, both in short supply. It is estimated that the white death killed more soldiers on the Alpine front than bullets or shells. On one day alone, 13 December 1916, known as White Friday, some 10,000 soldiers perished in avalanches.

For soldiers on the Alpine front, the elements were a third army, one that would kill them all, given a chance. This plight connected soldiers who often came from the same region, sharing the same customs and dialects. For politicians, mountains symbolised the lofty values that justified the war. For the men fighting among them, they were a very present danger, beyond politics altogether. Carlo Salsa's reflection on the mutual anonymity that made trench war possible is worth quoting again: 'If I knew something about that poor lad, if I could once hear him speak, if I could read the letters that he carries near his heart, only then would killing him like this seem like a crime.' Veterans' memoirs show that this subjunctive state of mind arose more easily in the mountains than on the Carso. Long months of inaction induced more thoughtfulness than soldiers' conditions usually allowed. Amid the silence, it was easier to realise that the enemies were men like themselves.

Unlike the war on the Isonzo, the war in the Dolomites did not obliterate the individual. What did character matter on the Carso, where sheer numbers and mass were decisive? Here, individuals could influence the outcome of an action. And, despite everything, the mountains were magnificent and the soldiers were young men. This explains the transcendental undertone of veterans' letters and memoirs, the sense of communing with nature at her most sublime. Living above the tree line, surrounded for months on end by a silence that was intensified rather than broken by the moaning wind, repeating a routine of simple duties, the soldiers could forget that war was more than an occasional disturbance. H. G. Wells was struck by the sight of 'Alpini sitting restfully and staring with speculative eyes across the mountain gulfs towards unseen and unaccountable enemies'. The sporadic violence could even merge with the natural cycle. For Paolo Monelli, an Alpino officer, the bright cloudlets left by bursting shells were in perfect harmony with the sky around them.

At the same time, these letters and memoirs express a boyish zest for adventure amid the mighty peaks. The small scale of most operations on this front meant that they easily resembled stunts. Luis Trenker, a mountain guide turned Habsburg soldier, described an attempt to capture a machine gun on a solitary ledge, reachable only by climbing a 'chimney' or narrow cleft up a sheer rockface. The account reads like mountaineering literature: war as sport.

Despite these differences, the Italian strategy was the same as on the Isonzo. Taking and holding as much ground as possible, regardless of its strategic value, entailed colossal effort for little or no benefit. Colonel Giulio Douhet, chief of staff in the Carnia sector and an implacable critic of Cadorna's methods, noted that 900 porters working in relay were needed to maintain a garrison of 100 men on a 3,000-metre peak. Munitions, too, were wasted on a grand scale. On one occasion, Italian gunners fired 950 rounds to drive a dozen Austrians off a small turret of rock. Two Austrians were killed ('4 tonnes of steel per dead man', as Douhet drily calculated), and the remainder withdrew. The Italians occupied the spur, but as so often were unable to hold it.

Around 1980, when the Cold War was in full swing, Mary Kaldor described the 'feats of tremendous ingenuity, talent and organisation' needed to produce modern armaments as *baroque*, meaning essentially decorative rather than functional. These weapons 'can inflict unimaginable destruction', but 'are incapable of achieving limited military objectives'. In this sense, the war in the Dolomites was baroque:

complex, expensive (in life and resources), and ineffectual. So great was
the Austrians' defensive advantage that the Italians' courage, stamina
and triumphs of engineering could not break through. Mining offered
a way to make the landscape work in their favour: the Austrians shot
down on them, but they burrowed underneath the Austrians. It did not
succeed; the mines altered details of the landscape for ever without
affecting the strategic picture.[3] No technical fix could solve the
contradiction between ends and means on the Alpine front.

3 Perhaps the Italians should have laid even bigger mines. More than 1,400 mines were
fired on the Western Front during 1916 alone, compared with 34 on the Italian front. In the
following year, 1917, more than 400 tonnes of explosive were detonated in 19 separate
mines at the Battle of Messines, killing an estimated 10,000 men. But where were the
Italians to get more gelignite? In 1916, they could only produce 80 tonnes a month.

EIGHTEEN

Forging Victory

*I do not remember much about the days, except
that they were very hot and that there were many
victories in the papers.*
HEMINGWAY

Arriving on the Alpine front from the Isonzo valley and the Carso, journalists felt they had escaped to another war altogether. They were quick to capitalise on the difference. One of them exclaimed that 'up here the soul of Italy is as pure as the snow that covers all the valleys'. Another wrote that 'life is healthy here, the war is gentle, even death is beautiful'. The journalists' relief was genuine, but their reports were full of fakery.

The chief fraudster was Luigi Barzini, perhaps the most famous journalist in the world when the war started. He was the star correspondent of Italy's most prestigious newspaper, *Corriere della Sera*, helping it to sell 350,000 copies a day. The Boxer uprising in China, the Russo-Japanese War, the Peking to Paris rally, the coronation of King George V in London, the Balkan Wars and the Mexican Revolution: he covered them all. Newsboys hawking *Corriere* boosted their sales by shouting 'Barzini's latest!' Female readers sent him ardent letters. His fame and talent for evocative description made him the obvious choice to cover the outbreak of war in 1914, and he was the first Italian journalist into occupied Belgium. His son remembered him as a provincial gentleman of the old school, handsome, spruce, chain-smoking, devoted to his family, masking self-doubt with courtesy. Like other *Corriere* staffers, he was radicalised by the Libyan war of 1911–12. His new-found convictions led to a series of lurid articles on the 'tragic and sublime battle' for Italian identity being waged 'at the frontiers of the race', across the Adriatic Sea. Propagating such views, Barzini would have shared his newspaper's commitment to intervention in 1915. He worked very hard throughout the war, spending long periods at the front where he became 'a sort of institution . . . as well-known by sight as the King or General Cadorna', churning out despatches that were collected into instant books which sold by the thousand.

Yet reporting the war turned out to be fraught with painful dilemmas. Barzini went to the front wanting to produce patriotic journalism that would increase public support for the war. As he told Albertini at the end of May 1915, the 'soul of the country' was in the care of the newspapers. 'We have to create pride and optimism,' he added. Publicly, he said that wartime journalism could 'give the national soul the nourishment of enlightening truth'. He was dismayed when army censors initially hacked his copy to shreds in their determination to suppress any information that could prove useful to the enemy – not that such information was easy to come by. 'They don't let us see much,' he complained to his wife in August. A few weeks into the war, he asked Albertini to let him come home; the 'ferocious severity' of the censors made it pointless. Albertini knew his man; he kept him at the front, and Barzini adapted. By mid-September, the censors were 'very polite' with Barzini: 'they never touch a word'.

What he lacked in bread-and-butter detail was made up with verbose description. The war in the mountains brought out the purple worst in his style; his despatches from the Dolomites were closer to travel writing or penny-dreadful fiction than reporting. 'Reaching the hut, we found ourselves facing a panorama of horror, above an incredible world of titanic walls, fascinating, frightful, sublime . . . ' The limestone peaks and ridges soar like ruins of mythic ramparts where the Olympians once fought the Titans, and men now scurry like ants. He wildly exaggerated the importance of the relatively minor clashes above the snow line, and nourished a myth of the Alpini as 'hunters of men', authentic warriors who had reconnected with their 'primordial soul'. His accounts of combat are unreal and undifferentiated; the infantry attacks magnificently and irresistibly; gunsmoke rolls over the lines; men die with smiles on their faces. If setbacks are mentioned, they are not explained or analysed. Even the practical outcome seems of little account; what matters is martial spirit. Barzini's comments on tactics were cut from the same cloth. He assured readers that the 1915 battles on the Isonzo proved 'It is much easier to attack uphill against dominant positions than downhill against dominated positions . . . The theory of the offensive appears to be irrefutable.' His fawning descriptions of the

Supreme Command focus on the superhuman figure of Cadorna. Staff officers emerge from the generalissimo's office transformed by contact with Italy's strategic genius. 'Armed with an indefinable new strength, with certainty in their eyes, a serene firmness on their faces, their brows lofty and as it were clarified, their worries are dissipated, their doubts are banished, one feels that each of them has found the solution to his problems on the far side of that magical door.' No wonder Barzini was so popular at the Supreme Command that other journalists protested, obliging him to use his access more discreetly.

Privately, he developed grave doubts. When Albertini arrived at the start of the Fourth Battle, Barzini gave him an earful about Cadorna's organisational and tactical failures. His letters to his editor could be equally blunt. The forward positions along the middle Isonzo were, he confided, 'held by a miracle, or because they have never been attacked', and noted the delay in supplies ('nothing arrives on time'). His wife also received frank correspondence.

I got up to the positions, and you will see something in today's *Corriere* [he wrote in July 1916] but I cannot do anything good, in my own style . . . I am very tired today. The journey was exhausting, I wrote like a lunatic, without even time for lunch, and anyway, with the stink of corpses still clinging to me, my appetite isn't exactly hearty. What an impossible life! And all I really want is to be left alone. For a month at least.

The self-pity was due to more than fatigue and frustration. Barzini felt the stress of his false position without being able to identify its cause, which lay out of sight, hidden in his conception of journalism. This conception did not recognise a public entitlement to know what was happening, or an obligation on journalists to seek out and tell the truth. As long as the truth was 'enlightening', he could avoid the conclusion that he was a military propagandist. When the bare facts condemned the war, it was harder to square his conscience with his copy. This is what happened in June 1917, at the end of the Tenth Battle, when the slaughter defied Barzini's usual cosmetic techniques. After a week, he told his editor that he could not file any more reports, because he would have to lie or be censored. In other words, he had reached the limit of self-censorship. 'Ortigara alone has cost us 20,000 men!' he exclaimed, in a recently discovered letter to Albertini. The Italians were incapable of concentrating their offensive. Cadorna's staff officers could only reach him through his deputy Porro, 'whose studied imbecility is beyond dispute'. 'We lurch from one disastrous action to the next,' he went on angrily, 'massacring whole divisions without inflicting equal damage on the enemy. We are wearing ourselves out when everything advises prudence, husbanding all our strength.'

He stayed at Ortigara, filing reports about the infantry attacking uphill in torrential rain that turns into snow. When darkness cloaks the scene, he tries to follow the ebb and flow of battle by its sounds. The atmosphere is tragic, yet there is no critique of Italian tactics. Events unroll with the inevitability of nature, as if human decisions play no part. His resources of self-censorship were not, after all, exhausted. Perhaps the letters to Albertini were a valve for perfidious feelings.[1]

When reporters face this dilemma today, they can usually write about it. Pressure to toe a censor's line enters the story as a topic for coverage. But this technique was hardly available in the First World War, and apparently it never crossed Barzini's mind to entrust the reader with his doubts. The primary censorship was internal, performed by himself on his own copy. He buried his misgivings under words, ever more positive words about Italy's noble warriors on land, at sea and in the air. And the more he wrote, the more the warriors themselves detested him. Whatever his standing *outside* the war zone, many of the men in the trenches thought his articles were more putrid than those corpses which spoiled his appetite. 'If I see that Barzino, I'll shoot him myself' was the pithy comment by a nameless infantryman that passed into legend. Lauding failed operations and heaping hosannas on incompetent officers, the journalists became hated figures. 'In the journalists' version of events,' wrote the pro-war publicist Giuseppe Prezzolini, 'Italy had become the most important country in the world and the Italian war the centre of the European conflict.' More than anyone else, Barzini was responsible for the ordinary soldiers' weary disgust with the press – an outlook caught by Giulio Barni, a tough-minded volunteer from Trieste, in a little poem called 'Propaganda'.

> Newspapers arrived
> in the trenches
> – so-called 'propaganda' –

1 Another journalist who kept his public and private accounts of the war in separate boxes was Rino Alessi of *Il Secolo*. Alessi's 'secret letters' to his editor form a fascinating parallel chronicle that often bears little resemblance to the war described in his articles. For example, he criticised Cadorna's decimations privately ('unacceptable from any point of view'), not in his reports.

and since there was no other paper
the soldiers took them
to wipe their arses

None of this was unique to Barzini or Italy. Across Europe, journalists believed their overriding duty was to the army, right or wrong. The chiefs of staff wanted to ban the press from the front and force it to rely exclusively on official bulletins. In Germany and Russia, the generals got their way. In Britain, the government and the leading newspapers quickly reached an informal understanding; the press would co-ordinate the dissemination of official news from the front, and in exchange, the government would keep censorship to a minimum. The press then tested the army's patience by using freelancers who hurried to France, where they played cat-and-mouse with the army around northern France. Their coverage supplemented the official version of events with colour and detail. Later, the British army agreed to accredit five British correspondents at the front. Dressed in officers' uniforms, lent a château and a fleet of cars, they were flattered and controlled. One of their censors described the process of co-optation: the five correspondents 'lived in the Staff world, its joys and sorrows, not in the combatant world. The Staff was both their friend and their censor. How could they show it up when it failed?' Among the rules under which they worked was this: 'There must be no criticism of authority or command.' They toed the line, filing bland and hopeful accounts of battles that they had not been allowed to see, untouched by the 'helpless anger' that their reports stirred among the infantry.

The Italian 'system of lies' was based on a similar arrangement. On 23 May 1915, when they realised that Cadorna wanted to ban all journalists from the front, the leading newspapers petitioned the government and general staff to give selected correspondents access, and let them file their copy after the Supreme Command had approved it. This privilege should be granted to newspapers with the 'attitudes' and 'moral capacity' needed for 'such a delicate task'. The correspondents should be 'rigorously militarised', and subject to military discipline. How could Cadorna resist? Correspondents were allowed to visit the front in large groups, under close military escort. (On his first tour, Barzini travelled with 60 other journalists.) Later, a corps of nine journalists plus three foreign correspondents were allowed to remain.

The scope of military censorship of the press, post, telephones and telegrams was set out in the war powers law (22 May 1915), authorising the government to examine the contents of any post and the regional prefects to seize any publications that might be 'gravely prejudicial to the supreme national interests'. Crucially, the publication of 'military information not from official sources' was forbidden. A catch-all decree on 20 June banned 'false news'. The prefect of Naples used this decree to arrest and fine newsboys who shouted about Italian losses. Reinforcing the message, Salandra stated that criticism of Italy's actions and aims was impermissible; nothing could be allowed to shake public trust in ultimate victory. The press did not object in principle to these constraints. What galled them, as we saw with Barzini, was their crude imposition.

One reason why this patriotic consensus was so sturdy is that it had been forged in 1911, when the press acclaimed the invasion of Libya. Editors had shared and reinforced public impatience with Giolitti's reforms, and hailed the invasion as a great enterprise that would unite the nation. The press conjured up a vision of Libya as a Promised Land where grateful natives eagerly awaited Italy's troops, and nature's bounty would pour into Italy's coffers. The half-dozen correspondents who felt that the Libyan campaign was '*their* endeavour', and who shaped public perceptions of it, were hardcore interventionists in 1914–15.

The central figure in this consensus was Luigi Albertini, editor of *Corriere della Sera*, mouthpiece of Milanese business and industrial interests, the only newspaper that could aspire to the grand manner of *The Times* of London, where Albertini himself had trained. He was Italy's nearest equivalent to Lord Northcliffe, the British newspaper tycoon, though the differences are more revealing than the parallels. Northcliffe told Haig to drop him a line if *The Times* printed anything he disliked. Albertini would have done the same for Cadorna, but he did not confront the established authorities as Northcliffe famously did with his campaigns against Kitchener and Asquith and over the production of shells. His intimacy with ministers was much more deferential than Northcliffe's; he rarely tested his power to challenge the government, and when he did so, could easily be tamed again, as we shall see in a later chapter. He wanted his paper to be 'not only the mirror but the soul and stimulus of a young nation, searching for its identity and for modernity'. As a free-trade conservative with a social outlook that combined populism with paternalism, he opposed Giolitti (except over Libya) and favoured his successor, Salandra. In 1914, sharing Salandra's view that 'sacred egoism' should steer Italy in the European crisis, he shadowed the prime minister's evolution from neutralism to interventionism and later boasted of being one of the people most responsible for getting Italy into the war. The government showed its appreciation by making him a senator.

During the war, the three-way links between *Corriere*, the government and the Supreme Command were astonishingly close. In all but name, the national newspaper of record – now selling 600,000 copies daily – became a parallel ministry of information, propaganda and intelligence. It saw itself, and was seen by the government and the Supreme Command, as part and parcel of the war effort. Albertini's mission was to nurture patriotism, support the men at the front, and expose profiteers. His correspondents in Europe and Africa sometimes served as a parallel intelligence network, even a parallel diplomatic service, more efficient than the real thing. Favoured papers were exempt from the Supreme Command's rule that newspapers could not accredit more than two correspondents; *Corriere della Sera* had some 20 correspondents along the front. Colonel Gatti, who ran the Historical Office at the Supreme Command, was one of the paper's military advisors. *Corriere* journalists drafted Cadorna's florid bulletins. Another staffer, Giuseppe Borgese, left the paper after Caporetto to organise Italian propaganda in Allied countries. And a *Corriere* man drafted General Diaz's famous Victory Bulletin at the war's end.

At the start of the war Cadorna was blind to public opinion and let his deputy deal with journalists. Addressing correspondents in Trentino, General Porro urged them to see their reports as supplements to the daily bulletins issued by the Supreme Command. For no army can march willingly to victory unless it has a united, enthusiastic nation at its back. 'Our mission', he intoned, 'is *to forge victory*. Keep that well fixed in your minds.' The journalists did as they were asked, with little prompting by the military. Until the end of 1915, the only official source of information was the daily bulletin, which was usually too rhetorical and phoney to be much use; even Sonnino, who had no time for journalists, thought they reflected badly on Italy's cause, but Cadorna disliked the foreign minister and rejected his plea to make the bulletins more credible. If the press found them unappetising, that was their problem.[2]

Only in December, facing political rumbles in Rome and disillusion around the country, did he accept that the Supreme Command needed a press office. The man chosen to design this new unit was a professional writer, Ugo Ojetti. As a middle-aged volunteer in the Territorial Militia, Ojetti had pulled strings to get sent to the Supreme Command, and was waiting for just this opportunity. 'In Rome, Cadorna felt troubled – at last! – about public opinion,' Ojetti explained to his wife, referring to the generalissimo's difficult sojourn in the capital over Christmas. 'For the first time since the start of the war he found himself – just a little – in contact with "public opinion". Now he wants the press to tackle this peril resolutely.' Ojetti formulated a strategy to provide the press with material that would be 'more moral and social than practical and military', and tailored to the city or region for which it was intended. At the same time, the output should be more informative about the operations at the front, covering 'the difficulties overcome, those that still have to be overcome, the purpose of particular actions'. This was too sophisticated for Cadorna, who simply wanted a more efficient way to get official statements disseminated by obedient reporters. Ojetti was replaced by a colonel on Cadorna's staff and put in charge of the photograph library.

If Cadorna was reluctant to accept the importance of the media, he flatly refused to see why the soldiers should need an information service of their own. Asked why no trench newspapers were produced for the infantry, he said there was no money. His conception of soldiering was too abstract and inhumane to accommodate the idea that his men would be better soldiers if they understood why they had to risk death for their country. Soldiers must obey and criticism must be punished harshly.

By today's standards, what most war correspondents filed in the First World War was hardly journalism at all. The combination of flattery,

---

2 In substance, Cadorna's bulletins were not more misleading than Haig's. British GHQ after the first day of the Somme notoriously assured readers that 'Thanks to the very complete and effective artillery preparation, thanks also to the dash of our infantry, our losses have been very slight . . . '

coercion and patriotism was fatal to free inquiry, as it often still is. Reporters now tend to take a more modest view of their role; they should take care of reporting, and leave the mustering of support for war to politicians, or at least to the leader writers. This distinction hardly existed during the Great War. There was no conception that the journalists' first duty is to report what they see truthfully and honestly.

Journalists who believed nothing was more important than winning the war, and that truthful reporting might discourage the public, easily persuaded themselves that they should serve the 'higher truth' of Italy's national mission. They expressed few misgivings about this price. Prezzolini noted privately in December 1915 that soldiers on home leave were spreading anti-war propaganda among the masses, while the officers did the same among the middle classes. 'I too inevitably make propaganda against the war if I tell the truth,' he added, 'given all the reasons we have to be dissatisfied with how it is being waged.' When truth and defeatism looked identical, patriotic journalists made decisions which posterity judges with a severity that would have bewildered them.

The Supreme Command's conduct of the war from 1915 to 1917 was a classic example of what can go wrong without the scrutiny of a sceptical press. Servile journalists relayed the lies and misjudgements of the Supreme Command, which welcomed their reports as evidence of its wisdom. This closed loop encouraged the Command's arrogance, hatred of criticism, brutal treatment of the troops, and a zero-sum attitude to its relations with government. The commission of inquiry after Caporetto found that hospitality and access had been repaid with friendly coverage; as a result, 'the public at large was given a false and exaggerated opinion about our successes . . . Not a few soldiers have brought to our attention the damage done to the morale of officers and men by the inaccuracies and exaggerations of the war correspondents.'

This was true, but incomplete. The Socialist leader Turati was closer to the mark when he told parliament that censorship (not flattery) had produced Caporetto. The commission also failed to mention that the Supreme Command was not the sole responsible party. For the government had outlawed criticism, and the journalists *wanted* to conspire against what is now called the public's right to know. They believed they were acting for the best, and would have been baffled by the principle – generally acknowledged if not always honoured – that 'there are certain rules of hygiene in the relationship between a

newspaper correspondent and high officials, people in authority . . .
Newspapermen cannot be cronies of great men.'

One of the first to grapple with the political implications of public
opinion was Giulio Douhet, Italy's most innovative military thinker
since Machiavelli. He argued that the Russo-Japanese War of 1904–5
had confirmed the power of public opinion. This aspect of modern war
was, he warned, particularly dangerous in Italy, where people's
'emotional sensitivity' made them vulnerable to the 'exaggerated
motions of the childish soul of crowds'. Easily swayed, the Italians
should be protected from harmful influences. The Supreme Command
took the same view of the average citizen's unfitness to be treated as an
adult. The corollary of paternalism is infantilisation. What bound
journalists, ministers and staff officers was a deep conservative
assumption that ordinary people – unlike themselves – were incapable
of grasping their true interests.

NINETEEN

Not Dying for the Fatherland

*'It's a silly front,' she said. 'But it's very beautiful.
Are you going to have an offensive?'*
HEMINGWAY

The Seventh, Eighth and Ninth Battles of the Isonzo

Despite his victory at Gorizia in August 1916, Cadorna was still at loggerheads with Rome. After Salandra lost the vote of confidence in parliament in June, a new government was formed under the 78-year-old Paolo Boselli. With ministers drawn from across the political spectrum, Boselli's was in effect a 'national unity government' under weak leadership.

One of the new ministers without portfolio was Leonida Bissolati, a former socialist. After the death of Cesare Battisti in July, he was the most prominent 'democratic interventionist'. He had argued passionately for Italy to join Britain and France, volunteered for the Alpini at the ripe age of 58, won two silver medals for valour and been wounded. Later in the year, he would became the first senior Allied politician to call for the destruction of Austria-Hungary. Boselli gave him special responsibility for relations with the military and sent him on a fact-finding mission to the front. At their first meeting, the Supreme Commander 'intuited' that Bissolati held him partly responsible for the near disaster in Trentino. 'He began to see me as the worst of enemies,' Bissolati reported. After the triumphant Sixth Battle, Cadorna wrote imperiously to Boselli that unauthorised visits by ministers to the front must stop. The Prime Minister agreed at once, but a week later he blundered by mentioning to journalists that Bissolati gave the Duke of Aosta much of the credit for taking Gorizia. The incandescent commander banned Bissolati outright from the war zone.

The next upset came at the end of August, and involved Colonel Douhet, chief of staff in the Carnia Corps, mentioned in earlier chapters. Even before the war, he was a prophet of air warfare, urging Italy to set up a military air force, seek command of the air, and practise high-altitude bombing long before these ideas had currency. Under Mussolini, Douhet would develop his thinking on terror bombing and total war. For now, he was an appalled observer of Cadorna's tactical traditionalism and ineffectiveness. The low-intensity conflict on the Carnian front gave him time to keep a diary, copiously analysing the Supreme Command's faults. He also corresponded with ministers and deputies – anyone in a position of influence who would listen. One of these was Bissolati; visiting Rome in July, Douhet handed the new minister a blistering assessment of Cadorna's performance: his thinking was 45 years out of date; the 'absurd concept' of the frontal attack had wiped out the country's 'best soldiers, those who really knew their profession'; the insistence on holding every bit of conquered ground, regardless of losses, was unjustifiable; the soldiers were treated as so much 'raw material'. In sum, Cadorna had no strategic vision, had lost the army's trust, and the government was duty-bound to act accordingly.

It was all true, and very provocative. But Douhet, who had the intransigence as well as the foresight of a prophet, would not be discreet. At the end of August, an anonymous memorandum written for Sonnino and Bissolati – arguing that the capture of Gorizia had not improved Italy's strategic situation by a jot – found its way by mishap to the Supreme Command. The mixture of expertise and contempt left no doubt that Douhet was the author; he was arrested for spreading false information, breaching confidentiality, and denigrating the Supreme Command. A court martial jailed him for a year.

Bissolati was also the real target in Cadorna's third feud at this time. Jealous of the credit that the press and public opinion gave to Capello after the capture of Gorizia, Cadorna became convinced that certain ministers were intriguing to replace him with the other man. So he banished Capello to a remote command on the Asiago plateau.

In mid-September 1916, with Capello cooling his heels far from the limelight, Douhet under arrest and Bissolati's independence buckling if not yet broken, Cadorna launched the Seventh Battle of the Isonzo. The Italians now had corpses behind as well as before them. A fetor of death hung over the land captured in August, and westerly breezes made life even more repulsive in the front lines. Cadorna had always known that winning Gorizia would not change the strategic balance on the Isonzo. 'There are other fortified lines right behind the city', he wrote to his daughter late in 1915. 'This war can only be ended through the exhaustion of men and resources . . . It's frightful, but that's how it is.' The King knew it, too. Observing the Fourth Battle from a hilltop in the rear, he had remarked: 'Who knows what people in Italy will think when we *do* take Gorizia! Militarily, Gorizia means nothing in itself.'

Following the Sixth Battle, fresh recruits and munitions had poured across the Isonzo. While the Second Army consolidated around Gorizia, the Third Army geared up for another offensive on the Carso, to strike down towards Trieste across the Vallone. Cadorna wanted to catch the Austrians before they had recovered from their first real defeat and fortified their new positions. He also wanted to capitalise on their distraction by Romania's entry into the war on the Allied side at the end of August.

Boroević was better placed than Cadorna knew. Alarmed by the loss of Gorizia, the Austrian high command granted reinforcements and better equipment. Steel helmets, mortars and gas-masks were rushed to the Isonzo. The high command also stood firm against German requests to release units from the Isonzo for the campaign against Romania. By early September, the Austrians had 152 battalions on the Isonzo, as well as 168 medium and heavy artillery pieces and 606 field guns. As for strengthening the new lines on the Carso, Boroević had 40,000 men at his disposal for construction work, including 20,000 Russian prisoners of war. Working around the clock, they dug trenches, laid wire, built roads and gun emplacements in the rear. By early September, he had four defensive lines – two more than the Italians realised.

Italy's hopes of a Romanian dividend burst in the first week of September, along with the storm clouds over the Carso, marking summer's end. Both sides' trenches were awash with mud and filth. Cadorna had to postpone the attack, but started the preparatory bombardment anyway. He had 430 medium and heavy guns, 600 mortars, and 130 battalions on the Carso, facing 62 enemy battalions with a hundred guns. For several days his gunners fired blind into the fog, doing little damage. On 13 September, the skies cleared; that afternoon, with the sun at their backs, the Italians sighted their targets. With the help of aerial observers, the heavy batteries reduced much of the Austrian front line to rubble, blowing broad holes in the wire, shattering their communications. Cadorna took heart; he believed the

Austrians were packed into their front-line bunkers. In fact they had left only a token force in the front lines, so their losses were relatively slight; their men were nearby, and ready. So were their skilfully disguised batteries.

The infantry attacked at 13:30. The Duke of Aosta had amassed 100,000 men on a front of eight kilometres, an unprecedented density. Emerging through smoke and dust in compact blocks, they presented ideal targets, like the British on the Somme a few weeks earlier. With no shells to spare, and not knowing the Italian batteries' new locations, the Austrian gunners had waited for this moment. Now they opened up, inflicting terrible losses. The Italians kept coming, wave after wave, across open ground in close-order formation, shoulder to shoulder, against field guns and machine guns. To one Austrian artillery officer, 'it looked like an attempt at mass suicide'. Those who reached the deserted Austrian line met flame-throwers, tear gas, and machine-gun and rifle fire emanating from hollows and outcrops on the crumpled Carso. When dusk fell, their only significant gain was a hilltop, wrested from the Polish infantry of the 16th Division. Bad weather returned, rain scouring the battlefield.

Over the following days, repeated attacks brought few durable gains. The Austrian VII Corps, ably led by Archduke Josef von Habsburg and well positioned on the eastern rim of the Vallone, bested the weary regiments probing uphill. A few scraps of ground were taken here and there. For the most part, where the Italians broke through, inexorable counter-attacks drove them back before they could dig in and bring up reserves. An isolated attack on Mount Rombon, at the northern end of the front, met with no greater success.

Austrian casualties kept pace, and by the time Cadorna suspended the attack late on the 17th, Boroević's army was in tatters. As Italian production increased, the artillery gap had widened. The quality of Austrian rations was slipping. The draft was despatching middle-aged intakes to the front after little training. Ominously, combat performance was starting to fracture along ethnic lines. On the Eastern Front, desertion rates were always high among the Bosnian Serbs, Russophile by culture and Eastern Orthodox faith; this pattern began to repeat itself on the Isonzo. The Czechs, on the other hand, fought tenaciously on the Isonzo, by contrast with their showing against the Russians. Most dependable of all were the Slovenes, Croatians and Bosnian Muslims, who usually wore their fez and tassel even when steel helmets were available. The ferocity of Bosnian regiments was legendary, and other Habsburg units sometimes donned fezzes before counter-attacking, to put the wind up the Italians. Croatian units that performed poorly in Galicia were formidable on the Isonzo. As for the Slovenes, whose alleged pacifism would be a stock joke in Tito's Yugoslavia, they excelled against the Italians wherever they were sent.

When the guns fell silent, the Supreme Command was already planning the next offensive. Aware of what was pending, Boroević begged for extra forces. The empire was still heavily engaged on the Eastern Front, and now committed against Romania as well. Even when Conrad released two more divisions, the Austrians were outnumbered almost three to one on the Carso. At least Boroević's units were among the best: hardened Hungarian, Czech and Transylvanian infantry, and a German–Slovene alpine regiment. Smashed trenches and bunkers were rebuilt, wire re-laid, communications repaired.

A senior staff officer arrived from Vienna to inspect the defences. He proposed a new fortified line to run the length of the Carso, three kilometres behind the current front line, from the Vipacco valley to the Hermada massif, a labyrinth of ridges sloping steeply to the Adriatic – the last natural bastion before Trieste. Grottoes in the limestone would be enlarged and linked. Hamlets on the new line would be razed. This was a project for the future; there was no time to get these works under way before the next attack.

On the Italian side, fresh men and munitions were hurried to the front. Commencing on 30 September with a bombardment that lasted more than a week, counting interruptions for bad weather, the Eighth Battle replayed the Seventh, except that Cadorna involved the Second Army more actively, attacking from the north while the Duke of Aosta's men pushed eastwards. The epicentre would be 800 metres wide, around the village of Nova Vas, where 10,000 men were massed. On 9 October, the shelling intensified into so-called 'annihilation fire', marking the climax before the infantry attacked. Even with more than a thousand guns, it was less than half the weight of equivalent bombardments on the Western Front.

The Austrians contained the first assault on the central Carso. In the north, however, the Second Army made dramatic gains, driving back the Austrians a couple of kilometres. The next day, 11 October, Cadorna widened the front to 18 kilometres, diluting the Austrian fire.

The Italians had a very good day, capturing several villages beyond the Vallone. If the Czech riflemen had not mounted a spectacular charge on Hill 144, at the southern edge of the Carso, the road would have lain open to Hermada, which was not ready to withstand a major offensive. Fog settled overnight, slowing the next Italian assault and favouring the counter-attacks. The Austrians clawed back some of the lost ground. The danger of a breakthrough was averted. Again, the price was appalling; by the day's end, the Eighth Battle had cost 24,000 Habsburg casualties. More than 40 guns were captured or destroyed. The best Habsburg chronicler of the Isonzo front reckoned that with 12 fresh divisions, the Italians would have broken through. But Cadorna did not have anything like those reserves to bolster his exhausted forces. He may also have been deceived by disinformation from Habsburg prisoners about the imminent arrival of extra Austrian divisions and even some German forces. Late on 12 October, he amazed his enemies by answering their prayers: the Italians stood down.

Again, the halt was intended as a pause for regrouping. The Duke of Aosta thought ten days would suffice. New artillery and trench mortars rolled to the front from the factories of northern Italy. The Germans let Conrad transfer another division from the Eastern Front, and fresh regiments of Bosnian, Hungarian and Tyrolese infantry were scraped together. The Russian prisoners and middle-aged militiamen set to work on the new defensive line down to Hermada.

The foul weather continued, and neither side had constructed effective shelters on the Carso. Men huddled in flooded trenches under icy gales. The sky began to clear in the last week of October, and the artillery opened up from Gorizia to the sea. With 1,350 guns, the Italians had three times the firepower of the Austrians. Deserters told the Austrians that the infantry would attack on the first fine day. This was 1 November. Annihilation fire demolished the Austrian front-line positions. At 11:30, the infantry attacked. With almost 200,000 men, Cadorna said he could crack the Carso and open the road to Trieste before winter. And indeed, on the northern Carso, the Third Army proved irresistible. Such was the Italian preponderance that the Duke of Aosta could afford to pack a single division (12,000 men) into 400 metres of front.

The Austrians were forced back, giving the Italians a salient five kilometres wide and three deep. The hill of Fajti, bulwark of Habsburg defence on the northern Carso, had fallen. The flood was stemmed on one flank by the Habsburg 43rd Division, clinging to its positions between Gorizia and the Vipacco valley, and on the other by a tough Czech regiment. But for how long? Was this the breakthrough? When the counter-attack came, eight Austrian battalions tore forward from their second line wielding any weapons to hand: rifles, grenades, tear-gas bombs, iron-tipped clubs. With both sides' gunners trying to stop fresh units from reaching the line, their forces clashed on the pitted moonscape of the Carso amid shellbursts and hissing fragments of limestone. Cadorna had kept back 22 regiments for this, the second day, and they determined its outcome. Despite regaining a few positions, the Austrians had to fall behind their second line, accepting the Italian salient as accomplished fact. By 3 November, even this line looked untenable. As John Schindler finely recounts, the focal point was Hill 464, a few hundred metres east of Fajti. Boroević sent his last reserve battalion into the fray. This was the 4th Battalion of the 61st Infantry, a rich ethnic mix from the Banat region, today divided among Romania, Hungary and Serbia. Although they were outnumbered by six to one, their rampaging counter-attack triggered one of those failures of nerve that overtook Cadorna's men. This turned the tide, and the arrival of an extra division from Galicia a few hours later clinched Cadorna's decision to halt the Ninth Battle. The Italians had lost 39,000 men, some 6,000 more than the enemy, and he refused to throw his last reserves into the battle. The Austrians were astounded; did he not know how close he was to breaking through?

Cadorna recognised that the ratio of losses and gains in the autumn campaigns was horrific, which explains why the account in his memoir is unreliable even by the general standard of that book. But it does not follow that he was battering blindly at a door that showed no sign of yielding, learning nothing from experience.

He revised his battle plan before the Ninth Battle. While he still paid lip-service to the aim of reaching Trieste before winter, his goal was more modest: an improvement in Italy's position on the Carso, reaching an imaginary line between the hills of Trstelj and Hermada – at least 15 kilometres north of Trieste – without incurring huge casualties. By providing the army, the government and the nation with limited but secure territorial gains, without colossal bloodletting, he would build on the capture of Gorizia, disarm his critics and end the year on a positive note, well placed for spring 1917. He formalised this thinking in a circular to his divisional generals on 17 October. After achieving 'total destruction' of the enemy front line, the infantry would attack across the Carso. The offensive would halt at the 'critical point' before the enemy had time to regroup.

It was hard to do these things singly, let alone in a tightly timed sequence amid the chaos of battle. Even with their trench mortars, the Italians could not be sure of breaching barbed wire. A tactic of holding back the infantry until this had been achieved, in order to launch a simultaneous assault, was sure to fail. And how to identify that 'critical point'? Cadorna's new realism rested on some highly unrealistic foundations.

Making matters worse, the Austrians had adapted their tactics to turn static defence into dynamic counter-attack. Instead of trying to hold their front line against the shelling and frontal attack, they waited in their second line, then rushed forward to clash with the enemy around the almost deserted front line. The element of surprise and enhanced morale made this method effective enough to be worth using, though the depth and improved accuracy of Italian fire ensured that initial casualties stayed high.

Cadorna had finally done what his critics wanted: he had concentrated his forces on a narrow front, and employed his batteries more effectively. Yet, in other respects, these offensives repeated the errors of 1915. The outcome confirmed that defensive superiority could be overturned only by a combination of patient preparatory sapping, artillery fire that was both colossal and precisely accurate, and the timely deployment of reserves. Worst of all, Cadorna had discovered a knack for abandoning offensives when Boroević had committed his last reserves. The steely exterior concealed a vacillating spirit.

Nevertheless, these battles brought the Italians within sight of the goal of attritional warfare: exhausting the enemy to the point of collapse. The Austrians had no hope of replenishing their losses. Since August, at least 130,000 had been killed, wounded or captured on the Isonzo. Many divisions were shadows of themselves; almost all had been completely reconstructed half a dozen times.

Yet Cadorna's advantages were less solid than they appeared to the enemy. His recruits were poorly trained, incoming officers likewise, and the army's material superiority did not nullify the defenders' advantage.[1] As for his actual gains on the Carso, they amounted to several villages and a couple of kilometres of limestone, won at a cost of 80,000 casualties. The Italians were nowhere near the Trstelj–Hermada line. This was far from a limited success at reasonable cost. By blaming these results on the infantry's lack of fighting spirit, among other factors, he twisted a consequence of his tactics into a cause of their failure. His claim that all three battles were halted as soon as the casualties became disproportionate to the results was equally cynical, for the impact of these campaigns on morale was clear at the time. Douhet put his finger on the problem when he said that none of Cadorna's offensives gave the troops 'the feeling that they had really won'. As Italy was fighting an aggressive war, success had to be measured by a different scale than resistance or endurance. The men knew this very well, and mocked the shortfall between ambition and performance with a little rhyme that they chanted when their officers were out of earshot:

> See Cadorna rampage, hear him roar!
> He's killed all the mice on the kitchen floor.

If the Italians were not driving ahead, they were, by definition, failing. The finest trench-memoir was written by a lieutenant who fought on the Carso in the winter of 1916. 'It is not dying that is the demoralising thing, the thing that grinds you down', he recalled. 'It is dying so uselessly, for nothing. This is not dying for the fatherland; it is dying for the stupidity of specific orders and the cowardice of specific commanding officers.' The mood of incipient despair grew during the last months of 1916, and found expression. On 1 November, as the Ninth Battle got underway, the Duke of Aosta had six men summarily executed for mutiny. Cadorna seized on this grim incident to issue a directive that commanders were duty-bound to decimate mutinous units. While he had no authority to revise the military penal code, nobody was prepared to challenge him.

---

1 For example, use of the creeping barrage – allowing infantry to advance behind a curtain of artillery fire – was standard practice on the Western Front by the end of 1916. By March 1917, it was still unknown on the Italian front, due to the relative inaccuracy of Italian guns and poor co-ordination between infantry and artillery. The mountainous landscape posed insuperable problems to communications at the front. Capello boasted that his artillery, around Gorizia, had mastered the creeping barrage, but it was not true.

TWENTY

The Gospel of Energy

*Only an immense force of will, which
manifests itself in perseverance admired by
present and future generations, can conduct
us to our goal.*
CARL VON CLAUSEWITZ

During the Eighth Battle, an officer behind the jump-off trench watches
the little black figures scramble over the parapet clutching their rifles,
then pause, 'calm and steadfast'. He is fascinated by this moment: surely
the men halt to focus 'their stalwart spirits' on the task ahead, for each
soldier is 'like a small thing with a single will, which is stronger than the
metal that breaks it'. Then they set off, across the Carso. The line ripples
under enemy fire, the men flinch, set off again in a crouching run, stop
to aim and fire, run again. 'If they don't fall, they get there. If they don't
get there, they don't come back.' This particular attack succeeds, despite
furious bombardment. For, the officer intones, 'the will of man is
stronger than all the guns'.

What starts as a deeply felt description turns into scripted rhetoric.
The clue to the officer's identity as an educated man, an intellectual, is
his interpretation of that moment on the parapet. Although veterans'
memoirs say little about the frontal attack – the core of the infantry's
unspeakable experience, and the reason why their casualty rates over
the war were 40 per cent (ten times worse than for cavalry and gunners)
– one man still remembered that precise moment nearly ninety years
later. Antonio Di Nardo (1896–2005) described the 'absurd' moment of
'pleasure at liberation from all that anxiety' when he got out of 'that
muddy ditch'. Rather than steeling their resolve, the infantry halted to
savour their relief that the waiting was over, and delay a moment longer
their plunge into the lethal unknown.

The countdown was excruciating; after fixing bayonets and draining
the double tot of grappa, the men had to get through endless minutes

before their officer shouted 'Avanti Savoia!' and led them into the smoking din. Another long-lived veteran remembered how his heart hammered, his 'whole body racked by terror', while comrades mumbled prayers or rehearsed their battle-cries, 'thinking of nothing but death'. Guido Favetti noted how 'the blood chills before an assault, the troops fall silent. Iron discipline! Whoever questions their orders by so much as a word will be shot immediately.' The attack was the moment of truth, the ultimate test of discipline and resolve. For Emilio Lussu, a junior officer in the Sassari Brigade, this interval was worse than the attack itself. 'Those who have not been through such moments do not know what war is.'

The men knew an attack was imminent when the military police mounted their machine guns behind the trench, ready to shoot at soldiers who lingered when the cry of 'Savoy!' went up. There are no data on the casualties caused by the carabinieri, but an impression emerges from memoirs and diaries. After a minor action in the Dolomites, an army doctor matter-of-factly recorded treating 80 casualties of enemy machine-gun fire, and another 25 shot in the buttocks by the carabinieri. This practice had no equivalent on the Western Front, where the British military police merely set up 'straggler posts' as a barrier to stop men leaving the front line before or during battle. If anything, it anticipated the Red Army 'blocking units', which gunned down soldiers who tried to escape in the Russian Civil War.

When zero hour came, the men knew that failure was the likeliest outcome. A failed attack on the Carso felt like this:

Voices and shouting on all sides: a torture of sounds. You don't understand a thing, but you intuit from the noises and whistles all around that things are not going well. You drop to the ground. The rain keeps falling, a thousand snakes hissing in your ears; a confusion of people coming and going; deafening clamour. Then, solemn silence. Slithering on your stomach, you regain the track in twos and threes. But you have no clear idea what happened: whether you were cowardly or brave, or whether, turning back, you would meet the same officers and men as before or another unit, or even the Austrians.

In common with their allies and enemies, the Italians had expected a war of manoeuvre: bold operations along the valleys, then sweeping victories on the lowlands beyond the Alps and the Carso. What they could not foresee or explain was how the infantry should prevail against machine guns in dominating positions protected by barbed wire that was, for the most part, still stubbornly intact after heavy bombardment. This omission did not trouble the staff officers, because the Supreme Commander had solved the conundrum in his famous tract, *Frontal Attack and Tactical Training*, discussed in an earlier chapter. 'The outcome of war will always', Cadorna wrote, 'be decided by manoeuvre.' Cadorna's guidance to attacking troops was childish: 'Infantry that finds itself under fire during an attack must remove itself from this fire *as quickly as possible* in the only way permitted: by proceeding with all speed . . . Stopping and lying down would be *a very serious mistake.*' Convinced that attrition could not alter the scope for manoeuvre, Cadorna was not interested in how to get from here (attrition) to there (victorious manoeuvre). Instead of treating this tremendous question on its merits, he dismissed it with a stunningly simple solution: willpower, or morale. 'When a soldier lacks the spirit and will to fight,' he wrote to the prime minister, 'he lacks everything.' By the same token, possession of this spirit and will make the soldier unstoppable. In the simpler language of the *Libretto personale*, a military service document issued to every soldier: 'A soldier who has faith and courage almost always triumphs over the difficulties and dangers presented by war.' What really mattered was to go forward wherever and whenever possible.

According to traditional doctrine, before machine guns, barbed wire and concrete dug-outs changed the battlefield for ever, infantry should attack after superiority of fire had been achieved. Cadorna agreed in principle, but insisted that attacks 'should proceed without such certainty'. There was realism, too, in his observation that the assault 'does not have to be carried out by a *mass* of men'. Given the efficacy of modern artillery and their power of concentration, masses of men 'would face certain destruction'. The assault should therefore be carried out by 'waves' of men in lines that were 'not dense'. In practice, he ignored this precept or did not take it far enough, preferring to promote the will as a total solution to tactical challenges, capable of making up for any technical or geographical disadvantages. 'Victory is determined', he wrote in his tract, 'by the demoralisation of the enemy.' This would only be true if demoralisation and defeat were one and the same.

Military thinkers have always emphasised the importance of morale and willpower, for the logical reason that soldiers who strongly want to win are more likely to prevail. In the decades before 1914, this emphasis became inflamed and fanatical. The argument ran that machine guns, barbed wire and concrete dug-outs did not knock willpower (or morale) off its pedestal as the decisive factor on the battlefield. On the contrary, by isolating willpower they confirmed its primacy. For French strategists, the key to success was '*élan*', passionate ardour or flair. The Italian equivalent was '*slancio*', one of Cadorna's favourite words. The British general staff was less poetical, as befits Anglo-Saxons, but the substance was the same: every leader in an attack must be 'imbued with a determination to close with the enemy', for success depended on 'the exercise of human qualities directed by the willpower of individuals'. A British general proposed that war was essentially the 'triumph' of 'one will over a weaker will'. In the same year, 1911, the Director of Military Operations at the French general staff advocated the development of 'a conquering state of mind'.

Faith in the will belonged to a set of powerful convictions that can be linked under the umbrella term 'vitalism', a matrix of assumptions about existence and value that influenced thinking in many fields. Vitalism championed impulses and intuitions over abstract ideas, character over structure, irrationalism over intellect, energy over fixity, soul or will over materialism, 'life force' over inherited forms. The French philosopher Henri Bergson, hugely influential in the prewar decade, coined the term *élan vital* as a tag for 'the inner force that cannot be rationally grasped or articulated, which thrusts its way into the empty and unknowable future, and moulds both biological growth and human activity'. Depending on context, vitalism was a banner for genuine innovation, a cloak for fear of technology, an alibi for egoism on the smallest (personal) or largest (collective) scale, and even a charter for racial hatred and killing.

For vitalists, action supplants virtue or utility as the measure of value. Action is not a substitute for knowledge but a higher mode of knowledge, soaring above the pedantry of investigation and research. From this angle, concepts are the enemy of understanding, because they separate us from the flow of sensations and intuitions that make up life's substance. Vitalism appealed to the anti-intellectual bent of intellectuals who already doubted the rationalist rules of their game. Trapped in the vast dynamics of nationalism, imperialism, militarism, industrialisation and commerce, and by the theories of natural evolution, human history and the unconscious mind discovered by Darwin, Marx and Freud, what room was left for individual reason and moral will? How should men not succumb to the dark currents running below Progress (justly called 'the political principle of the nineteenth century'), namely a gnawing sense of degeneration and impotence, merging fear of technology with fear of women? In hindsight, vitalism was a resistance movement, a late-romantic defence of the individual male and his solitary resources, a consolation after the 'death of God' in the mid-nineteenth century and before the birth of 'human rights' after 1945. For the vitalist vision is self-deifying, promising to restore mankind to his rightful place in the scheme of things, able to master all species and materials through mystical life-force.

The shrillness of military vitalist thinking around 1910 showed the urgency of the problem confronting the general staffs. Arguing that soldiers' morale was detachable from the quality of training, equipment and command, or the mere probability of survival, was a strange endeavour for the military mind. In this case, it was a resort adopted under great pressure. How else to reconcile the drastic improvements in defensive power since the American Civil War with the tactical necessity of infantry attacks? The staffs were well aware that modern weaponry had created what General Foch called a 'death zone' between armies. How could large numbers of men cross this zone intact? Before tanks and parachutes they had to use their legs, and before lightweight body armour they had no significant protection against bullets.

Frontal attack was the military expression of vitalist beliefs about nation and society. Denying the dominance of technology over the human spirit and boasting about the sovereignty of the will were axiomatic in vitalist thinking. And from a Social Darwinist perspective, victory *should* be costly. This doctrine was irresistible to commanders who needed to encourage their troops before operations that were likely to get them killed. Inspired by vitalist ideas, the generals could celebrate the offence as inherently superior to the defence and reassure their men that the enemy's advantages were trivial beside their own spiritual ascendancy. For the nation – weakened by modern urban living – must be ready for sacrifice in order to strengthen its moral fibre. This benefit would follow from the sacrifice; it did not depend on the soldiers' consciousness of why they had to lay down their lives. This helps to explain why the Supreme Command paid so little attention to the psychological welfare of the soldiers.

This neglect looks contradictory; if the soldiers' will could be eroded by defeatist propaganda, as Cadorna complained was happening, surely it could be built up by positive measures? Yet, if the soldiers were intended for sacrifice, why use up resources on educating and amusing them? Only after Caporetto would the penny drop: if the men did not understand, their motivation suffered. Vitalism also formed the mental background of the politicians who blocked aid packages to Italian prisoners of war. Captured men were not worth assisting; even if they had not betrayed the nation, they had let it down. The calculation that the benefit of discouraging potential deserters (by demonstrating the horrors of captivity) outweighed the prisoners' own rights, was premised on vitalist contempt.

Of all the prominent Italians discussed in this book, perhaps only two were immune to vitalism: the poet Rebora and the liberal leader Giolitti. Catholics inveighed against materialism and burned with contempt for the moral nullity of science, while reactionaries and Marxists alike preached faith in revolutionary action and the necessity of conflict for spiritual renewal or social progress. The compromises of parliamentary democracy were reviled. Perhaps Italian vitalism was the index of three volatile quantities: nationalist anxiety, territorial appetite, and military inefficiency. The reality of the unified kingdom – Giolitti's despised *Italietta* – felt to many Italians like a betrayal of Risorgimento dreams. Italy had lost in battle to Ethiopia and struggled with the tribes of Libya. Its industrialisation was half-baked; its per capita income was half that of Germany, Europe's other recently unified state, and one-third of Great Britain's; its cultural contribution to modern Europe was uncertain. No place, then, at the table of great powers. This situation seemed especially unjust to generations that grew up with the myth of a 'glorious minority' that had 'decided the destiny of Italy' by 'its own will'. With this achievement at their backs, those born since the 1870s felt that Italy's vitalist credentials were in better shape than other nations', and merited a leading role on the world stage.

The pressure of this background shapes the memoirs of veterans who could express their deeper assumptions. During failed offensives on the eastern Carso, Mario Puccini fantasised that the very vegetation 'did not want to become Italian'. Revisiting this location after it had been captured, he noticed the plants 'twisted, shorn, uprooted' by the fighting, and realised that 'if he only wants to, man can overcome any natural obstacle, however strong and stubborn it may be'. Vitalist ideas were palpable, too, in the army training manual, called *Military Life and Discipline*. Written in 1917 for use in military colleges, it is a primer of applied Social Darwinism. 'Outside the struggle there is only putrefaction, dissolution, death', wrote the author, an infantry lieutenant, for the benefit of teenaged cadets. 'The struggle is synonymous with life.' Combat and sacrifice are essential to the moral life and health of the state. In war, force must be disciplined if it is to be used effectively. This is why the army is the nation's school, its physical force, the test of its fitness for life, the cure for 'civic illiteracy'. All the 'individual wills which compose the army' must be unified 'under the supreme will of the commander'. What matters is action: 'faith in reality, in what we do: *activity*, that is our good'.

Looking back at Cadorna's prestige during the war, Carlo Sforza was caustic: 'The Italian middle classes wanted to believe that a harsh mask and hermetic silence were the sure signs of genius, and that brutality was energy.' The vogue for vitalism encouraged people to believe that a great commander has certain qualities of energy and will. Italy's supreme warlord must be great, therefore Cadorna possessed these qualities: youthful zest, tenacity, strength, manliness and decisiveness, but also modesty, goodness and simplicity. While he possessed some of these qualities in some degree, they recur so often in descriptions because the authors saw what they wanted to see. During the tragic last phase of the Eleventh Battle, Gatti was fascinated by Cadorna's self-possession: 'tranquil, serene, rested', the Supreme Commander appears happy. 'He speaks slowly, but is sure of himself: he sees nothing but his own thought. Everything that others say or do slides off Cadorna like waves off a rock. It leaves no trace. His energy is simple, primitive, infinite.' These were hallmarks of true greatness. When Luigi Barzini paid tribute to Cadorna's magical charisma, he took a cue from the generalissimo's own tract on tactics, which stated that a 'firm and indestructible will must descend from above to permeate and assiduously incite all levels of the hierarchy'.

Compared to the cult surrounding Mussolini in the 1920s and 1930s, Cadorna's was modest, even frugal. It is impossible to imagine Cadorna fondling lions for the camera or making his generals sprint in their parade uniforms, sabres and medals a-jangle. For stunts of that kind, D'Annunzio was the model. Cadorna's aristocratic hauteur, always with an air of *noblesse oblige*, was quite unlike Mussolini's chosen style. The Duce's charisma was crafted to maximise his communication with the masses, something that Cadorna did not have to do and would not stoop to attempt.

Still, there were seeds of the later cult in the earlier. If Cadorna was the first to be acclaimed as *Duce* or 'Leader', the second was D'Annunzio (as 'commandant' of the city-state of Fiume in 1919–20), and the last was Mussolini. The press promoted Cadorna as the nation's best champion, above political squabbling, indeed above politics as such, perhaps to fill a vacuum; for nobody in government could inspire people to sacrifice. Mussolini's energy, will, dedication, serene self-possession, virility, strength, decisiveness, simplicity, health, youth – and all the rest – dwarfed Cadorna's. For Fascism was the vitalist regime par excellence, enthroning energy as the gauge of political value and the pretext for what one of its most penetrating critics – writing, as it happens, within a stone's throw of the Isonzo – would call 'a permanent revolution, emancipating action from the principle of responsibility, exempting it from the embarrassing specificity of a *purpose*'.

The most startling form of cultural vitalism was Italian. This was Futurism, launched in 1909 by Filippo Tommaso Marinetti (1876–1944) as a campaign to promote new ways of writing poetry, liberated from rhyme and metre. Though he was a gifted writer, Marinetti's real talent was for publicity and provocation, using his private fortune to win huge exposure for events that would otherwise have gained little attention.

With Napoleonic self-confidence, Marinetti identified a tension in the cultural values of western Europe. Humanism and nationalism had promoted each other while keeping each other in check. An Italian patriot was supposed to take pride in Rome and Venice, Julius Caesar and Michelangelo. Marinetti cancelled the debt to humanism; condemning Venice as a sordid disgrace, he refused to venerate the great artistic achievements of the past. Denouncing tradition, museums, prudence, moderation and peace, the Futurists celebrated dynamism, energy, speed, novelty, mechanisation and violence, the last not so much as a political means, rather as an end in itself. 'We will glorify war – the world's only hygiene – militarism, patriotism, the destructive gesture of the freedom-bringer, beautiful ideas worth dying for, and scorn for women.' The last phrase was crucial: the Futurists mocked the fear of technology, but fear of women still lurked.

They claimed the Italian national character was innately attuned to life itself, *la vita*: flexible, quick, anti-intellectual, fiery, sensuous – all Futurist virtues. War was no mournful necessity; it was an incredible expression of energy, a source of renewal, the ultimate happening.[1] Futurist events were calculated to outrage and amuse. The flippancy of their declarations was part of a populist style; Marinetti realised that cultural statements can be snappy and accessible like newspaper headlines.

With his moustache, bowler hat and jaunty air, Marinetti looked like a music-hall impresario. Recruits had flocked to his banner and Futurism branched into painting, sculpture, discordant music ('the art of noises') and an architecture of 'fearless audacity'. In Futurist theory, every object has an 'interior force' that art should disclose. Seeking forms that could record or embody not fixed moments but dynamic sensations, they produced a few of the most memorable images of twentieth-century art. Bright canvases of charging cavalry, armoured trains, shattering detonations or crowded urban life, rendered with neo-impressionist techniques for splitting the spectrum into planes or dots of primary colour, rendering movement by 'velocity-lines' that trace motion through space; these have a permanent place in the great galleries of the world.

The Futurists spat on liberal ideals. According to Antonio Gramsci, the communist leader from Turin, they enjoyed a following among workers before the war. This esteem was not reciprocated. The Futurists proclaimed a contempt for ordinary people that pro-war politicians expressed by their decisions and generals by their tactics. 'Down with democracy!' was their refrain. For democracy was slow, middle-aged, the dismal kingdom of slaves. It was fit only for 'democretins', not free spirits. Freedom should be the preserve of an élite; it 'is only for those who know what to do with it and how to live it'. Elected chambers should be abolished: 'The time has come to finish with parliament. We did not need parliament in order to wage war. We shall know how to make peace without parliament.' The 'chamber of plotters, babblers and incompetents' should be replaced with a 'technical corps' that would know how to direct 'the corporation of the state'. It was a proto-fascist vision.

The Futurists have not lost their power to disturb. Their delight in the mayhem of war offends our conviction that violence must be abominated. We have confined that delight to the realm of simulation

1 The composer Stockhausen's scandalous comment on the destruction of New York's twin towers on 11 September 2001 – 'the greatest work of art imaginable for the whole cosmos' – was pure Marinetti.

and virtual fantasy – the violence of movies and computer games, or the vignettes of real but remote horror delivered by television. Marinetti and his friends proved their commitment in 1914, when they became red-hot interventionists, imploring a 'great fraternal sacrifice of all Italians', and raising the temperature of anti-German polemics (for the stolid, collectivised Germans were devoid of Futurist virtues). They were truly prophetic about war and technology; their monstrous vision matched the enormity of what was about to happen. The cartoonish terrorism of their rhetoric showed how difficult it was to escape from the sonorous clichés, genteel emotions and pasteboard décor of Italian culture. In the event, war reunited the Futurists with their old enemies under the banner of aggressive nationalism. Marinetti and D'Annunzio stood side by side, in uniform, despite their artistic differences.

For Marinetti, the war was 'the culminating and perfect synthesis of progress (aggressive velocity + violent simplification . . .)', and 'the most beautiful Futurist poem that has yet seen the light of day'. He became a fairly familiar figure along the Isonzo front; General Capello asked him to give pep talks to the Second Army before the Tenth Battle. What the men made of his 'violent Futurist speeches', as he proudly called them, declaiming poems called 'The Pope's Aeroplane' and 'The Song of the Pederasts', is not known, though a sardonic officer from Turin told an American Red Cross volunteer that Italy was famous for three things: 'D'Annunzio because he was immoral, Caruso because he was a bad singer, and Marinetti because he was mad'.

Mad or not, he was persona grata with the more intellectual commanders during the war, such as Capello. While he was the only top-flight commander to challenge Cadorna's tactics, and often showed better judgement of battlefield realities, Capello was banally conventional in his commitment to frontal offensives. 'Victory lies beyond the last trench' was a maxim that must have provoked inward groans among his men. He considered the average Italian soldier was 'too southern' to be 'spontaneously and voluntarily active', hence 'his spirit must be warmed to white heat'. Boasting about his own brute strength and 'splendid optimism', he liked to remind his officers that *his will* was *their fate.* (It was no less than the truth, but why rub it in?) He was notorious for devising an exhausting routine of exercises and fatigue duties for troops out of the line. One regiment was put to laying barbed wire, and suffered twice as many deaths during a week as during 40 days at the front. The commission of inquiry after Caporetto found that the Second Army troops often returned to the line in worse condition than they had left it. Capello wanted the men to look forward to returning to the front line. The main effect was something else: exhaustion and resentment, mounting into hatred.

On 22 April 1917, Marinetti lunched with Capello and his corps commanders. Badoglio ingratiated himself with the celebrity guest: 'I like your whole campaign against Italian "commemorative patriotism". I'm with you there. All our wars of independence from '48 to '70 only cost about 6,000 dead!' Capello interrupted: 'I had more than that at Oslavia', referring to a village near Gorizia, the site of ferocious fighting. Was the general's tone sorrowful, thoughtful or proud? Marinetti's diary does not say. Capello pounced on an officer for using the word 'hope'. 'What what what! What was that word?' Marinetti interjected helpfully: 'It was a passéist word.' Capello agreed: 'Yes, a passéist word. "Hope" indeed! I *want* victory, and it *will* be.'

For all the talk of ardour and will, battle turned out to provide above all 'an experience of supreme helplessness' for the front-line troops. This was an irony that patriotic vitalists could not afford to admit, even if they let themselves notice it.

The most troubling Futurist artwork is a small sculpture created just before the war by Umberto Boccioni (1882–1916). Ambitious, competitive, with a 'restless, aggressive mind', Boccioni wanted Italy to commit itself to 'ferocious conquest', and was arrested at an interventionist rally in Milan in September 1914, along with Marinetti. Once he set fire to an Austrian flag in a theatre, a favourite Futurist stunt. Called up in July 1915, he joined Marinetti, the Futurist musician Luigi Russolo, and the Futurist architect Antonio Sant'Elia in the Lombardy Battalion of Volunteer Cyclists, the only volunteer unit in the army. 'My Futurist ideals, my love of Italy, and my infinite pride in being Italian drive me irresistibly to do my duty.' He practised sculpting in dough when the mess sergeant allowed. The Futurists fought bravely, and Boccioni's diaries record keen exhilaration as well as hunger and cold at their posting high in the Trentino. 'The life we lead', he wrote, 'is a thrilling continuous effort of will.'

Returning to active service in summer 1916, after a long gap, was difficult. Weary, and missing his creative life, he wrote to a friend: 'Nothing is more terrible than art. . . . There is only art.' That, and the bathos of death. A proper Futurist extinction would come while storming a trench, atomised by a heavy calibre shell, or perhaps crushed by an armoured train. Instead, Boccioni, who had been assigned to an artillery regiment, died from injuries sustained after his horse shied at a car. He was not a skilled horseman and reacted to the creature's panic by digging his new shiny spurs into its flanks. It was an ironic end, nature's revenge on a champion of mechanistic beauty. If he had lived, he would have surely followed Marinetti into the Fascist Party.

Defiantly titled 'Unique Forms of Continuity in Space', like a laboratory specimen, Boccioni's sculpture is a male figure striding forward, superbly balanced, poised as he thrusts – an emblem of virile determination, needing no weapon because he himself is 'a living gun'. The angles and planes of his shoulders, spine, hips and thighs convey the tension of a coiled spring. While it recalls the French artist Millet's striding 'Sower' and nods to the Renaissance statue of the warrior Colleoni, and further back to the Winged Victory of Samothrace,[2] the figure's robotic smoothness and anonymity – its 'reproducibility' – are modern. The muscled hero strides forward in a nimbus of resolution, invisible currents flaming around his limbs, safe inside the force-field of his will. No wonder that the government of Silvio Berlusconi, bent on impressing the world with Italian vigour, put Boccioni's figure on one of the new Euro coins in 2002.

Boccioni modelled the piece in plaster; bronze casts were only made after his death. Even so, he knew it was his sculptural masterpiece, the closest he had come to conveying 'pure plastic rhythm'. Pure in form, however, rather than motive, for his figure is imbued with violent Futurist purpose. It has been compared with Marinetti's vision of a superman, a 'nonhuman and mechanical being, constructed for an omnipresent velocity . . . cruel, omniscient and combative . . . endowed with surprising organs adapted to the needs of a world of ceaseless shocks'. Boccioni's figure even has the protrusion 'in the form of a prow from the outward swell of the breastbone' that Marinetti foresaw as the evolutionary result of modern life.

Art historians praise its 'bursting vitality' and 'vital tension' for 'representing an epoch', 'the dynamic anxiety of our time'. This does not

---

2 The Futurists were obsessed with the headless statue of Nike, Greek goddess of victory, in the Louvre. Marinetti proclaimed that a racing car was more beautiful, and a plaster reproduction was smashed at the wedding feast of the painter Gino Severini. Were they disturbed because they could not reconcile her contemptible prestige as a cultural treasure with her splendid (Futuristic) attitude of surging and sensuous affirmation?

go far enough: Boccioni prefigured the infantry attack, not as it really would be, but as generals and intellectuals imagined it. The sculpture was only a year old when its posture began to be replicated by soldiers on the Western Front. In this sense, Boccioni's nameless, mutilated figure, storming unstoppably ahead, as if propelled by 'extreme resolution', was, in Nietzsche's phrase, born posthumously. And after all, had not Nietzsche himself ruled that 'the magnitude of an "advance" is even to be measured by the mass of things that had to be sacrificed to it'? In the First World War, the image of infantry as masses of 'things' was more than a metaphor. Father Gemelli, who had Cadorna's ear, argued in his influential studies that a 'good soldier' must lose his identity; for the price of complete obedience was depersonalisation, isolated from familiar bonds and affections. With hindsight, Gemelli's theory and Boccioni's figure anticipate the Fascist myth of a 'new Man', the 'soldier citizen' who would be stripped of 'individual autonomy and consciousness . . . trained to consider himself as a mere instrument of the State, and prepared to sacrifice his life for it.' Has a sculpture ever dramatised more memorably its creator's contempt for the 'brutalised and cowardly race' of ordinary people, the 'rabble whom we must lead into slavery'? Has an omen of the avant-garde ever been fulfilled on such a scale?

It is delightful that the best Italian critique of vitalism should be a comic novel, written in and about Trieste, the powder-keg city itself. Italo Svevo's masterpiece, *The Confessions of Zeno* (1923), recounts the decidedly unheroic adventures of a man who is inept, irresolute, unsuited to the battle of life, but generous, and truthful to the paradoxes of his nature, which is also ours. But Svevo wrote his novel in the war's aftermath. While researching this book, I found one solitary insight about vitalism written at the Italian front. It came from John Dos Passos, the future novelist. He came to Europe in 1916 as a Harvard graduate, naïvely intent on cultural tourism, then volunteered for the American Red Cross. After a few months of driving ambulances on the Western Front, he was transferred to Italy, arriving at the end of 1917. He spent seven months on the plain near Venice, watching the Italians strengthen their defensive line between Padua and the sea. The landscape was dreary in winter, its horizontal lines broken by rows of pollarded trees, 'black and gnarled in the mist'.

With little to do, time weighed heavily. The war seemed far away; distant gunfire rattled the windows of the café where he wrote letters.

Amid the monotony, an air raid was 'wonderfully exciting . . . the quiet sing song of an aeroplane overhead with all the guns in creation lighting out at it, and searchlights feeling their way across the sky like antennae, and the earthshaking snort of the bombs and the whimper of shrapnel pieces when they come down to patter on the roof.'

Dos Passos's letters and diaries are perceptive in a democratic American vein. The Italian officers' contempt for the other ranks outrages him; their 'overbearing nastiness to anyone they don't lick the boots of is disgusting'. Intrigued by the abstract motives and forces that bind people to the war, he is shocked by the power of nationalism with its 'patriotic cant'; it is 'the one thing that enslaves people more than any other to the servitude of war'. Near the end of his tour, he dropped a startling remark into a letter home: 'No I believe no more in the gospel of energy – One thing the last year has taught me has been to drop my old sentimentalising over action.' Among eyewitness accounts from the front, this is a sentence in a million. It took an American volunteer to notice something so fundamental about Italy's war.

TWENTY-ONE

Into a Cauldron

*If victory is long in coming, the men's weapons
will grow dull and their ardour will be
damped.*
SUN TZU

The Tenth Battle of the Isonzo

Boroević was certain that Cadorna wanted to attack again before the
end of 1916. He was right: an attack was planned for early December.
On the 7th, a break in the bad weather allowed the artillery to warm up.
But the winter soon closed in again and the infantry stood down.
(Someone joked that even the weather was Austrian.) According to
Cadorna, the troops in the Vipacco valley were drowning in mud. The
postponement would last five months. Minor actions flared here and
there as the Austrians tried to wrest back the territory they had lost
since August. Still, the front was relatively calm and sometimes
completely so. General Robertson was struck by the 'absolute quiet',
broken by an occasional rifle shot: 'a very different state of affairs from
what we were accustomed to on the Western Front'.

Meanwhile, much was happening across Europe that affected the
Italian war. Joffre hosted another inter-Allied conference in mid-
November, where the chiefs of staff agreed that the Allies' decisive blow
should involve combined offensives in May 1917. Cadorna's task was
to draw the maximum number of Austrian divisions away from the
Eastern Front. He was also asked to help the French and British by
sending more units to Albania and Salonika. This request was refused,
but he pledged to support an offensive in France.

Italy was again treated as capable at best of diversionary action. But
things were about to change for the better. When David Lloyd George
replaced Herbert Asquith as British prime minister in early December
1916, he was bent on carrying out what he would call a 'fundamental

reconstruction of Allied strategy on all fronts'. He planned to launch the process at a conference of Allied prime ministers, ministers of war, and chiefs of staff. In the first week of January 1917, the British and French prime ministers travelled to the conference in Rome by train from Paris. Lloyd George was nurturing a pet project with huge implications for the coming year's campaigns. He wanted Britain and France to lend the Italians so much artillery in the early part of the year, up to 400 medium and heavy guns, that Cadorna would retake the initiative on the Isonzo, capture Trieste, 'get astride the Istrian peninsula', and knock out the Austrian fleet. His logic ran like this: the events of 1916, including the bloodbaths on the Somme and at Verdun, had confirmed there was no prospect of breaking through on the Western Front, where both sides had massed their strongest forces. Yet the Allied military leaders were so obsessed with Flanders that they failed to realise how weak Germany's ally now was; Austria's subject nationalities were not whole-hearted about the war; and it was fighting alone against Italy. If the Italians could land a solid blow, their tottering enemy would have to transfer forces from the Eastern Front, weakening the Germans. This would strengthen the Allies everywhere. In the best of outcomes, the reinvigorated Italians would knock the Habsburg empire out of the war altogether.

While the cabinet agreed to let him float his idea in Rome, Lloyd George was well aware that the British and French military would resist any scheme that diminished the Western Front. The French were now committed to launching a vast offensive no later than April 1917. As conceived by the new French commander-in-chief, Robert Nivelle, who had recently replaced Joffre, this could produce a breakthrough that would cripple the Central Powers. Lloyd George, much taken by Nivelle, was ready to accept French leadership in a joint operational command, but Douglas Haig, the British commander-in-chief, bridled at playing second fiddle to 'a junior *foreign* commanding officer', as he complained to the cabinet.

Robertson was also travelling to Rome. Although he and Haig had their differences, they both deplored Lloyd George's attempts to find a way around the Western Front, and resented his loathing of the doctrine that cost so many lives for so little gain. They were convinced he was toying with public dismay at the scale of killing in Flanders, only pretending not to understand why the enemy must be attacked frontally, where he was strongest. At various times, after all, he had promoted the Balkans, the Eastern Front and the Middle East as alternative theatres. Now he was doing the same with Italy, and Robertson would have none of it. Sensibly, he neither trusted the Italian estimates of their own potential nor believed that Germany would let Austria-Hungary reach a separate peace with the Allies, regardless of how well the reinforced Italians might perform.

In this situation, Lloyd George might have been expected to exercise his legendary powers of persuasion on the French prime minister, Aristide Briand, and his minister of war during their hours on the train. He did nothing of the sort. He did not even show them his memorandum outlining Allied options for 1917. When the party reached Rome, he sent the cabinet secretary to brief Cadorna. But the canny Robertson got to him first.

When Lloyd George made his case, next day, the British and French generals' scepticism was deepened by the overdone praise of Cadorna. The French objected that lending batteries to Italy would jeopardise the Nivelle offensive, so Lloyd George promised that the 300 guns would 'absolutely' be returned in good time. When Cadorna's turn came to speak, he showed no enthusiasm. Guns that had to be returned in May were, he said, not worth having. Haughtily reluctant to plead his own cause, confused by the Anglo-French tensions, and anxious not to raise expectations, he ducked and quibbled. An onlooker who knew him quite well was Sir Rennell Rodd, Britain's ambassador to Rome. Watching Cadorna pass up a unique chance of substantial Allied support, Rodd reflected that it was a moment when character shapes outcome.

Undaunted, Lloyd George offered to let Cadorna keep the *British* guns for longer. This off-the-cuff contradiction of policy infuriated Robertson without reassuring Cadorna, who was haunted by the spectre of a second Austrian attack out of the Trentino, dismayed that the Allies would lend no troops, and troubled that he would have to attack, inviting German reprisals, without simultaneous offensives on other fronts. These were not negligible problems, yet another man would have sensed that nothing was to be gained by rubbing a would-be benefactor's nose in his own shortcomings. Lloyd George did not forgive Cadorna for squandering 'the most promising chance afforded to him to win a great triumph for his country'. Publicly, however, Italy's eligibility for military aid was on the table, and the Anglo-French commanders could not wish it off again.

Cadorna's sense of Austro-German intentions was sound. Conrad could be counted on to argue for a combined attack from the Trentino and across the Isonzo. In December 1916, he had won influential support from the chief of operations at the German Supreme Command. General Ludendorff, however, still rejected the idea. When Conrad raised it again in January, the Germans offered to discuss it after the next Allied offensive.

From Cadorna's point of view, the danger remained real and present. When the Germans shortened their line in France at the beginning of 1917, he worried that the spare troops would be sent in his direction, and sent urgent pleas to the Allies for 20 divisions plus artillery. Even Robertson conceded that contingency plans for Italy's defence should be prepared. When he visited the front at the end of March, he was dismayed by the makeshift condition of the defences; it was with a view to bolstering these, not to support an offensive, that planning began in April to move six British divisions to Italy by rail, to strengthen the rear lines around Padua. Also in April, ten British batteries of 6-inch howitzers were despatched to the Carso.

Lloyd George's argument in Rome is familiar to every scholar of British policy and planning in the war. What has not been clear is the source of his conviction that Italy held the key to a transformation of the war. Robertson decided the whole harebrained scheme was Lloyd George's invention, of a piece with his detestable 'indifference to military opinion on military matters'.[1]

There may be a missing link, in the form of Brigadier-General Charles Delmé-Radcliffe, who led the British Military Mission to the Italian army in the field. Contemptuous of politicians and desk-wallahs, arrogant and rude, jealous of his patch and well regarded by Victor Emanuel, Delmé-Radcliffe resembled the generalissimo himself. His quarrel with the British ambassador in Rome could have been modelled on Cadorna's feuds with any number of politicians. Long on gossip and short on crisp assessment, his communiqués to the highest levels of government perhaps baffled their recipients. What did Lloyd George make of the telegram of 26 December 1916, warning against alleged

---

1 Explaining this harsh judgement, Robertson added: 'For two years past he [Lloyd George] had repeatedly shown that he regarded British methods of making war as commonplace, costly, and ineffective.' Perhaps it took a field marshal to overlook so grandly the chance that readers might share Lloyd George's opinion.

anti-war elements in Rome, particularly 'the Caillaux–Giolitti–Tittoni intrigue'? Or his sideswipe at Sonnino's 'suspicious and bargaining nature, due perhaps to the Jewish blood in his veins'? Was Lloyd George impressed by expressions like 'the internal enemy' and the promotion of maximal Italian war aims? Whatever the answer, he surely approved Delmé-Radcliffe's perennial optimism about Italy's performance, putting the best spin on every setback, lobbying the Prince of Wales and Lord Northcliffe to support calls for Allied machine guns and artillery. 'I have no doubt that the second phase of the battle will produce even better results than the first phase', he reported to the War Office in late August 1917, just as the Italians were running out of steam in the Eleventh Battle; 'All the prospects on the Carso are also satisfactory', he added in the teeth of all evidence; 'The spirit of all the Italian troops is excellent' – an astonishing claim. He maintained that most Italians were strongly pro-war, and blamed 'this damned anti-war propaganda' for spreading defeatism.

Although they heartily detested each other, he and Ambassador Rodd saw eye to eye on the need to promote Italy's cause. Rodd suspected the British of undervaluing Italy's effort. Asquith, Kitchener and the Prince of Wales had all visited the Supreme Command, but something more was needed to catch the popular interest. As a well-connected mandarin with artistic interests, Rodd persuaded Arthur Conan Doyle, H. G. Wells, Rudyard Kipling and others to tour the front and pay tribute in articles and instant books. Wells opined that 'Italy is not merely fighting a first-class war in first-class fashion but she is doing a big, dangerous, generous and far-sighted thing in fighting at all.' Visiting in June 1916, before the Sixth Battle, the creator of Sherlock Holmes saw 'Trieste or death!' scrawled on walls all over northern Italy and had a close call with a shellburst. ('Had the Ostro-Boches dropped a high explosive upon us they would have had a good mixed bag.') Barred from the Carso, he went to Carnia instead, where the war was 'a most picturesque business'. Picturesque is the key word in British impressions, usually as part of a comparison with France and Flanders. Kipling was impressed by the feats of engineering in the mountains, as everyone was, and also by the generals he met: 'wide browed, bull-necked devils, lean narrow hook-nosed Romans – the whole original gallery with a new spirit behind it'. (Comparisons with ancient Romans came naturally to Englishmen with a classical education. Cadorna struck Conan Doyle as 'an old Roman, a man cast in the big simple mould of antiquity'.) He wrote five cheerleading essays for the *Daily Telegraph* and the *New York Tribune*. A sixth article, which mentioned that the Italians had sometimes oversold their military achievements, did not see print.

It was hard even for such prestigious writers to engage the British and American public, when all the Allied armies were making huge efforts amid terrible conditions. What might have caught the British imagination was resounding, unambiguous success on the battlefield. Gorizia was hardly enough. Such success was what Cadorna now set about preparing. He had lost 400,000 dead and wounded in 1916. Proportionally this was an improvement over 1915, but – leaving aside its impact on the survivors' morale – it left yawning gaps. No fewer than 151 new battalions were created, mostly in the infantry, bringing the total to 860. This was achieved by calling up classes back to 1873 and forward to 1898, while relaxing the entrance qualifications. By spring 1917, Italy had 59 divisions under arms; in all, there were nearly two million men at the front – some 200,000 more than in November 1916. In artillery, the army gained 52 new field batteries, 44 mountain batteries, and 166 heavy batteries. The number of medium and heavy guns doubled over the year to May 1917. (Even then, there were four times more Allied guns per kilometre of the Western Front than Italian guns on the Isonzo.) Trench mortars continued to arrive in large numbers. Even now, production of machine guns and shells lagged far behind needs; during the Tenth Battle, the siege artillery fired six rounds per gun per hour, contrasting with 30 rounds for British guns on the Western Front.

At the front, positions on the Carso and around Gorizia were strengthened. Mount Sabotino was turned into a battery, with dozens of guns hidden in the tunnel complex that the Austrians had excavated below the summit ridge. Sabotino faced Monte Santo across the Isonzo, still held by the Austrians, so the gunners on the two mountains could blast away like men o' war firing broadsides. The defensive lines in Trentino and the Asiago plateau were strengthened; by spring 1917, there were six lines on the plateau.

Politically, too, Cadorna shored up his position over the winter. By March, he had the cabinet eating out of his hand. Bissolati, his conversion complete, seemed infatuated by him. Another minister referred to him admiringly as *il Duce supremo*, the 'supreme Leader'. The problem of troop morale remained. The gloom that settled over the army towards the end of 1916 thickened like fog along the Isonzo valley, and little was done to identify its causes, let alone address them. As the army prepared for another winter, visitors noticed a sullen weariness at the front. A reduction in rations in December did nothing for the soldiers' spirits. The new year brought several worrying incidents where new recruits protested at the draft. Infantry shouted abuse at passing staff cars. When a journalist mentioned these omens to Cadorna, he waved them away. 'It is like that everywhere, and of course the soldiers are tired after two years.' A few serious cases of insubordination had been handled in the only proper way: by shooting the malefactors, 'to prevent sparks from becoming fires'. The Supreme Command was in denial, the press supported the Supreme Command, and the government was too distracted by its own weakness to challenge their combined version of events: that Italy was on the right track, making steady progress.

As before, the Supreme Command and the government worried that public morale would plummet when the soldiers came home for Christmas. In November, the Ministry of the Interior warned Italy's regional governors that 'subversive elements' might stir up discontent, and even incite men to desert or mutiny. In the event, many men's leave was cancelled due to anxiety over a possible Austrian attack from Trentino. The public mood was darkening, too, as people suffered the effects of Germany's submarine blockade of Allied shipping. Butter, sugar and petroleum were running low, rationing was introduced, and a crisis over wheat supplies in summer 1917 would lead to violent demonstrations. Civilian mortality rates climbed, as unheard-of numbers succumbed to malaria and tuberculosis. Nevertheless, the soldiers' and civilians' dedication to the struggle remained intact and was bolstered in early April, when the United States of America declared war on Germany. President Wilson had been forced off his neutralist fence by 'the gross misconduct of the Germans' in killing American citizens travelling on American and Allied ships. Ordinary Europeans could at last imagine that the war might end.

For the Austrians, the winter began with the death of the old emperor on 21 November. Like their fathers and their fathers' fathers, this generation of Habsburg soldiers had fought for that slim, impassive figure with his pendulous lip and muttonchop whiskers. Unchanging, utterly dependable, his Imperial and Royal Apostolic Majesty Franz

Josef had personified the empire. 'Uncle Joe' was as familiar to the Italians as to the Austrians. All of Italy's wars of independence had been fought against him. His mystique was irreplaceable, and its loss gradually revealed the empire as being, after all, a state like any other, and sillier than most.

His successor, Karl, nephew of the assassinated Archduke Franz Ferdinand, married to an Italian princess, realised that the empire was heading for disaster. Whether Austria-Hungary became a vassal of victorious Germany or disintegrated under the shock of defeat, it was probably doomed. His foreign minister, Count Czernin, warned that the army was on the brink of exhaustion, and popular despair might lead to proletarian revolution and national uprising, for the Habsburg Slavs were much affected by the unrest in Russia, which would soon lead to the first of the revolutions that brought down the Tsar.

Karl, an instinctive liberal, relaxed the severe controls on civilian life and marginalised the bellicose Conrad. Abroad, he explored whether he could extricate the empire from the war that threatened to destroy it. By chance, in the same month, December 1916, the German chancellor, Bethmann Hollweg, tried to forestall American intervention on the Allied side by proposing terms to discuss peace. Having crushed Romania, and as Russia was sucked into crisis, the German Supreme Command was in no mood for compromise. With the Kaiser's acquiescence, Ludendorff attached such tough conditions to the proposal that it became an ultimatum. The result was a minor coup for Allied propaganda.

A week later, President Wilson asked all parties to state their war aims. While Germany reiterated Bethmann Hollweg's hollow offer, the Allies began to talk about liberating the subject nations of the Habsburg empire – something that had never been a war aim. Alarmed, Karl made sure that the Allies were aware of his interest in a separate peace. Having ousted Conrad in March 1917, he let the Allies know that Austria sought peace on the basis of the restoration of Belgian and (on certain conditions) Serbian independence, and the award of Alsace-Lorraine to France.

French Prime Minister Alexandre Ribot was doubtful, while Lloyd George was intrigued. France and Britain had very few men in the field against Austria-Hungary; even so, they would benefit if Germany were alone on the Eastern Front. A bigger problem with Karl's initiative was its omission of any reference to Italy, for he opposed any concessions to the 'traitor', and argued that the Austrian élite would not accept them in any case. When the Allies said that Rome must be consulted, Karl's envoy explained that Austria would not give the Italians any territory that they had not conquered. Lloyd George demurred; the Italians should, he said, get the south Tyrol up to Bozen. The envoy wondered if they might not be offered a piece of south-eastern Anatolia instead.

On 19 April, with this crucial point unresolved, the British and French premiers met Sonnino in a railway carriage in the Alps, and – without showing him the emperor's letter – sounded him on the notion of a separate peace with Austria. Sonnino rejected requests for flexibility over the terms of the Treaty of London. Stubborn, 'hot-tempered and not easily soothed', harbouring 'vast ambitions for Italy, which he hoped to see realised as a result of the combined effort of all the Allies', he was not much liked in Paris and London. But he was respected; the Allies recognised that he had done more than anyone to bring Italy into the war on their side, and they knew he was the strongest figure in the government. Predictably, Sonnino now insisted that Italy's war aims necessitated the full defeat of the Central Powers; anything less would dishonour Italy's fallen. He did not comment on Lloyd George's suggestion that, with Austria out of the picture, Italy could concentrate on her aims in Asia Minor. Italy had gone to war for the 'unredeemed lands'; how could it make peace without liberating Trento and Trieste? He warned that Italy would be swept by revolution if the Allies reneged on their Adriatic pledges. While rejecting a separate peace, he pocketed the promise of territory in Anatolia and the port of Smyrna.

Karl's overtures did not recover from that encounter in the railway carriage. Back in London, digesting his second Italian snub since the start of the year, Lloyd George told the cabinet that Italy might be 'compelled' to accept an Allied agreement with Austria. He was reluctant to destroy Karl's illusion, just as he refused to give up the idea of supporting the Italians with guns. For now, however, Sonnino prevailed, at the price of confirming London's view that Italy's claims were 'unjust and unrealistic'.

When Cadorna learned about these feelers at the end of April 1917, he demanded assurances that nothing would prevent the army's 'imminent operations'. Boselli gave his word and urged Cadorna to make the next action 'decisive, in the sense that it virtually gives us Trieste'. By this time, the Eastern Front too had fallen quiet. Spinning in the vortex of revolution, Russia had lost its tsar in March. The offensive capacity of its army was dwindling fast, and the Central Powers stood back. Germany fuelled the fire with propaganda (telling the Russian soldiers that their government was against peace) and by helping Bolshevik exiles to return to Russia. (Lenin had reached St Petersburg three days before the secret summit in the Alps.) The prospect of Austrian divisions transferring to the Italian front, and the hope of inducing Cadorna to support their offensive in France, spurred the Allies to lend Cadorna 100 heavy guns.

Domestically, Austria was in dire straits. There had been food riots as early as 1915, and the harsh winter of 1916–17 aggravated shortages. Hunger was widespread; by March 1917, soldiers were volunteering for the front in order to get the better rations that were served in the line. Hungary supplied the army with grain, but not Austrian civilians. Economic conditions worsened; industrial output declined sharply over 1917. So many miners had been drafted that coal was in short supply.

The military picture was mixed. Romania had been subdued by the end of 1916, and Russia's internal crisis almost paralysed the Eastern Front. (A final botched offensive in the summer would finish off the Russian army.) On the Italian front, patches of territory around Gorizia were reclaimed in minor actions over the winter. The new defensive line down to Hermada was completed. Turning the Carso's geology to excellent account, the Austrians concealed billets, munitions and telephone wires deep in the limestone. The Imperial forces had taken 1,700,000 casualties during 1916, however, and there was no way to replace them. In the short term, transfers from Galicia could make up Boroević's shortfall, but they would not close the widening gap with the Italians.

On 1 February, General Nivelle visited Cadorna, seeking assurances that Italy would attack when the French and British offensive commenced in April. Cadorna, bristling at the Frenchman's careless reference to 'the hills' on the upper Isonzo, was not to be drawn. He still feared an Austrian attack out of Trentino.

Launched on 16 April, the Nivelle offensive went badly. Fielding 174 divisions, the Allies took almost 350,000 casualties before the operation was halted in mid-May. On 20 April, the French military attaché in Udine demanded that Cadorna must attack 'très instamment'. He was told that the offensive could not begin before early May. For the Italians had to transfer artillery from Trentino to the Isonzo, which could not be done until the Supreme Command was confident that the Austrians would not attack. In fact the Supreme Command had already assessed that this risk was acceptable, and detailed planning for the Tenth Battle was in hand. As Cadorna intended the next offensive to be decisive, it would be much more ambitious than the campaigns of autumn 1916. On the Carso, the Third Army would drive once again towards the Trstelj–Hermada line. Further north, three corps would target the heights behind Gorizia. General Capello, who was rehabilitated in March, would lead these corps. Cadorna had decided he could not do without Capello; he might be 'a rogue', but his energy and flair made him irreplaceable.

The Tenth Battle has to be understood in terms of ridges and summits. Mount San Gabriele, east of Gorizia, stands as an isolated summit. Monte Santo, further north, is the southern tip – and highest point – of a ridge that runs south-east for six or seven kilometres from Hill 383, above the Italian bridgehead at Plava. On its three other sides, Monte Santo falls away steeply. Italian shelling had reduced the church and monastery on its summit to ruins.

The battle would start on the Carso. After several days, the onus would switch to the 12 divisions under Capello's Gorizia Zone Command. Five days later, when Boroević had taken forces away from the Carso to strengthen the lines north of Gorizia, Capello would send 200 guns to the Carso, so that the Third Army could attack a depleted enemy. If Boroević did not take the bait, he would risk losing ground north of Gorizia, where the Austrians were vulnerable. The sole exceptions were Hill 383 above Plava and Monte Santo itself, both swathed with wire, riddled with caverns, and defended by batteries in the rear. Elsewhere, the trenches were shallow and discontinuous, and the positions exposed.

Capello proposed an audacious variation on this plan. He would attack across the river between Plava and Tolmein, creating a new bridgehead 10 kilometres north of Hill 383. The shortest route to Monte Santo lay southwards across arid highlands called the Bainsizza plateau.[2] Reasonably, Boroević had assumed that the Italians would not dedicate major resources to breaking onto the Bainsizza, which had

2 Given the pitch and roll of the gradients, the name 'plateau' is misleading (as it is for the 'Asiago plateau'). Mountainous by British standards, the Bainsizza was almost a trackless wilderness – there were no proper roads and very few paths. And it was almost waterless.

played no part in the war. If Capello could get substantial forces onto the Bainsizza, they would have several clear days to drive down behind Monte Santo and Mount San Gabriele, outflanking the Austrians all the way to the Vipacco valley. At the same time, he would attack the ridge between Plava and Monte Santo, east of the Isonzo. Secondary attacks would take place further south, between Gorizia and the Vipava valley.

As usual, Italian deserters were Boroević's best source of information. In early May, they swore that a major operation was imminent. Thanks to transfers from the Eastern Front, the Habsburg army on the Isonzo comprised 200,000 men in 215 battalions, with 1,700 machine guns and over 1,300 artillery pieces. Still outnumbered by roughly two to one, they were a ragtag force in some ways, with scrappy uniforms and worn-out weapons. Yet they were still disciplined and resolute, aware that any retreat on the Carso would threaten the empire and open the way to Italian conquest of the Slovene lands and Dalmatia.

The initial bombardment, when it started on 12 May, was more intense than anything the Austrians had seen before. With more than 3,000 guns, it was on a scale familiar in France and Flanders, and it built to a fearsome climax. Crossing into the Isonzo valley at dawn on the 14th, the Scottish Quaker volunteer George Barbour was struck by the contrast between the serenity of the Bainsizza plateau, stretching away in front of him, and 'this extraordinary strip of hell, right down 2,000 feet below like a volcanic rift in the ground, full of noise and black smoke with the silver stream of the river waggling like a snake in the underbrush'. Descending towards Plava,

... the road seems to be going straight down into a cauldron, screened alternately on left and right by wicker screens as it zigzags. At one point I stopped the car and looked down through a gap in the screening right down onto the nose of Monte Kuk which was having a heavy dose from the Italian large calibre guns, so that the [Austrian] trench line stood out as the base of a continuous smoking wall of dirty black fumes.

Zero hour followed at 12:00. By now, the mercurial Capello had been convinced by intelligence reports that a frontal assault on the ridge to Monte Santo held the key to glory. Five regiments were launched against the lone Habsburg battalion on Hill 383. Outnumbered by 15 to 1, the Austrians still inflicted 50 per cent casualties on the attackers before succumbing. Italian interdiction fire played a part: reinforcements could not reach the beleaguered defenders. A kilometre to the south, the Avellino Brigade crossed the Isonzo and wiped out the Dalmatian infantry of the 22nd Regiment. So violent were these clashes that the Avellino took 60 per cent casualties, losing 3,000 men.

The next summit along the ridge was Mount Kuk, a steep-sided cone with excellent sight-lines into the Isonzo valley. The Florence Brigade, edging up the hillside, was held at bay. Better results were achieved further south, on Monte Santo. After a devastating bombardment, involving the batteries hidden in the summit of Sabotino, the Austrians could not resist the Campobasso Brigade. The summit was taken but could not be held. For the next 24 hours, attackers and counter-attackers chased each other across the summit in increasingly ragged waves. As for the new bridgehead north of Kanal, Capello decided to spare only two battalions for this bold action. They crossed the river easily but could not penetrate the Bainsizza. There would be no flanking operation behind the Kuk–Vodice–Monte Santo ridge.

On the central Carso, the Duke of Aosta threw 60 battalions at the fortified line beyond the Vallone, aiming to deepen the salient that was carved out during the Ninth Battle. The Duke had dramatically increased the reserves, ready to exploit any success. But there was nothing to exploit. To their amazement, the Italians found they were outgunned on the central Carso. With their usual pinpoint accuracy, the Austrian batteries barred the way. Halfway through the second day, the Third Army's losses stood at 25,000 men. The offensive was scaled down.

At this point, the feeling at the Supreme Command was that Capello had made 'very slight progress' at a heavy price: 5,000 or 6,000 dead and wounded in three days. Cadorna was rattled. He had not expected such fierce resistance. Accusations were flung around, and heads rolled. In keeping with his original plan, Cadorna was minded to halt operations on the middle Isonzo and bolster the Third Army with mobile batteries. Capello promised that if he could keep the 200 medium and heavy guns, he would capture Vodice and Monte Santo. Cadorna let himself be talked around. As soon as Monte Santo had fallen, the guns would be sent to the Third Army.

Capello's flaws were on a scale with his talent. By letting him sweep aside the sober assessment of tactical realities, Cadorna reduced the prospects of a breakthrough on the Carso. For a couple of days, Capello made impressive progress. Kuk fell on the 17th. Fresh forces attacked the line below Mount Vodice, the last peak before Monte Santo itself.

On the 18th, several Italian divisions attacked a few thousand Austrians, remnants of various regiments. The Italians were separated from the summit ridge by 250 metres of open ground, with rudimentary defences – no wire or foxholes – but enfiladed by machine guns. Despite immense losses, they pushed the Polish militiamen off the summit in the late afternoon. There was no breakthrough, however: the Italians were stopped on the ridge, unable to push down its eastern flank. At the same time, Capello's secondary action – further south, along the six-kilometre front between Monte Santo and the Vipava valley – came to nothing. He had hoped that surprise would compensate for the lack of artillery preparation or support. Predictably, the Italians were driven back with heavy losses.

Early on the 20th, Capello's artillery opened up against Monte Santo. Ten or twelve waves of infantry were flung uphill. Eventually the Italians overran the summit, only to be forced back yet again by a counter-attack. Vodice had fallen at last, but efforts to proceed along the ridge to Monte Santo were unavailing. With the men back in their jumping-off line, Capello called a halt, judging that exhaustion had cancelled the advantage of numbers.

A price was paid for rewriting the battle plan. For Cadorna's original gambit had succeeded. Boroević reacted to the preparatory bombardment on the middle Isonzo by correctly suspecting a diversion from the Carso. When the infantry attacked the Kuk–Monte Santo ridge on the 14th and 15th, however, he changed his mind and rushed five divisions up to the ridge and the Bainsizza plateau. By 18 May, the Austrian force on the central Carso was cut to a single division. But the Third Army was unable to take advantage; it sat on its hands while Capello failed to capture Monte Santo.

On the 23rd, the Third Army batteries belatedly opened the second phase of the battle. Although still lacking those 200 extra guns, the shelling was fiercer than anything before on the Carso. Supported from the air and by floating batteries at the mouth of the Isonzo, the infantry's surprise attacks on the 24th and 25th widened the salient, rolling over three Austrian lines to capture a band of territory two kilometres deep from the central Carso to the sea. The Austrians melted away in front of the Italian right. Habsburg prisoners reported a crisis of morale, yet the Austrians did not buckle. The Third Army was still several kilometres from the Hermada–Trstelj line, but real progress had been made. By the 26th, Boroević was moving units south from Gorizia to contain the Italian thrust. A few extra regiments were transferred from the Tyrol, and the Germans allowed the Austrian high command to transfer two more divisions from the Eastern Front. Meanwhile the Italians ran out of energy and resolve, and almost out of shells, just when the enemy was at the point of collapse.

The Austrians would, though, have the last word. On 4 June, Boroević used his reinforcements from the East to launch surprise attacks north of Hermada, regaining some of the ground lost to the Third Army. The Italian losses were huge: 22,000 men, including 10,000 prisoners. Rumour had it that three regiments had surrendered without fighting, complete with their officers and equipment. Cadorna railed at the treachery of men who chose surrender rather than death. Privately, he wished he could ask Boroević to have them flogged. Officially, he wrote a furious letter to Prime Minister Boselli, blaming the government for laxity towards domestic opponents of the war.[3] After three weeks, the Italians had taken more than 150,000 casualties, including 36,000 killed. The Austrians had only 7,300 killed.

One of the last operations in the Tenth Battle took place on 28 May, near a tiny place called San Giovanni, on the coast road to Trieste. A church in a grove of trees, a few houses, a war memorial: if you blink, you miss it. Below the road, Italy's shortest river surges from under a limestone cliff. This is the Timavo: green, glassy, gelid, some thirty metres across and scarcely a couple of kilometres long, but deep.

The advance since 24 May had stalled here. Inland, the Austrians held firm on the Hermada massif. Ahead, the way was blocked by Hill 28, a thinly wooded knoll on the coast. A battalion of the 77th Infantry, the 'Tuscan Wolves', would cross the river on plank bridges below Hill 28 and capture it. A detachment would then cross two kilometres of low, open ground to the cliff-top village of Duino and hoist a huge Italian flag on the castle ramparts. The Italians of Trieste would take heart while the Austrians lost it.

The chances of success were negligible. The ground on both sides of the Timavo was a dreary marsh, with no tree cover. It would be impossible to infiltrate enough men across a plank bridge, under fire,

---

3 A full account of these surrenders did not appear until 1938. Even after their line was broken and they were encircled from the rear, the Italians had 'fought well until their generals were killed and they were completely cut off'.

quickly enough to reach the target. Even if by a double miracle the Italians took the hill and reached Duino castle, their flag would have been invisible from Trieste, nearly 20 kilometres away.

This ridiculous plan was partly conceived by a 54-year-old captain in the Novara Lancers. This was Gabriele D'Annunzio, Italy's celebrity bard and all-round decadent. Sharing the Futurists' fascination with aeroplanes, he had made daring flights over Austrian territory. He also milked events for personal publicity, lobbying far and wide for medals. He admired Cadorna, composing odes in his honour. Unofficially, many in the army found him comical and even hateful.

For this operation D'Annunzio was adjutant to the battalion commander, a Major Randaccio. The poet's diary is thick with omens. The weather is overcast, threatening rain. The men are exhausted after 'suffering and fighting for 24 days!' Only one of the planned bridges has been constructed: a line of planks 40 centimetres wide lashed to oil drums, with no handrail or cable. Observers have spotted barbed wire and snares on the objective. The 'enormous difficulties' have disheartened Randaccio: 'He does not seem to have much faith. I comfort him.' Rumours that the operation may be postponed send D'Annunzio hurrying to the high command, where he gains instant access to the Duke of Aosta, and authorisation to proceed.

Back at the Timavo, he can see the lightning conductor on the castle of Duino. The river fascinates him, and he is thrilled to see soldiers washing where mythical Castor or Pollux once watered a white horse. He is woken at a quarter to midnight from a delicious dream of his lover's breasts. (She is a Triestine lady, installed in Venice with complaisant husband.) Off in single file to the riverbank, with the poet carrying the flag. A small force manages to cross the planks under fire and some men reach the hilltop but cannot secure it. Randaccio sends for reinforcements which, as ever, are lacking. Austrian machine gunners concealed on the hillside enfilade the riverbank and bridge.

When the remaining troops on the riverbank see what they are expected to do, forty of them mutiny. Tying white shirts to their bayonets, they shout back at the officers who call them cowards. 'We don't want to be led to the slaughter!' 'Even the men who were taken prisoner write that it's fine in Austria!' The men who reached the hilltop are surrendering. Randaccio orders a retreat. Men stagger back across the planks, under fire. Some fall into the water. D'Annunzio, who apparently has not crossed though the official bulletin will say otherwise, helps them to clamber out. Randaccio is badly wounded; the poet pillows his bleeding head on the flag.

The survivors' sullen faces make D'Annunzio wonder if these 'traitors' will shoot him. Consoled by the certainty that any Italian blade or bullet will turn into diamond the moment it pierces his heart or shatters his brow, he is determined to punish the renegades. For he is convinced the objective could have been held if only 'a small unit of *real men*' had got there. So he orders the nearest battery to fire on the column of Italian prisoners across the river. Later, he notes that 'battle leaves in the sensual man a melancholy similar to that following great pleasure'. The infantry feel sad as well, though in a different way. The impact of this fiasco on their morale can be gauged from the fact that 800 officers and men of the Puglie Brigade surrendered on the Timavo later on the 29th, complete with rifles and knapsacks.

D'Annunzio alone profited from the operation, futile even by Cadorna's standards: a miniature version and indictment of the great offensives that had cost half a million casualties. For D'Annunzio was a propagandist more than a soldier, and propaganda is a realm where gesture is substance and words are deeds. The Timavo operation was a gesture, and in his terms it succeeded brilliantly, culminating beside Randaccio's grave in Aquileia, where the poet gave an oration that launched the major's posthumous career as a legend. The Duke of Aosta had copies of the speech distributed to the men of the Third Army.

Randaccio fulfilled the poet's criteria of heroism: leading a 'heroic' action, dying in the attempt, then depending on the poet for transfiguration. On his deathbed, Randaccio begged for the capsule of poison that he knew the poet always carried into battle. He asked three times and was, biblically, thrice refused. Why? D'Annunzio explained in his funeral oration: 'It was necessary that he suffered so that his life could become sublime in the immortality of death.' Legend also required a final, ruthless illusion; D'Annunzio swore to the dying man that Hill 28 had been taken and held, making Randaccio 'the victor'. For a loser to die in battle was merely banal; for a winner to do so, on the other hand, was 'beautiful'. His reported last words, inevitably, were '*Viva l'Italia.*'

The action was written up rapturously in the official bulletin, which stated that the 'audacious few' were ordered to retreat on the brink of achieving their objective, despite 'the violent storm of bullets'.

Surprisingly, D'Annunzio's biographers make little of this episode, even the boast about firing at his own men. Maybe they suspect he made it up, though he had the rank to do it and was vicious enough. It would, also, have been fully in keeping with Cadorna's notion of military discipline.[4] Perhaps he invented Randaccio's deathbed scene. What he did not fabricate was the pointless slaughter of the men of the 77th Infantry. Yet the poet's irresponsibility pales beside that of the Duke of Aosta and the Supreme Command, seduced out of thought by charisma, whether Capello's blustery vitalism or D'Annunzio's flattering glamour.

A greatly outnumbered and completely multiethnic Habsburg force – comprising Dalmatians, Ruthenes, German Austrians, Hungarians, Romanians, Czechs and Poles – had repulsed the biggest Italian attack yet mounted. Austrian artillery fire was still accurate and effective against regiments that still advanced slowly over difficult terrain, in compact masses. The Austrians, by contrast, used highly mobile assault forces, which proved their worth during counter-attacks.

Following events from his cell, the implacable Colonel Douhet concluded that the Tenth Battle had failed to achieve a single strategic goal. Gorizia had not been secured, key objectives on the Carso or the coast had not been captured and the Hermada massif had not been touched, let alone conquered. More surprisingly, this bleak judgement was echoed at the highest level of command. The Duke of Aosta, leading the Third Army, cut an imposing figure. Tall, handsome, melancholy, he was not given to airing controversial views or large conceptions. The bright young things around Cadorna at the Supreme Command thought he was diffident and dull-witted. Colonel Gatti, the brightest of the bright, liked him but judged him 'uncultured' because his grammar was faulty.

When the two men met on the evening of 26 May, Gatti was startled to hear the Duke say that, while the battle had gone well, at this rate it

---

4 Among the documented cases of a corps firing on its own men, the most notorious involved a company of the Salerno Brigade. On 1 July 1916, this company was caught in no-man's land after repulsing an Austrian attack above the Isonzo. Pinned down by machine guns, more than 200 men were unable to move or be helped, even at night. After a couple of days, voices in the Italian front line shouted that the men should surrender to save themselves. When some of the survivors crawled towards enemy lines, the corps commander carried out to the letter Cadorna's directive of September 1915, ordering machine-gun and artillery fire against the deserters.

would take more than ten years to win the war. Final victory could only come by crushing the Central Powers, which would always recover from smaller defeats. But how could this be achieved? People had had enough of the war; at some point they would rebel. The Allies could not be expected to give more help. The army would press ahead, taking bits of territory here and there, until the peoples of the warring states cried 'Enough!'

He is absolutely right, Gatti thought. *There is no military solution. American intervention may make a difference, but who knows when?* This hopeless vista was widely shared. The mood on the Isonzo front was resigned, or worse. The journalist Rino Alessi wrote to his editor on 6 June that the troops seemed 'depressed beyond measure'. Gatti was haunted by something the commander of the 120th Infantry told him at the end of the battle. 'They did not rebel: when they were pushed out of the trenches, they went; but they wept.' *Something new is starting to appear,* Gatti reflected in his diary, *something that was not there at the beginning of spring.* The Tenth Battle had knocked the stuffing out of the army. *It might carry on like this for months or years, just like – so they say – in Germany and Austria, where each illusion of victory has yielded to the next, down to the present day.* Or it might not. He wondered if the Italians were still paying for Cadorna's original decision not to attack the Tyrol in 1915. For the Tenth Battle had involved fewer than half the Italian divisions: '149 splendid battalions and 500 guns' remained in Trentino.

The Tenth Battle had a codicil elsewhere, far from the Carso. The Austrian counter-attack around Hermada in early May led Cadorna to bring forward a long-planned offensive on the Asiago plateau. After the failure of the Punishment Expedition in 1916, the Austrians had not been driven off the plateau. In fact, they re-created their strategic advantage on the Isonzo, by holding firm on a chain of hills that bisected the plateau. The northern end of this chain overlooks the Sugana valley, like the gable end of a house that towers 2,000 metres high. This is Ortigara, a wilderness as rocky as the Carso but steeper, and with even better sight-lines onto the approaches.

Cadorna's first assault, in November 1916, had come to nothing. Now he resolved to overwhelm the Austrians with sheer weight of shells and men. A new force was created for this purpose, the Sixth Army, under General Mambretti. Eventually the date of 20 June was set; Mambretti would have 200,000 men with 100,000 reserves. When the Austrians counter-attacked on the Carso, the attack was brought forward to 9 June. On the 7th, the weather turned: summer storms lashed the plateau. The following day, a mine under the Austrian front line exploded a day early, killing 130 Italians. By this point, the Austrian action on the Carso had petered out, so Mambretti could have reverted to his original timetable. Instead he attacked on the 10th. The target was a chain of four peaks that had to be approached over open, steep terrain.

It was a catastrophe: Italy's equivalent of the first day on the Somme. Low cloud cover meant that Italy's 430 guns and 220 mortars could not target the enemy wire. The general commanding the division directly below Ortigara realised the implications, and asked permission to delay the assault. This was refused by Mambretti, who was unaware that, as on the Carso, the Austrians had abandoned their trenches and excavated deep caverns for men and artillery, often three metres under the surface. The Austrian gunners on the adjacent summits had excellent sight of the Italian positions and the ground where the Sixth Army had to pass.

At 15:00 hours the men of 52nd and 29th Divisions went over the top. Torrential rain had turned the mountainsides to quagmires. The effect was like flypaper: the infantry were trapped under the machine guns, in front of intact wire. Some battalions took 70 per cent losses. After three waves of attack, progress was made elsewhere on the line, at immense cost. The survivors spent the night on the mountainside, trapped in front of the wire, pressing their bodies into the gaps between boulders, playing dead under Austrian flares, waiting for the order to retreat. No order came. Next day the clouds closed in again, and rain turned to snow on the heights. Cadorna arrived after lunch with his entourage, fresh from their hotel. Even Gatti was incredulous: 'He is perfectly calm, serene, even smiling. He discusses the fighting yesterday with Mambretti as if everything had gone splendidly.' The two men agree that yesterday's little difficulties will be investigated. If they can be overcome, the offensive will be re-launched. The men stay on the mountainside for eight days. When the skies clear on 18 June, the artillery opens up and the infantry attack again, with air support from Caproni bombers. That afternoon the clouds return. Next day, men of the 52nd Division hack their way to the summit of Ortigara with daggers and bayonets, capturing a thousand prisoners and several guns. They hang on until the 25th, resisting bombardments and counter-attacks, until stormtroopers sweep them off with gas and flame-throwers. The Austrians repeat their success elsewhere on the line. On the evening of the 29th, Mambretti orders a withdrawal to the original positions. The Italians have taken at least 25,000 casualties over the 19 days of the battle, on a front of three kilometres, for no gains whatever.

A captain in the Alpini, Paolo Monelli, recalled that when the last enemy bombardment stopped,

. . . a vast silence spreads . . . Then groans from the wounded. Then silence once more. And the mountain is infinitely taciturn, like a dead world, with its snowfields soiled, the shell-craters, the burnt pines. But the breath of battle wafts over all – a stench of excrement and dead bodies.

The Supreme Command blurred the scale of the disaster, calling in favours from journalists to help conceal the casualties and withholding an internal report from the government. Despite privately admitting that it had been a 'proper fiasco', Cadorna's analysis was predictably coarse. The infantry, he complained, did not attack as they should have done, they had no faith, they were indecisive, they lacked 'dash', the famous *slancio*.

This same infantry would supply the battle's most durable legacy, in the form of trench songs:

> Battalion of all the dead,
> We swear to save Italy . . .

> When the battalion goes back to the valley,
> there will be no soldiers left . . .

At the end of the century, still an emblem of pointless carnage, Ortigara inspired a new anti-war song:

> My granddad went to Ortigara,
> Nineteen years old, in Alpino green . . .

TWENTY-TWO

Mystical Sadism

The power of punishment is to silence, not to confute.
SAMUEL JOHNSON (1709–84)

Summary Justice in Cadorna's Army

By July 1917, the Catanzaro Brigade was brittle with exhaustion. The southern peasants who made up the 141st and 142nd Infantry had fought on the Carso and the Asiago plateau for two years, taking heavy casualties. Many men had not received a fortnight's leave since the winter of 1915–16. Rations were bad and scanty. Bloody losses on Mount Hermada at the end of the Tenth Battle left the survivors depressed and desperate for rest.

After more than forty days at the front, the brigade was relieved and sent to the village of Santa Maria la Longa, a logistics base of the Third Army. Word had it that the Catanzaro would be sent to Carnia or the Dolomites – mountain sectors, relatively quiet after the Carso. Instead, it was ordered back to Hermada after a few days. Furious muttering in the barracks tipped into open revolt, involving both regiments but centred on 6th Company of the 142nd Infantry. Shots were fired. The mutiny was contained with cavalry, armoured cars and light field artillery, despatched by Third Army headquarters. Even so, eleven men died, including two officers. A third officer had a lucky escape, for, according to one version of events, a band of rebels went to a nearby villa where they thought Gabriele D'Annunzio was staying, crying 'Death to D'Annunzio!' Luckily for himself, the poet was staying at a nearby airfield, preparing a bombing raid over Istria.

Next day, 28 men were charged with rebellion and executed on the spot. Of these, 12 were chosen by lot from 6th Company. Another 123 were sent for court martial. It was not the brigade's first clash with military justice, but it was by far the worst. Historians describe the episode at Santa Maria as the only real mutiny in the Italian army throughout the war. D'Annunzio hurried back to witness the executions. The men were lined against a cemetery wall beside a field of maize, chanting a hymn or prayer. Nettles grew by the wall. 'Sultry heat. Skylarks singing.' Short, dark-skinned, the men come from Campania, Calabria, Puglia and Sicily. The poet looks away as their bodies slump to the ground. His notes include no emotional response, merely details after the event: 'helmets, shreds of brain swarming with flies, and dried rivulets of blood'. Writing up the experience later, he addresses the dead men: 'You are peasants. I know you by your hands. I know you by your way of planting your feet on the earth. I do not want to know if you were innocent or guilty. I know you were valiant, I know you were true.' Like Major Randaccio, they are sublimated by extinction.

D'Annunzio's indifference to the men's innocence or guilt was in Cadorna's own spirit. What mattered was the deterrent effect. Other commanders-in-chief during the First World War shared this instrumental view of military justice. They, too, were angry when the penal code hindered the swift application of extreme measures, especially against deserters. What set Cadorna apart was his assumption that he was entitled to adapt the justice system to his convenience.

The Supreme Command's directives on discipline passed from severity to depravity. Cadorna's first directive to the army, on 19 May 1915, was wholly concerned with discipline. Order, authority and obedience would be maintained with indestructible firmness. Unit commanders would be held responsible if they hesitated to apply 'extreme measures of coercion and repression'. The implied threat of summary execution became explicit in a September directive. 'The summary justice of the bullet' awaited anyone who tried to surrender or retreat, instead of 'taking the way of honour that leads to victory or death'. Whoever escaped this 'salutary justice' would face court martial, then execution in front of their comrades.

Within a few months, Cadorna had the court-martial system in his sights. He openly deplored the courts' reluctance to pass capital sentences, and called for maximum severity. The Justice Department at the Supreme Command followed up with a statement that proper courts martial should only be convened if they were sure to pass severe sentences. Otherwise, improvised tribunals in the field would suffice, with no requirement for a military magistrate to take part, and sentences that could not be appealed

The crisis caused by Conrad's attack in spring 1916 hardened Cadorna's views still further. On 26 May, as the Austrians poured across the Asiago plateau, an infantry regiment was routed. When several hundred men failed to regroup, Cadorna urged the immediate execution of any soldier whose actions were 'unworthy of an army that upholds the cult of military honour', regardless of rank. The letter was given the widest circulation. When the missing men crept back to their position next day, the colonel commanding the regiment chose 12 members of the company by lot and had them shot for desertion. For this achievement he was mentioned in the daily bulletin – the first officer singled out for this honour. It was the first documented case of *decimation*, a punishment that became the dreadful emblem of Italian military justice. Historically, decimation was the Roman practice of killing every tenth member of a mutinous legion. When Cadorna revived the ancient term, he did not insist on this ratio. What mattered was the procedure of pulling names out of a helmet or knapsack, practically guaranteeing that innocent men would die. This, the most unacceptable element of decimation, was the one that Cadorna most prized. When the soldiers realised that they could be murdered randomly, regardless of their individual actions, if their unit offended their commanding officer, they would be terrified into complete obedience.

This was Cadorna's theory, presented with his usual candour in a letter to Salandra in January 1916, regretting that the military penal code did not authorise decimation to punish serious collective offences. After the mass desertions at the end of the Tenth Battle, he complained to Boselli that this punishment had been 'irresponsibly' deleted from the penal code. In fact, decimation had never been mentioned in the code. He took it on himself to authorise this 'supreme act of repression': a November 1916 directive stated that commanding officers had the duty to decimate guilty units. This caused a commotion that rippled as far as Rome; Cadorna wrote to Boselli on 20 November, protesting that all armies practised decimation. This was false. While the drawing of straws was not unknown in the French army, especially in putting down the 1917 mutinies, and may well have occurred in other armies as well, only in Italy did the commander-in-chief *urge* this punishment.

1917 was the year of decimation. In March, nine men of the Ravenna Brigade were chosen for execution after their regiment protested over the cancellation of leave. More is known about this atrocity than most others because the brigade commander's aide de camp (ADC) gave a statement to the commission of inquiry set up after Caporetto. Deployed on a notorious sector of the Carso, the brigade's two regiments alternated their front-line tours with fatigue and labour duties in the rear. To keep up their spirits, the men were promised perks in the form of extra leave, which never materialised. When one of the regiments was ordered to relieve another unit elsewhere on the Carso, 'there was a moment of discontent' in one battalion, whose men had been drinking. The battalion commander informed the brigade head-quarters 'as a matter of duty, but more to offload the responsibility'. The general commanding the Ravenna Brigade hurried to the battalion barracks. 'We found the men a bit annoyed, tired, and almost all in dreadful physical condition, officers included.'

The CO and his ADC let the men air their grievances. For the most part they were amenable to reason, but a few shots were fired in the air. This prompted the ADC to telephone division HQ, which despatched 'lots of carabinieri'. While the men calmed down and set off for their new posting, Division HQ sent staff officers to the spot and informed the corps commander, who telephoned the brigade ADC and thundered that the barracks should be burned to the ground and the offenders shot. The ADC tried to assure him that order had already been restored.

The divisional CO now got involved, presumably to cover himself vis-à-vis the corps commander. By the time he reached the barracks, they were empty; it was late at night and raining hard. The brigade CO reported that everything was in order and the troops were on their way to their new posting. 'How many did you shoot?' asked the divisional CO. 'None,' came the answer. 'That's bad, very bad!' exclaimed the divisional CO. Then the carabinieri found two soldiers asleep in the barracks. They had no idea that their company had left, nobody had woken them. The brigade CO told the carabinieri to put the men up against a wall and shoot them. One of the soldiers howled so desperately ('What have I done to make you shoot me? I've got seven children!') that the carabinieri hesitated. The divisional CO spoke up: 'Let us be done with this jabbering. Shoot them at once. Orders are orders.'

The brigade CO was relieved the following day. The corps commander ordered 20 soldiers to be picked by lot from the most rebellious company. Five of these men were selected for execution. This process presumably doubled the agony of those compelled to take part, and therefore also – in the corps commander's view – the salutary deterrent effect. The firing squad shook so badly that six volleys were needed to finish the job. The ADC told the incoming brigade CO that the measures taken 'seemed a little exaggerated', and had shattered the men's morale. 'The soldiers trembled at the mere sight of me.'

A fortnight later the Ravenna Brigade was transferred to the middle Isonzo, near Gorizia. To his astonishment, the ADC was called in to divisional HQ along with his new CO and told that he would be a member in a court martial of nine men involved in the rebellion. ('What!, I thought, won't you let it drop?') Before the court martial convened, the corps commander urged severity. The brigade commander's reaction was terse: 'That's easily said. We each of us have a conscience.' Charged with reluctance (not refusal) to take up their new position, the men could not defend themselves because the court martial required no proof either way. According to the ADC, 'nothing was established'. The prosecution called no witnesses. One defendant was a corporal who had fought in Libya, volunteered in 1915, and already been acquitted on similar charges over a different episode. His bearing impressed the court, which nonetheless sentenced him to death along with three infantrymen. The others were given ten years in prison. Refusing a blindfold, the corporal urged the firing squad to 'Aim at the breast, and always serve your country. Long live Italy!' The brigade commander muttered in distress that he should have been promoted to colonel, not shot as a criminal.

The bloodletting was not over. The corps commander now ruled that all those men who had received capital sentences for desertion – due to returning late from leave – should be executed, as it would be wrong to show clemency when the brigade was 'disturbed'. Consequently another 18 men were shot. The brigade commander reported that the entire brigade felt terrorised; it should be sent out of the line for a spell. The corps commander refused; if the measures taken did not restore discipline, he would take others. The brigade commander – 'perhaps more concerned for his career than anything else', as the ADC boldly remarked to the commission – raised no further objection.

A total of 29 men died to punish a minor rebellion in one battalion that lasted a few hours, causing no casualties. To put this in perspective, consider the French reaction to the widespread mutinies in spring 1917, following the Nivelle Offensive. More than 30,000 soldiers were caught up in the mutinies, which were for the most part peaceful protests, with unarmed soldiers chanting their refusal to return to the trenches. Even in the most mutinous division, the 5th, officers were 'almost universally treated with respect (probably because they returned the compliment)'. The contrast with the Italian case could not be clearer. Nivelle blamed pacifist propaganda, just as Cadorna had done in Italy, and with as little basis. The French reaction did not, however, involve a ruthless crackdown. While the ringleaders were court-martialled, careful efforts were made to rebuild the relationship between officers and men. In this way, discipline was restored before the capital sentences were carried out. Courts martial sentenced 554 mutineers to death, of whom 49 were executed. Records indicate that only three summary executions occurred during the turbulence – an official figure that is not much disputed. Given that fully half the French divisions were affected, this was an impressively low number. The Italians, on the other hand, shot 54 men in May 1917 alone, not counting 'numerous' summary executions, for infractions that were almost certainly less grave.

The monstrous treatment of the Ravenna Brigade says much about military justice in the 'war zone', a jurisdiction which eventually included most of northern Italy and much of central and southern Italy too, where the army had legislative as well as judicial power. From battalion to brigade, then up to division and corps, the commanding officers were governed by fear of seeming lenient. Otherwise the matter would have rested with the battalion commander or, at most, the general commanding the brigade. In a hierarchy that respected its own penal code, few if any of the 29 victims would have been put to death. At no point did the officers responsible for the executions argue that capital punishments were needed to re-establish order. These punishments were exemplary in a different sense; they were intended to demonstrate unflinching rigour to these officers' peers and seniors, especially in the Supreme Command.

Other decimations followed. On 15 August, in a trench above Caporetto occupied by two companies of IV Corps, a piece of doggerel was scrawled on a piece of cardboard. The gist was that the soldiers would surrender to the enemy unless their unit was relieved. (Their tour had been extended by 20 days, so their mood was not surprising.) This came to the notice of the corps commander, General Cavaciocchi, who ordered an investigation. When no culprits could be traced, he ordered four men to be chosen by lot and shot without ado. In September, the 3rd Battalion of the 58th Infantry (Abruzzi Brigade) was deployed on

Mount San Gabriele, east of Gorizia. One night, a five-man patrol moved around no-man's land, hoping to take prisoners who would spill details about the Austrians' rumoured offensive. When the patrol returned empty-handed, the battalion commander tore into them: so they thought they could save their skins by hiding in a crater, did they? Ignoring the men's protest that they simply had not met any enemy patrols, the major ordered two of them to be shot at once. Other men were present, and someone shot the major. The divisional commander moved the regiment several kilometres behind the lines where 14 men were chosen by lot from the 3rd Battalion, and executed.

The Justice Department at the Supreme Command, which should have defended the penal code, supported Cadorna's illegal directives. As for the staff officers who could have tried to oppose the butchery, their attitude was perhaps illustrated by Ugo Ojetti's comment to his wife after the Catanzaro Brigade's first decimation, in May 1916. 'If they do not noisily shoot ten or twelve cowards and runaways, they cannot restore stability. The soldiers are like horses: they know when a rider says "forward" but thinks "back": and they won't jump.'

Under Cadorna, discipline was corrupted by arrogance. In some brigades, minor offences were punished by tying up the miscreant in view of enemy positions – 'saving bullets', as General Carignani, commanding VII Corps, put it. Officers were encouraged to treat the men brutally. If they refused to send their men to pointless slaughter or criticised the conditions and equipment, they could be court-martialled themselves, or even shot summarily. Notorious sadists included General Saporiti of the Second Army, so incensed by the sight of a soup tureen overturned in a trench that seven men were court-martialled for 'causing harm to equipment of the Royal Army and insufficient concern for the cleanliness of the trench'. (The trench was littered with corpses, torn sandbags and broken planks.) Ignoring an explicit request for harsh sentences, the court martial bravely acquitted the men. Saporiti then sacked the colonel who had presided over the court.

The worst was General Andrea Graziani, who beat a soldier so savagely for dropping his rifle while entraining that the man lost the use of his hand. A court martial dismissed Graziani's grotesque accusation of attempted mutiny. When the presiding officer reproached him for maiming an innocent man, the general replied that he could not care less. 'The minister of war has assured me in writing that a commendation has been entered in my record.' On 2 November 1917, five months after the incident in Bologna, Cadorna made Graziani responsible for restoring discipline among the troops retreating from Caporetto. The wolf was now in charge of the sheep; he had 19 men shot in the back for sundry offences on the morning of 16 November alone; another man was shot for saluting without taking his pipe out of his mouth[1] and two more for hiding a couple of kilos of flour in their knapsacks. The total number of summary executions in the weeks after Caporetto can only be guessed at.

Despite these examples of courts martial showing independence, there were few acquittals for other ranks. Cases were often heard collectively, with as many as 40 men herded before a court martial, giving little opportunity for details to be discussed. Life sentences were frequent, and sentences of 15–25 years were common. In British and French courts martial, the presumption of innocence was often weaker than it should have been, and was occasionally discarded altogether. In Italy, this presumption was turned on its head; the accused were guilty because they had been charged. As in other armies, officers were much more likely to avoid severe sentences. Before 1917, the courts martial sometimes even criticised the conduct of the war, as mitigating the offences committed by junior or reserve officers.

As the government was too cowed and the press too patriotic to challenge the use of decimation, parliament was the only source of potential pressure on Cadorna to stop killing quantities of innocent men. Opposition deputies occasionally raised their voice, in vain. In June 1917, a Socialist deputy told the chamber that Cadorna was 'a century behind the times, also in his manner of maintaining military discipline – with terror and shootings by lot and decimation'. There was no reaction; the government did not even pretend to have oversight of Cadorna's regime. In December, after Caporetto, another Socialist deputy asked the government to investigate the decimations, given their importance in sapping the army's morale, 'rather than the alleged Socialist propaganda'. The government was reluctant, and there was no investigation until after the war. The result was a whitewash: the investigators concluded that some 140 summary executions were

---

1 When the Socialist newspaper *Avanti!* exposed this crime in 1919, the minister of war rejected calls for Graziani to be sacked or prosecuted. Graziani, a list of whose excesses would fill pages, became an enthusiastic Fascist, and was rising to the highest levels of the military when he died in mysterious circumstances in 1931.

carried out from October 1915 to November 1917 – fewer even than the executions that were officially reported in this period. While the commission of inquiry did not offer a number, at least its language was honourable: decimation was a 'savage measure that nothing can justify'.

The military penal code did permit 'summary justice', bypassing courts martial, in specified circumstances. Acts of 'cowardice' or 'revolt' could be punished summarily when they posed 'grave and imminent danger' to the army in whole or part. Crucially, such offences had to be 'flagrant' – conspicuous, egregious, and ongoing. Hence the punishment must be carried out on the spot. Any delay would delegitimate the execution. Even so, the code also stated that every act of summary justice must be preceded by 'a conscientious, albeit rapid, assessment of responsibilities'. Of the summary executions that were reported in sufficient detail, very few met these narrow conditions. Cadorna did not worry, informing the prime minister in June 1917 that summary executions had been carried out 'on a vast scale', without regard for legal niceties, in order to cut out the evil of indiscipline at the roots. He added that if the contagion spread, he would be forced to resort to decimation – a step he had taken the previous November. This murderous policy had no equivalent in other countries. Summary executions in the French army were rare: around a dozen for the whole war according to the evidence, which is incomplete. In the British army, summary punishments could not exceed imprisonment or field punishment for 28 days.

As in other armies, the majority of capital sentences were given for desertion, the form of indiscipline that most worried all commanders. Punishment was harsher than in Britain, France or Germany. The military penal code defined the offence very widely, to encompass evasion of the draft. Of 189,000 soldiers charged with desertion, only 7.4 per cent were accused of desertion in the face of the enemy. Most charges were factitious, concerned with late return from home leave and such like. The code was also exceptional in disallowing a defence in terms of intention (which British military law, for example, permitted). A prosecutor had only to demonstrate the defendant's absence from his unit.

The scope for imposing the death sentence for desertion was widened during the war. Again, 1917 was the nadir. Early that year, capital sentences became mandatory for third-time deserters. In April 1917, disregarding the military penal code, under which a capital sentence could be passed after five days' unauthorised absence, the death penalty was decreed for any soldier who was more than three days late returning from leave. From June, state assistance could be denied to the families of deserters. In August, the Supreme Command slashed the period of grace to 24 hours.

Terrible as the burden was of knowing that a day's delay in returning from leave could be fatal, the non-capital offences may have caused more misery. Charges of insubordination could be laid for so trivial a 'lack of deference, of civil and military education' as a shrug or an irreverent tone of voice, picked up by an irritable officer.

Consider, too, the censorship of private letters. On 28 July 1915, Cadorna made it a military crime to denigrate war operations, scorn or vilify the army, mention news 'other than that which had been made public', or write anything at all which might 'disturb public tranquillity and lower public spirits'. It was not enough to omit details that might be considered sensitive, because the military censors did not distinguish between opinions and information, as British and French censorship tried to do. This latitude was used to suppress any kind of criticism. The government wanted to examine all private correspondence. When this proved impossible, censorship was limited to correspondence to and from the front, and abroad. This, too, was far beyond their resources; by summer 1917, soldiers were sending nearly three million letters and cards daily from the front. Still, the censors' net had mesh fine enough to land many soldiers in prison for long terms. Military censors in other countries used soldiers' letters to gauge the mood at the front. In Italy, the sole purpose was repression.

The more thoughtful the criticism, the graver the consequences. Simple complaints about officers or rations could lead to six months or a year in prison. A 25-year-old private got four years for writing that newspaper stories about the valiant troops were full of lies. 'They don't fight with pride, no, nor with ardour. They go to the slaughter because they are led to it, and are frightened of being shot.' A 21-year-old gunner from Viterbo got 22 months for urging his father to tell people the war was unjust 'because [only] a minority wanted it . . . It is the people who make this war, the workers, the men with callused hands, and they are the ones who do the dying.' The court martial found that the defendant put himself beyond clemency by calling the war unjust when 'by universal consent the whole nation wanted it'. Although every democracy in the world wanted to overthrow German imperialism, the defendant – who claims to champion the working class – opposes this aim!

By August 1917, when this sentence was handed down, the Supreme Command had convinced itself that sole responsibility for sinking morale at the front lay with Socialists, pacifists and others who wanted Italy to lose the war, and with the government that tolerated them. These defeatists infiltrated the front with propaganda and corroded the resolve of soldiers on leave. 'Internal enemy' was one of Cadorna's stock phrases, a catch-all for civilians who questioned or criticised the war. In June and August, he sent a series of astonishing letters to the Prime Minister, accusing him of letting Italy's internal enemies go about their evil business with impunity, urging him to match the 'inexorable severity' of the military penal regime in the rest of the country.

Boselli chose not to reply. The attacks were unjustified, for Italy had functioned as a police or martial state since 1915. Military encroachment on civil jurisdiction peaked in March 1917, when the Supreme Command announced that civilians living *outside* the war zone could be tried by courts martial. Socialist deputies tried vainly to muster resistance in parliament.

Besides, Cadorna's thesis about defeatist propaganda does not stand examination. Salandra, the prime minister when Italy intervened, wrote in 1917 that 'only children believe the newspapers' when they blame 'pacifist tendencies' on Socialists and followers of Giolitti. The Italian front was no more saturated with Socialist leaflets than other fronts. The difference is that Italy was divided over the war, as it had been from the beginning. The carnage had deepened the divisions, and stained them with class hatred. It was indeed the people who made this war, the horny-handed workers, and they were indeed, overwhelmingly, the ones who did the dying; no fewer than 65 per cent of war orphans were the children of peasants. This situation was a gift to Socialist agitators, especially in Turin, the country's only proletarian city. Discontent was ably exploited by Marxists at the newspaper *New Order*. In August 1917, soldiers put down a protest against food shortages that turned into a riot. Around 40 people died. The unrest was more ominous because it was not simply about wages or shortages; these complaints focused a more political discontent and a smouldering sense of injustice over who was making the greatest sacrifice in the war. Workers in different industries organised joint stoppages, as when the iron, steel, metal and engineering workers demanded a single contract. Workers' councils were set up in some factories, as embryonic structures of self-government. This went on even though war-related industries came under military direction; by summer 1918, some 900,000 workers were in this position.

To Italy's nervous élite, especially the entrepreneurs who flourished thanks to war contracts, this solidarity portended a revolution that might forge an alliance between the 'reds' and 'blacks' – Socialists and clerical Catholics. For the Pope had dropped a bombshell of his own. In a note to the warring powers, released on 9 August after consultation with Vienna, Benedict XV mooted the conditions for ending a war that 'looks more like useless slaughter every day'. Cadorna was aghast; the Vatican was punishing him again for his father's part in liberating Rome! The Supreme Command tried to prevent the statement reaching the front, in vain. If this was the last gasp of Emperor Karl's diffident peace initiative, it was much the most effective. Amid the gloom after the Tenth Battle, the damning phrase 'useless slaughter' struck a chord.

Cadorna's network of military police and civilian agents kept tabs on public figures who were suspected of undermining the war effort. Presumably this network helped to organise the rallies in Milan and elsewhere over the summer, supporting the war and calling for Cadorna to be made dictator. The generalissimo's relish of this acclaim fed suspicions that he was involved in a plot to carry out a military coup. (Allegations were made over the summer by a pro-Giolitti deputy.) The target would be the Minister of the Interior, Vittorio Orlando, viewed in some quarters as dangerously liberal and cunning with it. A coup would oust him, opening the way to a clamp-down on Cadorna's critics in parliament, striking workers in northern cities, families of deserters and other malcontents. If Boselli resisted, he too would be removed. General Giardino, the minister of war, was also suspected by some of toying with scenarios for a coup, putting Orlando under arrest and installing a military dictatorship.

Given Cadorna's record since 1915, these jitters were not surprising, yet there is no definite evidence against him. He bullied, ignored, manipulated and harangued the government, usually with eye-watering bluntness, and would have rejoiced at Orlando's downfall. After the war, he blandly denied having ever wanted a 'reign of terror'. On the contrary, order could have been ensured by rounding up a few hundred ringleaders and propagandists and transporting them to Eritrea or Somalia, as well as suppressing the newspapers that the government allowed to whinge the length and breadth of the country. How a regime of arbitrary arrests, banishment and increased censorship could have been instituted without a coup, he did not say.

After a decent interval, at the end of September, Boselli convened a cabinet meeting with Cadorna to discuss the matters raised in his letters. Cadorna said the army was verminous with defeatism, and urged drastic steps. If he had really wanted to alert the government to Socialist agitation, he would have claimed that the riots in Turin directly hurt morale at the front. But, as Boselli knew, Cadorna's real purpose was twofold: to shift the blame for poor morale away from the Supreme Command, and to target Orlando. The despised minister happened to be a Sicilian, so Cadorna's letters to Boselli focused on Sicily, painting it as a hotbed of Socialist propaganda, an allegation that Orlando easily rebutted. Any crisis of morale in our army, he said, had nothing to do with propaganda; rather, it 'stems from the fact that the Supreme Command has killed too many soldiers, too quickly'.

Nevertheless, Cadorna got his way. The minister of justice prepared a decree to criminalise 'defeatism', an elusive target for prosecution. Issued on 4 October 1917, the Sacchi Decree was as draconian as the military measures (though the punishments were less severe). It dovetailed with Cadorna's military penal regime to form a solid wall of repression. For example, it was used to jail a civilian for six months for chanting a satirical rhyme from the trenches:

> General Cadorna sent a postcard to the Queen:
> 'Here's a picture of Trieste, so you can say: Trieste I've seen!'

Complete data on military justice are still not available. What is clear is that at least one Italian soldier in 12 was subject to disciplinary investigation during the war: a much higher proportion than in other Allied armies. More than half of the 870,000 charges related to absenteeism, leaving some 400,000 offences committed under arms. By the time a general amnesty for deserters was issued in September 1919, courts martial had heard 350,000 cases. Of the 210,000 sentences passed, 100,000 were for desertion, 24,500 for 'indiscipline', and 10,000 for self-mutilation. Of the 4,028 capital sentences, 729 were carried out. As for summary executions, the unflagging research of Marco Pluviano and Irene Guerrini discovered records of more than

300, but the real total may run to several thousand. For comparison: the French army was roughly twice the size of the Italian, and the British army mobilised approximately the same number of men in Britain. Around 350 British and 600 French soldiers were executed after courts martial, and summary executions were very rare. In France, parliamentary concern over executions was so strong that the army lost the authority to approve death sentences; the government gained a right to review every capital sentence, and each one had to be approved by the president of the republic. Only in the emergency of June 1917 did General Pétain succeed in wresting back this authority. In the British army, both the theatre judge advocate general and commander-in-chief had to review capital sentences.

There were no such safeguards in the Italian army. Nor was there any equivalent in Italy of a prime minister like Lloyd George, prepared to challenge the commander-in-chief, or cabinet ministers like Churchill, who publicly criticised the huge loss of life, or a bridging figure like General Robertson, quite capable of delivering unwanted messages from the government to the commander-in-chief and vice-versa. The best checks against abuse of military power were political or institutional, not dependent on the letter of the law. In the last analysis, these checks are cultural; Haig was annoyed by the Australian government's refusal to let Australians serving with the British army be shot for desertion, but it did not occur to him to ignore that veto. British and French courts martial were sometimes pressured to hand down harsh sentences and curtail defendants' rights, but due process was not disregarded routinely, with impunity, at the insistence of the commander-in-chief.

After the war, the Italian army's judge advocate general (responsible for the conduct of courts martial) ruled that most of Cadorna's directives on military justice were illegitimate. Cadorna would surely retort that, if he had led the British or French army, he would not have needed to take such measures. He had little respect for many of his senior commanders (who often deserved none) or their brigades. Italy was committed to a war that placed unprecedented demands on officers and men alike. This situation was what it was; he had to deal with it, and he did so by remaking the military justice system in his own image: intolerant, confrontational, devoid of empathy. Terror and barbarous punishment were not his last resort for getting soldiers to obey; they were his preferred means. Obedience was a beautifully simple requirement, not to be contaminated with notions of education or motivation. The soldiers did not need to reason; they merely had to do and die.

Count Carlo Sforza, foreign minister in the early 1920s and again after 1945, wrote witheringly of Cadorna's 'mystical sadism', implying that the penal regime was more expressive than practical, satisfying the warped appetite of a single man. To be sure, the regime did not crush all disobedience. Violent misbehaviour by troops going to and from the front became so widespread in summer 1917 – firing on carabinieri in the railway stations, shooting out of the windows, hurling stones and bottles – that the men's rifles had to be taken away for the duration of the journeys. And this was at the apex of Cadorna's terror.

The draconian measures against desertion also had little effect. The number of deserters almost trebled between April and August 1917. Would-be deserters became more astute; rather than escaping at the front, they failed to return from home leave. By October, more than 100,000 deserters and draft-dodgers were hiding in the interior of the country. Overall, desertion rates doubled during 1917, then diminished in 1918. The average rate of desertion was significantly higher than in other western European armies.[2] Indeed, an internal report in March 1918 admitted a connection between the penal regime and desertion; punishments that were perceived as savagely unjust, could encourage disaffected soldiers to take the ultimate risk.

Even so, historians believe that Cadorna's harshness was functional, not mystical. The scholar Bruna Bianchi, no admirer of Cadorna, argues that summary execution kept a lid on potential rebellion; without it, mutinies on a French scale would have erupted. Yet terror was a 'cure' with disastrous side-effects; evidence that soldiers' morale was harmed by the almost arbitrary killing of their comrades is strong and ample. All that can be said for Cadorna's methods is that they reinforced the obedience which almost all soldiers already displayed.

That humbling, haunting obedience: what are we to make of it, so long after the event? The historian Giovanna Procacci argues that the

2 The Italian army found 101,685 men guilty of desertion, rising from 10,000 in the first year of war to 55,000 in the last year. In the British army around 38,000 soldiers were tried on desertion charges. (Over 2,000 were sentenced to death, of whom 266 were executed.) The French army had 509 desertions in 1914, rising fivefold in 1915, then to 8,924 in 1916, and soaring to 27,000 in 1917. (Figures based on successful charges brought.) Germany mobilised 13.5 million soldiers, three times more than Italy, and convicted 130,000 to 150,000 men of desertion or absence without leave, up to 50,000 of them in the field army.

archive of censored letters proves that loathing of the war and hostility to the state and its institutions were 'very widespread', much more so than in other armies. It was above all 'the certainty of ferocious repression' that deterred the troops from acting out their feelings of 'internal rebellion'. Giorgio Rochat, on the other hand, argues that their obedience mainly reflected 'the dearth of cultural alternatives which would provide legitimation and external support for rebellion'. Disobedience lay beyond the conception of men who had grown up in a world where absolute authority was personified by the priest and the mayor. Rochat believes the deepest sources of obedience are unknowable; a historian should accept this, and salute the men's sacrifice.

To an outsider, this divergence is more political than scholarly. Procacci in particular frames her argument with a larger contention; the war, she says, exposed the authoritarian bones of the Italian state, and confirmed that 'the working class had never shared in patriotic sentiments'. Although the structure of the state was liberal, with a constitutional monarchy, elected parliament and formal separation of powers, the relations between state and society, government and citizens, were absolutist: closer to Germany and Austria-Hungary than to Britain and France.

The state still protects Cadorna's bloody regime. In 1990, a descendant of Corporal Silvio Ortis, who was executed in a blatant miscarriage of justice in 1916, tried to clear his forebear's name by seeking a pardon. After eight months, the military court in Rome replied ineffably that under applicable law, only the 'interested party' may seek a pardon. As Silvio Ortis had not filed this request himself, it was 'inadmissible'. When his appeal was rejected, the descendant wrote to the president of the republic. In 1998, his persistence bore fruit: a deputy in parliament agreed to propose an amendment allowing a spouse or relative to request a pardon. The amendment was presented to parliament in 2001, when the deputies agreed that a sub-committee would consider it in June 2006. In other words they kicked it into the long grass – where it remains to this day.

TWENTY-THREE

Another Second of Life

*The Italians were using up an awful amount
of men. I did not see how it could go on. Even
if they took all the Bainsizza and Monte San
Gabriele there were plenty of mountains
beyond for the Austrians. I had seen them.*
HEMINGWAY

The Eleventh Battle of the Isonzo

A diffused fear of revolution had been felt since the early spring of 1917.
The governing class worried that news of events in Russia might set
light to discontent over living conditions and the endless war. In June,
the government yielded to pressure in parliament for a debate on the
conduct of the war. Disappointed by the Tenth Battle and frustrated by
Boselli's feeble leadership, Sonnino's clam-like silence and Cadorna's
unaccountability, and in some cases suspicious of Orlando's ambitions,
many deputies were spoiling to have their say. Now they could have it,
albeit – this being the government's condition – in closed session.

The debate filled the last week of June. On the final day, a general
took the floor. This was Fortunato Marazzi, a pro-war Liberal deputy
who had served as a divisional commander (without much distinction,
as we saw in chapter 11). In a marathon speech, he enumerated many
of the blunders that Cadorna and both wartime governments had
committed since 1915. Why had Italy learned nothing from the first
campaigns on the Western Front? Why was the artillery dispersed along
the front instead of massed on the Isonzo? Why had the government
not held the Supreme Command responsible for its decisions? Why did
the Supreme Command persist with the 'simultaneous general attack'
despite disastrous results? The questions rolled pitilessly on. Deputies
were unused to such candour; according to one, no admirer of Marazzi,
the indictment 'grievously impressed' them. Yet it made no difference to

the outcome. The government survived a vote of confidence, Orlando and Sonnino basked in unexpected approval, and Boselli reaffirmed his trust in Cadorna. In truth, the chamber had little choice. With Sonnino and Bissolati, his most influential ministers, publicly committed to resigning if Cadorna went, Boselli was safe for the moment.

As usual, Cadorna paid no attention to grumbling deputies. He had been looking ahead to the Eleventh Battle even before the Tenth petered to a halt, in early June. Next time, he would commit as many men and guns as possible on the Isonzo. As he no longer feared an Austrian breakout from the Trentino, he brought 12 divisions from the Alpine front, leaving a minimal presence. He would throw 51 divisions at the line between Tolmein and the sea: a vast force, distributed along a front of 60 kilometres. Estimating that three months would be needed to stockpile two million medium and heavy shells – sufficient to ensure the batteries would not run short – he planned to attack in August.

The focal area would be the Bainsizza plateau, between Gorizia and Tolmein. Since the Tenth Battle, these thinly populated highlands had formed the Austrian front line on the middle Isonzo. Cadorna believed an element of surprise could be preserved here, which was impossible further south. He also assessed that the Austrian defences on the plateau were relatively light. This was correct: the Bainsizza had never been fortified or strongly garrisoned. Watching the build-up in July, Boroević decided not to bolster the Bainsizza at the price of diverting resources from elsewhere. If the Italians broke through, their impetus would dissipate like waves on sand; the terrain was its own defence. The Italians were aware of these factors but took no account of how they might affect their plans. Having taken the Bainsizza, they proposed to swing south and cut off Monte Santo and San Gabriele, the high hills that the Austrians still held behind Gorizia. But if the force on the Bainsizza became stuck there, for whatever reason, the Second Army units facing Monte Santo and San Gabriele would be in the familiar position of attacking up steep gradients, against solid defences, without flanking support.

Once again, Cadorna let General Capello – now commanding the Second Army – add a new element to the plan without caring how this affected the whole design. For Capello decided that the Second Army, once the Bainsizza had been secured, should wheel northwards toward Tolmein, the only point on the front where Austria still held both banks of the Isonzo. Even with their enlarged forces, however, the Italians could not expect to reduce the Tolmein bridgehead and the hills behind Gorizia while also attacking Mount Hermada, on the southern edge of the Carso.

By early August, Cadorna had more than half a million men ranged along the front, maintaining but not exceeding the 10:4 advantage in manpower that he had enjoyed since 1915. What was new was a crushing superiority in firepower. The factories were working flat out to supply the front with guns and munitions, while Austrian heavy industry had ground almost to a halt. The Italians had 3,750 guns on the Isonzo, including a handful of British and French batteries, and 1,900 mortars, against the Austrians' 430 heavy guns and 1,250 field guns. For the first time, the Italians could match the power of offensives on the Western Front.

The bombardment got under way in the first week of August. By the middle of the month, it was in full swing. The gunners had learned how to register on their targets, and the effect along the 12-kilometre Bainsizza front was devastating. Italian pilots controlled the sky, and their raids added to the Austrian sense that there was no protection to be had. From Tolmein to the sea, the Habsburg lines and rear positions were shrouded in smoke and fire, roaring day and night with shellbursts. Hermada was pounded from floating batteries, fixed on rafts near the mouth of the Isonzo.

Zero hour was 05:30 on the 19th. The infantry attacked along the whole front. On the Carso, the Third Army dented the Austrian lines in three places. The biggest advance was at the hamlet of Selo, long since pulverised, several kilometres inland. The Hermada massif was still impregnable. A push up the Vipacco valley, between the Carso and Gorizia, gained some ground before Habsburg counter-attacks forced the Italians back to their starting point.

So far, so familiar. Above Gorizia, however, something novel was happening; the Second Army had stormed across the Isonzo and made dramatic progress on the Bainsizza, where Boroević's skeleton force was overwhelmed. Capello was exultant: 'They do not know what a torrent of men I am unleashing.' Four corps were poised to exploit the opening. He realised the troops might soon run short of rations, water and even munitions; however, they were ordered to press ahead regardless. For several days the Italians made dream-like progress across the Bainsizza, rolling forward for two, three, four, five kilometres, smashing 45 Austrian battalions as they went, capturing dozens of guns and 11,000 prisoners. Italy had seen nothing like this. Was it too good to be true? Colonel Gatti, already worried that the whole offensive was unnecessary, was perplexed. Why did the Austrians not bring up their reserves? If they weren't here, where were they? Could it be that they had none? What else were they planning . . . ?

The Italians did not know that the Emperor Karl had visited Boroević's headquarters in Postojna, half way to Ljubljana, on 22 August. It was, they agreed, a moment of crisis. Long-range fire blocked their supply routes to the front; the troops were running short of munitions. The Bainsizza was untenable, and Karl prevailed on his general to fall back. Only the sovereign could have wrung this compromise from 'the lion of the Isonzo'. Under imperial pressure, Boroević utilised the elastic defence, or defence in depth. It was risky; a tactical withdrawal from the Bainsizza would lengthen the front around an Italian salient and boost enemy morale. On the other hand, given the Austrians' excellent defensive record, it should be possible to block the enemy when they reached the eastern limit of the plateau. As an extra inducement to flexibility, the Emperor reportedly pledged that the next operation on the Isonzo would be an Austrian offensive out of the Tolmein bridgehead. This promise revitalised Boroević and his staff; for the prospect of endless defence, with no chance of turning the tables, had a peculiar effect even on the hardiest soldiers. It was like watching their own death draw closer day by day. The stimulus to resist, in this condition, might at any moment flip into its opposite: a doomed fatalism, with a collapse of will. Karl's army on the Isonzo was poised on a razor's edge; the discussion at Postojna shows that he realised this. Before dawn on the 24th, the 12 Austrian regiments on the Bainsizza silently pulled back to the eastern edge of the plateau, with their guns. Secrecy was maintained, and a few hours later the weary Austrians had the satisfaction of seeing the Italian artillery hammer their empty positions.

From then on, the Italians fulfilled Boroević's hopes to the letter. Capello's divisions washed across the plateau, and subsided there. The Supreme Command had not prepared for such progress. The strategic reserves were centred on the front, ready to move wherever an opportunity arose. This was mistaken, as a breakthrough was much less likely south of Gorizia than north of it. As a result, the Second Army could not exploit the Austrian withdrawal. With the artillery toiling along rough tracks far behind, the infantry's scope for manoeuvre was limited. Instead of reinforcing his forward units, Capello launched several half-baked sorties towards Tolmein, which the Austrians swatted back. The flanking movement to the south, towards Monte Santo and San Gabriele, never transpired: the Austrians' cordon around the plateau contained it.

The pull-back also affected the defence behind Gorizia. Capello's assault on Monte Santo had groped upwards into the blaze of shellfire crowning the hill. Since the Italians captured it in May, only to lose it again, the Marian shrine on the summit had been razed. The imminent Italian occupation of the Bainsizza would expose another of Monte Santo's flanks, rendering it indefensible. Accordingly, the last Habsburg defenders quietly pulled back from their foxholes in the rubble, down the eastern flank of the mountain, and across the narrow pass to Mount San Gabriele. The nearest Italian regiment was only 40 metres from the ruins; when its colonel realised what had happened, he led his men to the summit. Monte Santo was Italian, once and for all.[1]

The 24th was a great day, and word of the army's achievements flashed to Rome. Ambassador Rodd telegraphed Lloyd George that the offensive might end in 'a complete smashing of the Austrian army'. The Prime Minister was jubilant; Cadorna's breakthrough (for such it seemed) confirmed his earlier hunch about the Italians. On the 26th, he re-launched his scheme to help them 'convert the Austrian retreat into a rout', as he put it. Again, General Robertson and the top brass dug in. By the time London and Paris agreed how many guns to send Cadorna, the Italians had stalled.

For a few days, however, anything seemed possible. Gatti joined in the acclaim for Cadorna: he alone had wanted the battle, and he 'has held everything together with his iron fist'. By the 28th, with the Bainsizza more like a cul-de-sac than a gateway, doubts were creeping back. Cadorna suspended operations on the plateau. The capture of Monte Santo was a spectacular success with great propaganda benefits, but it did not alter the strategic balance. Loyal as ever to the Supreme Command, General Delmé-Radcliffe blamed the 'extraordinary difficulty of the ground and the lack of roads'.

---

1 The great conductor Arturo Toscanini, who happened to be visiting the front, formed a military band and climbed to the top of Monte Santo the day after its liberation. 'We played in the Austrians' faces and sang our national anthems,' he wrote proudly to his wife. When General Capello awarded him the silver medal for valour at a ceremony in front of a bersaglieri brigade, the maestro was overcome by 'violent emotion' and 'cried like a baby'.

The Carso was quiescent. The Third Army had scaled down its operations around the 23rd, releasing Austrian forces for transfer to San Gabriele, which was now the major obstacle between the Bainsizza and the Carso. If the Italians took it, they should quickly reduce the remaining Austrian strongholds north of the Vipacco valley, break through towards Laibach and outflank Hermada. By the same token, if the Austrians held on to it, the advance on the Bainsizza would have little meaning.

After the exhilarating advance over the Bainsizza, the attack on San Gabriele brought a reversion to type. Compact blocks of infantry were sent up mountainsides, into field-gun and machine-gun fire, proving yet again that weight of numbers could not substitute for planning and preparation. One brigade after another assaulted San Gabriele for more than a fortnight. The hilltop caverns were impregnable, even against the 420-millimetre batteries which made San Gabriele look like a volcano, spewing fire and rock. The fire was so intense that the mountain lost 10 metres in altitude during the battle. Teams of Italian *arditi* – newly formed shock troops – came close to seizing the summit. At one point, Boroević believed it could not be held.

On 19 September, Cadorna halted the battle and ordered all units onto the defensive. The Italians had taken 166,000 casualties, including 40,000 dead, of whom 25,000 died on San Gabriele for trivial gains. Some 400 of the 600 battalions involved in the battle had lost one-half to two-thirds of their strength. Cadorna's and Capello's actions in the Eleventh Battle were so careless and self-destructive that historians have struggled to account for them. In truth, the two men acted fully in character. Cadorna's battle plans always tended to incoherence, his command often slackened fatally in the course of offensives, and he had never been able to control Capello (except by banishing him from the Isonzo). Capello's disobedience at critical moments was equally familiar.

The Eleventh Battle was a technical victory that felt like defeat. A close bystander who grasped the enormity of this failure without identifying its source (his mind refused to follow the evidence) was Colonel Gatti, the official historian at the Supreme Command. As the corpses piled up on San Gabriele, he wrote despairingly in his diary: 'I feel something collapsing inside me; I shall not be able to endure this war, none of us will; it is too gigantic, truly limitless, it will crush us all.' He found solace in the men's morale, which was holding up well, he thought. Yet he picked up a sense that their stamina was linked to a mysterious expectation that this would be the final battle. They were making a last colossal effort. What will happen, he mused, when they see that this is *not* the end?

Proportionately, Boroević's losses – at around 140,000 men – were even heavier, and could not be made good. The next Italian thrust would likely smash the line between Gorizia and the sea. This probability was not lost on Austria's ally. Ultimately, the strategic significance of the Eleventh Battle is that it forced Germany to pay urgent attention to the Italian front for the first time. The German Supreme Command realised that further loss of ground would lead to the loss of Trieste, which held the key to Austria's economic independence. 'Trieste must therefore be saved, with German help if not otherwise.'

One of the men ferrying cartridges up San Gabriele was Private Antonio Pardi of the 247th Infantry: slogging uphill with a crate on his back, clambering over the dead, hunching under continual explosions, dumping his crate by the forward positions and half running, half sliding down again in a panic, grabbing at corpses to keep his balance, arriving at the bottom 'clotted with filth, blood and mud'. Pardi set down his memories fifty years after the event, 'not out of love for a just and terrible war', but so that later generations could know what it had been like. 'Death was so certain that you almost stopped thinking how to avoid it, yet every passing second was another second of life.' This obliquely answers Gatti's question: when the soldiers realised this battle was not the last, they would carry on, living for the next second of life.

TWENTY-FOUR

The Traitor of Carzano

Is this a tragedy or an operetta?
MAJOR CESARE FINZI (1917)

While the Eleventh Battle raged and waned beyond the Isonzo valley, something extraordinary happened 200 kilometres away, on a quiet sector of the front near the city of Trent.

The River Brenta curves tightly around the Asiago plateau before making for the plains and the Venetian lagoon. The northern part of its course – called the Sugana valley – passes below the plateau on one side (the heights of Ortigara) and the Dolomite foothills on the other. Here and there the valley broadens out, and the lower flanks are dotted with settlements. One of these is the unremarkable village of Carzano, surrounded by woods and vineyards, where the little River Maso flows to the Brenta.

As one of the easiest routes from the Veneto plains to the Tyrol, the Austrians should have fortified the Sugana valley. Instead they had strengthened the Asiago plateau. In summer 1915, the Italians penetrated the Sugana valley to within a dozen kilometres of Trent. Conrad's Punishment Expedition pushed them back, before the counter-attack in June 1916 regained some of the lost ground. The new front stabilised near Carzano.

This sector lay in the operational zone of Cadorna's First Army, responsible for most of the Trentino front. Despite its strategic importance, it was generally quiet. Days passed without a shot fired; weeks passed without glimpsing the enemy. The soldiers manning the forward positions facing Carzano had no reason to expect anything unusual when, on a moonless night in July 1917, a Habsburg non-commissioned officer slipped through the wire and presented himself at a dug-out. The Italian officer who scrambled out of the dug-out looked in astonishment at the man calmly saluting him. True, he was unarmed and carried a sealed envelope, but he wore a fez, showing that he belonged to a Bosnian regiment. The fez had the same effect on Italians that the Scottish kilt had on Germans: it meant primeval savagery. How could a Bosnian intend anything except harm? When the Italian tried to take the envelope the other man refused, insisting it was for someone more senior. 'Io essere parlamentario', he repeated: it was bad Italian for 'I have come to parley.' Nonplussed, the officer blindfolded the Bosnian and led him to the sector command. He turned out to be a Czech sergeant in the 5th Battalion, 1st Infantry Regiment of Bosnia & Herzegovina.

His envelope made its way to the divisional chief of staff, who realised the documents were detailed plans of Habsburg defences around Carzano. There was a covering note signed by one 'Paolino': 'We are ready to help you. If you accept, fire two 152-mm shells at the church tower in Carzano at noon, then shine a searchlight from Levre mountain at dusk. A junior officer will appear at midnight.' The staff officers were extremely doubtful. They let the mysterious envoy return to the Habsburg line, and referred the matter to the Information Office at Sixth Army headquarters in Vicenza.

The head of information was Major Cesare Finzi, probably the only intelligence officer in the army who would not assume the contact was a trap. For he was part Hungarian, and understood the complex workings of nationality politics in the empire. The maps were authentic: Italian data proved it. If the Austrians were setting a trap, why had 'Paolino' asked for nothing more than another meeting? And if it was not a trap, what was it? He decided to take the bait. The signals were sent, the Czech sergeant arrived again, and Finzi proposed a nocturnal meeting in the apple orchards of no-man's land. 'Paolino' turned out to be a Slovene lieutenant, interim commander of the 5th Battalion, who introduced himself as Dr Ljudevit Pivko. A bespectacled schoolmaster from Marburg (now Maribor), Pivko explained that the Slovenes and Italians should be allies against the empire. He wanted to 'redeem' Slovenia for the Slovenes, he said, just as the Italians wanted to redeem Trent and Trieste.

Finzi was intrigued. Everyone knew that the Slovenes were outstandingly loyal to the empire, like the Croats and Bosnian Muslims. Inquisitive as well as cautious, he asks the other man to say more. Pivko complies, unburdening himself. 'I used to think my fatherland and the empire were one and the same. No longer. Today I understand that we Slavs have nothing in common with the Germans. You do not know how

the Austrians and Hungarians treat us; we are slaves, cannon fodder.'
He wants the Italians to achieve something important. The whole of
Trentino is, he says, thinly defended. Breaking through the Sugana valley
would lead straight westwards to the trophy of Trento itself. That
triumph would, though, be short-lived unless the Italians attacked
simultaneously from the west, chopping the Trentino salient in half.

He has discussed these ideas with a few sympathetic officers – Czechs
and Bosnian Serbs. Not, however, with his men, who are good but
simple. The Serbs, who hate the empire to a man, would support him;
others – Muslims and Croats – would kill him if they thought he was
plotting against the Emperor. Pivko's sincerity shines through; Finzi
trusts him, but can he convince the higher levels? Only if he shows them
a flow of accurate data from his Habsburg source. He tells Pivko that
if he can feed him information about the situation and developments on
his side of the line, while recruiting supporters among the battalion's
Serbs and Czechs, they can do something momentous.

After the meeting, Finzi is euphoric. The more he thinks about it, the
greater the opportunity becomes in his mind. At their next meeting,
Pivko brings two Czech officers, who gravely offer Finzi their services.
It is a surreal situation. Pivko hands over a wad of documents: field
orders, transfer lists, artillery dispositions. Finzi presses for details of
troop numbers, dispositions and movements throughout Trentino; also
on garrisons, communications, the traffic in and out of Trento railway
station. Pivko agrees to procure all this, and they devise an elaborate
code of signals: flares, machine-gun fire, coloured smoke trails by
aeroplanes.

Something else has been on Finzi's mind; it is important, but he does
not know how to broach it. Italy's goals in the war include the
annexation of territory where Slovenes and other South Slavs
(Yugoslavs) make up a majority of the population. As a Slovene
nationalist, Pivko is bound to oppose Italy's expansion around the
Adriatic. By betraying the empire, he will support that project. Finzi
cannot contain his curiosity; how does Pivko see this sensitive matter?
In whispered discussions, they agree that their views on the best
settlement on the eastern Adriatic coast are different rather than
irreconcilable, and need not hamper their collaboration. This
pragmatism seals the men's mutual liking. Finzi is unusual among
Italian officers in wanting to see the empire destroyed; this was not an
Allied war aim at the time, still less an Italian policy.

Pivko is as good as his word. By August, he has widened his network of contacts along the valley and onto the Asiago plateau, where Italian labourers and Russian prisoners are ready to talk. Pivko outlines a tremendous plan: he and his supporters can open the front at Carzano. The Italians should mount a surprise attack on Trento with 30 or 40 battalions (30,000 to 40,000 men), cutting off the garrison there. If they can overrun the city before reinforcements arrive from the Isonzo front, the lower Trentino will drop into their hands. The Italians can then pour up the Adige valley to Bolzano and the Brenner Pass. The loss of South Tyrol would be a devastating blow, lifting Italian spirits for the first time since August 1916. Britain and France will be grateful instead of grudging Allies. The moment is ripe for this operation, but Finzi fears that word will get out if he takes the idea to the Supreme Command through the usual channels. He approaches Cadorna directly, but the Supreme Commander is absorbed in preparations for the Eleventh Battle and Finzi cannot get past his chef de cabinet, Colonel Bencivenga, who sneers at the idea. Finzi tries to assure Bencivenga that the operation could be attempted without weakening the forces on the Isonzo, but the other man is not listening. Finzi is referred to his sector commander, General Etna.

Finzi is not easily discouraged. Contact has been authorised between the front-line units, and men from both sides are scampering like rabbits across no-man's land. He sends two Czech deserters back across the line in their Habsburg uniforms (it is their idea) to gather intelligence. He hits on the idea of making Romanian deserters loiter near the enemy line, calling out in their own language to see if their compatriots can be tempted to make contact. These initiatives seem obvious, but were not so in the Italian army before 1918.

In mid-August, Pivko signals for an urgent meeting. The Habsburg high command has anticipated Cadorna's attack on the Bainsizza plateau and is concentrating 30 divisions and as many guns as possible on the middle and lower Isonzo, sapping the forces in Tyrol. There is a golden opportunity to attack at Carzano, if the Italians hurry. Pivko has recruited three battalion commanders, three battery commanders, a machine-gun unit commander and 32 junior officers to the cause. He has a network of 52 informants across the Trentino.

But Finzi has a problem; he cannot persuade General Etna to take the idea seriously. The general thinks in terms of a local breakthrough to seize a few hundred prisoners. Finzi naturally conceals this difficulty from Pivko, who is working on a full-scale plan for a surprise attack on a front of two and a half kilometres. He hands this plan to Finzi in early September; it tells the Italians how many men they need, identifies their Habsburg guides, suggests timelines for a nocturnal advance, and even suggests passwords they should use. Small assault teams will infiltrate the lines at Carzano, and quickly widen this ingress to a breach. As the Italians move into no-man's land, the electric current in the Austrian barbed wire will be switched off, telephone lines will be cut, munitions dumps will mysteriously blow up, the artillery will not fire. The loyal Bosnians will find bottles of brandy on their mess-tables, spiked with opiates. The forward patrols will be silenced with chloroform. The Italian gunners will have the Austrian firing tables.

Finzi knows it is only a matter of time before the plot is discovered, and anyway the Bosnians are likely to be transferred away from Carzano in the near future. He redoubles his efforts to get a meeting with Cadorna. On 4 September, he is shown into the generalissimo's office. Cadorna listens closely, asks the right questions, takes Pivko's documents and tells Finzi to come back in three days. On the 7th, Finzi briefs a staff meeting with Etna in attendance. He describes Pivko as a Czech, because Czech nationalists are beginning to be trusted by the Italian military, which Yugoslavs never are. The sceptical Etna proposes a minimal alternative; there should be no simultaneous thrust by the First Army from the west, merely a sortie along the Sugana valley without a strong intention to reach Trento. This proposal carries the day. Finzi is crestfallen. When an unknown brigadier is put in charge and assault troops with no combat experience are chosen to lead the way, he realises the operation is probably doomed. Still, he is hopeful by nature and preparations continue.

In the second week of September, the plot is denounced by a Czech acquaintance of Pivko, who is instantly suspended. Luckily the investigators decide the informant is lying and Pivko returns to his post. The next day, he is sent to Trent to represent the battalion at an inspection by Emperor Karl. Pausing in front of Pivko, the Emperor murmurs a few kind words: 'I regret that somebody wished to cast a shadow over one of my most valiant officers. Greet my brave Bosnians for me.' It is an incredible, Schweik-like moment. The unflappable schoolteacher from Maribor surely wonders how long his luck can hold. Finzi, meanwhile, tries to prevent Brigadier Zincone from rewriting Pivko's plan. The brigadier wants to widen the breach at once, rather than penetrate rapidly beyond Carzano. Finzi even takes his concerns to Cadorna, who brushes them aside.

On 15 September, Pivko brings worrying news: his battalion is about to be transferred. If the Italians do not strike now, it may be too late. Finzi promises it will happen within 48 hours. Zincone agrees to move on the night of 17 September. Despite Finzi's misgivings, the Italians have seven well-equipped corps plus their batteries against two under-strength Habsburg corps, one under-strength division (comprising ten instead of twelve battalions), some mountain units, and a single infantry regiment in reserve. If the operation goes to plan, the Austrians will get a very nasty shock.

On the Austrian side, everything goes like clockwork; the road across no-man's land is wide open. But the assault troops advance gingerly, as if on manoeuvres. Finzi realises the officers do not trust their Austrian guides. They take Carzano and its garrison more or less punctually, but the main force is nowhere to be seen. The road should be filled with infantry; instead it is empty. Finzi runs back, cursing, to ask Zincone what has happened. 'The men are all on their way,' the brigadier confirms.

'But the road is deserted!'

'They are using the trenches.'

'Trenches! What trenches?' blurts Finzi, turning cold, realising the brigadier has sent the troops in single file along a narrow lateral trench that twists towards Carzano, instead of four abreast along the undefended road. Troops that should have been pressing on beyond Carzano are still only a few minutes from the Italian lines. He is speechless.

As he scurries to and fro on the road, urging the uncertain officers forward, he runs into Pivko, ashen-faced. It is almost dawn and only five of the 12 Italian columns are where they should be. The Austrians still do not know what is afoot. A few guns are firing towards the Italian lines, alerted by the telephone silence. A machine-gun unit spots shadows moving on the road and enfilades the entrance to Carzano. Just when Finzi tells the columns to carry on regardless, an order arrives from Brigadier Zincone: fall back, the operation is suspended. The forward troops and their guides are abandoned.

Pivko stands pale and rigid, as if turned to stone. He and 300 of his Bosnians are taken prisoner. As if to justify his decision, Zincone makes a slighting remark about the guides. Finzi is in a trance of despair; the

Italians' indifference is inexplicable. As he returns to sector HQ, he sees the Italian artillery open fire on bersaglieri in Carzano, who are cut off and surrendering to the Austrians. It is the final horror. The Italians lose 360 dead – fighting to get back to their lines – and more than 900 prisoners. Cadorna orders an inquiry. Etna and Zincone are relieved of their command, without explanation. Finzi ensures that Pivko's talents are put to good use in the Italian army.

Long after the war, Cadorna told Finzi that nothing had angered him more during the entire war than the fiasco at Carzano. Yet the dysfunctional system or 'culture' at the Supreme Command was largely responsible. In his jealousy and obsession with unified command, Cadorna made himself the lynchpin of all significant decisions. Bencivenga was Saint Peter, authorised to reject supplicants. When Finzi eventually gained access, Cadorna approved a minimal version of the proposal. He dismissed Finzi's well-founded worries about the commanding officer and unit assigned to the operation. There was no alternative address for these concerns. Another reason for the fiasco is that the Italian military never believed in the Pivko–Finzi plan, not because of distraction by the Eleventh Battle, rather because the concept did not conform to the Supreme Command's notion of offensive operations. Senior commanders understood that an attack might rely heavily on intelligence, subterfuge and infiltration; in practice, they did not trust such methods or know how to plan them.

Ultimately, Finzi's plan was distrusted for political reasons. Italy was fighting heart and soul to enlarge its national territory at the expense of non-Italian peoples – Germans in south Tyrol, Slavs around the Adriatic. Those peoples were twofold enemies: now as soldiers dressed in the Habsburg pike-grey uniform, and in future as more or less resentful victims of Italian force majeure. Viewed through a nationalist lens, this was a zero-sum struggle. Foreign Secretary Sonnino saw no merit in finessing the contradiction between Italian and Yugoslav aims. Translated into practice, this meant there was little point in threading the labyrinth of Habsburg nationality politics. Why bother, if it made no difference to your actions and aims?

Even before the war, according to a well-placed observer, Sonnino's views of the Austro-Hungarian Empire were 'antiquated'; he had had 'little notion of the strength of the national movements among the subject Habsburg races'. For he 'shared, to a degree surprising in a man so cultivated', the nationalist illusion that the eastern shore of the Adriatic 'was mainly Italian in spirit and in racial character'. Enlightened nationalists from Mazzini to Slataper tried to understand the aspirations of Habsburg Slavs. This was the tradition behind democratic interventionism, an important strand of opinion in the first year of war. Under Sonnino, 'an obstinate, unimaginative man, ensconced in the clauses of his London Treaty as in a besieged bastion', ignorance of Italy's eastern neighbours became a patriotic virtue.

Sonnino despised propaganda and wanted nothing to do with it. This goes far to explain why Italian propaganda towards the South Slavs until the end of 1917 was, in one historian's phrase, 'violently anti-Yugoslav'. Leaflets were dropped over enemy lines with undoctored translations from Italian nationalist newspapers. For the Italians mistook the motives behind the Slovenes' and Croats' ferocity on the Isonzo, wrongly assuming they were infinitely devoted to the empire, even more so than the German Austrians. In fact, the defence on the Isonzo depended increasingly on Slavic nationalism, a force which corroded the empire. This dialectical irony was lost on Italy's opinion-makers, who, instead of driving a wedge between the South Slavs and the empire, confirmed that Italian motives were as wicked as Habsburg propaganda had painted them.

The army had no excuse for neglecting nationality politics: as early as October 1915, Czech and Moravian prisoners had thanked their captors for liberating them from 'the Germans'. An officer who fought on the Carso in October 1916 described the hundreds of enemies who lurched out of the smoke and dust of the Italian bombardment, 'mad with terror, throwing their guns away, holding their hands up, shouting that they were Serbs or Romanians, taking [Italian] tricolour ribbons out of their pockets, sticking them in their berets and buttonholes, all while the artillery made such a racket that I cannot tell you, the wounded screaming and blood everywhere'. Such scenes should have triggered a reassessment of the situation in the empire, investigating the impact of Vienna's policy towards the non-German peoples, whose loyalty was repaid with steadily worsening conditions. The closure of parliament in Vienna and the provincial assemblies had denied the nationalities a legitimate voice, and tough censorship affected them disproportionately. Emperor Karl's efforts to restore constitutional government did not restore the trust of the non-German nationalities, which were ripe for Allied propaganda, but Italy's leaders were not interested. When H. G. Wells visited Italy in summer 1916, he found 'thoughtful men talking everywhere of the Yugoslav riddle'. Everywhere, it seems, except the cabinet and the Supreme Command, which were in denial.

The Yugoslavs, by contrast, had not stood still. A number of Croat and Slovene politicians fled abroad in 1914 and organised the Yugoslav Committee. This group lobbied the Allies to support the cause of Yugoslav unification, merging the Habsburg lands where Slovenes, Croats, Serbs and Bosniaks lived, with the independent kingdoms of Serbia and Montenegro. The same cause was argued passionately by the government of Serbia, which found itself exiled on the island of Corfu after Austria and Bulgaria conquered the Serbian kingdom in autumn 1915. The Yugoslav Committee and the Serbian government agreed that the Slavs living between the Alps and Greece should be united in a sovereign state. Their views on the nature of this state were, however, antithetical. The exiled Serbs could not accept the Committee's vision of national unity on a federal basis with full equality for Serbs, Croats and Slovenes.

Events in 1917 increased the pressure on both groups to compromise. Representing the Slovenes and Croats, as well as the large community of Habsburg Serbs from Croatia, who were directly threatened by Italian expansion, the Yugoslav Committee needed the promise of protection by the Serbian army. The Serbian government, facing the loss of its imperial Russian mentor, was driven to acknowledge the equal rights of non-Serb peoples. At the same time, Emperor Karl's peace feelers to the Allies threatened to revive an option that alarmed both the Committee and the Serbs: namely, self-government for the Habsburg Yugoslavs inside the empire.

Against this background, in mid-July 1917, the Serbian prime minister and the leader of the Yugoslav Committee agreed a blueprint for a postwar Yugoslav state, to be called the Kingdom of Serbs, Croats and Slovenes, under the Serbian monarchy and comprising 'all territory compactly inhabited by our people'. This pact between monarchist Serbs seeking to expand their kingdom to the Alps and the Adriatic coast, and on the other side republican Croats and Slovenes seeking a federal route to national independence, would not ensure harmony after the war, but it showed a united front to the world, outflanking the pro-Austrian Yugoslavs with their schemes for self-government within the empire, and – of course – dealing a blow to Italian nationalists. Sonnino was bitterly disappointed; he had hoped that tensions between Habsburg Yugoslavs and the Serbian government would deepen under pressure.

Touring the Allied capitals a fortnight later to drum up support, Sonnino called on Asquith, who as British prime minister in 1915 had helped bring Italy into the war. Territorial outcomes were, more than ever, preying on the foreign minister's mind. He stressed the 'great difference' between 'what Italy *needs*', meaning the unredeemed lands and 'such territories on the E. of the Adriatic as will make her secure', and on the other hand 'what she would *like* to have (in Asia Minor etc.).' He added that he was 'all for a deal with the Yugoslavs'. This flexibility was specious. For if Sonnino counted 'the harbours, bays and islands' on the eastern Adriatic coast as must-haves for Italy, what could he offer the Yugoslavs in exchange? There was no basis here for a deal. Events made Sonnino's fundamentalism about the Treaty of London look increasingly out of touch. By October, the timorous Boselli was ready to replace him with someone more adaptable. Before he could follow through, Italy was overwhelmed by its worst disaster since unification.

TWENTY-FIVE

Caporetto:
The Flashing Sword of Vengeance

The onrush of a conquering force is like the
bursting of pent-up waters into a chasm a
thousand fathoms deep.
SUN TZU

The Twelfth Battle of the Isonzo

October brought weeks of rain to the upper Isonzo valley, turning to sleet on the heights. Italian observers on both sides of the valley glimpsed the river through ragged gaps in the fog. One morning, they saw Habsburg soldiers move steadily up the valley, two abreast on the narrow road, towards the little town of Caporetto. No cause for alarm; they had to be prisoners marching to the rear. Otherwise . . .

For the Italians, the Twelfth Battle began as something unthinkable. By the time they realised what was happening, they were powerless to stop it. Cadorna liked to say that he led the greatest army in Italy since the Caesars. The last week of October 1917 turned this epic boast inside out; no single defeat in battle had placed Italy in such peril since Hannibal destroyed the Roman legions at Cannae, more than two thousand years before.

The unthinkable had a name: infiltration. On the other side of Europe, while Capello's Second Army died in droves behind Gorizia, the German Eighth Army rewrote the tactical playbook. It happened on 1 September 1917, around the city of Riga, where the River Dvina flows into the Baltic Sea. Aiming to paralyse the Russian lines rather than demolish them, the preliminary bombardment was abrupt – no ranging shots – and deep, preventing the movement of reserves. Protected by a creeping barrage, the assault troops crossed the river upstream and took

Italian infantry attack on the Carso, 1917: an experience of 'extreme resolution' or 'supreme helplessness'? (The soldier on the right carries gelignite tubes to blow up enemy wire.)

Boccioni's *Unique Forms of Continuity in Space* (1913). The bronze muscled figure strides forward, 'a living gun', safe inside the forcefield of his will.

The Italian first line on the southern Carso, near Mount Hermada, in 1917.

Emperor Karl studies the Italian positions beyond Mount Hermada, through binoculars, watched by the last Austrian governor of the imperial Adriatic provinces (Baron Fries-Skene, in plumed hat). On the right, General Boroević converses with the Emperor's aide. The date is 1 June 1917.

Italian wounded at the foot of Mount San Gabriele. Private Pardi carried ammunition up the mountain during the Eleventh Battle, when 'death was so certain that you almost stopped thinking how to avoid it'.

Bosnian prisoners of war. These were the 'lurid Turks' of Italian propaganda.

— M. NERO mk 2245 —

Ladra   Smasti   Libussina

Looking north across the Isonzo valley towards Mount Krn, 'Monte Nero' to the Italians, the highest point on the horizon. Caporetto is just out of sight to the left. This was 'the mighty mountain world' that Rommel and his Württemberg troops admired on 26 October 1917, two months after this panorama was photographed by an Italian officer, and only two days after Italian observers on this spot noticed enemy troops moving up the valley towards Caporetto, and assumed they must be

prisoners under escort to the rear. Lieutenant Gadda's battery was on the Krasji ridge, below the word 'Nero'. Corporal Borroni's platoon clashed with German troops near the river, between Ladra and Caporetto. No wonder that, as Ludendorff remarked, the communications in this sector were 'as bad as could be imagined'.

Italian dead after the German gas attack, Flitsch, 24 October 1917.

Third Army units retreating to the River Piave, early November 1917.

Italian prisoners of war.

Italian cavalry crossing the River Monticano. Here, according to Lord Cavan, commander of British forces in Italy, the enemy 'offered his last serious resistance', on 29 October 1918.

The Italian army entering Gorizia in triumph, early November 1918.

The Big Four in Paris, 1919. From left to right, Lloyd George, Orlando, Clemenceau and Wilson.

The Adriatic Sea, from the edge of the Carso.

the Russians by surprise, punching through their lines from several angles, attacking the weak points without trying to overwhelm all positions at once. The Germans' mobility and devolved command let them exploit this method to the full.

Their success did not take emerge from a vacuum. Since early 1916, if not before, the warring commanders had searched for tactical norms that could, in Hew Strachan's phrase, 're-establish the links between fire and movement which trench warfare had sundered'. Falkenhayn's initial bid for breakthrough at Verdun sent stormtroopers ahead in groups after massive bombardments that had destroyed French communications. The Russians discovered other elements of infiltration with Brusilov's brilliant offensive of May 1916. The British tested different attack formations, turning infantry lines into 'blobs' or, later, diamonds. Although there was no magic key, infiltration tactics emerged as a solution to attritional deadlock against defences that were 'crumbling or incomplete'. This was the situation in the Riga salient, where the Russians were preparing to withdraw as the battle began, and the garrison in the city escaped. And it was certainly the situation on Cadorna's upper Isonzo.

A week before the Riga operation, Emperor Karl wrote to the Kaiser 'in faithful friendship'. The Eleventh Battle of the Isonzo 'has led me to believe we should fare worse in a twelfth'. Austria wished to take the offensive, and would be grateful if Germany could replace Austrian divisions in the east and lend him artillery, 'especially heavy batteries'. He did not ask for direct German participation; indeed he excluded it, for fear of cooling the Austrian troops' rage against 'the ancestral foe'. The Kaiser replied curtly and referred the request to Ludendorff. The German general staff had already assessed that the Austrians would be broken by the next Italian offensive, which they expected before the end of the year. If Austria-Hungary collapsed, as it probably would, Germany would be alone: an outcome that had to be prevented. Meanwhile the Austrian high command – ignoring the Emperor's scruple – had separately suggested a combined offensive.

Ludendorff decided he could spare six to eight divisions until the winter. He dusted off Conrad's idea for an offensive across the upper Isonzo between Tolmein and Flitsch. Hindenburg, the chief of the general staff, sent one of his most able officers to reconnoitre the ground. An expert in mountain warfare, Lieutenant General Krafft von

Dellmensingen had served in the Dolomites in 1915 and seen the emergence of fast-moving assault tactics against Romania. He now prepared a plan to drive the Italian Second Army some 40 kilometres back from the Isonzo to the Tagliamento and perhaps beyond, depending on the breakthrough and its collateral impact on the lower Isonzo. It was not intended as a fatal blow; the Germans believed the Italians were so dependent on British and French coal, ore and grain that nothing short of total occupation – which was out of the question – could make them sue for peace. Success would be measured by Italy's inability to attack again before the following spring or summer.

The first target was a wedge of mountainous territory, five kilometres wide between Flitsch and Saga (now Žaga) in the north, then 25 kilometres long, from this line to the Austrian bridgehead at Tolmein. The little town of Caporetto lies midway between Saga and Tolmein, near a gap in the Isonzo valley's western wall of mountains. This breach, leading to the lowlands of Friuli, gave Caporetto a strategic importance quite out of proportion to its size. This had been recognised a century earlier by Napoleon, when he warned his commander in Friuli that if the Austrians broke through here, the next defensible line was the River Piave. South of Caporetto, the valley is a kilometre wide; northwards, the river snakes through a gorge of cliffs and steep hillsides, then broadens again at Saga, where the river angles sharply eastwards. At Flitsch, the valley splays open like a bowl, flanked on the north by Mount Rombon.

Since Austrian military intelligence had cracked the Italian codes earlier in the year, the Central Powers were well informed about enemy dispositions in this labyrinth of ridges rising 2,000 metres, where communications were 'as bad as could be imagined'. Krafft thought the Italian defences were so shallow that losing this wedge of ground could crack open the front from Gorizia to the Carnian Alps. Eight to 10 divisions at Tolmein and three more at Flitsch should suffice. As at Riga, the artillery would deliver a very violent bombardment, then support the assault by laying down box barrages to isolate enemy units.

Hindenburg created a combined Austro-German force for the purpose, the Fourteenth Army, led by a German general, Otto von Below, with Krafft as his chief of staff. Seven German divisions, all of high quality, would join the three Austrian divisions already on the ground plus an additional two from the Eastern Front, backed by a reserve of five divisions: a total of 17 divisions, supported by 1,076 guns, 174 mortars and 31 engineering companies. It was an Austrian general who proposed applying the new tactics. Alfred Krauss, appointed to command a corps at the northern end of the sector, argued that the attack should proceed along the valley floors, avoiding the high ridges in order to isolate and encircle them. He had made a similar proposal to Conrad in 1916, in vain. This time, his advice was taken. For Cadorna, obsessed with attacking high ground and retaining it at all costs, this proposition would have made no sense. Yet it was appropriate to the terrain north of Tolmein, where the mountain ranges loosely interlock, with the Isonzo threading between them.

The attack was scheduled for mid-October, leaving only five or six weeks to prepare. The roads from the assembly areas beyond the Alps were few and poor, especially from the north; two passes linked Flitsch to the Austrian hinterland, but the roads were narrow. Fortunately the Austrians had a railhead near Tolmein. Some 2,400 convoys brought 140,000 men, a million and a half artillery shells, three million fuses, two million flares, nearly 800 tonnes of explosive, 230,000 steel helmets, 100,000 pairs of boots, 60,000 horses. Then October brought its downpours. The sodden roads sagged under the ceaseless traffic of boots, wheels and hooves. By veiling the massive concentration, however, the bad weather served the Central Powers well. The Germans went to great lengths to keep their presence secret. Transports arrived by night, some units wore Austrian uniforms, others were taken openly to Trentino then secretly moved eastwards. Fake orders were communicated by radio. The Austrian lines on the Carso, 40 kilometres away, were ostentatiously weakened to deter the Italians from transferring men northwards. The German air force, brought in for the first time, photographed the Italian lines and prevented Italian planes from overflying the Austrian lines. The gunners bracketed their targets over a six-day period, to avoid alerting the enemy.

If the Italian observers noticed nothing unusual, this was partly because they expected the front to remain quiet until spring 1918. Austrian deserters talked about an attack in the offing, but their warnings were ignored. By the 24th, the Central Powers had a huge advantage in artillery, trench mortars, machine guns and poison gas on the upper Isonzo, and roughly a 3:2 superiority in men. The Germans crouched like tigers, ready to spring. As for the Austrians, far from being demoralised by sharing their front, they were inspired by the scale of German involvement. Without knowing the whole plan, the troops realised something big was up. The possibility of moving beyond the hated mountains stirred their hearts.

On 18 September, Cadorna put the forces on the Isonzo front on a defensive footing. Without ensuring that his order was implemented, he let himself be absorbed by other matters. He was incensed to discover that Colonel Bencivenga, his chef de cabinet until the end of August (and who was so unhelpful over the Carzano initiative), had criticised his command in high places in Rome. This mattered because Cadorna's Socialist and Liberal critics were finally making common cause, preparing to challenge his command when parliament opened in mid-October.

He was also vexed by an article in an Austrian newspaper. Cadorna filed every press clipping about himself, with references underlined in crayon. Several months earlier, a Swiss journalist had written that the Austrian lines on the Isonzo were impregnable. After the Tenth Battle, Cadorna sent his card to the journalist with a sarcastic inscription: 'With spirited compliments on such penetrating prophecies about the strength of the Austrian lines, and hopes that you will never desist from similar insights.' The insecurity betrayed by this gesture swallowed more urgent priorities. Now he did it again. A provincial newspaper in the Tyrol had commented that Cadorna wasted the first month after Italy's intervention in May 1915. This criticism was too painfully true to pass; Colonel Gatti had to prepare a rebuttal explaining to readers in Innsbruck that Cadorna had not wasted even a day. (Would his revered Napoleon have written to an English provincial newspaper to explain why he decided not to invade Britain?)

Then he went on holiday with his wife near Venice. The rain was so heavy that he returned early, on 19 October, 'in excellent spirits: calm, rested, tranquil'. By this point, the Supreme Command had been aware for at least three weeks that an attack was imminent on the upper Isonzo. The presence of Germans was rumoured. Even so, Cadorna's staff did not take the threat seriously. The Austrians had never launched a big offensive across the Isonzo; why would they do so now, with winter at the door?

As late as 20 October, Cadorna did not expect an Austrian offensive before 1918. On the 21st, two Romanian deserters told the Italians the place and time of the attack. They, too, were ignored. Next day,

Cadorna escorted the King to the top of Mount Stol, one of the ridges above Caporetto that link the Isonzo valley to Friuli. They agreed there was no reason to expect anything exceptional. On the 23rd, he predicted there would be no major attack, and said the Austrians would be mad to launch operations out of the Flitsch basin. Even on the morning of the 24th, when the enemy bombardment was under way, Cadorna advised his artillery commanders to spare their munitions, in view of the attack on the Carso that would inevitably follow. Rarely has a commander been exposed so completely as the prisoner of his preconceptions. What Clausewitz called 'the flashing sword of vengeance' was poised above his head, and he was unaware. He had little idea what was going on in the minds of his own soldiers; imagining the enemy's intentions was far beyond him.

At 02:00 on 24 October, the German and Austrian batteries opened up along the 30-kilometre front. The weight and accuracy of fire were unprecedented, smashing the Italian gun lines, observation posts and communications, 'as if the mountains themselves were collapsing'. According to Krafft von Dellmensingen, even the German veterans of Verdun and the Somme had seen nothing like it. Rather than softening up the enemy, the purpose was to atomise the defence. It succeeded with terrible effect, helped by fog and freezing rain, and more significantly by Italian negligence. For the lines on the upper Isonzo were in a sorry state.

After 18 September, the Duke of Aosta put Cadorna's order into effect on the Carso, placing the Third Army on the defensive. The lines after the Eleventh Battle were incomplete in many places and lacked depth in most. Batteries had to be moved to less vulnerable locations. Communications along and between the lines were poor, especially at the juncture of command areas; they had to be improved. These humdrum tasks also awaited the Second Army, by far the biggest Italian force, deployed between Gorizia and Mount Rombon. Yet its commander, General Capello, was reluctant; he convened his corps commanders and paid lip-service to 'the defensive concept' while urging them to hold 'the spirit of the counter-offensive' ever-present in their minds. Capello enjoyed a mystical turn of phrase, and what he meant here was not clear. Probably Krafft von Dellmensingen was right when he wrote in his memoirs that Capello had no idea what was meant by a modern defensive battle. He followed up with an order that his commanders must convince the enemy of 'our offensive intentions'.

Again, Capello wanted to go his own way, and again Cadorna shrank from confronting him.

This confusion was most harmful on the Tolmein–Rombon sector, which was woefully undermanned. Of the Second Army's 30 divisions, comprising 670,000 men, only ten were deployed north of the Bainsizza plateau. The northern sector had seen little significant action since 1916, and the Supreme Command judged that the mountains formed their own defence. For the same reason, none of the Second Army's 13 reserve divisions was located north of Tolmein. East of the Isonzo, the troops were concentrated in the front line, depriving the second and third lines of strength, while the mountainous terrain would make it difficult to bring reserves forward, even supposing they could be transferred in time to be effective.

Despite these defects, nothing much was done until the second week of October. By this time, Capello was laid low with a recurrent gastric infection and nephritis. Sometimes he relinquished command and retired to bed or to a military hospital in Padua. This did not improve the efficiency of his headquarters, however. With Capello breathing down his neck and the Supreme Commander ignoring him, the interim commander's grip was less than assured.

Illness did not shake Capello's conceit. On 15 October, he was still talking about 'the thunderbolt of the counter-offensive'. Four more days elapsed before Cadorna unambiguously rejected his request for extra reserves to bolster a visionary operation to push the Austrians back by six kilometres. Another four days passed before Capello explicitly dropped the idea of a counter-offensive. He did not commit himself to Cadorna's defensive design until late afternoon on 23 October: less than 12 hours before the start of the Twelfth Battle. Incredibly, Cadorna failed to see that the practical unity of his command had been compromised, perhaps beyond repair. There was no clenched fist in charge of the army, as his father had insisted there must be. His worst nightmare had come true, and he could not see it.

The weakest section of the front was strategically the most important, around the Tolmein bridgehead. Commands were blurred; brigades and regiments came and went, and commanding officers were shuffled like playing cards. On the Kolovrat ridge and Mount Matajur, many units that faced the German army on the afternoon of the 24th only reached their positions that morning.

On 10 October, Cadorna ordered the 19th Division to move most of its forces west of the Isonzo. This was significant, for the 19th straddled the valley at Tolmein. The lines in the valley bottom, and on the hills to the west, were in better shape than the lines further east. Cadorna saw that the distribution of men and guns favoured offensive action, and wanted this to be corrected without delay. As the 19th Division was part of XXVII Corps, responsibility for implementing this order lay with the corps commander, Pietro Badoglio. Since his men stormed the summit of Mount Sabotino in August 1916, Badoglio's career had been meteoric, raising him from lieutenant colonel to general within a year, making him the best-known soldier in the country after Cadorna, Capello, the Duke of Aosta and D'Annunzio. Now, inexplicably, he waited 12 days before implementing Cadorna's critical order. When the Germans attacked out of Tolmein, fewer than half of the division's battalions were west of the river, with an even smaller proportion of its medium and heavy guns. Badoglio had ordered the valley bottom to be 'watched' (as distinct from defended) by a minimal force. He had also instructed the corps artillery commander not to open fire without his authorisation. Around 02:30 on 24 October, this commander called for permission to fire. Badoglio refused: 'We only have three days' worth of shells.' By 06:30, the telephone link between the corps commander's quarters and his artillery headquarters, five kilometres away, had been destroyed. The artillery commander stuck to his orders, so there was no defensive fire around Tolmein.

At the northern end of the sector, the Italians were tucked into strong positions along the valley bottom between Flitsch and Saga. If Krauss were to capture this stretch of the river and take the mountain ridge beyond Saga, the Italians had to be rapidly overwhelmed. After knocking out the Italian guns, the Germans fired 2,000 poison-gas shells into the Flitsch basin. The gas was a mixture of phosgene and diphenylchloroarsine; the Italian masks could withstand chlorine gas, but not this. Blending with fog, the yellowish fumes went undetected until too late. As many as 700 men of the Friuli Brigade died at their posts. Observers on the far side of the basin scanned the valley positions, saw soldiers at their posts, and reported that the attack had failed. The dead men were found later, leaning against the walls of their dug-outs and trenches, faces white and swollen, rifles gripped between stiff knees.

(In Udine, 40 kilometres from Flitsch, Cadorna rises at 05:00, as always, to find his boots polished and uniform ironed by his bedside. After breakfasting on milk, coffee and savoyard biscuits with butter, he writes the daily letter to his family. This morning, he remarks that the worsening weather favours the defence. He is, he adds, perfectly calm and confident. At the 06:00 briefing, he learns that the second line on the upper Isonzo is under heavy shelling. He interprets the fact that there has been no assault as support for his view that this attack is a feint, intended to divert attention from the Carso.)

Zero hour was 07:30. The Austrian units spread into the fogbound valley below Mount Rombon. There was not much fighting; the powerful batteries at the bend in the river, by Saga, had been silenced. In mid-afternoon, the Italian forward units on Rombon were ordered to fall back to Saga after dark. With Austrians above and below them, their position was untenable. After burning everything that could not be carried, the three alpini battalions traversed the northern valley slopes while their attackers felt their way south of the river.

The Austrians reached Saga at dawn on the 25th to find it empty: the Italians had pulled back overnight to higher ground. For Saga guards the entrance to the pass of Uccea, leading westward. The southern side of this pass is formed by Mount Stol. The Italians hoped to block access to the Uccea pass from positions on Stol. Daylight illumines the high ridges before the valleys emerge from shadow. The Austrians entering Saga would look up at the Italian positions on Stol, and know that very little stood between them and the plains of Friuli.

It was a spectacular day's work by the Krauss Corps. At the other end of the wedge, around Tolmein, progress had been even more dramatic. As we move there, let us pause over the sharp ridges that radiate like spokes from Mount Krn, and look more closely at one of the batteries that stayed silent on 24 October.

The Italian third line between Flitsch and Tolmein ran along one of these ridges. One of the crags was occupied by an anti-aircraft battery under Lieutenant Carlo Emilio Gadda, 5th Regiment of Alpini, whom we met in an earlier chapter. No more eccentric character fought on the front. Later in life, he became modern Italy's most original writer of fiction, the author of labyrinthine (and virtually untranslatable) novels that manage to be confessional and evasive, playful and melancholy, learned and rawly emotional all at once. His work weaves rich patterns of neurotic digression; the narrative escapes from a compelling, intolerable memory or emotion by fastening onto some unrelated motif which meanders helplessly back toward the source of pain, obliging the next brilliant deviation.

Born in Milan in 1893, Gadda broke off his studies in engineering to volunteer in 1915. He was an unhappy son of the repressed middle class, one of many in his generation for whom the war meant escape from claustrophobic homes, protective mothers, dull prospects and the general powerlessness of young men in a world ruled by grey beards and wing-collars. Idealistic, upright and naïve, distracted 'to the point of cretinism' as he said of himself, Gadda kept his real views on the war hidden from fellow officers and his men. For he was privately scathing about incompetent commanders, politicians and 'that stuttering idiot of a King'. Nor was he sentimental about the other ranks; their low cunning (*furberia*) and lack of discipline would, he feared, lead the country to fail its first great test since unification. Yet he loved the comradeship and heroism of war, and dreaded returning to the muddles of civilian life. By October 1917, he had seen action in the Alps and on the Carso.[1] He was perching on a crag above the Isonzo in October 1917 because he wanted to be there; he had let another officer take the spell of leave to which he was entitled.

Looking north, towards the enemy, Gadda would have seen the Italian first line on the opposite ridge, roughly two kilometres away. The second line was a thousand metres below, on the valley floor. On the map, it all looked convincing enough. In fact, the lines were extremely vulnerable. Word came down the wire from sector HQ at 02:00 on 23 October that enemy artillery fire would commence at once, beginning with gas shells. It did not happen; the sector stayed quiet all day, which Gadda and his 30 men – who had only recently arrived on their crag – spent in strengthening positions along the eastern ridge, leading to Krn. The weather had been bad for days, and that night the temperature dropped below zero.

They are awoken at 02:00 on the 24th by the 'very violent' bombardment of Flitsch, four or five kilometres north. Dawn breaks in thick fog and sleet, and is followed by enemy fire of pinpoint accuracy. Gadda realises that the Austrians want to break the telephone wire

1 Gadda served on the eastern Carso in August 1916, when Ungaretti was on Mount San Michele. It is as if James Joyce and T. S. Eliot – equivalent innovators in English prose and poetry – both volunteered, fought on the Somme, and survived.

linking the batteries along the ridge. They soon succeed. The fog partly disperses, though it still shrouds the first and second lines. The men peer into it. No sounds reach them. Gadda interprets the eerie silence as proof that the Genoa Brigade, in front of them, is putting up a poor show. He worries about hitting his own forward lines if he opens fire in the fog. Several nerve-straining hours later, they hear machine guns further along their ridge towards Flitsch and glimpse men a few hundred metres away: either the Italians retreating or the Austrians giving chase.

Around 15:00, the small-arms fire is drowned out by massive detonations from the Isonzo valley, at their backs. This fills the men with dread. (The Italians are blowing up the munitions dumps and bridge at Caporetto before withdrawing.) Then silence settles again. (They do not know it, but their divisional commander has just ordered all the troops in their sector to fall back. Too late! The only bridges over the Isonzo have been blown or captured.) That night, the men lie down beside their machine guns, expecting the enemy to storm the ridge at every moment.

Further south, around Tolmein, zero hour on the 24th loosed an attack with several prongs. The main thrust was directed against high ground west of the Isonzo. Two German divisions and an Austrian division radiated out of the bridgehead and over the river, striking up the steep flanks and spurs that lead to the high ridges. Again the initial bombardment was highly effective, smashing the Italian cordon around the bridgehead. By nightfall, despite stiff resistance at some points, the attackers had captured the summits that Krafft identified as keys to Italian control.

North of Tolmein and east of the Isonzo, an Austrian division overran the fragile lines below the summit of Mount Mrzli, which the Italians had tried so hard to capture since 1915. With Badoglio's artillery standing silent, the Italians were rolled back towards the valley bottom, where six German battalions advanced on both sides of the river, meeting little resistance. By noon, the rain had turned to sleet and the Germans occupied Kamno, a hamlet halfway to Caporetto.

Around midday, between Kamno and Caporetto, the Germans clashed with a platoon of the 14th Regiment, 4th Bersaglieri Brigade. One of the Italians involved in that firefight, Delfino Borroni, is the last Italian veteran of the Twelfth Battle, still alive at this time of writing. His regiment reached Cividale on the 22nd and marched through the rainy night to the second line. They got to Livek, overlooking the Isonzo, very early on the 24th. Wet and hungry, the men found a store of chestnuts in one of the buildings and roasted them over a fire. Corporal Borroni (b. 1898) gorged himself, and had to run outside at the double. As he crouched in the bushes, trousers round his knees, the commanding officer called his platoon to fall in. 'Fix bayonets, boys, we're going down!' They crept towards the valley bottom in the darkness and waited for several hours, wondering what was going on. Eventually the Germans loom out of the mist. In Borroni's memory, they are a grey swarm, a cloud. With the advantage of surprise, the Italians take them all prisoner: a detachment of some 80 men. The next German unit arrives at noon with machine guns and forces the Italians back up the hill to Livek.

At 12:15, as Borroni and his men are ducking the machine-gun fire near Caporetto, Cadorna is still asking how many guns the Second Army can spare for the Third Army, to parry the expected thrust on the Carso.

The enemy reaches the edge of Caporetto at 13:55. A few Italian officers try to stem the flood of troops retreating through the town. Those with rifles are pulled out of the crowd; the rest are allowed to go on their way, so as not to clog up the streets. When the men see this, they start throwing away their rifles. They look as if they hate the war more than the enemy. At 15:30, the retreating Italians blow the bridge over the Isonzo. Caporetto is captured half an hour later, along with 2,000 Italian prisoners. When German bugles sound in the main square, the Slovene citizens pour onto the street 'to welcome their German liberators'.

The right flank of the force that attacked westwards out of Tolmein at 08:00 was formed by the Alpine Corps, a specialist mountain unit of division size, comprising Bavarian regiments and the Württemberg Mountain Battalion. The WMB included nine companies, staffed and equipped to operate autonomously. One of the company commanders was a 25-year-old lieutenant, a born soldier and natural leader, clear-headed, physically tough and avid for glory. His name was Erwin Rommel. Twenty-five years later, he would be one of the most famous soldiers in the world, admired by Hitler, adored by his men and respected by his enemies. This morning, Rommel was poised to grasp the sort of opportunity that does not come twice in a lifetime. His company of 200 men, deployed on the outer edge of the formation, was tasked to protect the right flank of the Bavarian Life Guards as they attacked the Kolovrat ridge opposite Tolmein.

Moving to the jump-off line, he is surprised by the lack of interdiction fire. The Italian heavy batteries were active on the 23rd; what has happened to them? His company reaches the Isonzo 'frozen and soaked to the skin' by heavy rain. They could be stopped by machine guns, but there are none. Again, the preparatory shelling has done its job; the surviving Italians emerge from the rubble with hands high and faces 'twisted in fear'.

Rommel traverses up the hillside while the Bavarians to his left attack the hill head-on. The trees have not yet shed their leaves, and the undergrowth is dense. This gives cover from the Italian lines above – all the more welcome as the Württembergers have no artillery support: the Austro-German batteries are all helping the frontal attack. Advancing at the speed of the machine gunners, each carrying more than 45 kilograms, the company 'worked its way forward in the pouring rain, moving from bush to bush, climbing up concealed in hollows and gullies'. They capture a series of isolated Italian forward positions. 'There was no organised resistance and we usually took a hostile position from the rear. Those who did not surrender fled head over heels into the lower woods, leaving their weapons behind.'

Moving on, they find intact batteries, deserted by their crews. Fuelling themselves with Italian rations, they press on to the crest of the Kolovrat. Here they encounter their first real obstacle: Hill 1114, well fortified and defended, is the next bump or summit on the ridge, blocking their advance. The Bavarians are already on the saddle below the hill, and their commander tries to assert himself over the Württembergers. Rommel insists that he takes orders from his battalion commander (who, conveniently, is far behind).

Overnight, his mind works on the problem ahead. A frontal attack on the hill would need artillery support. A bold alternative occurs: he could lead a small detachment in a flanking movement around Hill 1114, then break on to the ridge above the enemy stronghold and continue the attack along the ridge, leaving the Bavarians to mop up. This plan – in effect, a local application of infiltration tactics – appeals to 'the aggressive officers and men' of the WMB. It has another advantage, too: 'A successful breakthrough west of Hill 1114 would have an effect on the positions lower down.' In other words, isolating the enemy would demoralise him. This reasoning, characteristic of Rommel, gives a measure of the Germans' advantage.

During this tumultuous day, the Supreme Command receives essential information after hours of delay or not at all. By late morning, word reaches Udine through Capello's headquarters that the enemy has attacked out of Tolmein. During the afternoon, dribs of news indicate that the Isonzo valley has been occupied and the hills west of Tolmein are falling like dominoes. Along the front, telephone lines go dead or are answered by guttural voices. Staff officers are in denial, and corps commanders start to trade blame. Capello orders his reserves to the front, unaware that any fresh forces will arrive too late to make a difference. (The speed of the enemy advance is still unimaginable.) Several divisions collapse. In some places, the reserves push their way to the line against a current of abusive comrades. Almost nothing of this is known at the Supreme Command, where Cadorna telegraphs all Second Army units: 'The great enemy offensive has begun.' The Supreme Command puts its trust in the heroic spirit of all commanders, officers and men, who will know how to 'win or die'. But the Second Army officers do not know how to win, and the men do not want to die.

In Rome, parliament debates a Socialist motion for an official inquiry into alleged secret foreign funding of pro-war newspapers in 1914 and 1915. In the words of a Socialist deputy, 'The country has the right to know if the hands of those who are responsible for the war, who incited it and urged it on, are filthy not with blood, but with money.' In the late afternoon, the minister of war, General Giardino, takes the floor. The chamber is packed. Instead of defending the interventionist press, however, Giardino argues against an unrelated proposal to demobilise some of the older draft classes. After reading out parts of Cadorna's bulletin about enemy preparations for an attack, he warns that this is not the time to reduce strength. The enemy is poised to exploit dissension. 'Let them attack,' he perorates, 'we are not afraid.' The deputies thunder approval. (The next day, *Corriere della Sera* reports that the delirium in parliament was like the heady days of May 1915.) Back at his ministry, Giardino finds an urgent telegram from Udine: the enemy are attacking Caporetto, they have taken thousands of prisoners and huge quantities of weapons.

*

Around 18:00, Gatti sees Cadorna 'serene and smiling' amid the tumult at the Supreme Command, still half-convinced the real attack will follow on the Carso. He reviews the daily bulletin, which claims that the enemy has concentrated his forces on the front for an attack which 'finds us strong and well prepared' – a phrase that makes Gatti wince. The Italian guns are responding with 'violent salvoes'.

Cadorna does not know that the batteries have been silent all day. By 22:00, the scales are falling from his eyes. The Italians have been forced back to Saga and Kolovrat. Maybe 20,000 men have been captured. It is unlikely that the line can be held. He orders Capello to prepare the withdrawal of all forces on the Bainsizza plateau. Then he retires to take a strategic decision: should the Second Army retreat? Instead of assessing the situation on its merits, he lets hope persuade him that all may not be lost. He defines three new defensive lines, west of the Isonzo. On paper they look viable; in reality, even a highly disciplined army would be challenged to build secure positions while retreating through mountains. In a separate order, he instructs Capello and the Duke of Aosta to strengthen the defences on the River Tagliamento.

By now, some 14 infantry regiments and many battalions of alpini and bersaglieri have succumbed. As one of the staff officers milling around the Supreme Command, picking up snippets of news each more appalling than the last, Gatti cannot believe what he hears. 'Monstrous,' he writes helplessly in his diary, 'inconceivable'. Surely he will wake tomorrow and find it is all a dream.

The skies cleared overnight, as wind thinned the fog and low cloud. Very few telephone lines were still working. Cadorna took solace in writing to his family: 'If things go badly now, how they'll pounce on me. What a wonderful country this is! Let God's will be done.' At 07:00, he ordered a withdrawal from Mount Korada, south of Tolmein. This was a strategic position, protecting the Bainsizza line and blocking enemy access to Friuli. He still hesitated to order a general retreat to the Tagliamento; he knew how fragile the rear defences were, and feared that the Third and Fourth Armies, and the Carnia Corps, might be cut off. At 08:30 he took Gatti aside. This might look like the Austrian attack in Trentino in spring 1916, he said, but it was much more serious. 'Napoleon himself could not do anything in these conditions.' He blamed the soldiers. 'My personal influence cannot reach two million men,' he protested. 'Not even Napoleon could do that, in his Russian campaign.'

In the north, the Krauss Corps pressed westwards to the pass of Uccea and south to join up with the Germans at Caporetto. Italian forces east of the Isonzo were trapped, whether they knew it or not. The night passed quietly for Lieutenant Gadda and his gunners on their crag, except for occasional explosions and flares in the valley behind them. Lacking information and orders, Gadda did not know what to think or do. Yesterday's bombardment of their ridge was heavy, but he had survived much worse on the Carso. Their munitions were almost exhausted, so they could not expect to resist for long. Or might they use the fog to trick the Austrians into thinking the ridge was strongly defended? Gadda and his men could not know it, but they were victims of a perfect application of the Riga tactics. Isolated and confused, they could be left to surrender in their own time while the enemy pressed ahead.

Around 03:00 on the 25th, a messenger brings orders to retreat across the Isonzo. Caporetto has fallen: it is in enemy hands. Gadda leads his men down the mountain an hour later, carrying all their equipment, in complete darkness. 'My heart was broken,' he wrote later. Italian positions on the surrounding ridges are in flames. They pass groups of men from the Genoa Brigade with no officers, and hundreds of mules abandoned or killed in yesterday's shelling. They reach the river around 11:00 and see Italian troops, unarmed, on the far side of the river, apparently heading for Caporetto. Can it still be in Italian hands after all, or has it been recaptured? His unit of 30 has grown to a thousand or so. Enemy troops are converging towards them, they have to cross the river which runs through a steep gorge, and is in spate, five or six metres wide and very fast, barring the way. Their dream of pushing Italy's frontier beyond 'this cursed Isonzo' returns to mock them.

Ranging along the bank, they find a rickety bridge of planks lashed together with telephone wire, swaying over the torrent with a metal cable as railing. It would take all day to file across. He moves upstream, hoping the enemy has not broken through further north, towards Flitsch. Soldiers coming the other way tell him the next bridge upstream has been dropped. He cannot bear to believe them, and harangues them for spreading defeatist rumours. Then he sees the blown bridge and leads his men back to the plank bridge, their only hope.

There are troops in black uniforms on the far side of the river, moving up from Caporetto. His heart leaps: 'Look! Reinforcements!' Then he hears machine-gun and rifle fire, and realises the appalling truth: the Germans are on both sides of the river. Some soldiers try to cross the plank bridge and are targeted by machine guns concealed across the valley. The Italians throw their rifles away and cross the planks to surrender, obeying German officers who direct the movement of men with whistles, like football referees. The heap of rifles, machine guns, cartridge clips and ammunition belts at the water's edge rises higher. Even if they hid until nightfall, Gadda's unit would not be able to cross 'the terrible, insuperable Isonzo'. It would be pointless to hold out, childish even. With a heavy heart, he orders his men to put their guns beyond use. They walk the plank one by one.

The prisoners are marched to Caporetto. The Germans treat them correctly; there is no brutality. A drunken Italian soldier drops his bottle of wine at the edge of the village, staining the dust crimson. Gadda and a fellow officer manage to steal some shirts and a uniform from abandoned houses. Later, he will wish he had stuffed his pockets with biscuit from an abandoned wagon. The Germans are setting up offices, using captured Italian staff cars as well as their own to move along the valley. Groups of soldiers wander around, German and Italian, some of them drunk. Dead men and mules litter the streets. It is a fine warm afternoon. Two whores stop them and ask for introductions to the German officers. Gadda's gallant comrade asks the girls what plans they have now. 'Italians or Germans,' they say, 'it is all the same to us!' Their carefree answer mortifies Gadda, who realises that the day's evil has not yet been drained.

Soon he is on his way to prison camp in Austria, 'marching from midnight to 8 a.m.: horror, extremely sleepy and exhausted . . . The end of hope, annihilation of interior life. Extreme anguish for the fatherland.' Capture is, above all, *shameful*. Over the next year, as he slowly starves, disgrace feeds on him. Reflecting endlessly on the defeat, he blames it on the Italian generals and their lack of foresight. Yet Gadda feels that prison is a justified punishment; the army has not risen to meet history's challenge. Marches, battles and retreats haunt his sleep. He imagines family and friends reproaching him: 'You let them get past . . . '

Rommel looks up at the ridge, sparkling in the sunrise on 25 October. The battalion commander has arrived and approved his plan. He leads his detachment along the hillside, traversing below the ridge. They stumble on an enemy outpost, fast asleep in a clump of bushes. His tally of prisoners is mounting. The Italians higher up the ridge are no better prepared; the possibility of being attacked before lower positions have fallen has not occurred to them.

Beyond the next summit, called Kuk, the ridge falls sharply to the village of Livek. The Italians on Kuk expect a frontal attack. Instead Rommel swerves out of view across the southern flank of the hill, bypassing Kuk entirely. The German machine gunners sweat and gasp in the noonday sun. Soon he can look down onto Livek, swarming with Italians trying to fend off the German units that are pressing up the hillside from the Isonzo valley. Beyond Livek, the ridge rises again towards the goal: Mount Matajur, overlooking Friuli. Whoever captures Matajur will win the Pour le Mérite, the Blue Max, Prussia's highest military honour.

As his detachment catches up, he decides that Mount Kuk can be left to others. He moves down to the road connecting Livek to the rear, and starts to capture Italian traffic. 'Everyone was having fun and there was no shooting,' Rommel recalled gaily. 'Soon we had more than a hundred prisoners and fifty vehicles. Business was booming.' Things get more serious when a bersaglieri unit hoves into sight. After a fierce exchange of fire, he and his 150 Württembergers convince the 50 officers and 2,000 men of the 4th Bersaglieri Brigade to surrender.

During the morning of the 25th, an image of disaster emerged from the information reaching the Supreme Command: breakthroughs all along the front; morale collapsing; thousands of men making their way to the rear. The first towns west of the mountains were already threatened. Defence on the hoof was not working. Cadorna's best if not only chance of avoiding catastrophe was to pull back the Second Army to a line far enough west to regroup before the enemy reached them. Capello advised a general retreat to the River Torre or the Tagliamento. When Cadorna disagreed, Capello took himself off to hospital in Padua. Next morning, he offered to return; Cadorna declined: he had enough on his plate without an ailing and probably sulking Capello. Where the two men saw eye to eye was in blaming many regiments for not doing their duty. Late in the afternoon, Cadorna wrote to his son:

The men are not fighting. That's the situation, and plainly a disaster is imminent . . . Do not worry about me, my conscience is wholly clean . . . I am very calm indeed and too proud to be affected by anything that anybody can say. I shall go and live somewhere far away and not ask anything of anyone.

By the end of the second day, the Central Powers controlled the Isonzo north of Tolmein. Mount Stol and the Kolovrat–Matajur ridge were on the point of falling. In the south, Badoglio had apparently abandoned his divisions after, or even before, they disintegrated, putting the middle Isonzo in jeopardy. The Duke of Aosta continued to prepare a retreat, moving his heavy batteries westward.

Still Cadorna procrastinated. He painted an encouraging view in the daily bulletin, claiming falsely that Saga had not fallen and that the enemy had made headway further south because Italian interdiction fire had been negated by fog. Then he telegraphed the government: 'Losses are very heavy. Around ten regiments have surrendered without fighting. A disaster is looming, I shall resist to the last.' Before this grim message reached Rome, the government lost a vote of confidence by 314 to 96 votes. The Socialists and anti-war Liberals had brought Boselli down. Cadorna predicted correctly that the new prime minister would be his main enemy in the cabinet, Vittorio Orlando.

Meanwhile soldiers streamed westwards, throwing away their rifles and chanting 'The war's over! We're going home! Up with the Pope! Up with Russia!' Around midnight Cadorna, Porro and the King were in a car together, returning to Udine from the front, when thousands of troops enveloped them, singing the 'Internationale' as they passed. Cadorna turned to his deputy: 'Why doesn't someone shoot them?' Porro shrugged.

Nervous tension kept Rommel awake. Before midnight, a report arrived that Italian troops were moving towards a hamlet higher up the ridge. Enemy reinforcements could prove fatal to his endeavour; Rommel scrambled out of his sleeping bag and led his detachment (now seven companies) up a narrow path to the hamlet. 'The great disk of the moon shone brightly on the slope, steep as a roof.'

The next Italian line lay above the hamlet, apparently still unoccupied. Rommel decided to encircle the line. 'I felt that the god of War was once more offering his hand.' Despite heavy fire from positions on Mount Cragonza, the next hill along the ridge, Rommel's assault teams climbed around the village unscathed until they looked down on the unsuspecting Italians. 'We shouted down and told them to surrender.

Frightened, the Italian soldiers stared up at us to the rear. Their rifles fell from their hands.' The Württembergers did not fire a shot. Without pausing, they attacked Cragonza. By 07:15, it was theirs.

It is late morning on the 26th, and Rommel looks up at Hill 1356, the last bump on the ridge before Matajur (1,641 metres). Using a heliograph, he signals a request for German batteries on the other side of the Isonzo to target the hill. As the Italians react to the accurate bombardment, he swings south, turns the Italians' flank and attacks from the rear. The Italians rapidly withdraw, and Rommel halts. Hundreds of Italian soldiers are standing about on the hilltop, nearly two kilometres away, 'seemingly irresolute and inactive'. As the crowd swells into thousands, he makes a lightning decision. 'Since they did not come out fighting, I moved nearer, waving a handkerchief', with his detachment spread out in echelons behind him. 'We approached within 1,000 metres and nothing happened.' The enemy 'had no intention of fighting although his position was far from hopeless! Had he committed all his forces, he would have crushed my weak detachment.' Instead, 'The hostile formation stood there as though petrified and did not budge.'

The Germans have to follow a road through a wooded cleft that separates them from the summit. Rommel and a small team hurry ahead, reducing the Italians' time to recalculate the odds. Far ahead of his detachment, he breaks cover and walks steadily forward, waving his handkerchief and calling on the Italians to lay down their arms. 'The mass of men stared at me and did not move. I had the impression that I must not stand still or we were lost.' When the gap between them has narrowed to 150 metres, the Italians rush forward, throwing away their rifles, shouting 'Evviva Germania!' They hoist the incredulous Rommel on their shoulders. Both regiments of the Salerno Brigade surrender en masse. Their commander sits by the road with his staff, weeping.

Rommel never understood the Salerno Brigade's behaviour. Twenty years later, he still marvelled at their surrender, given that 'even a single machine gun operated by an officer could have saved the situation'. He could not conceive the condition of infantry who had been bundled to the top of a mountain and ordered to defend it to the death against some of the best soldiers in the world, without benefit of proper positions, artillery support, communications or confident leadership. Nor, to judge by his memoir, was he aware of the Italian infantry's experience since 1915. The seeds of the Salerno Brigade's defeat were sown long before October 1917.

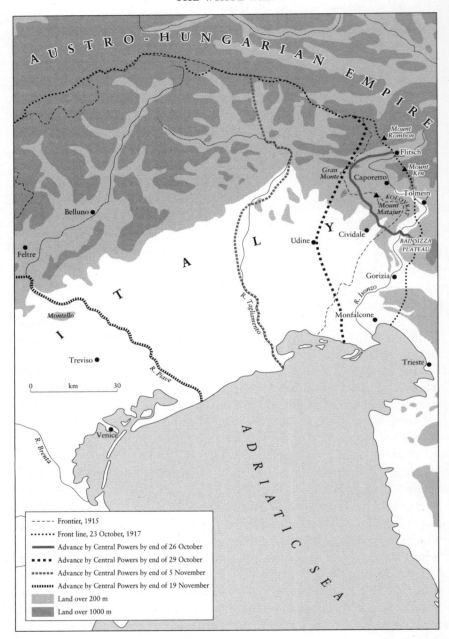

The Twelfth Battle (Caporetto), October–November 1917

An order arrives from Rommel's battalion commander: he must pull back to Mount Cragonza. He decides the major must be poorly informed about the situation ahead, and ignores the order. The stakes are too high, and success will justify his disobedience. The conquest of Mount Matajur is relatively simple. He and his men surprise an Italian company from the rear, near the rocky summit, then divert the force on the summit while Rommel circles around. Before the Germans have set up their machine guns for the final assault, the Italians surrender. By 11:40, Matajur is in German hands. In little over two days, Rommel and his men have covered 18 kilometres of ridge, as the crow flies, involving nearly 3,000 metres of ascent, capturing 150 officers and 9,000 men at a cost of 6 dead and 30 wounded. Operating in harmony with the landscape, moving at extraordinary speed, Rommel's men have swooped along the hillsides, weaving across the ridge between Italian strongholds, mopping up resistance as they go, protected as well as empowered by their own momentum.

The Württembergers gaze around at 'the mighty mountain world', laid out in radiant sunshine. The last ridges and spurs of the Julian Alps slope down to the lowlands of Friuli and the Veneto. There is Udine amid fertile fields. Far away to the south, 'the Adriatic glittered'. Like Rommel's own future. He wore the cross and ribbon of the Blue Max around his neck until the day in 1944 when Hitler, suspecting him of complicity in the so-called generals' plot, gave him a choice: commit suicide, be buried as a hero and save your family, or be arrested, executed and disgraced. As on the sunlit mountains long before, he did not flinch.

The fine weather, the enemy advance, the Italian rout, and Cadorna's hesitancy all persisted throughout the 26th. Survivors of the Second Army were in full retreat; vast numbers of men funnelled through the few roads leading westwards, throwing away their weapons, burning whatever could not be carried, blowing up bridges and looting as they went: 'infantry, alpini, gunners, endlessly', as one of them remembered. 'They move on, move on, not saying a word, with only one idea in their head: to reach the lowland, to get away from the nightmare.' The hillsides below the roads were littered with wagons that had tumbled off the roads; 'The horses lay still, alive or dead, hooves in the air.'

Civilians joined the stampede; the roads were clogged with carts, often drawn by oxen, piled high with chattels. The British volunteer ambulance unit watched the 'long dejected stream' pass along the road to Udine all day: 'soldiers, guns, endless Red Cross ambulances, women and children, carts with household goods, and always more guns and more soldiers – all going towards the rear'. A British Red Cross volunteer saw how 'the panic blast ran through the blocked columns – "They're coming!"' The command made no apparent effort to control the movement or clear the roads for guns and troops.

Cadorna issued an order of the day, warning that the only choice was victory or death. The harshest means would be used to maintain discipline. 'Whoever does not feel that he wins or falls with honour on the line of resistance, is not fit to live.' He elaborated his instructions to the Second and Third Armies for an eventual retreat, and put the Carnia Corps and the Fourth Army on notice to retire beyond the River Piave.

What forced his hand was the loss that evening of Gran Monte, a summit west of Stol. At 02:50 on the 27th, he ordered the Third Army to retreat to the River Tagliamento. The same order went out to the Second Army an hour later. Yet 20 of the Second Army's divisions were still in reasonable order, withdrawing from the Bainsizza and Gorizia. Cadorna's priority should have been the safe retirement of these divisions – more than 400,000 men – behind the River Tagliamento. In his mind, however, the Second Army in its entirety was guilty. Perhaps this explains his decision to make the Second Army use only the northern bridges across the Tagliamento, reserving the more accessible routes for the ten divisions of the Third Army, which retreated 'in good order, unbroken and undefeated', burning the villages as well as its own ammunition dumps as it went, so that 'the whole countryside was blazing and exploding'. This question of the bridges was critical, for the bed of the Tagliamento is up to three kilometres wide and the river was high after the rain, hence impassable by foot.

Between the Isonzo and the Tagliamento, the decomposing Second Army was left to its own devices. In the absence of proper plans for a retreat, there was nothing to arrest its fall. As commanding officers melted away in the tumult, key decisions were taken by any officer on hand, using his own impressions and whatever scraps of information came his way. According to a captain who testified to the Caporetto commission, the soldiers appeared to think the war was over; they were on their way home, mostly in high spirits, *as if they had found the solution to a difficult problem.*

A minor episode described in a letter to the press in 1918 illustrates the point. A lieutenant told the surviving members of his battalion that they would counter-attack soon, orders were on the way. Instead of orders, a sergeant came cycling along the road. When they stopped him and asked what was going on, he said the general and all the other bigwigs had run away.

'Then we're going too,' someone said, and we all shouted 'That's right, we have had enough of the war, we're going home.' The lieutenant said 'You've gone mad, I'll shoot you', but we took his pistol away. We threw our rifles away and started marching to the rear. Soldiers were pouring along the other paths and we told them all we were going home and they should come with us and throw their guns away. I was worried at first, but then I thought I had nothing to lose, I'd have been killed if I'd stayed in the trenches and anything was better than that. And then I felt so angry because I'd put up with everything like a slave till now, I'd never even thought of getting away. But I was happy too, we were all happy, all saying 'it's home or prison, but no more war'.

All along the front, variants on this scene convey a sense that a contract had been violated, dissolving the army's right to command obedience. Nearly 400 years before, in his 'Exhortation to liberate Italy from the barbarians', Niccolò Machiavelli had warned his Prince that 'all-Italian armies' performed badly 'because of the weakness of the leaders' and the unreliability of mercenaries. The best course was 'to raise a citizen army; for there can be no more loyal, more true, or better troops'. They are even better, he added, 'when they find themselves under the command of their own prince and honoured and maintained by him'. Machiavelli the great realist would not have been surprised by the size of the bill that Cadorna was served after dishonouring his troops so consistently, and neglecting their maintenance so blatantly, for two and a half years.

On the third day of the offensive, the Austrians and Germans gave the first signs that they would not convert a brilliant success into crushing victory. Demoted in spring 1917 from chief of the general staff to commander on the Tyrol front, Field Marshal Conrad von Hötzendorf had to sit and watch as von Below's Fourteenth Army turned the tables on the hated enemy. Now he called for reinforcements so he could attack the Italian left flank. At best, Cadorna's Second, Third and Fourth Armies and Carnia Corps would be trapped behind a line from Asiago to Venice, perhaps forcing Italy to accept an armistice. At the least, the Italians would be too distracted by the new threat to establish viable lines on the River Tagliamento.

Although Conrad's reasoning was excellent, the Germans were not ready to increase their commitment or let the Austrians pull more divisions from the Eastern Front. Any Habsburg units which might be released by Russia's virtual withdrawal from the war had to be sent to the Western Front, where the Germans were hard pressed by the British in the Third Battle of Ypres (Passchendaele). All Conrad got were two divisions and a promise that any others no longer needed on the Isonzo would be sent to the Trentino for an offensive by five divisions, to commence on 10 November. But five divisions were pathetically few for the task, and 10 November would be too late.

Cadorna's enemies had not expected such a breakthrough. As late as the 29th, Ludendorff stated that German units would not cross the Tagliamento. By this point, Boroević's First Army (on the Carso) and Second Army (around the Bainsizza) should have been storming after the Italian Third Army. This did not happen, due to bad liaison between commanders, exhaustion, and the temptations of looting. As a result, the Third Army crossed the Tagliamento in good order at the end of October. Both divisions of the Carnia Corps also reached safety with few losses. Von Below would characterise the Austrian Tenth Army, that should have outflanked the Carnia Corps, as not 'very vigorous in combat'.

On the afternoon of the 27th, the Supreme Command decamped from Udine to Treviso. Cadorna did not leave a deputy to organise the retreat. Was this an oversight or a logical expression of his belief that he was irreplaceable? Or was he punishing soldiers who had, as he believed, freely chosen not to fight? Let the cowards and traitors of the Second Army make their own shameful ways to the Tagliamento; they had forfeited the right to assistance.

By the following morning, the Supreme Command was installed in a palazzo in Treviso, more than 100 kilometres from the front. Over breakfast in his new headquarters, the chief talked about the art and landscape of Umbria, impressing his entourage with his serenity, a mood that presumably owed something to the King's and the government's affirmations of complete confidence in his leadership. (Meanwhile the enemy reached the outskirts of Udine, finding them 'almost deserted with broken windows, plundered shops, dead drunk Italian soldiers and dead citizens'.) Before lunch Cadorna released the daily bulletin, blaming the enemy breakthrough on unnamed units of the Second Army, which had 'retreated contemptibly without fighting or surrendered ignominiously'. Realising how incendiary these allegations were, the government watered down the text. It was too late: the original version had gone abroad and was already filtering back into Italy.

Late on the 28th, the enemy crossed the prewar border into Italy. The Austrian military bulletin was gleeful: 'After five days of fighting, all the territory was reconquered that the enemy had laboriously taken in eleven bloody battles, paying for every square kilometre with the lives of 5,400 men.' The Isonzo front ceased to exist. By the 29th, the Second and Third Armies were being showered with Austrian leaflets about Cadorna's scandalous bulletin. 'This is how he repays your valour! You have shed your blood in so many battles, your enemy will always respect you . . . It is your own generalissimo who dishonours and insults you, simply to excuse himself!'

An order on 31 October authorised any officer to shoot any soldier who was separated from his unit or offered the least resistance. This made a target of ten divisions of the Second Army. The worst abuses occurred near the northern bridges over the Tagliamento, where commanders who had abandoned their men days earlier saw a chance to redeem themselves.

The executions at Codroipo would provide a climactic scene in the only world-famous book about the Italian front: Ernest Hemingway's *A Farewell to Arms*.

The wooden bridge was nearly three-quarters of a mile across, and the river, that usually ran in narrow channels in the wide stony bed far below the bridge, was close under the wooden planking . . . No one was talking. They were all trying to get across as soon as they could: thinking only of that. We were almost across. At the far end of the bridge there were officers and carabinieri standing on both sides flashing lights. I saw them silhouetted against the skyline. As we came close to them I saw one of the officers point to a man in the column. A carabiniere went in after him and came out holding the man by the arm . . . The questioners had all the efficiency, coldness and command of themselves of Italians who are firing and are not being fired on . . . They were executing officers of the rank of major and above who were separated from their troops . . . So far they had shot everyone they had questioned.

The narrator is Lieutenant Frederic Henry, an American volunteer with the Second Army ambulance unit. Caught up in the retreat from the Bainsizza, he is arrested on the bridge as a German spy. As he waits his turn with the firing squad, Henry escapes by diving into the river. 'There were shots when I ran and shots when I came up the first time.' He is swept downstream, away from the front and out of the war. Immersion in the Tagliamento breaks the spell of his loyalty to Italy. 'Anger was washed away in the river along with any obligation . . . I had taken off the stars, but that was for convenience. It was no point of honour. I was not against them. I was through . . . it was not my show any more.'

The deaths in Hemingway's chapter on Caporetto involve Italians killing each other. The enemy guns are off-stage, heard but not seen, while German troops are glimpsed from a distance, moving 'smoothly, almost supernaturally, along' – a brilliant snapshot of Italian awe. Henry shoots and wounds a sergeant who refuses to obey orders; his driver, a socialist, then finishes the wounded man off ('I never killed anybody in this war, and all my life I've wanted to kill a sergeant'). The driver later deserts to the Austrians, a second driver dies under friendly fire, then there is the scene at the Tagliamento. It is a panorama of internecine brutality and betrayal, devoid of heroism. With the army self-destructing, nothing makes sense except Henry's passion for an English nurse. Caporetto is much more than a vivid backdrop for a love story: it is an immense allegory of the disillusion that, in Hemingway's world, everyone faces sooner or later. Henry's desertion becomes a grand refusal, a *nolo contendere* untainted by cowardice, motivated by a disenchantment so complete that it feels romantic: a new, negative ideal which holds more truth than all the politics and patriotism in the world.

By 1 November, there were no Italian soldiers east of the Tagliamento. Cadorna had hoped to hold the line long enough to regroup much of the Second Army. Instead, early next day, an Austrian division forced its way across a bridge on the upper Tagliamento that had not been completely destroyed. This gave heart to a German division trying to ford the river further south. When both bridgeheads were consolidated, Cadorna faced the danger that most of his Second Army and all of his Third Army could be enveloped from the north. On the morning of 4 November, he ordered a retreat to the Piave line. The Austro-German commanders redefined their objectives: the Italians should be driven across the River Brenta – beyond Venice! However, Ludendorff was not yet convinced. By the time he changed his mind, on 12 November, approving a combined attack from the Trentino, the Italians had stabilised a new line on the River Piave and Anglo-French divisions were arriving from the Western Front.

Haig commented privately on 26 October that, 'The Italians seem a wretched people, useless as fighting men but greedy for money. Moreover, I doubt whether they are really in earnest about this war. Many of them, too,' he added for good measure, 'are German spies.' Although these prejudices were widely shared in London and France, the Allies were shocked by the speed of the disintegration and alarmed at its potential impact: if Italy were to be neutralised along with Russia, Austria would be free to support Germany on the Western Front. On 28 October, with Friuli 'ablaze from end to end', Britain and France agreed to send troops. Robertson and Foch, the respective chiefs of staff, offered six divisions: hardly enough to bail out their ally, but sufficient to bolster the defence and buy London and Paris political leverage that could be used to unseat the generalissimo.

The deed was done at an inter-Allied meeting in Rapallo, on 6 November. General Porro's presentation dismayed the British and French; his vagueness about the facts of the situation and his pessimism confirmed that change at the top was overdue. There was even talk of retreating beyond the Piave to the River Mincio, losing the whole of the Veneto. In a stinging rebuff to the Supreme Command, and specifically to Cadorna's allegations of 28 October, the British stated that they were ready to trust their troops to the bravery of the Italian soldiers but not to the efficiency of their commanders. When Porro tried to speak, Foch told him to shut up. On behalf of Britain and France, Lloyd George insisted on 'the immediate riddance of Cadorna'. This gave cover to Orlando's government of 'national resistance', which wanted Cadorna to go but feared a showdown. In return for an Italian pledge to hold the line on the Piave, the British and French increased their promised support to five and six divisions respectively.

As the flood of Italian troops ebbed towards the Piave and the Supreme Command reasserted control over shattered units, the Central Powers made errors. Instead of striking from the north-west as von Below and Boroević swept in from the east, Conrad's underpowered army advanced to the southern edge of the Asiago plateau and no further.

The Krauss Corps was sent north to secure Carnia instead of pursuing the Italians westward.

After the war, Hindenburg described his disappointment over Caporetto. 'At the last the great victory had not been consummated.' Krauss accused Boroević of failing to clinch victory over the Third Army. These recriminations reflect the bitterness of overall defeat in the World War, which made Caporetto look like a missed opportunity. Piero Pieri, the first notable historian of the Italian war, put his finger on the problem: the Central Powers had, on this occasion, lacked 'the annihilating mentality'.

King Victor Emanuel had his finest hour on 8 November, rising to the moment with a speech affirming his faith in Italy's destiny. That day, the Second and Third Armies completed their crossing of the River Piave, which was running high after heavy rain. At noon on the 9th, the engineers dropped the bridges.

The new line lay some 150 kilometres west of the Isonzo. The fulcrum of the line was a rugged massif called Grappa, some 20 kilometres square. If Grappa fell, the Italians would be vulnerable both from the north and the east. After the Austrian attack of May and June 1916, Cadorna had planned to fortify Mount Grappa with roads, tunnels and trenches. In effect it was the fifth defensive line from the Isonzo. Engineering in mountainous terrain was what the Italian army did best, yet these works were hardly in hand when the Twelfth Battle began: a single track and two cableways to the summit, a water-pumping station, some barbed wire, and gun emplacements facing the wrong way (westwards).

When the Krauss Corps and then von Below's Fourteenth Army hit the Grappa massif in mid-November, like the last blows of a sledge-hammer, the Italians were almost knocked back onto the plains. Conrad quipped that they hung on to the south-western edge of Grappa like a man to a window-ledge. The Supreme Command packed 50 battalions onto Grappa – around 50,000 men, including many recruits from the latest draft class. The ensuing struggle was a battle in itself; the situation was only saved at the end of December, with timely help from a French division – the Allies' sole active contribution to the defence after Caporetto. This achievement gave birth to two new, much-needed myths: the defence of Mount Grappa was acclaimed as a victory that saved the kingdom, and the 'boys of '99', sent straight from training to perform miracles, proved that Italian fighting mettle was alive and well.

Foch and Robertson would have preferred the Duke of Aosta to replace Cadorna. This was said to be inappropriate because the Duke was a cousin of the King; in truth, it was impossible because Victor Emanuel loathed his tall, handsome cousin. So they accepted the government's proposal of General Armando Diaz, with Badoglio and Giardino as joint deputies.[2]

Diaz, a 57-year-old Neapolitan, had risen steadily through the ranks. After the Libyan war, in which he showed a rare talent for winning the affection and respect of his regiment, he served as General Pollio's chef de cabinet. After a year in the Supreme Command, he asked to be sent to the front, where his calm good humour was noticed by the King, among others. He led the XXIII Corps on the Carso with no particular distinction. A brother general described him as a fine man and a good soldier but completely adaptable, 'like pasta', with no ideas of his own. Cadorna's court journalists scoffed at the appointment, and Gatti was withering ('Who knows Diaz?').

Diaz would vindicate the King's trust. News of his promotion, on 8 November, struck him like a bolt of lightning. Accepting the 'sacred duty', he said: 'You are ordering me to fight with a broken sword. Very well, we shall fight all the same.' And fight he did, though in a different way from his predecessor. He proved to be an exceptional administrator and skilful mediator, reconciling the government and the Supreme Command to each other, and rival generals to his own appointment. Journalists were told that 'with this man, there will be no dangerous independence. State operations will be kept united at all times.' In other words, no more 'government in Udine'. His first statement to the troops urged them to fight for their land, home, family and honour – in that order. He was what the army and the country needed after Cadorna,

2 Badoglio's promotion less than a fortnight after abandoning his command and his corps disintegrated, leading to the suicide of two generals, has never been fully explained. The records of XXVII Corps were lost in the retreat and, uniquely among senior commanders, he never publicly discussed his role. Criticism at his expense was dropped from the report of the official commission of inquiry into the causes of Caporetto, published in 1919; this was General Diaz's reward for Badoglio's efficient performance as his deputy in 1918. The deleted chapter has not been recovered; presumably it was mislaid during Badoglio's long tenure as chief of the general staff (1924–40). Badoglio, limitlessly vain, was also a Marshal of Italy, the Marquis of Sabotino, the first Viceroy of Ethiopia and Duke of Addis Ababa, and Prime Minister (1943–44).

and while he showed no brilliance as a strategist, he made no crucial mistakes and took the decisions that led to victory.

On 7 November, hosting his last supper at the Supreme Command, Cadorna addressed posterity over the plates: 'I, with my will and my fist, created and sustained this organism, this army of 3,000,000 men, until yesterday. If I had not done it, we would never have made our voice heard in Europe . . . ' Early the following day, the King arrived to persuade Cadorna to leave quietly. They conferred for two hours. Cadorna knew he could not survive, yet the humiliation was too much. There was no graceful exit. Diaz arrived late that evening. When he presented a letter from the minister of war announcing his appointment as chief of staff with immediate effect, Cadorna broke off the meeting and telegraphed the minister: he would not go without a written dismissal. The order arrived early next morning. A new regime took over at the Supreme Command.[3]

The phrase 'doing a Cadorna' became British soldiers' slang for coming unstuck, perpetrating an utter fuck-up and paying the price.

The statistics of defeat were dizzying. The Italians lost nearly 12,000 dead, 30,000 wounded and 294,000 prisoners. In addition, there were 350,000 disbanded men, roaming around or making for home. Only half of the army's 65 divisions survived intact, and half the artillery had been lost: more than 3,000 guns, as well as 300,000 rifles, 3,000 machine guns, 1,600 motor vehicles and so forth. Territorially, some 14,000 square kilometres were lost, with a population of 1,150,000 people.

The Austro-German offensive was prepared with a meticulousness that the Supreme Command could hardly imagine. The execution, too, was incomparably efficient. Cadorna's general method, as he once explained to the King, was to use as many troops as possible along a sector as broad as possible, hoping the enemy lines would crack somewhere. The Italian insistence on retaining centralised control at senior levels was also archaic beside the German devolution of authority to

3 Cadorna spent his retirement writing mendacious memoirs, a biography of his father, and sparring with his critics in print. He died in 1928, a month after the tenth anniversary of Italy's victory, when 'almost nobody remembered that I'm still alive . . . I am supremely indifferent,' he wrote, self-deceiving to the last.

assault team level. (How high would a Rommel have risen in Cadorna's army?) Caporetto was the outcome when innovative tactics were expertly used against an army that was, in doctrine and organisation, one of the most hidebound in Europe.

The Twelfth Battle was a *Blitzkrieg* before the concept existed. An Austrian officer who fought in the Krauss Corps described the assault on 24 October as a fist punching through a barrier, then unclenching to spread its fingers. This is very like a recent description of *Blitzkrieg* as resembling 'a shaped charge, penetrating through a relatively tiny hole in a tank's armor and then exploding outwardly to achieve a maximum cone of damage against the unarmored or less protected innards'. Those innards had, in the Italian case, been weakened by a combination of savage discipline, mediocre leadership, second-rate equipment and arduous terrain. Without this debilitation, the Second Army would not have collapsed almost on impact.

Naturally, Cadorna could not see or accept that he had undermined the troops. But he knew that others would make this charge, which is why he launched, pre-emptively, the self-serving myth that traitors and cowards were responsible for the defeat. This myth became Cadorna's most durable legacy, thanks in part to a prompt endorsement by Leonida Bissolati, the cabinet minister. Adding a nuance to Cadorna's lie, Bissolati claimed that a sort of 'military strike' had taken place. Probably he was scoring points against his rivals on the political left; instead he deepened a stain on the army that still lingers. By likening the events on the Isonzo to the recent workers' protests in Turin, Bissolati put a political complexion on the defeat. The ease with which discipline was restored by the end of 1917 would have scotched these allegations if it had not suited Italy's leaders to keep them alive. It also suited the Allies, who wanted to minimise the responsibility of their Italian colleagues and had their own doubts about Italian martial spirit. Ambassador Rodd and General Delmé-Radcliffe parroted the conspiracy theory in their reports to London. For the historian George Trevelyan, leading the British Red Cross volunteers who retreated with the Third Army, there was 'positive treachery at Caporetto'; Cadorna's infamous bulletin had told the salutary truth. For the novelist John Buchan, working as a senior propagandist in London, treachery had 'contributed to the disaster', for a 'secret campaign was conducted throughout Italy' in 1917, producing a 'poison' that 'infected certain parts of the army to an extent of which the military authorities were wholly ignorant'.

For some, a more dreadful possibility underlay these accusations. Was 'Italy' a middle-class illusion? Instead of forging a stronger nation-state, the furnace of war had almost dissolved it. What would happen at the next test? Disaffection with the state might be wider and deeper than they had thought possible. Had the mass of Italians somehow been left out of the nation-building process? If so, what further disasters still lay in store? It was a moment when everything solid seemed to melt away. The philosopher Croce, usually imperturbable to a fault, wrote during the Twelfth Battle: 'The fate of Italy is being decided for centuries to come.' Even politicians who did not swallow the 'military strike' thesis, and knew that Socialist members of parliament were too patriotic to want peace at any price, feared the outcome if popular disaffection became politically focused. After all, Lenin had taken power in Russia in early November. For weeks after Caporetto, many officials believed that revolution or sheer exhaustion would force Italy out of the war.

This mood of shaken self-questioning subsided as the army was rebuilt in late 1917 and early 1918. It would be driven underground, into the national unconscious, first by the victories of 1918, then by Fascist suppression. Yet those who took part never forgot the fearful dreamlike days when the world turned upside down. For the essence of Caporetto lay in the wrenching uncertainty of late October, when the commanders did not know what was happening, the officers did not know what to do, the soldiers did not know where the enemy was, the government did not know if Italy was on the brink of losing the war, and ordinary citizens did not know if their country might cease to exist. All Italians dreamed that dream; the nation was haunted by an image of men fleeing the front in hundreds of thousands, throwing away their rifles, overcome by disgust with the army, the state and all its works, wanting nothing more (or less) than to go home. When the anti-fascist Piero Gobetti wrote in the 1920s that the Italians were still 'a people of stragglers, not yet a nation', he evoked that fortnight when the country threatened to come apart at the seams.

Under Mussolini, the myth of a military strike was discouraged; it undermined the Fascists' very different myth of the war as the foundation of modern Italy, a blood rite that re-created the nation. The fact of defeat at Caporetto had to be swallowed: a sour pill that could be sweetened by blaming the government's weakness. Fascist accounts of the Twelfth Battle tended to whitewash Cadorna and defend the honour of the army ('great even in misfortune') while incriminating

Capello and indicting the government in Rome for tolerating defeatists, profiteers and bourgeois draft-dodgers. Boselli ('tearful helmsman of the ship of state') and his successor Orlando were particularly lampooned. One valiant historian in the 1930s turned the narrative of defeat inside out by hailing Caporetto as a deliberate trap set and sprung by Cadorna, 'the greatest strategist of our times'. The Duce himself called Caporetto 'a reverse' that was 'absolutely military in nature', produced by 'an initial tactical success of the enemy'. Britain and France could also be condemned for recalling, in early October 1917, most of the 140 guns they had lent Cadorna earlier in the year. Even so, the defeat was not to be examined too closely. When Colonel Gatti wanted to write a history of Caporetto, in 1925, Mussolini granted access to the archives in the Ministry of War. Then he had second thoughts; summoning Gatti to Rome, he said it was a time for myths, not history. After 1945, leftist historians argued that large parts of the army had indeed 'gone on strike', not due to cowardice or socialism, but as a spontaneous rebellion against the war as it was led by Cadorna and the government.

That primal fear of dissolution survives in metaphor. Corruption scandals are still branded 'a moral Caporetto'. Politicians accuse each other of facing an 'electoral Caporetto'. When small businesses are snarled up in Italy's notorious red tape, they complain about an 'administrative Caporetto'. When England lost to Northern Ireland at football, it was 'the English Caporetto'. This figure of speech stands for more than simple defeat; it involves a hint of stomach-churning exposure – rottenness laid bare.

TWENTY-SIX

Resurrection

*Troops are never in better spirits for fighting
than when they have to wipe out a stain*
Carl von Clausewitz

The new lines had settled by the end of the year. From the Swiss border to the Asiago plateau, the front was unchanged. From Asiago to the sea, it now ran east to Mount Grappa, then swung south-eastwards for 130 kilometres along the River Piave. Fortunately for Diaz, defeat had cropped 170 kilometres from the front: otherwise his much-reduced army might not have blocked the last Austro-German thrusts at the Piave line.

The German guns were transferred to the Western Front during November, followed in mid-December by the troops. The Austrians were on their own again. Not so the Italians, who benefited from several Allied divisions and their batteries: 130,000 French and 110,000 British troops by the end of the year, deployed as a strategic reserve. Other Allied support in the form of munitions, shipping and extra loans ensured that coal and food shortages did not become acute.

Arriving from France and Flanders, the British soldiers were touched by their warm welcome. Battalions of the Royal Fusiliers were greeted at Ventimiglia with 'extravagant fervour', 'showered with carnations, and barrels of wine stood waiting for them at the official welcoming ceremony'. After the dull tones of Flanders, the Britons were captivated by the scenery. Moving along the Riviera to Genoa, Gunner James Blackburn (197th Siege Battery, Royal Garrison Artillery) gazed at the 'red tiled roofs, pale pink and pale green buildings, the blue sky, green fields, greener trees and hedgerows'. The longest-lived British veteran to serve in Italy was Gunner Alfred Finnigan, who in 2005 still remembered the 'absolute joy' of seeing the Mediterranean and the sun in December. The Italians, too, were fascinating: the carabinieri on Monte Carlo station who conjured oranges from under their capes, and the shopkeeper in Genoa who 'danced with delight' when she saw the Tommies and, having nothing else, gave away straw hats.

Some, like Captain L. Ferguson (1st Battalion, Cheshire Regiment), felt embarrassed by the largesse – 'we found the troops getting pelted with oranges and figs' – and distributed corned beef and biscuits to the children around the train. After the dismal sight of Italian soldiers begging for bread at Verona station, he was cheered to meet some alpini who spoke enough English to blame southerners for Caporetto and to promise that 'the armies now have no idea of retreating an inch more'.

To Major Arthur Acland (Duke of Cornwall's Light Infantry), the land up to the Piave was 'flatter than you would think it possible for any country to be'. South of Mount Grappa, where the Piave emerged onto the plains, the river flowed to the sea in tresses or braids along a wide stony course, around low islets of shingle and boulders, sometimes topped with scrubby vegetation. In spate, the Piave was several kilometres wide in some places, 'a mighty expanse of water'. In summer, it could safely be waded. A river that rose and fell by a metre or more in a day was a tricky proposition for bridging engineers.

The soft muddy banks of the Piave presented other problems after Carso limestone. Water constantly seeped into the trenches, which collapsed without constant revetting. The men appreciated the distance between the front lines, but keeping healthy was another challenge; it was almost impossible to stay dry, and the swamps on the lower Piave were malarial. Things were easier further from the sea. Acland's division was deployed on a whaleback hill called the Montello, 'some seven miles long, broadening to four miles at its widest and rising to about 800 feet, a pleasant hill, covered with vineyards and cultivated fields, interspersed with small woods . . . The northern slopes fell steeply to the river bank, above which they towered like cliffs.' This was the last Alpine ripple before the maritime plain, and it gave good observation of the enemy lines. The Tommies liked the posting; by day, they strengthened the communications and defences on the hill; by night, they 'played in the waters of the Piave'. The Indian summer days were hot, the nights bitingly clear, and there was ample wood to burn. Christmas Day was so warm that 'we could sit around with our shirts off to deal with our vermin'. The rear lines were of poor quality, but it hardly seemed to matter: the enemy showed no intention of attacking again, and Allied planes controlled the sky. All in all, 'it was such a gorgeous rest after Flanders'. Until Haig recalled two of the five British divisions at the end of February, the main challenge, much of the time, was to keep the men busy.

The British troops only knew the Italians had taken a hard knock, not how close they had come to collapse or the scale of the task facing Diaz, who had to consolidate the new line with only 33 intact divisions, half the number before Caporetto. His priorities were to restore discipline, rebuild disintegrated units, then raise morale. The first task was unexpectedly straightforward. The fear early in November that the army might unravel had passed by the end of the month. After the front settled in December, Diaz rounded up the soldiers who had dispersed, resurrecting 25 infantry divisions and more than 30 artillery regiments by the end of February 1918. Some of the men who were judged less reliable were sent to serve in labour units in France. He restructured his forces into six armies, none of them unmanageably huge as Capello's Second Army had been. He reinstated the organic connection between divisional infantry and their artillery. Taking a leaf out of the German book, he devolved more operational decision-making authority to lower levels. Training and equipment were improved.

At the Supreme Command, Diaz restored responsibility to the competent offices, decentralising the authority that Cadorna had gathered in his fist. The Operations Office could play its proper part for the first time. A network of liaison officers ensured a flow of information between the Supreme Command and the front-line units. Badoglio became a trusted and effective deputy, not a stuffed shirt as General Porro had been. Although he had never been interested in politics, or perhaps because of this, Diaz's attitude to the state authorities was co-operative without being submissive. He lunched with the King twice a week and met the Prime Minister several times a month. He had no objection to the formation of a war committee inside the cabinet, and was always ready to brief politicians.

Diaz's strategic priority was purely defensive, so he did not need to devise offensive tactics. On the other hand, he could not yield any ground: if the Piave line broke, the Italians would probably lose Venice, Padua and Vicenza – the whole of the Veneto, maybe more. Also, he faced an imminent shortage of manpower; after the class of 1899 was drafted at the end of 1917, he had only the 260,000-strong class of 1900 (called up in February) as a reserve for the following year. Diaz knew that his overall strength would probably decline over the coming months, and that substantial losses could not be made good.

In the first months of 1918, while the rear defences were prepared behind Venice, Diaz tested his army by launching limited operations to strengthen the crucial sector between the Asiago plateau and Mount Grappa. Involving the specialist assault teams called *arditi*, these operations succeeded well enough to raise the army's self-confidence. Otherwise, he would not be drawn into offensive action before he was ready. When General Foch, as Allied Supreme Commander, hard-pressed by the German spring offensives, implored Diaz to launch a diversionary action in May, he refused.

Diaz took steps to reform the conditions and treatment of his men. In December 1917, the rations were increased and made more varied. Pay was increased. Canteens were placed near the front, selling food and useful goods at discounted prices. Annual leave was raised from 15 to 25 days, and older draft classes were granted extra leave to work their land. All soldiers were provided with free insurance policies, and death benefits were paid to the families without delay. From May 1918, soldiers' families in hardship could apply for emergency relief. As for discipline, Diaz did not repeal Cadorna's rulings; he simply forbore to use his most savage methods. There would be no more decimations.

He took a rational approach to military morale. Although morale was seen as the key to victory, the men had been expected to supply their own. Under Diaz, the soldiers' attitude to the war – hitherto a vast neglected hinterland – became a bright arena, crowded with officers taking notes. An internal report in November and December 1917 found that the men were physically inert and morally apathetic; their letters home proved that they did not identify with the war and its aims; while there was no organised anti-war propaganda, passivity and resignation were widespread. Many of them believed rumours that the government would sue for peace before the year was out. There was no conviction that the war was necessary and must be won.

Against this alarming background, Diaz issued directives and guidelines on vigilance, propaganda and care for the troops. Propaganda would be channelled through newspapers, posters and leaflets, theatre and cinema. Meetings should be organised to learn the men's views and to impart 'a healthy, fortifying word'. Each army should have its own newspaper, with a humorous angle on army life, written by the men themselves where possible. 'Care' referred to material and moral wellbeing, such as hygienic accommodation and palatable rations. 'The best system for fighting anti-war propaganda', Diaz stated, 'is the elimination, as far as possible, of the causes of discontent.' This approach was unthinkable before Caporetto.

A new structure called 'P Service' was set up to co-ordinate all this. Its task was to spread 'the conviction of the absolute necessity of our war' among the troops and bolster civilian morale. Its officers included many gifted and sometimes eccentric figures who took deep pride in their work. This, after all, was a time when, as one officer said, 'the flower of the Italian intelligentsia [was] in a fervour of moral renewal'. These men were the commissars of national recovery.

Military and civilian surveillance were, at last, connected. The Information Service in each army was tasked to develop networks of informants from different social groups, starting with the police and extending to mayors, doctors, teachers and – naturally – journalists. 'Every movement in civic life' was to be turned towards a single goal: 'the triumph of the aspirations and demands of the Fatherland'. Propaganda should be adapted to its audience; the days of all-purpose rhetoric were over. In some situations, the men would gain most from discussions with a 'P' officer; in others, a musical revue would be the best way to build faith in 'our growing superiority over the enemy and our inevitable victory'. Photographs from the front were exhibited around the country, while films and plays toured the land. At the end of November, Diaz set new ground-rules for war correspondents; from now on, they could file up to 500 words a day, 'without rhetoric'. The Italian army became, of all things, a model of integrated information management.

Naturally, the authorities talked up the impact of these measures. Father Gemelli believed that the eight months after Caporetto saw 'a profound transformation' of soldiers' 'souls', involving the growth of a 'national soul'. Exalted claims of this kind set a tone that patriotic historians accepted without examination for decades.

The real story of morale after Caporetto is more complex. The governing class and the middle classes did experience a defining moment or apotheosis, and shelved their political quarrels to resist the threat as effectively as possible. For these groups, as the American ambassador noted, the scale of the disaster brought the remedy. 'To be or not to be': this was now Italy's choice, as Orlando thundered in parliament, relishing the roar of cross-party acclaim. The historian Giovanna Procacci argues that Italy's rulers and bourgeoisie were now united in dedication to a supreme purpose, something like the mood of other western European countries in August 1914. In the words of Francesco Nitti, Orlando's minister of finance, a war of political adventure turned into a war of national defence. All manner of patriotic committees and 'national associations for victory' sprang up. Politically conservative, intensely motivated, these citizens' groups were determined to root out defeatism in all its slippery forms. The Anti-German League, perhaps the most extreme group, offered cash rewards for denouncing 'defeatists' and spies. The government played the same game, promising rewards to state employees who sniffed uncertainty among their colleagues.

Vigilance easily warped into vigilantism. Citizens' committees worked with the police to identify fainthearts or appeasers. The press bayed for strong government to crush the 'enemy within', with no quarter for the filthy neutralists, socialists and Giolittians. Down with them all! In Rome, 158 pro-war deputies formed a Parliamentary Group (*Fascio*) for National Defence. With an eye on this powerful bloc, the Prime Minister took on the colours of the radical nationalists who had been his sharpest critics over the summer. Still holding the home affairs portfolio, Orlando urged the judges to apply the Sacchi Decree with relentless severity. A woman in Bologna was jailed for six months for saying that the Germans were invincible and Britain was to blame for the war. In April 1918, a priest in Florence got four months for 'not believing in Italian victory'. A man from Viterbo got three months for saying in a restaurant that Italians were cowards.

Food riots began again in February 1918, when wheat rationing was introduced. (The 1917 harvest was poor.) While labour unrest was muted compared to summer 1917, statistics on labour stoppages show there is little ground for arguing that a *union sacrée* was forged after Caporetto. Strikes increased during spring and summer, drawing in the more experienced, skilled workers (by contrast with 1917). Industrial action continued throughout June, showing no deference to the army during the Austrian offensive. The strikers had learned from the bloody clashes of 1917: these actions were better organised, often involving women, less violent, and often successful in wresting concessions. The workers understood their own importance to the war effort; it was harder to intimidate them. Ironically, they took encouragement from

[333]

politicians like Orlando and Salandra who promised that a better world would rise from the ashes of war. Industrial troubles in the north were matched by unrest in the southern countryside. Soothing promises were made of granting land to the peasants after the war, a gesture that backfired by reducing the peasants' age-old deference to landowners and awakening a sense of political rights.

This is why some historians see 'repression of dissent, rather than the creation of consensus' as the government's priority after Caporetto. And there was plenty to repress, especially outside the cities. Diaz knew this already from other sources; on 24 November, he warned Orlando that the rural population of north-east Italy was broadly against the war. Women were especially outspoken, saying it would be better to be occupied by the Austrians because then the war would be over and 'anyway everyone knows the Austrians treat people well'. At the end of October, a journalist reported that people around Milan were celebrating 'the arrival of the Austrians in Italy – who had come, according to the peasants, to chop off the heads of the gentlemen who wanted the war, and then to help the poor'. Worrying reports also arrived from further south, indicating that many Italians were not at all distressed by the emergency. Tuscan farmers were seen carousing over the defeat, and Neapolitans were overheard grumbling that if the Germans were in charge, at least there would be bread in the shops.

High levels of disaffection were suggested by an incident at a primary school near Mantua. The teacher set her class an essay topic: 'For Italy to win, we must resist to the end.' Most of her pupils – farmers' children – took issue with the title. One boy wrote that the officers ('the ones who give orders') were 'not tired yet of killing the poor people who aren't guilty of anything. To make it a just war, they should 1. send all those who want war to the front, because if they want it they should fight it. 2. send the rich people who give money for war bonds. 3. send the poor men home. Then it would be a just war!' The scandalised teacher reported her pupils' 'subversive' tendencies to the military police and the local magistrate.

The 'military model' that had encroached on Italian society since 1915 was now fully imposed, involving 'submission, the demonstration of absolute loyalty, and the elimination of all criticism'. Far from healing divisions in society, this process may have deepened them. Especially in the south, the state was felt increasingly as an incubus, a predatory master, not much different from the Bourbon tyrants of old. Orlando and his ministers, for their part, were doing what they believed was necessary to reverse the effects of Caporetto. A key to success would be the arms industry. General Alfredo Dallolio, an effective Under-Secretary of Arms and Munitions since 1915, was promoted to Minister in June 1917 with a staff of 6,000. Even so, the Boselli government had not reversed the cautious conservative policy that it inherited from Salandra. Over the summer and autumn of 1917, Francesco Nitti, a deputy who had been Giolitti's last minister for industry and trade, denounced Italy's partial economic mobilisation. As Orlando's minister of finance, subsidised by lavish credits from the USA, he loosened the government's purse-strings and deluged the arms manufacturers with fresh orders. Military production restored the huge losses after Caporetto and supplied the army for the final battles.

It was a fine achievement, and by no means inevitable. Yet pricing policy was slack, the large companies practically wrote their own contracts, profits were exorbitant, and corruption flourished. The discovery of accounting irregularities at his ministry led to Dallolio's resignation in May 1918. On the other hand, industries had incentives to plough back their profits into improving their plant and equipment. The northern engineering companies grew apace: Alfa-Romeo's 200 workers became 4,000; Fiat's 4,300 multiplied tenfold; Ansaldo's workforce grew from 6,000 to 56,000. The aeronautical industry grew from scratch to employ 100,000 people by the war's end. The great names of Italian engineering made their breakthroughs thanks to lavish state subventions and militarised management of the workforce.

Unfortunately for Orlando, no sooner had the political class stopped feuding over intervention and the conduct of the war than another source of contention opened up. This was the ever more delicate question of Italy's aims on the farther shore of the Adriatic Sea. The rout in the Twelfth Battle had harmed the Italians' prospects of getting their full dividend of territory after the war. Allied statesmen on both sides of the Atlantic 'now looked upon Italian war aims with even less deference than before'. In a speech on war aims in early January, Lloyd George kept silent about Italy's expansion across the Adriatic.

The European acclaim for Lloyd George's speech irked President Woodrow Wilson, who was putting the final touches to a statement of his own. He need not have minded, for his speech on 8 January became the best-known blueprint for a just peace, the rallying cry for millions who dreamed of a new postwar order. After reiterating his calls for open diplomacy (no more 'secret covenants'), free trade, a global reduction of arms to the lowest possible level and a 'general association of nations', Wilson called for the open-minded review of all colonial claims, taking equal account of 'the interests of the populations concerned': a warning to the Allies. Among their specific interests, absolute support was only given to Belgium, which 'must be evacuated and restored'. For the rest, the conditional was used: France, Serbia and Montenegro should be evacuated, and so forth.

Dismayingly for Rome, the ninth of Wilson's fourteen points was a shot across the bows: 'A readjustment of the frontiers of Italy should be effected along clearly recognizable lines of nationality.' On this basis, Italy would have little claim to Istria, less to Dalmatia, and none to the Alto Adige or the Isonzo valley above Gorizia, let alone the Greek islands or Asia Minor. This affront to the Treaty of London was rammed home by Wilson's tenth point: 'The peoples of Austria-Hungary, whose place among the nations we wish to see safeguarded and assured, should be accorded the freest opportunity to autonomous development.' Publicly, Orlando and Sonnino ignored this call for the empire to become some sort of federation. Privately, Sonnino complained to the American ambassador that Wilson had 'made no mention whatever of our aspirations, which are not at all imperialistic but simply defensive, for our security and independence, especially in the Adriatic'.

The background to Wilson's speech was an inter-Allied meeting in Paris several weeks earlier, where President Wilson's emissary – the diminutive Texan, Edward House – wanted the Allies to agree a new, liberal statement of their aims, pledging that they were 'not waging war for the purpose of aggression or indemnity'. The idea was to neutralise the peace proposals emanating from Bolshevik Russia and undercut domestic propaganda in Germany. While the British and French dragged their feet, fearing bad publicity if they were seen as going soft, only Italy strongly resisted. House was left feeling that 'it is perfectly hopeless trying to get Sonnino into anything progressive or constructive'. Sonnino's problem was that the United States was not bound by the Treaty of London, which was one of those 'secret covenants' denounced in the Fourteen Points speech. Wilson's only interest in the territorial issues turned on their implications for the postwar world. For he had overcome neutralist opinion in the United States by promising to fight for a new liberal international system, to eradicate many traditional causes of war. If Italy's claims promoted instability, he was duty-bound to resist them.

Both parties were careful not to let latent disagreement get in the way of practical alliance. A few days after the unsatisfactory meeting in Paris, the United States declared war on Austria-Hungary. The empire had not attacked America, nor did Wilson intend to fight Habsburg troops. This step had been requested by Orlando's government after Caporetto, and urged by the American ambassador in Rome. Wilson complied, both to aid Italian morale and to satisfy domestic critics who wanted the United States to show more grit. The declaration was muted, however, and reassured Vienna that the USA had no wish to 'impair' or 'rearrange' the empire.

Rome welcomed this signal of support. A month later, the Fourteen Points speech came as a cold shower. In truth, American opinion always had misgivings about Italy's aims, which seemed typical of sneaky European statecraft, singing with the anti-imperialist chorus while pursuing a quasi-imperial role. The tone of misgiving was caught by journalist Walter Lippmann, a liberal interventionist and advisor to Wilson: 'More and more the war has ceased to look like a clean-cut fight between right and wrong, between democracy and absolutism, between public faith and international lawlessness. Italy, Romania, Russia with their aggressive programs confuse the situation too much.'

Orlando tried to defuse the problem by denying there was one, blandly summarising Italy's aims: 'the completion of her national unity and the security of her borders on land and sea'. But he hurried to Britain for reassurance at the end of January, when both governments solemnly reaffirmed the Treaty of London. British liberal opinion was not convinced; the editor of *The Nation* queried the discrepancy between that 'most cynical' of all the secret treaties and the increasingly anti-imperialist flavour of Allied war aims. The treaty could only be implemented by cancelling the emergent aim of autonomy for the Habsburg nations. By forcing injustice onto non-Italians, this would have bad repercussions inside Italy: 'By the acquisition of German, Slovene, Serbo-Croat, Albanian, Greek, Turkish and possibly Abyssinian subjects, Italy would become an Empire doomed to racial unrest and firm government.'

This sort of prophecy cut no ice with Allied policy-makers, who needed to defeat the Central Powers. The Italians were keeping 44 Austrian divisions away from the Western Front. Insofar as London and Paris could assuage Rome, they would do so. But they were still persuaded that the Habsburg empire should emerge more or less intact in any settlement. National aspirations were encouraged, within limits; 'autonomy' fell far short of self-determination. Apart from diplomatic caution, it made no sense to question the empire's existence as long as there was a chance of tempting Emperor Karl to break with Germany.

The Allies' attitude suited Rome very well. If the empire did not survive the war, Italy would have to compete for territory with at least one new national state on the eastern Adriatic. This explains why Sonnino, jealous father of the London Treaty, his 'paltry masterpiece', refused to sanction the use of propaganda to reassure Yugoslav soldiers on the Isonzo front that Italy supported their dream of independence. He also blocked the formation of a Czech and Slovak volunteer brigade in Italy, even though his government had no designs on Czech lands. In his view, the cohesion of the empire should not be weakened any more than necessary.

On 3 March 1918, the Treaty of Brest-Litovsk took Russia out of the war on terms that strengthened Germany. Three weeks later, the Germans launched their spring offensive in the west, which made shattering progress for a couple of weeks. Then, in a political tit-for-tat with Vienna, Clemenceau revealed Karl's peace initiative of March 1917, with its friendly reference to French claims on Alsace and Lorraine. German fury at this betrayal had large consequences. When the two emperors met a month later at Spa, in occupied Belgium, Wilhelm tested Karl's loyalty with a double demand: the Central Powers should form a pan-Germanic political, economic and military union, and the Austrians should support the continuing German offensive by attacking Italy once more.

Germany was riding high. Apart from the accomplishment of Brest-Litovsk, Romania had been forced to accept humiliating terms for peace; it was hard to remember the last Allied triumph in Europe; Ludendorff's spring offensives had not yet stalled. Wilhelm's comments at Spa reveal an impossibly arrogant cast of mind, still bent on the mastery of Europe; the resemblance to Hitler's mindset in 1944 is striking. Neither he nor Karl grasped that Germany's recent successes veiled an imminent exhaustion. Unable to resist Wilhelm's pressure,

Karl pledged a two-pronged attack from Asiago in the north and across the River Piave towards Venice.

Karl's consent more or less ended British and French hopes that Austria-Hungary could be split away from Germany, and the Allies became more willing to contemplate the dissolution of the empire, though not yet self-determination for the Slav nations. This turn in Allied thinking coincided with an influential new campaign of pro-Yugoslav propaganda. In February, the British government had set up a Department of Propaganda in Enemy Countries, under the brilliant press baron Lord Northcliffe, whose primary target was the Habsburg empire. With Northcliffe telling the government that self-determination was a powerful tool against the Austrians, the department embraced the idea that a Yugoslav state would be a viable successor to the empire between the middle Danube and the Adriatic Sea. Inevitably, this had an impact on Italian designs. British propaganda urged a policy that challenged the fundamental aims of a British ally.

The first practical outcome was a conference in Rome, in April. The Congress of the Oppressed Nationalities of Austria-Hungary was meant to demonstrate a harmonious commitment to self-determination for the Habsburg nations. Top-heavy with journalists and artists, it was a noisy event. The Italian government did not take part, but Orlando was discreetly supportive and persuaded Albertini to help organise and perhaps subsidise the congress through *Corriere della Sera*. Sonnino hoped the participants would fail to reach a common position. Instead they affirmed the right of each people (counting the Yugoslavs as one) to 'set up a national State entity of its own', and pledged respect for the rights of minorities. There was a tactful, circle-squaring paragraph on Italian–Yugoslav relations, committing both sides to 'devote all their efforts' to achieving Yugoslav unity and independence, and also 'the completion of Italian unity'.

While the government chose not to recognise the congress, Orlando met its members, urging them to overcome 'the inexplicable and grievous misunderstanding' over Italy's war aims and to remember that no country sympathised more keenly with the Habsburg nations. He was eloquent about 'generous Poland' and the Czech cause; on the Yugoslav issue, however, he merely urged the Italians and 'the southern and Adriatic Slavs' to make common cause against their common enemy. This effort to soften the impact of the congress declaration before it was published (after a mysterious delay of nearly two months) was unavailing, for a new body was set up to milk this breakthrough. The Central Inter-Allied Propaganda Commission prepared colossal quantities of material: some 60 million copies of 643 manifestos and two million copies of 80 news-sheets in numerous Habsburg languages, skilfully crafted to undermine enemy unity and resolve. Deserting officers put their names to leaflets that were dropped over the Habsburg lines, with cunning messages: 'The Italians and Yugoslavs are in complete agreement and the Italians receive us and accept us as allies and brothers. Everyone who comes here is sorry that he did not come before, for here hunger and misery, fear and slavery, are unknown.'

Italian civilians were meanwhile exposed to a very different propaganda campaign. Jubilation at Wilson's declaration of war against Austria had curdled when no American troops arrived. Wilson's administration responded with a campaign to win hearts and minds. Except for the intervention campaign in 1914–15, it was the first time the public had been exposed to modern techniques, with pamphlets, postcards, ribbons, badges, and articles commissioned for the press. Families of emigrants who volunteered for the US Army were sent substantial grants. Trades unions, the American Red Cross, Italian-American community leaders – all sent the same message: that the United States would commit its huge resources to fighting for peace.

Given that ordinary Italians never saw proof positive of this commitment – for only one in every thousand of the 'doughboys' served in Italy – this campaign should have been an uphill struggle. Nevertheless, it succeeded. Many Italians saw the United States as a promised land where emigrants could make a new life, and Wilsonian ideals filled a vacuum in the labour movement since the Socialist Second International had split in 1914. Popular faith in American intervention showed again that the national division over the war had not healed; most Italians wanted peace more than territory.

This campaign encouraged a strand of liberal opinion, including the so-called 'democratic interventionists', to take up the cause of the Habsburg nationalities. (It was the same strand that had been disturbed to learn – after the Bolsheviks mischievously leaked the terms of the Treaty of London late in 1917 – that Italians were dying not only for 'Trento and Trieste' but also for the eastern Adriatic seaboard and its overwhelmingly Slav population.) This led to a press campaign for a Czechoslovak Legion to be formed. Permission was granted in May:

the volunteer division of 14,000 Czech and Slovak deserters and prisoners of war fought the last two battles of the war alongside the Italians. Sonnino still blocked the formation of a Yugoslav Legion; better that 18,000 Croat and Slovene prisoners of war languish in camps than fight for the Allied cause.

Italian realists were coming to accept what liberals such as Bissolati and Giolitti already believed: that Yugoslav pressure for self-determination had to be accommodated. Orlando, learning the new script, marked the third anniversary of intervention by declaring that, by fighting for Trento and Trieste, the Italians were also fighting on behalf of Warsaw, Prague and Zagreb. By June, Allied propaganda addressed the 'Yugoslavs' and urged the 'resurrection' (*sic*) of 'a free 'Yugoslavia". At the end of June, Wilson's secretary of state declared that 'All branches of the Slav race should be completely freed from German and Austrian rule.' The French foreign minister then broke new ground by referring to the future Czechoslovak, Polish and Yugoslav *states*. Britain supported this statement. The Allies had almost embraced the radical position that the empire would have to go.

The Italians still hesitated. Britain turned the screws by signalling that the London terms might have to be revised. Around the same time, Diaz asked Orlando to increase the flow of pro-Yugoslav propaganda, which was proving very valuable. In mid-August, under this pressure, the government pledged support for the Allied aim of 'a free and united Yugoslav state, embracing Serbs, Croats and Slovenes'. Sonnino's abiding hostility was common knowledge, and by early September, Albertini was convinced that Italy was paying an excessive price for its foreign minister's intransigence. *Corriere della Sera* challenged the censorship regime by attacking the foreign minister openly. (Orlando probably encouraged this unwonted boldness.) Denying the army an alliance with the Yugoslavs, wrote Albertini, meant depriving it of a powerful weapon.

As a sop to more liberal colleagues, Sonnino did not block a cabinet statement that Yugoslav independence and unity were 'consonant with the principles for which the Entente is fighting, as well as with the aims of a just and durable peace'. His real view was expressed later in September to the American ambassador: that Austria would emerge from the war as a great power once again, able to dominate and even absorb the Yugoslavs.

[341]

Karl's promise of a two-pronged offensive flew in the face of warnings that Field Marshal Boroević (his new rank) had sent to the high command since the end of March. Karl and his chief of staff hoped to make Rome negotiate, and enlarge their spoils when Germany won the war. Boroević did not believe the Central Powers could win. Instead of wasting its strength on needless offensives, Austria should conserve it to deal with the turmoil that peace would unleash in the empire.

But Karl and the high command were adamant: there must be an offensive. Boroević prepared a plan to attack across the River Piave, towards Venice and Padua. Yet again, Conrad argued for an attack from the Asiago plateau: if successful, this would make the Piave line indefensible and force another Italian retreat. He urged the Emperor to attack on both sectors, and Karl gave way. Preparations began on 1 April with a view to attacking on 11 June.

Boroević had seen Cadorna make this very mistake time and again, attacking on too broad a front. He spoke up again: if they had to attack on both sectors, the high command should send reinforcements. In mid-May, he repeated his warning that it was irresponsible to attack without enough shells and with troops ill-equipped and famished. By way of reply, the high command told Boroević to confirm that he would be ready by 11 June. Not before the 25th, he replied. The date was set for 15 June.

On paper, the Austrian army looked strong enough. With Russia out of the war, most of the 53 divisions with a further ten in reserve could be kept in Italy, which was now the empire's major front. However, the infantry divisions were down from 12,000 to 8,000 or even 5,000 men. New battalions were at roughly half strength. Some 200,000 Hungarian soldiers had deserted in the first three months of 1918. In the spring, Karl approved the call-up of the class of 1900; the new intake would be boys of 17, plus older men returning after convalescence. Cavalry divisions were even more depleted. The railways were dilapidated from over use, and motor vehicles lacked fuel.

The industrial capacity of the empire had never been strong; by 1917, output was declining under the double impact of battlefield casualties and the Allied blockade. In 1918, the decline became a slump. Production of artillery weapons and shells halved in the first half of the year, compared with 1917. Production of rifles fell by 80 per cent in the same period. Uniforms were tattered, there was no new underwear, and worn-out boots could not be replaced. Food shortages helped to trigger a general strike in January. The stoppages spread until 700,000 workers were crying for peace, justice and bread. Radical Socialists exploited the hardship caused by hunger, war taxes and inflation. ('In Russia, the land, the factories and the mines are being given to the people.') The mainstream Social Democrats, however, decided not to support the calls for revolution; instead they negotiated with the government. Even so, the army had to send forces from the front to ensure order. February brought the first significant mutiny, by naval crews in Montenegro. Food shortages and officers' privileges were the trigger, and the unrest spread up the Adriatic coast. Hopes that co-operation with newly independent Ukraine would unlock huge imports of grain came to nothing. April brought food riots in Laibach and 'mass rallies at which oaths for unity and independence were being sworn'. By now, seven divisions were deployed in the interior of the empire.

The army was not cushioned against the shortages. By 1918, it was getting only half the flour it needed. The daily rations of front-line troops in Italy were reduced in January to 300 grams of bread and 200 grams of meat. Even these statistics only tell half the story. A Czech NCO, Jan Triska of the 13th Artillery Regiment, recorded the real conditions. The rations had run out during the Caporetto offensive, and matters had grown much worse since then. The army was ordered to provision itself from the occupied territory. This was only possible for a month or two; in February, Boroević told the Army High Command that the situation was critical: the men had been hungry for four weeks, and were 'no longer moved by incessant empty phrases that the hinterland is starving or that we must hold out'. They must be properly fed if they were to fight.

By late April, the men were starving. Bread and polenta were very scarce, and often mixed with sawdust or even sand. Meat practically disappeared. Soldiers stole the prime cuts from horses killed by enemy fire, and orders went out for carcasses to be delivered directly to the slaughterhouse. Triska's battery horses were dying; only six of 36 were healthy. Even the coffee made of chicory was in short supply. 'Salt was only a memory.' The men were often given money instead of food, but there was nothing to spend it on. The men grew so weak during May that they could only walk with difficulty. Triska risked punishment by trading his service revolver and ammunition for horsemeat. He collected stems of grass to boil and eat, and picked mulberries when they could be found. Such was the condition of the men who were sent against the Italians in June.

*

With 23 undersized divisions on the Asiago plateau, another 15 on the line of the Piave and 22 more in reserve, the Habsburg force barely outnumbered the Italians, who had a clear advantage in firepower and in the air. The offensive would start on the Piave, where Boroević's divisions would attack across the river. Conrad's divisions were to follow up by striking from the north.

Addressing his officers, Boroević openly criticised the shortages of men and supplies. Due to Conrad's stubbornness, he implied, the Piave line was short of ten divisions. After this rare indiscretion, the field marshal did his duty, ordering his battalion commanders to attack like a hurricane and not pause until they reached the River Adige. 'For this, gentlemen, could well be the last battle. The fate of our monarchy and the survival of the empire depend on your victory and the sacrifice of your men.' It has been claimed that, despite everything, Habsburg morale ran high in June. Certainly, there are reports of soldiers marching to the line with maps of Treviso in their pockets, gaily asking the bystanders how far it was to Rome. They would have taken heart from the order to plunder the Allied lines (no shortages there). Different testimony came from Pero Blašković, commanding a Bosnian battalion on the Piave. According to Blašković, a Habsburg loyalist to the bone, everyone without exception hoped the offensive would be postponed, for they were all aware of Karl's muted search for a separate peace. It was this, more than hunger or lack of munitions, Blašković says, that took the men's minds off victory, making them reflect that defeat would cost fewer lives, letting more of them get safely home in the end.

The bombardment began at 03:00 on 15 June. As at Caporetto, the Austrians aimed to incapacitate the enemy batteries with a pinpoint attack, including gas shells. However, their accuracy was poor, due to Allied control of the skies; many of the shells may have been time-expired, and the Italians had been supplied with superior British gas-masks. Too many Austrian guns were deployed in the Trentino, a secondary sector; some heavy batteries had no shells at all; and there was no element of surprise, for Diaz's army had agents in the occupied territory, and deserters were talkative. The Austrian gunners only had the advantage on the Asiago plateau, where thick fog blanketed the preparations.

At 05:10, the guns lengthened their fire to strike the Italian rear lines and reserves. The pontoons were dragged out from behind the gravel islands near the river's eastern shore. The enemy batteries were still silent; perhaps the gas shells had knocked them out? No such luck; the Italian guns opened up, pounding the Austrian jump-off positions. The Italian riverbank was still wreathed in gas fumes when the assault teams jumped ashore, quickly taking the Italian forward positions amid the chatter of machine guns.

The morning went well; the Austrians moved 100,000 men across the river under heavy rain. Watching the infantry pour over the pontoons, Jan Triska and his gunners wondered if this time they would reach Venice. Enlarging the bridgeheads proved more difficult. Progress was made on the Montello, where the four divisions pushed forward several kilometres, and around San Donà, near the sea. Elsewhere, the attackers were pinned down near the river. Further north, Conrad's divisions attacked from Asiago towards Mount Grappa. Slight initial gains could not be held; the Italians had learned how to use the 'elastic defence', absorbing enemy thrusts in a deep system of trenches, then counter-attacking. By the end of the day, Blašković realised, 'our paper house had been blown down'. The Emperor sent Boroević a desperate telegram: 'Hold your positions, I implore you in the name of the monarchy!' The answer was curt: 'We shall do our best.'

Progress on the second day was no easier. Conrad was in retreat; his batteries – more than a third of all the Habsburg guns in Italy – were out of the fight. Boroević ordered his commanders to hunker down while forces were transferred from the north. Meanwhile the Piave rose again, washing away many of the pontoons. Supplying the bridgeheads across the torrent became even more dangerous. The Austrians were too close to exhaustion and their supplies too uncertain for a sustained battle to run in their favour. By the first afternoon, Major Blašković realised that the Austrian artillery, laying down a rolling barrage for the assault troops, were already husbanding their shells. If the under-used Italian units further north were to be redeployed around Montello, the Habsburg goose would soon be cooked. Overhead, the Caproni aeroplanes chased away the Habsburg planes and British Sopwith Camels proved their worth, bombing along the river. ('In aviation, too, morale is very important,' Blašković remarked sadly, 'but technology is even more so.') The pontoons and columns of men on the riverbank, waiting to cross, offered easy targets. While the Austrians ran out of shells, the Allied artillery and air bombardment were unrelenting. The fate of Jan Triska's battery on the Piave was indicative: over the week of battle, it lost 58 men, half its strength.

Conrad's divisions were too hard pressed to transfer men to the Piave. In fact, the opposite happened: the Italians transferred forces from the mountains to the river. When these reinforcements arrived, on 19 June, the Italians counter-attacked along the Piave. They failed to crack the bridgeheads, but the Austrian position was untenable. Pontoons that had survived the bombing were damaged by high water and debris. Blašković's regiment (the 3rd Bosnia & Herzegovina Infantry) ran out of shells and bullets; the men fought on with bayonets and hand-grenades until a Hungarian regiment managed to bring up a few crates of ammunition from the river.

Boroević told the Emperor that if the Montello could be secured, it should be the springboard for a new offensive. Securing it would need at least three more divisions, including artillery. If the high command did not intend to renew the offensive from the Montello, it was pointless to retain the bridgeheads; they should be abandoned and all efforts dedicated to strengthening the defences east of the river. As Karl wondered what to do, the German high command stepped in, ordering a cessation of hostilities so that the Austrians could despatch their six strongest divisions to the Western Front. For Ludendorff's spring offensives were running out of steam and 250,000 American troops were arriving every month. Karl consulted his commanders in the field, who echoed Boroević's stark choice: either reinforce or withdraw. Then he consulted his chief of the general staff, General Arz von Straussenberg. A new offensive within a few weeks was, they agreed, not a realistic prospect. Their reserves were almost used up; even if enough divisions could be transferred to the Piave from elsewhere – and none could safely be spared from Ukraine or the Balkans – the Italians would match them. It would not be possible to recapture the zest of 15 June without a lengthy recovery.

Late on the 20th, Karl ordered the right bank of the Piave to be abandoned. General Goiginger, commanding the corps that had performed so well on the Montello, refused to obey. They had taken 12,000 prisoners and 84 guns; how could they retreat? Eventually he submitted, and the withdrawal began. Both sides were exhausted, and the manoeuvre was completed without much fighting. The Bosnians and Hungarians on the Montello worked their way back to the river. The last Austrians crossed on 23 June, ending the Battle of the Solstice. The Italians had lost around 10,000 dead, 35,000 wounded and more than 40,000 prisoners, against 118,000 Habsburg dead, wounded, sick, captured and missing. Early in July, Third Army units capped the achievement by seizing the swampy delta at the mouth of the Piave which the Austrians had held since Caporetto.

The rejoicing was widespread and spontaneous. For many soldiers, the Battle of the Solstice cleansed the stain of Caporetto, and the name of the Piave has ever since evoked a glow of fulfilment, as smooth as the sound of its utterance, untouched by the horrors of the Isonzo front or the controversy that overshadowed Italy's victory in November. Ferruccio Parri, a much-decorated veteran who became a leading anti-fascist, said at the end of his long life that the Battle of the Solstice was 'the only proper *national battle* of which our country can truly be proud'.

For the Allies, two things were clear: the Italians were a fighting force again, and the Austro-Hungarian army was still dangerous: its morale had not collapsed and the soldiers were still loyal. The view inside Boroević's army was different; to their eyes, the civilian system had let them down. They were still better soldiers than the Italians, but what could they do without food or munitions? The spectacle of his own men after the battle filled the genial Blašković with despair: 'weary, dejected and starving, their tattered uniforms crusted with reddish dry clay. Their weapons alone gave them any likeness to soldiers, for otherwise they looked like beggars roaming from pillar to post.' Gloom settled over the Austrian lines.

The failure of the Piave offensive made life even harder for the civilians under Austrian occupation.

Looking confidently ahead after Caporetto, the Habsburg high command had proposed that the postwar border between Austria and Italy should run along the River Tagliamento. Boroević mooted an even more vengeful settlement: the border should be pushed back to the line of the rivers Adige and Mincio, restoring *all* the Veneto to Austria, undoing the 1866 war of unification. By July 1918, these ambitions had gone up in smoke.

When Cadorna's army retreated after Caporetto, most of the urban population packed its belongings: as many as 400,000 civilians fled across the Piave, including the state employees, landowners, lawyers and so forth. The exception was the clergy, for many priests were glad to see the return of Habsburg power. (Relations between the Vatican and the government in Rome, always difficult, had not recovered from the Pope's condemnation of 'useless slaughter'.) Beyond the Piave, these refugees were joined by a quarter of a million civilians from the new front-line areas – Venice, Padua, Treviso.

A much higher proportion of people in the villages and countryside stayed, and waited for the enemy. When the new front stabilised, the occupiers and the local civilians were roughly equal in number: about 800,000 of each. Except for 30,000 Slovenes around Gorizia and a few German-speaking pockets, the locals were Italian, while the occupiers came from all the lands of the Habsburg empire. The Central Powers were ill-prepared to take over the civil administration, and the territory came under military government led by Boroević, headquartered at Udine. The portion of territory under German control was ceded to the Austrians in March.

It was a martial regime. Railways, post and telegraph were subject to exclusive use by the military. Citizens needed a permit to move from one district to another. All Italian patriotic images were removed from public places and schools, and people were forced to celebrate the birthday of Empress Zita, charming emblem of Austrian–Italian unity. The military penal code was applied throughout the territory. There are no statistics for sentences passed by the courts martial; an Italian commission, set up after the war to investigate abuses under the occupation, concluded that death sentences were seldom passed. Exceptions included two civilians hanged for lighting lanterns at night. Their corpses were left on the gibbet for several days, to drive home the message that spies could expect no leniency.

Capital sentences were probably rare because the population was co-operative. Many people were not sorry to see the Austrians take control; they felt let down by the Italian army and tricked by the civilian authorities, which gave no warning or help in October 1917. Besides, communal memories of Habsburg rule before 1866 were not so bad. This attitude could not last. The first wave of plunder and pillage was followed by requisitions that stripped the population of almost everything edible. Livestock was confiscated in January. Vegetables, nuts, wine and oil were next to be seized, followed by the dry forage. All the manure was stolen. Despite these predations, and the benefit of a good local harvest, the occupiers could no longer feed themselves by February, when the requisitions extended to fabric, leather and other material. Household linen was taken in March; people could keep three sets of underwear, two pillow-slips, three sheets and three towels each. In at least one case, soldiers went from house to house, leaving people with nothing but the clothes on their backs. The loot was inventoried, in Habsburg style: the army took 95,000 sheets, 65,000 shirts, 39,000 items of underwear, 47,000 towels, 56,000 pillow-slips and 3,400 'unspecified items'.

The 'Italian traitors' were supposed to be left enough for their own needs. This did not happen, and by April severe malnutrition was common. Soldiers and civilians alike ate anything they lay their hands on – mice, acacia flowers, vineleaves, wild chicory from the hedgerows. Stray dogs and cats were skinned for the pot. Desperate mothers took their children as close to the front as they could get, hoping to beg food from kindly officers. By the end of the war, almost 10,000 civilians had starved to death. The situation was hardly better for the Slovene evacuees from the Isonzo valley who returned after the Twelfth Battle to find their homes ransacked and fields picked bare of anything that could be eaten or sold. The very landscape had altered. One woman, returning to her village near Tolmein, recorded the desolation:

... the mountains were bare and the trees broken and destroyed by shells, it was sad to see them. There was a soldiers' cemetery at the foot of Mount Mrzli, reaching as far as the eye could see, grave after grave, each marked with a little wooden cross and covered with moss and ivy. Wherever I looked in the valley all I could see were graves.

Boroević knew the brutal treatment of civilians was counter-productive. People hid whatever they could, depriving his front-line troops of victuals. He opened public kitchens, but his administration lacked the resources and, at lower levels, the will to ensure that people did not starve. Despite his efforts to provide a basic health service, more than 12,500 civilians perished for lack of medical care. Even the censorship office was too short-staffed to be much use, though it caught a woman from Pordenone who described the occupying army, in a letter, as 'a mass of famished barbarians who have come to Italy to steal everything'.

For Italian nationalists safe on the other side of the Piave, the multiple identity of the occupying force proved its wickedness. One journalist wrote of 'heterogeneous masses' of 'Germans, Austrians, Bulgarians, even the lurid Turks set foot on that sacred ground'. She meant the befezzed troops from Bosnia and Herzegovina, many of them Muslim by confession. One of these 'lurid Turks' was Pero Blašković who, though not a Muslim, wore the fez as the emblem of his beloved regiment. Compared to his native land, Friuli and the Veneto were highly developed, and the handsome towns, rich countryside and dignified people impressed him. He enthused about the fine straight edges of the fields, with wheat and rice, vineyards and mulberry groves, separated by tidy ditches, neat as a chessboard. Even the military graveyard at Redipuglia, near Gorizia, was evidence of 'the high level of Italian culture'. The Austrians were 'literally starving' when they arrived in this 'blessed land'; even so, Blašković deplored the scale of pillage, with everyone 'from the commanding officers to the chauffeurs' stealing whatever could be grabbed, ripped out or dismantled. Everything that could be melted down for munitions, from factory plant to church bells, was sent to Austria and Germany.

Boroević's regime could not seal the area against Italian propaganda,[1] which naturally portrayed the invasion as a primeval nightmare of rape and pillage, like the Germans in Belgium or – a local legend of mindless atrocity – the ancient Huns in Friuli (where Attila had sacked Aquileia in AD 452). Trench newspapers focused the soldiers' minds on images of 'the barbarian violating the women of Italy', married women dishonoured beside the corpses of their husbands, girls throwing themselves out of windows rather than submit. 'Protect them, soldier of Italy, for if you give way, your wife too will be defiled.' Postcards and posters conveyed the same frightful message, which had an added charge because Italian pro-war images of 'Italia' had from the start been 'very erotic', portrayed as 'a young, soft, rather sad girl'.

Given this grisly propaganda, ordinary Italians would have been surprised to learn that their government refused to help civilians who wanted to leave the occupied territory. The Supreme Command argued that the local people were more useful at home: they obstructed Habsburg control, strengthened Italian claims to the territory, and provided camouflage for spies. Orlando concurred, and refused to repatriate Italians from the occupied territory, except in extreme need.

The real scale of sexual crime during the occupation will never be known. The postwar royal commission found that rape was widespread in the first few weeks and continued to the end. The victims often preferred to keep silent, deterred by shame and social stigma from

[1] D'Annunzio's finest exploit was his flight over Vienna in August 1918, when his squadron dropped 150,000 leaflets on the astonished citizens. When the news reached the occupied Veneto, civilian morale rose.

admitting the crimes against them. There is evidence that 'most rapes were carried out in the absolute certainty of impunity, above all when officers or NCOs took part'. In these conditions, Boroević's personal honesty had little impact on lawlessness and corruption. Even the attitude of the pro-Habsburg clergy hardened over the summer. Occasional acts of sabotage led the administration to fear an uprising. Secret lists were prepared of people to seize as hostages. They were not needed: smouldering anger did not crystallise into active resistance, however hopeless things became, partly because people believed that time was on their side. In October, a foreign ministry official reported to Vienna that if the administration did not improve, 1919 would bring 'an economic collapse that will swallow up human lives as well as our reputation'. Too late! Their reputation had already perished. Allied troops advancing beyond the Piave in early November found destitution, dereliction, 'an air of utter emptiness . . . completely cleaned out of food'. Brutal, arrogant and predatory, the occupation did Rome the favour of destroying any trace of nostalgia in north-eastern Italy for Habsburg law and order. In the empire's last year of existence, imperial rule finally became as bad as Italian nationalists said it had always been.

Civilian life under the occupation was hardly studied until the 1980s. The whole topic jarred too uncomfortably against the narrative of triumphal recovery. Patriotic historians were troubled by the lack of 'heroic' resistance, repelled by the webs of collaboration and profiteering, and perplexed by the postwar polemics between returnees and civilians who never left.

This lack of curiosity looks trivial, however, beside the oblivion that shrouded an even more sensitive subject until the 1990s. This was the official attitude to Italian prisoners of war in Austrian and German camps. The 300,000 men taken during the Twelfth Battle joined the 200,000 or more in camps across the empire. If these men had known that it was more dangerous to be taken prisoner than to serve on the front line, fewer of them would have welcomed their capture. For the Italian government, uniquely, refused to send food parcels to its prisoners of war. As a result, more than 100,000 of the 600,000 Italian prisoners died in captivity – a rate nine times worse than for Habsburg captives in Italy. Only 550 of these were officers, dying of tuberculosis or wounds; the remainder died directly or indirectly of cold and hunger.

Provision of food and other aid to prisoners had been accepted practice since the Central Powers announced in late 1914 that, due to the Allied blockade, they would no longer be responsible for feeding and clothing Allied prisoners of war. While Britain and France subsidised the aid to their captured soldiers, Italy refused to take such measures, or even, except in extreme cases, to allow the exchange of sick prisoners. Fearful that soldiers would desert en masse if they believed they would be safe in captivity, the government treated Italian POWs as cowards or defectors who should be punished. This unpublicised policy was bolstered by a propaganda campaign against prisoners of war. (D'Annunzio, dependably odious, branded them 'sinners against the Fatherland, the Spirit, and Heaven'.) Charity subscriptions for captured soldiers were prohibited. As a concession, the Red Cross was permitted to take aid for officers only. Private packages were permitted, but few were sent – due to the penury in which many soldiers' families lived – and even fewer arrived.

This heinous policy was proposed by the Supreme Command and supported by successive governments thanks above all to Sonnino, who insisted that, under international law, responsibility lay with the captors. The worst effects were felt after Caporetto, when the vast flood of prisoners strained the camp system in Austria and Germany beyond its limits. Over the terrible winter of 1917–18, hundreds of prisoners died every day. According to Carlo Salsa, an inmate in Theresienstadt camp, prisoners concealed the corpses in their barracks, so the dead men's rations would keep arriving. The Red Cross appealed to the government in Rome, but nothing was done until summer 1918, when hard-tack rations were sent. They reached the camps in November, when the war was already over.

The Austro-Hungarian army in Italy shrank from 650,000 to 400,000 between July and October. Few of these men were combat casualties. Many deserted; others succumbed to the malaria that ravaged the coastal areas and the lower Piave, to dysentery or the so-called Spanish flu that appeared around Padua in July and spread eastwards. In their weakened condition, starving, with their uniforms in shreds, lacking boots and underclothes, they were prey to every illness. The average body weight in one division had sunk by August to 50 kilograms, less than 8 stones.

Despite blizzards of propaganda by Czech, Yugoslav, Polish and other separatist groups; half a million POWs returning from Russia, many of them newly politicised and loudly critical; extremely degrading conditions at the front, and the disappearance of any hope of victory – despite all this, the Habsburg army remained loyal. There were no mutinies on the Italian front until late October, just before the last battle; even these were limited to a few units. This testifies to the effectiveness of military discipline, the power of habit, the unthinkability of historic change, and the grip on soldiers' minds of their immediate circumstances. Perhaps the anticipation of a final decisive Italian attack was another binding element.

The army's endurance is more striking because the erosion of morale was unstoppable. A battalion commander on Mount Grappa explained the pressures on his men, in a stoical letter of 1 July:

We have been officially notified to expect that men of the [Allied] Czechoslovak brigade will dress in Austrian uniforms and attack our positions – this, when half our regiment is Czech. I won't go into the miserable state of our position except to mention some key words: 8 degrees Centigrade, heat and light forbidden, no water, ice-cold food, no caves, no shelter etc. – repeated desertions, countless Italian propaganda leaflets, but no press reports of our own.

Far from producing counter-propaganda, the Austrian newspapers were part of the problem; Boroević warned that journalism about the 'miserable internal state of Monarchy' amounted to enemy propaganda. The Army High Command went further: the normal language in the newspapers was indistinguishable from enemy propaganda: namely, 'self-determination', 'persecution' and 'demands of oppressed peoples'. Little could be done: the machinery of government was too decayed for censorship to be effective.

Increasingly, morale could only be raised by appealing to nationalist emotion, which begged the question of why the men should fight for the empire at all. A divisional commander on the Piave reported in mid-July that 'mental and physical depression' gripped his soldiers, 'regardless of nationality, rank or intelligence'. Few men's morale was proof against the combination of nationalist agitation at home, shortages on the front, and enemy propaganda. Desertions increased over the summer, usually to the interior. A staff officer, inspecting a corps in the Tenth Army in September, found no enthusiasm.

Most of the men are apathetic, but they will fulfil their duty bravely and unflaggingly . . . The longing for peace is widespread . . . Efforts of the company commanders to put heart into the ranks by patriotic instruction are unsuccessful largely because of news from the hinterland.

By July, many non-German regions of the empire were shearing away. Separatist goals were promoted by emerging leaders from Poland to Slovenia. Even token reference to the dynasty was often lacking at public rallies. The German ambassador estimated that two-thirds of people in Vienna believed the Allies would win the war. Morale at the front had been partly cordoned against this encroaching gloom, but there was now a feedback loop: troops demoralised by news from home would desert and spread news of disillusion at the front. Morale had depended on junior officers who by this stage were more likely than their men to sympathise with the nationalist arguments raging across the empire.

The 56 divisions now in Italy had a fighting strength of less than 37 divisions. In August, General Arz informed the German high command that the empire could only stay in the war until the end of the year; the army would then be needed to resolve 'internal political questions'. On 8 August, the Allies took the initiative in France: following a French counter-offensive on the Marne, British forces broke through near Amiens. A string of victories brought the end of the war into sight. At the end of the month, Foch asked Diaz to support the operations in France by attacking across the Piave. Diaz refused: his army was not ready. Orlando agreed, but changed his mind by mid-September when it dawned that the Allied breach of the Hindenburg Line meant that German defeat was close. His impatience mounted along with Allied pressure, and Orlando pressed Diaz to plan an attack in early October, or by the end of October at the latest. Diaz found Orlando's advice confusing and unreliable. He insisted that it would be reckless to attack in the near future. Senior commanders were told to expect the final push in spring 1919.

Sonnino suspected that dread of 'doing a Cadorna' was making Diaz – whom he admired – overly cautious. For his part, the Foreign Minister saw that Bulgaria's collapse at the end of September and Ottoman Turkey's imminent capitulation had shifted the balance: with their south-eastern flank wide open and the Allies poised to attack, the Central Powers would not hold out much longer. If the Italians were left digging in for the winter while the Allies drove the Germans out of France and Belgium, their negotiating position would be feeble. If they were to win the territory pledged in 1915, they had to defeat the Austrians once and for all, knocking them out of the war.

Diaz awoke to these realities when Austria and Germany sought a rapid negotiated end to the war in the first week of October. Within a few hours of each other, first Vienna and then Berlin asked Wilson for an armistice on the basis of his Fourteen Points. When Wilson made no answer, Karl announced that the empire would become a confederated monarchy. He tried to win time and favour by proclaiming that the Austrian half of the empire would be a federation where every 'ethnic group' formed its own 'state community'. It was too vague, too little, and much too late to save his inheritance by magically reconciling dynastic survival with national self-determination.

Diaz prepared to attack in the second half of October. His plan was ready by 9 October. When they met three days later, Orlando was smarting from his latest interrogation by Allied leaders in Paris; Clemenceau, easily irritated by the Italians, was galled by their inaction. Diaz issued the first orders for the offensive. By now, Germany was corresponding with Wilson; a peace based on the Fourteen Points was infinitely preferable to full-scale defeat and occupation. On the 14th, Wilson said any armistice must guarantee Allied military superiority and democratic government in Germany. A few days later he answered Karl's request; 'certain events of utmost importance' had overtaken the tenth of the Fourteen Points; instead of 'autonomous development', the peoples of Austria-Hungary would decide their own future.

The Italians were worried to learn on 19 October that Austria was working on a proposal to sue for peace on the basis of a unilateral retreat from Italian territory. This would steal their thunder, and Orlando – now so vexed by the chief of staff's prudence that he wondered if he could replace him – telegraphed Diaz at once: 'Between inaction and defeat, I prefer defeat. Get moving!' Wilson fuelled the fire under Diaz with a statement on 21 October supporting the Habsburg Slavs' bid for independence. Diaz decided that zero hour would be 03:00 on the 24th.

Orlando busied himself wringing renewed British and French commitment to the Treaty of London. Statements were splashed in the press, but Washington would not be drawn; the Department of State said only that 'Italy was entitled to the irredenta and also entitled to establish proper strategic boundaries.' Orlando's government explained coolly that this meant American support for its claims to the whole of the south Tyrol, Trieste, Istria and the Albanian coast. As the infantry on Grappa moved to the jump-off trenches and the gunners on the Piave

waited in their pits, the government knew that the dividend of victory
was still uncertain.

The plan of attack centred on the upper and middle Piave. Diaz would
punch through the enemy lines around the road to Vittorio Veneto and
Sacile, splitting Boroević's Sixth and Fifth armies, deployed respectively
on the northern and southern halves of the Piave. This would make the
Austrian positions on the Asiago plateau and Mount Grappa untenable.

Of Diaz's 57 infantry divisions and four cavalry divisions, including
three British, two French and one of Czechoslovak volunteers, some 33
would be committed in the Battle of Vittorio Veneto. The spearhead
would be the Eighth Army, comprising 14 divisions under General
Caviglia. Its right flank would be protected by the Tenth Army: two
British and two Italian divisions, under Lord Cavan. To its left, the small
Twelfth Army (one French and two Italian divisions, under a French
general) would secure the Piave below Mount Grappa and cross the
river at the same time as the Eighth Army. Grappa itself was the
responsibility of General Giardino's Fourth Army, which had to support
the Twelfth Army with counter-battery fire. The other armies in the
battle, the Sixth on the Asiago plateau (six divisions, including one
British and one French) and the Third on the southern portion of the
front, were to await developments.

Much depended on the river. Even if the Piave behaved itself, infantry
columns made easy targets, silhouetted against expanses of shingle.
When Diaz drew up his operational orders on 12 October, the river was
running high. Under mounting pressure to move, he made a crucial
decision: the attack would start on Mount Grappa instead of the Piave.
Strengthened with three extra divisions and 400 extra guns, the Fourth
Army would drive the Austrians off Grappa and then thrust northwards
up the valley of the River Brenta, enveloping the Austrian force on the
Asiago plateau. The operation on the Piave would begin overnight, less
than 24 hours after Giardino's attack in the mountains.

The Allies started with every advantage. Apart from infantry strength,
their superiority in guns and aircraft had increased since June. Boroević
decided to cede ground where he must, in the hope of counter-attacking
later. This was a desperate gamble; if morale was as fragile as he
suspected, the second and third lines and reserves might crumble when
the enemy overwhelmed the first line. But there was no alternative. On
17 October, his order of the day exhorted the army to fight for 'an

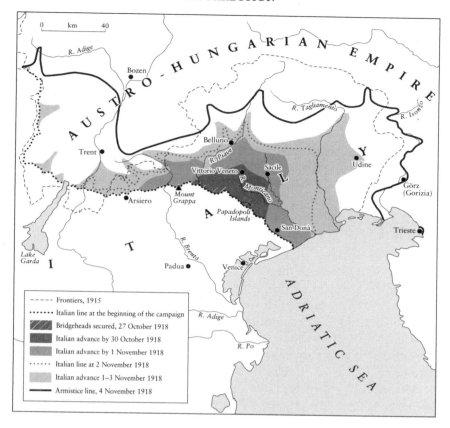

The Battle of Vittorio Veneto, October–November 1918

honourable peace'. Privately anticipating a catastrophe, he laid plans for an orderly retreat with mobile rearguard protection. A dynastic loyalist to the end, his priority was to preserve his forces so that they could defend the empire against its internal enemies after the armistice. And these enemies were multiplying: on the 23rd, hours before the Italians attacked, several Hungarian units refused to go up the line, and two Bosnian companies mutinied.

Attacking on schedule, the Fourth Army quickly ran into trouble. Giardino had less than a week to prepare an operation for which no studies existed, and the Austrian positions on Mount Grappa were strong. Boroević had expected the attack to begin on the high ground,

[357]

and Italian artillery had been shelling the Austrian lines on Grappa for days, so there was no surprise. When more rain fell on the 24th, Diaz had to delay the Eighth Army's attack – by 48 hours, as it turned out – which deprived Giardino of support on the right. Worst of all, the Italian tactics were primitive: infantry units were spread evenly, regardless of terrain, and advanced in lines. The fighting degenerated into a bloodbath, in Cadorna's worst style. Austria's initial resistance let Karl hope that all might not yet be lost. But he was not a fantasist; on the 26th, he informed Wilhelm that he would have to seek an armistice and a separate peace.

After six days' hard fighting, Giardino had 'no success' to show for nearly 25,000 casualties: two-thirds of the Italian losses in the battle. Fortunately, operations on the Piave were going to plan after a delayed start. A British corps commander had proposed that the Papadopoli islands, a shingle archipelago south of the Montello, should be occupied before the main attack. This was done on 23 October,[2] leaving the Tenth Army well placed for the next stage. Still, the island was separated from the Austrian lines by the main channels of the river, almost a mile wide, brimming and raging after days of rain. There was little that Cavan could do but wait.

Eventually, under cover of night on the 26th, the Tenth Army moved in strength across to the islands. Norman Gladden, a private in the 11th Northumberland Fusiliers (23rd Division) who had survived the Somme and Passchendaele, was among the troops waiting on the western shore. Over his shoulder, he saw 'thousands of gun flashes coalescing to form a continuous blaze of light along the bank'. In front, the pontoon bridge was a frightening sight.

A string of small boats had been thrown across the river in such a way that the powerful current tended to force them closer together, and they supported a planked gangway, which was roped across their gunwales. Over this bridge the assault troops had to pass, regulated by an Italian boatman to ensure that the structure should not become overloaded at any point. We were to proceed at three-pace intervals. I saw a steel-helmeted figure mount the bridge and stride slowly forward; and another, and another. The gangway stood some feet above the water and in the darkness seemed to be hung high in the air. The flaming horizon beyond threw the dark figures into relief, while shrapnel shells stabbed the darkness above.

2 First across the channel to Papadopoli was a battalion of Gordon Highlanders, rowed by Venetian gondoliers.

The Austrian forward positions on the far shore were thinly manned behind the wire entanglements, and half-heartedly defended after a shattering bombardment by British gunners. A British divisional history recorded that 'Not many Austrians stayed to fight, the majority, surprised and dismayed at the failure of the wire to hold up the attack, streamed back inland in disorder, almost too fast to give the riflemen and Lewis gunners much chance to shoot them down.' Further north, protected by a ferocious barrage, the Eighth and Twelfth Army engineers threw 11 pontoon bridges across the river. During the night of 26–27 October, the Piave tore most of them down; Austrian artillery demolished the rest. A few Eighth Army units that had crossed the river were trapped in bridgeheads between Grappa and Montello, helpless to assist Giardino. The Twelfth Army was no better off.

In this predicament, the role of spearhead fell to the British divisions of the Tenth Army, not an outcome that has won much recognition from Italian historians. Cavan sent these divisions beyond the river at dawn on the 27th. The troops' mood lightened as they moved eastward in the morning sunshine, meeting little resistance. 'A new carefree attitude was taking control. We were no longer the frightened troops nailed to the earth by a storm of steel. We were advancing into enemy-held territory, victors at last.' The Austrian 7th Infantry Division apparently panicked at the sight of the British (whose presence during the preparations had been carefully concealed), and the disarray spread to adjacent divisions. Some reserve units refused to move up when ordered.

Caviglia was stuck; high water as well as accurate Austrian shelling stopped him from enlarging his bridgehead. As had been agreed for this eventuality, he lent a reserve corps to the Tenth Army; this was sent southwards to use Cavan's bridges. The Italian–British force crossed overnight; the northern bridgeheads of the Eighth and Twelfth Armies were linked during the 28th and extended against a patchy defence. Major Blašković's battalion, deployed opposite a French bridgehead, was encircled and captured when a Hungarian regiment on their flank ran forward waving white rags. His men, filthy and pot-bellied with hunger, were a pitiful sight beside the smart, well-fed *poilus*.

That morning, Boroević reported to the high command that resistance by non-German troops was weakening and incidents of mutiny were increasing. 'He was informed that the government had asked President Wilson for an Armistice, and commented that this news would hardly raise morale.' Diaz's original plan was taking shape: the Allies were moving towards Vittorio Veneto and Sacile, the axis that should split the Austrians. To protect his Sixth Army, Boroević ordered four reserve divisions to prepare to engage the enemy. One division refused to budge; the other three took up positions on a stream called the Monticano, between the Piave and the Livenza. He also feared the envelopment of the Fifth Army, which had not been tested because the Duke of Aosta's men were still on the right bank, though crossings were now imminent. So he ordered the Fifth to withdraw to the Monticano line. Here the empire made its last stand.

Late in the day, Lord Cavan ordered his divisions across the Monticano. Except for an Italian battery, the British lacked artillery support; it took the whole of 29 October to knock out Austrian machine guns above the steep riverbank and in isolated farms. The issue was settled by nightfall, and Boroević ordered a retreat to the River Livenza, a few kilometres further east. He had urged the high command to tell the Italians that Habsburg forces would pull back behind the 1866 border, unilaterally evacuating the Veneto. (Preparations for this contingency had been in hand since 14 October, when the high command ordered the armies in Italy to send all inessential equipment and infrastructure to the interior of the empire.) General Arz, conceding that the army in Italy was finished, ordered Boroević to withdraw at once, as a token of goodwill. Cavan's forward units saw the sky light up as the Austrians burned their ammunition dumps. In Austrian accounts the retreat was dreadful but not headlong; 'a semblance of order' was 'maintained by sheer force of habit, a march into nothingness'.

Back on the Piave, the bridgeheads were enlarged all along the river. The final stage of the battle began on the 30th, with Italians pouring across the river in strength. Allied heavy guns crossed as well, which cheered the advance units, though resistance faded so quickly that artillery support was superfluous. Civilians emerged from their cottages, their faces taut with starvation, to cheer the Allies. In the morning, cyclists and bersaglieri of the Eighth Army occupied Vittorio Veneto, some 16 kilometres beyond the Piave. Later that day, forward units reached the River Livenza.

As per Diaz's plan, divisions of the Eighth and Twelfth Armies swung northwards, forcing the Austrians to withdraw from the Grappa massif or be encircled. The manoeuvre succeeded; with the Fourth Army advancing at last, the Austrian Eleventh Army was exposed on the Asiago plateau. That night, it withdrew from front-line positions. The

Sixth Army turned this tactical retreat into a rout. Over the next three days, the British 48th Division took more than 20,000 prisoners for the loss of 26 killed and 129 wounded.

Let us pick up the story of Jan Triska, the Czech artillery officer, who returned from home leave in mid-September. On 30 October, with the Italians less than 10 kilometres away, Jan's regiment prepared to retreat. For the first time ever, the men were ordered to fall in, in national groups. A second shock followed: the officers canvassed views on the future of the empire. Who was for the Emperor? Sixty hands went up. Who was for a republic? Eighty-six hands. And who wanted a national state of their own? Some forty Czechs raised their hands.

On the last day of October, the Italian line moved steadily eastwards. Cavan's 23rd Division liberated Sacile. Austrian rearguards tried to delay the Allies as huge numbers of soldiers made for the River Tagliamento, abandoning everything, burning the bridges as they went. Writing to his wife, Diaz allowed himself, for once, to exult. It was, he said, 'Caporetto in reverse'. Victory was assured. 'I have won the war more by the strength of my heart and nerves than by any intellectual gifts, and I feel stronger, more balanced, than all of them' – meaning the politicians who had carped at his caution.

A woman on the road from Conegliano to Vittorio Veneto was seen shouting triumphantly 'Now it's goodbye, Caporetto, and good riddance!' Across the empire, nations emerged or re-emerged into history. Karl refused on principle to approve the use of force against the separatists.

The Italians were in no hurry to reach an armistice, and Karl's negotiators were not received at Padua until the 31st. General Badoglio treated his opposite number, General Viktor Weber von Webenau, with cold formality. That morning, representatives of the American, British, French and Italian governments – the 'Big Four' – had met in Paris to discuss armistices with Germany and Austria. They agreed that the Italians, acting on behalf of the Allies, should occupy Habsburg territory along the eastern Adriatic, according to the Treaty of London. Some good historians have accused Italy's partners of missing a crucial opportunity; instead of handing the Italians control over the territory pledged in the Treaty of London, they should have raised the Treaty's incompatibility with Wilson's principles. It is an unhistorical objection, for the Central Powers were still undefeated and the Allies were still bound by the Treaty, which Wilson himself would not dispute before a full-dress peace conference. It may be that Wilson's envoy in Paris, Colonel House, 'knew literally nothing about the Adriatic and cared even less', in the bitter judgement of one of these historians; this does not mean his decisions on the last day of October were wrong or cynical.

While the talks continued in Paris and Padua, the Allies attacked the rearguards and retreating columns. The road from Sacile to Pordenone was packed with Austrian troops 'in headlong retreat . . . bombarded, bombed and machine-gunned from the air'. The future Marxist critic Ernst Fischer, commanding a half-battery of howitzers on the Piave, observed the Allied planes strafing the highway with a sharp eye: 'Under the impact of the hail of metal the road puckered like the skin of a freezing man.' They were freezing, too, unable to sleep for cold. Next day, Lieutenant Hugh Dalton of the Royal Artillery – who would serve as chancellor of the exchequer in the great reforming Labour government after the Second World War – saw the ditches full of dead men and horses. 'The loss in wrecked and abandoned material of every kind had been immense.' People were already eating the dead horses.

Elsewhere, the last Habsburg governor of Trieste received a cable from Vienna at 19:30 on the 31st, announcing that Austrian rule on the Adriatic Sea was over. He left by train the following day, shortly before Diaz ordered a general advance along the whole length of the front.[3] By 2 November, the Asiago plateau was completely in Italian hands. Advance units crossed the Tagliamento in the afternoon. Several Tyrolean regiments – the last Habsburg units still fighting – surrendered. Boroević telephoned the high command: as it had become impossible to 'defend our borders', what should he do? He was ordered to move as many intact units as possible to the hinterland so they could be transferred to their new national states.

At the Villa Giusti, Badoglio handed over Italy's terms for an armistice. The Austro-Hungarians must stop fighting at once; the imperial army must be reduced to 20 divisions and surrender half its artillery; all the occupied territories (corresponding to the Treaty of

---

3 One of the last Austrian tourists in Trieste was Field Marshal Conrad, who had been sacked from his last command (in the Trentino) after the disastrous Battle of the Solstice. As always, he enjoyed himself in Trieste by sea-bathing and sketching. He did not leave until 29 October – 'the last possible moment', as he told a friend. Was he savouring memories of his first visit to the city as a young man, when he had been 'filled with a sense of joy and freedom'?

London) must be evacuated within a period to be decided by the Allies; all German troops must leave the empire within 15 days; all Allied prisoners of war must be liberated at once; and the Allies must have free use of all imperial transport networks. The terms were non-negotiable and the Austrians had until midnight on 3 November to accept.

In the echoing halls of the Schönbrunn palace, Karl conferred late into the night with his prime minister, foreign minister, and chief of staff. He was especially troubled by the prospect that the Allies would use their freedom of movement to attack Germany from imperial territory – an eventuality he had promised to forestall. Arz advised him to accept as the only way to save hundreds of thousands of lives. This was an appeal he could not resist, but he still wanted his government's approval. Some form of assent was obtained, and the commanders at the front were informed; rashly, they were ordered to cease hostilities at once. At this point, early on 3 November, the high command was unaware of an Italian stipulation that the ceasefire should come into effect with a 24-hour delay, so their forward units could be informed. General Weber realised the discrepancy would be disastrous for Austrian troops, but the high command refused to amend the order. In desperation, Weber asked Badoglio to suspend hostilities immediately. His request was brushed aside, and the Italians signed the armistice at 15:20. It would come into force at 15:00 on 4 November.

As if bent on confirming, with its last breath, every accusation of haughty negligence towards the common people, the Habsburg élite had bungled the armistice. The Italians had 24 hours to round up unresisting Austrian soldiers who believed the war was over. Some 350,000 prisoners were taken in the last day of the war. One-third of this haul were German Austrians; 83,000 were Czechs and Slovaks, 60,000 were South Slavs, 40,000 were Polish; tens of thousands more were Romanian, Ruthenian and even – 7,000 of them – Italian. One of the Czechs was Jan Triska. At 07:00 on 3 November, his brigade was called by the high command. Italy had agreed an armistice, and all hostilities on the south-western front should halt with immediate effect. Nobody told them the Italians were still fighting, and Jan awoke on 4 November as a prisoner. Civilians lined the roads to hit and spit at them as they were marched to the rear. By 11 November, the Italians held 430,000 Habsburg prisoners. Their harsh treatment led to some 30,000 deaths, as needless as any on this front. Conditions for the soldiers who escaped capture were not much easier; the roads and railways away from the front were in pandemonium, food was nowhere to be had, and newly formed Yugoslav militias barred the retreating troops from towns and villages in Slovenia.

The Austrians kept their word and emptied their POW camps. When retreating Habsburg troops met Italians coming the other way, there was no hostility; indeed, 'we talked to them as to old friends'. The Italians' official reception was often less friendly. As Carlo Salsa's train thundered into Padua station, the returning prisoners embraced each other: 'We're in Italy! Italy! *Viva l'Italia!*' But soldiers with bayonets refused to let them off the train. Former prisoners were interned for weeks in poor conditions, and interrogated on the reason for their capture. The Supreme Command wondered at one point if they might not be sent directly to Libya, prolonging their punishment and populating the colonies in one stroke.

After three days and nights 'on the gun' behind the Piave, Gunner Blackburn and his mates had been idle since 28 October. 'It was hard for any of us to realise that the enemy had gone.' There was very little information from the front, and 'Nobody seems to know what is going to happen.' The men played cards and went ratting with stray dogs. Civilians began to return to the village: 'How they will manage to exist is their problem.' On 2 November, there were 'strong rumours of peace, the Italians are marching up and down the village, singing and shouting'. On the 3rd, curiosity overcame four of the Tommies. Deciding they 'were out of the war, as far as this front is concerned', they ventured across one of the pontoons. The Austrian first line was eerily intact, as if the men had vanished at a touch: 'On the parapet were rifles laid in a row, just as they had been left, alongside them were heaps of expended cartridge cases. The machine guns were still in position, the belts of ammunition still in the guns.' In a nearby field, they saw 32 battery horses in teams of eight, with their drivers still mounted, all killed by the bombardment. Other dead had already been collected and buried in graves so shallow that their boots stuck out. There was not another living soul anywhere in the wide landscape.

The Battle of Vittorio Veneto meant something to Italians that cannot be found in a summary of operations. It brought the balm of victory and the promise of peace. Piero Pieri, the war veteran and historian, would hail it as a masterly breakthrough, 'our purest glory'. The Italians had defeated an Austrian army in a straight fight – something that eluded them during the Risorgimento. More than this: 'After fifteen centuries, an Italian army drove back and destroyed a larger and completely foreign army.' Along with the empire, victory had destroyed the myth that Italians were incapable of waging war. A joke going around at the time caught the infantry's rueful pride: 'Just when we learned how to fight – the war is over!'

Boroević's postwar life was to be sad and brief. Denied permission to live in Yugoslavia, he survived in destitution in southern Austria, 'longing for death' as he told a friend. According to legend, he lived on gifts of food from veterans. The Yugoslavs refused to pay his pension, supposedly because he had ordered his retreating army to occupy Ljubljana in November 1918. He died in May 1920.

When I compare my fate with that of my good German comrades [he wrote in the last weeks of his life] I cannot help but be envious. They were all able to save their fatherland from catastrophe. I could not. The Yugoslavs, whose kingdom would not have emerged if I had not fought the battles on the Isonzo, cannot forgive my role in prolonging the war . . . I am likewise a stranger to Austria, Czechoslovakia and Hungary. Thus, for now, I have no country and am living for the sixth year out of my military chest.

Diaz's Victory Bulletin, issued on 4 November, exaggerated the strength of enemy forces and minimised the Allied contribution. It became a sort of national scripture, displayed in barracks as a bronze relief cast from the metal of Austrian guns and fixed to the walls of schools for pupils to learn. When people read its artful boast that 'the remains of what was once one of the most powerful armies in the world' were in retreat, they could not know that 'once' meant a long time ago. (On 9 November, Orlando suppressed a draft communiqué by Diaz that described the 'disastrous condition' of the Austrian army in its last days.) This false account of the last battle was not contested by the military, whom it flattered, or the journalists, who were still censored and self-censoring. Within a few years it merged seamlessly with Fascist glorification of the war. Under Mussolini, historians who knew better wrote that Italy had defeated the Austrians 'alone'.

The 24 hours of grace were used to put Italian boots on as much territory as possible around the northern Adriatic and in the Alto Adige.

At 16:20 on 3 November, an Italian destroyer nosed into the bay of Trieste. An officer in Austrian uniform led the ship through the mines guarding the harbour towards the quay, packed with excited citizens.[4] The officer was Lieutenant Guido Tedaldi, an Italian from one of the Adriatic islands. Someone asked if he would not rather change his uniform. No, he said, he had to *redeem* this one, by making it serve the fatherland. Redemption was the word of the day. Standing at the prow of the *Audace* was the tall, corpulent figure of General Pettiti di Roreto, who would be Trieste's first Italian governor. 'From today', he cried, 'our dead are dead no longer!' The crowd roared '*Viva l'Italia!* Welcome! At last!' A band played the royal march of the House of Savoy. 'In the name of His Majesty the King of Italy, I take possession of the city of Trieste!' the general declared.

Trento was liberated on the same day, and the first patrols entered Udine and Gorizia, closely followed by refugees who had been counting the hours before they could go home. A lady from Gorizia described the scene:

... such ruins were unimaginable ... Munitions boxes, heaps of stones, rags, furniture, stoves ... The windows are all barricaded with sandbags or bricks and you can still see the machine guns poking out of the garret windows. Barbed wire, bits of furniture, piles of wreckage, stones, block the street to the city centre. The square in front of the cathedral looks like a rubbish tip. The shops have all been gutted, everything tossed on the ground in complete confusion; a heavy-calibre shell has destroyed our house. The only movement, the only sign of life, is the rats. They rush about the streets by the dozen, outside the houses, between your legs.

Even making all haste, by 15:00 on 4 November the army was far short of the Brenner Pass. On the Adriatic, when the armistice came into force, the line of control ran short of Monfalcone, let alone Trieste. The problem was not resistance – Austrian authority melted at the touch, like snowflakes; it was mechanical. Diaz had no means to get his men far enough forward in the short time available. As long as the Italians were merely advancing, however, rather than fighting, the armistice did not oblige them to stop. Valentino Coda, a volunteer from Genoa who became the first Fascist deputy in parliament, spoke to joyful crowds in Trento: 'The dream has come true, our hundred-year effort has been crowned, and exultant Italy gathers you to her breast.' Pressing beyond Trento, the first troops in the Alto Adige passed Italian

4 Among the crowd was Trieste's great novelist, Italo Svevo.

prisoners of war on the long road home, looking like ghosts, smiling and weeping. A unit of the 75th Alpino Division reached the Brenner Pass on 7 November. Two days later, the last Austrian troops made their way north across the pass. On the 10th, an Italian battery climbed to the summit and ran the national flag up an improvised flagpole. The Italians stood on their 'natural border' at last.

Torpedo boats overloaded with infantry were sent from Venice to the ports of Pola, Zara and Sebenico. Facing no resistance, a single platoon could 'occupy' a town. Warships docked at the larger Dalmatian islands and the Albanian port of Valona. Troops even landed at Cattaro (Kotor), down in Montenegro. South of Istria, the Italians were 'received with open hostility' except in Zara, the only city with an Italian majority. Nonetheless, they behaved like masters with inalienable rights of conquest. An admiral claimed the title 'Governor of Dalmatia'. An American envoy warned that Italy's bullying attitude threatened 'to produce an open collision with the Yugoslavs . . . the population is in no way hostile to a joint landing of the Entente forces but only to the Italians being allowed to act alone'. Yugoslav leaders begged the Allies to land forces of their own in Dalmatia. A few units were sent, including an American regiment. As they came under Diaz's command, these units could hardly address the problem. Indeed, Italian commanders learned to send American platoons ahead, in order to defuse anti-Italian feeling. The Americans were then withdrawn overnight and replaced with Italians.

Fatefully, in mid-November, Orlando authorised the occupation of Fiume, a port between Trieste and Zara that had been developed as a Hungarian alternative to Austrian Trieste, 70 kilometres away. With good connections to central Europe, the port had grown rapidly. By the end of the nineteenth century, imperial buildings lined the harbour-front. Italian immigration was encouraged, to dilute the Croat population; by 1910, two-thirds of the old town (with 25,000 inhabitants) was Italian. The wider urban area remained overwhelmingly Croat. Before the war, Fiume had not figured prominently on the irredentists' wish-list; the Treaty of London granted it to the South Slavs, as a guarantee that they would not be deprived of a modern port.

By an ancient prerogative – preserved through centuries of Habsburg rule, like many other constitutional flora and fauna – Fiume was a 'corpus separatum', a distinct entity within the empire. On this basis, local Italian leaders claimed the town's right to self-determination in mid-October. When the Hungarian authorities abandoned Fiume at the end of the month, local irredentists staged a plebiscite on the city's future and proclaimed its annexation to Italy. This was the situation when a Sardinian brigade disembarked on 17 November, shoring up the self-proclaimed authorities and ensuring that the issue of Fiume would envenom the Paris conference in 1919.

The government approved a plan drawn up by Badoglio to break Slovene and Croat resistance in the occupied territories, and subvert the fragile Yugoslav state with black propaganda and paid agents. Orlando and Sonnino hoped to weaken the Yugoslav authorities-in-waiting while justifying Italy's occupation. Inland, the Italians ignored the demarcation line agreed in the armistice. The 83rd Company of Engineers marched on and on, beyond the Carso, stopping at a little village where they erected an obelisk with a Latin inscription, expressing the White Man's Burden of Italian greatness: 'Consul Aulus Postumius reached this point 2,000 years ago. Today Italy returns with her civilisation.'[5] Other units pushed further eastwards still, and were only deterred from occupying the Slovenian capital, Ljubljana, when Serbian army units threatened to attack.

The Americans and French were troubled. To clip Italian pretensions, France made Fiume the logistics base of the Allied Armies of the Orient. Indignant at this bid to loosen their grip on Fiume, the Italians refused to comply. The quarrel spiralled up to the highest level, and the Allies sent a quartet of admirals to investigate. Foch resolved the matter shortly before Christmas: the Yugoslavs should control Ljubljana and the Italians, Fiume. The Yugoslav state had already been proclaimed, thanks in part to Italy's threatening posture in the Adriatic, driving the Slovenes and Croats into the arms of Serbia, accelerating the very process of state-formation that Sonnino wanted to abort. Sonnino dedicated himself to preventing the new state's recognition by the Allies while suffocating it with an economic blockade. The United States recognised Yugoslavia nonetheless in February 1919, while Britain and France delayed doing so merely 'to please the Italians', as Clemenceau put it. By then Italy's leaders had squandered their credit with the other Allies, mismanaging their role at the Paris conference so spectacularly that Cadorna's campaigns look almost judicious by comparison.

5 In 229 BC, Aulus Postumius led a Roman army around the northern Adriatic to wage war against Queen Teuta of Illyria. Victory gave Rome control over much of the eastern Adriatic.

TWENTY-SEVEN

From Victory to Disaster

There is no instance of a country having benefited from prolonged warfare.
SUN TZU

There are things awaiting us which are in some senses more difficult than those we have undertaken.
PRESIDENT WILSON, to the Italian parliament, 3 JANUARY 1919

It comes down to this: a book-lined study in Paris, where three or four men design a peace treaty that shapes the postwar world. Over the course of several hundred meetings they and their assistants define borders, calculate reparations and debts, assign responsibility for the worst carnage in history, transfer colonies, and develop international law and trade.

Public hopes after a war had never run so broad and high. The four were expected, as an American advisor recalled, 'to produce a plan of permanent peace satisfactory to thirty-odd allied states, five enemy states, to say nothing of the neutrals, at the same time that they acted as an executive commission settling the turbulent current affairs of the entire world'.

For six months, between January and June 1919, sub-committees sat late into the night; ministers, generals and geographers were summoned to advise; drafting committees laboured over nuances of text; thousands of experts wrote thousands of briefing papers; thousands of petitioners, from Romanian royalty to Vietnamese and pan-African radicals, sought access to 'the Olympians', as the press dubbed the Big Three, for ultimately three members of this quartet determined the settlement. Their discretionary powers were fantastic; a snippet from their session on 13 May gives the flavour, with Wilson magisterial, Lloyd George teasing and Clemenceau wry or gruff:

PRESIDENT WILSON: If you were able, in the offers which might be made to Italy in the name of the League of Nations, to add that of Somaliland, that would help in the solutions we desire.

MR. LLOYD GEORGE: My intention is to give Greece the island of Cyprus also.

M. CLEMENCEAU: Don't forget that, according to the Treaty of Berlin, you need my authorisation for that.

MR. LLOYD GEORGE: I hope you'll give it me.

A journalist who covered the conference wrote that 'the crushing weight of the world' lay on these men's shoulders. 'They were supreme as perhaps no body of men in history has been supreme. No one could control them.' This was not quite true; they were accountable to legislatures which could reject their work. Mutual disagreement and rivalry also provided a kind of control. While they had agreed to build the peace on Wilson's Fourteen Points, the Europeans would not sacrifice their essential interests to an American notion of 'a new international morality'. In Wilson's view, this unprecedented war had to end with an unprecedented settlement, based on 'unselfish and unbiased justice'. Anything less would perpetuate the cycles of resentment, ensuring a bloody resumption in the future. Imperialism should crumble before the principle of national self-determination, creating states where government was legitimised by democratic consent. Relations among sovereign states should be conducted openly, without secret treaties. The 'balance of power', discredited for ever by the collapse of 1914, should be replaced with collective security, guaranteed by a new institution, the League of Nations. If states only entrusted their security to this non-existent organisation with hypothetical resources, humankind would move forward.

Lloyd George was touched by Wilson's idealism and partly supported it, though not at British expense. The 78-year-old Clemenceau, on the other hand, personified the outlook that had to be superseded if the new order was to emerge. He remembered the siege of Paris in 1870–1, and nothing could stop him straining every sinew to ensure that Germany would never be able to threaten France again. Wedded to the principle of the balance of power, he was immune to Wilson's vision, though not to the fascination of the man: professorial, messianic, martyred.

The fourth Olympian was Vittorio Orlando. Any Italian leader would have struggled to stand shoulder to shoulder with the Big Three; Orlando had no chance. Other delegates found him fawning and evasive, or as one American put it, 'obliging, courteous and impossible'. Lloyd George thought he had 'an attractive and amiable personality', faint praise indeed. Clemenceau was scathing: Orlando was 'all things to all men, very Italian'. While his affability contrasted pleasantly with the 'very hawklike, ferocious' demeanour of his foreign minister, Sonnino, it hardly weighed in the balance against Wilson's gravitas, Lloyd George's silver tongue and Clemenceau's salty charisma. Britain and France had forgotten neither Italy's mercenary intervention in 1915, nor her record on the battlefield. Politically, too, Orlando was more vulnerable. Lloyd George and Clemenceau had strong mandates from their cabinets; Wilson's Democratic Party had lost control of Congress, yet his global prestige when the conference opened gave him wide room for manoeuvre. Orlando led a minority government with a 'unity cabinet' that had only endured thanks to the crisis after Caporetto. He sat on the other side of the fireplace from the 'Big Three', in Wilson's study. This was fitting, for he acted as a semi-detached member, rarely commenting on business that did not touch Italy's claims. This was in deference to the others, with their greater resources, and an admission that nothing else concerned him.

A strange thing happened to Italy's war aims in November 1918. No sooner had it won than the government stopped treating the Treaty of London as the limit of its aspirations. The ink was hardly dry on the armistice when Orlando declared that Italy's victory was *one of the greatest that history had recorded.* A fortnight later, he told parliament that the victory *seemed to overshadow all others in recorded history* – a mad boast that implied a warning: what might happen if the nation were denied the fruit of such achievement? He told the upper chamber that Italy 'has revealed a power of action and will that compare with the greatest states in history and our time'. He was priming the country to demand more.

Tensions in his cabinet came to a head in December. As the leading 'democratic interventionist', Leonida Bissolati argued for renouncing those elements of the London Treaty that clashed with Wilson's famous Ninth Point. Specifically, Italy should not demand German-speaking south Tyrol or Dalmatia with its Croat majority. Nor should it keep the Dodecanese Islands, with their Greek majority. As quid pro quo, Italy should demand the Italian-majority cities of Zara, which had been pledged under the London terms, and Fiume, which the Treaty had promised to the Slavs, although many of its 25,000 Italian citizens had recently voted in a dubious plebiscite for annexation to Italy. Only one other minister supported Bissolati, who gained a powerful ally at the end of December when Diaz agreed that Italy should exchange Dalmatia for Fiume. (Like Cadorna, he believed that military bases on the eastern Adriatic coast would be a liability, 'militarily useless and dangerous'.) When Sonnino disagreed, Orlando wavered, then swung behind his foreign minister, reluctantly or with a show of reluctance. Bissolati resigned and three other ministers followed suit, including the influential minister of finance, Francesco Nitti.

Bissolati took his case to the people. He told the press that the United States would not support Italy's claims. On 11 January, he addressed a public meeting at La Scala theatre in Milan. Allied victory had opened the way to a new international order, based on the League of Nations. Italy's border with Yugoslavia should reflect nationality: Dalmatia to them, Zara and Fiume to us. Likewise the border with Austria. But a cabal of radical nationalists, 'war veterans, conspirators, police agents, and random souls undone and exasperated by the war', had packed the opera house and would not let him finish. Marinetti and his Futurists sat in a box, ready to lead the disruption. At a given moment,

... the infernal symphony began. Squeaks, shrieks, whistles, grumbles, nearly human ... but a human, nay a patriotic cry became distinguishable now and then and ruled the inarticulate mass with the rhythm of a brutal march. They said 'Croati no! Croati no!' meaning that they were not Croats, that they wanted no friendship with Croats or Yugoslavs; and they meant too that Bissolati was a Croat.

Bissolati raised his voice and spoke on, until he caught sight of Mussolini's pale, spade-like visage in the audience, and recognised 'that unmistakable voice, dishearteningly wooden, peremptorily insistent, like the clacking of castanets'. Bissolati turned to his companions on the stage and said 'Quell'uomo no!' 'I will not fight with that man.' He finished his speech in a low voice, as if reading to himself. There was no applause. The political campaign for a reasonable territorial settlement was over. Around the same time, Luigi Albertini came under pressure to stop attacking Orlando's claims in his newspaper, Corriere della Sera. Being Albertini, he dropped the liberal approach to the Adriatic that he had advocated since the summer and joined the outcry against the Allies. The Corriere even reversed its attitude to the League of Nations, discovering cynicism where it had praised idealism. Of Albertini's many disservices to his readers, the turnaround in 1919 may have been the worst.

It is easy to see why anti-fascists turned Bissolati's humiliation into a tragic myth. It signalled the silencing, by what has been called 'the first act of organised fascist violence', of principled resistance to maximal demands. These demands were unattainable, hence doomed; by dedicating himself to them, Orlando ensured that compromise – when it inevitably came – would bring him down. Behind this self-defeating strategy lay his partnership with Sonnino. As someone said in Paris, Sonnino was silent in all the languages he spoke, while Orlando was voluble in all the languages he didn't. The most perceptive critic of this odd couple was Carlo Sforza, who as foreign minister in 1920 negotiated a more equitable (though still unworkably pro-Italian) solution to the eastern Adriatic riddle. Orlando, he wrote acidly, understood everything and persisted in nothing. As for Sonnino, 'never was a foreign minister more stubborn and unintelligent, or more honest and sincere'. He could even drive the buttoned-up Wilson to clench his fist and use 'unparliamentary language'. Orlando's lack of principle reinforced Sonnino's doggedness.

Privately, the Prime Minister recognised that events had overtaken the Treaty of London, and a realistic settlement for the eastern Adriatic could not ignore nationality. Sonnino, on the other hand, wanted the literal execution of the Treaty. Incapable of controlling his foreign minister, Orlando accommodated him by demanding everything: the Treaty of London *plus* Fiume. When he tabled his demands at the conference in early February, he knew Wilson would reject them. At their first meeting, in Paris on 21 December, the President had warned that his Adriatic claims were unacceptable. Orlando reacted accordingly; when Wilson visited Rome early in January – at the height of his popularity in Europe – he was given no chance to address the waiting crowds. He spent his days in Italy pondering 'how far he could disappoint the Italian popular ambitions and still get through an amicable settlement'. It was the central question. He had already told Orlando that he would accept the demand for a 'natural border' in the north, on the Alpine watershed. Some American advisors and other delegates were appalled by this 'disastrous concession', which Wilson later attributed to 'insufficient study', though it was more likely calculated to win Italy's commitment to the League of Nations. He got that commitment, but Orlando's stance on the Adriatic hardened.

[373]

Ominously, D'Annunzio weighed in. Since the 'stench of peace' had offended his nostrils at the end of October 1918, the warrior-poet had been spoiling for a new melodrama to keep normality at bay. He published an 'open letter to the Dalmatians' in Mussolini's newspaper (Albertini's wobbly liberalism had made the *Corriere* uncongenial), championing maximal demands against 'that mishmash of southern Slavs'. Meanwhile the Italian land-grab continued apace. In February, they blocked the transport of American food aid to Yugoslavia, Czechoslovakia and Vienna. According to the outraged Americans, this led to 'acute starvation'. Threatened with the stoppage of American aid to Italy, Sonnino backed down. But the press continued to campaign for Fiume and officials still obstructed American aid to Yugoslavia. This ugly atmosphere made compromise more difficult.

Orlando raised the stakes again on 1 March, during a visit home. Italy was loyal to the Treaty of London, he told parliament, but it would not be deaf to appeals from Fiume, 'that most Italian city, the jewel of the Quarnero'.[1] This purple pledge brought deputies to their feet, crying '*Viva Fiume!*' Fiume could not be allowed to 'lose its nationality and its independence'. His tone with Italy's allies was rather different; he told House that Fiume was 'not very important' in itself, but 'as a symbol' it was 'vital to his continuance in office'. Moreover, 'we want to, we must, keep the Adriatic as a *mare clausum*, a closed sea'. It was typical of the man to blur a political plea with a nationalist ultimatum.

By April 1919, work on the Germany treaty was so advanced that the government in Berlin had to be invited. Orlando refused to proceed with German business before Italy's claims had been settled. Lloyd George tried to put him in his place; Britain, he said, 'had twice as many dead as Italy'. Orlando rightly countered that, in proportional terms, 'Italy's losses were heavier'.[2] Realising that Orlando was not to be brushed off, Lloyd George slyly remarked that he would accept any solution agreed by Orlando and Wilson. As Clemenceau took the same position, Wilson and Orlando were alone with each other. When they met on 14 April, Wilson proposed that Fiume should become a free port with 'very considerable autonomy', under the Yugoslav customs regime. Orlando shook his head. It was, Wilson reported, a difficult meeting. Two days later, playing his customary destructive role, the King urged Orlando to stand firm.

1 The Quarnero is the bay between Istria and northern Dalmatia.
2 Italy, with a population of 35 million, lost 689,000 soldiers in the war; Great Britain, with 46 million, lost 662,000 (plus another 140,000 missing).

The crunch came on 19 April, Easter Saturday, when Orlando made his case to the other three. Italy's border must 'coincide' with 'the natural frontier that God has given her'. In the north, the border should reach the Brenner Pass; in the north-east, it should reach beyond the Isonzo valley, the Julian Alps, the Carso, Trieste and Istria to a depth of 40 kilometres from the coast. This would give Italy even more Slovene territory than was promised in 1915. He demanded Fiume in the name of self-determination and the promised segment of Dalmatia in the name of Italy's strategic security, as well as its ancient Italian identity. If this all brought '100,000 foreigners' into Italy, he added, so be it. The real number of German-speakers in Austrian South Tyrol was nearly 250,000. Adding the 750,000 Slovenes and Croats, around a million non-Italians would be roped inside Victor Emanuel's kingdom.

Wilson made it clear that part of inland Istria, Dalmatia and Fiume (with its 'tiny island' of Italians) all had to go to Yugoslavia. The former Habsburg nations could not be treated as enemies. The Austrian navy had indeed attacked Italy from bases in the eastern Adriatic, but the Yugoslavs had neither means nor motive to pose any such threat. As for Fiume, the Yugoslavs had no other viable port for merchant shipping.

Sonnino said that Austria had offered them some Dalmatian islands in 1915 (he was lying); how could they now accept worse terms? Clemenceau said testily that it was 'impossible' to have the Treaty and other territory as well. Lloyd George added that the demand for Fiume was 'wrong' and appealed to their sense of proportion. In this charged atmosphere, Wilson stated flatly that the Treaty of London could not be reconciled 'with the peace that we wish to establish'. After the meeting, he suspended a US$50 million loan to Italy 'until the air clears – if it does'.

The quarrel escalated on Easter Sunday. Grotesquely, Orlando said that nothing would be more fatal to the peace of the world than denying him Fiume. Unless he got it, he would abandon the Conference and refuse to join the League of Nations. Stung, Wilson said Orlando's position was 'unbelievable'. With much hand-wringing, Orlando protested that he was 'acting for right and justice' and would 'brave all the consequences' of sticking to his position, 'up to and including death'. He stood up, walked over to the sealed window and wept. Faced with this operatic moment, the statesmen froze. Only Wilson went across to the distraught Orlando, and suggested that provisional acceptance of the London terms might be possible.

Despite this gesture, Wilson had no thought of climbing down. He set out his case in a statement for the press: Italy should not get Dalmatia, the offshore islands should be demilitarised, and minority rights should be guaranteed. Fiume 'must serve as the outlet of the commerce, not of Italy, but of the land to the north and northeast'. Lloyd George and Clemenceau warned him not to throw a stick of dynamite into the conference. Wilson disagreed; a 'moment of agitation will be followed by a depression in morale, with a feeling of hopelessness'.

Wilson released his statement on 23 April. Next morning, Orlando announced his departure for Rome (where he wished to be anyway for the opening of parliament). Radiating wounded dignity, he said that Wilson's statement had 'cast doubt' on his authority. In Rome, he found the city walls plastered with posters demanding Dalmatia and Fiume. The mayor told cheering crowds that Italians would never barter their national honour or insult the blood of their heroes. Streets that had been named in honour of Wilson the Liberator a few months earlier were renamed. Even the 'democratic interventionists' were angered by Wilson's high-handedness. D'Annunzio joined the show with a series of anti-Allied diatribes. His highly quotable insults to Wilson were picked up by hostile newspapers in the United States. (Probably these were the attacks that made Wilson 'white with anger', according to his worried wife.) Sonnino paid French newspapers 30 million francs to support Italy's claims. When one of Sonnino's juniors tried to impress Clemenceau with this outpouring, the old man pulled out a list of the journalists and the sums they had received.

Lloyd George laughed at Orlando's assumption that the conference would grind to a halt in his absence: 'They always believe that we people of the North bluff the way they do.' Ironically, Italy's victory had helped to destroy the continental balance of power that had given Rome such leverage in the past. Britain and France settled the fate of Germany's African colonies behind Orlando's back; they also took decisions over German reparations. Lloyd George told an Italian official that his prime minister should not bother to return if he would not give up Fiume.

The odd couple reappeared in Paris on 6 May. When Orlando took his seat, the others 'acted as though he had never been away', as Wilson told his wife. People agreed that Orlando looked worse, grey and weak. Lloyd George had worried that he would demand full execution of the Treaty of London; this would split the Big Three and lead to 'catastrophe'. In the event, the Italians had nothing new to suggest. Clemenceau foresaw all this on 19 April, predicting that if the Italians left the conference, 'they will soon come back to cold reality. All the friends of Italy will be alienated from her; they will suffer the effects of it – Italy, too, I fear . . . We would suffer greatly from it; Italy would perhaps suffer even more.'

How did the astute Sicilian come to overestimate his power so badly? He wanted to offer the public 'a compensation for the enormous sacrifices of war', no doubt, and a distraction from economic chaos.[3] Some American delegates may have led him to think that Wilson sympathised in his heart and would eventually give way. Perhaps he did not know that Wilson's regional experts strongly opposed any compromise over Fiume, or that some Italians from Fiume, brought to Paris to plead for annexation, privately told the Americans that the local Italians were against joining Italy, for economic reasons. Certainly he misunderstood Wilson's resolve, and to some extent the Allies' priorities. He took revenge in his memoirs, calling Wilson a *spontaneous hypocrite* who preached the general good as a cover for political trickery.

Orlando missed something more important about Wilson, the son of a Presbyterian minister: his *American* faith in divine providence and liberal progress, and in himself as their agent. In Orlando's view, Wilson had swallowed several toads and now strained at a gnat. He seemed unaware that, while the Big Four all bent the rules to suit their interests, only he wanted to trample on the principles of a just peace at the expense of a new national state in Europe, not out of strategic necessity (as could be claimed of French demands vis-à-vis Germany), but to satisfy nationalist vanity and political convenience. For Wilson, Yugoslavia's birth proved that anti-imperialist ideals could prevail: it was self-determination in action. He was adamant that the infant must be protected. A jotting on the back of a map of Italy, in mid-April, warning what would ensue if Fiume went to Italy, shows this consideration weighing on him:

3 The war had cost 148 billion lire, a sum equivalent, as John Schindler points out, to twice the Italian governments' total expenditures from 1861 to 1913. Italy was the only belligerent that did not increase tax levels during the war; this led to a huge public budget deficit. Foreign debt increased eightfold between 1916 and 1919 while government spending soared – as did inflation, after the relaxation of wartime price controls. Having prospered by the often corrupt allocation of wartime contracts, the northern industrialists had no interest in seeing a more honest system introduced.

THE WHITE WAR

At the very outset we shall have followed the fatal error of making Italy's nearest neighbors on her east her enemies, nursing just such a sense of injustice as has disturbed the peace of Europe for generations together with playing no small part in bringing on the dreadful conflict through which we have just passed.

This set Orlando apart from Clemenceau and his rapacious claims on the Rhineland. The other difference was that France was, after all, France. Allied condescension was no secret. 'It seems to the Italians that they are not quite being treated as equals,' Lloyd George observed. Rather than adapt, they became more obstinate.

Perhaps, too, they paid a price for incurable political incorrectness. As early as mid-November, when the delegations assembled in Paris, an Italian diplomat confided to an American that 'self-determination is applicable to many regions but not to the shores of the Adriatic'. Despite himself, the American was impressed by the other man's indifference to 'all the shibboleths and slogans which are resounding through the world today'. Amusing in doses, the Italians' refusal to pay even lip-service to higher ideals became repellent in the long run.

Finally, Orlando failed to reckon with Wilson's skilful timing. Did he notice that the President had one eye on his own electorate during their April showdown? By publishing his manifesto, Wilson sought to renew *American* faith in his principled leadership. The symmetry in their positions, with each man playing to his own public, escaped Orlando altogether.

With Orlando back on board, the Council of Four shelved further discussion of the Adriatic. By mid-May, Clemenceau thought the Italians were trying to save face. House organised 'proximity talks' between the Italians and the Yugoslavs; Wilson said he would accept any solution freely agreed. Now the Yugoslavs would not accept the Treaty of London line.

When the Big Four met on 26 May, Orlando agreed to give up Fiume in exchange for everything in the Treaty of London. When Wilson attacked the Treaty, Clemenceau advised Orlando not to insist on complete implementation. Under this pressure, the Italians cracked and the elements of a solution emerged: Fiume would be a separate state under the League of Nations, administered by a multinational council, with a plebiscite after 15 years; Zara and Sebenico would be free ports under Italian sovereignty or mandate; most of the islands would go to

Yugoslavia. On 6 June, Orlando wobbled again, provoking Wilson's contempt: 'His mind seems to me completely unstable.' Another variant was discussed and rejected. It was hopeless.

When Orlando duly fell from power on 19 June, Sonnino was dislodged from the foreign ministry at last. Yet the knot was tied too tightly for a new government to loosen it, and time ran out: the Paris conference ended on 28 June with no solution.[4] In mid-September, D'Annunzio led a band of war veterans to occupy Fiume. When the Italian general commanding the Allied garrison let him enter, a weird experiment in pastiche state-building began. As volunteers flocked to D'Annunzio, the government in Rome dithered. When the aged Giolitti became prime minister once again in June 1920, he withdrew from Albania: a bold move that built confidence with Yugoslavia. Not until November, when Wilson's Democratic Party lost the presidential election, compelling the Yugoslavs to accept that they would have to cope without Washington's help, did the conditions emerge for a bilateral settlement. The Treaty of Rapallo (November 1920) gave Italy a generous eastern frontier: the Julian Alps and the Carso, with a wide buffer zone beyond, halfway to Ljubljana; all of Istria, Zara, and several Adriatic islands. Fiume became a free state.

From his toy throne, D'Annunzio declared war on Italy: the logical outcome of his egomania. 'Either Fiume will be Italian or I too will leave Fiume', he raved, 'dead, wrapped in the flag of Giovanni Randaccio'. The government had no choice but to ring down the curtain on the self-styled 'Italian Regency of the Quarnero'. A well-placed shell from a battleship, directed at the bard's palace, drove him away. After a pro-independence party won the first free elections, Italian nationalists made Fiume ungovernable. They took over the municipal reins in 1922 and handed power to Mussolini's regime a year later. Formal annexation followed in 1924. For Italy to own Fiume, it had to become the world's first fascist dictatorship.

Italy's new borders enclosed at least 300,000 Slovenes, 200,000 Croats, and nearly 250,000 German-speaking Austrians: a total of some 750,000

---

4 Meeting on the 26th, the Big Three enjoyed deploring the Italians for one last time: 'WILSON: The truth is that Italy went to the highest bidder. LLOYD GEORGE: That is a harsh thing to say; but I fear there is some truth in it. WILSON: During this conference, Italy had no interest in anything that did not directly affect her . . . LLOYD GEORGE: I went through the entire war and, unfortunately, I always saw Italy trying to do as little as possible.' Etc.

non-Italians. Added to the 650,000 Italians, the extra population totalled around 1,400,000. Initially, the new minorities were treated with sensitivity but, by late November 1918, Orlando was complaining to Badoglio that the military government in Trieste was too lenient towards the 'Yugoslavs, clericals and socialists' who were 'conspiring against us'. Badoglio laid schemes to subvert Yugoslavia, mentioned above, and Trieste became a laboratory of proto-fascist misrule.

An American journalist reported that the liberated territories 'were treated like conquered provinces, which indeed they were. The majority of the population was certainly hostile to Italy. Hundreds of persons were therefore arrested for this hostility, defined as treason, and for spreading discontent and for imaginary plots.' After the Slovene cultural centre in Trieste was burned down in July 1920, 'beatings, pillagings, burnings, were daily events' in the occupied territories. Nationalists in Rome crowed that Trieste had shown how to deal with 'the new enemy that stabs the nation in the back'. Slovenes and Croats suspected of 'philo-Yugoslavism' or 'Slavophilia' were interned – a recourse that had been used with civilians in the war zone and would soon be extended countrywide, along with other forms of repression, against the enemies of Fascism.

Under Mussolini, the same treatment was meted out to Germans in the Alto Adige, Greeks on the Dodecanese Islands and the French minority in the Aosta valley. 'The abolition of personal rights and of freedom of speech, of the press and of association, the dissolution of non-Fascist associations and transference of their property to Fascist organisations, absence of impartiality in lawsuits, despotism of the police, a reign of terror against suspects, the suppression of free elections.' Place names were Italianised and war veterans were sent to live in the occupied areas. School reforms were designed to 'denationalise the racial minorities'. These policies were later relaxed in the Alto Adige, to avoid antagonising Austrian and German Nazis. The Slavs had no such defence; in the 1990s, a bilateral Italian–Slovenian commission agreed that the Fascist regime had 'attempted to realise a programme of complete destruction of the Slovene and Croatian identity'. In 1931, *Corriere della Sera* reported on the 'atmosphere of war' along the north-eastern border. 'No Italian who remains faithful to the principles that animated the makers of Italy in the last century', lamented the anti-fascist historian Gaetano Salvemini, in exile, 'can record without a feeling of grief and shame that Croatian and Slovene youths in Italy today are sentenced to life-imprisonment or death because they struggle for the same ideals.'

———————

The Italians paid a monstrous price for eastern Friuli, Trieste, Istria, the Trentino and Alto Adige. The nineteenth-century wars to unify the peninsula – the first three wars of independence – cost fewer than 10,000 lives. The war to annex these final territories killed 689,000 Italian soldiers: more than the total of Austro-Hungarian dead, missing and wounded on the Italian front (estimated at 650,000), and more, also, than the Habsburg Italian population that was 'redeemed' by the victory. Another million were seriously wounded, including 700,000 disabled veterans. Adding the estimated 600,000 civilians who died due to the hardships of war, the Italian death toll reached 1.3 million – around three times the number that would perish in the Second World War.

The price was also political. Orlando's and Sonnino's zero-sum strategy in Paris dealt a fatal wound to Italy's liberal system, already battered by the serial assaults of wartime. By stoking the appetite for unattainable demands, they encouraged Italians to despise their victory unless it led to the annexation of a small port on the other side of the Adriatic, with no historic connection to the motherland. Fiume became the first neuralgic point created by the Paris conference. Like the Sudetenland for Hitler's Germany and Transylvania for Hungary, it was a symbol of burning injustice. A sense of jeopardised identity and wounded pride fused with a toponym to produce an explosive compound.

The difference was that Germany and Hungary had lost the war. Uniquely among the winning states, political life in Italy perpetuated the prewar and wartime divisions. The former warmongers howled against Wilson and wept over Fiume, while the former neutralists were branded as 'Caporettists', collaborating in their country's humiliation. This suited the radical nationalist mindset which expected betrayal at the hands of bullying, ungrateful Allies. D'Annunzio had warned about the peril of a 'mutilated victory' as early as 24 October, when the Battle of Vittorio Veneto was scarcely under way. His grisly metaphor became a rallying cry.

In truth, victory was mutilated by Italy's own leaders. Twenty years later, from his voluntary exile in New York, the journalist Giuseppe

Borgese looked back in near disbelief at the 'unprecedented miracle of psychopathic alchemy' that had been performed at the end of the war. 'Italy, or at least the intellectual and political élite to which an evil destiny had entrusted Italy, had transubstantiated a victory into a disaster. The nation, masochism-stricken, exulted in frustration.' This enduring sense of bitterness, betrayal and loss was an essential ingredient in the rise of Mussolini and his Blackshirts.

After the Second World War, Italy lost everything to the east of Gorizia and south of Trieste. The Julian Alps, the Isonzo valley, Istria, Fiume, Zara: all were transferred to Communist Yugoslavia. The new border bisects the old battlefields on the Carso. Mount San Michele stayed in Italy, Monte Santo went to Yugoslavia, and they shared Mount Sabotino. The monumental ossuaries that Mussolini built near the Isonzo to honour the remains of fallen warriors now stand at Italy's outermost limit, within the sliver of land that Luigi Cadorna conquered in the first year of Italy's last war of independence.

The final demarcation around Trieste was agreed in 1954, almost 90 years after Raffaele Cadorna led the Italian V Corps in its race to the Isonzo. It had taken a century to work out a durable border settlement. Even then, the collision between nationalist fantasy and ethnic reality was only cut short by Italy's wholesale defeat and occupation in 1945. Pressure amounting to terror then drove 200,000–300,000 Italians out of Yugoslavia, across the Cold War frontier. The refugees' plight was made doubly bitter by their near-invisibility; when Tito's self-management reforms turned Yugoslavia into the West's favourite Communist state and tourists flocked to Dalmatia, nobody much cared to hear about the Italian victims of 'ethnic cleansing'. Only since May 2004, when Slovenia became the first former Yugoslav republic to join the European Union, has it been possible to see the sharp angles of the Isonzo valley as so many sutures, stitching the borderlands together.

TWENTY-EIGHT

End of the Line

everything we say
Of the past is description without place, a cast
Of the imagination, made in sound
WALLACE STEVENS

Looking south from the ski-lift at the head of the Isonzo valley, after summer storms, a striped tower glimmers in the farthest distance. It is the power-station at Monfalcone, more than 60 kilometres away, across a panorama of peaks and ridges; from this angle, the entire Isonzo front can be framed on the cover of a book.

The buzz of people fades when you take the path to Rombon, winding around boulders, through hollows filled with snow, across limestone amphitheatres. At this height the light is ultramarine, the air tingles. Your own breathing and the crunch of pebbles are the only sounds. Except for strands of rusty wire poking over the path, there is very little detritus. After the war, communities along the old front earned money by retrieving military scrap and human remains from the mountains. Corpses fetched 10 lire each, and 10 kilos of barbed wire sold for 1 lire. Steel, cast iron, brass and copper were more lucrative but harder to find. On the higher battlefields, foragers camped in old tunnels and dug-outs during the summer. Farmers dug up animal carcasses to sell the bones, fuelled their stoves with the stocks of old rifles, and sold the breeches and barrels. Today's foragers scour the hillsides for memorabilia. It is a risky pastime: someone dies every year from exploding ordnance.

A couple of hours' walking and scrambling get you to the top of Rombon, an airy field of boulders, halfway between the sky and the valley. Faint Habsburg trenches lead down towards the spur called Čukla, which overlooks Bovec, formerly Flitsch. The Isonzo is a silver line, nearly 2,000 metres below. The trenches are grooves in the rubble, more like a natural feature than man-made defences. Another hundred years will smooth these wrinkles away.

You get to Čukla by clambering down a rocky cleft, then running the scree at its base. Your boots turn up cartridge cases and bits of shell casing. Looking back, it is obvious why the Italians never took the summit. The path down to Bovec zigzags over the open hillside, then on mule tracks through woods that cloak the lower slopes. It is half an hour's drive to Kobarid, formerly Caporetto, where the valley opens out. Kobarid is recognisably the same town that changed hands so suddenly on 24 October 1917. The south-eastern skyline is dominated by the peak of Krn, soaring like a shark's fin.

A mule track loops up to Krn from a corrie above the valley floor. The route is popular with hikers; a hostel below the summit does a brisk trade in bean soup and beer. The summit is ten minutes away, a turret pointing at the Julian Alps. The onward path to Mount Mrzli passes a plaque to the handful of Yugoslav partisans – communist-led guerrilla forces – who died here in the Second World War. There is no plaque to the thousands of First World War dead; for more than seventy years, the nations that fought Italy from 1915 to 1918 did not care to recall the Great War. As well as the pain of defeat, there was embarrassment for the states that emerged from Austria-Hungary: their peoples had died defending the empire. The duty of remembrance fell to veterans, penning memoirs that burn with resentment at the official amnesia. After these states became Communist, they had even less incentive to examine their role as mainstays of the dynastic rule.

Matters only changed after the end of the Cold War. For Europe's 'new democracies', trying to recover their pre-fascist, pre-communist history, the imperial cause is no longer awkward. On the contrary, a mild Habsburg nostalgia pervades the area from Trieste to Vienna and Prague, flattered by tourist-board posters of art nouveau cafés and statues of Franz Josef's beautiful empress. New monuments have been added to the Habsburg cemeteries, paying respect where it is due, yet the polished marble facets look odd amid the mossy turf and lichen-covered crosses. These places remind us that states, too, have their life-span.

The information on the plaques – name, corps, rank and date of death in German ('the language of the army, in death as in life') – proves that the men came from all corners of the empire. 'What the state failed to achieve in time of peace became a reality in these war cemeteries. Here they all are, united by death in an indissoluble brotherhood.' The mystery of obedience hangs in the air.

The Isonzo has become a recreational river. Its turquoise waters are flecked with kayaks in summer; hikers throng the paths, and the cliffs are hung with climbers' ropes. The tree cover is thick on Mount Mrzli, above Tolmin; the stanchions of wartime cableways rot in the shade, sinking into the leaf mould. The summit is still jagged from Italian shellfire. Overhead, paragliders ride the thermals, unhurried; someone tells us they are Czechs, holding a competition. If their great-grandfathers could revisit the front, the greenery would amaze them. In their time, the tree line was lower and the grass much thinner. Even so, the grim beauty of the front made a deep impression on many of the troops, as their diaries show. Even in the worst situations, soldiers caught the scent of thyme high on the limestone ridges; the sight of comrades dying did not blot out the last patches of snow gleaming blue in the moonlight, or the constellations wheeling overhead. The 'indescribable joy' of battle that filled young Ferruccio Fabbrovich in June 1916 was a real thing, and it was felt more readily in the mountains. What one veteran called the 'exhilaration of extreme situations' could reach a pitch of ecstasy when vistas opened at your feet. The Austrian troops felt it when they went out of the line, marching to the edge of the Carso, and saw the Adriatic Sea below, azure to the horizon.

While soldiers in other theatres experienced this sensuous, heightened awareness of the natural world, it may have been more widespread on the Italian front. The Austrian novelist Robert Musil wrote a story, 'The Blackbird', about his service in the Tyrol.

... on every one of those nights I poked my head over the edge of the trench many times ... I saw the Brenta mountains light blue, as if formed of stiff-pleated glass, silhouetted ... the sky stayed blue all night ... sometimes I could stand it no longer, and giddy with joy and longing, I crept out for a little nightcrawl around, all the way to the golden-green blackness of the trees ... It is as if the fear of one's demise, which evidently lies on top of man forever like a stone, were suddenly rolled back, and in the uncertain proximity of death an unaccountable inner freedom blossoms forth.

This 'unaccountable inner freedom' enlivens much Italian literature about the war, offsetting the documentary element, the chronicling of unprecedented torment. Italian historians sometimes regret that their writers produced no classics to rank beside Jünger, Barbusse, Remarque or Hemingway. What sets their books apart is perhaps an inability to sustain the despair. Excitement keeps breaking through – not so much the Homeric bloodlust of Jünger, though this is present, as a sense of boyish adventure within an enterprise that is felt as essentially worthwhile, whatever its horrors. When the aged Emilio Lussu saw the fine film of his autobiographical novel, *A Year on the Plateau*, one of the best books about the Italian front, he objected that it was too grim. 'That's not all there is to war,' he said. 'Sometimes we even sang, joked and dreamed our dreams.'

Consider Eugenio Montale, Italy's greatest modern poet, stationed in the spectacular valley of Vallarsa in the Trentino, linking Mount Pasubio to the valley of the Adige. Today it is a green chasm with a narrow road unspooling along the northern side, plunging through tunnels and propped on stilts. Untouched by political passion, the young Montale felt uncomfortable in uniform, like 'an outcast'. The nearest settlement was a hamlet called Valmorbia. The valley sides were strewn with corpses, dead mules, slews of rock and mud, spilled munitions. Night transformed the brutal scene; Montale lay in the entrance of a cave, listening to the river. As the moon rose and sank, the valley seemed to set sail. Snuffling sounds and an acrid smell revealed the proximity of wolves. He turned this memory into a short poem, the only one he ever published about the front. Here is the last stanza:

> The lucid nights all through were dawn
> and brought wolves to my cavern.
> Valmorbia – a name – and now in wan
> remembrance, a land unknown to dusk.

Why does this feel patriotic when it dwells on a private moment, remote as a fairy-tale? Perhaps because the poet's survival enacts Italy's own, after the ravening threat of Caporetto.

The central British feeling about the First World War is elegiac indignation, fed by a certainty that the war was, in Siegfried Sassoon's phrase, 'a dirty trick which had been played on me and my generation', or what Hemingway called 'the most colossal, murderous, mismanaged butchery'. Although that phrase passes a fair judgement on Cadorna's leadership, Italian war writing does not by and large share this disillusion.

When the last British veterans were interviewed ninety years after the war, few had anything to say about politics or patriotism. Over time, the war had become a byword for futile sacrifice. 'The First World War was idiotic,' said one, typically. 'It started out idiotic and it stayed idiotic. It

[386]

was damned silly, all of it.' Whether their younger selves would have agreed with this verdict is, of course, another matter.

The last Italian veterans were not haunted by this sense of meaninglessness. One, in his 107th year, recalled his soldier self, 'a bit afraid, but full of hope and indomitable will'. The only woman interviewed spoke of carrying the love of her fatherland in her heart. Pasquale Costanzo (b. 1899) explained that people felt proud of the war, for 'the Italians repulsed the enemy with honour'. Paolo Bonomini (b. 1898) praised D'Annunzio's grandeur and charisma, and his power of discovering 'the will to believe in the highest values of the fatherland' in the 'farthest recesses of our soul'.

Testimony of this kind explains why the Great War was Italy's 'first true collective national experience'. More than five million Italians were mobilised, and many of them welcomed the collective endeavour as something precious which mitigated the hardship. A poet in the trenches, Piero Jahier, expressed his emotion at hearing the mixture of dialects. '*Brava Italia, che si lega per sempre nel sacrificio.*' 'Splendid Italy, binding herself forever in sacrifice.' These lines are displayed in the Museum of the Risorgimento, in Rome. Warm bonds of comradeship, which gave soldiers on all fronts an intimate motive for persevering, had an added political dimension in Italy. Nor was the experience limited to men in uniform. A teenaged boy from Friuli who spent the year after Caporetto as a refugee 'left as a Friulan and returned as an Italian'.

Were nationalists right, then, to say that the war completed the Risorgimento? Liberals denied it. A counter-argument was provided by the journalist Luigi Salvatorelli, another veteran of the Isonzo, for whom the Risorgimento was a project that would only be fulfilled by 'the formation of a national democracy'. The vision of Mazzini and Garibaldi had been dedicated to something greater than enlarging the territory under the House of Savoy. They had had a moral goal: the liberation and unification of a nation, realising rights to which other nations were equally entitled. Tragically, this project was opposed by a range of conservative and illiberal forces, clerical, landowning and nationalist.

On this view, far from completing the Risorgimento, the First World War had confirmed, by contrast, the lost greatness of that epoch. For May 1915 had seen the birth of 'a mixture of Nationalism and Fascism'. Hence the war, which 'was called – and in a sense, was – the last war of the Risorgimento', began with 'a profound moral scission, into which the anti-Risorgimento thrust its poisoned steel'. The Risorgimento was libertarian, patriotic, democratic, enlightened and still unfinished, forever wrestling with its antithetical twin: authoritarian, manipulative, nationalistic, conspiratorial and aggressive. From 1915 to 1944, the anti-Risorgimento had the upper hand. Perhaps the two still wrestle for mastery of Italy's dark heart.

The price of Italy's nation-building achievement in the war was a sense of betrayal by the state. The government and the newspapers lied to the common people while the army under-paid, under-equipped and under-fed them, before getting them killed in hopeless offensives; even the Church failed to protect them. It was an experience marked by brutality, contempt, corruption and oppression, fatigue duty like slave labour, rations filched or sold on. At the end of the war, their pensions were not paid, the economy was in melt-down, and they were at daggers drawn with their eastern neighbours, the Yugoslavs. It was as if national consciousness could only grow by undermining national institutions and sharpening political divisions. The interment of the Unknown Warrior in Rome was one occasion that focused these antagonisms. Socialist posters mocking the ceremony, in November 1921, were torn down by the police. If the nameless warrior could rise from his tomb, leftist agitators said, he would curse the war. Proletarians should honour him by cursing it themselves.

In this riven atmosphere, Mussolini offered a positive myth of the war. As early as December 1916, he had looked forward to the day when Italy would be governed by a '*trenchocracy*, a new and better élite'. Amid the chaos and uncertainty, he vowed to rebuild the state on the basis of the soldiers' achievement. This was a potent promise in a situation where, as the leading scholar of Italian fascism argues, 'Most veterans were convinced they were the aristocracy of "new men" bound to regenerate society and the State.' From the outset of his regime, Mussolini claimed a monopoly on the meaning of the Great War. Entering the Quirinale Palace on 30 October 1922, he bowed before his sovereign. According to Fascist myth, he said 'Sire, I bring you the Italy of Vittorio Veneto.' It meant that the mantle of victory – the one that, in Orlando's boast, overshadowed all others in recorded history – was in his gift and nobody else's. He then paid homage at the tomb of the Unknown Soldier.

For the Fascists, the war was a portal to revolution and rebirth. As a new political religion, Fascism needed a 'sacred history', and the dates of Italy's intervention and victory were celebrated with ritual pageantry.

The revolution had, in Mussolini's phrase, 'reconsecrated' the victory. The Duke of Aosta, who adapted seamlessly to the new regime, called the war 'the glorious epic of the great Redemption'. After the 'Golgotha' of Caporetto, Vittorio Veneto brought resurrection to 'crucified Italy'.

The place of the Great War in this ersatz theology is graphically clear at Redipuglia, site of Italy's biggest military cemetery, built in the 1930s, between Gorizia and Monfalcone. This 'shrine' to the 'undefeated' Third Army stretches implausibly up the western slope of Mount Sei Busi, scene of ferocious bloodletting in 1915 and 1916. It is a limestone landscape in itself: a geometrised model of the Carso, complete with its fatal gradient. Beyond a deep apron of stone, the Duke of Aosta lies at the foot of the slope within a 75-tonne block of porphyry: a tomb worthy of Achilles. Behind him, the bones of 100,187 soldiers are gathered inside 22 colossal terraces, each 140 metres wide, flanked by cypresses like dark flames. From below, visitors look like fleas on a stairway to Fascist heaven. In raised lettering on the edges of the terraces is the word PRESENTE, reiterated over and over: the soldier's reply at roll call. Ceaselessly summoning the dead to defend Italy's frontier, the monument taps into legends as old as warfare, of fallen soldiers returning to the battlefield. New accounts of such ghostly resurrection were heard during the war and for years afterwards, such as the tale of a labourer trudging home over the Asiago plateau and seeing an endless column of men move across the landscape. They were Italian and Austrian soldiers, pale and unarmed, marching noiselessly. All night the labourer watched them pass, until dawn dispersed them.

The original cemetery at Redipuglia was very different. Looking down from the terraces, you see a low green hill on the other side of the road to Trieste. At the end of the war, the regimental cemeteries on the Carso were emptied and the remains brought to that hill. The dead men's families fashioned little monuments from battlefield detritus: a broken propeller blade for a pilot, crossed pickaxe and shovel for a sapper, or simply a battered helmet, with a nameplate on a plinth of boulders and sprigs of wire like ivy. Infinitely sad and truthful, this cemetery expressed the native genius that nationalists had boasted about before the war ('We are for the ephemeral . . . We hate methods, we are for disorder against discipline.') Mussolini decided the Fascist myth about the Great War needed something more grandiose and streamlined, less ramshackle – and less honest. Redipuglia became the showpiece of Fascist commemorative architectonics, one of the few places where a visitor still feels the urgency of Walter Benjamin's warning in 1940: '*Even the dead will not be safe from the enemy if he wins.*'

By the end of 1923, nearly 6,000 committees were preparing commemorative pathways and parks in cities, towns and villages. Monuments appeared in front of town halls, cathedrals and village churches. The inscriptions commemorated the 'sons' who 'gave' (treacherous verb!) their lives to the Fatherland, often figured as a Mother. The expression *Madre Patria sacra*, confusing in English, turned the nation-state and its dead young men into a holy family. By 1938, there were 40 major monuments to the Great War dead. This civic activity did not mean that ordinary Italians wanted to remember. The anti-fascist Carlo Levi, exiled to remote Lucania in the 1930s, was struck that local people never mentioned the war. Nearly 50 names were carved in marble on the town hall; every family had lost someone. Even so, the war held no interest for the farmers; it had nothing to do with their way of life. The state, meaning 'Rome', had sent them off to fight for incomprehensible reasons. 'It had been a great misfortune, the people bore it as they always did.'

The Fascist visual language of commemoration has not been superseded; it is still definitive, embedded in the culture. Written history, by contrast, moved on. Even under Mussolini, serious work saw the light in a few specialised journals and privately published books. From the 1950s, historians began to dismantle the nationalist versions of the war. The most tenacious of these was the myth or cult of the '*umile fante*', the humble soldier, figured as a deferential patriot, superbly energetic and aggressive, scorning safety, meeting death with a song and a smile.

Even in its more intelligent guises, this cult was based on a presumption about the innermost motivations of several million men who, with few exceptions, did not or could not speak for themselves. A telltale sign is the attitude taken towards the other ranks' low level of awareness of Italy's reasons for fighting. Time and again, junior officers remarked that the men did not know why they were fighting at all. Standard accounts of the war did not condemn this ignorance as a failure of the Ministry of War, the Supreme Command or even the press; it was seen sentimentally as proof of the men's good-hearted innocence. One of the finest war memoirs is *Days of War* by Giovanni Comisso, a lieutenant in the engineers. He ends with a last description of the men: black as smoke, ragged, exhausted. Convinced that he will never see their like again, he stamps their image on his memory; they smile wearily, 'as if they themselves did not know what they had done, or why'.

The feeling of never-such-innocence-again was not uniquely Italian. In Britain, it refers to the volunteers of 1914 who expected a swift and glorious campaign; and it implies that the industrial slaughter on the Western Front stained our civilisation with a new kind of knowledge, some dark revelation about the human capacity for causing and enduring pain. Although Italy also expected a swashbuckling 'Garibaldian' war in 1915, the feeling about lost innocence that lingers in Comisso's and other memoirs was more insidious: never again, they implied regretfully, would vast numbers of conscripted peasants and workers sacrifice themselves on the basis of blind trust in their social, intellectual superiors. It is easy to see why officers might be moved by this feeling, and how the men's lack of understanding flattered the educated minority, confirming a sense of themselves as Italy's elect, destined to steer the nation onwards and upwards. To be sure, an officer's perception of his men as objects of the war was not necessarily self-serving. When the poet and future priest Clemente Rebora, whose sense of duty to the men glowed like a vocation, refers to 'the anonymous flesh of the infantry', he sounds quite unlike the agitator and future dictator Mussolini, praising 'the simple and primitive souls, who, despite everything, still make up a splendid human material', or the journalist Luigi Barzini, whose despatches did so much to propagate the myth of the humble soldier. 'Who are these valiant souls that spend their life's last spark in lighting a fuse?' Barzini asked. 'They can no longer be told apart, they have a single name, they are a single thing; they are the army.' It is the difference between empathy and presumption, or worse.

It is impossible not to bridle at the paternalism that refused to see the men's ignorance as a moral affront, or even as a practical problem. For there is no evidence that the infantry were charmed by their own blankness. Pasquale Costanzo (1899–2007), who served with the 119th Infantry throughout the war, told interviewers near the end of his life: 'I did not know why there was a war at all, for that matter they didn't let the troops in on anything. You had to find your reasons for yourself, on the spot.' This remark is worth quoting a second time because it says more about the infantry's real heroism than reams of memoirs, let alone monuments like Redipuglia.[1]

*

1 Captain Kurt Suckert of the 5th Alpine Regiment was one veteran who found seeds of hope in the soldiers' desolation. In *Viva Caporetto!*, still a startling book, Suckert – known by his pen-name, Curzio Malaparte – argued that the war had (continued on p. 392)

The most influential revisionist work was a movie. Mario Monicelli's *La grande guerra* (1959) follows the comical progress of two conscripts from the rigours of boot camp to the relative ease of life at the front, between battles. One is a naïve patriot, the other a cheeky slacker. On the Piave in 1918, they get separated from their platoon and are taken prisoner. A vicious Austrian officer will spare their lives if they reveal the Italian battle plans. Overcoming their terror, the bumbling pair choose death, so saving their honour and their country. The film's satire is mild by later standards, but the lack of piety was novel at the time. Its gallows humour resembles a folk ballad or a trench song, immune to official sentiment. The general staff took umbrage and the newspapers stirred up controversy.

When the movie showed in Rome, one of its older viewers was a corpulent, silver-haired man with startled eyes, slab cheeks, and dark furrows pulling down the corners of his mouth. Since we left him in Caporetto, as a prisoner of war in October 1917, Carlo Emilio Gadda had become a great writer, master of a baroque and multilayered style, more respected than read. An eccentric figure, persuaded against his better judgement to see the film, he was appalled. By scoring easy points against Italy's lack of military preparation in 1915, Monicelli disparaged 'the purity of intention and certainty of heroic sacrifice' that marked the tragedy. While some scenes at the front were accurate, others – dwelling on the squalor and bureaucratic pettiness – were 'too implacably severe' and above all *too late*. For 'duty' was felt at the time as an emotion and an obligation; only later did it turn into hollow rhetoric. As for the comedy, it was too derisive. 'Whoever lived through those "facts" and those years, whoever *wanted* to sacrifice himself, cannot endorse those facile gags and farce.' He was equally dismayed by the youthful audience. 'They split their sides laughing. No French or German public would laugh like this.'

Had he forgotten his own satire of the war as a ridiculous quarrel between 'Maradagals' and 'Parapagals'? Or was he claiming a veteran's privilege, as if nobody younger could strike the rightly anguished note?

humanised the soldiers by burning away their Catholic pieties about death, and teaching them 'how a man can create a new soul and a new life for himself'. Caporetto was the result of the growth of class consciousness among the infantry, 'the proletariat of the army', rebelling against the hierarchy personified by Cadorna, 'the enemy of the infantry'. Malaparte's thesis was too revolutionary for Giolitti's Liberal government, which suppressed his book. The Fascists banned it as well, even though Malaparte was a party member until 1931.

A veteran in Gadda's novel finds his service pistol in a chest in the attic, years after the war. Greased and glinting, the weapon fits his hand snugly, sparking instant recall of the Carso in summer, 'the noonday heat without trenches, ready, in the stink, among the scaly rocks, five minutes after the counter-attack'. Ambushed by memories that were better left undisturbed, the veteran's brain swarms with violent fantasy.

Perhaps, watching the film, Gadda could not bear the implication that the ideals of 1915 had been swallowed up by fascism, then discredited along with it, making the veterans' values incommunicable. His essay on the film included a swipe at Hemingway. Presumably he resented the fact that so many Italians got their idea of the war from *A Farewell to Arms*, with its debunking of patriotic ideals and indifference to Italy's victory. I would wager that Gadda, an expert self-tormentor, and ashamed of his own seduction by fascism, was haunted by the possibility that Hemingway's outsider vision was more accurate than his own, even if it was based on only a few weeks at the front as a Red Cross volunteer.

As soon as he was demobbed, in 1919, Gadda planned to write something that would 'break the circle of silence' about the reality of the war, and make it impossible for anything like it to happen again. Not surprisingly, he never wrote that book, though he managed a chapter of steely aphorisms for his novel, *The Castle of Udine* (1934), such as this: 'Speaking of war and peace as if they were myths, or earthquakes, is a disgusting thing in a man and a citizen.' Maybe *A Farewell to Arms* made him so uncomfortable because he had shared its anti-hero's distaste for patriotic rhetoric:

I was always embarrassed by the words sacred, glorious, and sacrifice and the expression, in vain . . . I had seen nothing sacred, and the things that were glorious had no glory . . . There were many words that you could not stand to hear and finally only the names of places had dignity . . . Abstract words such as glory, honor, courage, or hallow were obscene beside the concrete names of villages, the numbers of roads, the names of rivers, the numbers of regiments and the dates.

If it is true that nobody in the Europe of August 1914 would have understood what Hemingway was talking about in this famous passage, it is equally true that by 1916, even pro-war Italians were saying very similar things, in revulsion at the deceitful rhetoric that swilled around the nation like a polluting tide. That September, Gadda told a friend that, if he died, the announcement should be as laconic as possible, avoiding words and phrases like 'fatherland, honour, fervent youth, flower of his youth, hated enemy, proud and grieving, etc.' *Fell in the course of combat* would suffice. Another officer told his wife that he avoided using the word 'fatherland' in front of his men. 'I never use big words: faced with the real vision of death, my men are suspicious and unresponsive.' At the Supreme Command, Father Gemelli argued that the men's indifference to 'inspirational' speeches did not mean they were immune to high ideals. Rather, it confirmed that bourgeois rhetoric was of very limited use for communication with peasants and workers. Following events from afar, Professor Alfredo Panzini wondered with sharp flippancy if Italy's salvation depended on abolishing adjectives. It was in 1916, too, that Ungaretti wrote the pared-down poetry which passed a creative judgement on the bankruptcy of conventional expression. Unlike these men, Hemingway was not saturated in Italian war-language; but he did not need to be. His American artist's ear caught the poisoned sonorities of European nationalism, which his hard-bitten style satirised automatically in *A Farewell to Arms*, his best novel. It was a style that became influential around the world. Modern literature owes a debt-by-reaction to Italian war discourse.

Wandering over the Carso today, it is hard to recover much impression of the barren harshness that tormented the soldiers. Above the coast, the plateau has been scored with roads; traffic roars between the Rocca and Mount Cosich. The ambient temperature rose by two degrees over the last century, and the bora lost its edge. Sumac trees, planted as windbreaks, protected the thin soil; hornbeam, evergreens and stunted oak flourish. The undergrowth is like rainforest, impassable in summer. It is good to follow the old Habsburg highway from Redipuglia to Trieste on a clear afternoon, take the fork to Aurisina and find a path to the cliff top. Light flashing off the Adriatic sets crystal in the branches, like 'a cast of the imagination'.

Free from the Alps to the Adriatic

*Until Italy's eastern frontiers are all her own,
it is certain that her national independence
will not be complete. Thus, further wars will
be inevitable.*
PROSPERO ANTONINI (1865)

The Third War of Italian Independence, 1866

It is a summer evening in 1866. A coach sweeps along the highway from Cormons to Udine, splashing through streams, not slowing in the quiet hamlets. The postilion sways drunkenly in his saddle, but he has found excellent horses and the coach makes good time. The passenger has urgent news for his king and country. For he is an Italian general who arrived only two days before. Against the odds, he leaves with head high.

The date is 12 August. The Habsburg empire has just agreed that Italy should get the province of Venetia, including Venice. It is the latest twist in a summer of extraordinary reversals. Thanks to General Pettiti, the project to unify Italy looks in better shape today than anyone had expected 24 hours earlier. But it is still fragile, still incomplete.

Austria was not the only foreign power with a territorial stake in the Risorgimento. France coveted the Alpine portion of Savoy, near Geneva, and the coast at Nice. Europe's other great powers – Britain, Russia and Prussia – took a remoter interest, aiming to contain wider disruption and stop each other benefiting by the process too much. Emergent Italy's dispute with France was settled in January 1859, when they closed the last open territorial issue: France got Nice and Savoy in exchange for a military alliance to drive Austria out of the Italian lands. A few months later, in April, Austria provided a *casus belli* and lost to the allied forces at Magenta and Solferino. The French and Italian emperors had reasons of their own to negotiate peace before Austria was forced to its knees: Napoleon III was alarmed by his casualties and had one eye on averting Prussian intervention, while Franz Josef was shocked by his army's poor fighting form. So Piedmont gained Lombardy but not Venetia. This outcome was sealed by a treaty that pledged the Kingdom of Piedmont-Sardinia (i.e. Italy) to 'peace and perpetual friendship' with Austria.

The language deceived no one. The Austrians were obsessed by Italian unification. Although Lombardy and Venetia were a long way from the Germanic, Magyar and Slavic heartlands of their empire, they believed these provinces were crucial to its stature. More than anything else, Austrian hostility was the anvil on which Italy was hammered into existence.[1] The treaty opened half a century of duplicitous relations. The ink was hardly dry on the treaty when Camille Cavour, Piedmont's brilliant prime minister, said privately that he was ready to fight for Venetia.

The Kingdom of Italy was proclaimed the next year, threatening the 'Concert of Europe' that had endured more or less since 1815. The other European powers recognised the new arrival, reducing Austria's allies to two, both second-rate: Spain and the Pope. Cavour assured radicals in parliament that Rome and Venice would be annexed in the not too distant future. He also promised Garibaldi that Venice would be plucked from Austria when the time was right. The challenge of annexing the south Tyrol, Istria and Ticino (the Italian-speaking canton of Switzerland), not to mention the island of Malta (a standard claim, however far-fetched), would pass to future generations. When one of his provincial governors said that the port of Trieste and the coast of Dalmatia were Italian objectives, Cavour denied it. The governor was taken aside and warned that loose talk would alienate the great powers. A few weeks before his death in June 1861, Cavour told parliament there could be no lasting peace with Austria until Italy got Venetia. Privately, he predicted that this would probably happen the following year.

Austria's leaders were no more inclined than Italy's to accept the 1859 border as permanent. Convinced that Italy would always destabilise the empire's south-western corner, Franz Josef's generals dreamed of

[1] The struggle with Austria is fossilised in the Italian national anthem, which was formally adopted as recently as 2005, after a century and a half! The references to Legnano, Ferruccio and Balilla are more than obscure. As for 'the Austrian eagle' that had 'already lost its plumes', it was stuffed in a glass case ninety years ago. Full English and Italian text is available at http://en.wikipedia.org/wiki/Il_Canto_degli_Italiani#Lyrics.

reconquering Lombardy and garrisoned Venetia with 100,000 men. The shock of Magenta and Solferino wore off; old illusions of military competence returned. The Austrians knew they enjoyed Prussian backing, due to concern over pan-German use of Trieste and the Adriatic seaways.

Egged on by followers of Garibaldi and Mazzini, successive governments vowed to drive the Austrians out of Venetia. In 1864, King Victor Emanuel II announced that Venetia and Papal Rome would be gained for Italy. The army and navy were built up, but Italy was still weak. More than once, the government secretly offered to buy Venice with cash. Vienna was not interested. Count Rechberg, the Austrian foreign minister, wrote privately that Italian nationalism would destroy the 'monstrosity' called Italy if the empire waited patiently.

Unification could only proceed in linkage with stronger states whose interests coincided with Italy's. Prussia's sharpening rivalry with Austria held promise. All three states made token efforts to avoid war, but talks came to nothing. Victor Emanuel was ready to ally with Austria in exchange for Venetia and the south Tyrol, but the Austrians would not pay this price, and anyway were confident of defeating Prussia unaided. Bismarck, on the other hand, was interested; he had a better chance of knocking Austria off its pedestal as the senior Germanic power if Italy attacked in the south. In April 1866, Italy secretly pledged to open a second front in Venetia and South Tyrol as soon as Prussia declared war, in exchange for Bismarck's support over Venetia (though not the Tyrol). Austrian agents discovered the plan immediately. The Emperor ordered his generals to be ready for war against Prussia in the north and Italy in the south. The Austrians aimed to carry the fighting down the peninsula, exorcising what Metternich had called the 'phantom of Italian unity', replacing the kingdom with a federation or loose confederation of statelets. This scenario rattled Napoleon III, who saw France's interest as staying out of the war while preventing anything too dramatic happening to Italy or Austria. He wanted Italy to have Venetia, fulfilling France's commitment to unification while also diverting the Italian appetite for Rome. And he wanted the two Germanic powers to keep each other weak. Practically, this meant helping Austria to become a stronger counterbalance to Prussian power.

The opinion around Europe was that Austria could beat Prussia and Italy combined. Even so, a two-front war should always be avoided, and in early May the Austrians offered to trade Venetia for Italian neutrality. The Italians said they could not break their pledge to Prussia. In truth, they wanted to take Venetia and South Tyrol by arms. Nino Bixio, a hero of Garibaldi's campaigns, told parliament that he would rather 100,000 Italians died for Venice than accept it without fighting. The King agreed. The idea that national greatness required Italy to fight for something that might be obtained by diplomacy would prove disastrously durable. Year-on-year cuts in military spending since 1862 did not worry the pro-war faction. The mobilisation in May has been called 'a bureaucratic and logistical nightmare, which pointed anew to the difficulty of building a single new state from the wreckage of a half-dozen old ones in as many years'. The King and his prime minister, General La Marmora, waited several weeks before inviting Garibaldi out of retirement to muster a force against the Tyrol. The Liberator left at once for the north-east. Suspicious of volunteers and Garibaldi's popularity, the army laid not so subtle traps, giving the old hero what he called 'the usual defective rifles'. He had no artillery and many volunteers had to wear their own clothes. Austrian agents reported gleefully that Garibaldi's 20,000 volunteers were teenagers with no fighting experience. Historians put the number at 10,000.

With their confidence waning, the Austrians formalised their offer to cede Venetia peacefully, and were again rebuffed. In desperation, they promised that, even if they won, they would not change Italy's borders. The King and his generals were not listening. In an abrupt switch, the Austrians tried to involve Napoleon. On 12 June, they offered to let him mediate the transfer of Venetia to Italy in exchange for French neutrality. Napoleon was non-committal.

No one wanted to fire the first shot. Bismarck prevailed on the King of Prussia to mobilise on 15 June. With 350,000 men under arms, Prussia invaded Hanover and Saxony, crossed the Austrian frontier, occupied most of Bohemia and attacked Silesia. To Bismarck's lasting irritation, Victor Emanuel waited four days before declaring war on Austria 'for the honour of Italy and the rights of the nation'. Damning Italy's 'treachery and arrogance', Field Marshal Albrecht vowed not to let the King 'plant his standard on the Brenner Pass and the Carso'. With Austria's main force fighting the Prussians, Italy began its third war of independence with 200,000 men and 370 guns against 75,000 men and 168 guns. These numbers were misleading; La Marmora admitted that only half his troops could properly be called soldiers at all. Cadets with less than two months' training were sent to front-line companies. Desertion rates were high. Few of the divisional generals had any combat experience. An idea of the army's readiness can be gleaned from the fact that many officers flatly refused to believe their king would lead them into war in high summer. Even in camp, senior officers dressed like dandies in linen suits and silk cravats – a scandalised Prussian envoy called them 'voluptuous neckties'.

The King refused to clarify the command structure, rivalries among senior generals were not resolved, and communications were bad. Victor Emanuel tried to impose an incompetent chief of staff; when this proved impossible, he gave the position to La Marmora, already prime minister and foreign minister, but denied him full authority. The King and La Marmora took up their command only three days before Italy declared war. While there was no real battle plan, the idea was for a three-pronged attack. La Marmora would lead 12 divisions (some 120,000 men) across the River Mincio – marking the border with Venetia – towards the fortresses of the so-called Quadrilateral (Mantua, Peschiera, Verona and Legnano). His most talented general, Cialdini, was a hundred kilometres to the east, poised to lead eight divisions across the River Po, outflanking the Quadrilateral. Garibaldi would lead his volunteers into the Tyrol, where the Austrians had 16,000 men.

While La Marmora crossed the Mincio, Garibaldi led his volunteers up the western side of Lake Garda. Albrecht astonished the Italians by taking the offensive in the centre. La Marmora had made no defensive plans. The armies clashed at Custoza on 24 June. It was a messy collision along a ridge of rolling hills. La Marmora – leading only five and a half divisions – did not know the Austrians' location or strength. Many soldiers had not eaten for two days. Disoriented and demoralised, whole units surrendered at a jog, abandoning the wounded. The King tried in vain to rally his men, who doffed their hats as they ran away from the Polish Lancers, ignoring his appeals. Dispersal and collapse of morale were the problem, not casualties, for only 725 Italians died at Custoza: far fewer than the Austrian losses.

The King, La Marmora and Cialdini formed a bizarre trio, acting 'as though they could not order one another to do things; they just "requested" or "urgently begged" for action'. The situation could have been retrieved if Cialdini had crossed the Po, but he pulled back. The two parts of the army hardly co-ordinated with each other, let alone with the naval operations or Garibaldi. Panicking, the King and La

Marmora retreated 50 kilometres and ordered Garibaldi to fall back. The great basin of the River Po was there for the taking, but Albrecht's priority was to strengthen the front against Prussia. Some 60,000 men were transferred to Bohemia. By failing to exploit their victory, the Austrians let Italy profit from a war that it had already lost.

While Victor Emanuel and his generals tried to grasp what had gone wrong and wrestled over the post of chief of staff (honourably vacated by La Marmora), the Austrian commander in the north asked permission to seek an armistice. Vienna refused, and looked how to bring more reinforcements from Italy. When the Prussians won a clinching victory at Sadowa on 3 July, the road to Vienna lay open. Austria reacted by pulling its remaining forces out of Italy, and Bismarck told Victor Emanuel to attack at once. The price of refusal, he made clear, might include an unfavourable territorial settlement.

Napoleon III feared that Austria would not emerge strong enough to counterbalance Bismarck's Germany. On 4 July he urged Victor Emanuel to end the war. Picking up Austria's offer from 12 June, he promised that the Italians would get Venetia as a gift from France, but not the south Tyrol or Trieste. The Austrians welcomed this chance to hang the albatross of Venetia around Napoleon's neck.

For a king bent on a glorious campaign to unify his country, every outcome proffered humiliation. Failure to obey Bismarck could lead to a settlement that reflected all too faithfully his performance on the battlefield. If he obeyed Bismarck and attacked, he risked losing Napoleon's favour. At best, Italy would receive Venetia without conquering it – an 'intolerable' outcome, in La Marmora's judgement. As a sop to Bismarck, Cialdini launched a limited operation across the Po on 5 July, and Garibaldi's volunteers were let off the leash.

Unexpectedly, the cabinet asserted itself: Italy should prosecute the war with maximum force, creating facts on the ground to shape the settlement that Bismarck would soon impose. As well as Venetia and the south Tyrol, the army should make a grab for Istria. For without Istria, the new prime minister, Baron Ricasoli, said, 'We shall always have Austria as master of the Adriatic. It is right to profit from this occasion – not so much rare as unique – to undo every interference by Austria in the Adriatic.' Ricasoli told Cialdini that they must fight the Austrians in Venetia or be accused of bad faith; then they would be in no position to demand the south Tyrol. Admiral Persano, commanding the navy, was instructed absurdly to put to sea, sink the Austrian fleet and occupy

Istria within a week. For the Austrians might be forced to make peace any day now; whenever this happened, the Italians would have to stop. They could not count on getting any territory that they had not conquered.

This was fighting talk, but the King hesitated to offend Napoleon. Only on 14 July did the cabinet get his approval to try to clinch military control over Venetia and even drive Austria away from the northern Adriatic altogether. Seven corps would occupy Venetia. Five of these (around 150,000 men) would form an expeditionary force under General Cialdini and march the 200 kilometres to the River Isonzo, beating back any Austrian resistance as they went. After swinging south to take Trieste, they would – other things being equal – cross the Alps and march on Vienna. It was a madcap scheme or dream. If the fiasco of Custoza could not be undone, it could apparently be ignored.

Overly prudent and badly supplied, the expeditionary force made slow progress. Cialdini knew they were living on borrowed time; on 19 July he instructed V Corps to make all speed to Trieste, with cavalry support. A division under General Medici would double back north-westwards to help Garibaldi. The next day, Prussia and Austria agreed a five-day truce and started negotiating a settlement. When the Prussians accepted that the Habsburg empire would remain intact except for Venetia, the Austrians believed Trieste and south Tyrol were secure. The Italians were not informed of the truce beforehand, let alone of the negotiations. That same day, equally unknown to Cialdini, the Italian fleet was thrashed 'by an Austrian squadron half its size', near the Dalmatian island of Lissa (now Vis).

The Austrians kept transferring men northwards, hoping to bolster their negotiating position with Prussia. On the 21st, they moved their Italian headquarters eastwards across the River Isonzo to Gorizia. Meanwhile, under General Raffaele Cadorna (father of Luigi), the 30,000 men of V Corps made impressive progress across the plain. They reached the River Tagliamento on the morning of the 23rd to find the bridges had been dropped. Despite stifling heat and poor provisions, the men were in good fettle.[2] Cialdini told Cadorna to send a division across the Isonzo to occupy Gorizia, then push ahead to Trieste. Once there, he should camp outside the city, taking in enough troops to preserve order and take control of the port without antagonising the

2 Bread had to be brought from as far as Ferrara, south of the River Po, and went mouldy before it reached the men, who were more troubled by the shortage of tobacco.

citizens or disturbing business. He should break communications with the imperial hinterland, sequestrate Austrian government property, and stop the banks moving money out of the city.

None of this was to be. The Italians learned that the enemy still had some 30,000 troops on the Isonzo, 2,500 more at Palmanova, west of the river, and at least 10,000 more in Trieste. This was a far greater number than La Marmora (reinstated as chief of staff) had anticipated. Late on the 23rd, as his men threw pontoons over the Tagliamento, Cadorna was ordered to advance only as far as the village of San Giorgio di Nogaro, west of the Isonzo, and wait. The Austrians evacuated Udine that evening; further east again, the last Austrian brigade in Gorizia entrained for Vienna.

Braced by victory at sea, Austria sent half its garrison in Trieste to head off Cadorna's men. This force reached Monfalcone on 24 July. That day, Cadorna's V Corps almost reached Cervignano while Prussia and Austria cemented their truce into a formal armistice. La Marmora reacted cautiously, ordering Cialdini to suspend all operations for eight days. Cialdini replied astutely that he needed 24 hours – until early on the 26th – to execute this order, because he had no telegraph access to Cadorna and Medici. Meanwhile he sent word to Cadorna that La Marmora was contemplating 'ruinous' terms for a truce, so he (Cadorna) should make a dash for the Isonzo before he received official notice of the Austro-Prussian armistice. Cialdini would try to delay forwarding this notice until Cadorna had reached the Isonzo. The government helped by proposing unacceptable conditions for an armistice with Austria, demanding the south Tyrol as well as Venetia.

Cadorna decided to cross the Isonzo and cut the rail line from Trieste to Gorizia. Before he could start, he received orders to occupy several villages on the west bank of the river and wait for reinforcements that should arrive within 24 hours. One of these villages was Versa, on the far side of a bridge over a tributary of the Isonzo. The rivers were swollen by rain. When Cadorna's cavalry tried to take the bridge, the Austrians burned it and fell back to the village. Two thousand Italians waded across and took Versa from an Austrian regiment of 3,000 men at a cost of seven dead and 29 wounded. The Austrians (who lost 30 dead and 51 wounded) fell back towards the Isonzo. A dozen kilometres to the north, joyful crowds welcomed the Italian 14th Division as it marched into Udine. Meanwhile, the government in Rome buckled under Bismarck's pressure. As V Corps prepared to advance to the

Isonzo, La Marmora was told that Austria and Italy had agreed a truce. Formal notice reached Cadorna late the same day. He had already run out of reserves, provisions and boots; now he ran out of time.

Cadorna's opposite number, General Maroičić, called on the Italians to withdraw to the positions they had held when La Marmora was informed of the Austro-Prussian ceasefire. The final demarcation, he added, should be the provincial border between Venetia and the adjacent Austrian province, called the Küstenland, zigzagging between the Isonzo and the Tagliamento. Cadorna stood his ground at Versa, awaiting word from Cialdini, who duly proposed the Isonzo as the new border. Austrian troops were pouring back to the south, but Bismarck had already decided that the Italians should get Venetia and a sliver of Friuli, stopping well short of the Isonzo and the Alps. Apart from punishing them for botching their campaign, he wanted to prop up Austria as a bulwark against Italy and to keep Trieste safe for Germanic trade.

On 3 August, Austria rejected Italy's demand. The Ministry of War's position was clear: if Venetia had to be lost, then Austria 'must obtain an optimal redefinition of the southern limits of Tyrol. Whenever possible, we must insist on having the dominant positions.' Whenever the Italians on the plain looked up at the horizon, they must see Habsburg soldiers. La Marmora wanted to accept Bismarck's settlement but the King and Cialdini disagreed, not least because Garibaldi's volunteers and Medici's regulars were gaining ground in the Tyrol. On 21 July, Garibaldi had engaged the Austrians at Bezzecca, where two valleys meet near the northern tip of Lake Garda. Each side lost around 500 men, but the Italians held the village and prepared to push on to the city of Trento, 50 kilometres away. News of this success rallied the government. With Padua, Vicenza and Treviso secured and Venice surrounded, the government was tempted to defy French pressure, Prussian disapproval, and the Austrian build-up on the Isonzo. But dubious sources in Trieste reported that Austria now had 200,000 troops on the Isonzo – twice as many as La Marmora had thought. Albrecht gave notice that he was ready to sweep all the Italian forces out of South Tyrol and Friuli.

The Italians decided they could get no further without Prussian and French support. Early on 9 August, La Marmora ordered Garibaldi to evacuate the Tyrol and Cialdini to pull back behind the 'old Venetian border' within 48 hours. Garibaldi, still at Bezzecca, was astonished:

he had not been defeated and the enemy was in retreat! After pacing around his headquarters, he scrawled two words on La Marmora's telegram: '*Si annuisce*' – 'It is agreed.' But how could he agree with an order that stole victory from his volunteers? He scored through his reply and wrote '*Obbedisco!*' – 'I obey!' It was a gesture to inspire future generations. Legend has it that he turned to his companions: 'Whether there will be peace or war, it is up to you, young men, to liberate Italy from the foreigner, as long as a single one remains.' Garibaldi always insisted that he could have taken Trento with ease.

Cialdini said he could comply at once, but he feared the Austrians had their eye on the whole of Friuli and Venetia up to the River Tagliamento. La Marmora disagreed and trustingly drew most of his forces (including V Corps) behind the Tagliamento. It soon appeared that Cialdini was right. The outlook was grim for the Italians, who were outnumbered at their forward positions. When negotiations opened at Cormons on the 10th, Albrecht was adamant: the Tagliamento must be the border, and he had 140,000 men on the Isonzo to back him up. La Marmora's negotiator, General Pettiti, stood firm, but when he contacted the King and his government from Udine that evening, seeking guidance, they equivocated, leaving the mortified general alone with the responsibility. 'It is my misfortune', he wrote that night, 'that this will be called the Pettiti Armistice.' In the morning he made his dutiful way back to Cormons. A few days earlier, the Italians had dreamed of taking Trieste; now they risked not getting all of Venetia, never mind Friuli and the Isonzo.

Looking keenly about as he travelled through the disputed territory, Pettiti felt suddenly sure the Austrians did not really care about the portion of Venetia that Albrecht seemed bent on retaining. Fired with this conviction, he induced the Austrians to relent. By the end of 12 August, the old provincial border of Venetia was agreed as the new state border. Pettiti was entitled to feel proud as his coach rolled back to Udine. The agreement was ratified the following October. The prewar border of south Tyrol was maintained, nullifying Garibaldi's efforts. While this fell short of 'optimal redefinition', it was wholly to the Austrians' advantage.

Austria refused to negotiate the cession of Venetia with Italy; it had to be handled as a dynastic transaction between Franz Josef and Napoleon III, ignoring any idea that popular will was involved. (Where would the empire be if popular will or consent became requirements of sovereignty?) This was a finesse; in brute fact, Austria had been forced to accept that Italy was more than 'a geographical expression' (Metternich's put-down, still bitterly remembered); it was a nation-state, and here to stay. Austrian Venetia became the Italian Veneto on 19 October 1866, a few days after France received the province from Austria. Although he wanted a grand procession in the Piazza San Marco, the French envoy took advice that the crowds might jeer, so the ceremony was moved to a hotel. After making his speech to an Austrian official and a three-man Venetian committee, the Frenchman read out a letter from Napoleon III to Victor Emanuel, claiming credit for an act of democratic midwifery. 'Your Majesty knows that I accepted the offer of Venetia in order to preserve it from devastation and prevent a useless spilling of blood. My purpose has always been to give it to itself so that Italy might be free from the Alps to the Adriatic . . .'

The crowd outside San Marco cheered and waved flags while the ships of the Austrian merchant navy moved through the Lagoon for the last time, laden with troops heading across the sea to Trieste, Austria's last great guarantee of Adriatic power. The following day, the last Austrian governor of the Serenissima made his way to the waterfront. A large crowd applauded as he boarded a destroyer and was borne away. The Italian flag was hoisted in the piazza and troops made their way up the Grand Canal, accompanied by frenzied cries of 'Viva l'Italia!' and 'Viva l'unità d'Italia!' The French consul reported that no word of thanks to Italy's benefactor could be heard. A plebiscite in the Veneto showed 647,246 citizens in favour of union with the Kingdom of Italy, and only 69 against. The way was clear for Victor Emanuel to enter the city by royal gondola. Again, French diplomats were accorded no special recognition. The Italians were cutting the umbilical cord with Paris; gratitude, let alone deference, could no longer be expected.

The King's triumphal tour took him to Udine, capital of Friuli, festooned with flags for the occasion. Amid the colourful buzz a group of black-clad men stood in silence, holding up gloomy banners with the caption 'Italy has been made but not completed'. They were irredentists from Trento, Trieste, Istria and Dalmatia, reminding the carefree crowds that the nation still had unfinished business with the Austrians, and would not be allowed to forget it.

Notes

INTRODUCTION 'Italians! Go back!'

1 *'Nobody who hasn't seen it'*: Barbour, 14 May 1917. See also Dalton, 6.   1 *'We kill each other like this'*: Carlo Salsa, quoted by Bianchi [2001].   1 *the patterns of collusion*: Ashworth offers evidence that the 'live and let live system' emerged on the Western and Eastern Fronts, the Italian front and at Salonika, but not at Gallipoli. (Ashworth, 210–13.) Bianchi [2001] gives examples from the Italian front.   2 *'What do you want, to kill them all?'*: This witness was Adelmo Reatti. Foresti, Morisi & Resca.   2 *'like toads'*: Salsa, 85.   2 *A few weeks earlier*: This witness was Bersagliere Giuseppe Garzoni. Bianchi [2001], 356.   2 *As the survivors drew close*: Lussu, 97–8. This book is a lightly fictionalised memoir, not a journal or a work of scholarship.   2 *A Turkish officer*: See Patsy Adam-Smith, *The Anzacs* (West Melbourne: Thomas Nelson, 1978), Chapter 12.   2 *'offered such a target'*: A German source quoted by Warner, 45.   3 *'like a great wall'*: Wanda Newby, 65.   4 *'in Vienna for Christmas'*: General Porro, deputy supreme commander. De Simone, 202.   5 *'Our entire war is viewed'*: Isnenghi & Rochat, 446.   5 *The worst-paid infantry*: Schindler, 132.   6 *Italy's situation after the war*: Giuliano Procacci, 237.

ONE A Mania for Expansion

10 *'the most threatening salient'*: Martel.   11 *'a policy of expedients'*: Mack Smith [1997], 222.   12 *more spirit than man*: Bobbio, 71–2.   12 *Dante had ordained it*: Inferno, IX, 113.   14 *'mania for expansion'*: Mack Smith [1997], 149.   14 *'where not even the standard'*: Bosworth [1979], 11.   14 *the colony of Eritrea*: By 1913, Eritrea had only 61 permanent Italian colonists. Bosworth [1983], 52.   15 *'a large appetite'*: Bosworth [2007], 163.   16 *by manipulating elections*: Salvemini [1973], 82–3.   17 *least of the great powers*: Bosworth [1979]. The information in the rest of this paragraph is from Zamagni, 199, 205; Bosworth [2006], 37, and [2007], 164; Salvemini [1973], 4–6; Giuliano Procacci, 223–4; Forsyth, 27.   17 *'empirical politics . . . possible method'*: Gentile [2000].

TWO 'We Two Alone'

18 *a coup d'état in all but name*: Salvatorelli [1950].   19 *Isnenghi argues that*: Isnenghi [1999], 17.   19 *he wanted to cut the figure*: Bosworth [2007], 170.   19 *little faith in the future of the monarchy*: Martini, 393.   20 *the pledge by Italy's new chief*: Rusconi, 150.   21 *'Is it not more logical'*: Quotations and details about

Pollio and the Triple Alliance are from Rusconi, 27–41. *22 Italy wanted Austria's*: Rusconi, 93. *22 'the transport of the largest possible force'*: Rusconi, 90. *23 'So what should I do?'*: Rocca, 52. *23 'incompatible with the liberal principles'*: Rusconi, 83. *23 Italy depended on Britain and France*: Zamagni, 210. *24 'This may not be heroic'*: Rusconi, 96, 97, 94. *24 'Their famous lightning strike'*: Rusconi, 100. *24 'a hundred journalists'*: Rusconi, 106. *25 'complete and enlarge the fatherland'*: Rusconi, 104. *25 predicted with only partial exaggeration*: Rusconi, 91. *26 the retort was doubly irrelevant*: Rusconi, 121. *26 'a good deal'*: Rusconi, 122. *26 Why, then, go to war?*: Rusconi, 143–4. *27 ensure Balkan and Mediterranean markets*: Rochat & Massobrio, 177. *27 neutrality was 'suicide'*: Rusconi, 127. *28 a candid letter to Sonnino*: Monticone [1972], 63–4. *28 he predicted that it would be the turning point*: Rothwell, 23. *29 the Italians had 'blackmailed' them*: Mantoux, vol. I, 477. *29 'Russia is quite right'*: Asquith to Venetia Stanley in spring 1915. Cassar [1994]. *29 'the harlot of Europe'*: Rusconi, 24, 25. *29 'the most contemptible nation'*: Rothwell, 86. *29 'wretched "pound-of-flesh" convention'*: Wickham Steed, vol. 2, 66. *30 disperse the 'negative constellation'*: Rusconi, 146. *30 Salandra, meanwhile, instructed Italy's regional governors*: Monticone [1972]. Salandra later denied that he had ordered the 55 reports; they were, he claimed, part of a neutralist plot to keep Italy out of the war. Gibelli, 29. *31 This unconditional promise, not to be found*: Rothwell, 30. *31 home to some 230,000 German-speaking Austrians and up to 750,000 Slovenes and Croats*: Nicolson, 161; Kernek, 264. *31 one of Sonnino's advisors as 'derisory'*: Sforza [1944], 44. *31 'But this means immediate war!'*: Rocca, 66. *31 the port of Fiume was assigned to*: Mantoux, vol. I, 125. *33 He told a journalist, off the record*: Rusconi, 137. *33 'Salandra lied to me!'*: Rusconi, 137. *34 'What are we doing?'*: Rocca, 68. *34 Trevelyan saw 'hundreds of thousands'*: Trevelyan. *35 'it has all been a trick'*: Rusconi, 140. *35 'Either Parliament will defeat the Nation'*: Isnenghi & Rochat, 136. *35 decrees with the force of law*: Procacci [2006], 286. *35 Salandra's 'swinish and faithless'*: Rusconi, 139. *36 He later denied having ever believed*: Mack Smith [1978], 215. *36 building a new anti-Socialist bloc*: Procacci [1992]. *36 purge liberalism of its democratic 'dross'*: Rusconi, 147. *36 a solution to internal problems*: Giuliano Procacci, 229. *36 'only a war, with a phase of compulsory'*: Procacci [1992]. *36 'a modern plutocracy, unencumbered'*: From Croce's History of Italy from 1871 to 1915*, cited by Rusconi, 147. *37 proto-fascists shrieking*: Alfredo Rocca, the ideologist of Italian radical nationalism, quoted by Tranfaglia. *37 no German–Austrian plans*: Palumbo [1983]. *37 'we have been the horse'*: Rusconi, 141. *38 lacked strength or boldness*: Rusconi, 50. *38 'This whole war has been'*: Rusconi, 13.

THREE Free Spirits

40 'For almost thirty years': Woodhouse, 240. *40 an exchange from summer 1904*: Woodhouse, 218, 219. *42 he was thrilled by the Libyan campaign*: Woodhouse, 263, 264. *44 'in a species of lyric frenzy'*: According to Thomas Page, the US ambassador to Italy. *47 did not even mention D'Annunzio or his speech*: O'Brien [2004], 57. *47 'a new species of "free spirits"'*: O'Brien [2004],

NOTES TO PAGES 48–82

44.   48 *He drafted a manifesto on the 'profound antithesis'*: O'Brien [2004], 32.
48 *Mussolini was latently pro-intervention*: O'Brien [2004], 34.   49 *A former comrade in the Socialist Party later alleged*: Rossi.   50 *Mussolini waited to be called up*: O'Brien [2004], 68.   50 *'The people's heart is never in any war'*: Mussolini, 59–60, 110, 111.

FOUR Cadorna's Clenched Fist

52 *Who is Cadorna? What has he done*: Rocca, 179.   52/3 *The Ministry of War once wanted*: Rocca, 31–2.   53 *'length of service and reasons'*: Rocca, 24.
54 *Cadorna sent his pamphlet*: Rocca, 45–7.   55 *Cadorna issued a memorandum*: Rusconi, 162.   56 *Cadorna rejected the Minister of War's compromise*: Rochat [1991a].   56 *Italy's army was the weakest*: Gooch [1989], Rochat [1991a].   57 *Parliament, controlled by anti-war deputies, still refused*: Zamagni, 210.   57 *The artillery was in even worse shape*: De Simone, 162.   57 *'if another army were thrown into the fray'*: Rusconi, 115.   58 *the analysis arriving from his military attachés*: Rochat [1961].   58 *'the possibilities for successful offensives'*: Cadorna [1915], 32.   59 *'Gone are the wars of impetuous assaults'*: Labita.   59 *He warned readers in November*: Gatti [1915], 308.   59 *Gatti's end-of-year summary*: Gatti [1915], 343, 347.

FIVE The Solemn Hour Strikes

62 *only two of the army's 17 regular corps*: Rocca, 65.   63 *lack of 'offensive spirit'*: Cadorna [1950], 232–41.   63 *guarded in mid-May by only two divisions*: Sema, vol. I, 26.   63 *'We are on the eve of an enemy invasion'*: Flores, 35–6.
63 *An Austrian officer posted in the Dolomites*: Lt. Anton Moerl, quoted by Vianelli & Cenacchi, xxix.   64 *'We expected them to do just that'*: Vianelli & Cenacchi, xxix.   64 *So he attacked anyway, achieving no success*: Flores, 38.
64 *not admitted at the time, or under Fascism*: Alberti.   67 *Carlo Emilio Gadda, who fought on the Carso*: Gadda [1963].   71 *'Daddy, daddy, look at all the ladies'*: Pavan, 367.   71 *Other units, he was told, were active on Mrzli*: Details of operations on Mount Mrzli are from Alliney.   72 *This man, Lieutenant Colonel Negrotto*: Alliney, 30.   73 *urged the men to defend their 'Slavic soil'*: Schindler, 52; Sema, vol. I, 43.   73 *'It was like the end of the world'*: Faldella, 14.   74 *'hard Friulan faces'*: Mario Puccini, 114.   75 *He told his family*: Cadorna [1967], 104.

SIX A Gift from Heaven

77 *this particular story*: Weber, 11–13.   77 *losses that almost beggar belief*: Deák.
77 *'civilians in uniform'*: This is Deák's phrase.   77 *military spending, even at its zenith*: Rothenberg [1985].   78 *The only 'completely reliable' elements*: Spence [1985].   79 *at least one British Foreign Office mandarin*: Rothwell, 30.   80 *The last Habsburg census before the war*: Spence [1985].   80 *the purge of many Serbs early in the war*: Spence [1992].   81 *these 'schoolboys and grandfathers'*: Jung.
82 *The Italians had missed a chance to capture*: Del Bianco, vol. I, 402.   82 *'stop the Italians with all methods'*: As quoted on the webpage: http://www.austro-hungarian-army.co.uk/biog/wurm.htm, accessed in February 2008.   82 *as 'a gift*

[408]

from heaven': Farkas's phrase.   82 *'the water gleamed as if covered with silver'*: this was the description by Rilke's hostess, the Princess of Thurn and Taxis.   83 *Conrad 'believed that infantry could advance'*: Rothenberg [1985].   83 *Conrad's was a larger, more gifted and complex personality*: Information about and quotations by Conrad are from Sondhaus's excellent biographical study (Sondhaus, 2000).   85 *'be a hopeless struggle, but it must be pursued'*: Rothenberg [1985].   85 *'If we also have to fear Italy, then'*: Palumbo [1983].   86 *'a horrifying thought'*: Sondhaus [2000], 158–9.

SEVEN Walls of Iron, Clouds of Fire

90 *a junior officer in the Pisa Brigade*: Faldella, 18–20.   91 *'All at once the cry goes up'*: Albertazzi.   91 *The last veteran of the first battle on the Isonzo*: As well as interviewing Mr Carlo Orelli myself in May 2004, I have drawn on interviews by Paolo Rumiz of *La Repubblica* (unpublished); Aldo Cazzullo of *Corriere della Sera*, 1 November 2003; and Bultrini.

EIGHT Trento and Trieste!

95 *'For Trento. For Trieste. To get what was due'*: Borroni [2006b].   95 *'I did not know why there was a war'*: Pte. Pasquale Costanzo, quoted by Bultrini & Casarola, 65.   95 *'unaware of the existence'* of the words: O'Brien [2004], 75.   95 *'The profound ignorance of our masses'*: Malaparte [1981], 60.   96 *To the Triestine poet Umberto Saba*: Cortellessa, 85.   96 *'absolutely German'*: Maranelli.   98 *personified by Cesare Battisti*: Most details about Battisti are from Isnenghi [2005], 36–43.   99 *the first prominent Italian to call publicly*: Cornwall [2000], 113.   99 *'because it is not for me as an irredentist'*: Battisti.   101 *Joseph Roth gibed that 'national self-determination'*: Roth, 51–2.   102 *Mario Alberti, a high-profile irredentist*: Gross, 84.   102 *'Growing up in these parts meant growing up'*: Stuparich [1950].   103 *'Trieste is waking rawly'*: Joyce, 8.   104 *'slept the sleep of their prehistory'*: Federzoni.   104 *'Italianism is uncontaminated, full, generous, ardent'*: Barzini [1913].

NINE From Position to Attrition

107 *the men's nerves are shot*: Stuparich's published diary ends on this grim note.   113 *the Supreme Command did not realise*: Faldella quoted by Alliney, 43.

TEN The Dreaming Barbarian

114 *Fabio Todero has exposed this claim as a myth*: Todero [2005].   114 *a fifth of the population*: Cecotti, 67.   114 *'the soldiers look at us as if we were the reason'*: Alliney, 50.   115 *'Everything we hated about Austria'*: Arrigo Arneri, quoted by Fabio Todero [2005].   117 *'a man who lives by exhibiting to travellers his grandmother's corpse'*: Ellmann, 233.   122 *a silly pamphlet predicting that Trieste*: Slataper [1915].   123 *'We thought we knew all about the horrors of war'*: Oblath Stuparich, 32–3.

ELEVEN Walking Shapes of Mud

126 *'Where are the trenches?'*: Salsa, 49. 126/7 *'restore their strength with hot, abundant rations'*: Rocca, 102–3. 134 *'Don't you see I need more dead men'*: Balbi & Viazzi, 245. 134 *49,000 Italian casualties to the 67,000*: Isnenghi & Rochat, 167. 135 *'practically impossible' to destroy*: Alliney, 78.

TWELVE Year Zero

138 *the Ponton brothers, Massimiliano and Giuseppe*: Milocco & Milocco, 119–20. 138 *demonised in the nationalist press as a 'renegade'*: Pavan, 263. 139 *'always supported the Austrian government'*: Milocco & Milocco, 95. 140 *the tranquillity that they have lost'*: Cecotti, 141. 141 *D'Adamo spelled out the implications*: Milocco & Milocco, 75. 141 *'Pro-Austrian elements' were to be removed*: Cecotti, 25, 82. 142 *'The population is still hostile'*: Bonamore. 143 *forcing the local authorities to put on a show*: Milocco & Milocco, 34. 143 *'very hostile' to the men*: From a report by the colonel of the regiment that occupied Colle Santa Lucia, south of Cortina, in May 1915. Vianelli & Cenacchi, xxxv. 143 *'Wonderful! They have come to liberate us'*: Vianelli & Cenacchi, xxxiii. 144 *'the lands that will soon be ours'*: Albertazzi, 35. 144 *Mussolini's journal shows this outlook*: Svolšak [2003], 125. 145 *'They submit with resignation'*: Svolšak [2003], 307. 146 *like 'objects of administration'*: Cecotti, 113, 111. 146 *the verses of Simon Gregorčič*: Pavan, 225. 146 *'They do not stir that sense'*: Giovanni Del Bianco, quoted by Cecotti, 15. 147 *'What I think'*: Pavan, 374. 147 *'the glow of a more radiant future'*: Svolšak [2006], 158.

THIRTEEN A Necessary Holocaust?

148 *Amid the 'glacial silence', metaphors for the situation*: Favetti, 75, 78. 148 *'Is he not a true hero? They are all like this'*: Favetti, 114. 149 *Cadorna's losses in 1915 ran to 400,000*: Procacci [2000], 77. 149 *'going to be massacred'*: The pro-war liberal, Giovanni Amendola, writing to Luigi Albertini of *Corriere della Sera*, 11 November 1915. 149 *'mere garden secateurs'*: Giacomel [2003a], 65. 150 *'a good number of avoidable deaths'*: Barbour. Diary entry for 5 November 1915. 150 *made the soldiers' souls 'flabby'*: Franzina [1999], 69. 150 *'Standing inert with the prospect'*: De Simone, 155–6. 151 *'a necessary holocaust'*: Sema, vol. I, 143. 151 *'Nobody has a clue how to lay wire'*: Col. Douhet, cited by Procacci [2000], 75. 151 *'When told to advance'*: Barbour. Diary for 5 November 1915. 151 *This slack custom endured throughout the war*: The British Official History of operations in Italy recorded that, 'as noon approached Italian officers very obviously became uneasy and wanted to stop any work in hand.' Gladden, 30. 151 *'Shit of every size, shape, colour'*: Roscioni, 127. 151 *'literally a field of filth'*: Gladden, 26. 152 *two soldiers were shot*: Longo, 165 ff. 152 *The joke went around*: Gatti [1997], 117. 153 *Another incident occurred on 20 December*: Alliney, 90–2. 153 *'tendentious or exaggerated rumours'*: From a statement on 8 December 1915 by the Minister of War. Longo, 164. 154 *Sonnino, angling to get Cadorna replaced*: Rocca, 110–11.

154 *Cadorna solicited comments on tactics*: Longo, 170 ff. 155 *'Who would have believed two years ago'*: Rocca, 112. 155 *'intolerance of every judgement'*: De Simone, 144.

FOURTEEN The Return Blow

161 *'I have already reported that'*: Rocca, 119. 162 *'His Excellency the Supreme Commander of the Army'*: This incident was alleged by a parliamentary deputy in December 1917. Camera dei Deputati – Segretariato generale, 128. 163 *Brusati learned from the newspapers*: Rocca, 136. 165 *Ferruccio Fabbrovich, a 19-year-old volunteer*: Todero [2005]. 167 *When General Robertson*: Gatti [1921]. 167 *prove that he was greater than Bonaparte?*: De Simone, 33, citing an unnamed staff officer. 167 *'Why was Cadorna allowed to celebrate'*: Camera dei Deputati – Segretariato generale, 128. 168 *'wretched rivalry' with Falkenhayn*: Weber.

FIFTEEN Victory's Peak

173 *Fearful with reason*: Weber, 199. 173 *brass stars on their uniforms and the metal of their rifles*: Faldella, 45–6. 174 *'white and soft, wriggling towards'*: Longo. 175 *'wrapped in fire and steel'*: Frescura, 114. 176 *a wholly Italian army had defeated*: Pieri [1965], 117.

SIXTEEN Starlight from Violence

180 *not war poems but a soldier's poems*: Cortellessa, 297. Other poems cited in this chapter are from this superb anthology. 181 *'You smile upon the land that is your prey'*: Cortellessa, 78. *Laus vitae* means 'Praise of Life'. 182 *'kiss the noiseless vulva of the sky'*: Cortellessa, 142. 184 *some of the most radical propagandists for war*: Giovanni Papini, Giuseppe Prezzolini and Ardengo Soffici. 184 *'the holy city of modern man'*: Piccioni [1979], 79. 184 *'I don't like war,' he said*: Ungaretti [1981b]. 185 *'I'm a lost soul', he confessed*: Ungaretti [1981b]. 185 *'everything is at stake'*: Mauro. 186 *'a more heroic humanity'*: Piccioni [1979], 81. 186 *'I have never seen bluer waters'*: Mussolini cited by Svolšak [2003], 93. 186 *he petitioned the dictator for favours*: Piccioni [1980], 105. 186 *An excruciating letter came recently to light*: Zingone, 172. 188 *the memory of dead comrades' hands*: Albertazzi, 64; Salsa, 65. 189 *The other night I had to march'*: From a letter to Papini, 29 June 1916. Piccioni [1979] 189 *'if my knapsack is hurting'*: Ungaretti [1981b], 13–14, 38. 189 *'unfit for command' was the verdict*: Ungaretti [1981b]. 189 *'The least thing that would have distinguished'*: Ungaretti [1981a], 132. 190 *his beloved friend Apollinaire*: Piccioni [1980], 82. 190 *'My dear comrades have looked death'*: Piccioni [1980], 192. 190 *the 'community of suffering'*: Piccioni [1979], 86. 190 *'There was no time'*: Piccioni [1979], 86. 191 *'a fly-bitten, dusty little village'*: Dalton, 35. 191 *'I've lain down on muddy stones'*: Piccioni [1980], 95. 191 *'the almost savage exaltation'*: Cortellessa, 176. Ungaretti's *slancio vitale* (vital impulse) translated the French philosopher Henri Bergson's *élan vitale* or life force. See Chapter 20, 'The Gospel of Energy'. 191 *'burst like starlight from violence'*: Cortellessa, 37. 192 *'Where's this all leading? Where?'*: Dario Puccini, 250.

SEVENTEEN Whiteness

193 *'Snow is truly a sign of mourning'*: Ungaretti [1981b], 12.   196 *'No joking, no laughter any more.'*: Giacomel [2003a], 57.   198 *Hans Schneeberger, a 19-year-old ensign*: My account of the mine under the Castelletto draws on Schneeberger's description, 38–109.   201 *the Austrians regained the summit*: On 14 November 1915, Alfredo Panzini recorded a rumour that capturing Col di Lana cost 20,000 lives.   205 *'feats of tremendous ingenuity, talent and organisation'*: Kaldor.

EIGHTEEN Forging Victory

207 *'up here the soul of Italy is as pure'*: Fabio Todero [1999], 68.   207 *sell 350,000 copies a day*: Bosworth [2007], 175.   207 *'tragic and sublime battle'*: Barzini [1913].   208 *'a sort of institution'*: Price, 64.   208 *the 'soul of the country'*: Bricchetto, 170–1.   208 *the censors were 'very polite'*: Ojetti, 100. 208 *'Reaching the hut, we found ourselves'*: Fabio Todero [1999], 77. 208 *'hunters of men'*: Bricchetto, 172.   208 *'It is much easier to attack uphill'*: Bricchetto, 172.   209 *'Armed with an indefinable new strength'*: Isnenghi [2005], 191.   209 *'held by a miracle, or because'*: Bricchetto, 174.   209 *'I got up to the positions'*: Bricchetto, 174–5.   209 *'Ortigara alone has cost us 20,000 men!'*: Bricchetto, 177–8.   210 *'If I see that Barzino, I'll shoot him'*: Prezzolini. 210 *'unacceptable from any point of view'*: De Simone, 140.   211 *'lived in the Staff world, its joys and sorrows'*: Montague, 76–7.   211 *Italian 'system of lies'*: Prezzolini.   212 *'gravely prejudicial to'*: Ventrone [2003], 103.   212 *'their endeavour'*: Gualtiero Castellini of the *Gazzetta di Venezia*.   212 *hardcore interventionists in 1914–15*: Isnenghi [2005], 179–81.   212 *if The Times printed anything he disliked*: Macdonald, 179.   212/3 *'not only the mirror but the soul'*: According to Enzo Bettiza, 57.   213 *boasted of being one of the people most responsible*: Mack Smith [1978], 217.   213 *'Our mission', he intoned*: Fabio Todero [1999], 59.   214 *'In Rome, Cadorna felt troubled – at last!'*: Ojetti, 185. 214 *'the difficulties overcome'*: Gian Luigi Gatti, 39.   214 *hardly journalism at all*: Macdonald, 82–3.   214 *'Thanks to the very complete'*: Macdonald, 84. 215 *'I too inevitably make propaganda'*: Gian Luigi Gatti, 39.   215 *'the public at large was given a false and exaggerated'*: De Simone, 160.   215 *Turati was closer to the mark*: Orlando [1923], 140. Turati said this on 23 February 1918. 216 *'there are certain rules of hygiene'*: Walter Lippmann, quoted by Sevareid, 1. 216 *'emotional sensitivity' made them vulnerable*: Sema in Masau Dan & Porcedda.

NINETEEN Not Dying for the Fatherland

217 *'He began to see me as the worst of enemies'*: Melograni, 197.   217 *a week later he blundered*: Rocca, 176.   218 *a blistering assessment of Cadorna's performance*: Rocca, 179.   220 *'it looked like an attempt at mass suicide'*: Weber, 242.   220 *their only significant gain was a hilltop*: Schindler, 176.   221 *other Habsburg units sometimes donned fezzes*: From an unpublished memoir by Aleksandar Grlić.   222 *with 12 fresh divisions, the Italians*: Weber, 250.

222 *disinformation from Habsburg prisoners*: Sema, vol. II, 33. 224 *a circular to his divisional generals on 17 October*: Rocca, 171–2. 225 *blaming these results on the infantry's lack of fighting spirit*: Cadorna [1921], 318. 225 *equally cynical*: Cadorna [1921], 328. 225 *'the feeling that they had really won'*: Sema, vol. II, 28 225 *a little rhyme that they chanted*: Rocca, 238. 225 *'It is not dying that is the demoralising thing'*: Salsa, 63. 225 *the Duke of Aosta had six men*: Melograni, 218–19. 225 *Capello boasted that his artillery*: Sema, vol. II, 97.

TWENTY The Gospel of Energy

226 *'calm and steadfast'*: Frescura, 139–41. 226 *veterans' memoirs say little about the frontal attack*: This impression is confirmed by Isnenghi, who probably knows the veterans' literature better than anyone. Isnenghi [1997], 285–8. 226 *their casualty rates over the war*: Bosworth [1996], 66. 226 *the 'absurd' moment*: Bultrini & Casarola, 85. 227 *'whole body racked by terror'*: Bultrini & Casarola, 114, 149, 44. 227 *'the blood chills before an assault'*: Favetti, 113. 227 *'Those who have not been through'*: Lussu, 95. 227 *another 25 shot in the buttocks by the carabinieri*: Giacomel 2003a, 105. 227 *'straggler posts' as a barrier*: Sheffield, 74. 227 *'Voices and shouting on all sides'*: Mario Puccini. 228 *'The outcome of war will always'*: Cadorna [1915], 34. 228 *'Infantry that finds itself under fire'*: Cadorna [1915], 28. 228 *'When a soldier lacks the spirit'*: Cadorna to Orlando, 3 November 1917, in Orlando [1960], 501. 228 *'should proceed without such certainty'*: Cadorna [1915], 36, 27. 228 *'waves' of men*: Cadorna [1915], 31–2. 229 *'imbued with a determination'*: British Army General Staff, 141. 229 *'the exercise of human qualities'*: Howard. 229 *the 'triumph' of 'one will'*: Gen. Sir Ian Hamilton, in Howard. 229 *'a conquering state of mind'*: Howard. 229 *'the inner force that cannot be rationally grasped'*: Berlin, 317. 230 *'the political principle of the nineteenth century'*: Arendt, 178. 231 *a 'glorious minority'*: Missiroli [1932], 22. 231 *'did not want to become Italian'*: Mario Puccini. 231 *'Outside the struggle'*: Russo, 12, 47–8, 153–4. 232 *'The Italian middle classes wanted to believe'*: Sforza [1945], 136. 232 *'tranquil, serene, rested'*: Gatti [1997], 162. 232 *Luigi Barzini paid tribute to Cadorna's*: Isnenghi [2005], 191. 232 *'firm and indestructible will'*: Cadorna [1915], Premesse, para. 4. 233 *there were seeds of the later cult in the earlier*: Isnenghi [1999], 16; Ventrone [2003], 219. 233 *Fascism was the vitalist regime par excellence*: Bosworth [2007], 181. 233 *'a permanent revolution, emancipating action'*: Satta, 42. 234 *an architecture of 'fearless audacity'*: Antonio Sant'Elia, quoted by da Costa Mayer. 234 *they enjoyed a following among workers*: Ballo, 369. 234 *'is only for those who know what to do'*: Quotations from Schiavo. 235 *a 'great fraternal sacrifice of all Italians'*: Carrà. 235 *D'Annunzio because he was immoral*: Dos Passos. 235 *'splendid optimism'*: 'splendido ottimismo' was Marinetti's tribute. Marinetti [1987], 73. 235 *twice as many deaths during a week*: De Simone, 176. 236 *'I like your whole campaign'*: Marinetti [1978], 73–4. 236 *'an experience of supreme helplessness'*: Ousby, 84–5. 236 *'restless, aggressive mind'*: Golding's phrase. 236 *'ferocious conquest'*: Tallarico, 108. 236 *'My Futurist ideals, my love of Italy'*: Tallarico, 127. 236 *'The life we lead'*: Boccioni [1971], 318. 237 *'a living gun'*: from W. H. Auden's 1937 poem,

'Wrapped in a yielding air . . .' Auden in the 1930s was brilliantly perceptive about vitalism and its ambiguities.   237 *the Renaissance statue of the warrior Colleoni*: The masterpiece of Andrea del Verrocchio, made around 1480, this equestrian statue stands on a high plinth in Venice.   237 *'nonhuman and mechanical being'*: Marinetti [1971], 71. The comparison is suggested by an art historian, Marianne Martin.   237 *'bursting vitality'*: Tallarico, facing 121; Ballo, 366.   238 *propelled by 'extreme resolution'*: This is how Carlo Salsa interpreted the crouching run of the infantry during an attack. Like Frescura, Salsa was a vitalist intellectual who went on to support Fascism. Salsa, 84; Isnenghi [2005], 239.   238 *a 'good soldier' must lose his identity*: Procacci [2000], 81.   238 *Fascist myth of a 'new Man'*: Gentile [1986], 115.   238 *'brutalised and cowardly race'*: From Boccioni's Open Letter to Papini, dated 1 March 1914. Boccioni [1971], 74.

TWENTY-ONE Into a Cauldron

240 *According to Cadorna*: Cadorna [1921], 329.   242 *his memorandum outlining Allied options for 1917*: The relevant portion is excerpted in Lloyd George, 1422–5.   242 *Rodd reflected that it was a moment*: 'Cadorna need not have considered the obligation to return the guns as an insuperable obstacle, inasmuch as, if the Austrian defences had been successfully broken, the operations would obviously not have been arrested and the enemy man-power on the Western front would probably have been proportionately diminished.' Rodd, chapter XIII, 'Rome 1916–1917'.   243 *What has not been clear is the source of his conviction*: In his exhaustive study of Lloyd George's wartime premiership, John Grigg merely observes that his 'thoughts turned to the idea of an offensive on the Italian front' during December 1916. Grigg, 25.   243 *'indifference to military opinion'*: Robertson, 203.   243 *well regarded by Victor Emanuel*: Bosworth [1979], 265.   245 *four times more Allied guns per kilometre*: Dalton, 29.   245 *during the Tenth Battle, the siege artillery*: Dalton, 29.   245 *the 'supreme Leader'*: Rocca, 191.   246 *new recruits protested at the draft*: Sema, vol. II, 70.   246 *'subversive elements' might stir up discontent*: Sema, vol. II, 70.   246 *'the gross misconduct of the Germans'*: Secretary of State Lansing. Seymour [1935], 143.   248 *'hot-tempered and not easily soothed'*: Lloyd George, vol. 4, chapter 61.   248 *'unjust and unrealistic'*: Rothwell, 117.   248 *'imminent operations'. Boselli gave his word*: Sema, vol. II, 101.   252 *'very slight progress'*: Ojetti, 378.   254 *'fought well until their generals'*: Wilks & Wilks [2001], 30.   255/6 *the official bulletin will say otherwise*: The Official Bulletin of the Supreme Command, 29 May 1917.   256 *'battle leaves in the sensual man'*: D'Annunzio [2002], 360.   256 *800 officers and men of the Puglie Brigade*: Gatti [1997], 44.   258 *'They did not rebel'*: Gatti [1997], 48, 71.   258 *It might carry on like this for months*: Gatti [1997], 48.   259 *'He is perfectly calm, serene'*: Gatti [1997], 76.   260 *The Supreme Command blurred the scale*: De Simone, 178.   260 *'proper fiasco'*: Cadorna [1967], 207.   260 *The infantry, he complained, did not attack*: Gatti [1997], 113; *'slancio'* is from Cadorna [1967], 206.   260 *a new anti-war song*: 'Mio nonno parti per l'Ortigara, / Dicianovenne, vestito da Alpino ', by Chiara Riondino. Text available at http://www.obiezione.it/antiwarsongs.html, accessed in May 2007.

TWENTY-TWO Mystical Sadism

261 *'Death to D'Annunzio!'*: Alatri. 262 *'helmets, shreds of brain'*: Bonadeo [1995], 132. 262 *'You are peasants*: D'Annunzio [2005], 718–24. 262 *'The summary justice of the bullet'*: Directive dated 28 September 1915. Procacci [2000], 52; De Simone, 206. 262 *He openly deplored the courts' reluctance*: This was on 22 March 1916. 263 *'unworthy of an army that upholds'*: Procacci [2000], 52. 263 *a letter to Salandra in January 1916*: Procacci [2000], 52. 263 *not unknown in the French army*: Watt, 92, 201. 263 *nine men of the Ravenna Brigade*: Melograni, 296–8. 264 *gave a statement to the commission of inquiry*: Commissione di inchiesta, vol. 2, 359–65. 266 *'almost universally treated with respect'*: Smith, 183. 266 *shot 54 men in May 1917*: From Cadorna's letter to Boselli, 13 June 1917. Procacci [2000], 50–1. 266 *a piece of doggerel was scrawled*: De Simone, 166. 267 *'If they do not noisily shoot ten or twelve cowards'*: Ojetti, 308. 267 *'The minister of war has assured me'*: De Simone, 284. Ugo Ojetti, usually discreet to a fault, called Graziani 'that lunatic'. Ojetti, 424. 268 *can only be guessed at*: A Socialist deputy claimed after the war that the number exceeded 4,000. De Simone, 287. 268 *'a century behind the times'*: Rocca, 224. 269 *'on a vast scale'*: USSME, 653. 269 *the evidence, which is incomplete*: Offenstadt. 269 *Punishment was harsher than*: Franzina [2003], 130. 270 *'They don't fight with pride, no'*: Forcella & Monticone, 43. 270 *'because [only] a minority wanted it'*: Forcella & Monticone, 186. 270 *'by universal consent the whole nation wanted it'*: Forcella & Monticone, 186–78. 271 *a series of astonishing letters*: USSME, 653–62. 271 *civilians living* outside *the war zone*: Procacci [2006], 299. 271 *some 900,000 employees were in this position*: Zamagni, 219. 271 *'only children believe the newspapers'*: Salandra to Sonnino, quoted by Monticone [1972]. 271 *overwhelmingly, the ones who did the dying*: Giuliano Procacci, 235. 271 *a smouldering sense of injustice*: Procacci [1992]. 272 *'looks more like useless slaughter every day'*: Rocca, 246. 272 *plot to carry out*: Camera dei Deputati – Segretariato generale, 185. The deputy was Marcello Soleri. 272 *General Giardino, the minister of war*: Melograni, 350. 272 *denied having ever wanted a 'reign of terror'*: Melograni, 351. 273 *'stems from the fact that the Supreme Command'*: Calderoni, 182. 273 *a decree to criminalise 'defeatism'*: Bianchi [2006], 303. 273 *Complete data on military justice*: Cadorna [1967], 205; Forcella & Monticone, 441–2. 274 *real total may run to several thousand*: De Simone guesses that at least 2,000 were summarily shot between May 1915 and 24 October 1917, plus a further 5,000 among the troops retreating pell-mell after Caporetto. De Simone, 270. 274 *respected even in times of crisis*: Sheffield, 7. 275 *Cadorna's 'mystical sadism'*: Sforza [1945], 135. 275 *so widespread in summer 1917*: De Simone, 78. 275 *desertion rates doubled during 1917*: Cappellano & Carbone. 275 *an internal report in March 1918*: Procacci [2000], 83. 275 *Bruna Bianchi, no admirer of Cadorna, argues*: Bianchi [2003], 131. 275 *evidence that soldiers' morale was harmed*: for example De Simone, 198. 275 *The French army*: Watt, 170. 275 *Germany mobilised*: Jahr. 276 *Giovanna Procacci argues that the archive*: Procacci [2000], 97–105. 276 *'the working class had never shared'*: Procacci [1992], 170. 276 *relations*

between state and society: Procacci [2006], 301. 276 *'inadmissible'*: Calderoni, 166.

TWENTY-THREE Another Second of Life

277 *'grievously impressed'*: Martini, 941. 279 *'They do not know what a torrent'*: Gatti [1997], 134. 280 *the Emperor reportedly pledged that the next operation*: Weber, 234. 281 *'has held everything together'*: Gatti [1997], 159. 282 *Italians had taken 166,000 casualties*: De Simone, 128. 282 *'I feel something collapsing inside me'*: Gatti [1997], 161. 283 *What will happen, he mused, when*: Gatti [1997], 159. 283 *'Trieste must therefore be saved'*: Hindenburg, 285. 283 *'not out of love for a just and terrible war'*: Faldella, 74, 73.

TWENTY-FOUR The Traitor of Carzano

285 *'We are ready to help you'*: Pettorelli Lalatta, 22. My account of the Finzi–Pivko episode is drawn from this book by Finzi, who changed his name to Pettorelli Lalatta after the war. 288 *'I regret that somebody wished to cast'*: Pettorelli Lalatta, 118. 290 *'antiquated'*: Wickham Steed, vol. II, 59. 291 *'an obstinate, unimaginative man'*: Sforza [1966], 127. 291 *Sonnino despised propaganda*: Sforza [1944]. 291 *'violently anti-Yugoslav'*: Tosi, 96–8. 291 *wrongly assuming they were infinitely devoted*: Sema, vol. 2, 75. 291 *'mad with terror'*: Cicchino & Olivo, 150. 293 *Sonnino called on Asquith*: Asquith.

TWENTY-FIVE Caporetto: The Flashing Sword of Vengeance

294 *the greatest army in Italy since the Caesars*: Rocca, 3. 295 *'re-establish the links'*: Strachan, 182. 295 *Russians discovered other elements*: Stevenson, 165. 295 *'crumbling or incomplete'*: Griffith, 195. See also 53–7, 59–64, 97–100, 194, 196. 296 *recognised a century earlier by Napoleon*: Reynolds, 241. 296 *'as bad as could be imagined'*: Ludendorff, 212. 297 *the attack should proceed along the valley floors*: Weber, 378. 297 *over a six-day period, to avoid alerting*: Wilks & Wilks [2001], 16. 298 *'in excellent spirits'*: Gatti [1997], 196. 299 *'as if the mountains themselves'*: Krafft von Dellmensingen, quoted by Pavan, 104. 299 *'our offensive intentions'*: Wilks & Wilks [2001], 37. 300 *'the thunderbolt of the counter-offensive'*: Wilks & Wilks [2001], 39. 300 *Cadorna unambiguously rejected*: According to Gatti's diary for 20 October. Gatti [1997], 196. 301 *fewer than half of the division's battalions*: Wilks & Wilks [2001], 41. 301 *saw soldiers at their posts*: Comisso. 303 *'to the point of cretinism'*: Roscioni, 135. 303 *'that stuttering idiot of a King'*: Dombroski, 27. 303 *he had let another officer take*: Gorni, 163. 304 *the last Italian veteran of the Twelfth Battle*: From the *'Cime e trincee'* website http://www.cimeetrincee.it/delfino.htm, accessed June 2007. Also: Paolo Rumiz, 'Quei maledetti giorni che vissi a Caporetto', *La Repubblica*, 24 May 2005; Bultrini & Casarola, 33–6; Elena Percivaldi, interview with Borroni, October 2004, *'In Memoriam'* website, http://blog.libero.it/grandeguerra1418/, accessed June 2007. 305 *they start throwing away their rifles*: Frescura, 249. 305 *'to welcome their German liberators'*: Krafft von Dellmensingen, quoted by Pavan, 111. 307 *'The country*

has the right to know': De Simone, 38. 308 *'finds us strong and well prepared'*: Gatti [1997], 202. 308 *'Napoleon himself could not'*: Gatti [1997], 204. 310 *They walk the plank*: Ungarelli, 29–48. 311 *'The men are not fighting'*: De Simone, 45. 312 *'Why doesn't someone shoot them?'*: De Simone, 58. 315 *'infantry, alpini, gunners, endlessly'*: Frescura, 254, 253. 316 *'the panic blast ran through'*: Winthrop Young, 322, 323. 316 *'in good order, unbroken and undefeated'*: Quotations from Lt. Hugh Dalton, then serving with a British battery that was retreating with the Third Army. Dalton, 110, 108. 316 as if they had found the solution: De Simone, 74. From Freya Stark's diary, 29 October: 'Only the officers look unhappy about the war.' 317 *'Then we're going too,' someone said*: De Simone, 75. 318 *not 'very vigorous in combat'*: Wilks & Wilks [2001], 140. 318 *affirmations of complete confidence*: Gatti [1997], 212. 318 *'almost deserted with broken windows'*: Wilks & Wilks [2001], 121. 319 *'After five days of fighting'*: De Simone, 98. 319 *'This is how he repays your valour!'*: Cicchino & Olivo, 233–4. 319 *'The wooden bridge was nearly'*: Hemingway, 234. 320 *'Anger was washed away'*: Hemingway, 242. 320/1 *Ludendorff was not yet convinced*: On 3 November, Ludendorff stated that the River Piave had to be the final objective of the offensive. Stevenson, 379. 321 *'The Italians seem a wretched people'*: Winter, 26. 321 *'ablaze from end to end'*: From the diary of Giuseppina Bauzon, of Versa, quoted by Fabi [1991b], 108. 321 *ready to trust their troops to the bravery of the Italian soldiers but*: Sonnino's diary, quoted by Morselli. 322 *'At the last the great victory'*: Hindenburg, 287. 322 *Krauss accused Boroević*: Rothenberg [1976], 208. 322 *'the annihilating mentality'*: Pieri [1986], 355. 322 *these works were hardly in hand*: Pieri [1986], 315. 323 *loathed his tall, handsome cousin*: Bosworth [1979], 15. 323 *land, home, family and honour – in that order*: Minniti, 31. 324 *he once explained to the King*: De Simone, 96. 324 *'almost nobody remembered'*: Cadorna [1967]. 325 *a fist punching through a barrier*: Weber, 382. 325 *'a shaped charge'*: Ullman & Wade, 57. Available at http://www.dodccrp.org/files/pdf/Ullman_Shock.pdf, accessed in May 2007. 325 *Probably he was scoring points*: This is Isnenghi's argument in Cimprič. 325 *parroted the conspiracy theory*: Cornwall [2000], 75. 325 *'contributed to the disaster'*: Buchan, 326. For a recent contention that 'a widespread attitude of defeatism' was partly responsible for Caporetto, see Jonathan Dunnage, *Twentieth Century Italy: A Social History* (Harlow: Longman, 2002), 44. Dunnage, however, concedes that 'bad military leadership and training were equally to blame'. 326 *'The fate of Italy is being decided'*: Minniti, 106. 326 *many officials believed*: Procacci [1999], 134. 326 *the essence of Caporetto lay*: Isnenghi & Rochat, 396. 326 *'a people of stragglers'*: Revelli. 326 *'great even in misfortune'*: Piazzoni. 327 *One valiant historian*: Fabio Todero [1999], 22. The historian was Fernando Agnoletti. 327 *'a reverse'*: Preface to Alberti. 327 *it was a time for myths, not history*: Gatti [1997], xii. 327 *a spontaneous rebellion against the war*: De Simone, 46.

TWENTY-SIX Resurrection

328 *Allied support*: Wilks & Wilks [1998], 34–5. 328 *'extravagant fervour'*: Captions at the Royal Fusiliers Museum in the Tower of London. 328 *'red tiled*

roofs, pale pink': Blackburn. 328 *'absolute joy'*: Arthur, 103. 329 *'we found the troops getting pelted'*: L. I. L. Ferguson. 329 *'flatter than you would think'*: Acland. 329 *'a mighty expanse of water'*: Gladden, 67. 329 *'some seven miles long'*: Gladden, 29. 329 *'played in the waters'*: Acland. 329 *'we could sit around'*: Gladden, 38. 330 *men who were judged less reliable*: Schindler, 278. 330 *he devolved more operational decision-making*: Procacci [2000], 76. 330 *no objection to the formation*: Gratton, 24. 331 *An internal report in November*: Gian Luigi Gatti, 55. 332 *'The best system for fighting*: Gian Luigi Gatti, 71. 332 *'the conviction of the absolute'*: Gian Luigi Gatti, 69. 332 *'the flower of the Italian'*: Gian Luigi Gatti, 122. 332 *'Every movement in civic life'*: Gian Luigi Gatti, 72. 332 *'our growing superiority'*: Gian Luigi Gatti, 133. 332 *exhibited around the country, while propaganda*: Procacci [1989b]. 332 *'a profound transformation'*: Labita. 332 *'To be or not to be'*: Orlando [1923], 123. 333 *united in dedication to a supreme purpose*: Procacci [1999], 323. 333 *a war of political adventure turned*: Minniti, 25. 333 *The press bayed for strong government*: Procacci [1999], 309. 333 *158 pro-war deputies formed*: Pieri [1965], 171. 333 *A man from Viterbo got three months*: Procacci [2006], 302. 333 *Industrial action continued throughout June*: Procacci [1999], 138. 334 *a gesture that backfired*: Procacci [1989a] and Procacci [1989b]. 334 *'repression of dissent'*: Corner & Procacci. 334 *'anyway everyone knows'*: Labanca, Procacci, Tomassini, 31. 334 *'the arrival of the Austrians'*: Corner & Procacci. 334 *an incident at a primary school*: This episode occurred in October 1917, just before or after Caporetto. Franzina [2003], 13. 334 *'military model'*: Procacci [2006], 284. 335 *not much different from the Bourbon tyrants*: Monticone [1982], 37. 335 *Dallolio, an effective Under-Secretary*: Isnenghi & Rochat, 300. 335 *Francesco Nitti, a deputy*: Forsyth, 67–8. 335 *by no means inevitable*: L. Segreto quoted by Zamagni, 221. 335 *pricing policy was slack*: Forsyth, 85. 335 *industries had incentives*: Zamagni, 35, 221, 223, 225. 335 *aeronautical industry grew*: Toniolo, 129. 335 *'now looked upon Italian war aims'*: Rothwell, 158. 336 *'made no mention whatever of our aspirations'*: Sonnino, 252. 336 *'it is perfectly hopeless trying to get Sonnino'*: Seymour [1928], vol. 3, 287, 286, 290. 337 *urged by the American ambassador*: Zivojinovic, 95. 337 *'More and more the war has ceased'*: Lippmann. 337 *'the completion of her national unity'*: From a speech in February 1918. Orlando [1923], 122. 337 *'most cynical' of all the secret treaties*: H. W. Massingham, 'The Diplomacy of the Knock-out Blow', *The Nation*, 9 February 1918. Quoted by le Cornu. 338 *his 'paltry masterpiece'*: Sforza [1944], 46. 338 *refused to sanction the use of propaganda*: Sforza [1944], 49. 339 *persuaded Albertini to help organise*: Mack Smith [1978], 214. 339 *'inexplicable and grievous misunderstanding'*: Orlando [1923], 174–5. 340 *'The Italians and Yugoslavs are'*: Cornwall [2000], 290. 340 *only one in every thousand*: 3,800 from a total of 3,800,000. Melograni, 529. 340 *Wilsonian ideals filled a vacuum*: Melograni, 526 ff, quoting Harold Lasswell, *World Revolutionary Propaganda: a Chicago Study* (New York: Knopf, 1939), 114–15. 341 *'All branches of the Slav race'*: Cornwall [2000], 265, 323. 341 *'a free and united Yugoslav state'*: Cornwall [2000], 338. 341 *Orlando probably encouraged this*: Mack Smith [1978], 215. 341 *'consonant with the principles'*: Mamatey,

314; Lederer, 40. 342 *Boroević did not believe*: Bauer, 111. 342 *Some 200,000 Hungarian soldiers had deserted*: Bernardi, 115. 343 *'mass rallies at which oaths for unity'*: Cornwall [2000], 213. 343 *'no longer moved by incessant'*: Cornwall [2000], 281. 344 *Boroević openly criticised the shortages*: Blašković, 396. 344 *'For this, gentlemen, could well be'*: Bernardi, 128. 344 *despite everything, Habsburg morale ran high*: Schindler quotes General August von Cramon, chief German liaison officer with the Austrian army: 'The troops' offensive spirit was the best.' Schindler, 283. 344 *may have been time-expired*: Blašković, 396. 344 *The Austrian gunners only had the advantage*: Dalton, 206–7. 345 *'Hold your positions, I implore you'*: Bernardi, 129. 346 *the German high command stepped in*: Bauer, 122. 347 *'the only proper national battle'*: Minniti, 69. 349 *'the mountains were bare'*: Neža Rejec, quoted by Fortunat Černilogar, 217. 349 *'a mass of famished barbarians'*: Horvath-Mayerhofer, 153. 349 *'heterogeneous masses'*: Türr. 350 *images of 'Italia' had from the start*: This was observed by Robert Musil, the Austrian novelist, then serving in the Trentino. His sentence continued, 'who actually does not look Italian at all'. Musil [1999]. 350 *civilian morale rose*: Cornwall [2000], 398. 351 *'most rapes were carried out'*: Ceschin [2006b], 179. 351 *people believed that time was on their side*: Cornwall [2000], 361. 351 *'an air of utter emptiness'*: Gladden, 200, 202. 352 *when the war was already over*: Most of this information comes from Procacci [2000], a ground-breaking study. 352 *shrank from 650,000 to 400,000*: Cornwall [2000], 406. 352 *The average body weight*: Cornwall [2000], 406. 353 *'We have been officially notified'*: Cornwall [2000], 278. 353 *normal language in the newspapers*: Cornwall [2000], 286. 353 *'Most of the men are apathetic'*: Cornwall [1997]. 354 *German ambassador estimated*: Cornwall [2000], 429. 354 *'internal political questions'*: Rothenberg [1976], 214, 215. 354 *Foch asked Diaz to support*: Wilks & Wilks [1998], 90–1. 355 *'certain events of utmost importance'*: This reply was sent by Secretary of State Lansing on 19 October 1918. Albrecht-Carrié [1938], 350. 355 *Orlando's government explained coolly*: Zivojinovic, 66. 356 *were to await developments*: Wilks & Wilks [1998], 129. 356/7 *'an honourable peace'*: Schindler, 296. 358 *on the 26th, he informed*: Falls, 177. 358 *'no success'*: This is the judgement of the official Italian war history. Wilks & Wilks [1998], 160. 358 *British corps commander had proposed*: Wilks & Wilks [1998], 189. 358 *'A string of small boats had been'*: Gladden, 166–7. 358 *Gordon Highlanders, rowed by Venetian gondoliers*: Dalton, 242. 359 *'not many Austrians stayed'*: Wilks & Wilks [1998], 147. 359 *not an outcome that has won much recognition*: Gladden, 157; Wilks & Wilks [1998], 147, 153–4; Falls, 173. 359 *'A new carefree attitude was'*: Gladden, 178. 359 *Some reserve units refused*: Wilks & Wilks [1998], 151–2. 359 *'He was informed'*: Wilks & Wilks [1998], 152. 360 *since 14 October, when*: Primicerj, 50. 360 *the army in Italy was finished*: Rothenberg [1976], 217. 360 *'a semblance of order'*: Fischer. 360 *Civilians emerged from their cottages*: Testimony of Lt. Col. Alberto Genova and Capt. Alberto D'Isidoro, in Genova, 510. 361 *'Caporetto in reverse'*: Gratton, 27. 361 *'Now it's goodbye, Caporetto'*: Minniti, 24. 361 *Karl refused on principle*: Rothenberg [1976], 216. 362 *'knew literally nothing'*: Mamatey, 360. 362 *'in headlong retreat'*: Dalton, 256. 362 *Austrian rule on the Adriatic*

Sea: Fraccaroli, 76. 362 *last Habsburg units still fighting*: Rothenberg [1976], 217. 362 *ordered to move as many intact units*: Primicerj, 243. 362 *'the last possible moment'*: Sondhaus [2000]. 363 *even – 7,000 of them – Italian*: Deák. Research into the tens of thousands of Habsburg Italians who served in the Austrian army began only recently. Its latest fruit is Roberto Todero's study of Triestine Italians who fought for the Empire: *Dalla Galizia all'Isonzo. Storia e storie dei soldati triestini nella Grande Guerra* (Udine: Gaspari, 2006). 363 *the Italians held 430,000 Habsburg prisoners*: Wilks & Wilks [1998], 172. 364 *'we talked to them as to old friends'*: Fischer. 364 *Supreme Command wondered at one point*: Cortellessa, 25–6. 365 *'After fifteen centuries, an Italian army'*: Pieri [1986], 324–6. 365 *the myth that Italians were incapable of waging war*: Pieri [1965], 198. 365 *'Just when we learned how'*: Pieri [1986], 151. 365 *'When I compare my fate'*: Bernardi, 193. 365 *Victory Bulletin, issued on 4 November*: See O'Brien [2004] for an excellent explication, 157–9. 366 *he had to redeem this one*: Fraccaroli, 71. 366 *'such ruins were unimaginable'*: Lucio Fabi in Medeot, 109. 366 *'The dream has come true'*: Baldi. 367 *'received with open hostility'*: Lederer, 58, 106, 63. 368 *a plan drawn up by Badoglio*: Lederer, 71–75, 66. 368 *marched on and on, beyond the Carso*: Testimony of Capt. Alberto D'Isidoro, quoted in Genova, 480. 368 *France made Fiume the logistics base*: Lederer, 58, 68, 205.

TWENTY-SEVEN From Victory to Disaster

369 *'There are things awaiting us'*: Wilson, vol. 53, 598. 369 *'to produce a plan of permanent peace'*: Seymour [1951]. 369 *a snippet from their session on 13 May*: Mantoux, vol. II, 56. 370 *'the crushing weight'*: Huddleston, 103. 370 *'a new international morality'*: Wilson quoted by Bonsal, 103. 371 *'obliging, courteous and impossible'*: Bonsal, 100. 371 *'all things to all men, very Italian'*: MacMillan, 298. 371 *'very hawklike, ferocious'*: Seymour [1965], 273. 371 *the government stopped treating*: Mamatey, 359–60. 371 *one of the greatest that history*: Orlando [1923], 268. 371 *A fortnight later, he told*: Orlando [1923], 276–7. 371 *'has revealed a power of action'*: Orlando [1923], 331. 372 *'militarily useless and dangerous'*: This was Cadorna's judgement, though not his alone. Mack Smith [1978], 215. 372 *'war veterans, conspirators'*: Colapietra, 273. 372 *'that unmistakable voice'*: Borgese, 152–3. 372 *reversed its attitude to the League*: Mack Smith [1978], 223–6. 373 *'the first act of organised'*: O'Brien, [2004] 28, citing Mimmo Franzinelli, ed., *Squadristi. Protagonisti e tecniche della violenza fascista 1919–1922* (Milan: Mondadori, 2003). 373 *silent in all the languages he spoke*: Cervone, 260. 373 *Orlando, he wrote acidly*: Sforza [1966], 162. 373 *'never was a foreign minister'*: Sforza [1944], 48. 373 *'unparliamentary language'*: Wickham Steed, quoted by Kernek. 373 *Sonnino, on the other hand, wanted*: Albrecht-Carrié [1950], 123. 373 *no chance to address the waiting crowds*: Albrecht-Carrié [1938], 83–4. 373 *'how far he could disappoint'*: Wilson, vol. 53, 697. 373 *'disastrous concession'*: Bonsal, 104. See also Nicolson, 170. 373 *'insufficient study'*: Seymour [1928], vol. 4, 450 ff. 374 *'stench of peace'*: Cicchino & Olivo, 282. 374 *'that mishmash of southern Slavs'*: MacMillan, 304. 374 *'acute starvation'*: Hoover,

107. *374 officials still obstructed American aid*: Hoover, 174. *374 'that most Italian city'*: Orlando [1923], 339. *374 'not very important'*: Bonsal, 247. *374 the King urged Orlando*: Burgwyn, 274. *375 '100,000 foreigners'*: Mantoux, vol. I, 277, 279. *375 Sonnino said*: Mantoux, vol. I, 285–6, 288–9. *375 he would abandon the Conference*: Lansing [1922]. *375 suggested that provisional acceptance*: Mantoux, vol. I, 290–1, 293–5. *376 'moment of agitation will be followed'*: Mantoux, vol. I, 329. *376 'cast doubt'*: Mantoux, vol. I, 358. *376 'white with anger'*: Hoover, 206. *376 the old man pulled out a list*: Sforza [1944]. *376 'They always believe that we'*: Mantoux, entry for 2 May 1919. *377 'catastrophe'*: Mantoux, vol. I, 469. *377 'they will soon come back'*: Mantoux, vol. I, 286. *377 'a compensation for the enormous'*: Slovene–Italian Relations 1880–1956, 126. *377 think that Wilson sympathised*: Lansing [1922], 228. *377 some Italians from Fiume, brought to Paris*: Zivojinovic, 269. *377 a spontaneous hypocrite who*: Orlando [1960], 353. *377 The war had cost 148 billion lire*: Information in this footnote comes from Giuliano Procacci, 230–7; Schindler, 315–6; Toniolo, 124; Zamagni, 210 ff. *378 'At the very outset we shall have followed'*: Wilson, vol. 57, 271. *378 'It seems to the Italians'*: On 13 May. Mantoux, vol. II, 54. *378 'self-determination is applicable'*: Bonsal, 97. *378 Wilson sought to renew American faith*: I owe this insight to Kernek. *379 It was hopeless*: Seymour [1965], 247; Mantoux, vol. II, 323; Sonnino, 338. *379 he withdrew from Albania*: Lederer, 290–1. *379 enjoyed deploring the Italians*: Mantoux, vol. II, 571. *380 'Yugoslavs, clericals and socialists'*: Canavero, 18–19. *380 'were treated like conquered provinces'*: Mowrer, 351. *380 'the new enemy that stabs'*: Hametz, 22. *380 'The abolition of personal rights'*: Quotation and information from Salvemini [1934]. *380 'attempted to realise a programme'*: Slovene–Italian Relations 1880–1956, 135. *380 'atmosphere of war'*: a 'Fascist journalist' in Corriere della Sera, 4 April 1931, as quoted by Salvemini [1934], 20. *380 'No Italian who remains'*: Salvemini [1934], 19. *381 killed 689,000 Italian soldiers*: Schindler, 316. This includes the estimated 100,000 Italians who died in prisoner of war camps. (Procacci [2000], 78.) Other statistics are from Schindler, 324, 316; Bosworth [2007], 164. *381 perpetuated the prewar and wartime divisions*: Giuliano Procacci, 237. *381 victory was mutilated by Italy's own leaders*: Pieri [1965], 199. *382 'unprecedented miracle of psychopathic'*: Borgese, 159. *382 drove 200,000–300,000 Italians*: Slovene–Italian Relations 1880–1956, 159.

TWENTY-EIGHT End of the Line

383 'everything we say': Stevens, 302. *383 foragers camped in old tunnels and dug-outs*: Sacco, Monticone & Rigoni Stern, 105. *383 someone dies every year*: According to staff at the war museum in Kobarid. On one estimate, the war left 12,000 tonnes of Italian lead embedded in the Slovenian landscape. Pirc & Budkovič. *384 'the language of the army, in death as in life'*: Abel. *385 'exhilaration of extreme situations'*: Comisso. *385 soldiers in other theatres experienced*: See, e.g., Private Fred Hodges' memories in van Emden, 304. *385 'on every one of those nights'*: Musil [1995], 135–6. *385 Italian historians regret that*: Bonadeo [1989], 38; Fabio Todero [1999]. *386 'That's not all there is to war*': Rigoni Stern, 181. Lussu's book has been translated as *Sardinian Brigade* (London: Prion Books, 2000). Francesco Rosi's film, called *Uomini contro*, was released in 1970. 386 *valley seemed to set sail*: Cortellessa, 465. 386 *'a dirty trick which'*: Sassoon. 386 *'The First World War was idiotic'*: Arthur, 105. The other book of interviews is by van Emden. 387 *the 'farthest recesses of our soul'*: These quotations are from Bultrini & Casarola. 387 *'first true collective national experience'*: Minniti, 127; also Giuliano Procacci, 236. 387 *'left as a Friulan'*: Romano, 29. 387 *'a profound moral scission'*: Salvatorelli [1970], 188. 388 *an experience marked by brutality*: Malaparte [1967]. 388 *'trenchocracy, a new and better élite'*: O'Brien, [2004] 116. 388 *'Most veterans were convinced'*: Gentile [1986], 112. 388 *According to Fascist myth*: Bosworth [2002], 170. 388 *then paid homage at the tomb*: Schindler, 321. 388 *'sacred history'*: Gibelli, 361. 389 *'the glorious epic of the great Redemption'*: Gentile [1996], 38–9. 389 *New accounts of such ghostly resurrection*: Cortellessa, 356–7. 389 *until dawn dispersed them*: This story is told by Mario Rigoni Stern in his preface to Frescura, 5. 389 *'We are for the ephemeral'*: Carrà. 390 *'Even the dead will not be safe'*: Benjamin [1979], 257. 390 *into a holy family*: Canal. 390 *'It had been a great misfortune'*: Levi, 119. 391 *'the anonymous flesh of the infantry'*: Rebora, in a letter dated 28 November 1915. 391 *'the simple and primitive souls'*: O'Brien [2004], 117. 391 *'Who are these valiant souls'*: Fabio Todero [2003], 231. 391 *'I did not know why there was a war'*: Pte. Pasquale Costanzo, quoted by Bultrini & Casarola, 65. 391/2 *'how a man can create a new soul'*: Malaparte [1981], 54, 65. 392 *'the purity of intention and certainty'*: Ungarelli, 110–14. 393 *'the noonday heat without trenches'*: Gadda [1963]. 393 *a swipe at Hemingway*: 'Hemingway's was not the only eye that saw Italian soldiers marching to the trenches through the mire and driving rain'. Ungarelli, 110. 393 *'break the circle of silence'*: Roscioni, 126. 393 *nobody in the Europe of August 1914*: Fussell, 21. 394 Fell in the course of combat *would suffice*: Roscioni, 129. 394 *'I never use big words'*: This was the future historian, Adolfo Omodeo. Bonadeo [1989], 95–6. 394 *Father Gemelli argued*: Labita. 394 *Panzini wondered with sharp flippancy*: Panzini, 270.

APPENDIX Free from the Alps to the Adriatic

395 *'Until Italy's eastern frontiers'*: Marušič, 140. 397 *wrote privately that Italian nationalism*: Elrod, 152. 398 *'a bureaucratic and logistical'*: Wawro, 87. 398 *'for the honour of Italy'*: Wawro, 94. Other quotations in this paragraph are from Wawro, 95 and 27. 399 *ignoring his appeals*: Wawro, 110. 399 *'as though they could not order one another'*: Mack Smith [1971], 315. 401 *'by an Austrian squadron half its size'*: Wawro, 279. 403 *'must obtain an optimal redefinition'*: Wawro, 281. 404 *'Whether there will be peace or war'*: Zaniboni Ferino.

Bibliography

Dates in entries refer to the editions consulted, not to first publication.

Abel, Kornel, *Carso* (Milan: A. Corticelli, 1935) (trans. from *Karst: Ein Buch vom Isonzo*, 1934)

Acland, A., papers in the Department of Documents, Imperial War Museum, London

Addestramento della fanteria al combattimento: Istruzione della recluta (Rome: Tipografia del Senato, 1916)

Agnese, Gino, *Vita di Boccioni* (Florence: Camunia, 1996)

Alatri, Paolo, *D'Annunzio* (Turin: UTET, 1983)

Albertazzi, Amleto, *L'Inferno carsico* (Bologna: Licinio Cappelli, 1933)

Alberti, Gen. Adriano, preface by Benito Mussolini, *Testimonianze straniere sulla Guerra Italiana 1915–1918* (Rome: Ministero della Guerra, 1933)

Albertini, Luigi, *I giorni di un liberale* (Bologna: Il Mulino, 2000)

Albrecht-Carrié, René [1938], *Italy and the Paris Peace Conference* (New York: Columbia University Press)

– [1939], 'The Present Significance of the Treaty of London of 1915', *Political Science Quarterly*, vol. 54, no. 3 (September)

– [1950], *Italy from Napoleon to Mussolini* (New York: Columbia University Press)

Alessi, Rino, *Dall'Isonzo al Piave: Lettere clandestine di un corrispondente di guerra* (Milan: Mondadori, 1966)

Alliney, Guido, *Mrzli vrh: Una montagna in guerra* (Chiari: Nordpress, 2000)

Apih, Elio, et al., *Trieste* (Bari: Laterza, 1988)

Ara, A., 'Bissolati, Leonida', *Dizionario biografico degli Italiani*, vol. 10 (Rome: Istituto della Enciclopedia Italiana, 1968)

Ara, Angelo, and Claudio Magris, *Trieste: Un'identità di frontiera* (Turin: Einaudi, 1987)

Arendt, Hannah, *The Burden of Our Time* (London: Secker & Warburg, 1951)

Arthur, Max, *Last Post: The Final Word from our First World War Soldiers* (London: Weidenfeld & Nicolson, 2005)

Ashworth, Tony, *Trench Warfare, 1914–1918: The Live and Let Live System* (London and Basingstoke: Macmillan, 1980)

Asquith, H. H., Papers (Shelfmark: MS. Asquith 32, fol. 176), Bodleian Library, University of Oxford

Babington, Anthony, *For the Sake of Example: Capital Courts Martial 1914–1920* (London: Penguin, 2002)

Balbi, Marco, and Luciano Viazzi, *Spunta l'alba del seidici giugno* . . . (Milan: Mursia, 2000)

Baldi, Dedy, ed., *Valentino Coda: Tribuno-Soldato-Fascista* (Milan: Moderna, 1935)

Ballo, Guido, *Boccioni: La vita e l'opera* (Milan: Il Saggiatore, 1964)

Banac, Ivo, *The National Question in Yugoslavia: Origins, History, Politics* (Ithaca: Cornell University Press, 1984)

Barbour, G. B., papers in the Department of Documents, Imperial War Museum, London

Barenghi, Mario, *Ungaretti: Un ritratto e cinque studi* (Modena: Mucchi, 1999)

Barni, Giulio, *Anima di frontiera* (Milan: Scheiwiller All'Insegna del Pesce D'oro, 1966)

Barzini, Luigi [1913], 'Le condizioni degli Italiani in Austria', *Corriere della Sera*, 23, 24 and 25 September

– [1948], *Vita vagabonda*. Introduction by Luigi Barzini, Jr. (Milan: Rizzoli).

Battisti, Cesare, *Epistolario*, 2 vols. (Florence: Nuova Italia, 1966)

Bauer, Ernest, *Boroević: Il leone dell'Isonzo* (Gorizia: Libreria Editrice Goriziana, 2006)

Becker, Jean-Jacques, *La France en guerre 1914–1918: La grande mutation* (Brussels: Editions Complexe, 1988)

Benjamin, Walter, *Illuminations* (Glasgow: Fontana/Collins, 1979)

Berlin, Isaiah, 'Georges Sorel', *Against the Current* (London: Hogarth, 1979)

Bernardi, Mario, *Di qua e di là dal Piave: Da Caporetto a Vittorio Veneto* (Milan: Mursia, 1989)

Bertone, Manuela, and Robert S. Dombroski, eds., *Carlo Emilio Gadda: Contemporary Perspectives* (Toronto: University of Toronto Press, 1997)

Bettiza, Enzo, *Via Solferino: La vita del Corriere della Sera dal 1964 al 1974* (Milano: Rizzoli, 1982)

Bianchi, Bruna [2001], *La follia e la fuga: Nevrosi di guerra, diserzione e disobbedienza nell'esercito italiano (1915–1918)* (Rome: Bulzoni)

– [2003], 'La giustizia militare nell'esercito italiano', in Franzina [2003]

– [2006], ed., *La violenza contro la popolazione civile nella Grande Guerra: Deportati, profughi, internati* (Naples: Unicopli)

Bissolati, Leonida, *Diario di guerra* (Turin: Einaudi, 1935)

Blackburn, James, papers in the Department of Documents, Imperial War Museum, London

Blašković, Pero, *Sa Bošnjacima u Svjetskom ratu* (Vienna: Gesellschaft Bosnischer Akademiker in Österreich, 2000)

Bobbio, Norberto, *Liberalism and Democracy* (London: Verso, 2005)

Boccioni, Umberto [1971], *Gli scritti editi e inediti* (Milan: Feltrinelli)

– [2004], *taccuini futuristi* (Rome: mancosu)

Bonadeo, Alfredo [1989], *Mark of the Beast: Death and Degradation in the Literature of the Great War* (Lexington: University Press of Kentucky)

– [1995], *D'Annunzio and the Great War* (Cranbury, NJ and London: Associated University Presses)

Bonamore, Virgilio, *Diario*, translated by an unknown person for Channel 4 Television in London (kindly made available by the war museum in Kobarid)

Bonsal, Stephen, *Suitors and Supplicants: The Little Nations at Versailles* (New York: Prentice-Hall, 1946)

Borgese, G. A., *Goliath: The March of Fascism* (London: Gollancz, 1938)

Borroni, Delfino [2006a], interview by Luca Lippera, *Il Messaggero*, 3 November
- [2006b], interview in *La Voce online: Il portale della Comunità della Parrocchia Madonna dei Poveri*, December. Available at http://www.parrocchiamadonnadeipoveri.net/index.php?id=153, accessed in June 2007
- [n.d.], 'Il diario di Delfino Borroni', available at http://digilander.libero.it/lacorsainfinita/diari/borroni.htm, accessed in June 2007

Borsi, Giosuè, *Lettere dal fronte* (1916)

Bosworth, R. J. B. [1979], *Italy, the Least of the Great Powers: Italian Foreign Policy before the First World War* (Cambridge: CUP)
- [1983], *Italy and the Approach of the First World War* (London and Basingstoke: Macmillan)
- [1996], *Italy and the Wider World 1860–1960* (London: Routledge)
- [2002], *Mussolini* (London: Arnold)
- [2006], *Mussolini's Italy: Life under the Dictatorship 1915–1945* (London: Penguin)
- [2007], 'Italy', in Robert Gerwarth, ed., *Twisted Paths: Europe 1914–1945* (Oxford: OUP)

Bozzi, Carlo Luigi, *Gorizia nel 1918* (Gorizia: Studi goriziani, 1968)

Bricchetto, Enrica, '"Percorrendo il fronte da occidente a oriente": Luigi Barzini inviato speciale sul fronte alpino', in Franzina [2003]

British Army General Staff, War Office, *Field Service Regulations: Part I: Operations 1909: Reprinted, with amendments, 1914* and *Part II: Organization and Administration 1909: Reprinted, with amendments to October, 1914* (London: HMSO, 1914)

Buchan, John, *Episodes of the Great War* (London: Nelson, 1936)

Bultrini, Nicola, *L'Ultimo fante: La Grande Guerra sul Carso nelle memorie di Carlo Orelli* (Chiari: Nordpress, 2004)

Bultrini, Nicola, and Maurizio Casarola, *Gli Ultimi* (Chiari: Nordpress, 2005)

Burgwyn, H. James, *The Legend of the Mutilated Victory: Italy, the Great War, and the Paris Peace Conference, 1915–1919* (London: Greenwood, 1993)

Burwick, Frederick, and Paul Douglass, eds., *The Crisis in Modernism: Bergson and the Vitalist Controversy* (Cambridge: CUP, 1992)

Bush, John W., *Venetia Redeemed: Franco-Italian Relations 1864–1866* (Syracuse: Syracuse University Press, 1967)

Cadorna, Luigi [1915], *Attacco frontale e ammaestramento tattico* (Rome: Stato Maggiore)
- [1921], *La Guerra alla fronte italiana (24 maggio 1915 – 9 novembre 1917)* (Milan: Treves)
- [1922], *Il Generale Raffaele Cadorna nel Risorgimento italiano* (Milan: Treves)
- [1950], *Pagine polemiche* (Milan: Garzanti)
- [1967], *Lettere famigliari* (Milan: Mondadori)

Cadorna, Raffaele, *Liberazione di Roma nell'anno 1870 ed il plebiscito* (Turin: Roux, 1889)

Calderoni, Maria Rosa, *La fucilazione dell'alpino Ortis* (Milan: Mursia, 1999)

Camanni, Enrico, *La Guerra di Joseph* (Turin: Vivalda Editori, 1998)

Camera dei Deputati – Segretariato generale, *Comitati segreti sulla condotta della guerra (giugno–dicembre 1917)* (Rome: Archivio storico, 1967)

Canal, G., 'La retorica della morte. I monumenti ai caduti della Grande Guerra', *Rivista di storia contemporanea*, XI (4), 1982, 659–69

Canavero, A., 'Le "Terre liberate e redente" nel dibattito culturale e politico', in *Commissione parlamentare . . . ,* vol. I

Capello, Luigi, *Per la verità* (Milan: Treves, 1920).

Cappellano, Filippo, and Flavio Carbone, 'I Carabinieri reali al fronte nella Grande Guerra', in Nicola Labanca and Giorgio Rochat, eds., *Il soldato, la guerra e il rischio di morire* (Milan: Unicopli, 2006)

Caprin, Giulio, *L'ora di Trieste* (1915)

Carr, John Dickson, *The Life of Sir Arthur Conan Doyle* (London: John Murray, 1949)

Carrà [Carlo Carrà], *Guerrapittura* (Florence: Salimbeni, 1978)

Cassar, George (H.), *Asquith as War Leader* (London: Hambledon Press, 1994)

– *The Forgotten Front: The British Campaign in Italy, 1917–1918* (London: Hambledon Press, 1998)

Castellini, Gualtiero, *Trento e Trieste* (Milan: Treves, 1915)

Castronovo, Valerio, *La stampa italiana dall'Unità al fascismo* (Bari: Laterza, 1991)

Cecotti, Franco, ed., *'Un esilio che non ha pari': 1914–1918 Profughi, internati ed emigrati di Trieste, dell'Isontino e dell'Istria* (Gorizia: Libreria editrice Goriziana, 2001)

Cervone, Pier Paolo, *Vittorio Veneto, l'ultima battaglia* (Milan: Mursia, 1994)

Ceschin, Daniele [2003], 'La popolazione dell'Alto Vicentino di fronte alla Strafexpedition: l'esodo, il profugato, il ritorno', in Cora and Pozzato

– [2006a], 'I profughi in Italia dopo Caporetto: marginalità, pregiudizio, controllo sociale', in Bianchi [2006]

– [2006b], '"L'estremo oltraggio": la violenza alle donne in Friuli e in Veneto durante l'occupazione austro-germanica (1917–1918)', in Bianchi [2006]

Chiari, Joseph, 'Vitalism and contemporary thought', in Burwick and Douglass

Cicchino, Enzo Antonio, and Roberto Olivo, *La Grande Guerra dei piccoli uomini* (Milan: Ancora, 2005)

Cimprič, Željko, ed., *Kobarid Caporetto Karfreit 1917–1997* (Kobarid: Turistična agencija K.C.K., 1998)

Clausewitz, Carl von, *On War* (Ware: Wordsworth Editions, 1997)

Colapietra, Raffaele, *Leonida Bissolati* (Milan: Feltrinelli, 1958)

Colleoni, Angelo, *Monfalcone: Storia e leggende* (Monfalcone, 1984)

Comisso, Giovanni, *Giorni di guerra* (Milan: Mondadori, 1980)

Commissione di inchiesta, *Dall'Isonzo al Piave (24 ottobre–9 novembre 1917): Relazione della Commissione di inchiesta*: Vol. I, *Cenno schematico degli avvenimenti*, Vol. II, *Le cause e le responsabilità degli avvenimenti* (Rome: Stabilimento tipografico per l'Amministrazione della Guerra, 1919)

Commissione parlamentare di inchiesta sulle terre liberate e redente (luglio 1920– giugno 1922) (Rome: Camera dei deputati Archivio storico, 1991)

Conan Doyle, Arthur, *A Visit to Three Fronts* (London: Hodder & Stoughton, 1916)

– *Memories and Adventures* (Oxford: OUP, 1989)

Cora, Vittorio, and Paolo Pozzato, eds., *1916 – la Strafexpedition* (Udine: Gaspari, 2003)

Corner, Paul, and Giovanna Procacci, 'The Italian experience of "total" mobilisation, 1915–1920', in Horne

Corni, Gustavo, 'La società veneto-friulana durante l'occupazione militare austro-germanica 1917/1918', in Cimprič

Corns, Cathryn, and John Hughes-Wilson, *Blindfold and Alone: British Military Executions in the Great War* (London: Cassell, 2001)

Cornwall, Mark [1997], 'Morale and patriotism in the Austro-Hungarian army, 1914–1918', in Horne

– [2000], *The Undermining of Austria-Hungary* (Basingstoke: Macmillan)

Corsini, Umberto, Giulio Benedetti Emert and Hans Kramer, *Trentino e Alto Adige dall'Austria all'Italia* (Bolzano: Casa Editrice S.E.T.A., 1969)

Cortellessa, Andrea, ed., *Le notti chiari erano tutte un'alba: Antologia dei poeti italiani nella prima guerra mondiale* (Milan: Mondadori, 1998)

da Costa Mayer, Esther, *The Work of Antonio Sant'Elia: Retreat into the Future* (New Haven: Yale University Press, 1995)

Dalton, Hugh, *With British Guns in Italy* (London: Methuen, 1919)

D'Annunzio, Gabriele [2002], *Diari di guerra: 1914–1918* (Milan: Mondadori)

– [2005], *Prose di ricerca* (Milan: Mondadori)

Davies, Judy, 'The futures market: Marinetti and the Fascists of Milan', in Edward Timms and Peter Collier, eds., *Visions and Blueprints: Avant-Garde Culture and Radical Politics in Early Twentieth-Century Europe* (Manchester: Manchester University Press, 1988)

Davis, James C., *Rise from Want: A Peasant Family in the Machine Age* (Philadelphia: University of Pennsylvania Press, 1986)

Deák, István, 'The Habsburg Army in the First and Last Days of World War I: A Comparative Analysis', in Király and Dreisziger

De Cecco, Marcello, 'The economy from Liberalism to Fascism', in Adrian Lyttelton, ed., *Liberal and Fascist Italy 1900–1945* (Oxford: OUP, 2002)

Decsy, János, 'The Habsburg Army on the Threshold of Total War', in Király and Dreisziger

De Gasperi, Alcide, *De Gasperi scrive: corrispondenza con capi di Stato, cardinali, uomini politici, giornalisti, diplomatici* (Brescia: Morcelliana, 1974)

Del Bianco, Giuseppe, *La Guerra e il Friuli*, 3 vols. (Udine: Collezione Forum Julii, 1937–52)

Delmé-Radcliffe, Charles, papers in the Department of Documents, Imperial War Museum, London

De Simone, Cesare, *L'Isonzo mormorava: Fanti e generali a Caporetto* (Milan: Mursia, 1995)

Dombroski, Robert S., *Creative Entanglements: Gadda and the Baroque* (Toronto: University of Toronto Press, 1999)

Dos Passos, John, *The Fourteenth Chronicle: Letters and diaries* (London: Deutsch, 1974)

Douglas-Home, Charles, *Rommel* (London: Weidenfeld & Nicolson, 1973)

Dyer, Geoff, *The Missing of the Somme* (London: Hamish Hamilton, 1994)

Edmonds, Sir James E., and H. R. Davies, *Military Operations Italy 1915–1919* (London: HMSO, 1949)

Eksteins, Modris, *Rites of Spring: The Great War and the Birth of the Modern Age* (London: Bantam-Transworld, 1989)

Ellmann, Richard, *James Joyce* (Oxford: OUP, 1977)

Elrod, Richard B., 'Austria and the Venetian Question, 1860–1866', *Central European History*, vol. IV (1971), no. 2

Fabi, Lucio [1991a], *Storia di Gorizia* (Gorizia: il poligrafo / Edizioni della Laguna)

– ed. [1991b], *La guerra in casa 1914–1918: Soldati e popolazioni del Friuli austriaco nella Grande Guerra* (Romans d'Isonzo)

– *Sul Carso della Grande Guerra* (Udine: Gaspari, 2005)

Fabi, Lucio, Giancarlo L. Martina and Giacomo Viola, *Il Friuli del '15/18: Luoghi, itinerari, vicende di una Provincia nella Grande Guerra* (Udine: Provincia di Udine Assessorato alla Cultura, 2003)

Faldella, Emilio, ed., *I racconti della Grande Guerra* (Milan: Edizione dei Periodici Mondadori, 1966)

Faleschini, Antonio, 'Il 1866 in Friuli in cronache inedite e nel ricordo di contemporanei', *Il Friuli nel Risorgimento*, vol. 1 (Udine: Accademia di Scienze Lettere e Arti di Udine, 1966)

Falkenhayn, Erich von, *General Headquarters 1914–1916 and its Critical Decisions* (Nashville: War and Peace Books, 2000)

Falls, Cyril, *Caporetto 1917* (London: Weidenfeld & Nicolson, 1966)

Fambri, Paolo, *La Venezia-Giulia: Studii politico-militari* (Venice: Naratovich, 1880)

Farkas, Márton, 'Doberdo: the Habsburg Army on the Italian Front, 1915–16', in Király and Dreisziger

Fava, Andrea, 'War, 'National Education' and the Italian Primary School, 1915–1918', in Horne

Favetti, Guido, *L'esercito Della Morte: Dall'Africa Al Carso. Il Diario Di Un Volontario Irredento* (Udine: Gaspari, 2004)

Federzoni, Luigi, *La Dalmazia che aspetta* (Bologna: Zanichelli, 1915)

Ferguson, L. I. L., papers in the Department of Documents, Imperial War Museum, London

Ferguson, Niall, *The Pity of War 1914–1918* (London: Penguin Books, 1999)

Fettarappa Sandri, Carlo, 'La battaglia del Piave nuovo', *Gerarchia*, no. 7, July 1935

Ficalora, Tonino, *La presa di Gorizia* (Milan: Mursia, 2001)

Fischer, Ernst, *An Opposing Man* (London: Allen Lane, 1974)

Flores, Ildebrando, *La Guerra in alta montagna* (Milano: Corbaccio, 1934)

Forcella, Enzo, and Alberto Monticoni, *Plotone d'esecuzione: I processi della prima guerra mondiale* (Bari: Laterza, 1968)

Ford, Mark, 'Merry Kicks', *London Review of Books*, 20 May 2004

Foresti, Fabio, Paola Morisi and Maria Resca, eds., *Era come a mietere: Testimonianze orali e scritte di soldati sulla Grande Guerra con immagini inedite* (Bologna: Comune di San Giovanni in Persiceto, 1983)

Forsyth, Douglas J., *The Crisis of Liberal Italy: Monetary and Financial Policy, 1914–1922* (Cambridge: CUP, 1993)

Fortunat Černilogar, Damjana, 'Lo sfondamento di Caporetto e gli effetti della guerra sulla popolazione civile e sull'ambiente culturale', in Cimprič

Fraccaroli, Arnaldo, *L'Italia ha vinto* (Milan: Alfieri & Lacroix, 1919)
Franzina, Emilio [1999], *Casini di guerra: Il tempo libero dalla trincea e i postriboli militari nel primo conflitto mondiale* (Udine: Gaspari)
– ed. [2003], *Una trincea chiamata Dolomiti 1915–1917: Una guerra, due trincee* (Udine: Gaspari)
Fraser, David, *Knight's Cross: A Life of Field Marshal Erwin Rommel* (London: HarperCollins, 1993)
French, David, *The Strategy of the Lloyd George Coalition, 1916–1918* (Oxford: Clarendon Press, 1995)
Frescura, Attilio, *Diario di un imboscato* (Milan: Mursia, 1999)
Fussell, Paul, *The Great War and Modern Memory* (Oxford: OUP, 2000 [1975])
Gadda, Carlo Emilio [1963], *La cognizione del dolore*, translated by William Weaver as *Acquainted with Grief* (1969)
– [1999], *Giornale di guerra e di prigionia* (Milan: Garzanti)
Garibaldi, Giuseppe, *My Life* (London: Hesperus Classics, 2004)
Gatt Rutter, John, *Italo Svevo: A Double Life* (Oxford: Clarendon Press, 1988)
Gatti, Angelo [1915], *La Guerra senza confini. Osservata e commentata da Angelo Gatti, Capitano di Stato Maggiore. I primi cinque mesi (agosto-dicembre 1914)* (Milan: Treves)
– [1921], 'Il disegno di guerra del Generale Cadorna', in *Uomini e folle di guerra: Saggi* (Milan: Treves)
– [1957], *Un italiano a Versailles* (Milan: Ceschina)
– [1997], *Caporetto: Diario di guerra (maggio–dicembre 1917)* (Bologna: Il Mulino)
Gatti, Gian Luigi, *Dopo Caporetto: Gli ufficiali P nella Grande Guerra: propaganda, assistenza, vigilanza* (Gorizia: Libreria editrice Goriziana, 2000)
Genova, Alberto, *Noi combattenti a Caporetto e al Piave* (Treviso: Canova, 1969)
Gentile, Emilio [1986], 'From the Cultural Revolt of the Giolittian Era to the Ideology of Fascism', in Frank J. Coppa, ed., *Studies in Modern Italian History: From the Risorgimento to the Republic* (New York: Peter Lang)
– [1996], *The Sacralization of Politics in Fascist Italy*, translated by Keith Botsford (Cambridge, MA: Harvard University Press)
– [2000], 'Giolitti, Giovanni', *Dizionario biografico degli Italiani*, vol. 55 (Rome: Istituto della Enciclopedia Italiana)
Giacomel, Paolo [2003a], ed., *Avanti Savoia! La Grande Guerra vissuta da un romano, un sardo e un toscano della Brigata Reggio sul fronte delle Dolomiti* (Udine: Gaspari)
– [2003b], *Tu col cannone, io col fucile: Curzio Malaparte e Alessandro Suckert nella Grande Guerra* (Udine: Gaspari)
Gibelli, Antonio, *La Grande Guerra degli Italiani 1915–1918* (Milan: RCS Libri, 2007)
Gilmour, David, *The Long Recessional: The Imperial Life of Rudyard Kipling* (London: John Murray, 2002)
Giuliani, Sandro, *Interviste* (Milan: Popolo d'Italia, 1934)
Gladden, Norman, *Across the Piave* (London: HMSO, 1971)
Golding, John, *Boccioni: Unique Forms of Continuity in Space* (London: The Tate Gallery, 1985)

Gooch, John [1984], 'Italy before 1915: The Quandary of the Vulnerable', in Ernest R. May, ed., *Knowing One's Enemies: Intelligence Assessment before the Two World Wars* (Princeton: PUP)

– [1989], *Army, State and Society in Italy, 1870–1915* (Basingstoke: Macmillan)

Gorni, Guglielmo, 'Gadda, o il testamento del capitano', in Maria Antonietta Terzoli, *Le lingue di Gadda: Atti del Convegno di Basilea 10–12 dicembre 1993* (Rome: Salerno Editrice, 1996)

Gratton, Luigi, *Armando Diaz nell'ultimo anno della Grande Guerra* (Rivista Militare, 1994)

Griffith, Paddy, *Battle Tactics of the Western Front: The British Army's Art of Attack, 1916–1918* (New Haven: Yale University Press, 1994)

Grigg, John, *Lloyd George: War Leader 1916–1918* (Harmondsworth: Penguin, 2003)

Gross, Feliks, *Ethnics in a Borderland: An Inquiry into the Nature of Ethnicity and Reduction of Ethnic Tensions in a One-Time Genocide Area* (Westport: Greenwood Press, 1978)

Hametz, Maura, *Making Trieste Italian, 1918–1954* (Trowbridge: The Royal Historical Society / The Boydell Press, 2005)

Hansen, Major Eric G., 'The Italian military enigma', in http://www.global security.org/military/library/report/1988/HEG.htm, accessed in May 2007

Hemingway, Ernest, *The Essential Hemingway* (Harmondsworth: Penguin, 1964)

L'Herne, issue dedicated to Ungaretti (Paris: Editions de l'Herne, 1968)

Herwig, Holger H., 'Tunes of Glory at the Twilight Stage', *German Studies Review*, vol. VI, no. 3 (October 1983), 475–94

Hewitt, Andrew, *Fascist Modernism: Aesthetics, Politics, and the Avant-Garde* (Stanford: Stanford University Press, 1993)

Hindenburg, Paul von, *Out of My Life* (London: Cassell, 1920)

Hoover, Herbert, *The Ordeal of Woodrow Wilson* (London: Museum Press, 1958)

Horne, John, ed., *State, Society and Mobilisation in Europe during the First World War* (Cambridge: CUP, 1997)

Horvath-Mayerhofer, Christine, *L'Amministrazione militare austro-ungarica nei territori italiani occupati dall'ottobre 1917 al novembre 1918* (Udine: Istituto per la Storia del Risorgimento Italiano, 1985)

Howard, Michael, 'Men against Fire: The Doctrine of the Offensive in 1914', in Peter Paret, ed., *Makers of Modern Strategy from Macchiavelli to the Nuclear Age* (Oxford: Clarendon Press, 1986)

Huddleston, Sisley, *Peace-Making at Paris* (London: Fisher Unwin, 1919)

Isnenghi, Mario [1997], ed., *I luoghi della memoria: Strutture ed eventi dell'Italia unita* (Bari: Laterza)

– [1998], 'Un luogo del virtuale', in Cimprič

– [1999], *La tragedia necessaria: Da Caporetto all'otto settembre* (Bologna: Il Mulino)

– [2005], *Le guerre degli italiani: Parole, immagini, ricordi 1848–1945* (Bologna: Il Mulino)

Isnenghi, Mario, and Giorgio Rochat, *La Grande Guerra 1914–1918* (Milan: Sansoni, 2004)

Jahr, Christoph, essay on German executions in the First World War, available at http://www.shotatdawn.org.uk/page33.html, accessed in April 2006

Jones, Frederic J., *Ungaretti: Poet and Critic* (Edinburgh: Edinburgh University Press, 1977)

Joyce, James, *Giacomo Joyce* (London: Faber & Faber, 1984)

Jung, Peter, *The Austro-Hungarian Forces in World War I (1) 1914–16* (Oxford: Osprey, 2003)

Kaldor, Mary, *The Baroque Arsenal* (London: André Deutsch, 1981)

Kernek, Sterling J., 'Woodrow Wilson and National Self-determination Along Italy's Frontier: A Study of the Manipulation of Principles in the Pursuit of Political Interests', *Proceedings of the American Philosophical Society*, vol. 126, no. 4 (Aug. 1982), pp. 243–300

Király, Béla K., and Nandor F. Dreisziger, eds., *East Central European Society in World War I* (Boulder: Social Science Monographs, 1985)

Knightley, Phillip, *The First Casualty: From the Crimea to the Falklands: The War Correspondent as Hero, Propagandist and Myth Maker* (London: Pan Books, 1989)

Krleža, Miroslav, *Dnevnik 1914–17: Davni dani I* (Sarajevo: Oslobodjenje, 1981)

Labanca, Nicola, *Caporetto: Storia di una disfatta* (Florence: Giunti, 1997)

Labanca, Nicola, Giovanna Procacci and Luigi Tomassini, *Caporetto. Esercito, stato e società* (Florence: Giunti, 1997)

Labita, Vito, 'Un libro-simbolo: "Il nostro Soldato" di padre Agostino Gemelli', *Rivista di storia contemporanea*, XV, 1986, no. 3

Lancellotti, Arturo, *Giornalismo eroico* (Rome: Edizioni di Fiamma, 1924)

Lansing, Robert [1921], *The Peace Negotiations: A Personal Narrative* (Boston: Houghton Mifflin)

– [1922], *The Big Four and Others of the Peace Conference* (London: Hutchinson & Co.)

le Cornu, Daryl John, 'Bright Hope: British Radical Publicists, American Intervention and the Prospects of a Negotiated Peace, 1917'. PhD thesis, University of Western Sydney, Australia, 2005; available at http://library.uws.edu.au/adt-NUWS/uploads/approved/adt-NUWS20060123.103228/public/07Chapter5.pdf, accessed in June 2007

Lederer, Ivo J., *Yugoslavia at the Paris Peace Conference: A Study in Frontiermaking* (New Haven: Yale University Press, 1963)

Leicht, P. S., *Breve storia del Friuli* (Udine: Libreria Editrice 'Aquileia', 1951)

Leopardi, Giacomo, *The Canti with a Selection of his Prose*, translated with an introduction by J. G. Nichols (Manchester: Carcanet, 2003)

Levi, Carlo, *Cristo si è fermato a Eboli* (Turin: Einaudi, 1990)

Levin, N. Gordon, Jr., *Woodrow Wilson and World Politics: America's Response to War and Revolution* (New York: OUP, 1968)

Lewin, Ronald, *Rommel as Military Commander* (London: Batsford, 1968)

Licata, Glauco, *Storia del Corriere della Sera* (Milan: Rizzoli, 1976)

Liddell Hart, B. H., ed., *The Rommel Papers* (London: Collins, 1953)

Lippmann, Walter, *Force and Ideas* (New Brunswick: Transaction, 2000)

Lloyd George, David, *War Memoirs*, 6 vols. (London: Ivor Nicholson and Watson, 1933–7)

Longo, Giorgio, *Le battaglie dimenticate: La fanteria italiana nell' inferno carsico del S. Michele* (Bassano del Grappa: Itineri Progetti, 2002)

Lowe, C. J., 'Britain and Italian Intervention, 1914–1915', *The Historical Journal*, XII, 3 (1969)

Ludendorff, Erich, *The Concise Ludendorff Memoirs* (London: Hutchinson, n.d.)

Lussu, Emilio, *Sardinian Brigade* (London: Prion Books, 2000) [originally *Un anno sull'Altopiano* (1938)]

Lycett, Andrew, *Rudyard Kipling* (London: Phoenix, 2000)

Macdonald, Lyn, *Somme* (London: Penguin, 1993)

Machiavelli, Niccolò, *The Prince* (London: Penguin Books, 2004)

McKendrick, Jamie, ed., *The Faber Book of 20th-Century Italian Poems* (London: Faber & Faber, 2004)

Macksey, Kenneth, *Rommel: Battles and Campaigns* (London: Arms and Armour Press, 1979)

Mack Smith, Denis [1971], *Victor Emanuel, Cavour, and the Risorgimento* (Oxford: OUP)

– [1978], *Storia di cento anni di vita italiana visti attraverso il* Corriere della Sera (Milan: Rizzoli)

– [1985], *Cavour* (London: Weidenfeld & Nicolson)

– [1989], *Italy and its Monarchy* (New Haven: Yale University Press)

– [1997], *Modern Italy: A Political History* (New Haven: Yale University Press)

MacMillan, Margaret, *Peacemakers: Six Months That Changed the World* (London: John Murray, 2002)

Malaparte, Curzio [1967], *Battibecco* (Milano: Palazzi)

– [1981], *Viva Caporetto! La rivolta dei santi maledetti* (Milan: Mondadori)

Mamatey, Victor S., *The United States and East Central Europe 1914–1918* (Princeton: PUP, 1957)

Mantoux, Paul, *The Deliberations of the Council of Four (March 24–June 28, 1919)* translated and edited by Arthur S. Link with the assistance of Manfred F. Boemeke, 2 vols. (Princeton: PUP, 1992)

Maranelli, Carlo, *L'Italia irredenta: Dizionario geografico* (Bari: Laterza, 1915)

Marinetti, Filippo Tommaso [1971], *Selected Writings*, translated and introduced by R. W. Flint (New York: Farrar, Straus & Giroux)

– [1987], *Taccuini 1915/1921* (Bologna: Il Mulino)

– [1998], *Mafarka the Futurist: An African novel*, translated by Carol Diethe and Steve Cox (London: Middlesex University Press)

Martel, Charles [Charles à Court Repington of *The Times*], *Military Italy* (London: Macmillan & Co., 1884)

Martini, Ferdinando, *Diario 1914–1918* (Milan: Mondadori, 1966)

Marušič, Branko, 'Da Campoformido a Caporetto (1797–1917)', in Cimprič

Masau Dan, M., and D. Porcedda, *L'Arma della persuasione: Parole ed immagini di propaganda nella Grande Guerra* (Gorizia: Edizioni della Laguna, 1991)

Mauro, Walter, *Vita di Giuseppe Ungaretti* (Milan: Camunia, 1990)

Medeot, Camillo, ed., *Cronache Goriziane 1914–1918* (Gorizia, 1976)

Melograni, Piero, *Storia politica della Grande Guerra 1915–1918* (Bari: Laterza, 1972)

Messner-Sporšić, Ante, *1915–1918: Odlomci iz ratnih spomena* (Zagreb, 1934)

Milocco, Sara and Giorgio, 'Fratelli d'Italia': Gli internamenti degli Italiani nelle 'terre liberate' durante la Grande Guerra (Udine: Gaspari, 2002)

Minniti, Fortunato, Il Piave (Bologna: Il Mulino, 2002)

Missiroli, Mario [1924], Il Colpo di Stato (Turin: Gobetti)

– [1932], L'Italia Oggi (Bologna: Zanichelli)

Monelli, Paolo, Toes Up (London, 1930), translated from Le scarpe al sole (1920)

Montague, C. E., Disenchantment (London: MacGibbon & Kee, 1968)

Monticone, Alberto [1955], La Battaglia di Caporetto (Rome: Studium)

– [1972], Gli italiani in uniforme 1915/1918 (Bari: Laterza)

– [1982], 'Problemi e prospettive di una storia della cultura popolare dell'Italia nella prima guerra mondiale', in Mario Isnenghi, ed., Operai e contadini nella Grande Guerra (Bologna: Cappelli)

Morselli, Mario A., Caporetto 1917: Victory or Defeat? (London: Frank Cass, 2001)

Mosse, George, Masses and Man: Nationalist and Fascist Perceptions of Reality (Detroit: Wayne State University Press, 1987)

Mowrer, E. A., Immortal Italy (New York: Appleton, 1922)

Musil, Robert [1995], Posthumous Papers of a Living Author, translated by Peter Wortsman (London: Penguin)

– [1999], Diaries 1899–1941 (New York: Basic Books)

Mussolini, Benito, Memoirs 1942–1943 (London: Weidenfeld & Nicolson, 1949)

Mutterle, Anco Marzio, Scipio Slataper (Milan: Mursia, 1973)

Newby, Eric, On the Shores of the Mediterranean (London: Harvill, 1984)

Newby, Wanda, Peace and War: Growing up in Fascist Italy (London: Pan Books, 1992)

Nicolson, Harold, Peacemaking 1919 (London: Methuen, 1964)

Nietzsche, Friedrich, A Nietzsche Reader, edited and translated by R. J. Hollingdale (Harmondsworth: Penguin, 1977)

Novak, Bogdan C., Trieste 1941–1954: The Ethnic, Political, and Ideological Struggle (Chicago and London: University of Chicago Press, 1970)

Oblath Stuparich, Elody, Confessioni e lettere a Scipio (Turin: Fògola, 1979)

O'Brien, Paul [2004], Mussolini in the First World War: The Journalist, the Soldier, the Fascist (London: Hurst)

– [2006], 'Summary Executions in Italy During the First World War: Findings and Implications', in Modern Italy, vol. 11, no. 3, November

Offenstadt, Professor Nicolas, 'French executions', available at http://www.shotatdawn.org.uk/page34.html, accessed in July 2006

Ojetti, Ugo, Lettere alla moglie 1915–1919 (Florence: Sansoni, 1964)

Orlando, Vittorio Emanuele [1923], Discorsi per la guerra e per la pace (Foligno: Campitelli)

– [1960], Memorie (1915–1919) (Milan: Rizzoli)

Ostenc, Michel, '1915. L'Italie en guerre', Guerres mondiales et conflits contemporains, 219 / 2005

Ousby, Ian, The Road to Verdun (London: Jonathan Cape, 2002)

Page, Thomas Nelson, Italy and the World War (New York: Scribners, 1920); available online at http://net.lib.byu.edu/~rdh7/wwi/comment/Italy/PageTC.htm, accessed in July 2007

Palumbo, Michael [1979], 'German–Italian Military Relations', *Central European History*, December
– [1983], 'Italian–Austro-Hungarian Military Relations before World War I', in Samuel R. Williamson, Jr. and Peter Pastor, eds., *Essays on World War I: Origins and Prisoners of War* (New York: Social Science Monographs)
Panzini, Alfredo, *La Guerra del '15: Diario sentimentale* (Bologna: Massimiliano Boni, 1995)
Passerini, Luisa, 'L'immagine di Mussolini: specchio dell'immaginario e promessa di identità', *Rivista di storia contemporanea*, XV, 1986, no. 3
Pavan, Camillo, et al., *Grande Guerra e popolazione civile: Vol: 1: Caporetto* (Treviso, 1997)
Pettorelli Lalatta, Cesare, *L'occasione perduta: Carzano 1917* (Milan: Mursia, 1967)
Piazzoni, Sandro, 'La XII battaglia del Isonzo', *Gerarchia*, no. 7, July 1935
Piccioni, Leone [1979], *Vita di un poeta: Ungaretti* (Milan: Rizzoli)
– [1980], ed., *Ungarettiana* (Florence: Vallecchi)
Pieri, Piero [1962], *Storia militare del Risorgimento: Guerre e insurrezioni* (Turin: Einaudi)
– [1965], *L'Italia nella Prima Guerra Mondiale (1915–1918)* (Turin: Einaudi)
– [1986], *La Prima Guerra Mondiale, 1914–1918: Problemi di storia militare* (Rome: Stato Maggiore dell'Esercito Ufficio Storico)
Pierson, Lucia, *Mussolini visto da una scrittrice olandese* (Rome: Anonimo tipo-editoriale, 1933)
Pimlott, John, ed., *Rommel and his Art of War* (London: Greenhill Books, 2003)
Pinney, Thomas, ed., *The Letters of Rudyard Kipling* (Basingstoke: Macmillan, 1990)
Pirc, Simon, and Tomaž Budkovič, 'Remains of World War Geochemical Pollution in the Landscape', in Mervyn Richardson, ed., *Environmental Xenobiotics* (London: Taylor & Francis, 1996)
Plaschka, Richard Georg, 'The Army and Internal Conflict in the Austro-Hungarian Empire, 1918', in Király and Dreisziger
Pluviano, Marco, and Irene Guerrini, preface by Giorgio Rochat, *Le Fucilazioni sommarie nella Prima Guerra Mondiale* (Udine: Gaspari, 2004)
Pope, Stephen, and Elizabeth-Anne Wheal, *Dictionary of the First World War* (Barnsley: Pen & Sword Military Classics, 2003)
Portelli, Massimo, *La Campagna del 1866 nel Friuli Goriziano: Il combattimento di Versa e l'armistizio di Cormons* (Gorizia, 1966)
Prezzolini, Giuseppe, *Caporetto* (Rome: Quaderni della Voce, 1919)
Price, Julius M., *Six Months on the Italian Front* (London: Chapman & Hall, 1917)
Primicerj, Giulio, *1918: Cronaca di una disfatta: Testi e documenti austriaci sul crollo militare dell'impero absburgico* (Milan: Arcana, 1983)
Procacci, Giovanna [1989a], 'Popular protest and labour conflict in Italy, 1915–18', *Social History*, vol. 14, no. 1 (January)
– [1989b], 'Dalla rassegnazione alla rivolta: osservazioni sul comportamento popolare in Italia negli anni della Prima Guerra Mondiale', *Richerche storiche*, XIX (1), January–April

– [1992], 'State Coercion and Worker Solidarity in Italy (1915–1918): The Moral and Political Content of Social Unrest', in Leopold Haimson and Giulio Sapelli, eds., *Strikes, Social Conflict and the First World War* (Milan: Feltrinelli)

– [1998], 'L'impatto di Caporetto nell'opinione pubblica italiana', in Cimprič

– [1999], *Dalla rassegnazione alla rivolta: Mentalità e comportamenti popolari nella Grande Guerra* (Rome: Bulzoni)

– [2000], *Soldati e prigionieri italiani nella Grande Guerra* (Turin: Bollati Boringhieri)

– [2006], 'La società come una caserma. La svolta repressiva degli anni di guerra', in Bianchi [2006]

Procacci, Giuliano, 'Appunti in tema di crisi dello Stato liberale e di origini del fascismo', *Studi Storici*, VI (2), 1965, 221–37

Puccini, Dario, 'Ungaretti e la guerra (lettere inedite a Mario Puccini)', in Zingone

Puccini, Mario, *Come ho visto il Friuli* (Rome: Quaderni della Voce, 1919)

Putkowsi, Julian, and Julian Sykes, *Shot at Dawn* (Barnsley: Wharncliffe Publishing Ltd., 1989)

Rebora, Clemente, *La mia luce sepolta: Lettere di guerra* (Verona: Il Segno dei Gabrielli, 1996)

Revelli, Marco, 'Perche non piace a neo-liberali', in *La Repubblica*, 15 February 2006

Reynolds, Michael, *Hemingway's First War* (Oxford: Basil Blackwell, 1987)

Ridley, Jasper, *Garibaldi* (London: Weidenfeld & Nicolson, 2001)

Rigoni Stern, Mario, *Amore di confine* (Turin: Einaudi, 1986)

Robertson, Sir William, *Soldiers and Statesmen 1914–1918* (London: Cassell, 1926)

Rocca, Gianni, *Cadorna: Il generalissimo di Caporetto* (Milan: Mondadori, 2004)

Rochat, Giorgio [1961], 'La preparazione dell'esercito italiano nell'inverno 1914–15 in relazione alle informazioni disponibili sulla guerra di posizione', *Il Risorgimento* (1)

– [1973], 'Cadorna, Luigi', *Dizionario biografico degli Italiani*, vol. 16 (Rome: Istituto della Enciclopedia Italiana)

– [1991a], 'L'esercito italiano nell'estate 1914', in *L'esercito italiano in pace e in guerra* (Milan: R.A.R.A.)

– [1991b], 'Diaz, Armando', *Dizionario biografico degli Italiani*, vol. 39 (Rome: Istituto della Enciclopedia Italiana)

Rochat, Giorgio, and Giulio Massobrio, *Breve storia dell'Esercito Italiano dal 1861 al 1943* (Turin: Einaudi, 1978)

Rodd, Sir J. Rennell, *Social and Diplomatic Memories, 1902–1919*; available at http://net.lib.byu.edu/~rdh7/wwi/memoir/Rodd/Rodd13.htm, accessed in March 2006

Romano, Romano, *I ragazzi di Caporetto* (Milan: All'Insegna del Pesce D'oro, 1977)

Rommel, Erwin, *Infantry Attacks* (London: Greenhill, 1990)

Roscioni, Gian Carlo, *Il Duca di Sant'Aquila: Infanzia e giovinezza di Gadda* (Milan: Mondadori, 1997)

Rossi, A., *The Rise of Italian Fascism 1918–1922* (London: Methuen, 1938)

Roth, Joseph, *The Wandering Jews*, translated by Michael Hofmann (London: Granta, 2001)

Rothenberg, Gunther E. [1976], *The Army of Francis Joseph* (West Lafayette: Purdue University Press)

– [1985], 'The Habsburg Army in the First World War: 1914–1918', in Király and Dreisziger

Rothwell, V. H., *British War Aims 1914–1918* (Oxford: Clarendon Press, 1971)

Rusconi, Gian Enrico, *L'Azzardo del 1915: Come l'Italia decide la sua guerra* (Bologna: Il Mulino, 2005)

Russo, Luigi, *Vita e disciplina militare* (Bari: Laterza, 1946)

Sacco, Mimmo, Alberto Monticone and Mario Rigoni Stern, *Attualità della Grande Guerra* (Udine: Gaspari, 2005)

Salandra, Antonio, *I retroscena di Versailles*, ed. G. B. Gifuni (Milan: Pan, 1971)

Salsa, Carlo, *Trincee. Confidenze di un fante* (Milan: Mursia, 1995)

Salvatorelli, Luigi [1950], 'Tre colpi di stato', *Il Ponte* VI (4), April

– [1970], *The Risorgimento: Thought and Action* (New York: Harper & Row)

Salvemini, Gaetano [1934], *Racial Minorities under Fascism in Italy* (The Women's International League for Peace and Freedom / Conference on Minorities, Chicago)

– [1973], *The Origins of Fascism in Italy*, translated and introduced by Roberto Vivarelli (New York: Harper & Row)

Sapori, Francesco, *Il Duce nel mondo* (Rome: Novissima, 1937)

Sassoon, Siegfried, *Sherston's Progress* (London: Faber & Faber, 1936)

Satta, Salvatore, *De profundis* (Milan: Adelphi, 1980)

Schiavo, Alberto, ed., *Futurismo e fascismo* (Rome: Giovanni Volpe, 1981)

Schindler, John R., *Isonzo: The Forgotten Sacrifice of the Great War* (Westport: Praeger, 2001)

Schneeburger, Hans, et al., *La Montagna che esplode* (Udine: Gaspari, 2003)

Sema, Antonio, *La Grande Guerra sul fronte dell'Isonzo*, 3 vols. (Gorizia: Editrice Goriziana, 1995)

Serra, Renato, *Scritti letterari, morali e politici* (Turin: Einaudi, 1974)

Sevareid, Eric, *Conversations with Eric Sevareid: Interviews with Notable Americans* (Washington, DC: Public Affairs Press, 1976)

Severini, Gino, *The Life of a Painter: The Autobiography of Gino Severini* (Princeton: PUP, 1995)

Seymour, C. M. (Charles) [1928], ed., *The Intimate Papers of Colonel House*, 4 vols. (London: Ernest Benn)

– [1935], *American Neutrality 1914–1917* (New Haven: Yale University Press)

– [1951], *Geography, Justice, and Politics at the Paris Conference of 1919* (New York: The American Geographical Society)

– [1965], *Letters from the Paris Peace Conference* (New Haven: Yale University Press)

Sforza, Carlo [1944], *L'Italia dal 1914 al 1944 quale io la vidi* (Rome: Mondadori)

– [1945], *Costruttori e distruttori* (Rome: Donatello de Luigi)

– [1966], *Fifty Years of War and Diplomacy in the Balkans: Pashich and the Union of the Yugoslavs* (New York: AMS Press)

Sheffield, G. D., 'The Operational Role of British Military Police on the Western Front, 1914–18', in Paddy Griffith, ed., *British Fighting Methods in the Great War* (London: Frank Cass, 1996)

Silvestri, Mario, *Isonzo 1917* (Turin: Einaudi, 1965)

Sked, Alan, *The Decline and Fall of the Habsburg Empire 1815–1918* (Harlow: Longman, 2001)

Slataper, Scipio [1915], *Le strade d'invasione dall'Italia in Austria* (Florence: Bemporad)

– [1950], *Epistolario* (Milan: Mondadori)

– [1954], *Scritti politici* (Milan: Mondadori)

– [1958], *Lettere alle tre amiche* (Milan: Mondadori)

– [1980], *Il mio Carso* (Milan: Mondadori)

– [1981], *Lettere a Maria* (Volpe)

Slovene–Italian Relations 1880–1956: Report of the Slovene–Italian Historical and Cultural Commission (Koper-Capodistria, July 2000)

Sluga, Glenda, *The Problem of Trieste and the Italo-Yugoslav Border* (Albany: State University of New York Press, 2001)

Smith, L. V., *Between Mutiny and Obedience: The Case of the French Fifth Infantry Division during World War 1* (Princeton: PUP, 1994)

Somogyi, Eva, 'The Hungarian Honvéd Army and the Unity of the Habsburg Empire', in Király and Dreisziger

Sondhaus, Lawrence [1990], *In the Service of the Emperor: Italians in the Austrian Armed Forces 1814–1918* (Boulder, CO.: East European Monographs)

– [2000], *Franz Conrad von Hötzendorf: Architect of the Apocalypse* (Boston: Humanities Press)

Sonnino, Sidney, *Diario*, vol. 3 (1916–1922) (Bari: Laterza, 1972)

Spence, Richard B. [1985], 'The Yugoslav Role in the Austro-Hungarian Army, 1914–1918', in Király and Dreisziger.

– [1992], 'Die Bosniaken kommen!: The Bosnian-Herzegovinian Formations of the Austro-Hungarian Army, 1914–1918', in Richard B. Spence and Linda L. Nelson, eds., *Scholar, Patriot, Mentor: Historical Essays in Honor of Dimitrije Djordjevic* (Boulder: East European Monographs)

Staderini, Alessandra, 'L'amministrazione italiana nei territori occupati: il Segretariato Generale Affari Civili', in Franzina

Stallworthy, Jon, *War and Poetry* (Cheltenham: The Cyder Press, 2005)

Stark, Freya, *Traveller's Prelude* (London: John Murray, 1950)

Stevens, Wallace, 'Description without Place', *Collected Poems* (London: Faber, 2006)

Stevenson, David, *1914–1918: The History of the First World War* (London: Penguin Books, 2005)

Strachan, Hew, *The First World War* (London: Simon & Schuster, 2003)

Stuparich, Giani [1931], *Guerra del '15 (Dal taccuino d'un volontario)* (Milan: Treves)

– [1950], *Scipio Slataper* (Milan: Mondadori)

Suttie, Andrew, *Rewriting the First World War: Lloyd George, Politics and Strategy 1914–1918* (Basingstoke: Palgrave Macmillan, 2005)

Svolšak, Petra [1997], 'La popolazione civile nella zona di guerra', in Pavan

- [1998], 'L'occupazione italiana dell'Isontino dal maggio 1915 all'ottobre 1917 e gli sloveni', *Qualestoria*, no. 1/2, December
- [1998], 'La risonanza dello sfondamento di Caporetto nei giornali sloveni e nei mezzi di diffusione e informazione', in Cimprič
- [2003], *Soča, sveta reka* (Ljubljana: Nova revija)
- [2006], 'La popolazione civile nella Slovenia occupata', in Bianchi [2006]
Tallarico, Luigi, *Umberto Boccioni* (Reggio Calabria: Parallelo 38, 1985)
Taylor, A. J. P., *The Habsburg Monarchy 1809–1918* (Harmondsworth: Penguin, 1990)
Taylor, Philip M., *Munitions of the Mind* (Manchester: Manchester University Press, 1995)
Thomas, William Beach, *A Traveller in News* (London: Chapman & Hall, 1925)
Thompson, J. Lee, *Politicians, the Press, and Propaganda: Lord Northcliffe & the Great War, 1914–1919* (Kent, OH: Kent State University Press, 1999)
Todero, Fabio [1997], *Carlo e Giani Stuparich: Itinerari della Grande Guerra sulle tracce di due volontari triestini* (Trieste: LINT)
- [1999], *Pagine della Grande Guerra: Scrittori in grigioverde* (Milano: Mursia)
- [2003], *Le metamorfosi della memoria: La grande guerra tra modernità e tradizione* (Udine: Del Bianco)
- [2005], *Morire per la Patria* (Udine: Gaspari)
Todero, Roberto, *Fortezza Hermada 1915–1917: Storia e itinerari della Grande Guerra in Italia e Slovenia* (Udine: Gaspari, 2000)
Toniolo, Gianni, *An Economic History of Liberal Italy 1850–1918* (London: Routledge, 1990)
Toscanini, Arturo, *The Letters of Arturo Toscanini*, edited by Harvey Sachs (London: Faber, 2002)
Toscano, Mario, *Il Patto di Londra* (Bologna: Zanichelli, 1934)
Tosi, Luciano, *La propaganda italiana all'estero nella prima guerra mondiale: Rivendicazioni territoriali e politica delle nazionalità* (Udine: Del Bianco, 1977)
Tranfaglia, Nicola, *Dallo stato liberale al regime fascista* (Milan: Feltrinelli, 1973)
Travers, Tim, *The Killing Ground: The British Army, the Western Front and the Emergence of Modern Warfare, 1900–1918* (London: Unwin Hyman, 1987)
Trevelyan, G. M., *Scenes from Italy's War* (London: T. C. & E. C. Jack, 1919)
Triska, Jan F., *The Great War's Forgotten Front* (Boulder: EEM, 1998)
Türr, Stefania, *Alle trincee d'Italia: Note di guerra di una donna* (Milan: Antonio Cordani, 1918)
Ullman, Harlan K., and James P. Wade, *Shock and Awe: Achieving Rapid Dominance* (Washington, DC: National Defense University, 1996)
Ungarelli, Giulio, ed., *Le Carte militari di Gadda* (Milan: Scheiwiller, 1994)
Ungaretti, Giuseppe [1966], *Il Carso non è più un inferno* (Milan: Scheiwiller)
- [1978], *Lettere dal fronte a Gherardo Marone (1916–1918)* (Milan: Arnaldo Mondadori)
- [1981a], *Il Porto sepolto*, ed. Carlo Ossola (Milan: Il Saggiatore)
- [1981b], *Lettere a Soffici* (Florence: Sansoni)
- [2003], *Selected Poems*, translated by Andrew Frisardi (Manchester: Carcanet)
USSME / Ufficio Storico dello Stato Maggiore dell'Esercito, *L'Esercito Italiano nella Grande Guerra (1915–1918): vol: IV (1917), tomo 3* (Rome: Stato Maggiore dell'Esercito Ufficio Storico, 1967)

Valussi, Giorgio, *Il confine nord-orientale d'Italia* (Trieste: LINT, 1972)

van Emden, Richard, *Britain's Last Tommies: Final Memories from Soldiers of the 1914–1918 War, in their own Words* (London: Abacus, 2006)

Ventrone, Angelo [2003], *La seduzione totalitaria: Guerra, modernità, violenza politica (1914–1918)* (Rome: Donzelli)

– [2005], *Piccola storia della Grande Guerra* (Rome: Donzelli)

Vianelli, Mario, and Giovanni Cenacchi, *Teatri di guerra sulle Dolomiti* (Milan: Mondadori, 2006)

Vivarelli, Roberto, *Storia delle origini del fascismo: L'Italia dalla grande guerra alla marcia su Roma* (Bologna: Il Mulino, 1991)

Vivian, Herbert, *Italy at War* (London: Dent, 1917)

Warner, Philip, *The Battle of Loos* (London: Kimber, 1976)

Watt, Richard M., *Dare Call it Treason* (London: Chatto & Windus, 1964)

Wawro, Geoffrey, *The Austro-Prussian War: Austria's War with Prussia and Italy in 1866* (Cambridge: CUP, 1996)

Weber, Fritz, *Dal Monte Nero a Caporetto: Le dodici battaglie dell'Isonzo (1915–1917)* (Milan: Mursia, 1994)

Wells, H. G., *War and the Future* (London: Cassell, 1917)

Wickham Steed, Henry, *Through Thirty Years: 1892–1922: A Personal Narrative*, 2 vols. (London: Heinemann, 1924)

Wilks, John and Eileen [1998], *The British Army in Italy, 1917–1918* (Barnsley: Leo Cooper)

– [2001], *Rommel and Caporetto* (Barnsley: Leo Cooper)

Williams, Rowan A., 'The Czech Legion in Italy during World War I', in Samuel R. Williamson, Jr., and Peter Pastor, eds., *Essays on World War I: Origins and Prisoners of War* (New York: Social Science Monographs, 1983)

Wilmer, Clive, 'Hard to life', *The Guardian*, 31 May 2003

[Wilson, Woodrow] *The Papers of Woodrow Wilson* (Princeton: PUP, 1966 et seq.)

Winter, Denis, *Haig's Command: A Reassessment* (London: Penguin, 2001)

Winthrop Young, Geoffrey, *The Grace of Forgetting* (London: Country Life, 1953)

Woodhouse, John, *Gabriele D'Annunzio: Defiant Archangel* (Oxford: OUP, 1998)

Zamagni, Vera, *The Economic History of Italy 1860–1990* (Oxford: Clarendon Press, 1993)

Zaniboni Ferino, Ugo, *Bezzecca 1866: La campagna garibaldina fra l'Adda e il Garda* (Trento: Museo Trentino del Risorgimento e della Lotta per la Libertà, 1987)

Zingone, Alexandra, ed., *Giuseppe Ungaretti 1888–1970* (Napoli: Edizione Scientifiche Italiane, 1995)

Zivojinovic, Dragan R., *America, Italy and the Birth of Yugoslavia (1917–1919)* (Boulder: East European Quarterly, 1972)

Zorzi, Alvise, *Venezia austriaca, 1798–1866* (Bari: Laterza, 1985)

Acknowledgements

This is a narrative history, not based on methodical research into primary sources. Rather, it draws on original work by generations of scholars and writers. For all kinds of facts and figures, as well as for some interpretations, I am deeply and gratefully indebted to books and essays by René Albrecht-Carrié, Bruna Bianchi, Richard Bosworth, Mark Cornwall, Andrea Cortellessa, Cesare De Simone, Antonio Gibelli, John Gooch, Irene Guerrini, Mario Isnenghi, Ivo J. Lederer, Giorgio Longo, Denis Mack Smith, Piero Melograni, Alberto Monticone, Paul O'Brien, Piero Pieri, Marco Pluviano, Giovanna Procacci, Gianni Rocca, Giorgio Rochat, Gian Enrico Rusconi, John Schindler, Antonio Sema, David Stevenson, Hew Strachan, Petra Svolšak, Fabio Todero, Angelo Ventrone, Fritz Weber, Eileen Wilks, John Wilks, John Woodhouse and Dragan R. Zivojinovic. While the endnotes suggest the scale of this debt, they do not – could not – wholly contain it.

Ivo Banac, Cathie Carmichael, Miha Kovač, Lyn Macdonald, Paul O'Brien, Giovanna Procacci, Hew Strachan and John Woodhouse kindly answered questions and sent information. Noel Malcolm, Peter Morris, Paolo Pollanzi, the late Antonio Sema, Petra Svolšak, Roberto Todero, Angelo Ventrone, Eric Beckett Weaver and Mark Wheeler did the same, and sent books as well. Željko Cimprič provided the diary of Virgilio Bonamore. Vesna Domany-Hardy made available the memoir of her ancestor, Aleksandar Grlić. Bob Doneley and other contributors to the online Great War Forum (accessible at http://1914-1918.invisionzone.com/forums) discussed the incidents on the Italian front that are mentioned in my Introduction. The staff at the Bodleian Library (Oxford), the British Library (London), and the Biblioteca Civica 'Attilio Hortis' (Trieste) make those places a delight to work in. Tiziano Bertè at the Museo Storico Italiano della Guerra, Rovereto, went out of his way to help with the illustrations, as did the patient staff at the Photograph Archive of the Imperial War Museum, London. Mirjam and Ervin Hladnik-Milharčič took me up and down the Isonzo valley, some 20 years ago, telling stories about the First World War as we went. My title was suggested by the name of a fine website, devoted to the Italian front, http://www.guerrabianca.org, which is published by the Società Storica per la Guerra Bianca.

I am grateful to Richard Bosworth, Andrew Puddephatt and Hew Strachan for reading and commenting on one or another draft of the book, and to Paul Anderson, Patrick Burke, Cathie Carmichael, Jim McCue, Paul O'Brien, Alasdair Palmer, Paolo Pollanzi, Glenda Sluga and Ian Thomson for doing the same with chapters. Discussions with Alasdair Palmer and Mark Ellingham were heartening as always. Jamie McKendrick clarified my thoughts about translating Ungaretti, and let me use his fine version of 'Vigil'. Donald Sommerville's editing improved the draft in many ways. András Bereznay took great pains over the maps (the best that I have seen in any book about the Italian front). At Faber, Anne Owen and Kate

ACKNOWLEDGEMENTS

Murray Browne were the kindest of shepherds, herding everything towards publication.

Giani Cabrera, Richard Huckstep and Paolo Pollanzi added immeasurably to the pleasure and benefit of visits to Trieste and the old front lines between Mount Hermada and Trento. I am sure they influenced this book in even more ways than I realise. Peter Morris, generous companion, led the way up Mount Krn and Mount Mrzli; I'm sorry he could not stay to look down from Mount Rombon at the rainbow shimmering over the valley, like an arch to the Julian Alps. Paolo Rumiz, an excellent journalist, put me in touch with the late Carlo Orelli. Christine and Ronnie Bishop gave timely refuge and support. Without their and Divna Malbaša's help, the book would have taken another year to finish. Neil Belton had the idea in the first place; appreciation of his trust and acuity is surpassed only by my debt to the dedicatees.

MT

Index

10, 164, 330; French policy, 400,
404–5; German policy, 403; internees,
139; Italian forces, 62, 75; Italian gain,
7, 9, 11, 395, 404–5; Italian strategy,
321, 396, 397–8, 400–1, 402, 404;
landscape, 315, 350; plebiscite, 405
Venice: Austrian rule, 397; Austrian
strategy, 317, 320, 339, 342, 345;
Cavour's plans, 396; D'Annunzio in,
47, 255; defences, 9, 97, 331; Franz
Josef's visit, 13; Italian advance on,
403; Italian gain, 11, 395; Italian troop
movements, 367, 405; Italian retreat,
5; Marinetti's view of, 233; refugees,
348; Trieste relations, 100, 105
Verdi, Giuseppe, 39, 101
Verona Brigade, 130, 131–2
Victor Emanuel II, King, 8–9, 13, 397,
398, 399–401, 403–5
Victor Emanuel III, King: Aosta
relationship, 323; appeal to Tsar, 165;
appearance and character, 19, 39;
Cadorna relationship, 154–6, 163,
166, 318, 324; D'Annunzio
relationship, 43, 46; Delmé-Radcliffe
relationship, 243; Diaz appointment,
323, 330; Fiume issue, 374; at front,
172, 198, 199, 219, 299, 312; Gadda's
view of, 303; military role, 9, 53, 61,
152, 165; Mussolini relationship, 50,
388; political views, 19–20; population
of kingdom, 375; speech (23 May
1915), 61–2; speech (8 November
1917), 322; WWI entry, 18, 22, 27–8,
31, 33–5
Villesse, 142, 147n
Viola, Colonel, 131–2
Vipacco, River: Austrian defences, 177,
221, 251, 282; Austrian forces, 172,
223; Carso boundary, 66; Italian
advance, 279; Italian defence concerns,
9; San Michele, 89, 169; winter
weather, 240
vitalism, 186, 229–39, 257

Vittorio Veneto, Battle of, 356–61, 364,
381, 388–9
Vivante, Angelo, 105, 120
Voce, La, 117
Vodice, Mount, 252–3

Weber von Webenau, General Viktor,
361, 363
Wells, H. G., 167n, 194, 205, 244, 292
Western Front: Allied troops from, 321;
artillery, 154, 245, 279; Austrian
forces, 318, 338, 346; bombardments,
221; Cadorna, 58; creeping
barrage, 225n; deadlock, 5; focus on,
157, 159, 160; German guns, 328;
lessons of, 59, 277; Lloyd George's
policy, 241; military police, 227;
mines, 206n; relieving pressure on,
124; Robertson on, 240; slaughter, 1,
391; trenches, 59
Wilhelm II, Kaiser, 20, 84, 247, 295,
338, 358
Wilson, Woodrow: armistice
negotiations, 355, 359, 361–2;
declarations of war, 246, 337, 340;
Fourteen Points, 335–6, 355, 370;
Paris peace conference, 369–71, 373,
375–9, 381; propaganda campaign,
340; speech to Italian Parliament, 369;
war aims, 247, 341
Woodhouse, John, 40
Wurm, General Wenzel, 82

Yeats, W. B., 182
Yugoslav Committee, 292

Zara, 367, 371, 372, 378–9, 382
Zeidler, General Erwin: fortifications,
87–8; at Gorizia, 82, 87–8, 128, 134,
174; troops, 128, 157, 177
Zincone, Brigadier, 288–90
Zita, Empress of Austria, 348
Zuccari, General Luigi, 62
Zupelli, General Vittorio, 57, 124, 154–6